SOC

(SŌSH)

What makes *SOC* special?

SOC offers instructors **scholarly content** and *unmatched currency* in a succinct magazine format that engages students. *SOC* consistently encourages students to **foster their sociological imagination** and encourages them to get involved and MAKE A DIFFERENCE in the world around them.

What's Inside

Engaging pedagogy designed to be eye-catching and visually appealing can be found throughout the text. *SOC* shows students how they can apply sociological concepts to their everyday lives.

< **"From Me to You"** provides down-to-earth explanations of sociological concepts using the author's experiences as examples.

< **"At the Movies"** lists movies that relate to sociology.

< **"Hot or Not?"** boxes ask students to consider their opinion on a "hot" issue of current interest.

< **"Get Involved"** sections push students to actively participate in sociological issues that are relevant to them.

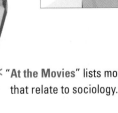

< **"Pop Soc"** teaches sociological concepts through popular culture.

SOC 2010

VICE PRESIDENT & EDITOR IN CHIEF **Michael Ryan**

AUTHOR **Jon Witt**

EDITOR AT LARGE **Gina Boedeker**

FIELD CORRESPONDENT **Richard T. Schaefer**

MANAGING EDITOR **Rhona Robbin**

DEVELOPMENT **Briana Porco**

STYLE DIRECTOR **Daniel Gonzalez**

FILM ADVISORS **Lindsey Jones and Alyssa Haak**

MARKETING MANAGER **Caroline McGillen**

SENIOR PRODUCTION EDITOR **Carey Eisner**

SENIOR PRODUCTION SUPERVISOR **Tandra Jorgensen**

COMPOSITOR **TBH Typecast, Inc.**

PRINTER **R. R. Donnelley & Sons**

ART MANAGER **Robin Mouat**

DESIGN MANAGER **Cassandra Chu**

INTERIOR DESIGNER **Maureen McCutcheon**

COVER DESIGNER **Linda Beaupré**

PHOTO WRANGLERS **Brian J. Pecko, Nora Agbayani, Sonia Brown**

ILLUSTRATION **Ayelet Arbel, Lineworks, John and Judy Waller, and Argosy Publishing, Inc.**

AUTHOR PORTRAIT **Arthur Mount**

To our esteemed author, Dr. Richard Schaefer: We thank you for your invaluable contributions to *SOC*.

To Lori: If I only had one friend left . . .

SOC 2010

Published by McGraw-Hill, an imprint of The McGraw-Hill Companies, Inc., 1221 Avenue of the Americas, New York, NY 10020. Copyright © 2010. All rights reserved. No part of this publication may be reproduced or distributed in any form or by any means, or stored in a database or retrieval system, without the prior written consent of The McGraw-Hill Companies, Inc., including, but not limited to, in any network or other electronic storage or transmission, or broadcast for distance learning.

This book is printed on acid-free paper.

1 2 3 4 5 6 7 8 9 0 BAM/BAM 0 9

ISBN 978-0-07-729065-8

MHID 0-07-729065-8

Front cover: (youths) Stockbyte/Getty Images; (sky) Paul Edmondson/Corbis
Back cover: Blend Images/Masterfile
Foldout: (left to right): Stockbyte/PunchStock; 2007 Getty Images; Nick White/Getty Images; Stockbyte/PunchStock

Library of Congress Cataloging-in-Publication Data

Witt, Jon.

Soc updated / Jon Witt. -- 2010 ed.
p. cm.
Rev. ed. of: Soc. 1st ed. c2009.
Includes bibliographical references and indexes.
ISBN-13: 978-0-07-729065-8 (pbk. : alk. paper)
ISBN-10: 0-07-729065-8
1. Sociology. I. Witt, Jon. Soc. II. Title.
HM586.W58 2010
301—dc22

2009033785

www.mhhe.com

WHAT'S NEW IN SOC

> New summary table on the three key perspectives in Chapter 1 provides a ready reference for students.

> New content related to the recent economic downturn, including coverage of rising unemployment rates, the Madoff scandal, and the impact of government intervention on the economy.

> Updated statistics and examples, including 2009 data, throughout.

> Expanded coverage of politics to include the 2008 election, current health care reform, the same-sex marriage debate, and recent protests of Iranian elections.

> New section on the rising role of community colleges.

TOP PHOTO: Bernie Madoff
BOTTOM PHOTO: Iranian protesters

SOC
2010 Edition

BRIEF CONTENTS

Name: Jon Witt (though my mom calls me Jonathan)

Education: I got my BA from Trinity College in Deerfield, IL, and earned my PhD from Loyola University in Chicago.

Occupations: Sociologist, father, and dog-walker

Hobbies: I like reading, writing, and messing around on computers—and I'm addicted to my iPhone

Childhood ambition: To be a printer like my dad—or, as I learned when I was old enough to say it, an offset lithographer

Family: Lori and I have been married for 25 years, and we have two daughters, Emily, 15, and Eleanor, 13

Last book read: Harper Lee's To Kill a Mockingbird

Favorite film: Right now it's Up

Favorite soundtrack: Playing Guitar Hero World Tour with Em & El

Latest accomplishment: This book!

Quote: There may be fields of sociological science quite beyond the average mind, and rightly left to the learned specialist; but that is no reason why we should not learn enough of the nature and habits of society to insure a more profitable and pleasant life.
—Charlotte Perkins Gilman, Human Work, 1904

My Blog: www.soc101.com

"What I like most about *SOC* is its layout; it seems to be more conducive to reading for my students. In addition, I believe the book is well-written and solidly covers the essence of each area—much better than some of the more lengthy textbooks out there."

–JUYEON SON, *University of Wisconsin, Oshkosh*

Thanks for your feedback. SOC was designed with students in mind. And one thing students appreciate is portability—content that can travel with them wherever they go.
—The Editors

"The Witt text helps me to accomplish my goals because most of my students are actually reading the text. Thus, they are better prepared for classroom lectures and discussions. Students can easily identify with the examples, illustrations, and visual presentations in the book, and they can better understand how the course material relates to real life."
– LORI MAIDA, *Westchester Community College*

That's great news! Jon Witt developed the narrative and features to reach students where they are, so that instructors can take them where they need them to be. SOC asks students to think critically about issues close to their lives. We're glad you think this will work well for your students.
—The Editors

"The design of *SOC* is most appealing. What is good is that substance is not sacrificed for style. The students get good information in an engaging design that still adheres to the traditional framework of sociology classes."
–JOHN TENUTO, *College of Lake County*

"I like how the Witt text looks like a magazine. It also has lots of graphs, interesting facts, and cool pictures to hold my attention."
–SKYE PETERS, *student at Parkland College*

From the cover to the interior design, images, graphs, charts, and pedagogy, SOC was designed to make sociology accessible and thought-provoking for students. The visuals reinforce the solid scholarship throughout.
—The Editors

Table of Contents

4 > Socialization 65

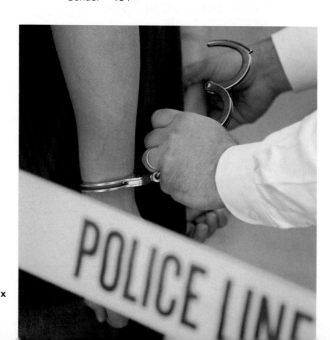

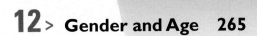

1

THE SOCIOLOG

THE INDIVIDUAL AND SOCIETY

George Bailey never got the chance to live the kind of life he wanted to live. He desperately wanted to escape small-town life, go to college, travel the world, design bridges, and achieve even more, but obligations and a sense of duty conspired against him. Now, feeling like a failure, he stands on a snowy bridge ready to commit suicide. So begins the holiday film classic *It's a Wonderful Life*.

Just as George prepares to jump, an angel named Clarence shows up and gives him a chance to see what the world would have been like had George never existed. It is not a pretty sight. People die whom George helped save, homes are lost that his family building-and-loan business helped finance, and life in the local community looks bleak largely due to the underhanded dealings of the evil banking tycoon Mr. Potter. George learns that he has had a major impact on family, friends, and community. In the words of Clarence, "One [person's] life touches so many others, when he [or she]'s not there, it leaves an awfully big hole." George changes his mind about suicide and rushes home to waiting family and friends, who unite to save his business from financial ruin.

The film's focus on the relationship between the individual and society is fundamentally sociological. On the one hand, the film presents a story about one of the lessons learned from sociology: that our individual actions matter and that it is through our actions that "society" is made. On the other hand, the film is also about the power of community, of family, and of social context. It is about the ways in which the options available to us are limited by position and circumstance.

Perhaps there is a bit of George Bailey in all of us. We create society by the choices we make and the things we do. At the same time, we are products of society, shaped by the people around us. For each of us, just as for George Bailey, many endings are possible—that is the nature of individual choice—but not all endings are equally probable—that is the nature of social position and the unequal distribution of resources. Throughout its history, sociology has sought to describe and explain this relationship between the individual and society.

ICAL IMAGINATION

As You READ >>

- What is sociology?
- How do sociologists look at the world?
- How might someone practice sociology?

>> What Is Sociology?

We need each other. We may like to think that we can make it on our own, but our individualism is made possible by our interdependence. We praise the Olympic gold medalist for her impressive skill, dedicated training, and single-minded determination. Yet, if it weren't for her mom driving her to the pool every day, for the building manager waking up at 4:00 A.M. to make sure the pool is open, for the women working overnight to make sure the locker room is clean and safe, and so many others who fade into the background in such moments of glory, she would never have had that chance to shine.

Sociology as a discipline is committed to investigating and understanding the full scope of our interdependence. **Sociology** is the systematic study of the relationship between the individual and society and of the consequences of difference. It focuses on social relationships, looking at how others influence our behavior; how major social institutions like the government, religion, and the economy affect us; and how we ourselves affect other individuals, groups, and even organizations. In doing this analysis, sociologists focus less on what one individual does or does not do than on what people do as members of a group or in interaction with one another, and on what that means for individuals and for society as a whole.

Through sociology we can ask and answer questions about our interdependence. With whom do we connect? How do we organize those connections? What gets in the way? Who benefits? Whether sitting in a classroom, working in an office or a factory, or exercising in a health club, we rely on others who shape how we think and act. As individuals, we do choose, but we cannot divorce our individual preferences from the influence of parents, teachers, friends, enemies, the media, and more, or from our access to resources such as money, social networks, and knowledge. We influence and are influenced by the world around us. Sociology studies those influences.

sociology The systematic study of the relationship between the individual and society and of the consequences of difference.

sociological imagination An awareness of the relationship between who we are as individuals and the social forces that shape our lives.

private troubles Obstacles that individuals face as individuals rather than as a consequence of their social position.

THE SOCIOLOGICAL IMAGINATION

Sociology helps us to see our place in the world in new ways. American sociologist C. Wright Mills (1959) created a concept called the **sociological imagination,** an awareness of the relationship between who we are as individuals and the social forces that shape our lives. Mills described the sociological imagination as our ability to see the interaction between history and biography. By "history" he meant not just the times in which we live but also our positions in society and the resources to which we have access. "Biography" encompasses our personal experience, our actions and thoughts, and the choices we make. As Mills put it, "neither the life of an individual nor the history of society can be understood without understanding both" (p. 3). We act within the confines of society.

One way to develop a sociological imagination is to view your own society as an outsider might. Consider sporting events, for example. In the United States, thousands of fans pack stadiums to cheer for well-trained football players. In Bali, Indonesia, dozens of spectators gather around a ring to cheer on well-trained roosters engaged in cockfights. In both instances, the spectators root for their favorites and might bet on the outcome. Yet what is considered a normal sporting event in one part of the world is considered unusual in another.

In applying the sociological imagination, Mills (1959) suggested that we distinguish between **private troubles,** obstacles that individuals face as individuals, and **public issues,** obstacles that individuals in similar positions face.

Unemployment, for example, is unquestionably a personal hardship (private trouble) for a man or woman without a job. But when millions of people lose their jobs, unemployment becomes a public issue. Social factors,

such as shifts in the economy, rather than individual failings contribute to large-scale unemployment. For example, from January 2008 to March 2009, the unemployment rate in the United States rose from 4.9 to 8.5 percent. This increase was tied to factors such as the banking crisis, the stock market plunge, and the decline in new home construction. At such times, blaming unemployment only on individuals is like treating symptoms without curing the disease that caused them. Discovering the larger patterns re-

lated to unemployment—in other words, treating it as a public issue—helps us to predict its impact on individuals and communities and to respond appropriately.

The sociological imagination is an empowering tool. It enables us to see the world and its people through a broader

> **public issues** Obstacles that individuals in similar positions face; also referred to by sociologists as "social problems."

lens. This might be as simple as understanding why a roommate prefers country music to hip-hop, or it may open up a whole new way of understanding other people around the world. For example, in the aftermath of the terrorist attacks of September 11, 2001, many Americans wanted to understand how Muslims throughout the world perceived their country. The sociological imagination can provide us with a more complete understanding of what happens and why.

THE HAMBURGER AS MIRACLE

Many people take for granted that it would be easy to provide for their needs if they had to, and they are eager to strike out on their own and prove themselves. As an example of using the sociological imagination, however, suppose you had to do something as seemingly simple as making a hamburger but had to do so without relying on any knowledge, skills, tools, or resources obtained from someone else. Without an interdependent network of people performing myriad small tasks that we take for granted, we would be hard-pressed to provide for ourselves. As we will see, like anything we might produce, a hamburger is a miracle because it is a symbol of our society's shared knowledge and skills.

How hard can it be to make a hamburger from scratch? Considering the ingredients, which seem fairly simple, there are any number of ways to proceed. Let's begin with the burger itself. First, you need to find a cow. How hard can that be? Well,

---

5 Movies on THE SOCIOLOGICAL IMAGINATION

Castaway
A man is isolated from society on a remote, deserted island.

Children of Men
A dystopian vision of society where humans can no longer reproduce.

The Class
A French film about the interactions between a teacher and his class of inner-city students.

The Curious Case of Benjamin Button
A man born into old age experiences life in reverse.

Transamerica
A transgender mom takes a road trip with her estranged son.

SOCthink

> > > Imagine spending the afternoon people watching at the mall. What differences might you observe in how people present themselves? What social factors might shape how they dress and talk, whether they are alone or in a group, and how much they buy? How might C. Wright Mills have explained such differences?

you can't buy one from a farmer, as doing so means relying on resources from others. For the same reason, you can't go out to the country (getting there itself might present something of a challenge) and steal one from a farm (which implies a farmer, which means dependence on another person). So you need to find a wild cow.

Assuming you do find a wild cow, you then have to kill it. Perhaps you might bash it with a large rock or stampede

for-grantedness of our human interdependence and to the knowledge we share collectively without even realizing it. Of course, this is true not just for hamburgers but for virtually any product we use. It could be a veggieburger, a book, a desk, a shirt, a car, a house, or a computer. Look around you and try to imagine making, by yourself, all the things that we as humans have produced. The knowledge and skill that these things represent is overwhelming. Thankfully,

> **The function of sociology, as of every science, is to reveal that which is hidden.**
>
> Pierre Bourdieu

it off a cliff. Next, you need to butcher it, but cow hide is tough. Imagine what it takes to produce a metal knife (finding ore, smelting, forging, tempering, and so on). Perhaps a sharp rock will do. Assuming you came up with a cutting tool, you now have a chunk of raw cow meat. Given that it's hamburger we're after (though you might want to settle for steak at this point), next you need to grind the meat. You might use a couple of those rocks to pulverize the meat into something of a meat mash, although a meat grinder would work better if it weren't so hard to make one. In any event, at last you have a raw hamburger patty.

Now you need to cook it. How will you do that? Where will you get the fire? Perhaps you could strike two rocks together in hopes of creating a spark, or maybe rub two sticks together. If you were allowed to get help from an outside source, you might check how Tom Hanks' character did it in the film *Cast Away*—but you aren't. Perhaps it would be easiest to wait around for lightning to strike a nearby tree. In any case, after you get fire, you still have to cook the meat. No frying pans are available, so either you make one or perhaps cook it on that handy rock you used to kill the cow. Or you could just put the meat on a stick that you cut down and whittled with the knife you made (or was that a "sharp" stone?) and roast it over the fire.

Assuming you are successful, you now have a cooked hamburger patty. But that's not enough. There are still many other steps that need to be completed. You need a bun, which involves figuring out how to come up with flour, water, salt, oil, sugar, and yeast. What about condiments such as ketchup, mustard, pickles, and onions? What if at the end of all that you decide to make it a cheeseburger?

Making something that seems so simple, that we take for granted, that we can get for a dollar at McDonald's, turns out to be quite complicated. The knowledge and skill to acquire all the ingredients in a hamburger is beyond the capacity of most individuals. Yet when we eat a burger, we think nothing of it. When you think about it—when you apply the sociological imagination—a hamburger is a miracle. It's miraculous, not in a supernatural sense but as a symbol pointing to the astonishing complexity and taken-

our interdependence means that we do not have to rely on our own knowledge and skill alone for our survival.

KEY COMPONENTS OF SOCIOLOGY

To better understand what sociology involves, we will look at each of the four key components of the definition in turn.

Systematic Study Sociologists are engaged with the world, gathering empirical data through systematic research. Relying on empirical data means that sociologists draw their conclusions about society based on experiences or observations rather than beliefs or the authority of others. If they want to understand the impact of television on community or the phenomenon of binge drinking on college campuses, they must gather data from those involved in these activities and base their conclusions upon that information.

Sociological research historically has been divided between quantitative and qualitative approaches to data collection. Quantitative approaches emphasize counting things and analyzing them mathematically or statistically. The most common way to collect this type of data is through surveys. In contrast, qualitative approaches focus on listening to and observing people and allowing them to interpret what is happening in their own lives. The most common way to collect this type of data is through participant observation, in which the researcher interacts with those she or he studies. In practice, sociologists often draw on both techniques in conducting their research. We will investigate these research techniques, along with others, in more detail in Chapter 2.

The Individual Although sociology is most commonly associated with the study of groups, there is no such thing as a group apart from the individuals who compose it. As individuals we are constantly choosing what do to next. Most of the time, we follow guidelines for behavior we have learned from others, but we have the ability to reject those guidelines at any time. A term sociologists sometimes use to describe this capacity is **agency,** meaning the freedom individuals have to choose and to act. In professional sports, for example, we use the term "free agent" to describe a player who has the power to negotiate with whatever team he or she wishes. We, too, have such freedom. We could choose not to go to class, not to go to work, not to get out of bed in the morning, not to obey traffic signals, not to respond when spoken to, not to read the next sentence in this book, and on and on.

Our self exists in an interactive relationship with

"*Actually, Lou, I think it was more than just my being in the right place at the right time. I think it was my being the right race, the right religion, the right sex, the right socioeconomic group, having the right accent, the right clothes, going to the right schools . . .*"

its environment, and we act within the context of our relationships. The same is true for that sports free agent. While he or she can choose any team, in order to get a big payday, he or she is limited to choosing within the confines of the league. Our choices, too, are constrained by our positions. Having access to varieties of resources, we choose among an array of options with knowledge of various possible outcomes. We usually follow "paths of least resistance"—the accepted and expected actions and beliefs—but the choice of whether to continue to follow them is ours each and every second of our lives (Johnson 1997).

Society The study of society is at the core of sociology. Although we will spend most of this book describing various aspects of society, we can begin by thinking of it as our social environment. Society consists of persistent patterns of relationships and social networks within which we oper-

ate. The social structure it provides is analogous to a building: the structure of a building both encourages and discourages different activities in different rooms (such as kitchens, bedrooms, and bathrooms), and many of the most essential operations of a building (such as heating and air conditioning) are mostly invisible to us. In the same way, the structure of our *institutions*—a term sociologists use to describe some of the key components of social structure, including economy, family, education, government, and religion—shapes what is expected of us. For example, the choices that are available to us in the context of the modern family, such as to go off and pursue our own education and career, are much different from the obligations we would face in more traditional family contexts. Nested within institutions are the groups, subgroups, and statuses that we occupy. Within the context of society, we construct culture and engage in social interaction. We will address the topics of structure, culture, and interaction in detail in coming chapters.

agency The freedom individuals have to choose and to act.

The Consequences of Difference The final part of the definition of sociology involves the consequences of difference. Sociology does more than just describe our structure, culture, and interaction; it also looks at how economic, social, and cultural resources are distributed and

at the implications of these patterns in terms of the opportunities and obstacles they create for individuals and groups. Since the founding of sociology, sociologists have been concerned with the impact our social positions have on our opportunities or lack thereof.

Sociologists have noted, for example, that the 2004 Indian Ocean tsunami affected Indonesian men and women differently. When the waves hit, following traditional cultural patterns, mothers and grandmothers were at home with the children; men were outside working, where they were more likely to become aware of the impending disaster. Moreover, most of the men knew how to swim, a survival skill that women in these traditional societies usually do not learn. As a result, many more men than women survived the catastrophe—about 10 men for every 1 woman. In one typical Indonesian village, 97 of 1300 people survived; only 4 were women. The impact of this gender imbalance will be felt for some time, given women's primary role as caregivers for children and the elderly (BBC 2005a).

The analysis of social power deserves particular attention because it shapes how and why we think and act as we do. The simple fact is that those who have access to and control over valued material, social, and cultural resources have different options available to them than do those without such access. One of the main tasks of sociology is to reveal and report the degree of **social inequality**—a condition in which members of society have differing amounts of wealth, prestige, or power. That is why the definition of sociology draws particular attention to the consequences of difference.

In combination, these four aspects of sociology help us to understand the things that influence our beliefs and actions and, in so doing, can help us to make choices that are more free. Failure to appreciate

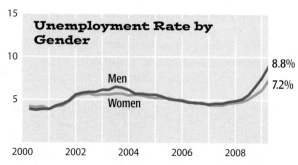

Unemployment rate

- 4.2%–6.5%
- 6.7%–7.8%
- 8.1%–9.6%
- 9.7%–12.6%

Categorical Trends in Unemployment

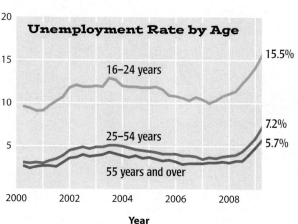

Unemployment Rate by Gender

Men
Women

8.8%
7.2%

Unemployment Rate by Age

16–24 years
25–54 years
55 years and over

15.5%
7.2%
5.7%

Year

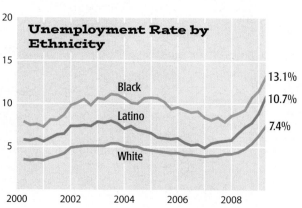

Overall Unemployment Rate, Ages 16 and Over

8.1%

Unemployment Rate by Ethnicity

Black
Latino
White

13.1%
10.7%
7.4%

Year

the relationship between the individual and society, for example, leads us to misdiagnose our individual and social problems, and so to develop inadequate cures for those things that ail us. French sociologist Pierre Bourdieu (1998a) put it this way: "Sociology teaches how groups function and how to make use of the laws governing the way they function so as to try to circumvent them" (p. 57). Only by appreciating the degree to which our thoughts and actions are determined by our social position and our lack of freedom are we able to make more realistic choices to change ourselves and our worlds.

SOCIOLOGY AND THE SOCIAL SCIENCES

Is sociology a science? The term **science** refers to the body of knowledge obtained by methods based on systematic observation. Just like other scientific disciplines, sociology involves the organized, systematic study of phenomena (in this case, human behavior) in order to enhance understanding. All scientists, whether studying mushrooms or murderers, attempt to collect precise information through methods of study that are as objective as possible. They rely on the careful recording of observations and the accumulation of data.

Of course, there is a great difference between sociology and physics, or between psychology and astronomy. For this reason, the sciences are commonly divided into natural and social sciences. **Natural science** is the study of the physical features of nature and the ways in which they interact and change. Astronomy, biology, chemistry, geology, and physics are all natural sciences. **Social science** is the study of the social features of humans and the ways in which they interact and change. The social sciences include sociology, anthropology, economics, history, psychology, and political science.

These social science disciplines have a common focus on the social behavior of people, yet each has a particular orientation. Anthropologists usually study past cultures and preindustrial societies that continue today, as well as the origins of humans. Economists explore the ways in which people produce and exchange goods and services, along with money and other resources. Historians are concerned with the peoples and events of the past and their significance for us today. Psychologists investigate personality and individual behavior. Political scientists study international relations, the workings of government, and the exercise of power and authority. Sociologists, as we have already seen, study the influence that society has on people's attitudes and behavior and the ways in which people interact and shape society.

Let's consider how different social sciences might study the impact of the global economic crisis that began in late 2008. Historians would compare recent events to those that occurred in previous crises such as the Great Depression of the 1930s. Economists would conduct research on the financial impact of the current crisis for individuals, nations, and the world as a whole. Psychologists would study the behavior and reactions of individuals to assess the emotional trauma such crises cause. And political scientists would study the stances taken by political leaders and their governments' responses to the crisis.

What approach would sociologists take? They would view the economic downturn as a public issue, and they would also seek to understand how the positions we occupy influence our experience of the crisis. This would include gathering data about the impact of this crisis on different categories of people based on factors such as social class, race and ethnicity, gender, age, and region of the country. We can get a glimpse of some of these effects on a person's likelihood of unemployment by viewing the graphs on page 6. Understanding how different groups are affected helps policy makers decide which actions to take to solve the crisis. A singular or universal solution is unlikely to be effective in addressing the different needs of the various groups. On a more local scale, sociologists would seek to understand the impact such changes have on communities, neighborhoods, families, and individuals.

natural science The study of the physical features of nature and the ways in which they interact and change.

social science The study of the social features of humans and the ways in which they interact and change.

Sociologists would take a similar approach in studying episodes of extreme violence. In April 2007, just as students at Virginia Tech were beginning to focus on the impending end of the semester, tragedy struck. In a two-hour shooting spree, a mentally disturbed senior armed with semi-automatic weapons killed a total of 32 students and faculty at Virginia's largest university. Observers struggled to describe the events and place them in some social context. For sociologists in particular, the event raised numerous issues and topics for study, including the role of the media in reporting breaking news events, the presence of violence in schools, the politics of gun control, concerns about gender, the inadequacy of the nation's mental health care system, and the stereotyping and stigmatizing of people who suffer from mental illness.

SOCIOLOGY AND COMMON SENSE

At times all of us practice some form of the sociological imagination, weighing the balance between individual and society. So what's the difference between sociology and common sense— the knowledge we get from our experiences and conversations, from what we read, from what we see on television, and so forth?

Sociological research shows that the choice of a marriage partner is heavily influenced by societal expectations.

Commonsense knowledge, although sometimes accurate, is not always reliable, because it rests on commonly held beliefs rather than on systematic analysis of facts.

Contrary to the common notion that women tend to be chatty compared to men, for instance, researchers have found little difference between the sexes in terms of their talkativeness. Over a five-year period, they placed unobtrusive microphones on 396 college students in various settings, on campuses in Mexico as well as the United States. They found that both men and women spoke about 16,000 words per day (Mehl et al. 2007).

theory In sociology a set of statements that seeks to explain problems, actions, or behavior.

Similarly, "common sense" tells us that in the United States today, military marriages are more likely to end in separation or divorce than in the past due to the strain of long deployments in Iraq and Afghanistan. Yet a study released in 2007 shows no significant increase in the divorce rate among U.S. soldiers over the past decade. In fact, the rate of marital dissolution among members of the military is comparable to that of nonmilitary families. Interestingly, this is not the first study to disprove the widely held notion that military service strains the marital bond. Two generations earlier, during the Vietnam era, researchers came to the same conclusion (Call and Teachman 1991; Karney and Crown 2007).

Like other social scientists, sociologists do not accept something as fact just because "everyone knows it." At times, the findings of sociologists may seem like common sense because they deal with familiar facets of everyday life. The difference is that such findings have been tested by researchers, analyzed in relation to other data, and evaluated in light of what is known by sociologists in the form of sociological theory.

>> What Is Sociological Theory?

Sociology, like all sciences, involves a conversation between theory and research. We gather data through systematic research, and we seek to describe and explain what we find using theories. Theories represent our attempts to tell the stories of our lives, but they do so in a particular way. Initially, theories might be general and vague. However, over time, as they become more fully informed by research, they are modified and refined into fuller, more accurate accounts of why we think and act as we do. We look first at theories and in Chapter 2 at methods.

FORMULATING SOCIOLOGICAL THEORIES

Why do people commit suicide? Émile Durkheim's answer to this question over a hundred years ago helped to establish sociology as a discipline. Among the traditional commonsense answers that Durkheim rejected were the notions that people inherit the desire to kill themselves or that sunspots drive people to take their own lives. He even suspected that psychological or biological explanations that pointed toward depression or chemical imbalance as causal factors were insufficient. He sought to prove that social forces existed that influenced an individual's likelihood of committing suicide.

In order to undertake this research, Durkheim developed a theory that offered a general explanation of suicidal behavior. We can think of theories as attempts to explain events, forces, materials, ideas, or behavior in a comprehensive manner. In sociology a **theory** is a set of statements that seeks to explain problems, actions, or behavior. An effective theory may have both explanatory and predictive power. That is, it can help us to see the relationships among seemingly isolated phenomena, as well as to understand how one type of change in an environment leads to other changes.

Durkheim theorized that people commit suicide because they lack the social integration to prevent them from taking this most final and individualistic of all acts. His hypothesis was this: "Suicide varies inversely with the degree of integration of the social groups of which the individual forms a part" ([1897] 1951:209). He chose religious affiliation as an indicator of social integration, arguing that Protestants are less socially integrated than are Roman Catholics. He claimed that Catholicism is a traditional faith with a hierarchical system of authority in which variation in belief (on such topics as birth control, abortion, married priests, and women priests) is not up to the individual. Protestantism, in contrast, puts the Bible into the believers' hands to interpret. The many schisms found among Protestants occurred as a consequence of individuals choosing to interpret matters of faith based on their own understanding of God's word. Whereas there is only one Roman Catholic Church, Protestantism includes Baptist, Methodist, Reformed, Episcopalian, Presbyterian, and many other denominational and nondenominational

churches. These contrasting contexts shaped the degree to which individuals were integrated into the religious community, leading Durkheim to predict that Protestants would be more likely to commit suicide than Catholics.

TESTING SOCIOLOGICAL THEORIES

In order to test his theory, Durkhiem gathered data from different countries to see if suicide rates varied. Looking at France, England, and Denmark, he found that England had 67 reported suicides per million inhabitants, France had 135 per million, and Denmark had 277 per million. Durkheim concluded that Denmark's comparatively high suicide rate was due to the fact that Denmark was a more Protestant nation than either France or England. In other words, it was the social makeup of these nations that shaped their suicide rates. More recent research focusing on individual rather than national rates continues to find this same relationship.

In extending his analysis to look at other indicators of social integration, Durkheim continued to obtain results that confirmed his underlying theory: the unmarried had much higher rates of suicide than married people; and soldiers were more likely to take their lives than civilians. In addition, there seemed to be higher rates of suicide in times of peace than in times of war and revolution, as well as higher rates in times of economic instability and recession rather than in times of prosperity. Durkheim concluded that his theory was correct: the suicide rate of a society reflects the extent to which people are or are not integrated into the group life of the society. Durkheim presented his results in his landmark work *Suicide*, published in 1897.

APPLYING SOCIOLOGICAL THEORIES

Built into Durkheim's theory is the presupposition that we find meaning in life through our interconnections with others. The more interconnected and interdependent we feel, the less likely we are to kill ourselves. Attempting to summarize the significance of our attachment to society, Durkheim put it this way: "The individual alone is not a sufficient end for his activity. He is too little. . . . When, therefore, we have no other object than ourselves we cannot avoid the thought that our efforts will finally end in nothingness. . . . Under these conditions one would lose the courage to live, that is, to act and struggle" ([1897] 1951:210).

SOCthink

> > > If Durkheim is correct and level of social integration influences the likelihood of suicide, why do rates vary for the groups listed in the Suicide Rates figure? Why is the rate for men four times higher than that for women? Why is the rate for non-Hispanic Whites higher than that for any other racial/ethnic groups? Why do White, non-Hispanic males have the highest suicide rate of all? Why is the rate for the elderly so high? Why is there a midlife suicide peak? What might the top-five or bottom-five states have in common? What might these patterns suggest about the social integration of people in these categories?

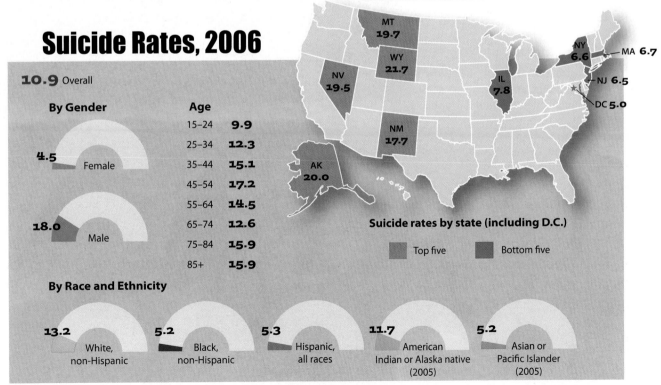

Suicide Rates, 2006

10.9 Overall

By Gender

4.5 Female

18.0 Male

Age	
15–24	9.9
25–34	12.3
35–44	15.1
45–54	17.2
55–64	14.5
65–74	12.6
75–84	15.9
85+	15.9

By Race and Ethnicity

13.2 White, non-Hispanic
5.2 Black, non-Hispanic
5.3 Hispanic, all races
11.7 American Indian or Alaska native (2005)
5.2 Asian or Pacific Islander (2005)

MT 19.7
WY 21.7
NV 19.5
NM 17.7
AK 20.0
IL 7.8
NY 6.6
MA 6.7
NJ 6.5
DC 5.0

Suicide rates by state (including D.C.)

Top five | Bottom five

Note: Rates are per 100,000, not percentage.

Source: National Center for Health Statistics 2007; Heron et al. 2009.

What Makes a Country Happy?

Looking on the bright side of life, happiness rates also vary from country to country. The five nations that score highest on the Happiness Index are Denmark, Switzerland, Austria, Iceland, and Finland. The bottom five are Tanzania, Zimbabwe, Moldova, Ukraine, and Armenia. The United States ranks 17th out of 95 nations. Researcher Stefan Klein (2006) suggests that societies that are characterized by a strong sense of social solidarity, active civic engagement, a commitment to social equality, and sufficient individual autonomy tend to be happier.

Human beings are, at their very foundation, social beings. According to Durkheim, we cannot consider what it means to be an individual apart from our position in society. This social dimension of individual behavior is what Durkheim wants sociology to explore, elaborate, and explain.

Durkheim's work on suicide provides a classic case of sociological theory at work. He theorized that social forces shape individual actions. He tested this theory by investigating suicide as one such individual choice—perhaps the most individual of all choices—and demonstrated that the likelihood of committing suicide varied based on group membership. Analysis of more recent data (see figure on page 9) shows that suicide rates continue to vary based on social position. Durkheim concluded that if social forces are at work in this most extreme example of individual choice, they similarly shape

all other individual choices. He argued that if social forces have such power in our lives, there should be a discipline dedicated to their study. As a result, Durkheim established Europe's first department of sociology at the University of Bordeaux in 1895.

>> The Development of Sociology

Given the complexity of human life, sociologists have developed a wide range of theories in which they describe and explain the diversity of social behavior. Sometimes their theories can be grand in scope, seeking to encompass the "big picture"; other times they can be more personal, intimate, and immediate. While we will spend most of the rest of this book investigating the insights sociological theories provide, here we will briefly address just five questions sociologists have frequently asked. These questions represent significant doors sociologists have opened to provide additional tools for the sociological imagination. The questions are these: How is social order maintained? How do power and inequality shape outcomes?

How do we construct our worlds and ourselves through everyday interaction? How does group membership (especially class, race, and gender) shape opportunity? What responsibility do sociologists bear to bring about positive social change?

HOW IS SOCIAL ORDER MAINTAINED?

The discipline of sociology grew up in the midst of significant social upheaval. The advent of the Industrial Revolution and urbanization in the early 19th century led to changes in patterns of government, thought, work, and everyday life. Aristocracy was on the decline while democracy was spreading; people were moving from a primary reliance on religious explanations to more scientific ones; and the world of the village and farm was rapidly giving way to life in the city and factory. It was in this context that Auguste Comte (1798–1857), in hopes of emulating what natural scientists did for nature, sought to establish a science of society that would reveal the basic "laws of society." Comte believed that knowing these laws would help us to understand what he referred to as "social statics"—the principles by which societies hold together and order is maintained—and "social dynamics"—the factors that bring about change and that shape the nature and direction of that change. Sociologists would then use their knowledge of these laws to help lead us toward the good society, balancing the needs for social order with positive social change. Comte coined the term *sociology*—which literally means "the study of the processes of companionship"—to describe this new science (Abercrombie, Hill, and Turner 2006:367).

Scholars learned of Comte's works largely through translations by the English sociologist Harriet Martineau (1802–1876). Seeking to systematize the research essential to conducting a science of society, Martineau ([1838] 1989) wrote the first book on sociological methods. She was also a pathbreaking theorist in her own right, introducing the significance of inequality and power into the discipline. Martineau's book *Society in America* ([1837] 1962) examined religion, politics, child rearing, and immigration in the young nation. It gave special attention to social class distinctions and to such factors as gender and race. In Martineau's ([1837] 1962) view, intellectuals and scholars should not simply offer observations of social conditions; they should act on their convictions in a manner that will benefit society. She spoke out in favor of the rights of women, the emancipation of slaves, and religious tolerance.

These two themes—analysis of social order and analysis of social inequality—have shaped the theoretical paths sociologists have pursued since this beginning. In early sociological theory, they find their fullest development in the works of Émile Durkheim and Karl Marx, respectively. As we will see throughout this book, they continue to be primary concerns for sociologists.

Émile Durkheim (1858–1917) emphasized the significance of social order. As we saw in his analysis of suicide, he saw society as a real, external force existing above the level of the individual and exerting its influence on individual behavior. Durkheim was particularly concerned about what happens when the influence of society declines, resulting in weakened social integration. He theorized that an increase in the division of labor, a defining characteristic of modern societies, meant that individuals shared

POPSOC

Harriet Martineau ([1838] 1989) argued that we could learn a lot about a culture by analyzing the ideas, images, and themes reflected in their popular songs. She wrote, "The Songs of every nation must always be the most familiar and truly popular part of its poetry.... They present also the most prevalent feelings on subjects of the highest popular interest. If it were not so, they would not have been popular songs." What might we learn about American culture based on analysis of the lyrics of the current top-10 songs? (Lists are available at "The Billboard Hot 100" or www.top10songs.com.)

fewer common experiences, ideas, and values. As workers became much more specialized in their tasks, they were at greater risk of what Durkheim called **anomie**—the loss of direction felt in a society when social control of individual behavior has become ineffective. Anomie increases the likelihood of alienation, loneliness, and isolation. Inspired by Comte's vision, Durkheim sought to establish sociology as a science to study these processes.

HOW DO POWER AND INEQUALITY SHAPE OUTCOMES?

Karl Marx (1818–1883) was also concerned about social order and integration, but his work particularly emphasized the significance of power and control over resources. Marx viewed our creative capacity to transform raw materials into products—for example, to take clay and make a pot, or a tree and make a desk—as the key factor distinguishing humans from other animals (whose behavior is ruled by their instincts). For Marx, human history is the progressive unfolding of human creativity in the form of new technology through which we establish our relationship to the natural world and with each other. Unfortunately, for most of human history, we lacked sufficient technology to provide enough material goods (such as food, clothes, and shelter) to meet everyone's needs, so not all people had enough.

Social inequality for Marx, then, is determined by ownership, or lack thereof, of key material resources. Those who own and control the means of production—the tools and resources necessary for that transformation to happen—rule the world. Members of the working class, in contrast, own only their capacity to transform raw mate-

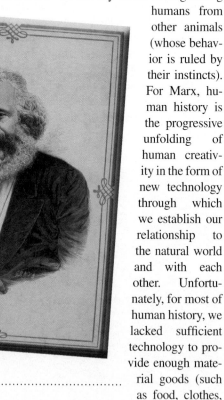

Karl Marx

Émile Durkheim

rials into products, which requires access to the means of production controlled by the ruling class. While Durkheim was concerned with anomie, Marx was concerned with alienation, by which he meant loss of control over our creative human capacity to produce, separation from the products we make, and isolation from our fellow workers. We will consider Marx's work as it relates to capitalism in more detail in a later chapter. His influence on sociological theory, however, extends beyond social class to an analysis of group identification and association, such as how class, gender, race, ethnicity, nationality, and age influence individual opportunity.

Seeking to expand sociological theory further, Max Weber (1864–1920; pronounced "VAY-ber") offered a more general theory of power that was less wedded to capitalism and ownership of the means of production. Weber argued that, although social class and its associated control over material resources may determine who has power in most instances, these are not the only possible foundations for power. Others he identified include social status, in which people defer to others out of respect for their social position or prestige, and organizational resources, in which members of a group gain power through their ability to organize to accomplish some specific goal by maximizing their available resources. Weber argued that these social resources draw their power from people's willingness to obey the authority of another person, which in turn is based on their perception of the legitimacy of that person's right to rule.

HOW DOES INTERACTION SHAPE OUR WORLDS?

Much of the work of Durkheim, Marx, and Weber involves **macro-sociology**, which concentrates on large-scale phenomena or entire civilizations. A later school of sociologists turned away from this approach in fa-

Max Weber

vor of **microsociology**, which stresses the study of small groups and the analysis of our everyday experiences and interactions. Microsociology emphasizes the significance of perception, of how we see others and how they see us. Sociologist Erving Goffman (1922–1982) popularized a method known as the *dramaturgical approach* (see Chapter 4), which compares everyday life to the setting of the theater and stage and sees people as theatrical performers. Just as actors project certain images to an audience, all of us seek to present particular features of our personalities to others even as we hide certain qualities. Thus, in a class, we may feel the need to project a serious image; at a party, we want to look relaxed and friendly. In this approach, sociologists must analyze our lived experience at the everyday level where our actions create, sustain, and modify our understanding of reality itself.

HOW DOES GROUP MEMBERSHIP INFLUENCE OPPORTUNITY?

Over time, sociologists came to more fully understand and appreciate the consequences that group membership, especially class, race, and gender, has for opportunity. Black sociologist W.E.B. Du Bois (1868–1963; pronounced "dew BOYS") combined an emphasis on the analysis of the everyday lived experience with a commitment to investigating power and inequality based on race. He was critical of those who relied on common sense or on all-too-brief investigations, arguing that a researcher has to be more than just a "car-window sociologist" because true understanding demands more than "the few leisure hours of a holiday trip to unravel the snarl of centuries" (Du Bois [1903] 1994:94). Through engaged and sustained research on the lives of African Americans, he documented their relatively low status in Philadelphia and Atlanta. His research revealed the social processes that contributed to the maintenance of racial separation, which extended beyond material differences to include social separation, which he referred to as the "color line."

Similarly, feminist scholarship has broadened our understanding of social behavior by extending the analysis beyond the male point of view that dominated classic sociology. An early example of this perspective can be seen in the life and writings of Ida Wells-Barnett (1862–1931). Carrying on a tradition begun with Mar-

Did You Know?

... According to the Thomas theorem, established by sociologists W. I. Thomas and Dorothy Swaine Thomas, "If men define situations as real, they are real in their consequences" (Thomas and Thomas 1928:571–572). In other words, our perceptions of what is real determine how we act more so than does reality itself.

tineau, Wells-Barnett argued that societies can be judged based on whether the principles they claim to believe in match their actions. Wells-Barnett found that when it came to the principles of equality and opportunity for women and African Americans, America came up short. Part of the task for the sociologist, then, is to bring to light such inconsistencies that may otherwise go largely unnoticed. This is something Wells-Barnett sought to do in her groundbreaking publications in the 1890s on the practice of lynching African Americans, as well as with her advocacy of women's rights, especially the struggle to win the vote for women. Like feminist theorists who succeeded her, Wells-Barnett used her analysis of society as a means of resisting oppression. In her case, she researched what it meant to be African American, a woman in the United States, and a Black woman in the United States (Wells-Barnett [1928] 1970).

Sociologists categorize and describe the above sociological insights by dividing them into three approaches: functionalist, conflict, and interactionist. Durkheim's work is considered an example of the **functionalist perspective,** which views society as akin to a living organism in which each part of the organism contributes to its survival. The various parts of a society, including institutions such as the family and government, are structured to maintain its stability. Whereas the functionalist approach focuses more on

anomie The loss of direction felt in a society when social control of individual behavior has become ineffective.

macrosociology Sociological investigation that concentrates on large-scale phenomena or entire civilizations.

microsociology Sociological investigation that stresses the study of small groups and the analysis of our everyday experiences and interactions.

functionalist perspective A sociological approach that emphasizes the way in which the parts of a society are structured to maintain its stability.

Did You Know?

... Michelle Obama majored in sociology at Princeton University in 1985. She used that degree as a stepping stone to law school at Harvard.

stability and consensus, the **conflict perspective** emphasizes the distribution of power and the allocation of resources in society. According to the conflict perspective, social order cannot be fully understood apart from a consideration of how the status quo is established and maintained and who benefits and who suffers from the existing system. Marx's work fits best within the conflict perspective. Finally, whereas functionalist and conflict theorists both analyze large-scale, society-wide patterns of behavior, theorists such as Goffman who take the **interactionist perspective** generalize about everyday forms of social interaction in order to explain society as a whole.

The three-perspectives model has the advantage of providing us with conceptual hooks that allow us to recall some of the key concerns and issues sociologists have raised. A disadvantage, however, is that it gives the illusion that these three are discrete categories with fundamentally different and incompatible ways of looking at the world. In practice, research rooted in one perspective almost inevitably should draw on or address insights from the other two.

DO SOCIOLOGISTS HAVE A RESPONSIBILITY TO PURSUE SOCIAL CHANGE?

Throughout sociology's history, a recurring theme common to all perspectives has been the idea that sociological theory and research should contribute to positive social change. In the early 1900s, many leading sociologists in the United States saw themselves as social reformers dedi-

SOCthink

> > > Sometimes it seems like we are experiencing "credential inflation," with more and more education needed to get decent entry-level jobs. Why do you think this has happened? How might looking at the issue from the functionalist, conflict, and interactionist perspectives shape how we frame an answer?

cated to systematically studying and then improving a corrupt society. They were genuinely concerned about the lives of immigrants in the nation's growing cities, whether those immigrants came from Europe or from the rural American South. Early female sociologists, in particular, often took active roles in poor urban areas as leaders of community centers known as settlement houses. For example, Jane Addams (1860–1935), an early member of the American Sociological Society, cofounded the famous Chicago settlement, Hull House. Addams and other pioneering female sociologists commonly combined intellectual inquiry, social service work, and political activism—all with the goal of assisting the underprivileged and creating a more egalitarian society. Working with Ida Wells-Barnett, Addams successfully prevented racial segregation in the Chicago public schools, and her efforts to establish a juvenile court system and a women's trade union reflect the practical fo-

Three Sociological Perspectives

	Functionalist	Conflict	Interactionist
View of society	Stable, well integrated	Characterized by tension and struggle between groups	Active in influencing and affecting everyday social interaction
Level of analysis emphasized	Macro	Macro	Micro, as a way of understanding the larger macro phenomena
Key concepts	Social integration Institutions Anomie	Inequality Capitalism Stratification	Symbols Nonverbal communication Face-to-face interaction
View of the individual	People are socialized to perform societal functions	People are shaped by power, coercion, and authority	People manipulate symbols and create their social worlds through interaction
View of the social order	Maintained through cooperation and consensus	Maintained through force and coercion	Maintained by shared understanding of everyday behavior
View of social change	Predictable, reinforcing	Change takes place all the time and may have positive consequences	Reflected in people's social positions and their communications with others
Example	Public punishments reinforce the social order	Laws enforce the positions of those in power	People respect laws or disobey them based on their own past experience
Proponents	Émile Durkheim Talcott Parsons Robert Merton	Karl Marx W.E.B. Du Bois Ida Wells-Barnett	George Herbert Mead Charles Horton Cooley Erving Goffman

From Me to You

When I took "Soc101" in college, it took me a long time to understand the sociological imagination. I still remember feeling overwhelmed by all the concepts, facts, and figures. Eventually, as we studied the impact of the media and the power of inheritance, things began to fall into place; I took another course and was hooked. As you begin your study of sociology, my advice is to stay focused on how our individual choices are shaped by our social positions and access to resources. How do our circumstances influence how we understand ourselves and others? I hope that after encountering sociology, you will come away with a new way of seeing, equipped to act in new and more informed ways.

cus of her work (Addams 1910, 1930; Lengermann and Niebrugge-Brantley 1998).

This commitment to positive social change was not unique to Addams and her colleagues. From the very beginning and on down to the present, sociologists have recognized an obligation to go beyond explaining how the world works and become actively engaged in making the world a better place. In the words of French sociologist Pierre Bourdieu, "I have come to believe that those who have the good fortune to be able to devote their lives to the study of the social world cannot stand aside, neutral and indifferent, from the struggles in which the future of that world is at stake" (1998a:11). For some this has meant releas-

Jane Addams

ing the results of their research to the public so that we might make more informed decisions; for others it has meant active engagement in establishing social policy or assisting in the lives of others. For example, Durkheim, who considered an educated citizenry essential to democratic success, used his appointment to the Department of Science of Education and Sociology at the Sorbonne in Paris, along with his political connections and appointments, to shape French educational policy and practice. Du Bois cofounded the National Association for the Advancement of Colored People, better known as the NAACP. In fact, one of the dominant reasons students choose to major in sociology is because they want to make a difference, and sociology provides a pathway to do just that.

conflict perspective A sociological approach that assumes that social behavior is best understood in terms of tension between groups over power or the allocation of resources, including housing, money, access to services, and political representation.

interactionist perspective A sociological approach that generalizes about everyday forms of social interaction in order to explain society as a whole.

applied sociology The use of the discipline of sociology with the specific intent of yielding practical applications for human behavior and organizations.

>> Practicing Sociology

For those who would like to pursue a career in sociology, a variety of paths are available. In recent decades, the number of U.S. college students who have graduated with a degree in sociology has risen steadily (see figure on page 16). While few occupations specifically require an undergraduate degree in sociology, sociological skills such as the ability to observe, interpret, and report on both macro- and micropatterns; to analyze and interpret data; and to work to bring about positive change are important assets in a wide range of occupations. Employment options for sociology majors include entry-level positions in business, social services, community organizations, not-for-profit groups, law enforcement, and more. The pie graph on page 16 summarizes the preferred career paths for those with B.A. or B.S. degrees in sociology. One way to investigate a possible future in sociology is through an internship. Studies show that students who choose an internship have less trouble finding jobs, obtain better jobs, and enjoy greater job satisfaction than students without internship placements (American Sociological Association 2006a; 2006b).

Hot or Not?

How much responsibility do individuals have to make things better for society?

APPLIED SOCIOLOGY

Applied sociology is the use of the discipline of sociology with the specific intent of yielding practical

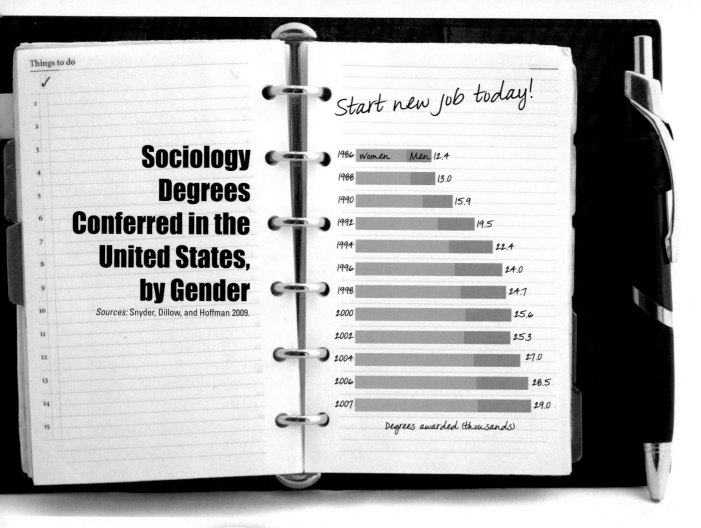

Sociology Degrees Conferred in the United States, by Gender

Sources: Snyder, Dillow, and Hoffman 2009.

Start new job today!

Year			Degrees awarded (thousands)
1986	Women	Men	12.4
1988			13.0
1990			15.9
1992			19.5
1994			22.4
1996			24.0
1998			24.7
2000			25.6
2002			25.3
2004			27.0
2006			28.5
2007			29.0

Degrees awarded (thousands)

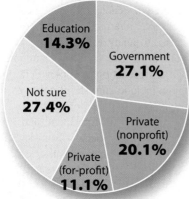

Education **14.3%**

Government **27.1%**

Not sure **27.4%**

Private (nonprofit) **20.1%**

Private (for-profit) **11.1%**

applications for human behavior and organizations. Often, the goal of such work is to assist in resolving a social problem. For example, in the past 40 years, eight presidents of the United States have established commissions to delve into major societal concerns facing our nation. Sociologists are often asked to apply their expertise to studying such issues as violence, pornography, crime, immigration, and population. In Europe both academic and governmental research departments are offering increasing financial support for applied studies.

One example of applied sociology involves the growing interest in the ways in which nationally recognized social problems manifest themselves locally. Since 2003, sociologist Greg Scott and his colleagues have been seeking to better understand the connection between illicit drug use and the spread of HIV/AIDS. The study, which will run through 2009, has so far employed 14 researchers from colleges and public health agencies, assisted by 15 graduate and 16 undergraduate students. By combining a variety of methods, including interviews and observa-

Preferred Employment Sector of Graduating Sociology Majors

Note: Based on spring 2005 national survey of 1248 college seniors majoring in sociology.

Source: Adapted from American Sociological Association 2006a:29.

tion, with photo and video documentation, these researchers have found that across all drug users, HIV/AIDS transmission is highest among users of crystal methamphetamine. Meth users are also most likely to engage in risky sexual behavior and to have partners who do so. Fortunately, of all drug users, meth users are the ones most closely connected to treatment programs, which allows them to receive substance abuse education and treatment from their health care providers. However, their cases, brought to the forefront by Scott and his team, highlight the need for public health officials to identify other individuals who engage in high-risk sexual behavior and to get them into appropriate treatment programs (G. Scott 2005).

Growing interest in applied sociology has led to such specializations as medical sociology and environmental sociology. The former includes research on how health care professionals and patients deal with disease. For example, medical sociologists have studied the social impact of the AIDS crisis on families, friends, and communities. Environmental sociologists examine the relationship between human societies and the physical environment. One focus of their work is the issue of "environmental justice," raised when researchers and community activists found that hazardous waste dumps are especially likely to be situated in poor and minority neighborhoods (Bullard 2007; Sze and London 2008).

CLINICAL SOCIOLOGY

The growing popularity of applied sociology has led to the rise of the specialty of clinical sociology. While applied sociology may involve simply evaluating social issues, **clinical sociology** is dedicated to facilitating change by altering organizations (as in family therapy) or restructuring social institutions (as in the reorganization of a medical center). Louis Wirth (1931) wrote about clinical sociology more than 75 years ago, but the term itself has become popular only in recent years. The Association for Applied Clinical Sociology was founded in 1978 to promote the application of sociological knowledge in interventions for individual and social change. This professional group has developed a procedure for certifying clinical sociologists—much as physical therapists or psychologists are certified.

Applied sociologists generally leave it to others to act on their evaluations, but clinical sociologists take direct responsibility for implementation and view those with whom they work as their clients. This specialty has become increasingly attractive to graduate students in sociology because it offers an opportunity to apply intellectual learning in practical ways. A competitive job market in the academic world has made such alternative career routes appealing.

clinical sociology The use of the discipline of sociology with the specific intent of altering organizations or restructuring social institutions.

globalization The worldwide integration of government policies, cultures, social movements, and financial markets through trade and the exchange of ideas.

For sociology graduates interested in academic careers, the road to a Ph.D. (or doctorate) can be long and difficult. This degree symbolizes competence in original research; each candidate must prepare a book-length study known as a dissertation. Typically, a doctoral student in sociology will engage in four to seven years of intensive work, including the time required to complete the dissertation. Yet even this effort is no guarantee of a job as a sociology professor.

Most people who take an introductory course in sociology will never take another sociology course, so what does sociology have to offer them? Practicing sociology is about so much more than a career;

it is a way of looking at the world around us and understanding its complexity and interconnections in a new way. It is about understanding others from their perspective and even understanding ourselves through their eyes. It is a way of assessing the accuracy of claims and refining our knowledge about why we think the way we think and act the way we act. Sociology is something you do; it's a way of life.

>> Developing a Sociological Imagination

Learning to apply the sociological imagination may be more important now than ever. Through **globalization**— the worldwide integration of government policies, cultures, social movements, and financial markets through trade and the exchange of ideas—our lives are more connected with and dependent upon diverse groups of people around the world whose beliefs and practices may be quite different from our own. University campuses often provide a microcosm of this trend, drawing together people from around the world with radically different values, political views, customs, and more into a relatively confined social space and providing opportunities for them to interact. If such interactions are to be meaningful, positive, and respectful, we must learn to use the sociological imagination to better understand ourselves and our culture.

SOCthink

> > > Consider the obstacles to cross-cultural interaction on college campuses. Why might people be unwilling to interact with others who have different cultural practices? How might it perpetuate inequality?

Sociologists expect the next quarter century to be perhaps the most exciting and critical period in the history of the discipline. That is because of a growing awareness—both in the United States and around the world—that current social problems can only be addressed by recognizing the full scope of our economic, political, and social interdependence. Through theory and research, sociologists offer us the tools we need.

For REVIEW

I. **What is sociology?**
    • Sociology is a way of seeing that joins theory and research to investigate the relationship between the individual and society and the impact unequal distribution of resources has on opportunity.

II. **How do sociologists look at the world?**
    • Sociologists develop theories that provide windows into our lives, allowing us to better understand social order, inequality, and interaction.

III. **How might someone practice sociology?**
    • Sociology can provide a pathway to a career in a related applied, clinical, or academic context. But more than that, we can practice sociology in our everyday lives by utilizing the sociological imagination to better understand ourselves and others.

Pop Quiz

1. Sociology is
   a. the analysis of individual motivations and internal struggles.
   b. concerned with predicting what particular individuals do or do not do.
   c. the systematic study of the relationship between the individual and society and of the consequences of difference.
   d. the integration of government policies, cultures, social movements, and financial markets through trade and the exchange of ideas.

2. According to C. Wright Mills, the sociological imagination focuses on the intersection between
   a. natural science and social science.
   b. power and access to resources.
   c. theory and research.
   d. history and biography.

3. What is the primary sociological lesson we learn from the hamburger as a miracle example?
   a. We take our interdependence and the knowledge we collectively share for granted.
   b. An individual could easily survive on his or her own without assistance from others.
   c. Modern technology makes it difficult for us to provide for our individual needs.
   d. Interdependence is no longer necessary because we can provide for our needs through modern technology.

4. In their attempts to describe the relationship between sociology and common sense, sociologists argue that
   a. common sense provides time-tested answers that are reliable most of the time whereas sociological facts change all the time.
   b. sociology depends on systematic analysis through research whereas common sense does not.
   c. sociology cannot assess or test the truthfulness of commonsense claims.
   d. there is no significant difference between the two.

5. Émile Durkheim's research on suicide found that
   a. Catholics had much higher suicide rates than Protestants.
   b. the more socially integrated someone is the less likely he or she is to commit suicide.
   c. married people are more likely to take their lives than single people.
   d. suicide is a solitary act, unrelated to group life.

6. Karl Marx argued that in order to understand social order we must include analysis of
   a. anomie.
   b. ownership of the means of production.
   c. the sociological imagination.
   d. microsociology.

7. Which sociologist made a major contribution to society through his in-depth studies of urban life, including both Blacks and Whites?
   a. W.E.B. Du Bois
   b. Robert Merton
   c. Auguste Comte
   d. Charles Horton Cooley

8. What is the sociological term for the loss of direction felt in a society when social control of individual behavior has become ineffective?
   a. suicide
   b. alienation
   c. anomie
   d. agency

9. Thinking of society as a living organism in which each part of the organism contributes to its survival is a reflection of which theoretical perspective?
   a. the functionalist perspective
   b. the conflict perspective
   c. the feminist perspective
   d. the interactionist perspective

10. The career path with the specific intent of altering social relationships or restructuring organizations is known as
    a. dramaturgical sociology.
    b. applied sociology.
    c. academic sociology.
    d. clinical sociology.

1 (c); 2 (d); 3 (a); 4 (b); 5 (b); 6 (b); 7 (a); 8 (c); 9 (a); 10 (d)

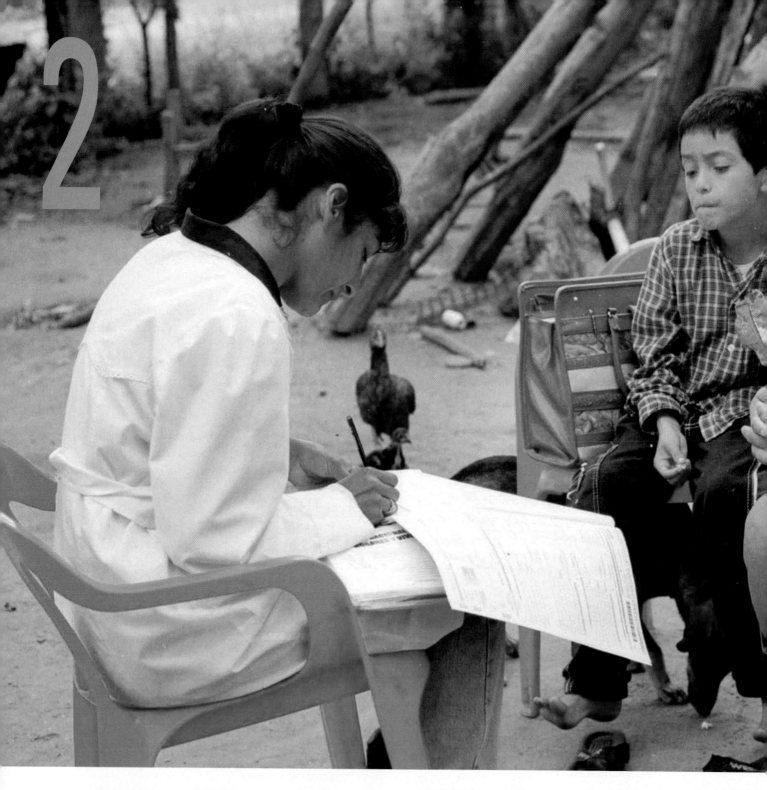

2

SOCIOLOG

ASKING QUESTIONS AND FINDING ANSWERS

Part of the fun of sociology is asking questions and finding answers, and sociologists Patricia and Peter Adler seem to have had more fun than most. Their search to understand our social lives has led them to spend extended periods of time with college athletes, drug dealers, school kids, Hawaiian resort workers, graduate students, self-injurers, and others. In each such study their underlying sociological commitment has remained the same: to answer the questions "Why do we think the way we think?" and "Why do we act the way we act?"

To better understand the tourism industry, for example, the Adlers spent eight years gathering information at five Hawaiian hotels, studying the staff and operations in minute detail (Adler and Adler 2004). This allowed them to better understand how tourist experiences are scripted (including the ceremonial lei provided upon arrival) and the significance of race, ethnicity, and social class when it comes to access to resources (including the kinds of jobs available to new immigrants such as Filipinos, Samoans, and Vietnamese).

Similarly, in their effort to better understand self-injury—including self-cutting, burning, branding, biting, and bone-breaking—the Adlers conducted lengthy, emotionally intense interviews with self-injurers over a six-year period, becoming friends with many. "Rather than remaining strictly detached from our subjects," they write, "we became involved in their lives, helping them and giving voice to their experiences and beliefs" (2007:542).

In other studies they found that college athletes go to big-time college sports schools with the best of intentions to be good students but get worn down by the obligations of being an athlete, and resign themselves to inferior academic performance (Adler and Adler 1985).

As is the case with all good sociological research, such studies seek to tell our stories and help us to understand ourselves in light of our interdependence. Sociologists such as the Adlers systematically gather our stories together through research and make sense of them with theory.

ICAL RESEARCH

As You READ >>

- What steps do sociologists take when seeking to answer why people think and act the way they do?
- What techniques do sociologists use to collect data?
- What ethical concerns must sociologists consider while conducting research?

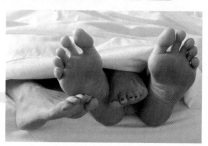

>> Steps in the Research Process

Sociology at its core represents a conversation between theory and research. Sociologists seek to describe and explain the patterns and practices of our lives through systematic investigation of what we do and why. If we want to know why people think and act the way they do, we need to know more about what they actually think and do. We need to observe them, ask them questions, participate

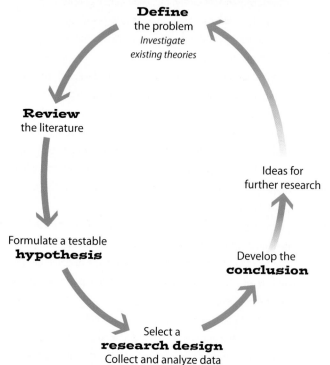

The Scientific Method

Define
the problem
Investigate existing theories

Review
the literature

Formulate a testable **hypothesis**

Select a
research design
Collect and analyze data
Survey • Observation • Experiment • Existing sources

Develop the
conclusion

Ideas for
further research

in their lives, or in other ways come to understand their experiences from their perspective. We cannot sit back and guess.

Sociology inherits this commitment in part from early attempts by some sociologists to emulate the scientific method. The **scientific method** is a systematic, organized series of steps that ensures maximum objectivity and consistency in researching a problem. Although not all sociologists today would tie the task of sociology as strongly to the natural science model, the commitment to making sense of the world through engagement with the world remains.

Conducting sociological research in the spirit of the scientific method requires adherence to a series of steps designed to ensure the accuracy of the results. Sociologists and other researchers follow five basic steps in the scientific method: (1) defining the problem, (2) reviewing the literature, (3) formulating the hypothesis, (4) selecting the research design and then collecting and analyzing data, and (5) developing the conclusion (see the figure at left). To better understand the process, we will follow an example about the relationship between education and income from start to finish.

DEFINING THE PROBLEM

Does it "pay" to go to college? Many people make great sacrifices and work hard to get a college degree. Parents borrow money for their children's tuition. Students work part-time or even take full-time jobs while attending evening or weekend classes. Does it pay off? Are there sufficient monetary returns for getting that degree?

The first step in any research project is to state as clearly as possible what you hope to investigate—that is, to define the problem. Typically, this means explicitly identifying both the concepts we are interested in learning more about and the nature of the relationship we suspect might exist between those concepts. In our example, we are interested in knowing if increased education influences economic position.

In defining the problem, we draw on existing theories about why people think and act the way they do. These theories might be fairly simple and tentative guesses about the relationships, or they might be more elaborate and fully formed, such as we saw in the works of Karl Marx, Max Weber, and Émile Durkheim. For example, Durkheim developed a prediction regarding suicide based on his theory that social integration influences individual action, and he set about to test this theory using social research. Through research we seek to assess and refine our theories so that the explanations and descriptions of the world we get through sociology are fuller and more complete, more accurately reflecting both the simplicity and the complexity of human behavior.

Several competing theories exist concerning the relationship between education and income. One approach states that society needs people to develop their skills in order for society to realize its full potential, so it rewards those who make the sacrifices necessary to develop those skills through education. Another theory states that education does not so much provide opportunity as reinforce the existing system of inequality by providing the illusion of opportunity. In this theory, people more or less end up in the same economic position in which they began their educational journey. Which theory we start with will shape the kind of data we collect. We will look into both of these theories about education in a later chapter, but for the purpose of our example, we will focus on the first.

Often the concepts in our theories are too general or abstract to study in a systematic fashion. In order to investigate those concepts, we need to move from the abstract to the concrete. To do so, social science researchers develop an operational definition of each concept being studied. An **operational definition** transforms an abstract concept into indicators that are observable and measurable, allowing researchers to assess the concept. For example, a sociologist interested in status might use membership in exclusive social clubs as an operational definition of status. Someone studying religiosity might consider the frequency of a person's participation in religious services or the amount of time spent in prayer or meditation as an operational definition of how religious the person is. In our example, we need operational definitions for both education and earnings. Although we could argue that education involves more than just years of schooling completed, it is conventional to operationalize it that way. Similarly, income is conventionally operationalized as the total income an individual reports having received in the last year.

scientific method A systematic, organized series of steps that ensures maximum objectivity and consistency in researching a problem.
operational definition Transformation of an abstract concept into indicators that are observable and measurable.

REVIEWING THE LITERATURE

The next phase of research involves a review of the literature: investigating previous research conducted by sociologists and others regarding the concepts we wish to study. Analyzing how others have studied these concepts allows researchers to refine the problem under study, clarify possible techniques for collecting data, and eliminate or reduce avoidable mistakes. An excellent place to start such research is the many sociological journals that regularly publish articles in which sociologists carefully document their findings. (See the "Finding Information" table on page 24 for more useful tips.)

In our example, we would need to seek out existing research about the relationship between education and income. In that literature we would find significant evidence

Begin with material you already have, including this text and others.

Check out Wikipedia, which can be a good place to start by pointing toward other materials, but don't stop there.

When using the Internet, consider the source; always doublecheck claims with a reputable source or organization.

Use newspapers.

Search using computerized periodical indexes to find related academic journal articles.

Use the library catalog.

Examine government documents (including the U.S. Census).

Contact people, organizations, and agencies related to your topic.

Consult with your instructor, teaching assistant, or reference librarian.

that the two are linked. We would also learn that other factors besides years of schooling influence earning potential. For example, a person's occupational category (such as plumber, tool-and-die worker, secretary, or professor) might shape her or his income in a way different than just educational level alone. We also find that additional background factors such as class, gender, and race affect income. For example, the children of rich parents are more likely to go to college than those from modest backgrounds, so we might consider the possibility that the same parents may later help their children secure better-paying jobs. This might lead us to consider adding additional concepts to our definition of the problem.

hypothesis A testable statement about the relationship between two or more variables.

cal theorists, we would next formulate our hypothesis. A **hypothesis** is more than just an educated guess; it is a testable statement about the relationship between two or more factors known as variables. Income, religion, occupation, and gender can all serve as variables in a study. We can define a **variable** as a measurable trait or characteristic that is subject to change under different conditions.

By formulating a hypothesis, we are trying to explain why something happens. In doing so, we must clearly define the potential variables that in-

Did You Know?

... U.S. government agencies regularly release reports with information on income, education, poverty, and health care. According to the Census Bureau, median household income in 2007 was $50,233. According to the U.S. Department of Education, of people ages 25–29, 86.1 percent had received their high school diploma or equivalent, and 27.4 percent had earned a bachelor's degree or more.

FORMULATING THE HYPOTHESIS

After reviewing earlier studies and drawing on the contributions of sociologi-

fluence the event we want to explain. This assumes that **causal logic,** the relationship between a variable and a particular event in which one leads to the other, is at work. Durkheim, for example, wanted to explain why people commit suicide, and he hypothesized that social integration is a powerful factor. In our example we are suggesting that increased education leads to higher income.

In hypotheses, the causal variable that brings about change is called the **independent variable.** The variable that is affected is known as the **dependent variable** because change in it depends on the influence of the independent variable. In other words, the researcher believes that the independent variable predicts or causes change in the dependent variable. For example, a researcher in sociology might anticipate that the availability of affordable housing (the independent variable; often referred to in equations as *x*) affects the level of homelessness in a community (the dependent variable; typically represented in equations as *y*).

We can put these pieces together to generate a generic hypothesis statement: knowledge of the independent variable (*x*) allows us to better explain or predict the value or position of the dependent variable (*y*). We could then place variables we are interested in studying, such as those in the figure to the right, into this statement to clearly present the nature of the relationships we expect to find between variables we wish to study.

Causal Logic

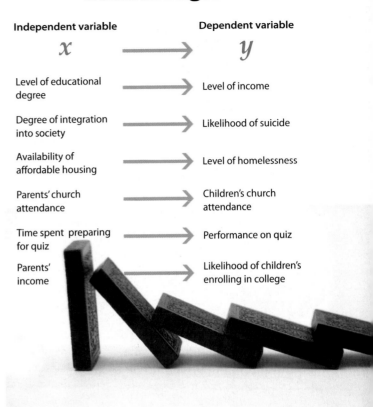

Independent variable	Dependent variable
x	y
Level of educational degree	Level of income
Degree of integration into society	Likelihood of suicide
Availability of affordable housing	Level of homelessness
Parents' church attendance	Children's church attendance
Time spent preparing for quiz	Performance on quiz
Parents' income	Likelihood of children's enrolling in college

SOCthink

> > > What independent variables do you think would best explain college grade point average (GPA)? To what extent do you think each of the independent variables listed in the figure "Causal Logic" would contribute to explaining GPA performance?

In our example, our hypothesis suggests that knowing how many years of schooling a person has completed will allow us to better predict how much money he or she will earn. Our independent variable is the level of education, and income is the dependent variable. Further, we expect that this relationship will be positive, meaning the higher a person's educational attainment, the more money she or he will make.

When interpreting results, however, we need to distinguish between correlation and causation. A **correlation** is a relationship between two variables in which a change in one coincides with a change in the other. Just because variables change in a way that appears related does not mean that the relationship is necessarily causal. For example, research shows that the source individuals use to get their news influences how knowledgeable they are. Those who watch television news are less knowledgeable than those who read newspapers and newsmagazines. The

correlation between the two variables is actually caused by a third variable, people's training in processing large amounts of information. People with poor reading skills are much more likely than others to get their news from television, whereas those who are more educated or skilled turn more often to the print media. Thus, although television viewing is correlated with lower news comprehension, it does not *cause* it. Correlation does not equal causation. Sociologists seek to identify the *causal* link between variables; the suspected causal link is generally described in the hypothesis (Neuman 2006).

variable A measurable trait or characteristic that is subject to change under different conditions.
causal logic The relationship between a condition or variable and a particular consequence with one event leading to the other.
independent variable The variable in a causal relationship that causes or influences a change in a second variable.
dependent variable The variable in a causal relationship that is subject to the influence of another variable.
correlation A relationship between two variables in which a change in one coincides with a change in the other.

COLLECTING AND ANALYZING DATA

To assess their hypotheses, sociologists, like all scientists, collect data. There are a variety of ways, known as research designs, that sociologists go about doing this, including surveys, observation, experiments, and use of existing data. Because the design selected is so critical to the research process, we will go into greater depth about each of those research designs later in this chapter. For now we will focus on some key issues that you must address regardless of which research design you select.

Selecting the Sample Sociologists cannot study everybody, so they seek ways to select individuals and groups that are representative of the population that is the subject of the research. In most large-scale studies, social scientists carefully choose what is known as a **sample**—a selection from a larger population that is statistically representative of that population. There are many kinds of samples, but the one social scientists use most frequently is the random sample. In a **random sample,** every member of the entire population being studied has the same chance of being selected. Thus, if researchers want to examine the opinions of people listed in a city directory (a book that, unlike the telephone directory, lists all households), they might use a computer to randomly select names from the directory. The results would constitute a random sample. The advantage of using specialized sampling techniques is that sociologists can be confident that the results they obtain will be representative of the larger population, freeing them from having to question everyone in the population (Igo 2007).

It is all too easy to confuse the careful scientific techniques used in representative sampling with the many nonscientific polls that receive so much more media attention. For example, television viewers are often encouraged to "visit our website and express your views" in an online poll

sample A selection from a larger population that is statistically representative of that population.
random sample A sample for which every member of an entire population has the same chance of being selected.

about headline news or political contests. Such polls reflect nothing more than the views of those who happened to see the television program and took the time to register their opinions. These data do not necessarily reflect (and indeed may distort) the views of the broader population. Not everyone has access to a television or radio, time to watch or listen to a program, or the means and/or inclination to vote in this way. Even when these techniques include answers from tens of thousands of people, they will be far less accurate than a carefully selected representative sample of 1500 respondents.

For the purposes of our research example of education and income, we will use information collected in the General Social Survey (GSS). Since 1972, the National Opinion Research Center (NORC) has conducted this national survey 26 times, most recently in 2006. In the GSS, administered in both English and Spanish, a representative sample of the adult population is interviewed in depth on a variety of topics. Our investigation of the relationship between education and income is based on analysis of the 4510 people interviewed in the 2006 GSS (Schaefer 2009).

Ensuring Validity and Reliability To have confidence in their findings, and in keeping with the scientific method, sociologists pursue research results that are both valid and reliable. **Validity** refers to the degree to which a measure or scale truly reflects the phenomenon under study. In our example, a valid measure of income would accurately represent how much money a person earned in a given year. Although income can be a touchy subject, various studies show that people are reasonably accurate in reporting how much money they earned in the most recent year. If a question is written unclearly, however, the resulting data might not be accurate. For example, respondents to an unclear question about income might report partial-year earnings or total household income (perhaps including their parents' or spouse's income as well as their own).

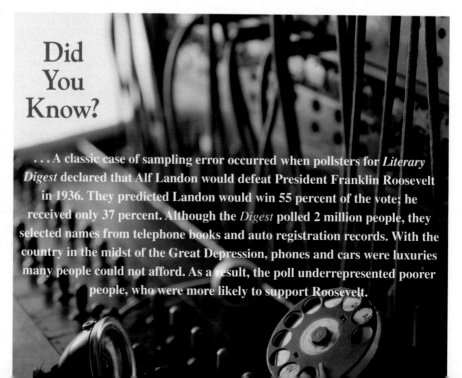

Did You Know?

...A classic case of sampling error occurred when pollsters for *Literary Digest* declared that Alf Landon would defeat President Franklin Roosevelt in 1936. They predicted Landon would win 55 percent of the vote; he received only 37 percent. Although the *Digest* polled 2 million people, they selected names from telephone books and auto registration records. With the country in the midst of the Great Depression, phones and cars were luxuries many people could not afford. As a result, the poll underrepresented poorer people, who were more likely to support Roosevelt.

Reliability refers to the extent to which a measure produces consistent results. Using the same instrument to collect data from the same people in similar circumstances should provide the same results. For example, if you give people the same questionnaire about income and education at two different times, unless something significant has changed between times, the responses should be the same.

DEVELOPING THE CONCLUSION

After conducting research, sociologists then assess their results. This can involve data entry, statistical testing, transcribing and coding interviews, and more, depending on the research method used. The key is to ensure that your conclusions are fully supported by your data.

Supporting Hypotheses In our example, we find that the data support our hypothesis: People with more formal schooling do earn more money than those with less schooling. Data consistently show that those with a high school diploma earn more than those who failed to complete high school, that those with some college earn more than do those with just a high school diploma, that those with a college degree earn still more, and on up the line so that those with graduate degrees earn the most. The figure below demonstrates this relationship. Those with a high school diploma or less have a very small portion of the high-income slice of the pie compared to those who have more education.

Of course, this is not true for all individuals. There are people who have a high school degree or less who end up with high incomes, and there are those with advanced degrees who earn modest incomes. A successful entrepreneur, for example, might not have much formal schooling, and a holder of a doctorate may choose to work for a low-paying, not-for-profit institution. Sociologically speaking, both these findings—that education shapes income and that the relationship is not perfect—are interesting and would likely lead to more questions about how and why such variation occurs.

SOCthink

> > > While education plays a significant role in explaining income, some people with minimal education earn high incomes, and some with advanced degrees earn relatively little. What additional social factors do you think might help to explain a person's income? What impact might a person's gender, race, ethnicity, religion, age, or social background have on income?

Sociological studies do not always generate data that support the original hypothesis. In many instances, the results refute the hypothesis, and researchers must reformulate their conclusions. This often leads to additional research in which sociologists reexamine their theory and methods, making appropriate changes in their research design.

validity The degree to which a measure or scale truly reflects the phenomenon under study.
reliability The extent to which a measure produces consistent results.
control variable A factor that is held constant to test the relative impact of an independent variable.

Controlling for Other Factors Given the complexity of human behavior, it is seldom sufficient to study only one independent and dependent variable. While such analyses can provide us with insight, we also need to consider other causal factors that might influence the dependent variable. One way to do this is to introduce a **control variable,** which is a factor that the researcher holds constant to test the relative impact of an independent variable. For example, if researchers wanted to explain neighborhood crime rates as a dependent variable, they might look at the neighborhood's poverty rate as an independent variable. It is likely, however, that additional factors influence crime rates, so they might introduce familiarity—the degree to which neighbors know and regularly interact with each other—as a control variable. They would find that neighborhoods with a high level of familiarity do have lower crime rates than those with low familiarity rates. The introduction of the control variable allows us to see that some of the variation in neighborhood crime rates

Impact of a College Education on Income

High school diploma or less

9%	$60,000 and over	31%
15%	$40,000–59,999	
24%		24%
21%	$25,000–39,999	19%
31%	$15,000–24,999	12%
	under $15,000	14%

Associate's degree or more

Source: Schaefer 2009.

Fifty-two percent of people with a high school diploma or less (left) earn under $25,000 a year, while only 26 percent earn $40,000 or more. In contrast, 55 percent of those with an associate's degree or higher (right) earn $40,000 or more, while only 26 percent earn less than $25,000.

that was initially assumed to be due to poverty is actually due to the influence of the control variable.

In our example, as we have already implied, we might want to control for the effect of additional variables that shape income. Not everyone enjoys equal educational opportunities, a disparity linked to income inequality. We might ask: What impact does a person's race or gender have? Is a woman with a college degree likely to earn as much as a man with similar schooling? In later chapters, we will consider such additional factors and variables. That is, we will examine the impact that education has on income while controlling for variables such as gender and race.

SOCthink

> > > Sticking with education as our independent variable, what other dependent variables might we study to see the impact of education on society? What do we hope to get out of education both individually and collectively?

IN SUMMARY: THE RESEARCH PROCESS

We began with a general question about the relationship between education and income. By following the steps in the research process—defining the problem, reviewing the literature, formulating a hypothesis, collecting and analyzing data, and developing a conclusion—we were able to show that education does pay. One of the ways we can check the validity of our findings is to share them with sociologists, policy makers, and others in a public forum in the form of a paper at a professional conference or an article in a refereed academic journal. By exposing what we did, how we did it, and what we found, others can serve as a useful check to make sure we did not miss anything and that we proceeded in an appropriate manner.

Research is cyclical in nature. At the end of the process, researchers almost always find that they have more questions they would like to pursue, and most research papers include a specific section addressing how they might define the problem and carry out the research next time. Along the way, researchers may have discovered new concepts they should consider, better ways to ask questions to get the information they need, individuals or groups they should include in the study, or a whole host of other possibilities. In the end, the studies researchers produce become part of the literature review for the next project, whether theirs or someone else's.

research design A detailed plan or method for obtaining data scientifically.

survey A study, generally in the form of an interview or questionnaire, that provides researchers with information about how people think and act.

>> Major Research Designs

As we have seen, sociologists go about gathering and making sense of the stories of our lives in a variety of ways. Sometimes sociologists want to tell our larger collective story; other times they want to tell the stories of individuals and groups who are often left out of such large-scale accounts. Different research designs are available to tell these different types of stories. For example, large national surveys allow us to get a sense of the national mood about issues such as politics or religion, and statistics can give insight into where we stand in relationship to each other on such issues. To explore the stories of individuals, researchers may employ methods, such as observation, that emphasize more direct and personal interaction with their subjects.

Sociologists draw on a variety of research designs when considering how to collect their data. A **research design** is a detailed plan or method for obtaining data scientifically. Often a research design is based on the theories and hypotheses the researcher starts with (Merton 1948). The choice requires creativity and ingenuity because it directly influences both the cost of the project and the time needed to collect the data. As noted previously, research designs that sociologists regularly use to generate data include surveys, observation, experiments, and existing sources.

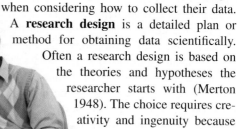

SURVEYS

Almost all of us have responded to surveys of one kind or another. We may have been asked what kind of detergent we use, which presidential candidate we intend to vote for, or what our favorite television program is. A **survey** is a study, generally in the form of an interview or questionnaire, that provides researchers with information about how people think and act. Among the United States' best-known opinion surveys are the Gallup poll and the Harris poll. As anyone who watches the news during presidential campaigns knows, these polls have become a staple of political life.

Issues in Designing Surveys As indicated earlier, a survey must be based on precise, representative sampling if it is to genuinely reflect a broad range of the population. We might be skeptical that feedback from just a few hundred people can provide an accurate picture of how 300 million people think, but correctly run surveys can do just that. When it comes to presidential polling, for example,

George W. Bush Approval Ratings:
Poll Results from Throughout His Presidency

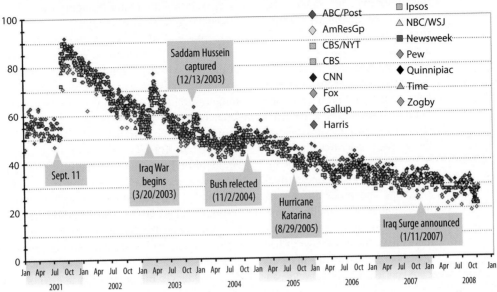

Legend:
- ◆ ABC/Post
- ◇ AmResGp
- ▢ CBS/NYT
- ▢ CBS
- ◆ CNN
- ◇ Fox
- ◇ Gallup
- ◇ Harris
- ▢ Ipsos
- △ NBC/WSJ
- ■ Newsweek
- ◆ Pew
- ◆ Quinnipiac
- △ Time
- ◇ Zogby

Chart annotations: Saddam Hussein captured (12/13/2003); Sept. 11; Iraq War begins (3/20/2003); Bush relected (11/2/2004); Hurricane Katarina (8/29/2005); Iraq Surge announced (1/11/2007)

Source:
www.pollkatz.homestead.com.

we can compare the results of such polls against actual election results. In a study of the historical accuracy of presidential polls, political scientist Michael W. Traugott (2005) reports that, based on one common measure of assessing results, the polls from 1956 to 2004 were, on average, within 2 percent of accurately predicting the final result. We can also get a sense of the accuracy of polls by looking at "polls of polls" that combine various results into a single report or graph to better see the pattern that the polls collectively demonstrate (see the figure above). Examples of such polls for presidential and congressional approval ratings are available at sites such as www.pollster.com. While the pollsters sometimes fail to "get it right" (for example, predicting that Dewey would defeat Truman in the 1948 presidential election), most often they do, and with amazing precision.

In addition to developing representative samples, sociologists must also exercise great care in the wording of questions. An effective survey question must be simple and clear enough for people to understand. It must also be specific enough that researchers have no problems interpreting the results. Open-ended questions ("What do you think

Going GLOBAL

Why Are We in Iraq?

Researchers can gather information even under difficult circumstances. In a 2006 nationwide survey in Iraq, Iraqis were asked about "the three main reasons for the U.S. invasion of Iraq." A large majority—76 percent—said the United States wanted "to control Iraqi oil." A sizable 41 percent thought the United States' intention was "to build military bases," and almost a third, 32 percent, thought it was "to help Israel." Fewer than 2 percent of the respondents thought the United States went to war "to bring democracy to Iraq."

of the programming on educational television?") must be carefully phrased to solicit the type of information desired. Surveys can be indispensable sources of information, but only if the sampling is done properly and the questions are worded accurately and without bias.

Studies have also shown that the characteristics of the interviewer have an impact on survey data. For example, female interviewers tend to receive more feminist responses from female subjects than do male researchers, and African American interviewers tend to receive more detailed responses about race-related issues from Black subjects than do White interviewers. The possible impact of gender and race indicates again how much care social research requires (D.W. Davis and Silver 2003).

Types of Surveys There are two main forms of the survey: the **interview,** in which a researcher obtains information through face-to-face or telephone questioning, and the **questionnaire,** in which a researcher uses a printed or written form to obtain information from a respondent. Each of these has its advantages. An interviewer can obtain a higher response rate because people find it more difficult to turn down a personal request for an interview than to throw away a written questionnaire. In addition, a skillful interviewer can go beyond written questions and probe for a subject's underlying feelings and reasons. For their part, questionnaires have the advantage of being cheaper, especially in large samples. Either way, what we can learn from surveys can be amazing.

Why, for example, do people have sex? A straightforward question, but until recently one that rarely was investigated scientifically, despite its significance to public health, marital counseling, and criminology. In an exploratory study published in 2007, researchers surveyed nearly 2000 undergraduates at the University of Texas at Austin. They began phase 1 of the research by asking approximately 400 students in a variety of psychology courses to answer this question: "Please list all the reasons you can think of why you, or someone you have known, has engaged in sexual intercourse in the past." The explanations were highly diverse, ranging from "I was drunk" to "I wanted to feel closer to God."

In phase 2 of the research, the team asked another sample of 1500 students to rate the importance of each of the 287 reasons given by the first group. Nearly every one of the reasons was rated most important by at least some respondents. Although there were some gender differences in the replies, there was significant consensus between men and women on the top 12 reasons (see the table below). Based on their overall results, the researchers identified four major categories of reasons why people have sex: Physical (pleasure, stress reduction), Goal Attainment (social status, revenge), Emotional (love, commitment), and Insecurity (self-esteem boost, duty/pressure) (Meston and Buss 2007). After reviewing the study results, critics argued that the researchers' sample was not sufficiently representative to permit generalizing their findings to the population as a whole. The researchers acknowledged as much from the beginning, having undertaken the project as exploratory research. They have since conducted research using a more representative sample, and their findings were largely the same (Melby 2007).

Quantitative and Qualitative Research Surveys most often represent an example of **quantitative research,** which collects and reports data primarily in numerical form. Analysis of these data depends upon statistics, from the simple to the complex, which provide basic summaries describing what variables look like and how they are related. Basic descriptive statistics, such as percentages, are likely familiar. The **mean,** or average, is a number calculated by adding a series of values and then dividing by the number of values. The **median,** or midpoint, is the number that divides a series of values into two groups of equal numbers of values. The median is most often used when there are extreme scores that would distort the mean. The **mode** is the single most common value in a series of scores and is seldom used in sociological research. The mean, median, and mode all seek to provide a single score that is representative of or provides a summary for the whole distribution of scores. When it comes to analyzing relationships between variables, researchers usually rely on computer programs to deal with more complex analysis of quantitative data.

While quantitative research can make use of large samples, it can't offer great depth and detail on a topic. That is why researchers also make use of **qualitative research,** which relies on what they see in field and naturalistic settings, often focusing on small groups and communities rather than on large groups or whole nations. Here, too, sociologists rely on computers to assist their analysis. Numerous software programs allow researchers not only to record observations but to identify common themes, con-

interview A face-to-face or telephone questioning of a respondent to obtain desired information.

questionnaire A printed or written form used to obtain information from a respondent.

quantitative research Research that collects and reports data primarily in numerical form.

mean A number calculated by adding a series of values and then dividing by the number of values.

median The midpoint, or number that divides a series of values into two groups of equal numbers of values.

Top 12 Reasons Why Men and Women Had Sex

Men	Reason	Women
1	I was attracted to the person	1
2	It feels good	3
3	I wanted to experience the physical pleasure	2
4	It's fun	8
5	I wanted to show my affection to the person	4
6	I was sexually aroused and wanted the release	6
7	I was "horny"	7
8	I wanted to express my love for the person	5
9	I wanted to achieve an orgasm	14
10	I wanted to please my partner	11
17	I realized I was in love	9
13	I was "in the heat of the moment"	10

Source: Meston and Buss 2007:506.

Research is formalized curiosity. It is poking and prying with a purpose.

Zora Neale Hurston

cepts, or concerns expressed in interviews. The most common form of qualitative research is observation.

OBSERVATION

Investigators who collect information by participating directly and/or by closely watching a group or community are engaged in **observation.** This method allows sociologists to examine behaviors and communities in greater depth than is possible using other methods. Though observation may seem a relatively informal method compared to surveys, researchers are careful to take detailed notes while observing their subjects.

An increasingly popular form of qualitative research in sociology today is **ethnography**—the study of an entire social setting through extended systematic observation. Typically, the emphasis is on how the subjects themselves view their social life in some setting. In some cases, the sociologist actually joins the group for a period to get an accurate sense of how it operates. This approach is called *participant observation.*

During the late 1930s, in a classic example of participant observation research, William F. Whyte moved into a low-income Italian neighborhood in Boston. For nearly four years, he was a member of the social circle of "corner boys" whom he described in his classic book *Street Corner Society.* Whyte revealed his identity to these men and joined in their conversations, bowling, and other leisure-time activities. His goal was to gain greater insight into the community that these men had established. As Whyte ([1943] 1981:303) listened to Doc, the leader of the group, he "learned the answers to questions that I would not even have had the sense to ask if I had been getting my information solely on an interviewing basis." Whyte's work was especially valuable since, at the time, the academic world had little direct knowledge of the poor and tended to rely for information on the records of social service agencies, hospitals, and courts (P. Adler, Adler, and Johnson 1992).

The initial challenge that Whyte faced—and that every participant observer encounters—was to gain acceptance into an unfamiliar group. It is no simple matter for a college-trained sociologist to win the trust of a religious cult, a youth gang, a poor Appalachian community, or a circle of skid row residents. It requires a great deal of patience and an accepting, nonthreatening type of personality on the part of the observer.

Observation research poses other complex challenges for investigators. Sociologists must be able to fully understand what they are observing. In a sense, then, researchers

mode The single most common value in a series of scores.
qualitative research Research that relies on what is seen in field or naturalistic settings more than on statistical data.
observation A research technique in which an investigator collects information through direct participation and/or by closely watching a group or community.
ethnography The study of an entire social setting through extended systematic observation.

must learn to see the world as the group sees it in order to fully comprehend the events taking place around them.

SOCthink

> > > What social group or setting (such as a religious group, political organization, sorority/fraternity, laboratory, or office) might you want to learn more about through in-depth participant observation? How would you go about making contact? How would you gain members' trust?

This raises a delicate issue. If the research is to be successful, the observer cannot allow the close associations or even friendships that inevitably develop to influence the subjects' behavior or the conclusions of the study. Anson Shupe and David Bromley (1980), two sociologists who have used participant observation, have likened this challenge to that of walking a tightrope. Even while working hard to gain acceptance from the group being studied, the participant observer *must* maintain some degree of detachment.

Recently, the issue of detachment became a controversial one for social scientists embedded with the U.S. military in Afghanistan and Iraq. Among other studies, researchers participated in the creation of the Army's Human Terrain System, a $4-million effort to identify the customs, kinship structures, and internal social conflicts in the two countries. The intention was to provide military leaders with information that would help them make better decisions. Although the idea of scholars cooperating in any way with soldiers struck many social science researchers as inappropriate, others countered that the information they developed would help the military to avoid needless violence and might even facilitate the withdrawal of troops from the region (Glenn 2007).

experiment An artificially created situation that allows a researcher to manipulate variables.

experimental group The subjects in an experiment who are exposed to an independent variable introduced by a researcher.

control group The subjects in an experiment who are not introduced to the independent variable by the researcher.

Hawthorne effect The unintended influence that observers of experiments can have on their subjects.

secondary analysis A variety of research techniques that make use of previously collected and publicly accessible information and data.

EXPERIMENTS

When scientists want to study a possible cause-and-effect relationship, they conduct an **experiment**—an artificially created situation that allows a researcher to manipulate variables. Researchers carefully control the experimental context in order to measure the degree to which the independent variable causes change in the dependent variable

From Me to You

Students in my sociology of religion course must conduct a semester-long research project on a religious group that is unlike their own. Combining observation and interviews, they must visit the group's religious services numerous times and meet with both leaders and followers. Initially, students are nervous about making first contact, concerned about what kind of people they might find, and worried that the group will try to convert them. By the end, however, they typically come away with a sense of respect for the believers, glad to have had the opportunity to get to know them. While research can seem scary, give it a try. It provides a pathway to greater knowledge and understanding.

under study. Although experiments can prove insightful, sociologists tend not to use them as frequently as the other research designs, because they are typically more interested in understanding people's natural responses.

In a classic experiment, researchers begin by dividing subjects with similar characteristics into two groups in order to see the impact of one independent variable. The **experimental group** is then exposed to an independent variable; the **control group** is not. Thus, if scientists were testing a new type of antibiotic, they would administer the drug to an experimental group but not to a control group.

One of the disadvantages of experiments, just as in observation research, is that the presence of a social scientist or other observer may affect the behavior of the people being studied. The recognition of this phenomenon grew out

SOCthink

> > > Imagine you are a researcher interested in the effect TV watching has on schoolchildren's grades. How might you go about setting up an experiment to measure this effect?

of an experiment conducted during the 1920s and 1930s at the Hawthorne plant of the Western Electric Company. A group of researchers set out to determine how to improve the productivity of workers at the plant. The investigators manipulated such variables as lighting and working hours to see what impact the changes would have on how much workers produce. To their surprise, they found that every step they took seemed to increase output. Even measures that seemed likely to have the opposite effect, such as reducing the amount of lighting in the plant, led to higher productivity.

Why did the plant's employees work harder even under less favorable conditions? The researchers concluded that the worker's modified their behavior because they knew they were being studied. They responded positively to the novelty of being subjects in an experiment and to the fact that researchers were interested in them. Since that time, sociologists have used the term **Hawthorne effect** to describe the unintended influence that observers of experiments can have on their subjects (Brannigan and Zwerman 2001). It highlights the difficulties experiments present in seeking to understand how people behave in their real-world environments.

Sociologists do sometimes try to approximate experimental conditions in the field. Sociologist Devah Pager (2003) devised an experiment to assess the impact of a criminal background on individuals' employment opportunities. She sent four polite, well-dressed young men out to look for an entry-level job in Milwaukee, Wisconsin. All four were 23-year-old college students, but they presented themselves as high school graduates with similar job histories. Two of the men were Black and two were White. One Black applicant and one White applicant claimed to have served 18 months in jail for a fel-

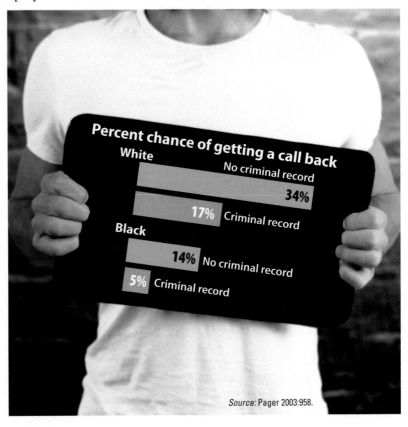

White Privilege in Job Seeking

Percent chance of getting a call back
White
No criminal record
34%
17% Criminal record
Black
14% No criminal record
5% Criminal record

Source: Pager 2003:958.

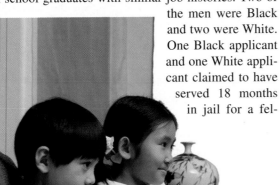

ony conviction—possession of cocaine with intent to distribute.

The experiences of the four men with 350 potential employers were vastly different. The White applicant with a purported prison record received only half as many callbacks as the other White applicant—17 percent compared to 34 percent (see the graphic above). But as dramatic as the effect of his criminal record was, the effect of his race was more significant. Despite his prison record, he received slightly more callbacks than the Black applicant with no criminal record (17 percent compared to 14 percent). Race, it seems, was more of a concern to potential employers than a criminal background.

USE OF EXISTING SOURCES

Sociologists do not necessarily need to collect new data in order to conduct research and test hypotheses. The term **secondary analysis** refers to a variety of research techniques that make use of previously collected and publicly accessible information and data. Generally, in conducting secondary analysis, researchers use data in ways that were unintended by the initial collectors of the informa-

What's in a Name?

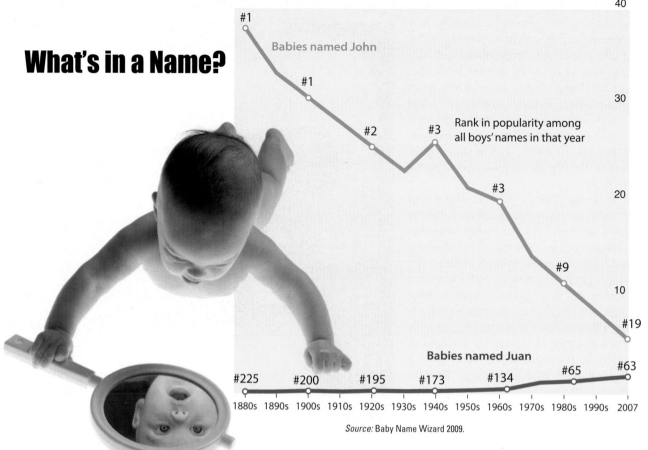

Number of babies (thousands)

Babies named John

Rank in popularity among all boys' names in that year

#1
#1
#2
#3
#3
#9
#19

Babies named Juan

#225   #200   #195   #173   #134   #65   #63

1880s 1890s 1900s 1910s 1920s 1930s 1940s 1950s 1960s 1970s 1980s 1990s 2007

40
30
20
10

Source: Baby Name Wizard 2009.

SOCthink

> > > "NameVoyager" at www.babynamewizard.com is a very cool application that allows you to type in any name to trace its popularity over time. Go there and enter several names to see how they have changed over time. Considering some of the specific names you tried, what factors might have contributed to their rise and fall? How popular is your first name? How and why has its popularity changed over time?

tion. For example, the federal government compiles census data for its own specific uses, but marketing specialists also find the data valuable for locating everything from bicycle stores to nursing homes (Weiss 2000).

Sociologists can learn a great deal using available information. For example, every year the Social Security Administration receives thousands of registrations for newborn babies. Using these data, we can recognize shifts in cultural trends in the population. As the figure "What's in a Name?" shows, for example, John has been an extremely popular boy's name for over a century. In 2007, over 5000 babies were named John, making it the 20th most popular name that year. Though only about half as many babies were named Juan in 2006, that name has been gaining in popularity in recent generations, reflect-

Major Research Designs

Method	Examples	Advantages	Limitations
Survey	Questionnaires Interviews	Yields information about specific issues	Can be expensive and time-consuming
Observation	Ethnography	Yields detailed information about specific groups or organizations	Involves months if not years of labor-intensive data collection
Experiment	Deliberate manipulation of people's social behavior	Yields direct measures of people's behavior	Has ethical limitations on the degree to which subjects' behavior can be manipulated
Existing sources/ Secondary analysis	Analysis of census or health data Analysis of films or TV commercials	Cost-efficiency; nonreactive	Limited to data collected for some other purpose

In examining these sources, researchers employ a technique known as **content analysis**—the systematic coding and objective recording of data, guided by a given rationale.

Using content analysis, Erving Goffman (1979) conducted a pioneering exploration of how advertisements portray women. The ads he studied typically showed women as subordinate to or dependent on others, or as taking instruction from men. Women engaged in caressing and touching gestures more than men. Even when presented in leadership roles, women were likely to be shown striking seductive poses or gazing out into space (Kilbourne 2000).

content analysis The systematic coding and objective recording of data, guided by some rationale.

You can observe a lot by just watching.

Yogi Berra

ing the growing impact of the Latino population in the United States.

Existing data from another source confirms this shift. Analysis of data released by the U.S. Census Bureau tracking people's family names in 2007 revealed that although Smith remained the most common surname in the United States, Garcia and Rodriguez had risen into the top 10. The announcement marked the first time in the nation's history that a non-Anglo name had been counted among the most common names. Such name changes reflect an overall shift in the U.S. population from a nation comprised primarily of European descendants to one that is more globally diverse, a trend sociologists expect will continue (Baby Name Wizard 2009; Levitt and Dubner 2005; Word et al. 2007).

Part of the appeal of secondary analysis to sociologists is that it is nonreactive—that is, doing this type of study does not influence what you find. For example, Émile Durkheim's statistical analysis of existing suicide data neither increased nor decreased human self-destruction. Researchers, then, can avoid the Hawthorne effect by using secondary analysis. However, there is one inherent problem: The researcher who relies on data collected by someone else may not find exactly what he or she needs. Social scientists who are studying family violence can use statistics from police and social service agencies on reported cases of spouse abuse and child abuse, but how many cases are not reported? Government bodies have no precise data on all cases of abuse.

Secondary analysis also allows us to study social contexts, both present and past, through careful analysis of cultural, economic, and political documents, including newspapers, periodicals, radio and television tapes, the Internet, scripts, diaries, songs, folklore, and legal papers.

Today researchers who analyze film content are finding an increase in smoking in motion pictures, despite heightened public health concerns (American Lung Association 2003). Research studying television programs demonstrates that sexual content on TV continues to rise (see the figure on next page). Other researchers have found a grow-

Percentage of Television Shows That Contain Sexual Content

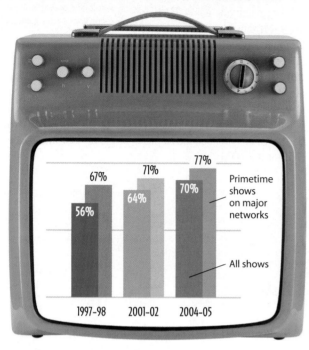

Primetime shows on major networks

All shows

67%
56%
71%
64%
77%
70%

1997-98 2001-02 2004-05

Source: Kaiser Family Foundation 2005:4.

Sociologists Stephen J. Scanlan and Seth L. Feinberg suggest that we can better understand key sociological concepts by analyzing the *The Simpsons.* One example they provide, among many, is the episode "Lisa vs. Malibu Stacy," in which eight-year-old Lisa is outraged because her talking doll says things like, "Let's buy makeup so the boys will like us." They say this raises sociological issues related to gender socialization, inequality, consumerism, and more. Additional issues raised in other episodes include social class, deviance, education, marriage and family, and religion. What might we learn about society by analyzing popular culture through the lens of sociology?

ing difference in the way men and women use sexually explicit language. For example, an analysis of the lyrics of *Billboard* magazine's top 100 hits indicates that, since 1958, male artists have increased their use of such language while female artists have decreased theirs (Dukes et al. 2003). In all such cases, content analysis allows us a better understanding of our cultural practices.

>> Research Ethics

A biochemist cannot inject a drug into a human being unless the drug has been thoroughly tested and the subject agrees to the shot. To do otherwise would be both unethical and illegal. Sociologists, too, must abide by certain specific standards in conducting research, called a **code of ethics.** The professional society of the discipline, the American Sociological Association (ASA), first published its *Code of Ethics* in 1971 and revised it most recently in 1997. It puts forth the following basic principles:

Content analysis of popular song lyrics shows that over the last 50 years, top female artists such as Beyoncé Knowles have used fewer sexually explicit words, while male artists like Jay-Z have used more.

- Maintain objectivity and integrity in research.
- Respect the subject's right to privacy and dignity.
- Protect subjects from personal harm.
- Preserve confidentiality.
- Seek informed consent when data are collected from research participants or when behavior occurs in a private context.
- Acknowledge research collaboration and assistance.
- Disclose all sources of financial support.

Because most sociological research uses people as sources of information—as respondents to survey questions, subjects of observation, or participants in experiments—these principles are important.

CONFIDENTIALITY

In all cases, sociologists need to be certain they are not invading their subjects' privacy. Generally, they do so by assuring subjects of anonymity or by guaranteeing the confidentiality of personal information. In addition, research proposals that involve human subjects are now subject to oversight by a review board, whose members seek to ensure that the research does not place subjects at an unreasonable level of risk. If necessary, the board may ask researchers to revise their research designs to conform to the *Code of Ethics*.

These basic principles and procedures may seem clear-cut in the abstract but can be difficult to adhere to in practice. For example, should a sociologist who is engaged in participant observation research always protect the confidentiality of subjects? What if the subjects are members of a group involved in unethical or illegal activities? What if the sociologist is interviewing political activists and is questioned by government authorities about the research?

Like journalists, sociologists occasionally find themselves facing the ethical dilemma of whether to reveal their sources to law enforcement authorities. In May 1993, sociologist Rik Scarce was jailed for contempt of court because he declined to tell a federal grand jury what he knew—or even whether he knew anything—about a 1991 raid on a university research laboratory by animal rights activists. At the time, Scarce was doing research for a book about environmental protestors and knew at least one suspect in the break-in. Although he was chastised by a federal judge, Scarce won respect from fellow prison inmates, who regarded him as a man who "wouldn't snitch" (Monaghan 1993:A8).

Hot or Not?

Should researchers sometimes deceive subjects, even if it might result in their emotional harm, in order to get more genuine responses?

The ASA, in defense of the principle of confidentiality, supported Scarce's position when he appealed his sentence. Scarce maintained his silence. Ultimately, the judge ruled that nothing would be gained by further incarceration, and Scarce was released after spending 159 days in jail. The U.S. Supreme Court ultimately declined to hear Scarce's case on appeal. The Court's failure to consider his case led Scarce (1994, 1995, 2005) to argue that federal legislation is needed to clarify the right of scholars and members of the press to preserve the confidentiality of those they interview.

RESEARCH FUNDING

An additional concern of the ASA's *Code of Ethics* is the possibility that funding sources could influence research findings. Accepting funds from a private organization or even a government agency that stands to benefit from a study's results can clash with the ASA's first principle of maintaining objectivity and integrity in research. As such, all sources of funding should be disclosed. The previously mentioned controversy surrounding the involvement of social scientists in the U.S. Army's Human Terrain System is one example of this conflict of interest.

> code of ethics The standards of acceptable behavior developed by and for members of a profession.

Another example is the Exxon Corporation's support for research on jury verdicts. On March 24, 1989, the Exxon oil tanker *Valdez* hit a reef off the coast of Alaska, spilling over 11 million gallons of oil into Prince William Sound. Two decades later, the *Valdez* disaster is still regarded as the world's worst oil spill in terms of its environmental impact. In 1994, a federal court ordered Exxon to pay $5.3 billion in damages for the accident. Exxon appealed the verdict and began approaching legal scholars, sociologists, and psychologists who might be willing to study jury deliberations. The corporation's objective was to develop academic support for its lawyers' contention that the punitive judgments in such cases result from faulty deliberations and do not deter future incidents.

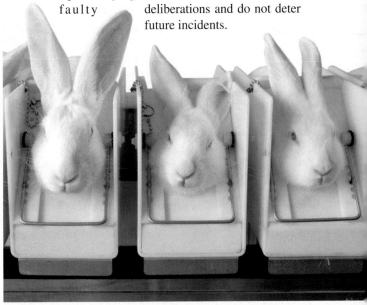

Some scholars have questioned the propriety of accepting funds under these circumstances, even if the source is disclosed. The scholars who accepted Exxon's support deny that it influenced their work or changed their conclusions. To date, Exxon has spent roughly $1 million on the research, and at least one compilation of studies congenial to the corporation's point of view has been published. As ethical considerations require, the academics who conducted the studies disclosed Exxon's role in funding the research. In 2006, drawing on these studies, Exxon's law-

Some sociologists believe that such neutrality is impossible. They worry that Weber's insistence on value-free sociology may lead the public to accept sociological conclusions without exploring researchers' biases. Others have suggested that sociologists may use objectivity as a justification for remaining uncritical of existing institutions and centers of power (Gouldner 1970). Despite the early work of W.E.B. Du Bois and Jane Addams, for example, sociologists still need to be reminded that the discipline often fails to adequately consider all people's social behavior.

> **If we knew what it was we were doing, it would not be called research, would it?**
>
> Albert Einstein

yers succeeded in persuading an appeals court to reduce the corporation's legal damages from $5.3 to $2.5 billion (Freudenburg 2005; Liptak 2008a, 2008b). Then, in 2008, the amount was reduced to a mere $500 million.

VALUE NEUTRALITY

The ethical considerations of sociologists lie not only in the methods they use and the funding they accept but in the way they interpret their results. Max Weber ([1904] 1949) recognized that personal values would influence the topics that sociologists select for research. In his view, that was perfectly acceptable, but he argued that researchers should not allow their personal feelings to influence the interpretation of data. In Weber's phrase, sociologists must practice **value neutrality** in their research.

value neutrality Max Weber's term for objectivity of sociologists in the interpretation of data.

As part of this neutrality, investigators have an ethical obligation to accept research findings even when the data run counter to their own personal views, to theoretically based explanations, or to widely accepted beliefs. For example, Émile Durkheim challenged popular conceptions when he reported that social (rather than supernatural) forces were an important factor in suicide.

Sociologists should not focus only on those in the majority but must also seek out the stories of those who are often invisible due to their relative lack of power and resources. In fact sociologists have learned much about society by listening to the voices of those who are excluded from mainstream sources of power and denied access to valuable resources. In her book *The Death of White Sociology* (1973), Joyce Ladner called attention to the tendency of mainstream sociologists to investigate the lives of African Americans only in the context of social problems. More recently, feminist sociologist Shulamit Reinharz (1992) has argued that sociological research should be not only inclusive but open to drawing on relevant research by nonsociologists who might provide additional depth and understanding of social life. The issue of value neutrality does not mean that sociologists can't have opinions, but it does mean that they must work to overcome any biases, however unintentional, that they may bring to their analysis of research.

FEMINIST METHODOLOGY

Although researchers must be objective, their theoretical orientation necessarily influences the questions they ask—or just as important, the questions they fail to ask. Because their contributions have opened up so many new lines of inquiry, sociologists using the feminist perspective have had perhaps the greatest impact on the current generation of social researchers. Until recently, for example, researchers frequently studied work and family separately, as if they were two discrete institutions. Feminist theorists, however, reject the notion that these are separate spheres. They were the first sociologists to look at housework as real work and to investigate the struggles people face in balancing the demands of work and family (Hochschild 1989; Lopata 1971).

Feminist theorists have also drawn attention to researchers' tendency to overlook women in sociological

SOCthink

> > > To what extent is it possible to maintain value neutrality when studying a social group with which you might disagree (such as White supremacists or convicted child molesters)? Why might sociologists choose to study such groups?

studies. For most of the history of sociology, researchers conducted studies of male subjects or male-led groups and organizations, then generalized their findings to all people. For many decades, for example, ethnographic studies of urban life focused on street corners, neighborhood taverns, and bowling alleys—places where men typically congregated. Although researchers gained valuable insights in this way, they did not form a true impression of city life, because they overlooked the areas where women were likely to gather, such as playgrounds, grocery stores, and front stoops. These are the arenas that the feminist perspective focuses on.

Feminist scholars have also contributed to a greater global awareness within sociology. To feminist theorists, the traditional distinction between industrial nations and developing countries overlooks the close relationship between these two supposedly separate worlds. Feminist theorists have called for more research on the special role that immigrant women play in maintaining their households, on the use of domestic workers from less developed nations by households in industrial countries, and on the global trafficking of sex workers (Cheng 2003; K. Cooper et al. 2007).

Finally, feminist researchers tend to involve and consult their subjects more than other researchers, contributing to a significant increase in more qualitative and participatory research. They are also more oriented toward seeking change, raising the public consciousness, and influencing policy, which represents a return to sociology's roots (Harding 2003; Naples 2003; Sprague 2005).

Sociologists must be engaged with the world. While there are numerous ways in which they accomplish this, first and foremost this involvement comes through research. As we have seen throughout this chapter, it is not enough for sociologists to stand back and theorize or even hypothesize about why we think and act the way we do. We must go out, collect data, and use it to inform our interpretations and explanations of human behavior. Having done so, we bear a responsibility for that knowledge, whether that means simply sharing it with other sociologists through conference presentations and journal articles or actively working for positive social change.

I. What steps do sociologists take when seeking to answer why people think and act the way they do?

- They need to define the problem, review existing literature, formulate a hypothesis, collect and analyze data, and develop a conclusion.

II. What techniques do they use to collect data?

- Research designs used to collect data include surveys, observation, experiments, and use of existing sources.

III. What ethical concerns must they consider while conducting research?

- They have a responsibility to follow the ASA *Code of Ethics*, particularly respecting confidentiality, revealing research funding, maintaining value neutrality, and overall, treating their subjects with respect.

Pop Quiz

1. The first step in any sociological research project is to
   a. collect data.
   b. define the problem.
   c. review previous research.
   d. formulate a hypothesis.

2. An explanation of an abstract concept that is specific enough to allow a researcher to measure the concept is a(n)
   a. hypothesis.
   b. correlation.
   c. operational definition.
   d. variable.

3. In sociological and scientific research, a hypothesis
   a. is an educated guess.
   b. is a testable statement about the relationship between two or more variables.
   c. insists that science can only deal with observable entities known directly to experience.
   d. ensures that the people being studied are representative of the population as a whole.

4. The variable hypothesized to cause or influence another is called the
   a. dependent variable.
   b. hypothetical variable.
   c. correlation variable.
   d. independent variable.

5. The degree to which a measure or scale truly reflects the phenomenon under study is known as
   a. reliability.
   b. sampling.
   c. validity.
   d. control.

6. Which research technique do sociologists use to ensure that data are statistically representative of the population being studied?
   a. sampling
   b. experiments
   c. correlation
   d. control variables

7. Ethnography is an example of which type of research design?
   a. surveys
   b. observation
   c. experiments
   d. use of existing resources

8. In the 1930s, William F. Whyte moved into a low-income Italian neighborhood in Boston. For nearly four years, he was a member of the social circle of "corner boys" whom he describes in *Street Corner Society*. His goal was to gain greater insight into the community established by these men. What type of research technique did Whyte use?
   a. experiment
   b. survey

1 (b); 2 (c); 3 (b); 4 (d); 5 (c); 6 (a); 7 (b):

c. secondary analysis

d. participant observation

9. The unintended influence that observers of experiments can have on their subjects is known as

   a. the correlation effect.

   b. confidentiality.

   c. validity.

   d. the Hawthorne effect.

10. According to Max Weber, researchers should not allow their personal feelings to influence the interpretation of data. He referred to this as

   a. the code of ethics.

   b. content analysis.

   c. value neutrality.

   d. secondary analysis.

3

CULTURE

BREAKING RULES AND LOWERING BARRIERS

Juan Mann was depressed. His fiancée had left him. His parents had just divorced. He had dropped out of college, and his friends had scattered. He felt all alone in the world. So on Wednesday, June 30, 2004, he decided to do something different. He took a homemade sign to the Pitt Street Mall in Sydney, Australia, that said "Free Hugs." Someone at a party had given him his first hug in a long time, and it had brightened his day. He figured that if he needed a hug like that more than he even knew, there were probably many other people out there feeling similarly isolated who might want one too. Every Thursday he would head back to the mall to offer more. Before long, with the help of a viral video on the Internet, Juan's "Free Hugs Campaign" went global with over 25 million views on YouTube alone. People were not just watching the video; in many countries and in many languages, they were making their own signs and heading out to a public place to offer hugs. (A YouTube or Google image search on "free hugs" will turn up the original video along with many other videos and images of people from around the world who were inspired by it.)

One of the interesting things about this movement is that it calls for us to go outside our comfort zones and act in ways that are not "normal." As children we are told not to talk to strangers, much less hug them. If we see a stranger offering a hug, we wonder if something suspicious is up. We have rules about such things—laws even. When people do things differently, we get nervous. It disrupts our sense of order. We want and need the actions of others to be predictable, so we create both formal and informal rules to guide our behaviors. Such rules are part of culture.

But culture is not set in stone. We create it, and we therefore have the power to change it. People doing new things, stepping outside the lines of expected behavior, is precisely how change happens. So, when confronted with the offer "Free Hugs," we face a choice: Act like the majority of people who pass free huggers by, thus reaffirming expected behaviors, or seize the opportunity to do the unexpected, thereby creating new pathways for us to follow. It is in such moments that new culture is born.

As You READ >>

- Why do humans create culture?
- What does culture consist of?
- How does culture both enable and constrain?

>> Culture and Society

We need culture. As humans, we lack the complex instincts other species are born with that enable them to survive. Unlike birds, for example, our genes do not provide us with the knowledge of how to build nests (or homes) for ourselves, and we lack the good sense to fly to warmer climates for the winter. In place of such instincts, we construct culture through which we establish relationships both to the natural world and with each other. **Culture** consists of the totality of our shared language, knowledge, material objects, and behavior.

culture The totality of our shared language, knowledge, material objects, and behavior.

Culture shapes our perception, knowledge, and understanding of the external world. While our senses experience the external world in a physical way, we must interpret the meaning and significance of those sensations. We do not perceive nature directly; we perceive the world around us through the lens of culture. Our retinas may send visual images to our brains, but recognition comes only through culture. We see this at work with optical illusions: We can look at the same thing over and over, but it is not until someone says to us, "No, look at it this way" that we recognize it.

SOCthink

> > > Sometimes we can see something over and over and still not recognize patterns until someone points them out (such as the arrow in the FedEx logo). What might this tell us about the importance of authorities for recognition?

Culture thus provides us with a kind of tool kit of habits, skills, and styles (Swidler 1986). It allows us to take for granted that others will understand what we mean, and it helps make it possible for us to get what we want. Shared culture simplifies day-to-day interactions. For example, when we say hello, we expect a similar response in return. If we buy a flat screen TV or an airline ticket, we expect that the clerk will accept a credit card rather than demand huge sums of cash. When we show up for the first day of class, we assume that students will sit at their desks and the professor will take his or her place up front. Our interactions are cultural exchanges in which we trust that our assumptions are shared by others.

Do you see the old woman or the young one?

Because our culture represents the core of who we are, including our knowledge, values, beliefs, rules for behavior, and more, we seek both to preserve it and to pass it along to others. We preserve it through books, art, video recordings, and other means of expression. We pass it along in families, through mass media, among peers, and, more formally, at school, investing substantial amounts of resources to do so. Were it not for the social transmission of culture, each generation would have to start from scratch, reinventing not just the wheel but all other forms of culture as well.

Although it is through culture that we establish a relationship to the external world, society provides the context within which those relationships develop. **Society** consists of the structure of relationships within which culture is

SOCthink

> > > How does social context influence how we relate to others? If you were talking about how school is going, how might you respond differently at home with your parents as compared to in a dorm with friends or at work with colleagues?

created and shared through regularized patterns of social interaction. How we structure society constrains the kind of culture we construct. Some ways of thinking, acting, and making are more acceptable, while others may not even be recognized as possible. People often confront this reality when they travel abroad and find their taken-for-granted ideas and actions to be out of place and inappropriate.

Cultural preferences vary across societies. Educational methods, marriage ceremonies, religious doctrines, and other aspects of culture are learned and transmitted through human interaction within specific societies. Parents in India are accustomed to arranging marriages for their children; in the United States parents typically leave marital decisions up to their children. Lifelong residents of Cairo consider it natural to speak Arabic; lifelong residents of Buenos Aires feel the same way about Spanish.

>> The Development of Culture Around the World

Through our creation of culture, we have come a long way from our prehistoric heritage. The human species has managed to produce such achievements as novels by Toni Morrison, paintings by Picasso, poems by Langston Hughes, and films such as *Schindler's List*. We now take for granted what once seemed impossible, from air travel, to the cloning of cells, to organ transplants. We can peer into the outermost reaches of the universe or analyze our innermost feelings. In all these ways, our cultural creativity sets us apart as remarkably different from other species of the animal kingdom.

CULTURAL UNIVERSALS

Given that we have a certain amount of freedom to construct culture in a multitude of ways, one of the early sociological questions was whether there are any aspects of culture shared by all people. Some sociologists sought to discover whether there are fundamental laws of society, equivalent to long-known laws of nature. Such patterns were referred to as **cultural universals**—common practices and beliefs shared by all societies. What this search revealed was that components of culture can be called universal only if they are expressed in the most general terms. Many cultural universals are, in fact, adaptations to meet essential human needs, such as the need for food, shelter, and clothing. Anthropologist George Murdock's (1945:124) list of cultural universals included sports, cooking, funeral ceremonies, medicine, marriage, and sexual restrictions.

> **society** The structure of relationships within which culture is created and shared through regularized patterns of social interaction.
>
> **cultural universal** A common practice or belief shared by all societies.

The foods people eat, and the customs around eating and preparation of food, reflect their culture as well as their economic circumstances.

The ways in which different groups address these human needs vary significantly. One group may not allow marriage between first cousins while another encourages it. Not only does the expression of cultural universals vary from one society to another, but it can change dramatically over time.

Sociobiology is a discipline committed to the systematic study of how biology affects human social behavior; it looks at cultural universals from a biological perspective. Sociobiologists argue that our thoughts and actions as a species can ultimately be explained through our genes and our biological makeup. While most sociologists would agree that our biology can certainly influence our social behavior, the degree of variability within and between societies suggests that sociobiological theories are limited as a means to explain complex human behavior.

sociobiology The systematic study of how biology affects human social behavior.

innovation The process of introducing a new idea or object to a culture through discovery or invention.

Part of the reason sociologists question biological explanations for human behavior is the fact that such claims have been used in the past to justify inequality—claims that were later revealed to be scientifically untrue. For example, it was once thought that women were not capable of success in college because their brains were too small and their uterus made them too emotional. Over time we learned that such presuppositions are false—women now make up almost 60 percent of college graduates—but at one time they were accepted as "natural" and therefore resistant to change. One of the lessons we learn about culture throughout human history is that variety and change are the norm.

INNOVATION

Humans have the ability to create new things. A robin's nest in the year 2009 looks very much like one in 1999 or 999 because robins act on a nest-building instinct. Human abodes, however, vary widely—we can live in a cave, a castle, a sod house, a pueblo, a high-rise apartment, a McMansion, or a dorm room. Such variation is possible because we are free to innovate. **Innovation**—the process of introducing a new idea or object to a culture—interests sociologists because it can have ripple effects across a society.

SOCthink

> > > How has the invention of the automobile changed our lives and our communities? How has the personal computer changed the way we interact?

There are two main forms of innovation: discovery and invention. **Discovery** involves making known or sharing the existence of an aspect of reality. The identification of the DNA molecule and the sighting of a new moon of Saturn are both acts of discovery. A significant factor in the process of discovery is the sharing of newfound knowledge with others. By contrast, an **invention** results when existing cultural items are combined into a form that did not exist before. The bow and arrow, the automobile, and the television are all examples of inventions, as are abstract concepts such as Protestantism and democracy.

Going GLOBAL

Communication, Corporations, and Consumerism

Communication, corporations, and consumerism combine to spread particular cultural preferences around the globe. What are the consequences of such diffusion for local cultures around the world?

GLOBALIZATION AND DIFFUSION

Cultural innovation can be highly globalized in today's world. Imagine walking into Starbucks with its familiar green logo and ordering a decaf latte and a cinnamon ring—only this Starbucks happens to be located in the heart of Beijing's Forbidden City, just outside the Palace of Heavenly Purity, former residence of Chinese emperors. The first Starbucks in mainland China opened in 1999, and by 2009 there were more than 350, with 69 stores in Beijing alone. The success of Starbucks in a country in which coffee drinking is still a novelty (most Chinese are tea drinkers) has been striking (Lu Haoting 2009).

The emergence of Starbucks in China demonstrates the cultural impact of globalization. Starbucks' expansion affects not only coffee consumption patterns but also the international trade in coffee beans, which are harvested mainly in developing countries. Our consumption-oriented culture supports a retail price of two to three dollars for a single cup of premium coffee. At the same time, the price of coffee beans on the world market has fallen so low that millions of farmers around the world can barely eke out a living. Worldwide, the growing demand for coffee, tea, chocolate, fruit, and other natural resources is straining the environment, as poor farmers in developing countries clear more and more forestland to enlarge their fields.

discovery The process of making known or sharing the existence of an aspect of reality.

invention The combination of existing cultural items into a form that did not exist before.

diffusion The process by which a cultural item spreads from group to group or society to society.

Even as people in Asia have begun to drink coffee, people in North America have discovered the Japanese cuisine known as sushi. More and more cultural expressions and practices are crossing national borders and influencing the traditions and customs of the societies exposed to them. Sociologists use the term **diffusion** to refer to the

process by which some aspect of culture spreads from group to group or society to society. Historically, diffusion typically occurred through a variety of means, including exploration, war, military conquest, and missionary work. Today, societal boundaries that were once relatively closed due to the constraints of transportation and communication have become more permeable, with cross-cultural exchange occurring more quickly. Through the mass media, the Internet, immigration, and tourism, we regularly confront the people, beliefs, practices, and artifacts of other cultures.

material culture The physical or technological aspects of our daily lives.

nonmaterial culture Ways of using material objects, as well as customs, ideas, expressions, beliefs, knowledge, philosophies, governments, and patterns of communication.

technology "Cultural information about how to use the material resources of the environment to satisfy human needs and desires."

Diffusion often comes at a cost. In practice, globalization has led to the cultural domination of developing nations by more affluent nations. In these encounters, people in developed nations often pick and choose the cultural practices they find intriguing or exotic, while people in developing nations often lose their traditional values and begin to identify with the culture of the dominant na-

tions. They may discard or neglect their native language and dress, attempting to imitate the icons of mass-market entertainment and fashion. In this way Western popular culture represents a threat to native cultures. As Sembene Ousmane, one of Africa's most prominent writers and filmmakers, noted, "[Today] we are more familiar with European fairy tales than with our own traditional stories" (World Development Forum 1990:4). So something is gained and something is lost through diffusion, and often it is the poorer societies that sacrifice more of their culture.

>> Elements of Culture

To better understand how culture operates, it is helpful to distinguish among its different forms. A classic two-fold model of culture was proposed by sociologist William F. Ogburn (1922). He drew a line between material and nonmaterial culture. **Material culture** refers to the physical or technological aspects of our daily lives, including food, houses, factories, and raw materials. **Nonmaterial culture** refers to ways of using material objects and to customs, ideas, expressions, beliefs, knowledge, philosophies, governments, and patterns of communica-

2008	**270.3 million subscribers**
2005	207.9
2000	109.5
1995	33.8
1990	5.3
1985	0.3

= 7 million subscribers

Wireless Phone Usage

Technology makes it possible for us to keep in touch with almost anyone anywhere, as these numbers showing the explosion in the number of wireless phone subscribers since 1985 demonstrates.

Source: CTIA 2009.

tion. While this simple division is helpful, the concept of nonmaterial culture is so inclusive that we break it down into four key components: language, values, norms, and sanctions.

MATERIAL CULTURE AND TECHNOLOGY

It is easy to underestimate the degree to which we live in a humanly constructed world. Even for those of us who live close to nature, material culture is everywhere. It includes the clothes we wear, the books we read, the chairs we sit in, the carpets we walk on, the lights we use, the buildings we live in, the cars we drive, the roads we drive on, and so much more. Even those things that seem natural, like yards or parks, are human constructs.

SOCthink

> > > In 2008 people sent an average of 3.5 billion text messages per day in the United States—almost 3 times as many as in 2007. How might frequent "texting" and less talking affect the nature of our relationships, both positively and negatively?

Technology is a form of material culture. We tend to think of it only as the physical object itself, but sociologist Gerhard Lenski suggests that it represents a way of knowing. He defined **technology** as "cultural information about how to use the material resources of the environment to satisfy human needs and desires" (Nolan and Lenski 2006:37). In other words, technology is a means of interacting with the world around us.

Technology enhances our human abilities, giving us power, speed, and even flight. The steam engine, for example, represented a critical turning point during the Industrial Revolution. It provided us with historically unprecedented strength and stamina—the ability to lift and move extremely heavy objects and to do so over sustained periods of time. It made modern coal mining practical, provided manufacturing machinery with the power needed for early factories, and powered early tractors and locomotives, setting the stage for modern global mobility.

What is sociologically important about material culture is the role it plays, like all forms of culture, in connecting individuals with one another and to the external environment. Advances in technology, especially when it comes to the revolutions in communication and transportation, have linked more individuals in a global network than was ever possible in the past. Cell phones, for example, enable us to stay in touch with friends and family from almost anywhere, and laptop computers allow us to bring the workplace with us wherever we go.

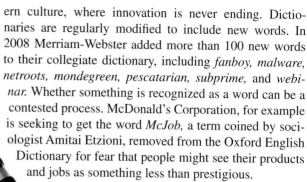

Culture, Technology, and Superheroes

Some superheroes (Superman and the X-Men) are born that way, but others gain their powers the old-fashioned way: they invent them. Characters such as Ironman and Batman appeal to us in part because they rely on human innovation for their strength and stamina. Technology makes them faster than a speeding bullet or more powerful than a locomotive. To what extent does technology provide us with superhuman powers?

ern culture, where innovation is never ending. Dictionaries are regularly modified to include new words. In 2008 Merriam-Webster added more than 100 new words to their collegiate dictionary, including *fanboy, malware, netroots, mondegreen, pescatarian, subprime,* and *webinar.* Whether something is recognized as a word can be a contested process. McDonald's Corporation, for example is seeking to get the word *McJob,* a term coined by sociologist Amitai Etzioni, removed from the Oxford English Dictionary for fear that people might see their products and jobs as something less than prestigious.

Analysis of language gives us insight into cultures. The English language, for example, makes extensive use of words related to war. We speak of "conquering" space, "fighting the battle" of the budget, "waging war" on drugs, making a "killing" in the stock market, and "bombing" an examination; something monumental or great is "the bomb." An observer from another culture could gauge the importance of warfare and the military in our culture simply by recognizing the prominence of militaristic terms in our language. As another example, in the Old West, words such as *gelding, stallion, mare, piebald,* and *sorrel* were all used to describe one animal—the horse. Even if we knew little about that period in history, we could conclude from the list of terms that horses were important to the culture. Similarly, the Slave Indians of northern Canada, who live in a frigid climate, have 14 terms to describe ice, including 8 for different kinds of "solid ice" and others for "seamed ice," "cracked ice," and "floating ice." Clearly, language reflects the values and priorities of a culture (Basso 1972; Haviland 2002).

Different languages express reality in different ways, and crossing one language with another can lead to embarrassment. To lend authenticity to his 1990 film *Dances with Wolves,* actor-director Kevin Costner hired a Lakota woman to teach the Lakota language to the cast. Lakota is a gendered language in which women and men speak slightly different dialects. The cast members found the language so difficult to learn that the teacher decided to dispense with the complexities of gendered speech. When members of the Lakota Sioux tribe saw the film, they could not help laughing at the men sounding like women (Haviland et al. 2005:109).

Because different groups share different languages, the ability to speak other languages is crucial to intercultural relations. Throughout the Cold War era, beginning in the 1950s and continuing well into the 1970s, the U.S. government

Sometimes technological change outstrips our capacity to interpret and understand the impact of such changes. Because it goes to the core of our perception of reality, nonmaterial culture is often more resistant to change than is the material culture. Ogburn introduced the term **culture lag** to refer to the period of adjustment when the nonmaterial culture is struggling to adapt to new conditions of the material culture. For example, the ethics of the Internet—particularly issues concerning privacy and censorship—have not yet caught up with the explosion in Internet use and technology.

LANGUAGE

Turning to nonmaterial culture, we begin with language, its most basic building block. **Language** is a system of shared symbols; it includes speech, written characters, numerals, symbols, and nonverbal gestures and expressions. It provides the foundation of a common culture because it facilitates day-to-day exchanges with others, making collective action possible.

Even as we learn the meanings of existing words through interactions with others, we create new words and modify old meanings—especially in our mod-

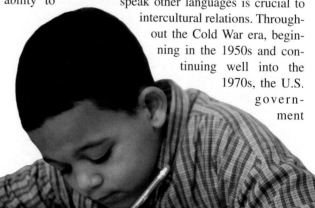

From Me to You

I was reminded of our ability to create new words while on a family hiking trip in Oregon. Eleanor, who was four at the time, was riding on my shoulders along the trail while her sister, Emily, and my wife, Lori, were falling behind. Eleanor turned and yelled as loud as she could, "Stop chickenjagging!" We knew immediately what she meant and have used this word ever since. Anyone can create words, but they become meaningful only when they are shared with others. For Eleanor's new word to become part of the common language, the chickenjagging network must extend beyond our immediate family into the wider world.

not a given. Rather, it is culturally determined and encourages a distinctive interpretation of reality by focusing our attention on certain phenomena.

In a literal sense, language may color how we see the world. Berlin and Kay (1991) noted that humans possess the physical ability to make millions of color distinctions, yet languages differ in the number of colors they recognize. For example, the English language distinguishes between yellow and orange, but some other languages do not. In the Dugum Dani language of New Guinea's West Highlands, there are only two basic color terms—*modla* for "white" and *mili* for "black." By contrast, there are 11 basic terms in English. Russian and Hungarian, though, have 12 color terms. Russians have terms for light blue and dark blue, while Hungarians have terms for two different shades of red (Roberson et al. 2000; Wierzbicka 2008).

Feminists have noted that gender-related language can reflect—although in itself it does not determine—the traditional acceptance of men and women in certain occupations. Each time we use a term such as *mailman, policeman,* or *fireman,* we are implying (especially to young children) that these occupations can be filled only by males. Yet many women work as *letter carriers, police officers,* and *firefighters*—a fact that is being increasingly recognized and legitimized through the use of such nonsexist language.

> **culture lag** A period of adjustment when the nonmaterial culture is still struggling to adapt to new material conditions.
>
> **language** A system of shared symbols; it includes speech, written characters, numerals, symbols, and nonverbal gestures and expressions.
>
> **Sapir-Whorf hypothesis** The idea that the language a person uses shapes his or her perception of reality and therefore his or her thoughts and actions.

encouraged the study of Russian by developing special language schools for diplomats, intelligence agents, and military advisors. And following the terrorist attacks of September 11, 2001, the nation recognized how few skilled translators it had for Arabic and other languages spoken in Muslim countries. Language quickly became a key not only to tracking potential terrorists but also to building diplomatic bridges with Muslim countries willing to help in the war against terrorism (Furman, Goldberg, and Lusin 2007; Taha 2007).

Sapir-Whorf Hypothesis Language does more than simply describe reality; it also shapes the reality of a culture. For example, most people in the United States cannot easily make the verbal distinctions concerning ice that are possible in the Slave Indian culture. As a result, they are less likely to notice differences in types of ice.

According to the **Sapir-Whorf hypothesis,** named for two linguists, the language a person uses shapes his or her perception of reality and therefore his or her thoughts and actions. Edward Sapir and Benjamin Whorf argued that since people can conceptualize the world only through language, language *precedes* thought. Thus, the word symbols and grammar of our language organize the world for us. The Sapir-Whorf hypothesis also holds that language is

Did You Know?

. . . There are approximately 7000 languages spoken in the world today. However, over 500 of them are considered nearly extinct because they have fewer than 100 living speakers. Another 3000 are endangered, with fewer than 10,000 speakers.

Language can also transmit stereotypes related to race. Look up the meanings of the adjective *black* in dictionaries published in the United States, and you will find "dismal, gloomy or forbidding, destitute of moral light or goodness, atrocious, evil, threatening, clouded with anger." By contrast, dictionaries list "pure" and "innocent" among the meanings of the adjective *white*. Through such patterns of language, our culture reinforces positive associations with the term (and skin color) *white* and negative associations with *black*. Is it surprising, then, that a list meant to prevent people from working in a profession is called a "blacklist," while a fib that we think of as somewhat acceptable is called a "white lie"?

SOCthink

> > > What are some slang terms we use to refer to men and to women? What images do such terms convey for what it means to be male or female?

Such examples demonstrate that language can shape how we see, taste, smell, feel, and hear. It also influences the way we think about the people, ideas, and objects around us.

Nonverbal Communication Of course, we communicate using more than just words. If you do not like the way a meeting is going, you might suddenly sit back,

fold your arms, and turn down the corners of your mouth. When you see a friend in tears, you may give her a quick hug. After winning a big game, you may high-five your teammates. These are all examples of **nonverbal communication**—the use of gestures, facial expressions, and other visual images to communicate. We are not born with these expressions. We learn them, just as we learn other forms of language, from people who share our culture. We learn how to show—and to recognize—happiness, sadness, pleasure, shame, distress, and other emotional states (Fridlund et al. 1987).

Like other forms of language, nonverbal communication is not the same in all cultures. For example, people from various cultures differ in the degree to which they touch others during the course of normal social interactions. Even experienced travelers are sometimes caught off guard by these differences. In Saudi Arabia a middle-aged man may want to hold hands with a male partner after closing a business deal. The gesture, which would surprise most Americans, is considered a compliment in that culture. The meaning of hand signals is another form of nonverbal communication that can differ from one culture to the next. For instance, in both Australia and Iraq the thumbs-up sign is considered rude (Koerner 2003; Passero 2002).

debates and billboards promoting conflicting causes tell us that much.

The values of a culture may change, but most remain relatively stable during any one person's lifetime. Socially shared, intensely felt values are a fundamental part of our lives in the United States. Sociologist Robin Williams (1970) has offered a list of U.S. basic values. These include achievement, efficiency, material comfort, nationalism, equality, and the supremacy of science and reason over faith. Obviously, not all 306 million people in the United States agree on all these values, but such a list serves as a starting point in defining America's national character.

SOCthink

> > > Consider Williams' list of basic values. Do you think most people value these things? How might some values, such as achievement and equality, conflict? How do we resolve such conflicts?

In recent decades, scholars have made extensive efforts to compare values in different nations, even while recognizing the challenges in interpreting value concepts in a similar manner across cultures. Psychologist Shalom Schwartz has measured values in more than 60 countries. Around the world, certain values are widely shared, including benevolence, which is defined as "forgiveness and loyalty." In contrast, power, defined as "control or dominance over people and resources," is a value that is endorsed much less often (Hitlin and Piliavin 2004; Schwartz and Bardi 2001).

nonverbal communication The use of gestures, facial expressions, and other visual images to communicate.

value A collective conception of what is considered good, desirable, and proper—or bad, undesirable, and improper—in a culture.

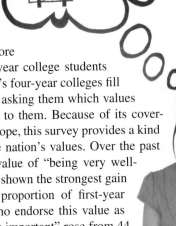

Each year more than 200,000 first-year college students at 440 of the nation's four-year colleges fill out a questionnaire asking them which values are most important to them. Because of its coverage, content, and scope, this survey provides a kind of barometer of the nation's values. Over the past four decades, the value of "being very well-off financially" has shown the strongest gain in popularity; the proportion of first-year college students who endorse this value as "essential" or "very important" rose from 44 percent in 1967 to 76.8 percent in 2008. By

In Arab cultures, men may hold hands as a sign of affection and friendship.

VALUES

Although each of us has our own personal set of standards—which may include caring or fitness or entrepreneurship—we also share a general set of objectives as members of a society. **Values** are these collective conceptions of what is considered good, desirable, and proper—or bad, undesirable, and improper—in a culture. Values may be specific, such as honoring one's parents and owning a home, or they may be more general, such as health, love, and democracy. Even individualism represents a collective value. As Richard Rodriguez points out, "American individualism is a communally derived value, not truly an expression of individuality. The teenager persists in rebelling against her parents, against tradition or custom, because she is shielded . . . by American culture from the knowledge that she inherited her rebellion from dead ancestors and living parents" (2002:130). Of course, all members of a society do not uniformly share its values. Angry political

Life Goals of First-Year College Students in the United States, 1966–2008

Percentage who identify goal as very important or essential

Develop a meaningful philosophy of life

Be very well-off financially

Help to promote racial understanding

1966 1970 1975 1980 1985 1990 1995 2000 2005 '08

Source: UCLA Higher Education Research Institute, as reported in Astin et al. 1994; Pryor et al. 2008.

contrast, the value that has shown the most striking decline in endorsement by students is "developing a meaningful philosophy of life." This value was the most popular in the 1967 survey, endorsed by more than 80 percent of respondents. However, it fell to 45 percent in 2005, but rebounded to 51.4 percent in 2008.

During the 1980s and 1990s, first-year college students expressed increased support for values having to do with money, power, and status. At the same time, their support for values having to do with social awareness and altruism, such as "helping others," declined. According to the 2008 nationwide survey, only 44.7 percent of students stated that "influencing social values" was an "essential" or "very important" goal. The proportion of students for whom "helping to promote racial understanding" was an essential or very important goal reached a record high of 42 percent in 1992, then fell to 33 percent in 2005, before rising to 37.3 percent in 2008. Like other aspects of nonmaterial culture, such as language and norms, a nation's values are not necessarily fixed.

Because it challenges honesty as a shared value, cheating is a significant concern on college campuses. Professors who take advantage of computerized services that can identify plagiarism, such as the search engine Google or TurnItIn.com, have found that many of the papers their students hand in are plagiarized, in whole or in part. When high school students were asked how many times they had copied an Internet document for a classroom assignment in the past year, 36 percent said that they had done so at least once. When asked how many times they had cheated during a test at school in the past year, 64 percent said that they had done so at least once (Josephson Institute of Ethics 2008). Perhaps cheating has become a normal part of student culture even if it is at odds with the dominant school values.

Sometimes values shift in response to historic events. Americans have always valued their right to privacy and resented government intrusions into their personal lives. In the aftermath of the terrorist attacks of September 11, 2001, however, many citizens called for greater protection against the threat of terrorism. In response, the federal government broadened its surveillance powers and increased its ability to monitor people's behavior without court approval. In 2001, shortly after the attacks, Congress passed the USA PATRIOT Act, which empowers the FBI to access individuals' medical, library, student, and phone records without informing them or obtaining a search warrant.

NORMS

While values express our core beliefs, norms provide guidance for how to act: "Wash your hands before dinner." "Thou shalt not kill." "Respect your elders." All societies have ways of encouraging and enforcing what they view as appropriate behavior while discouraging and sanctioning what they consider to be improper behavior. **Norms** are the established standards of behavior maintained by a society. However, they are more than just the rules we think about and know—we come to embody them as part of our everyday actions.

For a norm to become significant, it must be widely shared and understood. For example, in movie theaters in the United States, we typically expect that people will be quiet while the film is shown. Of course, context matters, and the application of this norm can vary, depending on the particular film and type of audience. People who are viewing a serious artistic film will be more likely to insist on the norm of silence than those who are watching a slapstick comedy or a horror movie.

Types of Norms Sociologists distinguish between norms in two ways. First, norms are classified as either formal or informal. **Formal norms** generally have been written down and specify strict punishments for violators. In the United States we often formalize norms

norm An established standard of behavior maintained by a society.

formal norm A norm that generally has been written down and that specifies strict punishments for violators.

laws Formal norms enforced by the state.

Hot or Not?

If you could cheat on your next sociology test and get away with it, would you? Why or why not?

into laws, which are very precise in defining proper and improper behavior. Sociologist Donald Black (1995) defined *law* as "governmental social control"; that is, **laws** are formal norms enforced by the state. But laws are just one example of formal norms. The requirements for a college major and the rules of a card game are also considered formal norms.

By contrast, **informal norms** are generally understood but not precisely recorded. We follow largely unspoken rules for all kinds of everyday interactions, such as how to ride on an elevator, how to pass someone on a sidewalk, and how to behave in a college classroom. Knowledge of such norms is often taken for granted.

SOCthink

> > > What norms are you abiding by right now, as you read this book?

Norms are also classified by their relative importance to society. When classified in this way, they are known as *mores* and *folkways*. **Mores** (pronounced "MOR-ays") are norms deemed highly necessary to the welfare of a society, often because they embody the most cherished principles of a people. Each society demands obedience to its mores; violation can lead to severe penalties. Thus, the United

Break-a-Norm Day

- Wearing formal clothes in an informal setting
- Eating with the wrong utensil or none at all
- Responding to friends or family the same as to a boss or teacher
- Having long gaps in speech when talking with someone
- Standing just a little too close to or far from someone when talking with him or her
- Facing the back of an elevator instead of getting in and turning around

Norms provide us with rules that guide our everyday behavior. All we need to do is step outside the lines even a little bit to see the influence they have over our lives. These are some examples of how people violate norms. How would you feel about violating any of these norms? How might others respond to you?

States has strong mores against murder, treason, and child abuse, which have been institutionalized into formal norms.

Folkways are norms governing everyday behavior. They play an important role in shaping the daily behavior of members of a culture. Society is less likely to formalize folkways than mores, and their violation raises comparatively little concern. For example, fashion is a folkway, and there is wide latitude in what we might wear. But what about not wearing *any* clothes in public? For most of us, most of the time, that would be crossing the line into the territory of mores, and we might expect a strong and swift response. However, this too may be undergoing a change: in April 2008, *The New York Times* reported that the nude vacation business is booming (Higgins 2008).

In many societies around the world, folkways reinforce patterns of male dominance. For example, various folkways reveal men's hierarchical position above women within the traditional Buddhist areas of Southeast Asia. In the sleeping cars of trains, women do not sleep in upper berths, above men. Hospitals that house men on the first floor do not place female patients on the second floor. Even on clotheslines, folkways in Southeast Asia dictate male dominance: women's attire is hung lower than that of men (Bulle 1987).

informal norm A norm that is generally understood but not precisely recorded.

mores Norms deemed highly necessary to the welfare of a society.

folkways Norms governing everyday behavior, whose violation raise comparatively little concern.

Acceptance of Norms People do not follow norms, whether mores or folkways, in all situations. In some cases they can evade a norm because they know it is weakly enforced. For instance, it is illegal for American teenagers to drink alcoholic beverages, yet drinking by minors is common throughout the nation. In fact, teenage alcoholism is a serious social problem.

In some instances behavior that appears to violate society's collective norms may actually represent adherence to

stances, can cause one to be viewed as either a hero or a villain. For instance, secretly taping telephone conversations is normally considered not just illegal but intrusive. However, it can be done with a court order to obtain valid evidence for a criminal trial. We would heap praise on a government agent who used such methods to convict an organized crime figure. In our culture we tolerate killing another human being in self-defense, and we actually reward killing in warfare.

> ## Strangers in a new culture see only what they know.
>
> Anonymous

the norms of a particular group. Teenage drinkers are often conforming to the standards of their peer group when they violate norms that condemn underage drinking. Similarly, business executives who use shady accounting techniques may be responding to a corporate culture that demands the maximization of profits at any cost, including the deception of investors and government regulatory agencies.

Norms are violated in some instances because one norm conflicts with another. For example, suppose you live in an apartment building and one night hear the screams of the woman next door, who is being beaten by her husband. If you decide to intervene by knocking on their door or calling the police, you are violating the norm of minding your own business while at the same time following the norm of assisting a victim of domestic violence.

Even if norms do not conflict, there are exceptions to any norm. The same action, under different circum-

Acceptance of norms is subject to change as the political, economic, and social conditions of a culture are transformed. Until the 1960s, for example, formal norms throughout much of the United States prohibited the marriage of people from different racial groups. Over the past half century, however, such legal prohibitions have been cast aside. The process of change can be seen today in the increasing acceptance of single parents and the growing support for the legalization of marriage for same-sex couples.

When circumstances require the sudden violation of longstanding cultural norms, the change can upset an entire population. In Iraq, where Muslim custom strictly forbids touching by strangers for men and especially for women, the war that began in 2003 has brought numerous daily violations of the norm. Outside mosques, government offices, and other facilities likely to be targeted by terrorists, visitors must now be patted down and have their bags searched by Iraqi security forces. To reduce the discomfort caused by the pro-

A female U.S. soldier searches Iraqi women.

cedure, women are searched by female guards and men by male guards. Despite that concession, and the fact that many Iraqis admit to or even insist on the need for such measures, people still wince at the invasion of their personal privacy. In reaction to the searches, Iraqi women have begun to limit the contents of the bags they carry or simply to leave them at home (Rubin 2003).

5 Movies on CULTURES OUTSIDE THE U.S.

City of God
Young kids growing up in the slums of Rio de Janeiro.

Waltz with Bashir
An animated story about the Israeli-Lebanese war.

Nobody Knows
Four children, abandoned by their parents, struggle to get by in Tokyo.

Persepolis
An animated coming-of-age film set during the Iranian Revolution.

4 Months 3 Weeks and 2 Days
The story of two young women living in communist Romania.

SANCTIONS

When norms are violated, we can expect a response designed to bring our behavior back into line. If a basketball coach sends a sixth player into the game, we count on the referee to call a foul. If a candidate shows up for a formal job interview in shorts and a T-shirt, we predict that a job offer will not follow. If we park without putting money into the meter, we should expect a ticket. In each of these cases, some form of negative repercussion results from our failure to abide by expected norms.

Sanctions are penalties and rewards for conduct concerning a social norm. They include both negative and positive responses to behavior; their purpose is to influence future behavior. Adhering to norms can lead to positive sanctions such as a pay raise, a medal, a word of gratitude, or a pat on the back. Negative sanctions might include fines, threats, imprisonment, and stares of contempt. In this way sanctions work to enforce the order that the norms represent. Most of the time we do not even need others to sanction our acts. Having internalized society's norms, we police ourselves, using such internal motivations as guilt or self-satisfaction to regulate our own behavior.

As we saw with the "Free Hugs" campaign, norms provide order, but norms change, and change can result in chaos. As social scientist Gustave Le Bon said in 1895,

"Civilization is impossible without traditions, and progress impossible without the destruction of those traditions. The difficulty, and it is an immense difficulty, is to find a proper equilibrium between stability and variability." In a world of norms, we constantly face this tension: to obey or not to obey.

> **sanction** A penalty or reward for conduct concerning a social norm.
>
> **dominant ideology** A set of cultural beliefs and practices that legitimates existing powerful social, economic, and political interests.

>> Culture and the Dominant Ideology

Together the elements of culture provide us with social coherence and order. Culture clarifies for us what we think is good and bad, and right and wrong, giving us a sense of direction. That is not to say, however, that there is universal agreement on values and norms or that culture works on behalf of all for the greater good. Culture helps to unify and provide meaning, but it also serves the interests of some individuals and groups to the detriment of others. Some people benefit from existing norms and values, while others are denied opportunities or access to resources simply due to the positions they occupy—positions we have culturally defined as inferior.

One of the ways culture can function to maintain the privileges of certain groups is through the establishment of a **dominant ideology**—the set of cultural beliefs and practices that legitimate existing powerful social, economic, and political interests. The dominant ideology helps to explain and justify who gets what and why in a way that supports and maintains the status quo. Dominant ideas

Agricultural strikes in the 1960s and 1970s alerted the nation to the harsh economic plight of migrant workers.

can even squelch alternative expressions of what might be, casting such alternatives as threats to the existing order. This concept was first proposed by Hungarian Marxist Georg Lukács (1923) and Italian Marxist Antonio Gramsci (1929), but it did not gain an audience in the United States until the early 1970s. In Karl Marx's view, a capitalist society has a dominant ideology that serves the interests of the ruling class.

subculture A segment of society that shares a distinctive pattern of mores, folkways, and values that differs from the pattern of the larger society.

argot Specialized language used by members of a group or subculture.

A society's most powerful groups and institutions control wealth and property. Armed with a dominant ideology, they can also shape beliefs about reality through religion, education, and the media. In so doing, they can influence what we come to accept as true. For example, feminists would argue that if all of society's most important institutions send the message that women should be subservient to men, this dominant ideology will help to control and subordinate women.

One of the limitations of the dominant ideology thesis is that, in the United States, it is not easy to identify a singular, all-inclusive "core culture." Studies report a lack of consensus on national values and a wide range of cultural traits from a variety of cultural traditions. In addition, as we saw in the surveys of young people's values, significant shifts in cultural values can occur. Yet there is no denying that certain expressions of values have greater influence than others, even in so complex a society as the United States. For example, the value of competition in the marketplace—a cornerstone of any capitalist economy—remains powerful, and we often look down on those who we suspect might be lazy.

>> Cultural Variation

Although societies can be defined in part by the culture their inhabitants share, culture varies both among and within societies. Inuit tribes in northern Canada, clad in furs and dieting on whale blubber, have little in common with farmers in Southeast Asia, who dress for the heat and subsist mainly on the rice they grow in their paddies. Cultures adapt to meet specific sets of circumstances, such as climate, level of technology, population, and geography. This adaptation to different conditions shows up in differences in all elements of culture, including language, values, norms, and sanctions. Thus, despite the presence of cultural universals such as courtship and religion, great diversity exists among the world's many cultures. Moreover, even within a single nation, certain segments of the populace develop cultural patterns that differ from the patterns of the dominant society.

ASPECTS OF CULTURAL VARIATION

Subcultures Rodeo riders, residents of a retirement community, workers on an offshore oil rig—all are examples of what sociologists refer to as *subcultures*. A **subculture** is a segment of society that shares a distinctive pattern of mores, folkways, and values that differs from the pattern of the larger society. In a sense, a subculture can be thought of as a culture existing within a larger, dominant culture. The existence of many subcultures is characteristic of complex societies such as the United States.

SOCthink

> > > Are people who participate in *World of Warcraft* or *Second Life* part of subcultures? What are some characteristics of these groups that typify subcultures?

Members of a subculture participate in the dominant culture while at the same time engaging in unique and dis-

tinctive forms of behavior. Frequently, a subculture will develop its own slang known as **argot**—specialized language that distinguishes it from the wider society. For example, back in the 1940s and 1950s, New York City's sanitation workers developed a humorous argot used to this day to describe the dirty and smelly aspects of their job. They call themselves *g-men* (a term more typically applied to government agents); a garbage scow or barge is known as a *honey boat;* and trash thrown from an upper-story window is called *airmail.* More recent coinages include *disco rice* (maggots) and *urban whitefish* (used condoms). Administrators at the Sanitation Department practice a more reserved humor than those who work on the trucks. When they send a *honey boat* to New Jersey, they are not dumping the city's garbage; they're *exporting* it. Policy makers at the department have also invented some novel acronyms to describe New Yorkers' attitude toward the construction of new sanitation facilities: *banana* (build absolutely nothing anywhere near anyone) and *nope* (not on planet earth) (Urbina 2004).

Such argot allows insiders—the members of the subculture—to understand words with special meanings and establishes patterns of communication that outsiders cannot understand. In so doing, it clarifies the boundary between "us" and "them" and reinforces a shared identity. We see something like this in the taken-for-granted words and acronyms in the instant-messaging and text-messaging world. There, abbreviations come fast and furious, from the well-known, such as *lol* (laughing out loud), *brb* (be right back), and *g2g* (got to go), to the more obscure, such as *1337* (meaning "elite" and referring to symbolic language or "leet-speak") or *pwned* (leet term meaning "defeated").

In India a new subculture has developed among employees at the international call centers established by multinational corporations. To serve customers in the United States and Europe, the young men and women who work there must be fluent speakers of English. But the corporations that employ them demand more than proficiency in a foreign language; they expect their Indian employees to adopt Western values and work habits, including the grueling pace that U.S. workers take for granted. In return, the corporations offer perks such as Western-style dinners and dances and coveted consumer goods. Ironically, they allow employees to take the day off only on American holidays like Labor Day and Thanksgiving—not on Indian holidays like Diwali, the Hindu festival of lights. While most Indian families are home celebrating, call center employees see mostly each other; when they have the day off, no one else is free to socialize with them. As a result, these employees have formed a tight-knit subculture based on hard work and a taste for Western luxury goods and leisure time pursuits. Increasingly, they are the object of criticism from Indians who live a more conventional Indian lifestyle centered on family and holiday traditions (Kalita 2006).

Subculture Slang

Anime and Manga Fans
Chibi eyes: the characteristic, big childlike eyes used in anime

Majoko: a girl anime character with magical powers who must save the world

Carnival Workers
86'ed: banned from carnival grounds

Blade glommer: a sword swallower

Flat store: a carnival game rigged so that it can't be won

Graffiti Writers
Bite: to copy another graffiti writer's work

Burner: a stylistically impressive, brilliantly colored piece of graffiti, usually written in a complex pattern of interlocking letters and other visual elements

Toy: an inexperienced or unskilled graffiti writer

Kill: to saturate an area with one's graffiti

Bikers (Motorcyclists)
Brain bucket: a helmet

Ink slinger: a tattoo artist

Pucker factor: the degree of panic felt during a near-accident

Yard shark: a dog that races out to attack passing motorcyclists

Skateboarders
Deck: a skateboard platform

Face plant: a face-first crash

Sketchy: in reference to a trick, poorly done

Subcultures often produce their own unique jargon. The words may be appropriate in those subcultures, but they have the effect of drawing a line between insiders and the rest of us.

Source: Reid. 2006.

Countercultures Sometimes a subculture can develop that seeks to set itself up as an alternative to the dominant culture. When a subculture conspicuously and deliberately opposes certain aspects of the larger culture, it is known as a **counterculture.** Countercultures typically thrive among the young, who have the least investment in the existing culture.

The 1960s, now often characterized by the phrase "sex and drugs and rock 'n' roll," provide a classic case of an extensive counterculture. Largely composed of young people, members of this counterculture were turned off by a society they believed was too materialistic and technological. It included many political radicals and "hippies" who had "dropped out" of mainstream social institutions, but its membership was extensive and diverse. The young people expressed

> **counterculture** A subculture that deliberately opposes certain aspects of the larger culture.

in their writings, speeches, and songs their visions, hopes, and dreams for a new society. These young women and men rejected the pressure to accumulate more expensive cars, larger homes, and an endless array of material goods. Instead, they expressed a desire to live in a culture based on more humanistic values, such as sharing, love, and co-existence with the environment. As a political force, they worked for peace—opposing U.S. involvement in the war in Vietnam and encouraging draft resistance—as well as racial and gender equality (Anderson 2007; Gitlin 1993).

In the wake of the attacks of September 11, 2001, people around the United States learned of the existence of

terrorist groups operating as a counterculture within their own country. In Northern Ireland, Israel, the Palestinian territory, and other parts of the world, many generations have lived in such circumstances. But terrorist cells are not necessarily fueled only by outsiders. Frequently, people become disenchanted with the policies of their own country, and a few take very violent steps (Juergensmeyer 2003).

Culture Shock Today we are more and more likely to come into contact with and even immerse ourselves in cultures unlike our own. For example, it has become increasingly common for students to study abroad. Though they may well have predeparture orientation sessions, when they get in-country, they often have a difficult time adjusting because so many of the little things that they took for granted, things they barely noticed before, no longer apply. Anyone who feels disoriented, uncertain, out of place, or even fearful when they encounter unfamiliar cultural practices may be experiencing **culture shock.** For example, a resident of the United States who visits certain areas in China and wants meat for dinner may be stunned to learn that the local specialty is dog meat. Similarly, someone from a strict Islamic culture may be shocked upon first

> **culture shock** The feelings of disorientation, uncertainty, and even fear that people experience when they encounter unfamiliar cultural practices.

seeing the comparatively provocative dress styles and open displays of affection that are common in the United States and other Western cultures.

Interestingly, once students who study abroad return home, they may experience a kind of reverse culture shock. Their time away has changed them, often in ways they were unaware of, and they find that they cannot so easily slip back into the old routines that those who remained at home expect of them. Culture shock reveals to us both the power and the taken-for-granted nature of culture. The rules we follow are so ingrained that we barely notice that we were following them until they are no longer there to provide the structure and order we assume as a given.

All of us, to some extent, take for granted the cultural practices of our society. As a result, it can be surprising and even disturbing to realize that other cultures do not follow our way of life. The fact is, customs that seem strange to us are considered normal and proper in other cultures, which may view our own mores and folk-ways as odd.

ATTITUDES TOWARD CULTURAL VARIATION

Ethnocentrism Because we are now more likely to encounter people from a whole range of cultural backgrounds than we were in the past, we are also more likely to struggle with what we think about the beliefs, values, and practices of others. When we hear people talking about "our" culture versus "their" culture, we are often confronted with statements that reflect the attitude that "our" culture is best. Terms such as *underdeveloped, backward,* and *primi-*

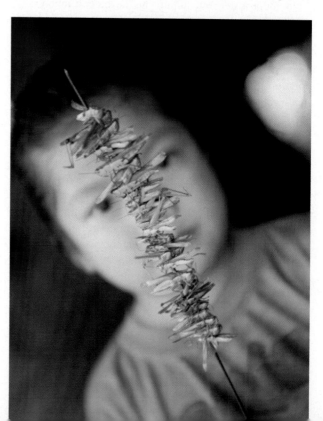

tive may be used to refer to other societies. What "we" believe is a religion; what "they" believe is superstition and mythology.

It is tempting to evaluate the practices of other cultures on the basis of our own perspectives. Sociologist William Graham Sumner (1906) coined the term **ethnocentrism** to refer to the tendency to assume that one's own culture and way of life represent what's normal or are superior to all others. The ethnocentric person sees his or her own group as the center or defining point of culture and views all other cultures as deviations from what is "normal." Thus, Westerners who see cattle as a food source might look down on the Hindu religion and culture, which view the cow as sacred. People in one culture may dismiss as unthinkable the mate selection or child-rearing practices of another culture.

Ethnocentric value judgments have complicated U.S. efforts at democratic reform of the Iraqi government. Prior to the 2003 war in Iraq, U.S. planners had assumed that Iraqis would adapt to a new form of government in the same way the Germans and Japanese did following World War II. But in the Iraqi culture, unlike the German and Japanese cultures, loyalty to the family and the extended clan comes before patriotism and the common good. In a country in which almost half of all people, even those in the cities, marry a first or second cousin, citizens are predisposed to favor their own kin in government and business dealings. Why trust a stranger from outside the family? What Westerners would criticize as nepotism, then, is actually an acceptable, even admirable, practice to Iraqis (J. Tierney 2003).

One of the reasons ethnocentrism develops is because it contributes to a sense of solidarity by promoting group pride. Denigrating other nations and cultures can enhance our own patriotic feelings and belief in our way of life. Yet this type of social stability is established at the expense of other peoples. One of the negative consequences of ethnocentric value judgments is that they serve to devalue groups and to deny equal opportunities.

Of course, ethnocentrism is hardly limited to citizens of the United States. Visitors from many African cultures are surprised at the disrespect that children in the United States show their parents. People from India may be repelled by our practice of living in the same household with dogs and cats. Many Islamic fundamentalists in the Arab world and Asia view the United States as corrupt, decadent, and doomed to destruction. All these people may feel comforted by membership in cultures that in their view are superior to ours (Juergensmeyer 2003).

Cultural Relativism Whereas ethnocentrism means evaluating foreign cultures using the familiar culture of the observer as a standard of correct behavior, **cultural relativism** means viewing people's behavior from the perspective of their own culture. It places a priority on understanding other cultures, rather than dismissing them as "strange" or "exotic." Unlike ethnocentrists, cultural relativists seek to employ the kind of value neutrality that Max Weber saw as so important.

Cultural relativism stresses that different social contexts give rise to different norms and values. Thus, we must examine practices such as polygamy, bullfighting, and monarchy within the particular contexts of the cultures in which they are found. Cultural relativism is not the same as moral relativism and thus does not suggest that we must unquestionably accept every cultural variation. But it does require a serious and unbiased effort to evaluate norms, values, and customs in light of their distinctive culture.

Practicing the sociological imagination calls for us to be more fully aware of the culture we as humans have created

> You never really understand a person until you consider things from his point of view . . . until you climb into his skin and walk around in it.
>
> Harper Lee, *To Kill a Mockingbird*

get involved! Learn about another culture. One of the most effective ways is to immerse yourself in one. Seek out opportunities for deep and prolonged interaction with a group of people from a culture unlike your own. Contact your school's service learning program or study-abroad office to find out what possibilities exist.

> **ethnocentrism** The tendency to assume that one's own culture and way of life represent what's normal or are superior to all others.
>
> **cultural relativism** The viewing of people's behavior from the perspective of their own culture.

for ourselves and to be better attuned to the varieties of culture other people have established for themselves. Culture shapes our everyday behaviors all the time, and we select from the tools it provides. For the most part, we are not aware of the degree to which we are immersed in a world of our own making. Whether that includes the capacity to read a book, make a meal, or hug a stranger on the street, it is through culture that we establish our relationship to the external world and with each other.

For REVIEW

I. **Why do humans create culture?**
- Humans lack the complex instincts present in other animals, and as such they must construct a relationship to nature and with each other. We do this through the construction of shared culture.

II. **What does culture consist of?**
- Culture can be broken down into two categories. The first is material culture, which consists of our modification of the physical environment and includes technology. The second is nonmaterial culture, which consists of a number of components including language, values, norms, and sanctions.

III. **How does culture both enable and constrain?**
- While culture provides us with the knowledge, rules, and artifacts we need to survive, it also limits our options. Words enable us to see, and tools enable us to make things, but both are designed for particular purposes and shield us from alternative possibilities. Further, with ethnocentrism, we cut ourselves off to new possibilities from different cultures.

Pop Quiz

1. What do sociologists refer to as the structure of relationships within which a culture is created and shared through regularized patterns of social interaction?
   a. culture
   b. diffusion
   c. globalization
   d. society

2. People's need for food, shelter, and clothing are examples of what George Murdock referred to as
   a. norms.
   b. folkways.
   c. cultural universals.
   d. cultural practices.

3. What is an invention?
   a. introducing a new idea or object to a culture
   b. combining existing cultural items into a form that did not exist before
   c. making known or sharing the existence of an aspect of reality
   d. the physical or technological aspects of our daily lives

4. What term do sociologists use to refer to the process by which a cultural item spreads from group to group or society to society?
   a. diffusion
   b. globalization
   c. innovation
   d. cultural relativism

5. Which of the following statements is true according to the Sapir-Whorf hypothesis?
   a. Language simply describes reality.
   b. Language legitimates existing social, economic, and political interests.
   c. Language shapes our perception of reality.
   d. Language is not an example of a cultural universal.

6. Values represent shared _____, whereas norms provide guidelines for shared _____.
   a. rules; ideas
   b. beliefs; behaviors
   c. language; technologies
   d. actions; knowledge

1 (d); 2 (c); 3 (b); 4 (a); 5 (c); 6 (b);

7. What type of norms are deemed highly necessary to the welfare of a society, often because they embody the most cherished principles of a people?
   a. formal norms
   b. informal norms
   c. mores
   d. folkways

8. Which of the following terms describes the set of cultural beliefs and practices that help to maintain powerful social, economic, and political interests?
   a. mores
   b. dominant ideology
   c. consensus
   d. values

9. Terrorist groups are examples of
   a. cultural universals.
   b. subcultures.
   c. countercultures.
   d. dominant ideologies.

10. What is the term used when one seeks to understand another culture from its perspective, rather than dismissing it as "strange" or "exotic"?
    a. ethnocentrism
    b. culture shock
    c. cultural relativism
    d. cultural value

7 (c); 8 (b); 9 (c); 10 (c)

4

SOCIALIZA

ISOLATION AND SOCIALIZATION

For the first six years of her life, Isabelle lived in almost total seclusion in a darkened room. She had little contact with other people, with the exception of her mother, who could neither speak nor hear. Isabelle's grandparents had been so deeply ashamed of Isabelle's illegitimate birth that they kept her hidden away from the world. Ohio authorities finally discovered Isabelle in 1938, when her mother escaped from her parents' home, taking Isabelle with her.

Six years old at the time of her rescue, Isabelle could not speak. While she could make various croaking sounds, her only communication with her mother involved simple gestures. Isabelle had been largely deprived of the typical interactions and socialization experiences of childhood. Since she had seen few people, she initially showed a strong fear of strangers and reacted almost like a wild animal when confronted with an unfamiliar person. As she became accustomed to seeing certain individuals, her reaction changed to one of extreme apathy. At first, observers believed that Isabelle was deaf, but she eventually began to react to nearby sounds. On tests of her educational development, she scored at the level of an infant rather than a six-year-old.

Specialists developed a systematic training program to help Isabelle adapt to human relationships and socialization. After a few days of training, she made her first attempt to verbalize. Although she started slowly, Isabelle quickly passed through six years of development. In a little over two months, she was speaking in complete sentences. Nine months later, she could identify both words and sentences. Before Isabelle reached the age of nine, she was ready to attend school with other children. By her 14th year she was in sixth grade, doing well in school, and emotionally well adjusted.

Yet without an opportunity to experience socialization in her first six years, Isabelle initially lacked what we often take for granted as natural human abilities. While we may be born with the propensity toward language and other social skills, Isabelle's inability to communicate at the time of her discovery—despite her physical and cognitive potential to learn—and her remarkable progress over the next few years underscore the importance of socialization in human development (K. Davis 1940, 1947).

TION

- How do we become ourselves?
- Who shapes our socialization?
- How does our development change over time?

>> The Role of Socialization

What makes us who we are? Is it the genes we are born with, or the environment in which we grow up? Researchers have traditionally clashed over the relative importance of biological inheritance and environmental factors in human development—a conflict called the nature versus nurture debate. Although most social scientists today acknowledge the significance of the interaction between these factors in shaping human development, sociologists come down more strongly on the side of nur-

socialization The lifelong process through which people learn the attitudes, values, and behaviors appropriate for members of a particular culture.

ture. They argue that the rules we follow, the language we speak, and the values we believe in have less to do with our DNA than with the cultural context into which we emerge. Parents, teachers, friends, co-workers, and even television personalities provide us with the cultural tools we require to survive and thrive. We need to internalize the culture that has been constructed by others who came before us,

SOCthink

> > > What skills that you learned before age two do you now take for granted? From whom did you learn them? In what contexts?

and we do this through **socialization**—the life-long process through which people learn the attitudes, values, and behaviors appropriate for members of a particular culture.

SOCIAL ENVIRONMENT: THE IMPACT OF ISOLATION

We can better appreciate how heredity and environment interact and influence the socialization process by examining situations in which one factor operates almost entirely without the other (Homans 1979). As we saw above, Isabelle was able to proceed through the typical stages of socialization with the help of experts. Unfortunately, many other cases of children raised in extreme isolation demonstrate that missing out on these critical years of childhood socialization creates difficult obstacles to overcome. We want and need early intimacy and interaction with others.

Extreme Childhood Isolation Children who have been isolated or severely neglected typically have a difficult time recovering from the loss of early childhood socialization. For example, in 1970, California authorities discovered a 14-year-old girl named Genie locked in a room where she had been confined since she was 20 months old. During her years of isolation, no family member had spoken to her, nor could she hear anything other than swearing. Since there was no television or radio in her home, she had never heard the sounds of normal human speech. One year after beginning extensive therapy, Genie's grammar resembled that of a typical 18-month-old. Though she made further advances with continued therapy, she never achieved full language ability. Today Genie, now in her early 50s, lives in a home for developmentally disabled adults (Curtiss 1977; James 2008; Rymer 1993).

While researchers know of only a few cases of children reared in near total isolation, they are aware of many cases of children raised in extremely neglectful social circumstances. Infants and young children in orphanages in the formerly communist countries of Eastern Europe often suffer from profound neglect. In many Romanian orphanages, babies once lay in their cribs for 18–20 hours a day, curled against their feeding bottles and receiving little adult care. Such minimal attention continued for the first five years of their lives.

Ten Modern Cases of Feral Children

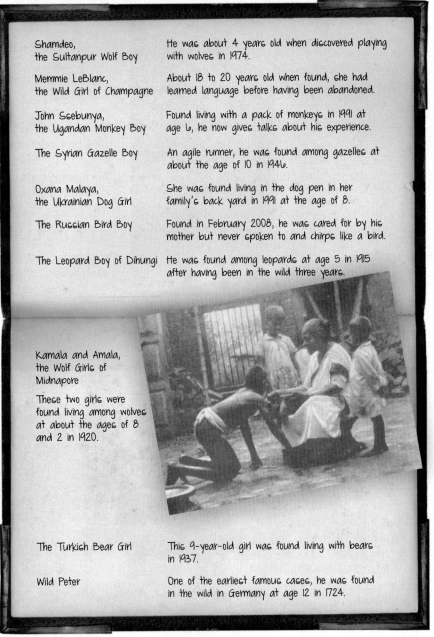

Shamdeo, the Sultanpur Wolf Boy	He was about 4 years old when discovered playing with wolves in 1974.
Memmie LeBlanc, the Wild Girl of Champagne	About 18 to 20 years old when found, she had learned language before having been abandoned.
John Ssebunya, the Ugandan Monkey Boy	Found living with a pack of monkeys in 1991 at age 6, he now gives talks about his experience.
The Syrian Gazelle Boy	An agile runner, he was found among gazelles at about the age of 10 in 1946.
Oxana Malaya, the Ukrainian Dog Girl	She was found living in the dog pen in her family's back yard in 1991 at the age of 8.
The Russian Bird Boy	Found in February 2008, he was cared for by his mother but never spoken to and chirps like a bird.
The Leopard Boy of Dihungi	He was found among leopards at age 5 in 1915 after having been in the wild three years.
Kamala and Amala, the Wolf Girls of Midnapore	These two girls were found living among wolves at about the ages of 8 and 2 in 1920.
The Turkish Bear Girl	This 9-year-old girl was found living with bears in 1937.
Wild Peter	One of the earliest famous cases, he was found in the wild in Germany at age 12 in 1724.

Source: www.feralchildren.com.

A cloth-covered "artificial mother" of the type used by Harry Harlow.

Cases of extreme isolation demonstrate the importance of the earliest socialization experiences for children. We now know that it is not enough to attend only to an infant's physical needs; parents must also concern themselves with children's social development. If parents discourage their children from having friends—even as toddlers—those children miss out on social interactions with peers that are critical for emotional growth.

Primate Studies Our need for early socialization is reinforced by studies of animals raised in isolation. Although we would never conduct such experiments on human babies, psychologist Harry Harlow (1971) conducted tests with rhesus monkeys that had been raised away from their mothers and away from contact with other monkeys. As was the case with Isabelle, the rhesus monkeys raised in isolation were fearful and easily frightened. They did not mate, and the females, who were artificially inseminated, became abusive mothers. Early isolation had long-term damaging effects on the monkeys.

A creative aspect of Harlow's experimentation was his use of "artificial mothers." In one such experiment, Harlow presented monkeys raised in isolation with two substitute mothers—one a cloth-covered replica and one a wire-covered model that had the capacity to offer milk. Monkey after monkey went to the wire mother for the life-giving milk, yet spent much more time clinging to the more motherlike cloth model. Apparently, the infant monkeys developed greater social attachments based on their need for warmth, comfort, and intimacy than their need for food.

THE INFLUENCE OF HEREDITY

Researchers who argue for a stronger role for biological explanations of our behavior point to different research to support their position—studies of twins, especially identical twins raised apart from each other. Oskar Stohr and Jack Yufe, identical twins who were separated soon after their birth, were raised on different continents and in very different cultural settings. Oskar was reared as a strict Catholic by his maternal grandmother in the Sudetenland of Czechoslovakia. As a member of the Hitler Youth movement in Nazi Germany, he learned to hate Jews. By contrast, his brother Jack was reared in Trinidad by the twins' Jewish father. Jack joined an Israeli kibbutz (a collective settlement) at age 17 and later served in the Israeli army. When the twins were reunited in middle age, however, some startling similarities emerged. They both wore wire-rimmed

Many of them were fearful of human contact and prone to unpredictable antisocial behavior.

This situation came to light only when families in North America and Europe began adopting thousands of these children in the 1990s. The adjustment problems were often so dramatic that about 20 percent of the adopting families concluded that they were ill-suited to be adoptive parents. Many of them have asked for assistance in dealing with the children. Since these conditions were brought to light by international aid workers, the Romanian government has made efforts to introduce the deprived youngsters to social interaction and its consequent feelings of attachment, which they have never experienced before (Groza et al. 2008; Ionescu 2005; Craig Smith 2006).

glasses and mustaches. They both liked spicy foods and sweet liqueurs, were absent-minded, flushed the toilet before using it, stored rubber bands on their wrists, and dipped buttered toast in their coffee (Holden 1980).

It is tempting in such cases to focus almost exclusively on such quirky similarities, but the twins also differed in many important respects. For example, Jack was a workaholic, and Oskar enjoyed leisure-time activities. Whereas

Researchers have also been impressed with the similar scores on intelligence tests of twins reared apart in *roughly similar* social settings. Most of the identical twins register scores even closer than those that would be expected if the same person took a test twice. However, identical twins brought up in *dramatically different* social environments score quite differently on intelligence tests—a finding that supports the importance of socialization in human devel-

It matters not what someone is born, but what they grow to be.

J. K. Rowling

Oskar was a traditionalist who was domineering toward women, Jack was a political liberal much more accepting of feminism. Finally, Jack was extremely proud of being Jewish, but Oskar never mentioned his Jewish heritage. Oskar and Jack are prime examples of the interplay of heredity and environment (Holden 1987).

To better understand the nature–nurture interplay, the Minnesota Twin Family Study has been following pairs of identical twins reared apart to determine what similarities, if any, they show in personality traits, behavior, and intelligence. Preliminary results from the available twin studies indicate that both genetic factors and socialization experiences are influential in human development. Certain characteristics—such as temperament, voice patterns, nervous habits, and leadership or dominance tendencies—appear to be strikingly similar even in twins reared apart, suggesting that these qualities may be linked to heredity. However, identical twins reared apart differ far more in their attitudes; values; chosen mates; need for intimacy, comfort and assistance; and even drinking habits. These qualities, it would seem, are influenced by environmental factors.

opment (Joseph 2004; McGue and Bouchard 1998; Minnesota Center for Twin and Family Research 2008).

Results from twin studies suggest that the nature–nurture debate is likely to continue. As sociologists we cannot dismiss the significance of biology in shaping human behavior.

> **self** A distinct identity that sets us apart from others.

It does appear, however, that although some general behavioral propensities may be shaped by our genes, their manifestation is dependent upon socialization and cultural context. For example, we may inherit tendencies toward temperament, but the ways we express anger (or other emotions) depend upon our environment.

>> The Self and Socialization

At the heart of this debate about nature versus nurture is the question "Who am I?" In both approaches the implicit assumption is that we are shaped by factors beyond our control. Sociologically speaking, however, we are not simply passive recipients of external forces. As individuals we are engaged in an ongoing dance with the world. We choose what to think and how to act, but we do so within the confines of the cultural resources to which we have access.

SOCIOLOGICAL APPROACHES TO THE SELF

Our concept of who we are, our self, emerges as we interact with others. The **self** is a distinct identity that sets us apart from others. It is not a static phenomenon but continues to develop and change throughout our lives. Sociologists and psychologists alike have expressed interest in how the individual develops and modifies his or her sense of self as a result of social interaction.

Cooley: The Looking-Glass Self In the early 1900s, American sociologist Charles Horton Cooley (1864–1929)

Did You Know?

... The birth rate for twins has risen 70 percent since 1980, and the birth rate for triplets-plus rose 400 percent from 1980 to 1998 (though it has declined in the years since then). Technological advances in both in vitro fertilization and embryo transfer are the primary cause for these increases, providing more cases for researchers to investigate to better understand the interplay between nature and nurture.

proposed that we learn who we are by interacting with others. Our view of ourselves, then, comes not only from direct contemplation of our personal qualities but also from others. Cooley appropriately termed his theory that we become who we are based on how we think others see us the **looking-glass self,** emphasizing the importance of social interaction on self-identity.

According to Cooley, the process of developing a self-identity, or self-concept, has three phases. First, we imagine how others see us—relatives, friends, even strangers on the street. Second, we imagine how others evaluate what we think they see—as intelligent, attractive, shy, or strange. Finally, we define our self as a result of these impressions—"I am smart" or "I am beautiful" (Cooley 1902). This process is ongoing; it happens during each and every one of our interactions. Our understanding of our self, then, involves a complex calculation in which we come to be who we are based not on how others actually see us or how they will judge us but on how we think they will see us and how we think they will judge us based on what we think they see.

According to Cooley, then, our self results from our "imagination" of how others view us. As a result, we can develop self-identities based on *incorrect* perceptions of how others see us. We can develop a sense of confidence or a sense of doubt based on how we think others react to our performance, but we might be completely wrong. Imagine you are on a first date. All the cues you receive throughout the evening are positive—your companion smiles, laughs, and seems to be having a genuinely good time. You go home feeling happy, confident that the evening went really well. But your date never returns your calls, and there is no second date. You go from a feeling of elation and confidence to a sense of disappointment and doubt, perhaps even asking, "What's wrong with me?"

Mead: Stages of the Self George Herbert Mead (1863–1931), another American sociologist, sought to expand upon Cooley's theory that we become our self through interaction with others. He argued that there are two core components of the self: the "I" and the "Me." The **I** is our acting self. It is the part of us that walks, reads, sings, smiles, speaks, or performs any other action we might undertake. The **Me** is our socialized self. Based on the standards we have learned from others, the Me plans action and then judges our performance afterward.

For Mead the self represents an ongoing interaction between our socialized self and our acting self. The Me plans. The I acts. The Me judges. Take participating in classroom discussions as an example. Our Me may have something to say but fears that the words won't come out quite right, which could lead to embarrassment, so our I stays silent. Our Me then kicks our self afterwards when someone else says exactly what we planned to say and receives praise from the professor for having said it.

It is through our interactions with others that we get the social expectations of the Me into our heads. According to Mead (1964b), when we are young, we see ourselves as the center of the universe and find it difficult to consider the perspectives of others. For example, when shown a mountain scene and asked to describe what an observer on the opposite side of the mountain might see, young children describe only objects visible from their own vantage point. Although we always retain a certain level of self-centeredness, as we mature, the self changes and begins to reflect greater concern with the reactions of others.

Parents, friends, co-workers, coaches, and teachers are often among those who play a major role in shaping a person's self. The term **significant others** refers to individuals who are most important in the development of the self. Many young people, for example, choose the same occupational field

> **I wanted to change the world. But I have found that the only thing one can be sure of changing is oneself.**
>
> **Aldous Huxley**

looking-glass self A theory that we become who we are based on how we think others see us.

I The acting self that exists in relation to the Me.

SOCthink

> > > What cues do you rely on to know if things are going well on a first date? How about on a job interview? To what extent do you think it is possible to fake such cues?

as their parents or adopt the same pop culture preferences as their friends (Sullivan [1953] 1968).

As we grow up, we develop a sense of who people are, how they fit together, and where we might fit into that map. Over time we begin to see that the positions these significant others occupy are part of a larger social network. Mead (1934, 1964a) described that transformation as a three-stage process of self-development: the preparatory stage, the play stage, and the game stage.

The Preparatory Stage

During the *preparatory stage,* which lasts until about age three, children merely imitate the people around them, especially family members with whom they continually interact. Thus, a small child will bang on a piece of wood while a parent is engaged in carpentry work or will try to throw a ball if an older sibling is doing so nearby. This imitation is largely mindless—simple parroting of the actions of others.

As they grow older, children begin to realize that we attach meanings to our actions, and they become more adept at using symbols to communicate with others. **Symbols** are the gestures, objects, and words that form the basis of human communication. By interacting with family and friends, as well as by watching cartoons on television and looking at picture books, children in the preparatory stage begin to develop interaction skills they will use throughout their lives. They learn that they can use symbols to get their way, such as saying please and thank you, or perhaps throwing a tantrum in the candy aisle of the local supermarket.

The Play Stage

As children develop skill in communicating through symbols, they gradually become more aware of social relationships out of which those symbols grow. During the *play stage*, from about ages three through five, they begin to pretend to be other people: a doctor, parent, superhero, or teacher. Such play need not make a lot of sense or be particularly coherent to adults, and children, especially when they are young, are able to move in and out of various characters with ease. For Mead, playing make-believe is more than just fun; it is a critical part of our self-development.

Mead, in fact, noted that an important aspect of the play stage is role playing. **Role taking** is the process of mentally assuming the perspective of another and responding from that imagined viewpoint. Through this process a young child internalizes the performances of other people and gradually learns, for example, when it is best to ask a parent for favors. If the parent usually comes home from work in a bad mood, the child will wait until after dinner, when the parent is more relaxed and approachable.

The Game Stage

In Mead's third stage, the *game stage,* the child of about six to nine years of age no longer merely plays roles but now begins to consider several tasks and relationships simultaneously. At this point in development, children grasp not only their own social positions but also those of others around them. The transition from play to game is evident when teaching kids to play team sports such as t-ball or soccer. When they are little, you will often see a clump of kids chasing after a ball or moving up the field together. They have yet to learn that different people play different positions and that they will be more successful as a team if everyone plays the position to which they are assigned. When they do, they can take for granted that someone will be covering a base so they can throw a runner out or that a goalie will be there to make a save if the ball gets behind them. This map of who should be where and who should do what serves as a kind of blueprint for society, and internalizing it represents the final stage of development in Mead's model; the child can now respond to numerous members of the social environment.

Mead uses the term **generalized other** to refer to the attitudes, viewpoints, and expectations of society as a whole that a child takes into account in his or her behavior. Simply put, this concept suggests that when an individual acts, he or she takes into account an entire group of people. For example, a child will not act courteously merely to please a particular parent. Rather, the child comes to understand that courtesy is a widespread social value endorsed by parents, teachers, and religious leaders.

At the game stage, children can take a more sophisticated view of people and the social environment. They now understand what specific occupations and social positions are and no longer equate Mr. Williams only with the role of "librarian" or Ms. Sanchez only with "principal." It has become clear to the child that Mr. Williams can be a librarian, a parent, and a marathon runner at the same time and that Ms.

Me The socialized self that plans actions and judges performances based on the standards we have learned from others.

significant other An individual who is most important in the development of the self, such as a parent, friend, or teacher.

symbol A gesture, object, or word that forms the basis of human communication.

role taking The process of mentally assuming the perspective of another and responding from that imagined viewpoint.

generalized other The attitudes, viewpoints, and expectations of society as a whole that a child takes into account in his or her behavior.

Sanchez is one of many principals in our society. Thus, the child has reached a new level of sophistication in observations of individuals and institutions.

Goffman: Presentation of the Self

Given that others play such a powerful role in shaping who we are and how we think about ourselves, the way we represent our self to others becomes a major concern for us and a significant interest to sociologists. Erving Goffman, a Canadian sociologist, provided a helpful model for better understanding how we go about constructing and maintaining our self through interactions with others. He suggested that each of us seeks to convey impressions of who we are to others even as those others are doing the same, creating a kind of performance that we can analyze and understand.

To study our everyday social interactions, Goffman offers the **dramaturgical approach,** which studies interaction as if we were all ac-

Momsense

From June Cleaver in the 1950s to Marge Simpson today, TV moms have shaped the scripts that modern mothers use as they perform their role. Comedian Anita Renfroe has taken this a step further. She condensed the things a mom would say in a 24-hour period down to 2 minutes and 35 seconds and set it to the William Tell Overture. A YouTube search on "Momsense" will take you there.

tors on a stage. All social encounters, according to Goffman, represent our attempts to carry out successful performances, equivalent to putting on a play. We perform front stage, largely following scripts, having already prepared for our performance backstage. We use appropriate props, including costumes, to make our performance believable. Although some improvisation is permissible, too much threatens the credibility of the character we are trying to play and may ruin the show. In order to give a successful performance, we also may need other cast members with whom we work as a team. Finally, our performance is carried out before an audience that judges how well we do. Whether in our role as students, restaurant servers, or even lovers, we all know that we have a part to play and that if we don't say the right lines or use the correct props the show will collapse, undermining our sense of self.

Early in life, the individual learns to slant his or her presentation of the self in order

to create distinctive appearances and satisfy particular audiences. Goffman (1959) referred to this altering of the presentation of the self as **impression management.** To maintain a proper image and avoid public embarrassment, we engage in **face-work.** How often do you initiate some kind of face-saving behavior when you feel flustered or rejected? In response to a rejection at a singles' bar, a person may engage in face-work by saying, "There really isn't an interesting person in this entire crowd." Or, if we do poorly on an exam, we may say to a friend who did likewise, "This professor is incompetent." We feel the need to maintain a proper image of the self if we are to continue social interaction.

In some cultures, people engage in elaborate deceptions to avoid losing face. In Japan, for example, where lifetime employment has until recently been the norm, "company men" thrown out of work during a severe economic recession may feign employment, rising as usual in the morning, donning suit and tie, and heading for the business district. But instead of going to the office, they congregate at places such as Tokyo's Hibiya Library, where they pass the time by reading before returning home at the usual hour. Many of these men are trying to protect family members, who would be shamed if neighbors discovered that the family

breadwinner was unemployed. Others are deceiving their wives and families as well (French 2000).

Goffman's work on the self represents a logical progression of sociological studies begun by Cooley and Mead on how personality is acquired through socialization and how we manage the presentation of our self to others. Cooley stressed the process by which we create a self; Mead focused on how the self develops as we learn to interact with others; Goffman emphasized the ways in which we consciously create images of ourselves for others.

PSYCHOLOGICAL APPROACHES TO THE SELF

Psychologists have shared the interest of Cooley, Mead, and other sociologists in the development of the self. Early work in psychology, such as that of Sigmund Freud (1856–1939), stressed the role of inborn drives—among them the drive for sexual gratification—in channeling human behavior. Later psychologists such as Jean Piaget emphasized the stages through which human beings progress as the self develops.

Like Cooley and Mead, Freud believed that the self is a social product and that aspects of one's personality are influenced by other people (especially one's parents). However, unlike Cooley and Mead, Freud suggested that the self has components that work in opposition to each other. According to Freud, we have a natural instinct that seeks limitless pleasure, but this is at odds with our societal needs for order and constraint. By interacting with others, we learn the expectations of society and then select behavior most appropriate to our own culture.

Through his research on children, including newborns, the

> **dramaturgical approach** A view of social interaction in which people are seen as theatrical performers.
>
> **impression management** The altering of the presentation of the self in order to create distinctive appearances and satisfy particular audiences.
>
> **face-work** The efforts people make to maintain a proper image and avoid public embarrassment.

Swiss child psychologist Jean Piaget (1896–1980) underscored the importance of social interactions in developing a sense of self. In his well-known **cognitive theory of development,** Piaget (1954) identified four stages in the development of children's thought processes. In the first, or *sensorimotor,* stage, young children use their senses to make discoveries. For example, through touching they discover that their hands are actually a part of themselves.

During the second, or *preoperational,* stage, children begin to use words and symbols to distinguish objects and ideas. The milestone in the third, or *concrete operational,* stage is that children engage in more logical thinking. For example, they learn that even when a formless lump of clay is shaped into a snake, it is still the same clay. Finally, in the fourth, or *formal operational,* stage, adolescents become capable of sophisticated abstract thought and can deal with ideas and values in a logical manner.

cognitive theory of development The theory that children's thought progresses through four stages of development.

Piaget suggested that moral development becomes an important part of socialization as children develop the ability to think more abstractly. When children learn the rules of a game such as hopscotch or Candy Land, they are learning to obey societal norms. Those under eight years of age display a rather basic level of morality: rules are rules, and there is no concept of "extenuating circumstances." As they mature, children become capable of greater au-

tonomy, and they begin to experience moral dilemmas and doubts as to what constitutes proper behavior.

According to Piaget, social interaction is the key to development. As children grow older, they pay increasing attention to how other people think and why they act in particular ways. In order to develop a distinct personality, each of us needs opportunities to interact with others. As we saw earlier, Isabelle was deprived of the chance for normal social interactions, and the consequences were severe (Kitchener 1991).

>> Agents of Socialization

The people with whom we interact influence how we think about ourselves and how we represent ourselves to others, and the positions they occupy determine the kind of influence they have. Family, friends, schools, peers, the mass media, the workplace, religion, and the state are among the agents of socialization that play the most powerful roles in shaping the self.

FAMILY

The family is the most important agent of socialization, especially for children. We can see the power of family socialization among the Amish. Children in Amish communities are raised in a highly structured and disciplined manner, but they are not immune to the temptations posed by their peers in the non-Amish world. During a period of discovery called *rumspringa,* a term that means "running around," Amish young people attend barn dances where taboos like drinking, smoking, and driving cars are commonly violated. Parents often react by looking the other way, sometimes literally, pretending not to notice. They remain secure in the knowledge that their children almost always return to the traditional Amish lifestyle. Research shows that only about 20 percent of Amish youths leave the fold, and most of them join one of the only somewhat more modern Mennonite groups. Rarely does a baptized adult leave (Schachtman 2006; Zellner and Schaefer 2006).

Although the Amish provide what seems like an extreme case, the truth is that all families play a powerful role in shaping their children. Although peer groups and the media do influence us, research shows that the role of the family in socializing a child cannot be overestimated (McDowell and Parke 2009). The lifelong process of learning begins shortly after birth. Since newborns can hear, see, smell, and taste, and can feel heat, cold, and pain, they are constantly orienting themselves to the surrounding world. Human beings, especially family members, constitute an important part of their social environment. People minister to the baby's needs by feeding, cleaning, carrying, and comforting her or him. It is in the context of families that we learn to talk, walk, feed ourselves, go to the bathroom, and so on—basic skills that we take for granted as natural but that we learned thanks to our families.

Cross Cultural Variation As both Cooley and Mead noted, the development of the self is a critical aspect of the early years of one's life. How children develop this sense of self, however, can vary from one society to another. For example, most parents in the United States do not send six-year-olds to school unsupervised. However, that is the norm in Japan, where parents push their children to commute to school on their own from an early age. In cities like Tokyo, first-graders must learn to negotiate buses, subways, and long walks. To ensure their safety, parents carefully lay out rules: never talk to strangers; check with a station attendant if you get off at the wrong stop; stay on to the end of the line, then call, if you miss your stop; take stairs, not escalators; don't fall asleep. Some parents equip the children with cell phones or pagers. One parent acknowledges that she worries, "but after they are 6, children are supposed to start being independent from the mother. If you're still taking your child to school after the first month, everyone looks at you funny" (Tolbert 2000:17).

Family structures also reproduce themselves through socialization. In the contexts of families, children learn expectations regarding marriage and parenthood. Children observe their parents expressing affection, dealing with finances, quarreling, complaining about in-laws, and so forth. Their learning represents an informal process of anticipatory socialization in which they develop a tenta-tive model of what being married and being a parent are like.

While we consider the family's role in socialization, we need to remember, however, that children are not simply robots who lack agency. They do not play a passive role in their socialization. As Mead's "I" implies, they choose, sometimes to the consternation of their parents, and in so doing are active participants in their self-creation. Through the choices they make, they influence and alter the families, schools, and communities of which they are a part.

The Impact of Race and Gender In the United States, social development includes exposure to cultural assumptions regarding gender and race. African American parents, for example, have learned that children as young as two years old can absorb negative messages about Blacks in children's books, toys, and television shows—the vast majority of which are designed primarily for White consumers. At the same time, African American children are

exposed more often than others to the inner-city youth gang culture. Because most Blacks, even those who are middle class, live near very poor neighborhoods, their children are susceptible to these influences, despite their parents' strong family values (Benhorin and McMahon 2008; Klewar and Sullivan 2009; Patillo 2005).

The term **gender roles** refers to expectations regarding the proper behavior, attitudes, and activities of males and females. For example, we traditionally think of "toughness" as masculine—and desirable only in men—while we view "tenderness" as feminine. As we will see in Chapter 12, other cultures do not necessarily assign these qualities to each gender in the way that our culture does. As the primary agents of childhood socialization, parents play a critical role in guiding children into those gender roles deemed appropriate in a society.

Other adults, older siblings, the mass media, and religious and educational institutions also have a noticeable impact on a child's socialization into feminine and masculine norms. A culture or subculture may require that one sex or the other take primary responsibility for the socialization of children, economic support of the family, or religious or intellectual leadership. In some societies girls are socialized mainly by their mothers and boys by their fathers—an arrangement that may prevent girls from learning critical survival skills. In South Asia, for example, fathers teach their sons to swim to prepare them for

a life as fishermen; girls typically do not learn to swim. When the deadly tsunami hit the coast of South Asia in 2004, many more men than women survived.

SCHOOL

In school we typically move beyond the more sheltered confines of our family and learn to become members of the larger social groups to which we belong. Schools teach us the taken-for-granted knowledge of the broader society—not only basic skills such as reading, writing, and 'rithmatic but also shared cultural knowledge such as the national anthem, the heroes of the American Revolution, and the pillars of good character. Like the family, schools have an explicit mandate to socialize people in the United States—and especially children—into the norms and values of U.S. culture.

Schools teach children the values and customs of the larger society because that shared culture provides the glue that holds us together as a society. If we did not transmit our knowledge and skills from one generation to the next, society would collapse. The knowledge we gain there, however, goes beyond just the official curriculum to include the more informal lessons we learn on the playground. We do learn the facts and figures of history, science, reading, math, and more, but we also learn how to stand up for ourselves when our parents or teachers are not there to hover over us or to bail us out.

In addition to providing social order, schools open doors for us as individuals. We are exposed to new ways of thinking and acting that allow us to make new choices about our future. While this can include training for careers that allow us to "get ahead," it also involves exposure to new cultures, ideas, practices, and possibilities. It might even lead us to an unexpected future such as a career in sociology!

While schools provide both social order and individual opportunity, they can also reinforce existing inequality through the ways students are socialized. As economists Samuel Bowles and Herbert Gintis (1976) have observed, schools produce teachable students who become manageable workers. They argue that schools have less to do with transmitting academic content than with socializing students into the proper attitudes and behaviors of the workplace. Schools teach students how to work for rewards, how to work in teams, how to meet deadlines, how to take responsibility for a task or work product, how to comply with instructions, and so on. The students who internalize these skills best are rewarded with opportunities in the workplace while others are left behind.

These differential outcomes are compounded by the fact that the positions we occupy when we enter school shape where we end up. For example, higher education in the United States is costly despite the existence of public colleges and universities and financial aid programs. Students from affluent backgrounds, therefore, have an advantage in gaining access to universities and professional training. At the same time, less affluent young people may never receive the preparation that would qualify them for the best-paying and most prestigious jobs.

PEER GROUPS

Families and schools do shape us, but if you ask any 13-year-old who matters most in his or her life, the likely answer is "friends." As children grow older, the family becomes somewhat less important in social development. Instead, peer groups increasingly assume the role of Mead's significant other. Within the peer group, young people associate with others who are approximately their own age and who often enjoy a similar social status (Giordano 2003).

In the context of peer groups, a hierarchy often develops. Sociologists Patricia and Peter Adler conducted participant observation at elementary schools to investigate how popularity works amongst fourth- through sixth-grade students. They found that, even this early, a pecking order is established ranging from the "popular clique" at the top that includes the "cool kids" on down to what they call the "social isolates" at the bottom, whom other kids sometimes call "dweebs" or "nerds" (Adler and Adler, 1996). Children get the message about where they fit and how they should behave.

gender role Expectations regarding the proper behavior, attitudes, and activities of males and females.

In other research the Adlers also found that popularity reinforces gender stereotypes. To be popular as a boy is to be athletic, tough, and not too academic. To be popular as a girl is to be attractive, to be able to manipulate others using social skills, and to come from a family wealthy enough to permit shopping for the latest cool stuff (Adler, Kless, and Adler 1992). In similar research, college students were asked to reflect on what made people popular in high school. Researchers found that male and female students named many of the same paths to popularity—such as physical attractiveness, participation in sports, and

High School Popularity

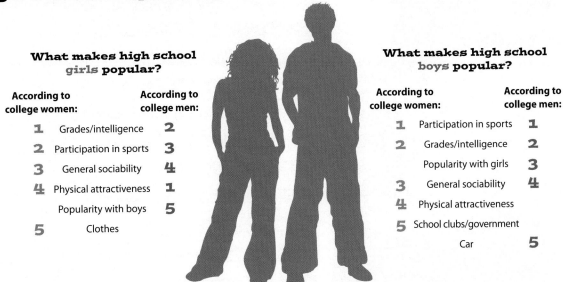

What makes high school girls popular?

According to college women:		According to college men:
1	Grades/intelligence	2
2	Participation in sports	3
3	General sociability	4
4	Physical attractiveness	1
	Popularity with boys	5
5	Clothes	

What makes high school boys popular?

According to college women:		According to college men:
1	Participation in sports	1
2	Grades/intelligence	2
	Popularity with girls	3
3	General sociability	4
4	Physical attractiveness	
5	School clubs/government	
	Car	5

Note: Students at the following universities were asked in which ways adolescents in their high schools had gained prestige with their peers: Cornell University, Louisiana State University, Southeastern Louisiana University, State University of New York at Albany, State University of New York at Stony Brook, the University of Georgia, and the University of New Hampshire.

Source: Suitor et al. 2001:445.

grades/intelligence—but gave them different orders of importance. While neither men nor women named sexual activity, drug use, or alcohol use as one of the top five paths, college men were much more likely than women to mention those behaviors as a means to becoming popular, for both boys and girls (Suitor et al. 2001).

Though we value the importance of kids establishing themselves as individuals, the irony is that peer culture is not very individualistic. Children, and especially adolescents, run in packs and look, talk, and act alike (often in the name of individualism). Of course, although parents often lecture their kids about not giving in to peer pressure, they don't really mean it. What they mean is to not give in to the *wrong kinds* of peer pressure. They love peer pressure if it makes their children more like the "good kids" or, even better, if the form of social pressure they give in to is parental pressure.

MASS MEDIA AND TECHNOLOGY

In the past 80 or so years, media innovations—radio, motion pictures, recorded music, television, and the Internet—have become important agents of socialization. One national survey indicates that 68 percent of U.S. children have a television in their bedroom, and nearly half of all youths ages 8–18 use the Internet every day (Rideout et al. 2005; Wartella et al. 2009). We are spending more and more of our time interacting with technology, which has an inevitable impact on our interactions with each other.

Television programs and even commercials can introduce young people to unfamiliar lifestyles and cultures.

... The average person in the United States is expected to watch 1728 hours of television in 2010. That works out to 4.7 hours per day.

On PBS alone, children are exposed to life in the city, on the farm, and across the world. The same thing happens in other countries and regions. In the Palestinian-held Gaza Strip, for example, Hamas—a group better known for its

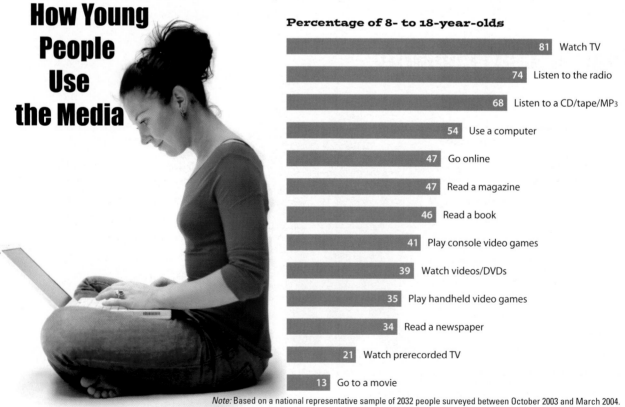

How Young People Use the Media

Percentage of 8- to 18-year-olds

81	Watch TV
74	Listen to the radio
68	Listen to a CD/tape/MP3
54	Use a computer
47	Go online
47	Read a magazine
46	Read a book
41	Play console video games
39	Watch videos/DVDs
35	Play handheld video games
34	Read a newspaper
21	Watch prerecorded TV
13	Go to a movie

Note: Based on a national representative sample of 2032 people surveyed between October 2003 and March 2004.
Source: Rideout et al. 2005:7.

suicide bombing campaigns—has launched a television program meant to familiarize children with the Palestinian position on the disputed territories. In between lectures on revered sites such as Nablus and Al Aksa Mosque, the show's host, known as Uncle Hazim, takes on-air phone calls from viewers and talks with animal characters reminiscent of those on *Sesame Street.* Designed with a child-age audience in mind, the show omits all mention of violence and armed conflict in pursuit of Hamas's goals (Craig Smith 2006).

New technologies are changing how we interact with family, friends, and even strangers. Through email, cell phones, texting, and instant messaging, we can maintain close, almost constant, connections with family and friends both near and far. Through Facebook and MySpace, we can establish and extend networks with "friends" both known and unknown. But new technologies can also lead to narrowcasting, in which we interact mainly with people who are most like ourselves. This can limit the number of significant relationships we have with people with whom we might share fundamental differences, thus weakening our conflict resolution skills. Other skills, however, may be strengthened. Researchers studying technology use among families in northern California's Silicon Valley (a technology corridor) found that families are socialized into multitasking (doing more than one task at a time) as the social norm; devoting one's full attention to one task—even eating or driving—is less and less common on a typical day (Silicon Valley Cultures Project 2004).

Around the world, including in Africa and other developing areas, people have been socialized into relying

SOCthink

> > > According to a recent commercial, "snurfing" involves surfing the Internet while you are talking to someone on the phone. To what extent does multitasking such as this have a negative impact on our interpersonal skills? How do you feel when people do this to you? Why might you have done it to others?

on new communications technologies. For instance, not long ago, if Zadhe Iyombe wanted to talk to his mother, he had to make an eight-day trip from the capital city of Kinshasa (in the Democratic Republic of the Congo) up the Congo River by boat to the rural town where he was born. Now both he and his mother have access to a cell phone, and they send text messages to each other daily. And Iyombe and his mother are not atypical. Although cell phones aren't cheap, 2.5 billion owners in developing countries have come to consider them a necessity. Today, there are more cell phones in developing countries than in industrial nations—the first time in history that developing countries have outpaced the developed world in the adoption of a telecommunications technology (LeClaire 2009; K. Sullivan 2006).

Access to media can also increase social cohesion by presenting a common, more or less standardized view of

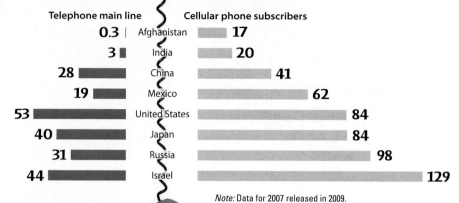

Telephones and Cell Phones by Country, 2007 (rates per 100 people)

Telephone main line		Cellular phone subscribers
0.3	Afghanistan	17
3	India	20
28	China	41
19	Mexico	62
53	United States	84
40	Japan	84
31	Russia	98
44	Israel	129

Note: Data for 2007 released in 2009.

Source: International Telecommunications Union 2009.

culture through mass communication. Sociologist Robert Park (1922) studied how newspapers helped immigrants to the United States adjust to their environment by changing their customary habits and teaching them the values and views of people in their new home country. Unquestionably, the mass media play a significant role in providing a collective experience for members of society. Think about how the mass media bring together members of a community or even a nation by broadcasting important events and ceremonies (such as inaugurations, press conferences, parades, state funerals, and the Olympics) and by covering disasters.

Which media outlets did people turn to in the aftermath of the September 11, 2001, terrorist attacks? Television and telephone were the primary means by which people in the United States bonded. But the Internet also played a prominent role. About half of all Internet users—more than 53 million people—received some kind of news about the attacks

online. Nearly three-fourths of Internet users communicated via email to show their patriotism, discuss events with their families, or reconnect with old friends. More than a third of Internet users read or posted material in online forums. In the first 30 days alone, the Library of Congress collected from one Internet site more than half a million pages having to do with the terrorist attacks. As a library director noted, "The Internet has become for many the public commons, a place where they can come together and talk" (D. L. Miller and Darlington 2002; Mirapaul 2001:E2; Rainie 2001).

THE WORKPLACE

Learning to behave appropriately in an occupation is a fundamental aspect of human socialization. In the United States, working full time confirms adult status; it indicates that one has passed out of adolescence. In a sense, socialization into an occupation can represent both a harsh reality ("I have to work in order to buy food and pay the rent") and the realization of an ambition ("I've always wanted to be an airline pilot") (W. Moore 1968:862; Simmons 2009).

It used to be that our work life began with the end of our formal schooling, but that is no longer necessarily the case, at least not in the United States. More and more young people work today, and not just for a parent or relative. Adolescents generally seek jobs in order to earn spending money; 80 percent of high school seniors say that little or none of what they earn goes to family expenses. These teens rarely look on their employment as a means of exploring vocational interests or getting on-the-job training (Hirschman and Voloshin 2007).

Did You Know?

. . . May 1, 2010 is **International Shutdown Day.** This is an annual event to encourage people to turn off their computer for 24 hours and reflect on the impact computers have on our lives and our communities. Participants are urged to spend the time they save interacting with friends, going for a hike, or volunteering in the community.

Child Care Arrangements for Preschoolers

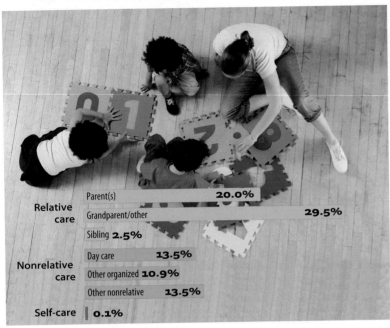

Relative care	Parent(s)	20.0%
	Grandparent/other	29.5%
	Sibling	2.5%
Nonrelative care	Day care	13.5%
	Other organized	10.9%
	Other nonrelative	13.5%
Self-care		0.1%

Source: U.S. Census Bureau 2008a.

Some observers feel that the increasing number of teenagers who are working earlier in life and for longer hours are finding the workplace to be almost as important an agent of socialization as school. In fact, a number of educators complain that time spent at work is adversely affecting students' schoolwork. The level of teenage employment in the United States is the highest among industrial countries, which may provide one explanation for why U.S. high school students lag behind those in other countries on international achievement tests.

Socialization in the workplace changes when it involves a more permanent shift from an after-school job to full-time employment. Occupational socialization can be most intense during the transition from school to job, but it continues throughout one's work history. Technological advances and corporate reorganization may alter the requirements of the position and necessitate new training. According to the Bureau of Labor Statistics (2008), between the ages of 18 to 42 alone, the typical person holds 11 different jobs. We can no longer assume that we will have a job-for-life, so whether by choice or by necessity, we must be open to ongoing occupational socialization.

RELIGION AND THE STATE

Increasingly, social scientists are recognizing the growing importance of government ("the state") and the continued significance of religion as agents of socialization. Traditionally, family members served as the primary caregivers in U.S. culture, but in the 20th century, the family's protective function was steadily transferred to outside agencies such as public schools, hospitals, mental health clinics, and child care centers, many of which are run by the state. Historically, religious groups also provided such care and protection. Despite early sociological predictions that religion would cease to play a substantial role in modern society, these groups continue to play a significant role in identity formation and collective life (Warner 2005).

Preschool children in particular are often cared for by someone other than a parent. Eighty-eight percent of employed mothers depend on others to care for their children, and 29 percent of mothers who aren't employed have regular care arrangements. Over a third of children under age five are cared for by nonrelatives in nursery schools, Head Start programs, day care centers, family day care, and other providers. Children this age are also more likely to be cared for on a daily basis by grandparents than by their parents (U.S. Census Bureau 2008a).

Both government and organized religion act to provide markers representing significant life course transitions. For example, religious organizations continue to celebrate meaningful ritual events—such as baptism, bismillah, or bar/bat mitzvah—that often bring together all the members of an extended family, even if they never meet

Hot or Not?

Should government play a larger role in socializing children by funding public education for all children starting at the age of two?

Leh Village, India school children.

Although many 18-year-olds choose not to vote, voter turnout in the 2008 presidential election was the highest it had been in decades, causing long lines at some polling stations.

borns to the world in the Soboa ceremony by stepping over the seven-day-old infant seven times. And Naval Academy seniors celebrate their graduation from college by hurling their hats skyward.

THE LIFE COURSE

Such specific ceremonies mark stages of development in the life course. They indicate that the process of socialization continues through all stages of the life cycle. In fact, some researchers have chosen to concentrate on socialization as a lifelong process. Sociologists and other social scientists who take such a **life course approach** look closely at the social factors, including gender and income, that influence people throughout their lives, from birth to death. They recognize that biological changes help mold but do not dictate human behavior.

In the transition from childhood to adulthood, we can identify certain markers that signify the passage from one life stage to the next. These milestones vary from one society and even one generation to the next. In the United States, according to one national survey, completion of

for any other reason. Government regulations stipulate the ages at which a person may drive a car, drink alcohol, vote in elections, marry without parental permission, work overtime, and retire. While these regulations do not constitute strict rites of passage—most 18-year-olds choose not to vote, and most people choose their age of retirement without reference to government dictates—they do symbolize the fact that we have moved on to a different stage of our life, with different expectations regarding our behavior.

rite of passage A ritual marking the symbolic transition from one social position to another.

life course approach A research orientation in which sociologists and other social scientists look closely at the social factors that influence people throughout their lives, from birth to death.

Body painting is a ritual marking the passage to puberty in some cultures.

>> Socialization Throughout the Life Course

Adolescents among the Kota people of the Congo in Africa paint themselves blue. Cuban American girls go on a day-long religious retreat before dancing the night away. These are both **rites of passage**—rituals that mark the symbolic transition from one social position to another, dramatizing and validating changes in a person's status.

In the Kota rite the color blue—the color of death— symbolizes the death of childhood and the passage to adulthood. For adolescent girls in Miami's Cuban American community, the *quinceañera* ceremony celebrating the attainment of womanhood at age 15 supports a network of party planners, caterers, dress designers, and the Miss Quinceañera Latina pageant. For thousands of years, Egyptian mothers have welcomed their new-

Milestones in the Transition to Adulthood

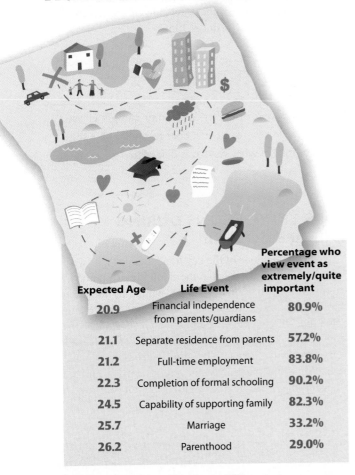

Expected Age	Life Event	Percentage who view event as extremely/quite important
20.9	Financial independence from parents/guardians	80.9%
21.1	Separate residence from parents	57.2%
21.2	Full-time employment	83.8%
22.3	Completion of formal schooling	90.2%
24.5	Capability of supporting family	82.3%
25.7	Marriage	33.2%
26.2	Parenthood	29.0%

Note: Based on the 2002 General Social Survey of 1398 people.
Source: T. Smith 2003.

formal schooling has risen to the top, with 90 percent of people identifying it as an important rite of passage. On average, Americans expect this milestone to be attained by a person's 23rd birthday. Other major events in the life course, such as getting married or becoming a parent, are expected to follow three or four years later. Interestingly, the significance of these markers has declined, with only about one-third of survey respondents identifying marriage and less than one-third identifying parenthood as important milestones representing adulthood (S. Furstenberg et al. 2004; T. Smith 2003).

One result of these staggered steps to independence is that in the United States, unlike some other societies, there is no clear dividing line between adolescence and adulthood. Nowadays, the number of years between childhood and adulthood has grown, and few young people finish school, get married, and leave home at about the same age, clearly establishing their transition to adulthood. The term *youthhood* has been coined to describe the prolonged ambiguous status that young people in their 20s experience (Côté 2000).

SOCthink

> > > What are some of the markers of youthhood? When does it begin? When does it end? To what extent do you feel like an adult? What characteristics of our society contribute to ambiguity in our passage into adulthood?

ANTICIPATORY SOCIALIZATION AND RESOCIALIZATION

In our journey through our lives, we seek to prepare ourselves for what is coming and to adapt to change as necessary. To prepare, we undergo **anticipatory socialization,** which refers to processes of socialization in which a person "rehearses" for future positions, occupations, and social relationships. A culture can function more efficiently and smoothly if members become acquainted with the norms, values, and behavior associated with a social position before actually assuming that status. Preparation for many aspects of adult life begins with anticipatory socialization during childhood and adolescence and continues throughout our lives as we prepare for new responsibilities (Levine and Hoffner 2006).

High school students experience a bit of anticipatory socialization when they prepare for college. They begin to imagine what college life will be like and what kind of person they will be when they get there. They may seek out information from friends and family in order to get a better sense of what to expect, but increasingly, they also rely on campus websites and Facebook entries. To assist in this process and to attract more students, colleges are investing more time and money in websites through which students can take "virtual" campus tours, listen to podcasts, and stream videos of everything from the school song to a sample zoology lecture.

Occasionally, assuming a new social or occupational position requires that we *unlearn* an established orientation. **Resocialization** refers to the process of discarding old behavior patterns and accepting new ones as part of a life transition. Often resocialization results from explicit efforts to transform an individual, as happens in reform schools, therapy groups, prisons, religious conversion settings, and political indoctrination camps. The process of resocialization typically involves considerable stress for the individual—much more so than socialization in general, or even anticipatory socialization (Hart, Miller, and Johnson 2003).

Resocialization is particularly effective when it occurs within a total institution. Erving Goffman (1961) coined the term **total institution** to refer to an institution that reg-

anticipatory socialization Processes of socialization in which a person "rehearses" for future positions, occupations, and social relationships.

resocialization The process of discarding former behavior patterns and accepting new ones as part of a transition in one's life.

total institution An institution that regulates all aspects of a person's life under a single authority, such as a prison, the military, a mental hospital, or a convent.

ulates all aspects of a person's life under a single authority. Examples can be more or less extreme, from summer camp or boarding school to prison, the military, a mental hospital, or a convent. Because the total institution is generally cut off from the rest of society, it provides for all the needs of its members. In its extreme form, so elaborate are its requirements, and so all-encompassing its activities, that the total institution represents a miniature society.

degradation ceremony An aspect of the socialization process within some total institutions, in which people are subjected to humiliating rituals.

Goffman (1961) identified several common traits of total institutions:

- All aspects of life are conducted in the same place under the control of a single authority.

- Any activities within the institution are conducted in the company of others in the same circumstances—for example, army recruits or novices in a convent.

- The authorities devise rules and schedule activities without consulting the participants.

- All aspects of life within a total institution are designed to fulfill the purpose of the organization. Thus, all activities in a monastery might be centered on prayer and communion with God (Malacrida 2005; Mapel 2007; Williams and Warren 2009).

People often lose their individuality within total institutions. For example, a person entering prison may experience the humiliation of a **degradation ceremony** as he or she is stripped of clothing, jewelry, and other personal possessions. From that point on, scheduled daily routines allow for little or no personal initiative. The individual becomes secondary and rather invisible in the overbearing social environment (Garfinkel 1956).

SOCthink

> > > To what extent is summer camp, a cruise, or even life at a residential college similar to a total institution? In what ways is it different?

ROLE TRANSITIONS DURING THE LIFE COURSE

As we have seen, one of the key transitional stages we pass through occurs as we enter the adult world, perhaps by moving out of the parental home, beginning a career, or entering a marriage. As we age, we move into the midlife transition, which typically begins at about age 40. Men and women often experience a stressful period of self-evaluation, commonly known as the **midlife crisis,** in which they realize that they have not achieved basic goals and ambitions and may feel they have little time left to do so. This

Life in prison is highly regulated—even recreation time.

conflict between their hopes and their outcomes causes strain. Compounding such stresses that are often associated with one's career or partner is the growing responsibility for caring for two generations at once (Mortimer and Shanahan 2006; Wethington 2000).

During the late 1990s, social scientists began focusing on the **sandwich generation**—adults who simultaneously try to meet the competing needs of their par-

5 Movies on SOCIALIZATION

49 Up
Documentary following 14 children as their lives progress from age 7 to 49.

In America
An Irish family adapts to life in New York City.

Children Underground
Documentary about children surviving in the subway systems of Romania.

Half Nelson
A young teacher in Brooklyn struggles in and out of the classroom.

Training Day
A day in the life of a rookie narcotics officer in the LAPD.

ents and their children. Their caregiving goes in two directions: to children, who even as young adults may still require significant support and direction, and to aging parents, whose health and economic problems may demand intervention by their adult children.

Like the role of caring for children, that of caring for aging parents falls disproportionately on women. Overall, women provide 60 percent of the care their parents receive, and even more as the demands of the role grow more intense and time consuming. Increasingly, middle-aged women and younger are finding themselves on the "daughter track," as their time and attention are diverted by the needs of their aging mothers and fathers (Gross 2005).

ADJUSTING TO RETIREMENT

Our last major life course transition generally occurs after age 60—sometimes well after that age, due to advances in health care, greater longevity, and gradual acceptance by society of older people. In fact, yesterday's 60 may be today's 70 or even 75. Nonetheless, at some point, most people eventually transition to a different lifestyle (Vincent 2006).

Retirement is a rite of passage that typically marks a transition out of active participation in the full-time labor market. Symbolic events are associated with this rite of passage, such as retirement gifts, a retirement party, and special moments on the last day on the job. The preretirement period itself can be emotionally charged, especially if the retiree is expected to train his or her successor (Reitzes and Mutran 2004).

From 1950 to the mid-1990s, the average age at retirement in the United States declined, but in recent years it has reversed direction. In 2007, 14 percent of women and 21 percent of men age 70 to 74 were still working (Gendall 2008). A variety of factors explains this reversal: changes in Social Security benefits, an economic shift away from hard manual labor, and workers' concern with maintaining their health insurance and pension benefits. At the same time, longevity has increased, and the quality of people's health has improved (He et al. 2005:89).

Gerontologist Robert Atchley (1976) has identified several phases of the retirement experience:

- *Preretirement,* a period of anticipatory socialization as the person prepares for retirement.
- *The near phase,* when the person establishes a specific departure date from his or her job.
- *The honeymoon phase,* an often euphoric period in which the person pursues activities that he or she never had time for before.
- *The disenchantment phase,* in which retirees feel a sense of letdown or even depression as they cope with their new lives, which may include illness or poverty.
- *The reorientation phase,* which involves the development of a more realistic view of retirement alternatives.
- *The stability phase,* in which the person has learned to deal with life after retirement in a reasonable and comfortable fashion.
- *The termination phase,* which begins when the person can no longer engage in basic, day-to-day activities such as self-care and housework.

Retirement is not a single transition, then, but a series of adjustments that varies from one person to another. The length and timing of each phase will differ for each individual, depending on such factors as financial and health status. In fact, a person will not necessarily go through all the phases identified by Atchley. For example, people who are forced to retire or who face financial difficulties may never experience a honeymoon phase. And many retirees continue to be part of the paid labor force of the United States, often taking part-time jobs to supplement their pensions. That is certainly the expectation of baby boomers, as fully 79 percent expect to work in some capacity after they retire (see "Retirement Expectations" on page 86).

> **midlife crisis** A stressful period of self-evaluation that begins at about age 40.
>
> **sandwich generation** The generation of adults who simultaneously try to meet the competing needs of their parents and their children.

Retirement Expectations

nic minority groups work intermittently after retirement more often than older Whites (Brown and Warner 2008; Ozawa and Choi 2002).

We encounter some of the most difficult socialization challenges (and rites of passage) in these later years of life. Retirement undermines the sense of self we had that was based in our occupation, a particularly significant source of identity in the United States. Similarly, taking stock of our accomplishments and disappointments, coping with declining physical abilities, and recognizing the inevitability of death may lead to painful adjustments. Part of the difficulty is that potential answers to the "Now what?" question that we might have asked in previous life stages are dwindling, and we begin to face the end of our days.

And yet, as we reflect on the story of our lives, we can look back to see all the people who shaped us into becoming who we are. Such relationships play a crucial role in our overall self-concept and self-satisfaction. As we have already seen, we are interdependent. And, though the influences of others on our life can be both a blessing and a curse, we wouldn't be who we are without them.

Other/don't know **4%**

Retire from your current job but work full-time doing something else **7%**

Start your own business/go into business for yourself **15%**

Not work at all **20%**

Work part-time mainly for interest or enjoyment **30%**

Work part-time mainly for needed income it provides **25%**

Note: Survey of the baby boom generation (people born from 1946 to 1964) conducted in 2003.
Source: AARP 2004.

Like other aspects of life in the United States, the experience of retirement varies according to gender, race, and ethnicity. White males are most likely to benefit from retirement wages, as well as to have participated in a formal retirement preparation program. As a result, anticipatory socialization for retirement is most systematic for White men. In contrast, members of racial and ethnic minority groups—especially African Americans—are more likely to exit the paid labor force through disability than through retirement. Because of their comparatively lower incomes and smaller savings, men and women from racial and eth-

get **involved!**

Stop! Go on a "technology fast," and give up email, blogs, Facebook, MySpace, texting, computers, and even your cell phone for a week. Keep a journal of how you respond.

For REVIEW

I. **How do we become our self?**
   - We are born with innate tendencies, but we depend upon the socializing influences of others with whom we interact to provide us with the cultural tools necessary for our survival.

II. **Who shapes our socialization?**
   - Although almost anyone with whom we interact can have a significant influence on us, particularly important to our development are the family, school, peer group, mass media, religion, and the state.

III. **How does our development change over time?**
   - We learn new things at various stages of our life course, experiencing significant transitions as we pass from childhood to adulthood and again from adulthood into retirement. At each stage, the kinds of things expected of us by others shift significantly.

Pop Quiz

1. The nurture side of the nature–nurture debate argues that
   a. socialization plays a critical role in shaping our attitudes, values, and behaviors.
   b. our attitudes, values, and behaviors are largely inherited biologically through our DNA.
   c. sociology has a limited role in explaining our behaviors before age two.
   d. we cannot determine the degree to which our behaviors are shaped by heredity or environment.

2. According to Charles Horton Cooley, the process of developing a self-identity by imagining how others see us is known as
   a. socialization.
   b. the looking-glass self.
   c. the Me.
   d. the generalized other.

3. In George Herbert Mead's *play stage* of socialization, people mentally assume the perspectives of others, thereby enabling them to respond from that imagined viewpoint. This process is referred to as
   a. symbolization.
   b. the significant other.
   c. impression management.
   d. role taking.

4. Suppose a clerk tries to appear busier than he or she actually is when a supervisor happens to be watching. Erving Goffman would say this is a form of what?
   a. degradation ceremony
   b. impression management
   c. resocialization
   d. looking-glass self

5. According to child psychologist Jean Piaget's cognitive theory of development, children begin to use words and symbols to distinguish objects and ideas during which stage in the development of the thought process?
   a. sensorimotor stage
   b. preoperational stage
   c. concrete operational stage
   d. formal operational stage

6. Which social institution is considered to be the most important agent of socialization in the United States, especially for children?
   a. family
   b. school
   c. peer group
   d. mass media

7. The term *gender role* refers to
   a. the biological fact that we are male or female.
   b. a role that is given to us by a teacher.
   c. a role that is given to us in a play.
   d. expectations regarding the proper behavior, attitudes, and activities of males and females.

8. On the first day of basic training in the army, a male recruit has his civilian clothes replaced with army "greens," has his hair shaved off, loses his privacy, and finds that he must use a communal bathroom. All of these humiliating activities are part of
   a. becoming a significant other.
   b. impression management.
   c. a degradation ceremony.
   d. face-work.

9. What do sociologists call the symbolic representations of major change in a person's status throughout their life course?
   a. rites of passage
   b. anticipatory socialization
   c. impression management
   d. role taking

10. The process of discarding former behavior patterns and taking on new ones is known as what?
    a. resocialization
    b. impression management
    c. anticipatory socialization
    d. the I

1. (a); 2. (b); 3. (d); 4. (b); 5. (b); 6. (a); 7. (d); 8. (c); 9. (a); 10. (a)

5

SOCIAL

BECOMING AN INDIVIDUAL IN SOCIETY

"Tattooing had really never entered my awareness very much. When it did, the associations were always with sailors first, ex-convicts second, and various toughs and gangsters last. . . . I had read in some obscure novel about the three signs of 'badness'—socks rolled down to the ankle, long sideburns, and a tattoo showing on the wrist. Robert Mitchum's demented killer had *Love* and *Hate* tattooed on the fingers of each hand." So writes Samuel M. Steward (1990:8) of his perception of tattoos back in the 1950s, a perception widely shared by others at the time. Steward had been a college professor for 20 years, but he decided to walk away from that to become a tattoo artist. You might say he was ahead of his time.

Times change, and so do we. Nowadays almost 40 percent of people 18–40 years old have at least one tattoo. So many people have them—including society's trendsetters and major sports figures—that mainstream culture accepts tattoos. Yet, for those who grew up in an earlier era, perhaps the stigma remains: Only 10 percent of people aged 41–64 have tattoos.

In fact, knowing a person's age allows us to predict a variety of things about how they think and what they do. Research on what has been called "Generation Next," which includes people born between 1981 and 1988, finds them less cynical about government and political leaders, less critical of business, and more tolerant on issues of immigration, race, and homosexuality than those from earlier generations. When it comes to technology, they were actually less likely to have sent or received an email within the past 24 hours than those ages 26–40. However, just over half had sent or received a text message, making them twice as likely to have done so (Kohut 2007a).

Although we like to think of our preferences as a matter of our own individual choice, when we are born shapes our tastes. Like age, our gender, race, class, ethnicity, nationality, education, religious affiliation, occupation, and income all shape how we think, what we do, and even how we feel. Sociology investigates how those positions combine to form our social structure.

STRUCTURE &INTERACTION

- What makes up society?
- How does social structure shape individual action?
- How do sociologists describe traditional versus modern societies?

>> Social Interaction

When we create culture—whether in the form of language, rules, or objects—we establish a relationship with each other and to the external world. The more we share culture with others, the more resistant it becomes to change, because change would involve getting all the people who now share that culture to think and act in new ways. Because shared culture tends to remain stable, over time we come to take certain cultural expectations for granted. In so doing, we construct the context or social environment within which we live. The result is society—the structure of relationships within which culture is created and shared through regularized patterns of social interaction.

social interaction The shared experiences through which people relate to one another.
social structure The way in which a society is organized into predictable relationships.

In working together to construct culture, we participate in **social interaction,** the shared experiences through which people relate to one another. It is through interaction that society comes alive. To use an analogy, think of society as a board game. The various components of the game—the board, game pieces, dice, rules, and so on—provide the structure of the game, but it is not truly a game until someone plays it. Society, too, must be enacted, embodied, and brought to life by individuals interacting.

How we interact with other people is shaped by our perception of their position relative to our own. According to sociologist Herbert Blumer (1969:79), the distinctive characteristic of social interaction is that "human beings interpret or 'define' each other's actions instead of merely reacting to each other's actions." In other words, we respond to someone's behavior based on the meaning we attach to his or her actions. Our perceptions, evaluations, and definitions shape our reality. The meanings we ascribe to others' actions typically reflect the norms and values of the dominant culture and our socialization experiences within that culture. Our understanding of social reality is liter-

ally constructed from our social interactions (Berger and Luckmann 1966).

The ability to define social reality reflects a group's power within a society. In fact, one of the crucial aspects of the relationship between dominant and subordinate groups is the ability of the former to define a society's values. Sociologists W. I. Thomas and Dorothy Swain Thomas (1928), critics of theories of inherent racial and gender differences, argued that our "definition of the situation" shapes our responses. In other words, we act based on what we perceive to be true rather than on what is objectively true, and our perceptions are shaped by socialization into society's dominant values.

Changing the meanings we attach to the positions people occupy often involves a struggle because those who wield power and influence in a society are reluctant to relinquish their positions of control. Since the mid-1900s—starting with the civil rights movement of the 1950s and 1960s and continuing among such groups as women, the elderly, gays and lesbians, and people with disabilities—an important aspect of the process of social change has involved redefining or reconstructing social reality.

Did You Know?

. . . Muhammad Ali was found guilty of draft evasion and sentenced to five years in prison. In 1967, he refused induction into the Army due to his pacifist religious convictions as a Muslim. Ultimately, the U.S. Supreme Court reversed his draft evasion conviction, and he avoided serving jail time.

When members of subordinate groups challenge traditional social assumptions, they can raise our consciousness about the consequences of group membership or social position and help us perceive and experience reality in a new way. For example, when Olympic gold medalist Muhammad Ali began his professional boxing career in the early 1960s, he was much like any other young Black fighter. He was managed and sponsored by a White syndicate and went by his given name, Cassius Clay. Soon, however, the young boxer rebelled against the old stereotypes of the self-effacing Black athlete and began to define his own social role. He converted to Islam, becoming a member of the U.S.-based Nation of Islam, and abandoned his "slave name" to take the name Muhammad Ali. He insisted on expressing his own political views, including refusing to fight in the Vietnam War. Ali changed the terms of social interaction for Black athletes by rebelling against racist thinking and terminology. In redefining social reality, he helped open up greater opportunities for himself and for other African Americans in the world of sports and beyond.

>> Elements of Social Structure

All social interaction takes place within a **social structure**—a series of predictable relationships composed of various positions that people occupy. Occupying those positions shapes how we think and act and what resources we have access to. For example, our position as parent, employee, or student exists in relation to other positions, such as child, boss, or professor. Further, each of these positions implies certain expectations and obligations on our part, such as discipline, labor, and studying. In short, how we interact with others is shaped by the positions we occupy.

For purposes of study, we can break down any social structure into six elements: statuses, social roles, groups, social networks, virtual worlds, and social institutions. These elements make up the social structure just as a foundation, walls, and ceilings make up a building's structure. The elements of social structure are internalized through the lifelong process of socialization described in Chapter 4.

STATUSES

We normally think of a person's "status" as having to do with influence, wealth, and fame. However, sociologists use the term **status** to refer to the social positions we occupy relative to others. Within our society, a person can occupy the status of president of the United States, fruit picker, son or daughter, violinist, teenager, resident of St. Louis, dental technician, or neighbor. A person can hold a number of statuses at the same time.

Ascribed and Achieved Status Sociologists categorize statuses as either ascribed or achieved. An **ascribed**

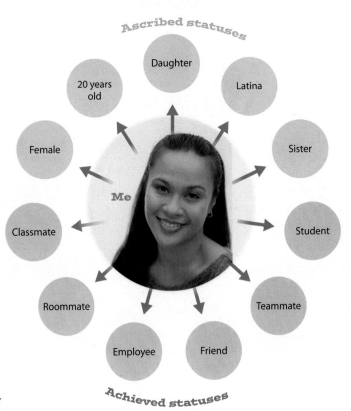

Social Statuses

Ascribed statuses

20 years old · Daughter · Latina · Female · Sister · Me · Classmate · Student · Roommate · Teammate · Employee · Friend

Achieved statuses

status is assigned to a person by society without regard for the person's unique talents or characteristics. Generally, the assignment takes place at birth; thus, a person's age, race/ethnicity, and gender are all considered ascribed statuses. Though such characteristics are biological in origin, the key is the social meaning we attach to such categories. Ascribed statuses are often used to justify privileges or reflect a person's membership in a subordinate group, and we will analyze the impacts of race, ethnicity, and gender as ascribed statuses in Chapters 12 and 13.

status The social positions we occupy relative to others.
ascribed status A social position assigned to a person by society without regard for the person's unique talents or characteristics.

In most cases, we can do little to change an ascribed status. We can, however, attempt to change the traditional constraints associated with it. For example, since its founding in 1971, the activist political group Gray Panthers has worked for the rights of older people and tried to modify society's negative and confining stereotypes of the elderly. As a result of their work and that of other groups supporting older citizens, the ascribed status of "senior citizen" is no longer as difficult for millions of older people.

An ascribed status does not necessarily have the same social meaning in every society. In a cross-cultural study, sociologist Gary Huang (1988) confirmed the long-held view that respect for the elderly is an important cultural norm in China. There, in many cases, the prefix "old" is used respectfully: calling someone "old teacher" or

that he was diagnosed with Parkinson's disease. He had a remarkable career in films and television, but now his status as a well-known personality with Parkinson's may outweigh his statuses as actor, author, and political activist.

People with disabilities frequently observe that the nondisabled see them only as blind, or only as wheelchair users, and so on, rather than as complex human beings with individual strengths and weaknesses whose disability is merely one aspect of their lives. Often people with disabilities find that their status as "disabled" receives undue weight, overshadowing their actual ability to hold meaningful employment and contributing to widespread prejudice, discrimination, and segregation. For example, most voting places are inaccessible to wheelchair users and fail to provide ballots that can be used by the blind. Activists argue that such unnecessary and discriminatory barriers present in the environment—both physical and attitudinal—restrict people with disabilities more than do any biological limitations.

"old person" is like calling a judge in the United States "your honor." Huang points out that such positive old-age-related language distinctions are uncommon in the United States; consequently, we view the term "old man" as more of an insult than a celebration of seniority and wisdom.

achieved status A social position that is within our power to change.

master status A status that dominates others and thereby determines a person's general position in society.

social role A set of expectations for people who occupy a given social position or status.

Unlike ascribed statuses, an **achieved status** is a social position that is within our power to change. Both bank president and prison guard are achieved statuses, as are lawyer, pianist, sorority member, convict, and social worker. We must do something to acquire an achieved status—go to school, learn a skill, establish a friendship, invent a new product, commit a crime, and so on. But our ascribed status can heavily influence our achieved status. Being male in the United States, for example, still decreases the likelihood that a person will consider child care as a career.

Master Status Each of us holds many different and sometimes conflicting statuses; some may connote a higher social position, and others a lower position. How, then, do others view our overall social position? According to sociologist Everett Hughes (1945), societies deal with inconsistencies by agreeing that certain statuses are more important than others. A **master status** is a status that dominates others and thereby determines a person's general position in society. For example, in 1998, Michael J. Fox revealed

SOCthink

> > > Why do factors such as race, gender, or disability become master statuses? What might master status tell us about how powerful our definition of "normal" is?

Ascribed statuses frequently influence our achieved status. The African American activist Malcolm X (1925–1965), an eloquent and controversial advocate of Black power and Black pride in the 1960s, recalled that his feelings and perspectives changed dramatically while in eighth grade. When his English teacher, a White man, advised him that his goal of becoming a lawyer was "no realistic goal for a nigger" and suggested he become a carpenter instead, Malcolm X (1964:37) found that his position as a Black man (ascribed status) was an obstacle to his dream of becoming a lawyer (achieved status). In the United States, the ascribed statuses of race and gender can function as master statuses that play an important part in one's efforts to achieve a desired professional and social status.

SOCIAL ROLES

Throughout our lives, we acquire what sociologists call social roles. A **social role** is a set of expectations for people who occupy a given social position or status. While we occupy a status, we play a role. Thus, in the United States, we expect that cab drivers will know how to get around a city, that receptionists will handle phone messages, and that police officers will take action if they see a citizen being threatened. With each distinctive social status—whether ascribed or achieved—come particular role expectations. However, actual performance varies from individual to individual. One secretary may assume extensive administrative responsibilities, whereas another may focus on clerical duties.

Roles are a significant component of social structure. Roles can contribute to a society's stability by enabling members to anticipate the behavior of others and to pattern their own actions accordingly. Yet social roles can also restrict people's interactions and relationships. If we view a person *only* as a police officer or a supervisor, it will be difficult to relate to him or her as a friend or neighbor.

Role Conflict Sometimes the statuses we occupy can clash. **Role conflict** occurs when incompatible expectations arise from two or more social statuses held by the same person. Fulfillment of the roles associated with one po-

Hot or Not?

Is there no such thing as our true self? Are we only actors performing roles based on the positions we occupy?

sition may directly violate the roles linked to a second status.

Imagine the delicate situation of a woman who has worked for a decade on an assembly line in an electrical plant and has recently been named supervisor of her unit. She now must balance her status as a friend with her status as the boss. How should she treat her longtime friends and co-workers? Should she still have lunch with them? Should she recommend the firing of an old friend who cannot keep up with the demands of the assembly line? She will most likely experience a sharp conflict between her friendship and supervisory roles. Such role conflicts involve difficult ethical choices. The new supervisor will have to make a difficult decision about how much allegiance she owes her friend and how much she owes her employers, who have given her supervisory responsibilities.

Another type of role conflict occurs when individuals move into occupations that are not common among people with their ascribed status. Male preschool teachers and female police officers experience this type of role conflict. In the latter case, the women must strive to reconcile their workplace role in law enforcement with the societal view of a woman's proper role, which historically has not embraced many skills associated with police work. And even as female police officers encounter sexual harassment, as women do throughout the labor force, they must also deal with the "code of silence,"

> **role conflict** The situation that occurs when incompatible expectations arise from two or more social statuses held by the same person.

an informal norm that precludes their implicating fellow officers in wrongdoing (Maher 2008; Pershing 2003).

Role Strain Role conflict describes the situation of a person dealing with the

SOCthink

> > > List the social statuses you occupy. Which ones are ascribed, and which are achieved? What roles are you expected to play as a consequence of the positions you occupy? How do you resolve possible role conflicts?

challenge of occupying two social positions simultaneously. However, even a single status can cause problems. Sociologists use the term **role strain** to describe the difficulty that arises when the same social status imposes conflicting demands and expectations.

People who belong to minority cultures may experience role strain while working in the mainstream culture. Criminologist Larry Gould (2002) interviewed officers of the Navajo Nation Police Department and found that they faced role strain when responding to the majority and minority communities. They were expected to follow the official policies and procedures defined by conventional law enforcement officials (sheriffs and FBI agents). At the same time, Navajo Nation officers practice an alternative form of justice known as Peacemaking, in which they seek reconciliation between the parties to a crime or grievance. The officers expressed great confidence in Peacemaking but worried that if they did not make arrests, other law enforcement officials would think they were too soft or were "just taking care of their own." All felt the strain of being considered "too Navajo" or "not Navajo enough."

role strain The difficulty that arises when the same social status imposes conflicting demands and expectations.

Role Exit Often, when we think of assuming a social role, we focus on the preparation and anticipatory socialization a person undergoes for that role. Such is true if a person is about to become an attorney, a chef, a spouse, or a parent. Yet, social scientists have paid less attention to the adjustments involved in leaving social roles.

Sociologist Helen Rose Fuchs Ebaugh (1988) used the term **role exit** to describe the process of disengagement from a role that is central to one's self-identity in order to establish a new role and identity. Drawing on interviews—with, among others, ex-convicts, divorced men and women, recovering alcoholics, ex-nuns, former doctors, retirees, and transsexuals—Ebaugh (herself a former nun) studied the process of voluntarily exiting from significant social roles.

Ebaugh has offered a four-stage model of role exit. The first stage begins with doubt. The person experiences frustration, burnout, or simply unhappiness with an accustomed status and the roles associated with that social position. The second stage involves a search for alternatives. An individual who is unhappy with his or her career may take a leave of absence; an unhappily married couple may begin what they see as a trial separation.

The third stage of role exit is the action stage, or departure. Ebaugh found that the vast majority of her respondents could identify a clear turning point when it became essential to take final action and leave their jobs, end their marriages, or engage in some other type of role exit. Only 20 percent of respondents saw their role exit as a gradual, evolutionary process that had no single turning point.

The last stage of role exit involves the creation of a new identity. Traditionally, students experience a form of role exit when they make the transition from high school to college. They may leave behind the role of a child living at home and take on the role of a somewhat independent college student living with peers in a dorm. Sociologist Ira Silver (1996) has studied the central role that material objects play in this transition. The objects students choose to leave at home (like stuffed animals and dolls) are associated with their prior identities. They may remain deeply attached to those objects but not want them to be seen as part of their new identities at college. The objects they bring with them symbolize how they now see themselves and how they wish to be perceived. iPods and wall posters, for example, are calculated to say, "This is me."

SOCthink

> > > Whether from a sports team, a religious group, the military, or some other close-knit group, what experience, if any, have you had with role exiting? To what extent does your experience match the four stages Ebaugh describes?

Sociologist Helen Rose Fuchs Ebaugh interviewed transsexuals (as pictured here) and others exiting from significant social roles in order to develop her four-stage model of role exit.

From Me to You

While I love teaching, I hate grading. When I mention that to students they say I have no one to blame but myself; if I didn't assign things I wouldn't have to grade them. But I don't teach in a vacuum. If I didn't assign papers and tests students would focus their time and energy on their looming chemistry test or their literature paper instead of reading for, participating in, or even attending my course. It is not that students aren't interested or sincere; it's that they are forced to budget their time according to their most pressing demands. Because we exist in social systems, the expectations of those systems limit the amount of innovation we might desire.

GROUPS

Statuses combine in various ways to form social groups. In sociological terms, a **group** is any number of people with shared norms, values, and goals who interact with one another on a regular basis. The members of a women's basketball team, a hospital's business office, a synagogue, or a symphony orchestra constitute a group. However, the residents of a suburb would not be considered a group, because they rarely interact with one another at one time.

Groups play a vital part in a society's social structure. Much of our social interaction takes place within groups and is influenced by their norms and sanctions. Being a teenager or a retired person, for example, takes on special meaning when we interact within groups designed for people with that particular status. The expectations associated with many social roles, including those accompanying the statuses of sibling and student, become more clearly defined in the context of a group.

Primary and Secondary Groups Charles Horton Cooley (1902) coined the term **primary group** to refer to a small group characterized by intimate, face-to-face association and cooperation. Such groups often entail long-term commitment and involve more of what we think of as our whole self. The members of a street gang can constitute a primary group; so can members of a family occupying the same household, or a group of "sisters" living in a college sorority.

Primary groups shape who we are and what we think about ourselves, thus playing a pivotal role both in the socialization process and in the development of our statuses and roles. Indeed, whether with family, friends, or teammates, primary groups can be instrumental in our day-to-day existence. When we find ourselves identifying closely with a group, it is probably a primary group.

We also participate in many groups that are not characterized by close bonds of friendship, such as large college classes and business associations. The term **secondary group** refers to a formal, impersonal group in which there is little social intimacy or mutual understanding. Participation in such groups is typically more instrumental or goal-directed, often involving only what we think of as one part of our self. Given these characteristics, we are more likely to move into and out of such groups as suits our needs. The distinction between primary and secondary groups is not always clear-cut, however. Some social clubs may become so large and impersonal that they no longer function as primary groups; similarly, some work groups can become so close-knit that they are experienced as primary groups (Hochschild 1989). The

role exit The process of disengagement from a role that is central to one's self-identity in order to establish a new role and identity.

group Any number of people with shared norms, values, and goals who interact with one another on a regular basis.

primary group A small group characterized by intimate, face-to-face association and cooperation.

secondary group A formal, impersonal group in which there is little social intimacy or mutual understanding.

Comparison of Primary and Secondary Groups

Primary group	Secondary group
Generally small	Usually large
Relatively long period of interaction	Relatively short duration, often temporary
Intimate, face-to-face association	Little social intimacy or mutual understanding
Some emotional depth to relationships	Relationships generally superficial
Cooperative, friendly	More formal and impersonal

accompanying table demonstrates some significant differences between primary and secondary groups.

In-Groups and Out-Groups In addition to degree of intimacy, groups can hold special meaning for members because of their relationship to other groups. For example, people in one group sometimes feel antagonistic toward or threatened by another group, especially if that group is perceived as being different either culturally or racially. To identify these "we" and "they" feelings, sociologists use two terms first employed by William Graham Sumner (1906): in-group and out-group.

An **in-group** can be defined as any group or category to which people feel they

belong. Simply put, it comprises everyone who is regarded as "we" or "us." The in-group may be as narrow as a teenage clique or as broad as an entire society. The very existence of an in-group implies the existence of an out-group that is viewed as "they" or "them." An **out-group** is a group or category to which people feel they do not belong.

In-group members typically feel distinct and superior, seeing themselves as better than people in the out-group. Proper behavior for the in-group is simultaneously viewed as unacceptable behavior for the out-group. This double standard enhances the sense of superiority. Sociologist Robert Merton (1968) described this process as the conversion of "in-group virtues" into "out-group vices." We can see this differential standard operating in the context of terrorism. When a group or a nation takes aggressive actions, it usually justifies them as necessary even if civilians are hurt or killed. Opponents are quick to assign the emotion-laden label of *terrorist* to such actions and to appeal to the world community for condemnation. Yet these same people may themselves retaliate with actions that hurt civilians, which the first group will then condemn (Juergensmeyer 2003).

Conflict between in-groups and out-groups can turn violent on a personal as well as a political level. In 1999 two disaffected students at Columbine High School in Littleton, Colorado, launched an attack in the school that left 15 students and teachers dead, including themselves. According to initial reports, the gunmen, members of an out-group that other students referred to as the Trenchcoat Mafia, apparently resented the continual taunting of an in-group known as the Jocks. Similar episodes have occurred in schools across the nation, where rejected adolescents, overwhelmed by personal and family problems, peer group pressure, academic responsibilities, or media images of violence, have lashed out against more popular classmates.

Every society honors its live conformists, and its dead troublemakers.

Mignon McLaughlin

SOCthink

> > > How do in-groups and out-groups function in a typical U.S. high school? What groups are common? How are boundaries separating insiders and outsiders maintained?

Reference Groups Both in-groups and primary groups can dramatically influence the way an individual thinks and behaves. Sociologists call any group that individuals use as a standard for evaluating themselves and their own behavior a **reference group.** For example, a high school student who aspires to join a social circle of hip-hop music devotees will pattern his or her behavior after that of the group. The student will begin dressing like these peers, listening to the same downloads and DVDs, and hanging out at the same stores and clubs.

Reference groups have two basic purposes. They serve a normative function by setting and enforcing standards of conduct and belief. The high school student who wants the approval of the hip-hop crowd will have to follow the group's dictates, at least to some extent. Reference groups also perform a comparison function by serving as a standard against

which people can measure themselves and others. An actor will evaluate him- or herself against a reference group composed of others in the acting profession (Merton and Kitt 1950).

Often, two or more reference groups influence us at the same time. Our family members, neighbors, and co-workers all shape different aspects of our self-evaluation. In addition, reference group attachments change during the life cycle. A corporate executive who quits the rat race at age 45 to become a social worker will find new reference groups to use as standards for evaluation. We shift reference groups as we take on different statuses during our lives.

in-group Any group or category to which people feel they belong.
out-group A group or category to which people feel they do not belong.
reference group Any group that individuals use as a standard for evaluating themselves and their own behavior.
coalition A temporary or permanent alliance geared toward a common goal.

Coalitions As groups grow larger, coalitions begin to develop. A **coalition** is an alliance, whether temporary or permanent, geared toward a common goal. Coalitions can be broad-based or narrow and can take on many different objectives. Sociologist William Julius Wilson (1999) has reported on community-based organizations in Texas that include Whites and Latinos, working-class and affluent, who banded together to work for improved sidewalks, better drainage systems, and comprehensive street paving. Out of this type of coalition building, Wilson hopes, will emerge better interracial understanding.

Some coalitions are intentionally short-lived. Short-term coalition building is a key to success in popular TV programs like *Survivor* and *Big Brother* in which players gain a strategic advantage by banding together to vote others off the island or out of the house. The political world is also the scene of many temporary coalitions. For example, in 2003, President George W. Bush established a "Coalition of the Willing": 45 nations dedicated to removing Saddam Hussein from power in Iraq and willing to provide troops to accomplish that goal. The Iraq invasion began in March 2003, and Hussein was captured in December 2003. As of May 2009, four active coalition partners remained: Australia, Romania, the United Kingdom, and the United States.

SOCIAL NETWORKS

Groups do not merely serve to define other elements of the social structure, such as roles and statuses; they also link the individual with the larger society. We all belong to a number of groups, and through our acquaintances, we connect with people in different social circles. Such connections comprise a **social network**—a series of social relationships that link individuals directly to others, and through them indirectly to still more people. Social networks can center on virtually any activity, from sharing job information to exchanging news and gossip. Some networks may constrain people by limiting the range of their interactions, yet networks can also empower people by making vast resources available to them (Watts 2004).

Sometimes the connections are intentional and public; other times networks can develop that link us together in ways that are not intentional or apparent. Sociologists Peter Bearman, James Moody, and Katherine Stovel (2004) investigated one such network, asking themselves this question: If you drew a chart of the romantic relationship network at a typical American high school, what would it look like? Using careful data collection techniques to enhance the validity of their findings, they found that 573 of the 832 students they surveyed had been either romantically or sexually involved in the previous 18 months. Of these, 63 couples connected only with each other as pairs with no other partners. Other students connected directly or indirectly with a handful of partners. One larger group, however, connected 288 students di-

Adolescent Sexual Networks

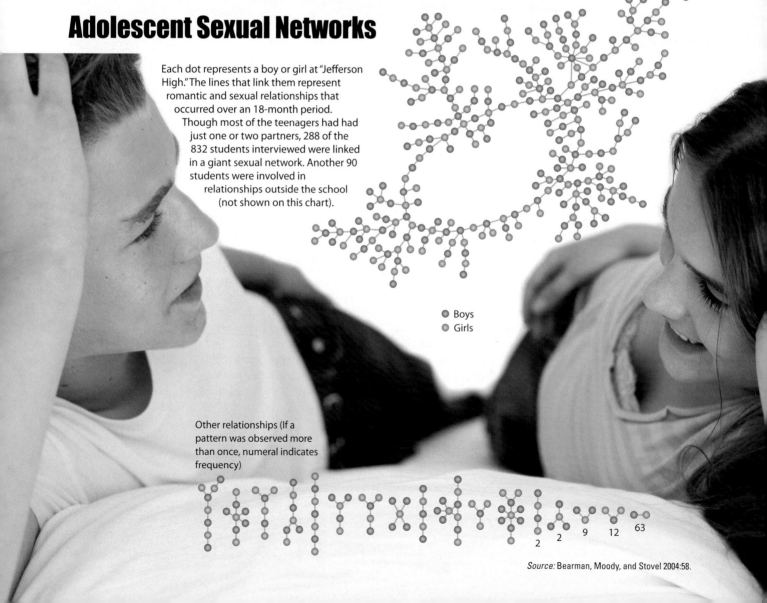

Each dot represents a boy or girl at "Jefferson High." The lines that link them represent romantic and sexual relationships that occurred over an 18-month period. Though most of the teenagers had had just one or two partners, 288 of the 832 students interviewed were linked in a giant sexual network. Another 90 students were involved in relationships outside the school (not shown on this chart).

● Boys
● Girls

Other relationships (If a pattern was observed more than once, numeral indicates frequency)

2   2   9   12   63

Source: Bearman, Moody, and Stovel 2004:58.

to enter the paid workforce found that networking was an effective tool in their search for employment. Informal networking also helped them to locate child care and better housing—keys to successful employment (Benschop 2009; Carey and McLean 1997).

VIRTUAL WORLDS

Today, with recent advances in technology, people can maintain their social networks electronically; they don't need face-to-face contacts. Whether through text messaging, Blackberry devices, or social networking sites like Facebook, a significant amount of networking occurs online. Adolescents can now interact freely with distant friends, even under close scrutiny by parents or teachers. And employees with a taste for adventure can escape their work environments without leaving their cubicles.

> **social network** A series of social relationships that links individuals directly to others, and through them indirectly to still more people.
> **avatar** A person's online representation as a character, whether in the form of a 2-D or 3-D image or simply through text.

The future of virtual networking and the effects it will have are difficult to imagine. Consider Second Life (SL), a virtual world that included over 15 million networked "players" as of May 2009. Over 540,000 of those players were active over a seven-day period. Participants in such virtual worlds typically create an **avatar** that is their online representation as a character, whether in the form of a 2-D or 3-D image or simply through text. The avatar that a player assumes may represent a very different looking-glass self from his or her actual identity. Once equipped with an avatar, the player goes about his or her life in the virtual world, establishing a business and even buying and decorating a home (Bainbridge 2007; Second Life 2009).

rectly or indirectly into a single extended network (see the figure on the previous page). Such an example points to the fact that the choices we make often link us with others both known and unknown.

Networks can also serve as a social resource that is every bit as valuable to us as economic resources when it comes to shaping our opportunities. Involvement in social networks—commonly known as "networking"—can be especially valuable in finding employment. For example, a 2009 survey of executives revealed that 73 percent found job opportunities through network connections, compared to 14 percent by responding to job postings, and 9 percent by posting a résumé to a database or maintaining an online profile (ExecuNet 2009).

In the workplace, networking pays off more for men than for women because of the traditional presence of men in leadership positions. One survey of executives found that 63 percent of the men used networking to find new jobs, compared to 41 percent of the women. Thirty-one percent of the women used classified ads to find jobs, compared to only 13 percent of the men. Still, women at all levels of the paid labor force are beginning to make effective use of social networks. A study of women who were leaving the welfare rolls

Just like real worlds, virtual worlds have become politicized and consumer-oriented. MySpace has been purchased by the global media giant News Corp, which has added targeted advertising to the site. If a MySpace user confesses to liking, say, tacos, a banner ad for Taco Bell may appear at the top the page. And SL is now open to real-world corporations that want to "build" their stores in SL. The commercialization of these spaces has been met with a good deal of antagonism: Reebok has weathered a virtual nuclear bomb attack, and "customers" have been "shot" outside the American Apparel store. Elsewhere in SL, virtual protesters have marched on behalf of a far-right French group in a confrontation with anti-Nazi protesters. In 2007, the Maldives became the first real-world country to place an "embassy" in SL (Burkeman 2007; A. Hamilton 2007; Semuels 2007).

Virtual life can and does migrate into real life. In 2007, college housing officials became worried when freshmen and their parents began checking out the Facebook profiles of prospective roommates. Soon, colleges were fielding requests for new roommates before students even arrived on campus. Concerns went

POPSOC

As something of a spoof, CNET's online game review site, GameSpot, offered a tongue-in-cheek review of "Real Life." They gave it a 9.6 out of 10, saying that it features "believable characters, plenty of lasting appeal, and a lot of challenge and variety," and they described the game play as "extremely open-ended." They concluded that "if you take a step back and look at the big picture, you'll see that real life is an impressive and exciting experience, despite its occasional and sometimes noticeable problems" (Kasavin 2003). Part of what makes such a post amusing is that there is a sense that the boundary between the "real world" and virtual reality continues to blur. What happens, for example, when someone who is married in real life weds someone else's virtual-world character (Alter 2007)?

far beyond tastes in music; the reservations expressed most often by parents included a potential roommate's race, religion, and sexual orientation (Collura 2007).

Sociologist Manuel Castells (1997, 1998, 2000) views these emerging electronic social networks as fundamental to new organizations and to the growth of existing businesses and associations; analysts such as Clay Shirky (2008) are trying to understand them. Shirky suggests that the Internet has radically transformed the possibilities for collective action. He argues that previous technologies either allowed two-way communication that was small-scale because it was limited to individuals (e.g., the telephone), or facilitated large-scale group formation through broadcasting but was limited to one-way communication (e.g., talk radio listeners or fans of *Lost*). With the Internet, he suggests, "group action just got easier" because it supports interactive, large-scale group formation. He identifies a series of steps toward that end (see the accompanying table).

Finally, virtual networks can help to preserve real-world networks interrupted by war and other dislocations.

Shirky's Four Steps Toward Increased Internet Interaction

Step	Site
Sharing	Flikr; Bit Torrent; Del.icio.us
Conversation	Forums; MAKE; How To
Collaboration	Linux; Aegisub
Collective action	Flash Mob activism; NetRoots activisism

Source: Based on Shirky, 2008.

In 2003 the deployment of U.S. troops in the Middle East increased many people's reliance on email. Today, digital photos and sound files accompany email messages between soldiers and their families and friends. GIs can even view siblings' graduations or children's birthday parties live, via webcams. And U.S. soldiers and Iraqi citizens have begun to post their opinions of the war in Iraq in online journals or blogs. Though critics are skeptical of the identity of some of the authors, these postings have become yet another source of news about the war (Faith 2005; O'Connor 2004; Sisson 2007).

SOCIAL INSTITUTIONS

Combinations of statuses, groups, and networks can coalesce to address the needs of a particular sector of society,

forming what sociologists refer to as institutions. A **social institution** is an organized pattern of beliefs and behavior centered on basic social needs. Sociologists have tended to focus on five major institutions that serve as key elements of the larger social structure: family, education, religion, economy, and government. Though these institutions frequently overlap and interact, considering each institution individually provides us with a perspective within which we can analyze the larger social system. We will look in depth at all five in future chapters, but we begin here by considering the contributions each makes to the social structure.

How we organize social interaction within each of these institutions helps contribute to social order. If a society is to survive, certain functions must be performed, and focusing on these institutions allows us to see how different societies fulfill these needs (Aberle et al. 1950). It is within the context of families, for example, that we ensure the society's continued existence by producing the next generation. Families carry out both biological reproduction (having children) and social reproduction (teaching them the culture they need for survival). Families also provide care and protection for members. Through education we teach the more formal and public culture necessary to be members of the larger society. This includes the formal curriculum (history, math, science, etc.) but also includes learning to interact with others outside our immediate families. We rely on religion to be the glue that holds society together by establishing a clear identity with shared beliefs and practices, answering basic questions about meaning, and enforcing both individual and collective discipline. Government helps to maintain internal order through laws, policing, and punishment and seeks to establish stable re-

lations with other societies through diplomacy. Finally, the economy regulates the production, distribution, and consumption of goods and services.

How societies choose to fulfill these functions can vary significantly, as can the degree to which these institutions overlap. For example, one society may protect itself from external attack by amassing a large arsenal of weaponry; another may make determined efforts to remain neutral in world politics and to promote cooperative relationships with its neighbors. No matter what its particular strategy, any society or relatively permanent group must address all these functional prerequisites for survival.

> **social institution** An organized pattern of beliefs and behavior centered on basic social needs.

Focusing on the functions institutions fulfill can help us to better understand social order, but it often implies that the way things are is the way things should be. Sociologists who focus more on power, the consequences of difference, and resource distribution suggest that we must also look at the ways our construction of these institutions reinforces inequality. We can meet these needs in a variety of ways, so we must address the interest some groups have in maintaining the status quo.

SOCthink

> > > How is it possible for education to represent both a path for opportunity and an instrument for maintaining inequality? Where in your experience have you seen both at work?

1400 Smith Street

halls or outside the washroom) and shared a critical view of the firm's attorneys and day-shift secretaries. Expressing their frustration about their relative lack of power and respect, the word processors routinely suggested that their assignments represented work that the "lazy" secretaries should have completed during the normal workday. One word processor, seeking to reclaim a sense of personal power, reacted against the lawyers' superior attitude and pointedly refused to recognize or speak with any attorney who would not address her by name (Duneier 1994b). Through such analysis, sociologists can better explain both how social order is attained and how social inequality is produced in the context of the economy.

Such approaches to viewing life in the contexts of social institutions allow us to better understand what it means to live in the world as it is structured today. Looking at society through the lens of social institutions gives us a sense of what is going on with regard to both the "big picture" and the intimate details of our daily interactions. One of the ways that sociologists have characterized the structure of our modern world is in terms of bureaucracy, which not only describes the social structure but also shapes our everyday experiences.

"Frankly, at this point in the flow chart, we don't know what happens to these people..."

Cartoon by Chris Wildt, www.CartoonStock.com.

Major institutions, such as education, help to maintain the privileges of the most powerful individuals and groups within a society while contributing to the powerlessness of others. To give one example, public schools in the United States are financed largely through property taxes. This arrangement allows more affluent areas to provide their children with better-equipped schools and better-paid teachers than low-income areas can afford. As a result, children from prosperous communities are better prepared to compete academically than children from impoverished communities. The structure of the nation's educational system permits and even promotes such unequal treatment of schoolchildren (Kozol 2005).

By focusing on everyday interactions within the contexts of these institutions, we can further understand why we think and act the way we do. Focusing on the economy, sociologist Mitchell Duneier (1994a, 1994b) studied the social behavior of the word processors, all women, who worked in the service center of a large Chicago law firm. Duneier was interested in the informal social norms that emerged in this work environment and the rich social network these female employees created.

Duneier learned that, despite working in a large office, these women found private moments to talk (often in the

>> Bureaucracy

A **bureaucracy** is a component of a formal organization that uses rules and hierarchical ranking to achieve efficiency. Rows of desks staffed by seemingly faceless people, endless lines and forms, impossibly complex language, and frustrating encounters with red tape—all these unpleasant images have combined to make "bureaucracy" a dirty word and an easy target in political campaigns. As a result, few people want to identify their occupation as "bureaucrat," despite the fact that all of us perform various bureaucratic tasks. In an industrial society, elements of bureaucracy enter into almost every occupation.

CHARACTERISTICS OF A BUREAUCRACY

Max Weber ([1913–1922] 1947) provided the first detailed sociological analysis of bureaucracy. He recognized that its underlying structure remained the same regardless of location, whether in religion, government, education, or business. Weber argued that bureaucracy was quite different from traditional forms of organization, such as those used to run a family business, and he set out to identify its core components. He did so by constructing what he called an **ideal type,** an abstract model of the essential characteristics of a phenomenon. In actuality, perfect bureaucracies do not exist; no real-world organization corresponds exactly to Weber's ideal type.

Weber proposed that whether the purpose is to run a church, a corporation, or an army, the ideal bureaucracy displays five basic characteristics: division of labor, hierarchy of authority, written rules and regulations, impersonality, and employment based on technical qualifications. Let's look at each in turn; the accompanying table provides a summary.

Division of Labor In bureaucracies, specialized experts perform specific tasks. In a college bureaucracy, for example, the admissions officer does not do the job of registrar; the academic advisor doesn't see to the maintenance of buildings. By working at a specific task, people are more likely to become highly skilled and carry out a job with maximum efficiency. This emphasis on specialization is so basic a part of our lives we may not realize that it is a fairly recent development in Western culture.

Division of labor has freed up people to specialize, enhancing their knowledge and skill and leading to significant advances and innovation. However, fragmenting work into smaller and smaller tasks can isolate workers from one another and weaken any connection they might feel to the overall objective of the bureaucracy. In *The Communist Manifesto* ([1847] 1955), Karl Marx and Friedrich Engels charged that capitalism's inherent drive toward increased efficiency and productivity reduces workers to a mere "appendage of the machine." Such a work arrangement, they wrote, produces extreme **alienation**—loss of control over our creative human capacity to produce, separation from the products we make, and isolation from our fellow producers. Restricting workers to very small tasks also can lessen their job security as new employees can easily be trained to replace them.

Another potential downside of the division of labor is that, even though it makes us more interdependent, our relative isolation can result in our failing to recognize our links with others. As we saw with the "hamburger as miracle" example in Chapter 1, we take other people's skills for granted and assume they will do their jobs, even though we are unaware of what most of those jobs are. In some cases this can lead to **trained incapacity**—a situation in which workers become so specialized that they develop blind

> **bureaucracy** A component of formal organization that uses rules and hierarchical ranking to achieve efficiency.
> **ideal type** An abstract model of the essential characteristics of a phenomenon.
> **alienation** Loss of control over our creative human capacity to produce, separation from the products we make, and isolation from our fellow producers.
> **trained incapacity** The tendency of workers in a bureaucracy to become so specialized that they develop blind spots and fail to notice potential problems.

Characteristics of a Bureaucracy

	Positive consequences	Negative consequences	
		For the individual	**For the organization**
Division of labor	Produces efficiency in a large-scale corporation	Produces trained incapacity	Produces a narrow perspective
Hierarchy of authority	Clarifies who is in command	Deprives employees of a voice in decision making	Permits concealment of mistakes
Written rules and regulations	Lets workers know what is expected of them	Stifles initiative and imagination	Leads to goal displacement
Impersonality	Reduces bias	Contributes to feelings of alienation	Discourages loyalty to company
Employment based on technical qualifications	Discourages favoritism and reduces petty rivalries	Discourages ambition to improve oneself elsewhere	Fosters "Peter principle"

spots and fail to notice potential problems. Even worse, workers can become so isolated that they may not care about what is happening in the next department. Some observers believe that such developments have caused workers in the United States to become less productive on the job (Wais 2005).

In some cases, the bureaucratic division of labor can have tragic results. In the wake of the terrorist attacks on the World Trade Center and the Pentagon on September 11, 2001, many Americans wondered how the FBI and CIA could have failed to detect the terrorists' elaborately planned operation. The problem, in part, turned out to be the division of labor between the FBI, which focuses on domestic matters, and the CIA, which operates overseas. Officials at these intelligence-gathering organizations, both of which are huge bureaucracies, are well known for jealously guarding information from one another. Subsequent investigation revealed that they knew about Osama bin Laden and his al Qaeda terrorist network in the early 1990s. Unfortunately, five federal agencies—the CIA, FBI, National Security Agency, Defense Intelligence Agency, and National Reconnaissance Office—failed to share their information on the network. Although the hijacking of the four commercial airliners used in the massive attacks may not have been preventable, the bureaucratic division of labor definitely hindered efforts to defend against terrorism, undermining U.S. national security.

goal displacement Overzealous conformity to official regulations of a bureaucracy.

The organizations of major corporations can be complex but most typically have a single CEO. Debra Lee, pictured here, is president and CEO of Black Entertainment Television.

Hierarchy of Authority Bureaucracies follow the principle of hierarchy; that is, each position is under the supervision of a higher authority. A president heads a college bureaucracy; he or she selects members of the administration, who in turn hire their own staff. In the Roman Catholic Church, the pope is the supreme authority; under him are cardinals, bishops, and so forth. In businesses, the most basic relation is between boss and worker, but in large corporations there are various levels of authority. To track relationships, such companies map those connections using organizational charts that identify all the links of who answers to whom, ultimately leading up to the president or CEO at the top.

Written Rules and Regulations Through written rules and regulations, bureaucracies generally offer employees clear standards for an adequate (or exceptional) performance. If situations arise that are not covered by the rules, bureaucracies are self-correcting. They have rules in place to ensure that new rules are established that make work expectations as clear and comprehensive as possible. Because bureaucracies are hierarchical systems of interrelated positions, such procedures provide a valuable sense of continuity for the organization. Individual workers may come and go, but the structure and past records of the organization give it a life of its own that outlives the services of any one particular person.

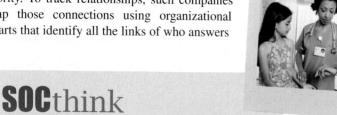

Of course, rules and regulations can overshadow the larger goals of an organization to the point that they become dysfunctional. What if a hospital emergency room physician failed to treat a seriously injured person because he or she had no valid proof of U.S. citizenship? If blindly applied, rules no longer serve as a means to achieving an objective but instead become important (perhaps too important) in their own right. Robert Merton (1968) used the term **goal displacement** to refer to overzealous conformity to official regulations in which we lose sight of the larger principle from which the rule was created.

Impersonality Max Weber wrote that, in a bureaucracy, work is carried out "without hatred or passion." Bureaucratic norms dictate that officials perform their duties without giving personal consideration to people as individuals. Although this norm is intended to guarantee equal treatment for each person, it also contributes to the cold, uncaring feeling often associated with modern organizations.

We typically think of big government and big business when we think of impersonal bureaucracies, and bureaucratic impersonality often produces frustration and disaffection. Whether it involves registering for college classes or getting tech support for a malfunctioning computer, most people have had some experience of feeling like a number and longing for some personal attention. The larger the organization or society, however, the less possible such personal care becomes because attending to individual wants and needs is inefficient.

Employment Based on Technical Qualifications Within the ideal bureaucracy, hiring is based on technical qualifications rather than on favoritism, and performance is measured against specific standards. Written personnel policies dictate who gets promoted, and people often have a right to appeal if they believe that particular rules have been violated. In combination with the principle of impersonality, the driving personnel principle is supposed to be that it is "what you know, not who you know" that counts. Such procedures protect bureaucrats against arbitrary dismissal, provide a measure of security, and encourage loyalty to the organization.

> Bureaucracy is . . . the most rational known means of exercising authority over human beings.
>
> Max Weber

Although any bureaucracy ideally will value technical and professional competence, personnel decisions do not always follow that ideal pattern. Dysfunctions within bureaucracies have become well publicized, particularly because of the work of Laurence J. Peter. According to the **Peter principle,** every employee within a hierarchy tends to rise to his or her level of incompetence (Peter and Hull 1969). This hypothesis, which has not been directly or systematically tested, reflects a possible dysfunctional ultimate outcome of advancement on the basis of merit. Talented people receive promotion after promotion until, sadly, some of them finally achieve positions that exceed their abilities (Blau and Meyer 1987).

Weber developed his five indicators of bureaucracy almost 100 years ago, and they describe an ideal type. Not every formal organization will fully realize all of Weber's characteristics. The underlying logic they represent, however, points toward a way of doing things that is typical of life in modern societies.

Peter principle A principle of organizational life according to which every employee within a hierarchy tends to rise to his or her level of incompetence.
bureaucratization The process by which a group, organization, or social movement increasingly relies on technical-rational decision making in the pursuit of efficiency.
McDonaldization The process by which the principles of efficiency, calculability, predictability, and control shape organization and decision making, in the United States and around the world.

BUREAUCRATIZATION AS A WAY OF LIFE

Bureaucracy for Weber was an indicator of a larger trend in modern society toward rational calculation of all decision making using efficiency and productivity as the primary standards of success. We recognize this pattern first at the level of businesses and organizations. More companies seek greater efficiency through **bureaucratization**—the process by which a group, organization, or social movement increasingly relies on technical-rational decision making in the pursuit of efficiency. Over time, however, the technical-rational approach pervades more and more areas of our lives.

The Spread of Bureaucratization One example of the expansion of bureaucratization is found in the spread of what sociologist George Ritzer (2008) calls **McDonaldization**—the process by which the principles

... The U.S. Census Bureau identifies 472 distinct occupational categories, such as Chief Executive and Crossing Guard, each of which contains at least 10,000 workers. They break these down into 14 occupational groups with 9 job categories.

Did You Know?

of efficiency, calculability, predictability, and control shape organization and decision making, in the United States and around the world. Ritzer argues that these principles, which are at the heart of the McDonald's

Normally, we think of bureaucratization in terms of large organizations, but bureaucratization also takes place within small-group settings. Sociologist Jennifer Bickman Mendez (1998) studied domestic houseworkers employed

> ## Civilization degrades the many to exalt the few.
>
> Amos Bronson Alcot

fast-food chain's success, have been emulated by many organizations, ranging from medical care to wedding planning to education. Even sporting events reflect the influence of McDonaldization. Around the world, stadiums are becoming increasingly similar, both physically and in the way they present the sport to spectators. Swipe cards, "sports city" garages and parking lots, and automated ticket sales maximize efficiency. All seats offer spectators an unrestricted view, and a big screen guarantees them access to instant replays. Scores, player statistics, and attendance figures are updated by computer and displayed on an automated scoreboard. Spectator enthusiasm is manufactured through video displays urging applause or rhythmic chanting. At food counters, refreshments include well-known brands whose customer loyalty has been nourished by advertisers for decades. And, of course, the merchandising of teams' and even players' names and images is highly controlled.

iron law of oligarchy The principle that all organizations, even democratic ones, tend to develop into a bureaucracy ruled by an elite few.

in central California by a nationwide franchise. She found that housekeeping tasks were minutely defined, to the point that employees had to follow 22 written steps for cleaning a bathroom. Complaints and special requests went not to the workers but to an office-based manager.

Weber predicted that eventually even the private sphere would become rationalized. That is, we would turn to rational techniques in an effort to manage our self in order to handle the many challenges of modern life. A trip to any bookstore would seem to prove his point: we find countless self-help books, each with its own system of steps to help us solve life's problems and reach our goals.

Weber was concerned about the depersonalizing consequences of such rationalization, but he saw no way out. Because it is guided by the principle of maximum efficiency, the only way to beat bureaucratization, he thought, was to be more bureaucratic. He argued that, unfortunately, something human was lost in the process. Culture critic Mike Daisey describes something like this through his experience working at Amazon.com. His job performance was measured based on five factors: time spent on

each call, number of phone contacts per hour, time spent on each customer email, number of email contacts per hour, and the sum total of phone and email contacts per hour. Of these calculations, he writes, "Those five numbers are who you are. They are, in fact, all you are. . . . Metrics will do exactly what it claims to do: it will track everything your employees do, say, and breathe, and consequently create a measurable increase in their productivity" (Daisey 2002:114). Metrics do work, but they do so by dehumanizing the worker. "The sad thing," Daisey continues, "is that metrics work so well precisely because it strips

5 Movies on SOCIAL STRUCTURE AND INTERACTION

Office Space
Comedy about the social structure and culture of office work in the United States.

Born Into Brothels
True life stories of children growing up in the red-light district of Calcutta.

The Lives of Others
Communist bureaucracy turns on its citizens in East Berlin.

Mean Girls
Social cliques run amok at a suburban American high school.

This Is England
An exploration of social structure and class among youths in 1980s Great Britain.

away dignity—it's that absence that makes it possible to see precisely who is pulling his weight and who is not" (p. 114). When workers' performance is measured only in numbers, the only part of the self that counts is that part that produces those numbers. Weber predicted that those parts of the self deemed not necessary to the job, such as emotional needs and family responsibilities, would be dismissed as irrelevant.

From Bureaucracy to Oligarchy One of the dangers, then, is that bureaucratization overwhelms other values and principles, that how we organize to accomplish our goals overwhelms and alters the goals themselves. Sociologist Robert Michels ([1915] 1949) studied socialist parties and labor unions in Europe prior to World War I and found that such organizations were becoming increasingly bureaucratic. The emerging leaders of the organizations—even some of the most egalitarian—had

a vested interest in clinging to power. If they lost their leadership posts, they would have to return to full-time work as manual laborers.

Through his research, Michels originated the idea of the **iron law of oligarchy,** the principle that all organizations, even democratic ones, tend to develop into a bureaucracy ruled by an elite few (called an oligarchy). Why do oligarchies emerge? People who achieve leadership roles usually have the skills, knowledge, or charisma to direct, if not control, others. Michels argued that the rank and file of a movement or organization look to leaders for direction and thereby reinforce the process of rule by a few. In addition, members of an oligarchy are strongly motivated to maintain their leadership roles, privileges, and power.

In such instances, actions that violate the core principles of bureaucracy can seep in. Ascribed statuses such as gender, race, and ethnicity can influence how people are treated in formal organizations. For example, a study of women lawyers in the nation's largest law firms found significant differences in the women's self-images, depending on the relative presence or absence of women in positions of power. In firms in which fewer than 15 percent of partners were women, the female lawyers were likely to believe that "feminine" traits were strongly devalued and that masculinity was equated with success. As one female attorney put it, "Let's face it: this is a man's environment, and it's sort of Jock City, especially at my firm." Women in firms where female lawyers were better represented in positions of power had a stronger desire for and higher expectations of promotion (Ely 1995:619).

BUREAUCRACY AND ORGANIZATIONAL CULTURE

Weber's model also predicted that bureaucratic organizations were self-correcting and would take steps to remedy worker concerns. Faced with sabotage and decreasingly productive workers, for example, early bureaucratic managers realized that they could not totally dismiss workers' emotional needs as irrelevant. As a result, new management philosophies arose to counter the negative effects of depersonalization.

According to the **classical theory** of formal organizations, also known as the **scientific management approach,** workers are motivated almost entirely by economic rewards.

> **classical theory** An approach to the study of formal organizations that views workers as being motivated almost entirely by economic rewards.
> **scientific management approach** Another name for the classical theory of formal organizations.

This theory stresses that only the physical constraints on workers limit their productivity. Therefore, workers may be treated as a resource, much like the machines that began to replace them in the 20th century. Under the scientific management approach, management attempts to achieve maximum work efficiency through scientific planning, established performance standards, and careful supervision of workers and production. Planning involves efficiency studies but not studies of workers' attitudes or job satisfaction.

Not until workers organized unions—and forced management to recognize that they were not objects—did theorists of formal organizations begin to revise the classical approach. Along with management and administrators, social scientists became aware that informal groups of workers have an important impact on organizations (Perrow 1986). An alternative management philosophy, the **human relations approach,** emphasizes the role of people, communication, and participation in a bureaucracy. This type of analysis reflects the significance of interaction and small-group behavior. Unlike planning under the scientific management approach, planning based on the human relations perspective focuses on workers' feelings, frustrations, and emotional need for job satisfaction. Today, many workplaces—primarily for those in higher-status occupations—have been transformed to more family-friendly environments. To the extent that managers are convinced that helping workers meet all their needs increases productivity, care and concern are instituted as a result of rational calculation.

human relations approach An approach to the study of formal organizations that emphasizes the role of people, communication, and participation in a bureaucracy and tends to focus on the informal structure of the organization.

Gemeinschaft A close-knit community, often found in rural areas, in which strong personal bonds unite members.

Gesellschaft A community, often urban, that is large and impersonal, with little commitment to the group or consensus on values.

mechanical solidarity Social cohesion based on shared experiences, knowledge, and skills in which things function more or less the way they always have, with minimal change.

>> Social Structure in Global Perspective

Principles of bureaucratization may influence more and more spheres of our lives today, but it has not always been thus. In fact, sociology arose as a discipline in order to better understand and direct the transition from traditional to modern society. Early sociologists sought to develop models that described the basic differences between the two. They hoped that by better understanding how traditional societies operate, we might more effectively identify the underlying factors that shape core concerns in modern society, such as social order, inequality, and interaction.

GEMEINSCHAFT AND GESELLSCHAFT

Ferdinand Tönnies (1855–1936) was appalled by the rise of industrial cities in his native Germany during the late 1800s. In his view, the city marked a dramatic change from the ideal of a close-knit community, which Tönnies termed a *Gemeinschaft,* to that of an impersonal mass society, or *Gesellschaft* (Tönnies [1887] 1988).

The *Gemeinschaft* (pronounced "guh-MINE-shoft") is typical of rural life. It is a small community in which people have similar backgrounds and life experiences. Virtually everyone knows one another, and social interactions are intimate and familiar, almost like an extended family. In this community there is a sense of commitment to the larger social group and a sense of togetherness among members. People relate to others in a personal way, not just as, say, clerk or manager. However, with such personal interaction comes little privacy and high expectations of individual sacrifice.

Social control in the *Gemeinschaft* is maintained through informal means such as moral persuasion, gossip, and even gestures. These techniques work effectively because people genuinely care how others feel about them. Social change is relatively limited in the *Gemeinschaft;* the lives of members of one generation may be quite similar to those of their parents, grandparents, and so on.

In contrast, the *Gesellschaft* (pronounced "guh-ZELL-shoft") is characteristic of modern urban life. In modern societies most people are strangers who feel little in common with other residents. Relationships are governed by social roles that grow out of immediate tasks, such as purchasing a product or arranging a business meeting. Self-interest dominates, and there is little consensus concerning values or commitment to the group. As a result, social control must rest on more formal techniques, such as laws and legally defined sanctions. Social change is a normal part of life in the *Gesellschaft,* with substantial shifts evident even within a single generation.

Sociologists have used these two terms to compare social structures that stress close relationships with those that feature less personal ties. It is easy to view the *Gemeinschaft* with nostalgia, as a far better way of life than the rat race of contemporary existence. However, the more intimate relationships of the *Gemeinschaft* come at a price. The prejudice and discrimination found there can be quite confining; ascribed statuses such as family background often outweigh a person's unique talents and achievements. In addition, the *Gemeinschaft* tends to distrust individuals who are creative or simply different.

SOCthink

> > > How would you classify the communities with which you are familiar? Are they more *Gemeinschaft* or *Gesellschaft?*

MECHANICAL AND ORGANIC SOLIDARITY

While Tönnies looked nostalgically back on the *Gemeinschaft,* Émile Durkheim was more interested in the transition to modern society, which he felt represented the birth of a new form of social order. Durkheim hoped to use sociology as a science to better understand this transition. In his book *The Division of Labor in Society* ([1893] 1933), Durkheim, not unlike Weber, highlighted the significance of the degree to which jobs are specialized in society. For Durkheim, however, the amount of division of labor that exists in a society shapes the degree to which people feel connected with each other.

In societies in which there is minimal division of labor, a shared way of thinking develops that emphasizes group solidarity. Durkheim termed this collective frame of mind **mechanical solidarity.** It involves a sense of social cohesion based on shared experiences, knowledge, and skill, in which things function more or less the way they always have, with minimal change. Most individuals perform the same basic tasks, and they do so together. In this type of society, no one needs to ask, "What do your parents do?" since all are engaged in similar work. Each person hunts, prepares food, makes clothing, builds homes, and so forth. As we see among the Amish, there is little concern for individual needs when people have few options regarding what to do with their lives. Instead, the group is the dominant force in society. Both social interaction and negotiation are based on close, intimate, face-to-face social contacts. Since there is little specialization, there are few social roles.

As societies become more advanced technologically, they rely on greater division of labor. The person who cuts down timber is not the same person who puts up your roof. With increasing specialization, many different tasks must be performed by many different individuals—even in manufacturing a single item, such as a radio or stove. In general, social interactions become less personal than in societies characterized by mechanical solidarity. People begin relating to others on the basis of their social positions (butcher, nurse, and so on) rather than on their distinctive human qualities. Because the overall social structure of the society continues to change, statuses and social roles are in perpetual flux.

As we saw in the "hamburger as miracle" example in Chapter 1, once society has become more complex and division of labor is greater, no individual can go it alone. Dependence on others becomes essential for group survival. In Durkheim's terms, mechanical solidarity is replaced by **organic solidarity**—a collective consciousness resting on the need a society's members have for one another. Durkheim chose the term *organic solidarity* because he believed that role specialization forces individuals to become interdependent in much the same way as the various organs of the human body: Each performs a vital function, but none can exist alone. Also, like a living organism, society can grow and adapt to change.

TECHNOLOGY AND SOCIETY

Some sociologists focus more explicitly on technology than on social organization, expressed as division of labor, to understand distinctions between traditional and modern societies. In sociologist Gerhard Lenski's view, a society's

level of technology is critical to the way it is organized. As we saw in Chapter 3, Lenski defines technology as "cultural information about the ways in which the material resources of the environment may be used to satisfy human needs and desires" (Nolan and Lenski 2006:361). As technology changes, new social forms arise, from preindustrial, to industrial, to postindustrial. The available technology does not completely define the form that a particular society and its social structure will take. Nevertheless, a low level of technology may limit the degree to which a society can depend on such things as irrigation or complex machinery.

Preindustrial Societies Perhaps the earliest form of preindustrial society to emerge in human history was the **hunting-and-gathering society,** in which people simply rely on whatever foods and fibers are readily available. Such groups are typically small and widely dispersed, and technology in such societies is minimal. Organized into groups, people move constantly in search of food. There is little division of labor into specialized tasks because everyone is engaged in the same basic activities. Since resources are scarce, there is relatively little inequality in terms of material goods.

In **horticultural societies,** people plant seeds and crops rather than merely subsist on available foods. Members of horticultural societies are much less nomadic than hunter-gatherers. They place greater emphasis on the production of tools and household objects. Yet technology remains rather limited in these societies, whose members cultivate crops with the aid of digging sticks or hoes (Wilford 1997).

The third type of preindustrial development is the **agrarian society.** As in horticultural societies, members of agrarian societies are engaged primarily in the production of food, but technological innovations such as the plow allow

organic solidarity A collective consciousness that rests on mutual interdependence, characteristic of societies with a complex division of labor.

hunting-and-gathering society A preindustrial society in which people rely on whatever foods and fibers are readily available in order to survive.

horticultural society A preindustrial society in which people plant seeds and crops rather than merely subsist on available foods.

agrarian society The most technologically advanced form of preindustrial society. Members are engaged primarily in the production of food, but they increase their crop yields through technological innovations such as the plow.

farmers to dramatically increase their crop yields and cultivate the same fields over generations. As a result it becomes possible for larger, more permanent settlements to develop.

Agrarian societies continue to rely on the physical power of humans and animals (as opposed to mechanical power).

industrial society A society that depends on mechanization to produce its goods and services.

postindustrial society A society whose economic system is engaged primarily in the processing and control of information.

Division of labor increases because technological advances free up some people from food production to focus on specialized tasks, such as the repair of fishing nets or blacksmithing. As human settlements become stabler and more established, social institutions become more elaborate and property rights more important. The comparative permanence and greater surpluses of an agrarian society allow members to specialize in creating artifacts such as statues, public monuments, and art objects and to pass them on from one generation to the next.

Industrial Societies The Industrial Revolution transformed social life in England during the late 1700s, and within a century its impact on society had extended around the world. An **industrial society** is one that depends on mechanization to produce its goods and services. The strength and stamina humans gained from new inventions such as the steam engine opened up a new world of possibilities by applying nonanimal (mechanical) sources of power to most labor tasks. As such, industrialization significantly altered the way people lived and worked, and it undercut taken-for-granted norms and values.

During the Industrial Revolution, many societies underwent an irrevocable shift from an agrarian-oriented economy to an industrial base. Specialization of tasks and manufacture of goods increasingly replaced the practice of individuals or families making an entire product in a home workshop. Workers, generally men but also women and even children, left their family homesteads to work in central locations such as urban factories.

The process of industrialization had distinctive social consequences. Families and communities could not continue to function as self-sufficient units. Individuals, villages, and regions began to exchange goods and services and to become interdependent. As people came to rely on the labor of members of other communities, the family lost its unique position as the main source of power and authority. The need for specialized knowledge led to more formalized schooling, and education emerged as a social institution distinct from the family.

Postindustrial Societies Mechanized production continues to play a substantial role in shaping social order, relationships, and opportunities, but technological innovation once again has reshaped social structure by freeing up some people from the demands of material production. This has led to the rise of the service sector of the economy in many technologically advanced countries. In the 1970s,

sociologist Daniel Bell wrote about the technologically advanced **postindustrial society,** whose economic system is engaged primarily in the processing and control of information. The main output of a postindustrial society is services rather than manufactured goods. Large numbers of people become involved in occupations devoted to the teaching, generation, or dissemination of ideas. Jobs in fields such as advertising, public relations, human resources, and computer information systems are typical of a postindustrial society (Bell 1999).

Some sociologists, including Bell, view this transition from industrial to postindustrial society as largely a positive development. Others, however, point to the often hidden consequences that result from differential access to resources in postindustrial society. For example, Michael Harrington (1980), who alerted the nation to the problems of the poor in his book *The Other America,* questions the significance that Bell attaches to the growing class of white-collar workers. Harrington concedes that scientists, engineers, and economists are involved in important political and economic decisions, but he disagrees with Bell's claim that they have a free hand in decision making, independent of the interests of the rich. Harrington follows in the tradition of Marx by arguing that conflict between social classes will continue in the postindustrial society.

POSTMODERN LIFE

Sociologists recently have gone beyond discussion of the postindustrial society to contemplate the emergence of postmodern society. A **postmodern society** is a technologically sophisticated, pluralistic, interconnected, globalized society. While it is difficult to summarize what a whole range of thinkers have said about postmodern life, four elements provide a sense of the key characteristics of such societies today: stories, images, choices, and networks.

Did You Know?

. . . TV talk-show host Regis Philbin was a sociology major. He graduated from the University of Notre Dame with a B.A. in sociology in 1953. Sociology, he says, "gave me a great insight into human nature."

Going GLOBAL

International U.S. Favorability Ratings

Ten lowest ratings		Ten highest ratings	
Germany	30%	Ivory Coast	88%
Indonesia	29%	Kenya	87%
Malaysia	27%	Ghana	80%
Egypt	21%	United States	80%
Jordan	20%	Mali	79%
Argentina	16%	Israel	78%
Morocco	15%	Ethiopia	77%
Pakistan	15%	Nigeria	70%
Palestinian Territories	13%	Senegal	69%
Turkey	9%	Uganda	64%

Source: Kohut 2007b.

Because we exist in an interdependent global network, the consequences of our actions, both large and small, reverberate throughout the world. In a global survey of 47 nations conducted in 2007, the Pew Research Center looked at international favorability ratings for the United States. How favorably do other nations view the United States? The average national score was 47.3 percent, but there was significant variation by country.

Stories Because postmodern societies are pluralistic and individualistic, people hold many different, often competing, sets of norms and values. Fewer people assume that a single, all-inclusive story—whether a particular religious tradition, or an all-encompassing scientific theory of everything, or even the faith many early sociologists had in the inevitability of modern progress—can unite us all under a common umbrella. Instead, we embrace the various individual and group stories that help us to make sense of the world and our place in it. We do so in the full knowledge that others out there are doing exactly the same thing and often coming to dramatically different conclusions. This multiplicity of stories undercuts the authority that singular accounts of reality have had in the past.

Images Postmodern society is also characterized by the explosion of the mass media, which emphasizes the importance of images. As we saw in Chapter 4, the average person in the United States watches almost five hours of television per day (Bureau of the Census 2008a). This works out to the equivalent of more than 71 full days per year. We are bombarded by images everywhere we turn, but in postmodern theory, the significance of the image goes much deeper than television and advertisements; it impacts our taken-for-granted notion of material reality itself. Theorists argue that we do not confront or interact with the material world directly. Just as language shapes our perception of reality according to the Sapir-Whorf hypothesis, our experience of "reality" is always mediated through representations of reality in the form of signs, symbols, and words. According to postmodernists, our images or models of reality come before reality itself.

Postmodern theorists use a geography metaphor to illuminate this concept: "the map precedes the territory" (Baudrillard [1981] 1994). In other words, the images we construct draw our attention to certain features that we might not otherwise single out. A road map, for example, highlights different features, and for different purposes, than does a topographical map or political map. In so doing, it shapes what we see. We cannot step around or look through such cultural constructs to approach the thing itself, and so our knowledge of what is real is always constrained by the images we construct.

Choices In a postmodern world, reality is not simply given; it is negotiated. We pick and choose our reality from the buffet of images and experiences presented to us. In fact, we *must* choose. In contrast to societies characterized by mechanical solidarity, where one's life path is virtually set at birth, members of postmodern societies must make life choices all the time. Assuming we have access to sufficient resources, we choose what to eat, what to wear, and what to drive. Shopping, which in the past would have been viewed primarily as an instrumental necessity to provide for our basic needs, becomes an act of self-creation. As James B. Twitchell (2000) put it, "We don't buy things, we buy meanings" (p. 47). An iPhone, a Coach purse, and a MINI Cooper are more than just a phone, a handbag, and a car. They are statements about the kind of person we are or want to be. The significance of choice goes much deeper than just consumer products. We also choose our partners, our schools, our jobs, our faith, and even our identities. As individuals, we may choose to affirm traditions, language, diet, and values we inherited from our family through socialization, but we can also choose to pursue our own path.

Networks Members of postmodern societies live in a globally interconnected world. The food we eat, the clothes we wear, the books we read, and the products we choose often come to us from the other side of the world. The computer technician we talk to for assistance in the United States may be located in India. McDonald's has even experimented with centralized drive-through attendants—who might even be located in another state—who take your order and transmit it to the restaurant you are ordering from (Richtel 2006). Increasingly, all corners of the globe are linked into a vast, interrelated social, cultural, political, and economic system. A rural Iowa farmer, for example, must be concerned with more than just the local weather and community concerns; he or she must know about international innovations in

> **postmodern society** A technologically sophisticated, pluralistic, interconnected, globalized society.

farming technology, including biotech, as well as the current and future state of international markets.

Whether in the form of traditional, modern, or postmodern society, social structure provides order, shaping the options that are available to us. It provides the context within which we interact with others. The statuses we occupy shape the roles we perform. What we think and do is influenced by the relationships we have with others in the contexts of groups, networks, and institutions. Sociology as a discipline is committed to making sense of our structural context and the impact it has on our lives.

Still, society and social structure are not singular things—as the turn toward the micro, bottom-up perspective in sociology has helped us to appreciate. Though we are, in many respects, products of society, socialized to think and act in appropriate ways, we always have the option to think and act in new ways and to construct new culture. The possibility for such change may be more apparent in our pluralistic world. Ours is a world not of "the" structure, "the" family, and "the" religion, but of structures, families, and religions. We have the possibility for more contact with more people who have more ways of thinking and acting than at any time in the past. As such, we can become aware of more alternatives for how we might think and act that might lead us to change our worlds.

get involved!

Explore! We occupy many statuses over the course of our lives, and they can both open and close doors for us. Ask five people in various positions—whether as parents, professors, child care providers, custodians, managers, religious leaders, or so on—how they came to be in those positions. How have the positions they occupy enabled them to accomplish their personal and collective goals? How have they been constrained by their positions?

For REVIEW

I. **What makes up society?**

- Society provides a structure that is built up out of the statuses we occupy, the roles we perform, and the groups, networks, and institutions that connect us.

II. **How does social structure shape individual action?**

- The positions we occupy shape our perceptions, the resources to which we have access, and the options that are available. For example, in the context of bureaucracies, our social position, connections, and performance expectations are clearly defined.

III. **How do sociologists describe traditional versus modern societies?**

- Sociologists highlight the impact that division of labor and technological development have on the organization of community, work, and social interaction in traditional and modern societies.

Pop Quiz

1. A social position we inherit and about which we can do little to change, such as age, race, or sex, is known as
   a. an ascribed status.
   b. role strain.
   c. an achieved status.
   d. a social role.

2. In the United States, we expect that cab drivers will know how to get around a city. This expectation is an example of which of the following?
   a. role conflict
   b. role strain
   c. social role
   d. master status

3. What occurs when incompatible expectations arise from two or more social positions held by the same person?
   a. role conflict
   b. role strain
   c. role exit
   d. both a and b

4. In sociological terms, what do we call any number of people with similar norms, values, and expectations who interact with one another on a regular basis?
   a. a category
   b. a group
   c. an aggregate
   d. a society

5. Primary groups are characterized by
   a. a series of relationships that link individuals directly to others and through them indirectly to still more people.
   b. formal, impersonal relationships with minimal social intimacy or mutual understanding.
   c. social positions that are within our power to change.
   d. intimate, face-to-face association and cooperation.

6. The U.S. Postal Service, Def Jam Records, and the college or university in which you are currently enrolled as a student are all examples of
   a. primary groups.
   b. reference groups.
   c. formal organizations.
   d. *Gemeinschaft.*

7. The principle of bureaucracy that establishes that work should be carried out "without hatred or passion" is known as
   a. impersonality.
   b. hierarchy of authority.
   c. written rules and regulations.
   d. division of labor.

8. What type of society did Ferdinand Tönnies describe as a close-knit community in which members have strong personal bonds?
   a. *Gesellschaft*
   b. mechanical
   c. *Gemeinschaft*
   d. organic

9. Sociologist Daniel Bell uses which of the following terms to refer to a society whose economic system is engaged primarily in the processing and control of information?
   a. postmodern
   b. horticultural
   c. industrial
   d. postindustrial

10. What characteristic of postmodern life emphasizes the importance of consumption on identity creation?
    a. stories
    b. images
    c. choices
    d. networks

1. (a); 2. (c); 3. (a); 4. (b); 5. (d); 6. (c); 7. (a); 8. (c); 9. (d); 10. (c)

6

DEVIANC

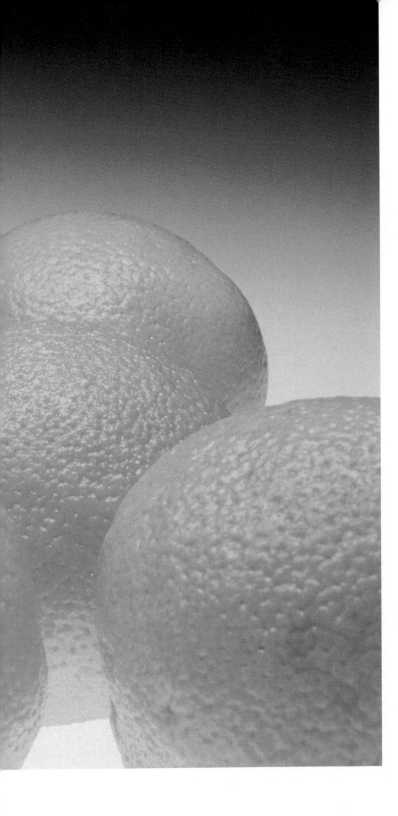

LIVING THE GANG LIFE

Sociology student Sudhir Venkatesh (2008), wanting to better understand the lives of poor African Americans, ventured into the housing projects in inner-city Chicago. After a rocky beginning, his naïveté and genuine curiosity helped to open the door to what became a seven-year, in-depth participation research project about gangs, drugs, crime, public housing, and more.

Venkatesh's commitment to going beyond what W.E.B. Du Bois dismissed as "car-window sociology" ultimately provided him access to information about crime and deviance that he could never have found through a survey. Through his research he learned that gangs have a highly organized structure, with those at the top of the gang hierarchy doing well financially, and the foot soldiers at the bottom, who make up 95 percent of the membership, averaging only $3.30 per hour (Levitt and Dubner 2005). They also have an astonishingly high death rate. These two facts together led one of Venkatesh's collaborators to say that selling drugs for a gang is perhaps "the worst job in all of America."

While it may not yield much money, dealing drugs does allow gang members to help support their families. Venkatesh argued that their willingness to work these jobs, even in the face of minimal return and high risk, demonstrated their desire to work, but they found so few viable options that some actually worked at McDonald's to supplement their drug-dealing income.

Venkatesh also found that gangs seek to contribute to the local community, giving money to women who work in the buildings looking after children and the elderly. They require their young members to stay in school, and prohibit members from using hard drugs—in part because they cannot be good at business if they are high, and in part because it is bad for the image of the gang.

Through research like Venkatesh's, sociologists can better understand crime and deviance. The gang Venkatesh studied tried to create a level of stability in their neighborhood, but they relied on crime and violence as tools of their trade. What social factors lead to such outcomes, and can those factors or outcomes be changed? In this chapter we will look at these questions and more.

As You READ

>>

- How do groups maintain social control?
- What is the difference between deviance and crime?
- How do sociologists explain deviance and crime?

>> Social Control

At some point all of us have wondered, "Should I do what *they* want or should I do what *I* want?" The tension between the individual and society is at the heart of sociology. To better understand the power that others wield over us, sociologists study social control, deviance, and crime.

As we saw in Chapter 3, we create norms—dress codes, game rules, dining etiquette—to provide social order and make our lives predictable. We enforce them through **social control**—the techniques and strategies for preventing deviant human behavior in any society. Social control occurs on all levels of society. In the family, we are socialized to obey our parents simply because they are our parents. Peer groups introduce us to informal norms, such as dress codes, that govern the behavior of their members. Colleges establish the standards they expect of students. In bureaucratic organizations, workers encounter a formal system of rules and regulations. Finally, the government of every society legislates and enforces social norms.

Most of us respect and accept basic social norms and assume that others will do the same. Even without thinking, we usually obey the instructions of police officers, follow the day-to-day rules at our jobs, and move to the rear of elevators when people enter. Such behavior reflects an effective process of socialization to the dominant standards of a culture. At the same time, we are well aware that others expect us to act "properly" and that failure to do so will result in consequences. **Sanctions** are the penalties and rewards we face for conduct concerning a social norm. For example, if we fail to live up to expectations at work, we might get fired. If we do a good job, we might get a promotion.

Sanctions point to the power that societies, institutions, and groups have over our lives. On the one hand, we want people to respect social norms so that the group or society can survive. Society is defined in part by people's willingness to accept shared beliefs and practices, even if doing so sometimes constrains their selfish pursuits. On the other hand, society can be oppressive, limiting individual freedom and advancing the interests of some at the expense of others. Entrenched interests seek to maintain the status quo and use their power over sanctions to do so. In fact, positive social change often comes through resistance to the status quo, with individuals and groups rejecting existing norms and following new paths. Such attempts may meet with significant opposition, as was evident in the civil rights movement. Similar struggles were necessary in America to win independence from England, to overturn the institution of slavery, to earn women the vote, and to force an end to the war in Vietnam.

CONFORMITY AND OBEDIENCE

Techniques for social control operate on both the group and the societal level. People we think of as peers or equals influence us to act in particular ways; the same is true of people who hold authority over us or whose positions we re-

spect. Social psychologist Stanley Milgram (1975) made a useful distinction between these two levels of social control.

According to Milgram, **conformity** means going along with peers—individuals of our own status who have no special right to direct our behavior. **Obedience,** on the other hand, is compliance with higher authorities in a hierarchical structure. A recruit entering military service will typically conform to the habits and language of other recruits and obey the orders of superiors. Students will conform to the drinking behavior of their peers and obey the requests of campus security officers.

In a classic experiment, Milgram (1963, 1975) sought to test how far people would go when obeying authority. Would they administer increasingly painful electric shocks to another person if asked to do so by a scientific researcher? Contrary to what we might believe about ourselves, Milgram found that most of us would obey the researcher. In his words, "Behavior that is unthinkable in an individual . . . acting on his own may be executed without hesitation when carried out under orders" (1975: xi).

To set up his experiment, Milgram placed ads in local newspapers to recruit subjects for an experiment at Yale University. His participants included postal clerks, engineers, high school teachers, and laborers. They were told that the purpose of the research was to investigate the effects of punishment on learning. The scientist, dressed in a gray technician's coat, explained that in each test, one subject would be randomly selected as the "learner" and another would function as the "teacher." However, the experiment was rigged so that the "real" subject would always be the teacher while an associate of Milgram's served as the learner.

To begin, each teacher was given a sample shock of 45 volts to convince him or her of the authenticity of the experiment. A learner was then strapped to an electric apparatus, and the teacher was taken to an electronic "shock generator" with 30 switches labeled from 15 to 450 volts. The experimenter then instructed the teacher to apply shocks of increasing voltage each time the learner gave an incorrect answer on a memory test. Teachers were told that "although the shocks can be extremely painful, they cause no permanent tissue damage." In reality, the learner did not receive any shocks.

In a prearranged script, the learner deliberately gave incorrect answers and pretended to be in pain when "shocked." For example, at 150 volts, the learner would cry out, "Get me out of here!" At 270 volts, the learner would scream in agony. When the shock reached 350 volts, the learner would fall silent. If the teacher wanted to stop the experiment, the experimenter would insist

---

social control The techniques and strategies for preventing deviant human behavior in any society.

sanction A penalty or reward for conduct concerning a social norm.

conformity The act of going along with peers—individuals of our own status who have no special right to direct our behavior.

obedience Compliance with higher authorities in a hierarchical structure.

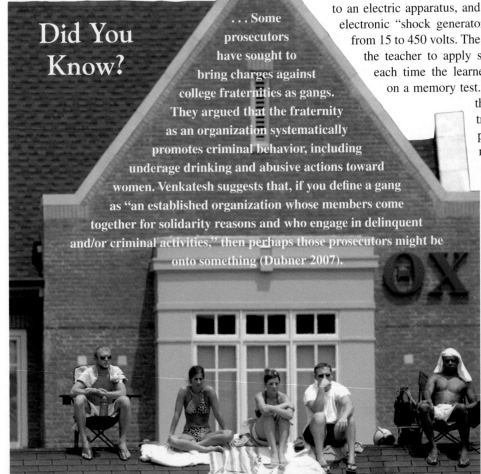

Did You Know?

. . . Some prosecutors have sought to bring charges against college fraternities as gangs. They argued that the fraternity as an organization systematically promotes criminal behavior, including underage drinking and abusive actions toward women. Venkatesh suggests that, if you define a gang as "an established organization whose members come together for solidarity reasons and who engage in delinquent and/or criminal activities," then perhaps those prosecutors might be onto something (Dubner 2007).

SOCthink

> > > According to the American Sociological Association *Code of Ethics*, researchers must "protect subjects from personal harm." To what extent might Milgram's subjects have experienced emotional harm? How and why might a researcher seek to justify such a risk?

that the teacher continue, using such statements as "The experiment requires that you continue" and "You have no other choice; you *must* go on" (Milgram 1975:19–23).

The results of this unusual experiment stunned and dismayed Milgram and other social scientists. A sample of psychiatrists had predicted that virtually all subjects would refuse to shock innocent victims. In their view, only a "pathological fringe" of fewer than 2 percent would continue administering shocks up to the maximum level. Yet almost two-thirds of participants fell into the category of "obedient subjects."

Why did these subjects obey? Why were they willing to inflict seemingly painful shocks on innocent victims who had never done them any harm? There is no evidence that these subjects were unusually sadistic; few seemed to enjoy administering the shocks. Instead, in Milgram's view, the key to obedience was the experimenter's social role as "scientist" and "seeker of knowledge."

Milgram pointed out that in the modern industrial world, we are accustomed to submitting to impersonal authority figures whose status is indicated by a title (professor, lieutenant, doctor) or by a uniform (the technician's coat). Because we view the authority as more important than the individual, we shift responsibility for our behavior to the authority figure. Afterwards, Milgram's subjects frequently stated, "If it were up to me, I would not have administered

A participant in the Milgram experiment.

shocks." They saw themselves as merely doing their duty (Milgram 1975).

Milgram launched his experimental study of obedience in part to better understand the involvement of Germans in the murder of 6 million Jews and millions of other people during World War II. In an interview conducted long after the publication of his study, he suggested that "if a system of death camps were set up in the United States of the sort we had seen in Nazi Germany, one would be able to find sufficient personnel for those camps in any medium-sized American town" (CBS News 1979:7–8). Though many people questioned this statement, the revealing photos taken at Iraq's Abu Ghraib prison in 2004, showing U.S. military guards humiliating if not torturing Iraqi prisoners, recalled the experiment Milgram had done two generations earlier. Under conducive circumstances, otherwise normal people can and often do treat one another inhumanely (Hayden 2004; Zimbardo 2007).

SOCthink

> > > Do you think a person's background factors would influence how far he or she would go in Milgram's experiment? How might age, gender, religion, or education make a difference?

INFORMAL AND FORMAL SOCIAL CONTROL

The sanctions that society uses to encourage conformity and obedience—and to discourage violation of social norms—are carried out through both informal and formal social control. As the term implies, people use **informal social control** casually to enforce norms. Examples include smiles, laughter, a raised eyebrow, and ridicule. We seek to read such cues in new situations such as a first date or a job interview so that we might adjust our behavior accordingly.

SOCthink

> > > All groups must use some form of social control if they are to maintain any sense of order. What mechanisms of formal and informal social control are evident in your college classes and in day-to-day life and social interactions at your school?

Formal social control is carried out by authorized agents, such as police officers, judges, school administrators, employers, military officers, and managers. It can serve as a last resort when socialization and informal sanctions do not bring about desired behavior. An increasingly significant means of formal social control in the United States is imprisonment. In 2007, over 7 million adults underwent some form of correctional supervision—jail, prison, probation, or parole. Put another way, 1 out of every 30 adult Americans was subject to this very formal type of social control (Glaze and Bonczar 2008).

In 2007, in the wake of the mass shootings at Virginia Tech, many college officials reviewed security measures on their campuses. Administrators were reluctant to end or even limit the relative freedom of movement students on their campuses enjoyed. Instead, they concentrated on improving emergency communications between campus police and students, faculty, and staff. Reflecting a reliance on technology to maintain social control, college leaders called for replacement of the "old" technology of email with instant alerts that could be sent to people's cell phones via instant messaging.

Six years earlier, in the aftermath of the terrorist attacks of September 11, 2001, new measures of social control became the norm in the United States. Some of them, such as stepped-up security at airports and high-rise buildings, were highly visible to the public. The federal government has also publicly urged citizens to engage in informal social control by watching for and reporting people whose actions seem suspicious. But many other measures taken by the government have increased the covert surveillance of private records and communications.

Only a month and a half after September 11, and with virtually no debate, Congress passed the USA PATRIOT Act of 2001. Sections of this sweeping legislation revoked legal checks on the power of law enforcement agencies. Without a warrant or probable cause, the FBI can now secretly access most private records, including medical histories, library accounts, and student registrations. In 2002, for example, the FBI searched the records of hundreds of dive shops and scuba organizations. Agents had been directed to identify every person who had taken diving lessons in the past three years because of speculation that terrorists might try to approach their targets underwater (Moss and Fessenden 2002).

Many people think that this kind of social control goes too far. Civil rights advocates also worry that the government's request for information on suspicious activities may encourage negative stereotyping of Muslims and Arab Americans. Clearly, there is a trade-off between the benefits of surveillance and violation of the right to privacy.

> **informal social control** Social control that is carried out casually by ordinary people through such means as laughter, smiles, and ridicule.
> **formal social control** Social control that is carried out by authorized agents, such as police officers, judges, school administrators, and employers.

The interplay between formal and informal social control can be complicated because we sometimes have to balance one source of control against another. College students, for example, receive conflicting messages about the acceptability of binge drinking. On the one hand, it represents deviance from the standards of conduct expected of those in an academic context. On the other hand, binge drinking shows conformity to the peer culture, especially in the context of sororities and fraternities (see the figure "Binge Drinking on Campus"). Increasingly, colleges and

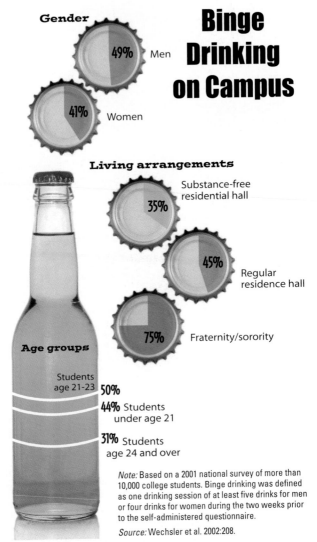

Binge Drinking on Campus

Gender
49% Men
41% Women

Living arrangements
35% Substance-free residential hall
45% Regular residence hall
75% Fraternity/sorority

Age groups
50% Students age 21–23
44% Students under age 21
31% Students age 24 and over

Note: Based on a 2001 national survey of more than 10,000 college students. Binge drinking was defined as one drinking session of at least five drinks for men or four drinks for women during the two weeks prior to the self-administered questionnaire.

Source: Wechsler et al. 2002:208.

universities are taking steps to exert greater social control by instituting rules banning kegs, closing fraternities and sororities, expelling students after multiple alcohol-related violations, and working with local liquor retailers to discourage high-volume sales to students (Wechsler and Nelson 2008).

law Governmental social control.
control theory A view of conformity and deviance that suggests that our connection to members of society leads us to systematically conform to society's norms.

LAW AND SOCIETY

Some norms are so important to a society that they are formalized into laws limiting people's behavior. **Law** may be defined as governmental social control (Black 1995). Some laws, such as the prohibition against murder, are directed at all members of society. Others, such as fishing and hunting regulations, primarily affect particular categories of people. Still others govern the behavior of social institutions (for instance, corporate law and laws regarding the taxing of nonprofit enterprises).

Sociologists see the creation of laws as a social process. Because laws are passed in response to a perceived need for formal social control, sociologists have sought to explain how and why such a perception arises. In their view, law is not merely a static body of rules handed down from generation to generation. Rather, it reflects continually changing standards of what is right and wrong, of how violations are to be determined, and of what sanctions are to be applied (Schur 1968).

Formal Procedure: How a Bill Becomes Law

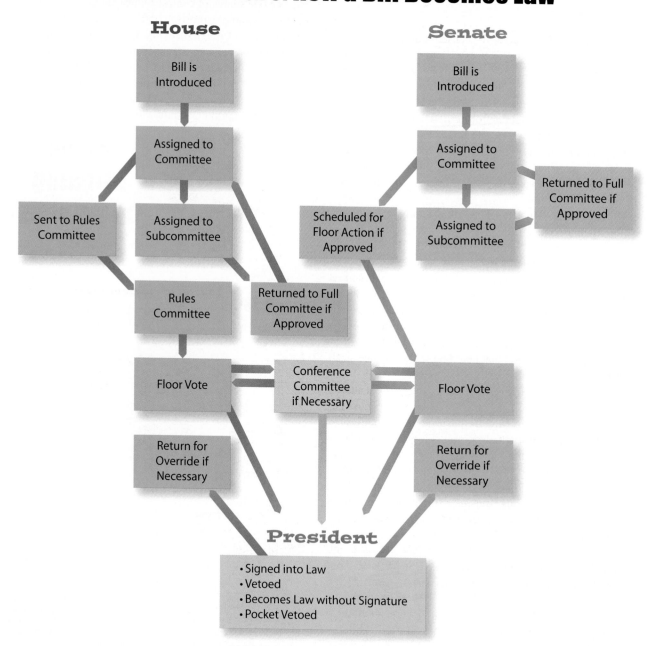

In diverse societies, the establishment of laws inevitably generates conflicts over whose values should prevail. As such, the creation of civil and criminal laws can be controversial. For example, should it be against the law to employ illegal immigrants? To have an abortion? To allow prayer in public schools? To smoke on an airplane? Such issues have been bitterly debated because they require a choice among competing values. Not surprisingly, unpopular laws—such as the Eighteenth Amendment, which prohibited the manufacture and sale of alcohol (ratified in 1919), or the nationwide 55-mile-per-hour speed limit that was imposed in 1974—become difficult to enforce when there is no consensus supporting the norms. In both cases, the public commonly violated the stated government policy, and the laws proved unenforceable; the states repealed Prohibition in 1933, and Congress overturned the national speed-limit policy in 1987.

The current debate over whether to allow people to use marijuana legally for medical purposes illustrates the difficulty in crafting laws that govern private behavior. Although approximately 70 percent of adults support such use, federal law prohibits all uses of marijuana (ProCon.org 2009). Nevertheless, as the map above shows, 13 states have granted citizens the right to use marijuana for medical purposes. In May 2009, the U.S. Supreme Court upheld the right of states to pass such statutes, despite existing federal laws.

Socialization is the primary vehicle for instilling conforming and obedient behavior, including obedience to law. Generally, it is not external pressure from a peer group or authority figure that makes us go along with social norms. Rather, we have internalized such norms as valid and desirable and are self-policing. In a profound sense, we want to see ourselves (and to be seen) as loyal, cooperative, responsible, and respectful of others. In the United States and other societies around the world, people are socialized both to want to belong and to fear being viewed as different or deviant.

Control theory suggests that our connection to other members of society leads us to conform systematically to

Maryland protects medical marijuana patients from jail, but not from the threat of arrest.

Washington, DC

13 states have laws that allow the cultivation of medical marijuana and that protect patients who possess medical marijuana (with their doctor's recommendations or certifications) from criminal penalties.

17 states and the District of Columbia have laws that recognize marijuana's medical value, but these laws are ineffective because they rely on federal cooperation.

Source: Marijuana Policy Project 2008.

Medical Marijuana Laws

society's norms. According to sociologist Travis Hirschi and other control theorists, our bonds to family members, friends, and peers induce us to follow the mores and folkways of our society. We give little conscious thought to whether we will be sanctioned if we fail to conform. Socialization develops our self-control so well that we don't need further pressure to obey social norms. Although control theory does not explain the rationale for every conforming act, it nevertheless reminds us that while the media may focus on crime and disorder, most members of most societies conform to and obey basic norms most of the time (Gottfredson and Hirschi 1990; Hirschi 1969).

>> Deviance

The flip side of social control is deviance. **Deviance** is behavior that violates the standards of conduct or expectations of a group or society (Wickman 1991:85). In the United States, most people classify those who are alcoholics, compulsive gamblers, or mentally ill as deviant. Being late for class is categorized as a deviant act, as is wearing jeans to a formal wedding. On the basis of the sociological definition, we are all devi-

> deviance Behavior that violates the standards of conduct or expectations of a group or society.

ant from time to time. Each of us violates common social norms in certain situations.

Hot or Not?

Should colleges and universities have a responsibility to crack down on file sharing over their networks?

WHAT BEHAVIOR IS DEVIANT?

Because deviance involves violation of some group's norms, defining an act as deviant depends on the context. File sharing on the Internet—including MP3s, movies, computer games, books, and almost anything else that can be digitized—provides an example of how deviance can be in the eye of the beholder. Sharing files, whether through Bit-Torrent, LimeWire, and eMule, has become widespread. New movies are sometimes available online even before they have been released in the theater. Because the "property" these files represent is not physical, it can be reproduced for virtually no cost. Anyone with a computer and an Internet connection can grab them from people who are willing to share, then pass them along to others. Just how deviant is this? Record and movie companies take it very seriously; they have actively pursued lawsuits against those who share files in part to scare those who might think of doing it. However, the widespread availability of these files suggests that many people do not view this practice as particularly deviant. Some even view it as an act of protest against what they consider unfair prices charged by big corporations.

In most instances, those individuals and groups with the greatest status and power define what is acceptable and what is deviant. For example, serious medical warnings

Present-day fans of bullfighting, which has a long and rich history in Spain and elsewhere, are now often stigmatized for their admiration of a sport that can result in pain and death for the bulls.

of the dangers of tobacco appeared as early as 1964, yet cigarette smoking continued to be accepted for decades—in good part because of the power of tobacco farmers and cigarette manufacturers. Only after public health and anticancer activists led a long campaign against cigarette smoking did smoking become more of a deviant activity. Today, many state and local laws limit where people can smoke.

Of course, deviation from norms is not always negative, let alone criminal. A member of an exclusive social club who speaks out against a traditional policy of excluding women, Blacks, and Jews from admittance is deviating from the club's norms. So is a police officer who blows the whistle on corruption or brutality within the department.

DEVIANCE AND SOCIAL STIGMA

Some people are unwillingly cast in negative social roles because of physical or behavioral characteristics. Whole groups of people—for instance, "short people" or "blondes"—may be labeled in this way. Once individuals have been assigned a deviant role, they can have trouble presenting a positive image to others and may even experience lowered self-esteem. Sociologist Erving Goffman coined the term **stigma** to describe the labels society uses to devalue members of certain social groups (Goffman 1963).

We face pressure not to deviate too far from expected norms. To avoid stigma, for example, women can feel pressured to approximate what Naomi Wolf (1992) refers to as the "beauty myth"—an exaggerated ideal of beauty, beyond the reach of all but a few females. As a result,

"ex-convict," "recovering alcoholic," and "ex–mental patient" can stick to a person for life. Goffman draws a useful distinction between a prestige symbol that calls attention to a positive aspect of one's identity, such as a wedding band or a badge, and a stigma symbol that discredits or debases one's identity, such as a conviction for child molestation. While stigma symbols may not always be obvious, they can become a matter of public knowledge. Starting in 1994, many states required convicted sex offenders to register with local police departments. Some communities publish the names and addresses, and in some instances even the pictures, of convicted sex offenders on the Web.

stigma A label used to devalue members of certain social groups.

crime A violation of criminal law for which some governmental authority applies formal penalties.

A person need not be guilty of a crime to be stigmatized. Homeless people often have trouble getting a job because employers are wary of applicants who cannot give a home address. Moreover, hiding one's homelessness is difficult because agencies generally use the telephone to contact applicants about job openings. If a homeless person has access to a telephone at a shelter, the staff generally answers the phone by announcing the name of the institution—a sure way to discourage prospective employers. Even if a homeless person surmounts these obstacles and manages to get a job, she or he is often fired when the employer learns of the situation. Regardless of a person's positive attributes, employers regard the negative connotation of homelessness as sufficient reason to dismiss an employee.

many of the 1.5 million cosmetic procedures done every year in the United States are performed on women who would be defined objectively as having a normal appearance. Although feminist sociologists have accurately noted that the beauty myth makes many women feel uncomfortable with themselves, men too lack confidence in their appearance. The number of males who choose to undergo cosmetic procedures has risen sharply over the years; men now account for 16 percent of such surgeries (American Academy of Cosmetic Surgery 2009).

Often people are stigmatized for deviant behaviors that they may no longer practice. The labels "former gambler,"

>> Crime

If deviance means breaking group norms, **crime** is a violation of law for which some governmental authority applies formal penalties. It is a type of deviance representing a violation of social norms administered by the state. Laws divide crimes into various categories, depending on the severity of the offense, the age of the offender, the potential

punishment, and the court that holds jurisdiction over the case.

OFFICIAL CRIME REPORTS

When we think of crime, the categories most likely to come to mind involve what we might think of as street crimes. The FBI breaks such crimes into two major categories: violent crimes and property crimes. They do not include all types of crime in these reports, focusing only on four major types within each category. Violent crimes include murder, forcible rape, robbery, and aggravated assault; property crimes include burglary, larceny-theft, motor vehicle theft, and arson. The FBI provides an annual account of the number of these crimes in their *Uniform Crime Reports* (UCR), which is available online. Because they are tracked so closely by the FBI and have been for a long time, these crimes have come to be known as **index crimes.**

index crimes The eight types of crime reported annually by the FBI in the *Uniform Crime Reports*: murder, forcible rape, robbery, aggravated assault, burglary, larceny-theft, motor vehicle theft, and arson.

As we can see in the accompanying table, property crimes occur at a much higher rate than do violent crimes. In fact, according to the "crime clock" that the FBI provides as part of its report, a property crime occurs on average every 3.2 seconds. The most frequent property crime is larceny-theft, which includes incidents such as shoplifting and stealing items from cars. By contrast, a violent crime occurs every 22.4 seconds. Robbery, which involves the use or threat of force, is the most frequent vi-

olent crime, with one occurring every 1.2 minutes. Murder is the least frequent of the index crimes, with one occurring every 31.0 minutes (U.S. Department of Justice 2008).

Trends in Crime Analysis of crime data reports reveals a significant decline in violent crime nationwide during the late 1990s after consistently high rates over many years. Sociologists have offered a number of explanations for this, including

- A booming economy and falling unemployment rates through most of the 1990s.
- Community-oriented policing and crime prevention programs.
- New gun control laws.
- A massive increase in the prison population, which at least prevents inmates from committing crimes outside prison.

In the past five years rates have held relatively steady, but even with the previous declines, rates of reported crime remain well above both those of other nations and those of the United States just 20 years earlier. Feminist scholars draw our attention to one significant variation: the proportion of major crimes committed by women has increased. In a recent 10-year period (1998–2007), female arrests for major reported crimes increased 6.6 percent, while comparable male arrests declined 6.1 percent (U.S. Department of Justice 2008:Table 33).

National Crime Rates and Percentage Change

Offenses in 2007	Number reported	Rate per 100,000 inhabitants	Percent change in rate Since 1998	Percent change in rate Since 2003
Violent crimes			decrease ← → increase	
Murder	16,929	6	-1.3	-10.6
Forcible rape	90,427	30	-7.1	-13.0
Robbery	445,125	148	3.6	-10.8
Aggravated assault	855,856	284	-3.9	-21.5
Total	1,408,337	467	-1.9	-17.7
Property crimes				
Burglary	2,179,140	723	-2.5	-16.3
Larceny-theft	6,568,572	2,178	-9.9	-20.2
Motor vehicle theft	1,095,769	363	-16.2	-21.0
Total	9,843,481	3,264	-9.1	-19.5

Notes: Arson was designated an index offense beginning in 1979; data on arson were still incomplete as of 2004. Because of rounding, the offenses may not add to totals.

Source: U.S. Department of Justice 2008a: Table 1.

Violent Crime Victimization Rates, 1973–2007

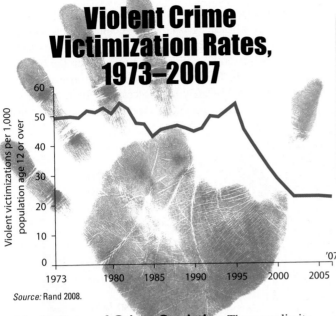

Violent victimizations per 1,000 population age 12 or over

(y-axis: 0, 10, 20, 30, 40, 50, 60)
(x-axis: 1973, 1980, 1985, 1990, 1995, 2000, 2005, '07)

Source: Rand 2008.

Limitations of Crime Statistics There are limitations to official crime statistics, the most serious of which is that they include only those crimes reported to law enforcement agencies. In addition, because members of racial and ethnic minority groups often distrust law enforcement agencies, they may not contact the police when they are victimized. Further, feminist sociologists and others have noted that many women do not report rape or spousal abuse out of fear they will be blamed for the crime.

Partly because of such deficiencies in official statistics, the U.S. Department of Justice initiated the National Crime Victimization Survey in 1972 (Rand 2008). In compiling this annual report, the department's Bureau of Justice Statistics not only gathers information from law enforcement agencies but also interviews over 70,000 individuals in 40,000 households to determine if they were victims of a specific set of crimes during the preceding year. In general, those who administer **victimization surveys** question ordinary people, not police officers, to determine whether they have been victims of crime.

Even using such surveys, the likelihood of underreporting the actual number of crimes remains. Surveys require that victims understand what has happened to them and that

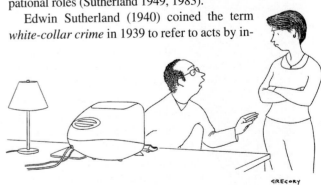
they be willing to disclose such information to interviewers. People are particularly reluctant to report crimes such as fraud, income tax evasion, and blackmail in victimization studies. Nevertheless, 90 percent of all households have been willing to cooperate with investigators for the National Crime Victimization Survey. As shown in the figure at left, data from these surveys reveal a fluctuating victimization rate with significant declines in both the early 1980s and the late 1990s (Rand 2008).

> **victimization survey** A questionnaire or interview given to a sample of the population to determine whether people have been victims of crime.
>
> **white-collar crime** Illegal acts committed by affluent, "respectable" individuals in the course of business activities.

Another limitation of the UCR official statistics is that they exclude many offenses that we would count as criminal. In so doing, they minimize the degree to which we see perpetrators of other types of crime as criminal in the same way as violators of the index crimes. We turn next to several such categories, including white-collar crime, victimless crimes, and organized crime.

WHITE-COLLAR CRIME

Income tax evasion, stock manipulation, consumer fraud, bribery and extraction of kickbacks, embezzlement, and misrepresentation in advertising—these are all examples of **white-collar crime,** or illegal acts committed in the course of business activities, often by affluent, "respectable" people. Historically, we have viewed such crimes differently because they are often perpetrated through respected occupational roles (Sutherland 1949, 1983).

Edwin Sutherland (1940) coined the term *white-collar crime* in 1939 to refer to acts by individuals, but the term is now used more broadly to include offenses by businesses and corporations as well. Corporate crime, or any act by a corporation that is punishable by the government, takes many forms and includes individuals, organizations, and institutions among its victims. Corporations may engage in anticompetitive behavior, environmental pollution, medical fraud, tax fraud, stock fraud and manipulation, accounting fraud, the production of unsafe goods, bribery and corruption, and health and safety violations (J. Coleman 2006).

The recent downfall of Bernie Madoff represents the largest case of white-collar crime of its type in history. Madoff, an American businessman who managed people's financial investments, promised investors annual returns of 15 to 20 percent and delivered on that promise for years. This enabled him to attract extremely wealthy clients from around the world, even charitable organizations. In the end, he was just running a scam. Madoff had provided investors with false statements showing nonexistent trades and profits. Estimates are that he defrauded his clients out of $65 billion in purported assets. Life savings and family fortunes were gone in an instant (Gaviria and Smith 2009).

The scheme collapsed in December 2008, after Madoff confessed to his sons that his investment company was a "giant Ponzi scheme." After consulting an attorney, they reported their father to the FBI. Madoff was arrested the next day. In a Ponzi scheme, the fraudulent investor uses money from new investors to pay off old ones rather than investing the money. The payoff is at higher-than-average rates of return, which encourages new investors who are attracted by the profits. The whole system topples if current investors want to pull their money out, or if there aren't enough new investors to cover profits and payouts to existing investors. Both happened with the economic collapse in late 2008. On March 12, 2009, Madoff pled guilty to 11 felony counts, including securities fraud, mail fraud, money laundering, and perjury. He was sent directly to jail and was sentenced to the maximum of 150 years in prison (Henriques and Healy 2009).

What is particularly interesting about the Madoff case is that officials at the Securities and Exchange Commission (SEC) were tipped off numerous times to the possibility that Madoff's investments were a scam. Finally, after receiving documented accusations that he was running a Ponzi scheme, the SEC launched an official investigation in 2006. Two years later they

concluded that there was "no evidence of fraud." The SEC failed to see what analysts now say should have been obvious. Red flags were ignored, but why? Sociologists suggest that white-collar criminals are often given the benefit of the doubt. In fact, during each previous investigation, Madoff deliberately and successfully used his status as a respected businessman as evidence of his

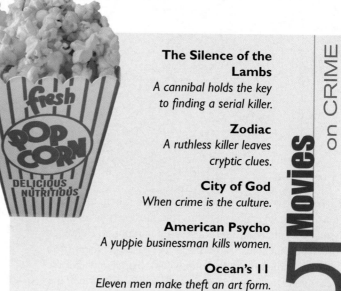

5 Movies on CRIME

The Silence of the Lambs
A cannibal holds the key to finding a serial killer.

Zodiac
A ruthless killer leaves cryptic clues.

City of God
When crime is the culture.

American Psycho
A yuppie businessman kills women.

Ocean's 11
Eleven men make theft an art form.

innocence. He might have avoided detection had it not been for his own confession (Berenson and Henriques 2008).

VICTIMLESS CRIMES

Another category of crimes that raises questions about how we define deviance consists of so-called victimless crimes. **Victimless crime** refers to the willing exchange among adults of widely desired, but illegal, goods and services, such as drugs or prostitution (Schur 1965, 1985). The fact that the parties involved are willing participants has led some people to suggest that such transactions should not constitute crimes.

Some activists are working to decriminalize many of these illegal practices. Supporters of decriminalization are troubled by the attempt to legislate a moral code for adults. In their view, prostitution, drug use, gambling, and other victimless crimes are impossible to prevent. The already overburdened criminal justice system should instead devote its resources to "street crimes" and other offenses with obvious victims.

Despite widespread use of the term *victimless crime,* however, many people object to the notion that there is no victim other than the offender in such crimes. Excessive drinking, compulsive gambling, and illegal drug use contribute to an enormous amount of personal and property damage. A person with a drinking problem can become abusive to a spouse or children; a compulsive gambler or drug user may steal to pursue his or her obsession. Feminist sociologists contend that prostitution, as well as the more

Hot or Not?

Should gambling, prostitution, and recreational drugs be legalized?

disturbing aspects of pornography, reinforce the misconception that women are "toys" who can be treated as objects rather than people. According to critics of decriminalization, society must not give tacit approval to conduct that has such harmful consequences (Farley and Malarek 2008; Meier and Geis 1997).

ORGANIZED CRIME

When it comes to organized crime, the name Tony Soprano is the first that comes to mind for many people. He was the fictional boss of the DiMeo crime family on HBO's hit series *The Sopranos*. In real life, examples of organized crime groups go beyond the Mafia to include the Japanese Yakuza, the Russian Organization, Colombian drug cartels, and many other international crime syndicates. For our purposes, we will consider **organized crime** to be the work of a group that regulates relations among criminal enterprises involved in illegal activities, including prostitution, gambling, and the smuggling and sale of illegal drugs (National Institute of Justice 2007).

Organized crime dominates the world of illegal business, just as large corporations dominate the conventional business world. It allocates territory, sets prices for goods and services, and acts as an arbiter in internal disputes. A secret, conspiratorial activity, organized crime generally evades law enforcement. It takes over legitimate businesses, gains influence over labor unions, corrupts public officials, intimidates witnesses in criminal trials, and even "taxes" merchants in exchange for "protection" (Federal Bureau of Investigation 2009).

Historically, organized crime has provided a means of upward mobility for groups of people struggling to escape poverty. Sociologist Daniel Bell (1953) used the term *ethnic succession* to describe the sequential passage of leadership from Irish Americans in the early 1900s to Jewish Americans in the 1920s and then to Italian Americans in the early 1930s. Recently, ethnic succession has become more complex, reflecting the diversity of the nation's latest immigrants. Colombian, Mexican, Russian, Chinese, Pakistani, and Nigerian immigrants are among those who have begun to play a significant role in organized crime activities (Friman 2004; Kleinknecht 1996).

> **victimless crime** A term used by sociologists to describe the willing exchange among adults of widely desired, but illegal, goods and services.
> **organized crime** The work of a group that regulates relations among criminal enterprises involved in illegal activities, including prostitution, gambling, and the smuggling and sale of illegal drugs.
> **transnational crime** Crime that occurs across multiple national borders.

There has always been a global element in organized crime. However, law enforcement officials and policy makers now acknowledge the emergence of a new form of organized crime that takes advantage of advances in electronic communications. International organized crime includes drug and arms smuggling, money laundering, and trafficking in illegal immigrants and stolen goods (Lumpe 2003; Office of Justice Programs 1999).

INTERNATIONAL CRIME

In the past, international crime was often limited to the clandestine shipment of goods across the border between

POPSOC

Where there are rules there will always be violations of those rules.

Joel M. Charon

The success of shows such as *The Sopranos, CSI, NCIS, Criminal Minds,* and *Without a Trace* continue a long tradition of TV crime shows.

two countries. Increasingly, however, crime is no more restricted by such borders than is legal commerce. Rather than concentrating on specific countries, international crime now spans the globe.

Transnational Crime More and more, scholars and law enforcement officials are turning their attention to **transnational crime,** or crime that occurs across multiple national borders. Historically, probably the most dreaded example of transnational crime has been slavery. At first, governments did not regard slavery as a crime but merely regulated it as they would trade in any other good. In the 20th century, transnational crime grew to embrace trafficking in endangered species, drugs, and stolen art and antiquities.

Transnational crime is not exclusive of some of the other types of crime we have discussed. For example, organized

Going GLOBAL

International Incarceration Rates

Rank
out of 217 nations

International incarceration rates
(prison population rates per 100,000 of the national population)

Rank	Nation	Rate
1	United States of America	760
3	Russian Federation	628
26	South Africa	335
31	Israel	325
59	Mexico	207
89	England and Wales	151
103	Kenya	130
115	China	119
117	Canada	116
164	Sweden	74
177	Japan	63
202	India	33

Prison Population Rates per 100,000 of the National Population, Selected Nations, 2009

Source: International Centre for Prison Studies 2009.

criminal networks are increasingly global. Technology definitely facilitates their illegal activities, such as trafficking in child pornography. Beginning in the 1990s, the United Nations began to categorize transnational crimes, such as hijacking, illegal drug trade, sea piracy, and terrorism.

One way to fight such crime has been through multilateral cooperation in which countries cooperate to pursue border-crossing crime. The first global effort to control international crime was the International Criminal Police Organization (Interpol), a cooperative network of European police forces founded to stem the movement of political revolutionaries across borders. While such efforts to fight transnational crime may seem lofty—an activity with which any government would want to cooperate—they are complicated by sensitive legal and security issues. Most nations that have signed protocols issued by the United Nations, including the United States, have expressed concern over potential encroachments on their national judicial systems, as well as concern over their national security. Thus, they have been reluctant to share certain types of intelligence data. The terrorist attacks of September 11, 2001, increased both the interest in combating transnational crime and sensitivity to the risks

anomie Durkheim's term for the loss of direction felt in a society when social control of individual behavior has become ineffective.

of sharing intelligence data (Deflem 2005; Felson and Kalaitzidis 2005).

International Crime Rates Taking an international perspective on crime reinforces one of the key sociological lessons about crime and deviance: Place matters. Although cross-national data comparison can be difficult, we can offer insight about how crime rates differ around the world.

During the 1980s and 1990s, violent crimes were much more common in the United States than in the nations of western Europe. Murders, rapes, and robberies were reported to the police at much higher rates in the United States. Yet the incidence of certain other types of crime appears to be higher elsewhere. For example, England, Italy, Australia, and New Zealand all have higher rates of car theft than the United States. Developing nations have significant rates of reported homicide due to civil unrest and political conflict among civilians (van Dijk et al. 2007; World Bank 2003a). But when it comes to putting offenders in jail, the United States tops them all. On a typical day, the United States imprisons 760 of every 100,000 adults, compared to 628 in Russia, fewer than 207 in Mexico, and 116 in Canada (International Centre for Prison Studies 2009).

Why are rates of violent crime so much higher in the United States than in western Europe? Sociologist Elliot Currie (1985, 1998) has suggested that our society places greater emphasis on individual economic achievement than other societies. At the same time, many observers have noted that the culture of the United States has long tolerated, if not condoned, many forms of violence. Coupled with sharp disparities between poor and affluent citizens, significant unemployment, and substantial alcohol and drug abuse, these factors combine to produce a climate conducive to crime.

However, disturbing increases in violent crime are evident in other Western societies. For example, crime has skyrocketed in Russia since the overthrow of Communist Party rule (with its strict controls on guns and criminals) in 1991. In 1998 there were fewer than 260 homicides in Moscow; now there are more than 1000 homicides a year. Organized crime has filled the power vacuum in Moscow: One result is that gangland shootouts and premeditated "contract hits" have become more common. Some prominent reformist politicians have been targeted as well. Russia incarcerates an extremely high proportion of its citizens—almost as high as the United States (Bush 2006; Pridemore 2003).

>> Sociological Perspectives on Deviance and Crime

Why do people violate social norms? We have seen that deviant acts are subject to both informal and formal social control. The nonconforming or disobedient person may face disapproval, loss of friends, fines, or even imprisonment. Why, then, does deviance occur?

Sociologists have been interested in crime and deviance from the very beginning and have generated numerous theories of deviance and crime. Though we might wish otherwise, there is no one, simple, universal theory that explains all such acts. Here we will look to just a few of the theories that sociologists have offered in order to identify significant factors that we must consider in our attempt to understand deviance and crime more fully.

5 Movies on DEVIANCE

V for Vendetta
An anarchist challenges totalitarian rule in near-future Great Britain.

Girl, Interrupted
A young girl enters a mental institution during the 1960s.

A Clockwork Orange
The success and failure of rehabilitating a delinquent.

The Devil and Daniel Johnston
The true story of a young musician who suffers from schizophrenia.

Mysterious Skin
Two teenage boys battle with the shared memories of sexual abuse.

SOCIAL ORDER, DEVIANCE, AND CRIME

Émile Durkheim's ([1895] 1964) emphasis on the importance of social order led him to investigate the nature and causes of deviance and crime. He wondered why deviance, which would seem to undermine order, is found in all societies. For Durkheim the answer rested with how such actions were perceived by others.

Durkheim's Theory of Deviance Durkheim argued that there is nothing inherently deviant or criminal in any act; the key is how society responds to the act. He put it this way: "We must not say that an action shocks the common consciousness because it is criminal, but rather that it is criminal because it shocks that consciousness" ([1895] 1964:123–24). In other words, nothing is criminal or worthy of condemnation unless we decide it is. For example, we do not regard killing in self-defense or in combat in the same way we view killing in cold blood. At least, that is the case until we change our minds about how we view wartime killing, as has happened at various times in our past. When it comes to war, for example, our attitudes about what is appropriate can shift. In both Vietnam and

Iraq, strong public support gave way to serious misgivings about U.S. involvement in these nations. In both cases, this was driven in part by images from the conflict, including, for example, the treatment of prisoners at Abu Ghraib. In this way, our understanding of what constitutes deviance and crime are tied to issues of social solidarity.

In fact, Durkheim concluded that deviance and crime actually can have a positive impact on society in a variety of ways. For example, identifying acts as deviant clarifies our shared beliefs and values and thus brings us closer together. We say, in effect, "This is who we are, and if you want to be one of us you cannot cross this line. Some things we might let go, but if you push the limits too far you will face sanctions." Punishment, too, can draw a group together, uniting members in their opposition to the offender. Sanctions also discourage others from similar violations, thus increasing conformity. When we see a driver receiving a speeding ticket, a department store cashier being fired for yelling at a customer, or a college student getting a failing grade for plagiarizing a term paper, we are reminded of our collective norms and values and of the consequences of their violation. Finally, Durkheim did recognize that deviant acts might also force us to recognize the limits of our existing beliefs and practices, opening up new doors and leading to cultural innovation.

Based on Durkheim's analysis, it is possible to conclude that all societies identify criminals for the sake of social order. No matter how much unity a society might appear to have, there will always be some who push the limits. Regardless of how "good" such people may appear to be to outsiders, they may face sanction within the group for the good of the whole.

SOCthink

> > > Durkheim argues that increased division of labor results in fewer shared experiences and thus a weakened sense of community. Might this imply that we need ever-more shocking violations of our remaining shared values in order to bring us together?

Durkheim did, however, also recognize that some social circumstances increase the likelihood of turning toward deviance and crime. As we have already seen, Durkheim ([1897] 1951) introduced the term **anomie** into the sociological literature to describe the loss of direction felt in a society when social control of individual behavior has become ineffective. Anomie is a state of normlessness that typically occurs during a period of profound social change and disorder, such as a time of economic collapse, political or social revolution, or even sudden prosperity. The power of society to constrain deviant action at such times is limited because there is no clear consensus on shared norms and values. Just as we saw with Durkheim's analysis of suicide, at times when social integration is weak, people are freer to pursue their own deviant paths.

Merton's Theory of Deviance Sociologist Robert Merton (1968) took Durkheim's theory a step further. He realized that sometimes members of a society share collective values or goals and other times they do not. He also realized that some people accept the means to attain those goals and others don't. To understand deviance and crime,

ating from such cultural expectations. His **anomie theory of deviance** posits five basic forms of adaptation.

Conformity to social norms, the most common adaptation in Merton's typology, is the opposite of deviance. The "conformist" accepts both the overall societal goal (for example, to become wealthy) and the approved means (hard work). In Merton's view, there must be some consensus regarding accepted cultural goals and the legitimate means for attaining them. Without such a consensus, societies could exist only as collectives of people rather than as unified cultures, and they might experience continual chaos.

The other four types of behavior all involve some departure from conformity. The "innovator" accepts the goals of

Law and justice are not always the same.

Gloria Steinem

he felt it was necessary to go beyond the general state of society to look more closely at where people fit in relationship to both goals and means.

We can better understand Merton's model by looking at economic success as an important goal in the United States. In addition to providing this goal for people, our society offers recommended pathways on how to pursue success—go to school, work hard, do not quit, take advantage of opportunities, and so forth. A mugger and a merchant may share the common goal of economic success, but their means of attaining it are radically different. What happens to individuals in a society with a heavy emphasis on wealth as a basic symbol of success? Merton reasoned that people adapt in certain ways, either by conforming to or by devi-

society but pursues them with means that are regarded as improper. For instance, a safecracker may steal money to buy consumer goods and expensive vacations.

In Merton's typology, the "ritualist" has abandoned the goal of material success and become compulsively committed to the institutional means. Work becomes simply a way of life rather than a means to the goal of success. An example would be the bureaucratic official who blindly applies rules and regulations without remembering the larger goals of the organization. Certainly, that would be true of a welfare caseworker who refuses to assist a homeless family because their last apartment was in another district.

The "retreatist," as described by Merton, has basically withdrawn (or retreated) from both the goals and the

means of society. In the United States, drug addicts and vagrants are typically portrayed as retreatists. Concern has been growing that adolescents who are addicted to alcohol will become retreatists at an early age.

The final adaptation identified by Merton reflects people's attempts to create a *new* social structure. The "rebel" feels alienated from the dominant means and goals and may seek a dramatically different social order. Members of a revolutionary political organization, such as a militia group, can be categorized as rebels according to Merton's model.

Merton's theory, though popular, does not fully account for patterns of deviance and crime. While it is useful in explaining certain types of behavior, such as illegal gambling by disadvantaged "innovators," it fails to explain key differences in crime rates. Why, for example, do some disadvantaged groups have lower rates of reported crime than others? Why do many people in adverse circumstances reject criminal activity as a viable alternative? Merton's theory does not easily answer such questions (Clinard and Miller 1998). In order to more fully appreciate such nuances, we must add to what we can learn from Merton by turning to additional theories that seek to better understand deviance and crime at an interpersonal level.

INTERPERSONAL INTERACTION AND LOCAL CONTEXT

Perhaps the likelihood of committing deviant acts is not solely shaped by social integration or the acceptance of society's larger goals and means to attain them. Maybe parents around the world were right all along that it really does depend on who your friends are. If we are to understand and explain such acts, we must also consider the importance of social interaction and the local context.

Cultural Transmission

As humans, we learn how to behave in social situations, whether properly or improperly. Sociologist Edwin Sutherland (1883–1950) proposed that, just as individuals are socialized to conform to society's basic norms and values, so also are they socialized to learn deviant acts. It's not that we are born to be wild; we learn to be wild.

Sutherland drew on the **cultural**

transmission school, which emphasizes that individuals learn criminal behavior by interacting with others. Such learning includes not only the techniques of lawbreaking (for example, how to break into a car quickly and quietly) but also the motives, drives, and rationalizations of the criminal. The cultural transmission approach can also be used to explain the behavior of those who habitually abuse alcohol or drugs.

Sutherland maintained that through interactions with a primary group and significant others, people acquire definitions of proper and improper behavior. He used the term **differential association** to describe the process through which exposure to attitudes favorable to criminal acts leads to the violation of rules. Research suggests that this view of differential association also applies to noncriminal deviant acts, such as smoking, binge drinking, and cheating (Higgins et al. 2007; Nofziger and Hye-Ryeon 2006; Vowell and Chen 2004).

To what extent will a given person engage in an activity that is regarded as proper or improper? For each individual, it will depend on the frequency, duration, and importance of two types of social interaction—those experiences that endorse deviant behavior and those that promote acceptance of social norms. People are more likely to engage in norm-defying behavior if they are part of a group or subculture that stresses deviant values, such as a street gang.

Sutherland offers the example of a boy who is sociable, outgoing, and athletic and who lives in an area with a high rate of delinquency. The youth is very likely to come into contact with peers who commit acts of vandalism, fail to attend school, and so forth, and he may come to adopt such behavior. However, an introverted boy who lives in the same neighborhood may stay away from his peers and avoid delinquency. In another community, an outgoing and athletic boy may join a Little League baseball team or a scout troop because of

anomie theory of deviance Merton's theory of deviance as an adaptation of socially prescribed goals or of the means governing their attainment, or both.

cultural transmission A school of criminology that argues that criminal behavior is learned through social interactions.

differential association A theory of deviance that holds that violation of rules results from exposure to attitudes favorable to criminal acts.

Did You Know?

... In a 2006 survey of over 5000 students at 32 graduate schools, 56 percent of master of business administration (MBA) students admitted to cheating within the past academic year. This contrasted with 47 percent of nonbusiness students. Considering goals and means, into which category of Merton's model might those MBA students belong?

his interactions with peers. Thus, Sutherland views improper behavior as the result of the types of groups to which one belongs and the kinds of friendships one has (Sutherland et al. 1992).

While the cultural transmission approach may not explain the conduct of the first-time, impulsive shoplifter or the impoverished person who steals out of necessity, it does help to explain the deviant behavior of juvenile delinquents or graffiti artists. It directs our attention to the paramount role of social interaction and context in increasing a person's motivation to engage in deviant behavior (Morselli et al. 2006; Sutherland et al. 1992).

Social Disorganization Theory The relative strength of social relationships in a community or neighborhood influences the behavior of its members. Social psychologist Philip Zimbardo (2007) studied the effect of these communal relationships by conducting the following experiment. He abandoned a car in each of two different neighborhoods, leaving its hood up and removing its hub caps. In one neighborhood, people started to strip the car for parts even before Zimbardo had finished setting up a remote video camera to record their behavior. In the other neighborhood, weeks passed without the car being touched, except for a pedestrian who stopped to close the hood during a rainstorm.

Social disorganization theory attributes increases in crime and deviance to the absence or breakdown of communal relationships and social institutions, such as the family, school, church, and local government. The lack of such local community connections, with their associated cross-age relationships, makes it difficult to exert informal control within the community, especially of children. Without community supervision and controls, playing outside becomes an opportunity for deviance, and older violators socialize children into inappropriate paths. Crime becomes a normal response to a local context.

This theory was developed at the University of Chicago in the early 1900s to describe the apparent disorganization that occurred as cities expanded with immigrants from abroad and migrants from rural areas. Using the latest survey techniques, Clifford Shaw and Henry McKay (1969) literally mapped the distribution of social problems in Chicago. They found high rates of social problems in neighborhoods where buildings had deteriorated and the population had declined. Interestingly, the patterns persisted over time, despite changes in the neighborhoods' ethnic and racial composition.

Labeling Theory Sometimes when it comes to deviance, what you see determines what you get. The Saints and Roughnecks were two groups of high school males who were continually en-

From Me to You

The cafeteria at the school where I teach has an all-you-can-eat policy, but you cannot take food with you when you leave. Most of my students admit they violate this policy. When I suggest that what they are doing might be criminal, they are offended. They justify their theft in any number of ways: They pay a lot for their meal plan, they sometimes miss meals, it wouldn't make sense to throw the food away, etc. Yet there are people in prison who have taken things costing less than the total value of food taken by the average student. Why is it that those of us, like me, who are guilty of having taken food do not view ourselves as criminal?

gaged in excessive drinking, reckless driving, truancy, petty theft, and vandalism. There the similarity ended. None of the Saints was ever arrested, but every Roughneck was frequently in trouble with police and townspeople. Why the disparity in their treatment? On the basis of observation research in their high school, sociologist William Chambliss (1973) concluded that how they were seen, as rooted in their social class positions, played an important role in the varying fortunes of the two groups.

The Saints hid behind a facade of respectability. They came from "good families," were active in school organizations, planned on attending college, and received good grades. People generally viewed their delinquent acts as a few isolated cases of sowing wild oats. The Roughnecks had no such aura of respectability. They drove around town in beat-up cars, were generally unsuccessful in school, and aroused suspicion no matter what they did.

We can understand such discrepancies by using an approach to deviance known as **labeling theory,** which emphasizes how a person comes to be labeled as deviant or to accept that label. Unlike Sutherland's work, labeling theory does not focus on why some individuals come to commit deviant acts. Instead, it attempts to explain why society views certain people (such as the Roughnecks) as deviants, delinquents, bad kids, losers, and criminals, while it sees others whose behavior is similar (such as the Saints) in less harsh terms. Sociologist Howard Becker (1963:9; 1964), who popularized this approach, summed up labeling theory with this statement: "Deviant behavior is behavior that people so label."

Labeling theory is also called the **societal-reaction approach,** reminding us that it is the response to an act, not the act itself, that determines deviance. Traditionally, research on deviance has focused on people who violate social norms. In contrast, labeling theory focuses on police, probation officers, psychiatrists, judges, teachers, employers, school officials, and other regulators of social control. These agents, it is argued, play a significant role in creating the deviant identity by designating certain people (and not others) as deviant (Bernburg et al. 2006). An important aspect of labeling theory is the recognition that some individuals or groups have the power to define labels and apply them to others. This view ties into the conflict perspective's emphasis on the social significance of power.

In recent years, the practice of racial profiling, in which people are identified as criminal suspects purely on the basis of their race, has come under public scrutiny. Studies confirm the public's suspicion that in some jurisdictions, police officers are much more likely to stop African American males than White males for routine traffic violations, in the expectation of finding drugs or guns in their cars. Civil rights activists refer to these cases sarcastically as DWB (Driving While Black) violations (Warren et al. 2006). Beginning in late 2001, profiling took a new turn as people who appeared to be Arab or Muslim came under special scrutiny.

While the labeling approach does not fully explain why certain people accept a label and others manage to reject it, labeling theorists do suggest that the power an individual has relative to others is important in determining his or her ability to resist an undesirable label. It opens the door to additional emphasis on the undeniably important actions of people with power who can shape what counts as deviance.

POWER AND INEQUALITY

In addition to its significance for labeling theory, the story of the Saints and Roughnecks points toward the role that power and control over valued resources can play in defining deviance. Sociologist Richard Quinney (1974, 1979, 1980) is a leading proponent of the view that the criminal justice system serves the interests of the powerful; people with power protect their own interests and define deviance to suit their own needs. Crime, according to Quinney (1970), is defined as such by legislators who may be influenced by the economic elites to advance their interests.

Race and Class Looking at crime from this perspective draws our attention to the effects that power and position might have throughout the criminal justice system in the United States. Researchers have found that the system treats suspects differently based on their racial, ethnic, or social class background. In many cases, officials using their own discretion make biased decisions about whether to press charges or drop them, whether to set bail and how much, and whether to offer parole or deny it. Researchers have found that this kind of **differential justice**—differences in the way social control is exercised over different groups—puts African Americans and Latinos at a disadvantage in the justice system, both as juveniles and as adults. On average, White offenders receive shorter sentences than comparable Latino and African American offenders, even when prior arrest records and the relative severity of the crime are taken into consideration (Brewer and Heitzeg 2008; Quinney 1974).

We see this pattern of differential justice at work with death penalty cases. Simply put, poor people cannot afford to hire the best lawyer and often must rely on court-appointed attorneys, who typically are overworked and underpaid. With capital punishment in place, these unequal resources may mean the difference between life and death for poor defendants. Indeed, the American Bar Association (2009) has repeatedly expressed concern about the limited defense most defendants facing the death penalty

> **social disorganization theory** The theory that attributes increases in crime and deviance to the absence or breakdown of communal relationships and social institutions, such as the family, school, church, and local government.
>
> **labeling theory** An approach to deviance that attempts to explain why certain people are viewed as deviants while others engaged in the same behavior are not.
>
> **societal-reaction approach** Another name for labeling theory.
>
> **differential justice** Differences in the way social control is exercised over different groups.

Executions by State Since 1976

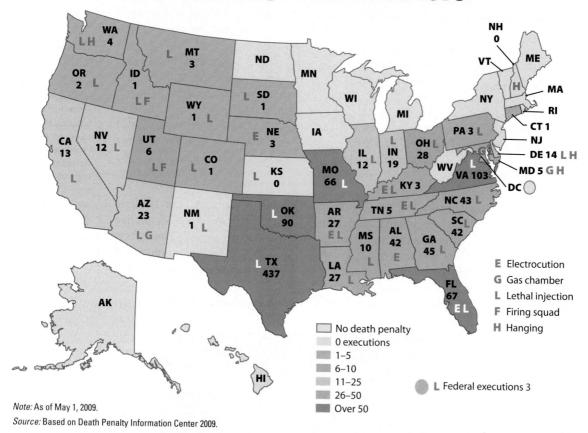

E Electrocution
G Gas chamber
L Lethal injection
F Firing squad
H Hanging

No death penalty
0 executions
1–5
6–10
11–25
26–50
Over 50

L Federal executions 3

Note: As of May 1, 2009.

Source: Based on Death Penalty Information Center 2009.

---

receive. Through mid-2009, DNA analysis and other new technologies had exonerated 17 death row inmates and 238 inmates overall (Innocence Project 2009).

Various studies show that defendants are more likely to be sentenced to death if their victims were White rather than Black. About 78 percent of the victims in death penalty cases are White, even though about half of *all* murder victims are White. There is some evidence that Black defendants, who constituted 42 percent of all death row inmates in 2008, are more likely to face execution than Whites in the same legal circumstances. About 70 percent of those who have been exonerated by DNA testing were members of minority groups. Evidence exists, too, that capital defendants receive poor legal services because of the racist attitudes of their own defense counsel. Apparently, discrimination and racism do not end even when the stakes are life and death (Death Penalty Information Center 2009; Innocence Project 2009; D. Jacobs et al. 2007).

Differential justice is not limited to the United States. In 2007, the people of India were alarmed to learn that police had never investigated a series of killings in the slums of New Delhi. Only after residents found 17 bodies of re-cently murdered children in a sewer drain on the edge of a slum were police moved to act. For many onlookers, it was just the latest example of the two-tier justice system found in India and many other countries (Gentleman 2007).

Such dramatic differences in social treatment may lead to heightened violence and crime. People who view themselves as the victims of unfair treatment may lash out, not against the powerful so much as against fellow victims. In studying crime in rural Mexico, Andrés Villarreal (2004) found that crime rates were high in the areas where land distribution was most inequitable. In areas where land was distributed more equally, communities appeared to suffer less violence and to enjoy greater social cohesion.

Gender Feminist criminologists such as Freda Adler and Meda Chesney-Lind have suggested that many of the existing approaches to deviance and crime were developed with only men in mind. For example, in the United States, for many years any husband who forced his wife to have sexual intercourse—without her consent and against her will—was not legally considered to have committed rape.

> Whenever you find yourself on the side of the majority, it is time to pause and reflect.
>
> **Mark Twain**

The law defined rape as pertaining only to sexual relations between people who were not married to each other, reflecting the overwhelmingly male composition of state legislatures at the time.

It took repeated protests by feminist organizations to get changes in the criminal law defining

rape. It was not until 1993 that husbands in all 50 states could be prosecuted under most circumstances for the rape of their wives. However, significant exceptions remain in no fewer than 30 states. For example, the husband is exempt when he does not need to use force because his wife is asleep, unconscious, or mentally or physically impaired. These interpretations rest on the notion that the marriage contract entitles a husband to have sex (Bergen 2006).

When it comes to crime and to deviance in general, society tends to treat women in a stereotypical fashion. For example, consider how women who have many and frequent sexual partners are more likely to be viewed with scorn than men who are promiscuous. Cultural views and attitudes toward women influence how they are perceived and labeled. The feminist perspective also empha-

sizes that deviance, including crime, tends to flow from economic relationships. Traditionally, men have had greater earning power than their wives. As a result, wives may be reluctant to report acts of abuse to the authorities and thereby lose what may be their primary or even sole source of income. In the workplace, men have exercised greater power than women in pricing, accounting, and product control, giving them greater opportunity to engage in such crimes as embezzlement and fraud. But as women have taken more active and powerful roles both in the household and in business, these gender differences in deviance and crime have narrowed (Bisi 2002; Chesney-Lind 1989; Kruttschnitt and Carbane-Lopez 2006).

Together, sociological perspectives on crime and deviance help us to better understand and explain such acts. No single explanation is sufficient. We must consider multiple factors from a variety of perspectives including: the extent to which deviance exists for the sake of social order, the degree of opportunity to attain both means and ends, the role of socialization in deviance, the strength of local community networks, the power to administer labels and make them stick, and differential access to valuable resources based on class, race, and gender. As Sudhir Venkatesh found in his research on gangs, if we are to fully understand something, we need to dig deep enough and consider what is going on from enough angles and with sufficient care, concern, and curiosity.

I. How do groups maintain social control?

- They use positive and negative sanctions in both formal and informal ways to bring about conformity and obedience.

II. What is the difference between deviance and crime?

- Deviance involves violating a group's expected norms, which may lead the offender to be stigmatized. Crime is a form of deviance that involves violating the formal norms administered by the state for which the offender may receive formal sanctions.

III. How do sociologists explain deviance and crime?

- Sociologists offer up a number of theories of crime, each of which provides additional factors to be considered—such as the need for social order, the significance of interpersonal relationships and local context, and the importance of power and access to resources—that help us to better understand why deviance and crime occur.

Pop Quiz

1. Society brings about acceptance of basic norms through techniques and strategies for preventing deviant human behavior. This process is termed
   a. stigmatization.
   b. labeling.
   c. law.
   d. social control.

2. The penalties and rewards we face for conduct concerning a social norm are known as
   a. informal social controls.
   b. stigmas.
   c. sanctions.
   d. conformities.

3. Stanley Milgram used the word *conformity* to mean
   a. going along with peers.
   b. compliance with higher authorities in a hierarchical structure.
   c. techniques and strategies for preventing deviant behavior in any society.
   d. penalties and rewards for conduct concerning a social norm.

4. According to Hirschi's control theory,
   a. deviance involves acceptance and/or rejection of society's goals and means.
   b. our connection to members of society leads us to systematically conform to society's norms.

   c. we come to view ourselves as deviant based on how others view us.
   d. power and access to resources shape whose norms and values determine individual action.

5. Which of the following statements is true of deviance?
   a. Deviance is always criminal behavior.
   b. Deviance is behavior that violates the standards of conduct or expectations of a group or society.
   c. Deviance is perverse behavior.
   d. Deviance is inappropriate behavior that cuts across all cultures and social orders.

6. The FBI reports which two major categories of crime in its annual *Uniform Crime Reports*?
   a. violent crime and property crime
   b. organized crime and white-collar crime
   c. victimless crime and transnational crime
   d. transnational crime and victimization crime

7. Which type of crime involves the willing exchange among adults of widely desired, but illegal, goods and services?
   a. index crimes
   b. white-collar crime
   c. victimless crime
   d. organized crime

1. (d); 2. (c); 3. (a); 4. (b); 5. (b); 6. (a); 7. (c);

8. Which of the following is *not* one of the basic forms of adaptation specified in Robert Merton's anomie theory of deviance?

    a. conformity

    b. innovation

    c. ritualism

    d. hostility

9. Which of the following theories contends that criminal victimization increases when communal relationships and social institutions break down?

    a. labeling theory

    b. conflict theory

    c. social disorganization theory

    d. differential association theory

10. Even though they committed the same deviant acts, the Saints and Roughnecks did not receive the same treatment from authorities. Sociologist William Chambliss suggests this was due to the fact that authorities viewed members of the groups differently. Which theory supports that conclusion?

    a. Merton's anomie theory

    b. culture transmission theory

    c. differential association theory

    d. labeling theory

8. (d); 9. (c); 10. (d)

7

FAMILIES

LOVE AND MARRIAGE

"Do you love me?" This is the question that Tevye asks Golde, his wife, in the musical *The Fiddler on the Roof* (Jewison 1971). A matchmaker had, as tradition demanded, arranged their marriage, and the two met for the first time on their wedding day. Tevye and Golde never really expected to love each other, but 25 years have passed. Times were changing in their small Russian village in the early 1900s, and now Tevye wants to know.

Tevye and Golde's questions about love and marriage arise because their three daughters all reject the matchmaker tradition, believing that they should follow their own hearts instead. Their eldest turns down the matchmaker's choice of an older, wealthy butcher, opting instead for a poor tailor her own age. Their next daughter falls in love with a revolutionary university student from the big city, and she seeks Tevye's blessing but not his permission. Finally, their youngest daughter seeks neither blessing nor permission in marrying a Russian who is outside their Jewish faith. Along the way, Tevye asks himself if he can accept such violations of "tradition."

In the story, the daughters' breaks with tradition are tied to the larger social, economic, and historical upheavals in Russia at the time. Tradition has always ruled in the community, and these changes in tradition challenge Tevye and Golde's ability to accept their daughters' relationships and even their ability to understand their own. Tevye and Golde decide that they do, in fact, love each other. But their affirmation of love emerges only with the decline of traditions that have guided village life for generations.

Such forces continue to shape our understanding of marriage and of families. We often think that the way things are is the way that things have always been, but when it comes to love, marriage, and families, there is significant variation over time and across cultures. Understanding our beliefs and actions from within the context of an institution such as the family allows us to better see and understand both the "big picture" of our interconnections and the intimate realities of our everyday interactions.

As You READ

>>

- What is the family?
- How do people pick partners?
- How do families vary?

>> Global View of the Family

Families vary around the world. Among Tibetans, a woman may be married simultaneously to more than one man, usually brothers. This system allows sons to share the limited amount of good land. Among the Betsileo of Madagascar, a man has multiple wives, each one living in a different village where he cultivates rice. Wherever he has the best rice field, that woman is considered his first or senior wife. Among the Yanomami of Brazil and Venezuela, it is considered proper to have sexual relations with one's opposite-sex cousins if they are the children of one's mother's brother or father's sister. But if one's opposite-sex cousins are the children of one's mother's sister or father's brother, the same practice is considered to be incest (Haviland et al. 2005; Kottak 2004).

In the United States, the family of today is not what it was a century or even a generation ago. New roles, new gender distinctions, and new child-rearing patterns have all combined to create new forms of family life. Today, for example, more and more women are taking the bread-winner's role, whether as a spouse or as a single parent. Blended families—the result of divorce and remarriage—

are common. And many people are seeking intimate relationships outside marriage, whether in gay or lesbian partnerships or in cohabiting arrangements.

We see such changes reflected in popular culture representations of families. The 1950s U.S. family was epitomized on television by shows such as *Leave It to Beaver* and *Father Knows Best* with a stay-at-home mom, working dad, and assorted kids. Times have changed. *Two and a Half Men* features a father, son, and uncle; *Hannah Montana* depicts a single father with his daughter and son; and then there's *Desperate Housewives*. Perhaps the closest you get these days to the 1950s family is *The Simpsons* with

Did You Know?

About 2.2 million couples get married in the United States every year. That works out to almost 6000 per day. In 2007, Nevada had by far the highest marriage rate with 126,354 couples tying the knot, so perhaps not everything that happens in Vegas stays in Vegas.

Homer, Marge, Lisa, Bart, and Maggie. This shift in how families are portrayed is consistent with changes we have seen both in practice and in our understanding of what constitutes a family.

Because families as we experience them are varied in structure and style, we need a sociological approach that is sufficiently broad to encompass all those things we experience as family. We will look at two different definitional approaches. The first is a substantive definition that focuses on what a family is, and the second is a functional definition that focuses on what families do.

SUBSTANCE: WHAT A FAMILY IS

Perhaps the most conventional approach to defining family is the **substantive definition,** which focuses on blood and law. Blood, in this case, means that people are related because they share a biological heritage passed on directly from parent to child, linking people indirectly to grandparents, aunts and uncles, and other biological relatives. Law means the formal social recognition and affirmation of a bond as family, particularly in the form of marriage and adoption.

The primary advantage of this definitional approach is that boundaries are clear; we can tell who is in and who is out. This makes it easier to count such families, so perhaps it is no surprise that the U.S. Census relies on a substantive approach: "A family is a group of two people or more (one of whom is the householder) related by birth, marriage, or adoption and residing together" (U.S. Census Bureau 2008). It also allows us to track who is related to whom over time.

Kinship Patterns Many of us can trace our roots by looking at a family tree or by listening to elderly family members talk about their lives—and about ancestors who lived and died long before we were born. Yet a person's lineage is more than simply a personal history; it also reflects societal traditions that govern descent. In every culture, children encounter relatives to whom they are expected to show an emotional attachment. The state of being related to others is called **kinship.** Kinship is culturally learned, however, and is not totally determined by biological or marital ties. For example, adoption creates a kinship tie that is legally acknowledged and socially accepted.

The family and the kin group are not necessarily one and the same. Whereas the family is a household unit, kin do not always live together or function as a collective body on a daily basis. Kin groups include aunts, uncles, cousins, in-laws, and so forth. In a society such as the United States, the kinship group may come together only rarely, for a wedding or funeral. However, kinship ties frequently involve obligations and responsibilities. We may feel compelled to assist our kin, and we feel free to call upon them for many types of aid, including loans and babysitting.

How do we identify kinship groups? The principle of descent assigns people to kinship groups according to their relationship to a mother or father. There are three primary ways of determining descent. The United States follows the system of **bilateral descent,** which means that both sides of a person's family are regarded as equally important. For example, no higher value is given to the brothers of one's

> **substantive definition of the family** A definition of the family based on blood, meaning shared genetic heritage, and law, meaning social recognition and affirmation of the bond including both marriage and adoption.
> **kinship** The state of being related to others.
> **bilateral descent** A kinship system in which both sides of a person's family are regarded as equally important.

father than to the brothers of one's mother. However, most societies—according to anthropologist George Murdock, 64 percent of societies—give preference to one side of the family or the other in tracing descent. In **patrilineal** (from the Latin *pater,* "father") **descent,** only the father's relatives are significant in terms of property, inheritance, and emotional ties. Conversely, in societies that favor **matrilineal** (from the Latin *mater,* "mother") **descent,** only the mother's relatives are significant.

SOCthink

> > > How important are intergenerational kinship networks and extended family members in your family? How has this changed since your parents' and grandparents' generations?

Family Types The substantive approach also shapes what we traditionally view as common family types. If we assume that we are connected through blood and law, we can analyze how we structure those relationships. Families might place greater emphasis on immediate family members or on extended family networks. They also are shaped by the number of partners deemed appropriate.

Historically, family connections served as a valuable resource, providing us with access to material, social, and cultural resources. We depended on relatives for food, shelter, opportunities, and knowledge. In fact, historian Stephanie Coontz (2005) argues that, historically, the primary reason to get married was to obtain not a partner but in-laws, thus extending one's network of cooperative relationships. This was the logic of the matchmaker tradition that not only brought Tevye and Golde together in *The Fiddler on the Roof* but brought their families together as well. The matchmaker, as a member of the community, sought to maximize social network connections for the good of the whole.

A family in which relatives—such as grandparents, aunts, or uncles—live in the same household as parents and their children is known as an **extended family.** Although not common, such living arrangements do exist in the United States. The structure of the extended family offers certain advantages over that of the nuclear family. Crises such as death, divorce, and illness put less strain on family members because more people can provide assistance and emotional support. In addition, the extended family constitutes a larger economic unit than the nuclear family. If the family is engaged in a common enterprise—a farm or a

patrilineal descent A kinship system in which only the father's relatives are significant.
matrilineal descent A kinship system in which only the mother's relatives are significant.
extended family A family in which relatives—such as grandparents, aunts, or uncles—live in the same household as parents and their children.
nuclear family A married couple and their unmarried children living together.

small business—the additional family members may represent the difference between prosperity and failure.

With the advent of the Industrial Revolution, the economy shifted away from agricultural production and its corresponding small-town life and toward industrial production in urban areas. Families became smaller and more mobile in response to these structural changes. The obligations of the extended family could hold individuals back, and so we saw a move toward a smaller family unit that came to be known as the nuclear family. The **nuclear family** includes a married couple and their unmarried children living together. The concept of nuclear family builds on the essence or nucleus of the substantive definition of blood and law, including as it does both the parent-to-child and the marriage relationship.

SOCthink

> > > How often do you communicate with your parents, grandparents, or siblings? How might advances in communications technology, especially the cell phone and the Internet, make it easier to maintain regular contacts with extended family members? What consequences might this have for how we view family?

Most people in the United States assume that the nuclear family is by far the most common arrangement. In fact, married couples with children under 18 make up 32 percent of total families. The breadwinner father and stay-at-home mom model idealized in 1950s television makes up only 9.8 percent of total families and 21 percent of families with children under 18 (Bureau of Labor Statistics 2008: Table 4). In contrast, the percentage of single-parent and nonfamily households has risen steadily over the past 50 years.

Types of Marriage

In considering these different family types, we have limited ourselves to the form of marriage that is characteristic of the United States—monogamy. The term **monogamy** describes a form of

U.S. Households by Family Type, 1940–2008

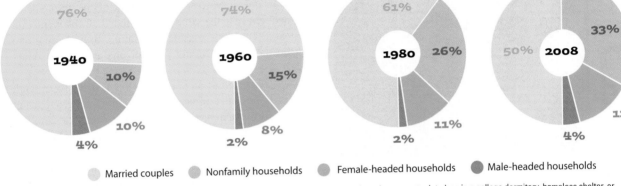

1940	1960	1980	2008
76%	74%	61%	50%
10%	15%	26%	33%
10%	8%	11%	12%
4%	2%	2%	4%

● Married couples ● Nonfamily households ● Female-headed households ● Male-headed households

Note: Nonfamily households include women and men living alone or exclusively with people to whom they are not related, as in a college dormitory, homeless shelter, or military base.

Source: U.S. Census Bureau, 2009a: Table HH-1.

marriage in which one woman and one man are married only to each other. Individuals in the United States are more likely to move into and out of a number of serious romantic relationships, what sociologist Andrew Cherlin (2009) refers to as the "marriage-go-round." Termed **serial monogamy,** a person may have several spouses in his or her lifetime, but only one spouse at a time.

Some cultures allow an individual to have several husbands or wives simultaneously. This form of marriage is known as **polygamy.** In fact, most societies throughout the world, past and present, have preferred polygamy to monogamy. Anthropologist George Murdock (1949, 1957) sampled 565 societies and found that in more than 80 percent, some type of polygamy was the preferred form. While polygamy declined steadily through most of the 20th century, in 28 sub-Saharan African countries, at least 10 percent of men still have polygamous marriages (Tertilt 2005).

There are two basic types of polygamy. The most common is **polygyny,** which refers to the marriage of a man to more than one woman at the same time. Less common is **polyandry,** in which a woman may have more than one husband at the same time. Such is the case, for example, in the Nyinba culture of Nepal and Tibet, in which brothers share a common wife. This arrangement provides a sufficient number of physical laborers in the difficult farming environment yet minimizes the number of offspring.

Most people assumed that polygamy was a thing of the past in the United States. However, in April 2008, law enforcement officials in Texas received an anonymous phone call purported to be from a 16-year-old girl who claimed that she had been forced into a polygamous marriage with an adult man. The girl also complained of having been beaten. Shortly thereafter, officials raided the Yearning for Zion ranch where the girl was living, taking a total of 462 children from the ranch and placing them into temporary legal custody. The ranch was run by members of the Fundamentalist Church of Jesus Christ of Latter Day Saints (FLDS), a group that practices polygamy even though it is illegal in the United States and was banned by the mainstream LDS denomination over 100 years ago. The state ordered DNA testing to ascertain who was related to whom. Ultimately, the children were returned to their families as there was insufficient evidence

monogamy A form of marriage in which one woman and one man are married only to each other.

serial monogamy A form of marriage in which a person may have several spouses in his or her lifetime but only one spouse at a time.

polygamy A form of marriage in which an individual may have several husbands or wives simultaneously.

polygyny A form of polygamy in which a man may have more than one wife at the same time.

polyandry A form of polygamy in which a woman may have more than one husband at the same time.

SOCthink

> > > Why do you think that polygamy was the most common form of marriage historically? Why has it given way to monogamy in modern societies?

Big Love, Long Life?

In 2008, the HBO television series *Big Love* was nominated for a Golden Globe award as the year's best television series, drama. It portrays a fictionalized account of a polygamous family, telling the story of Bill Henrickson, his three wives (Barb, Nicki, and Margene), and their eight children. It was a surprise success given its unconventional storyline. While uncommon in the United States, over 50 percent of men in Cameroon have multiple wives. One study found that men in nations that practice polygyny tend to have a longer life span, perhaps because they rely on multiple wives to lighten the workload of daily life (Callaway 2008; Tertilt 2005).

to demonstrate abuse or the immediate risk of abuse. However, the case did raise awareness of the fact that polygamy continues to exist in the United States.

Once we begin to look at the varieties of family types around the world, we see the main limitation of the substantive definition: There are people who seem to be family but who do not fit neatly into blood or law. For example, the biological parent-to-child tie was expanded by including adoption as part of law. We accept stepparents and stepsiblings as family members even when the children have not been formally adopted by the stepparent. We are currently debating whether to grant same-sex couples legal standing as families. But what about pushing the definition of family still further? Is dad's college friend "Uncle" Bob part of the family? New forms of reproductive tech-

nology, involving donated sperm and eggs and surrogate parents, also challenge conventional thinking. Any substantive definition we might come up with runs the risk of excluding those whom we think of as family members. In response sociologists turn toward the more inclusive functionalist definition of families to address such limitations.

FUNCTIONS: WHAT FAMILIES DO

People in the United States seem to agree that traditional definitions of family are too restrictive. When they are asked how they would define family, their conception is much more inclusive than the substantive definition implies. In one survey, only 22 percent of the respondents defined family in the same way as the U.S. Census Bureau. Instead, 74 percent considered a family to be "any group whose members love and care for one another" (Coontz 1992:21).

We need a definition of families that is inclusive enough to encompass the broad range of intimate groups that people form, such as extended families, nuclear families, single-parent families, blended or reconstituted or stepfamilies, gay and lesbian families, child-free families, racially and ethnically mixed families, commuter marriage families, surrogate or chosen families, and more. One way to avoid getting trapped into overly narrow conceptions of families and to embrace their diversity is to shift focus from a substantive definition of what families *are* to a **functionalist definition** of what families *do* for society and for their members.

Sociologist William F. Ogburn (Ogburn and Tibbits 1934) identified six primary functions that families perform for us:

- *Reproduction.* For a society to maintain itself, it must replace dying members. Families provide the context within which biological reproduction takes place.

- *Socialization.* Parents and other family members monitor a child's behavior and transmit the norms, values, and language of their culture to the child.

- *Protection.* Unlike the young of other animal species, human infants need constant care and economic secu-

PETS AS FAMILY

From Me to You

When discussing families in terms of what they do instead of what they are, students inevitably ask, "Do pets count as family?" Some strongly agree, while others think it is the most ridiculous thing they have ever heard. More and more students are coming down on the side of pets as family. When we "adopted" Jessie, our Pembroke Welsh corgi, I better understood why. Owners develop strong emotional bonds with their pets and some refer to them as their "fur kids." Pets provide a source of comfort and companionship. They give us someone to care about, and they care for us in their own ways. Isn't that what we want from family?

Hot or Not?

Should pets, including dogs, cats, birds, or others, count as family?

rity. In all cultures, the family assumes the ultimate responsibility for the protection and upbringing of children.

- *Regulation of sexual behavior.* Sexual norms are subject to change both over time (for instance, in the customs for dating) and across cultures (compare strict Saudi Arabia to the more permissive Denmark). However, whatever the time period or cultural values of a society, standards of sexual behavior are most clearly defined within the family circle.

- *Affection and companionship.* Ideally, families provide members with warm and intimate relationships, helping them to feel satisfied and secure. Of course, a family member may find such rewards outside the family—from peers, in school, at work—and may even perceive the home as an unpleasant or abusive setting. Nevertheless, we expect our relatives to understand us, to care for us, and to be there for us when we need them.

- *Provision of social status.* We inherit a social position because of the family background and reputation of our parents and siblings. For example, the race, ethnicity, social class, education level, occupation, and religion of our parents all shape the material, social, and cultural resources to which we have access and therefore the options we might have.

No matter how it is composed, any group that fulfills these functions is family to us. We might count teammates, close college dorm mates, or a long-term circle of friends as family. We look to such groups in moments of need for all kinds of support, including care and affection, guidance in how to think and act, dating advice, and sometimes even material support, whether borrowing a car or just some money for pizza. We may use the expression that they are "like family" to convey that sense, or we may even refer to such significant people in our lives as our sister, brother, mom, or dad. In fact, given the survey results above, people may already be defining as family any group that provides sufficient love and care for each other. According to this functionalist definition, a family *is* what a family *does.*

AUTHORITY PATTERNS: WHO RULES?

Regardless of what a family looks like, within the context of any group we define as family, we will inevitably have to address issues of power. Imagine, for example, that you have recently married and must begin to make decisions about the future of your new family. You and your partner face many questions: Where will you live? How will you furnish your home? Who will do the cooking, shopping, and cleaning? Whose friends will be invited to dinner? Each time a decision must be made, an issue is raised: Who has the power to make the decision? In simple terms, who rules the family?

Societies vary in the way that power is distributed within the family; historically, however, the answer to that question has largely been shaped by gender. A society that expects males to dominate in all family decision making is termed a **patriarchy.** In patriarchal societies, such as Iran, the eldest male often wields the greatest power, although wives are expected to be treated with respect and kindness. An Iranian woman's status is typically defined by her relationship to a male relative, usually as a wife or daughter. In many patriarchal societies, women find it more difficult to obtain a divorce than a man does (Farr 1999). In contrast, in a **matriarchy,** women have greater authority than men. Formal matriarchies, which are uncommon, emerged among Native American tribal societies and in nations in which men were absent for long periods because of warfare or food-gathering expeditions.

> **functionalist definition of families** A definition of families that focuses on what families do for society and for their members.
>
> **patriarchy** A society in which men dominate in family decision making.
>
> **matriarchy** A society in which women dominate in family decision making.

Over a century ago, Friedrich Engels ([1884] 1959), a colleague of Karl Marx, went so far as to say that the family is the ultimate source of social inequality because of its role in the transfer of power, property, and privilege. Historically, he argues, the family has legitimized and perpetuated male dominance. It has contributed to societal injustice, denied women opportunities that are extended to men, and limited freedom in sexual expression and mate selection. In the United States, it was not until the first wave of contemporary feminism, in the mid-1800s, that there was a substantial challenge to the historical status of wives and children as the legal property of husbands and fathers.

egalitarian family An authority pattern in which spouses are regarded as equals.

Due in part to the efforts of women and men in similar movements over the years, we have seen the rise of a third type of authority pattern. In the **egalitarian family,** spouses are regarded as equals. This shift has been driven at least in part by occupational and financial opportunities for women that previously had been denied them (Wills and Risman 2006). That does not mean, however, that all decisions are shared in such families. Wives may hold authority in some spheres, and husbands in others. For example, sociologists have found that, in terms of paid and unpaid labor in two-parent families, the total hours worked by mothers and fathers is roughly equal at about 65 hours per week, though the distribution of tasks varies (Bianchi, Robinson, and Milkie 2006).

Historian Stephanie Coontz (2008) suggests that, when it works, marriage today is better than ever. She writes that it "delivers more benefits to its members—adults and children—than ever before. A good marriage is fairer and more fulfilling for both men and women than couples of the past could ever have imagined." She points to shared decision making and housework, increases in time spent with children, and declines in violence and sexual coercion and in the likelihood of adultery.

While the egalitarian family has become a more common pattern in the United States in recent decades, male dominance over the family has hardly disappeared. Sociologists have found that although married men are increasing their involvement in child care, their wives still perform a disproportionate amount of it. Furthermore, for every stay-at-home dad there are 38 stay-at-home moms (Fields 2004:11–12; Garcia-Moreno et al. 2005; Sayer et al. 2004). And unfortunately, many husbands reinforce their power and control over wives and children through acts of domestic violence.

In addition to such internal power struggles, families also continue to provide a foundation for power within the larger society. Family serves as the basis for transferring power, property, and privilege from one generation to the next. Although the United States is widely viewed as a land of opportunity, social mobility is restricted in important ways. Children inherit the privileged or less-than-privileged social and economic status of their parents (and in some cases, of earlier generations as well). The social class of parents significantly influences children's socialization experiences and the degree of protection they receive. Thus, the socioeconomic status of a child's family will have a marked influence on his or her nutrition, health care, housing, educational opportunities, and in many respects, life chances as an adult. In many ways the family helps to maintain inequality.

>> Marriage and Family

In spite of concerns about power and inequality in the family sphere, people's faith in marriage continues (Cherlin 2009). Currently, over 95 percent of all men and women in the United States marry at least once during their lifetimes. Historically, the most consistent aspect of family life in this country has been the high rate of marriage. When it comes to picking partners in the United States, most of us assume that romantic love alone will guide our choice. We learn from sociology, however, that even if we no longer rely on a matchmaker to tell us which particular individual to choose, our social positions shape our choices.

SOCthink

> > > Matchmaker services still exist in the United States, and some charge as much as $20,000 for a membership with additional annual fees. Why might people turn to matchmaking services today? What are the disadvantages of relying on our own contacts and judgment when it comes to finding a romantic partner?

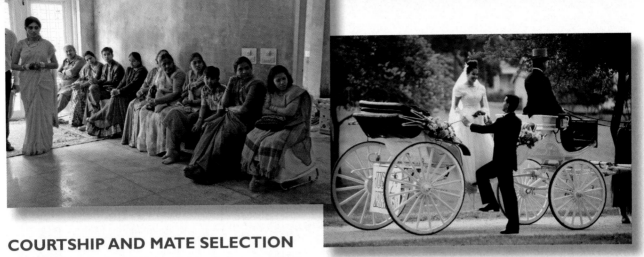

COURTSHIP AND MATE SELECTION

"My rugby mates would roll over in their graves," says Tom Buckley of his online courtship of and subsequent marriage to Terri Muir. But Tom and Terri are hardly alone these days in turning to the Internet for matchmaking services. A generation or two ago, most couples met in high school or college, but now that people are marrying later in life, the Internet has become the new meeting place for the romantically inclined. Today, thousands of websites offer to help people find mates. For example, eHarmony, which claims to be the first to use a "scientific approach" to matching people based on a variety of abilities and interests, says that it "facilitates" 236 marriages a day. A 2007 survey found that 19 percent of couples who married in 2006–2007 had met online (Logue 2009; Peel 2008).

Ten Questions Couples Should Ask (or Wish They Had) Before Marrying

Do you want to have children?

Who will do what when it comes to housework?

What are your expectations regarding sex?

What do you think about having a television in the bedroom?

What do you expect regarding religious training for our children?

How much money do you owe?

Do you like and respect my friends?

What do you really think about my parents?

What does my family do that annoys you?

Are there some things you are not willing to give up in the marriage?

Source: New York Times 2006.

Going GLOBAL

Percentage of People Ages 20–24 Ever Married, Selected Countries

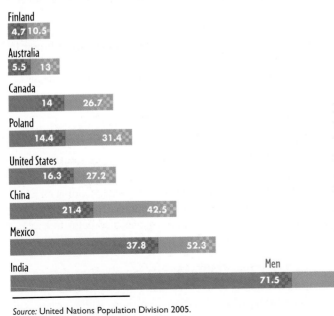

Finland
4.7 10.5

Australia
5.5 13

Canada
14 26.7

Poland
14.4 31.4

United States
16.3 27.2

China
21.4 42.5

Mexico
37.8 52.3

India
Men 71.5   Women 94.3

Source: United Nations Population Division 2005.

Internet romance is only the latest form of courtship. Many traditional cultures, including those of the central Asian nation of Uzbekistan, define courtship largely through the interaction of two sets of parents, who arrange marriages for their children. Typically, a young Uzbekistani woman is socialized to eagerly anticipate her marriage to a man whom she has met only once, when he is presented to her family at the time of the final inspection of her dowry. In the United States, by contrast, courtship occurs primarily by individuals who have a romantic interest in each other. In U.S. culture, courtship often requires these individuals to rely heavily on intricate games, gestures, and signals. Despite such differences, the norms and values of the larger society—whether in the United States, Uzbekistan, or elsewhere—influence courtship (Kemp 2008; Rand 2006).

One unmistakable trend in mate selection is that the process appears to be taking longer today than in the past. A variety of factors, including concerns about financial security and personal independence, has contributed to this delay in marriage. Most people are now well into their 20s before they marry, both in the United States and in other countries. In the United States, the median age at first marriage for women is 25.6, and for men is 27.4. Since 1970, this represents an increase of 4.8 years for women and 4.2 years for men (U.S. Census Bureau 2009a: Table MS-2).

When it comes to picking partners, our potential pool is shaped by social norms. These norms can be distinguished in terms of endogamy and exogamy. **Endogamy** (from the Greek *endon,* "within") specifies the groups within which a spouse must be found and prohibits marriage with outsiders. For example, in the United States, many people are expected to marry within their own racial, ethnic, or religious group and are strongly discouraged or even prohibited from marrying outside the group. Endogamy is intended to reinforce the cohesiveness of the group by suggesting to the young that they should marry someone "of their own kind."

endogamy The restriction of mate selection to people within the same group.
exogamy The requirement that people select a mate outside certain groups.
incest taboo The prohibition of sexual relationships between certain culturally specified relatives.

In contrast, **exogamy** (from the Greek *exo,* "outside") requires mate selection outside certain groups, usually one's own family or certain kinfolk. The **incest taboo,** a social norm common to virtually all societies, prohibits sexual relationships between certain culturally specified relatives. In the United States, this taboo means that we must marry outside the nuclear family. We cannot marry our siblings, and in most states, we cannot marry our first cousins.

Endogamous restrictions may be seen as preferences for one group over another. In the United States, such preferences are most obvious in racial barriers. Some states outlawed interracial marriage, until a 1967 Supreme Court decision overturned such laws. Nevertheless, the number of marriages between African Americans and Whites in

the United States has increased more than eight times in recent decades, jumping from 51,000 in 1960 to 403,000 in 2006. Moreover, 25 percent of married Asian American women and 12 percent of married

5 Movies on MARRIAGE

Far From Heaven
Subverting the ideal 1950s marriage.

Monsoon Wedding
An Indian wedding celebration.

The Squid and the Whale
How divorce affects children.

Little Children
Two suburban parents embark on an affair.

A Home at the End of the World
An alternative marriage and family.

Asian American men are married to a person who is not of Asian descent. Marriage across ethnic lines is even greater among Hispanics; 27 percent of all married Hispanics have a non-Hispanic spouse. Even though all these examples of racial exogamy are noteworthy, endogamy is still the social norm in the United States (Bureau of the Census 1998, 2007a:Table 59).

Even in places where endogamy is already the norm, we still tend to pick people like ourselves. This is known as **homogamy**—the conscious or unconscious tendency to select a mate with personal characteristics and interests similar to one's own. Internet dating services depend upon this principle to help find matches. Sociologist Pepper Schwartz, who works as a consultant for PerfectMatch.com, has developed a 48-question survey that covers everything from prospective mates' decision-making style to their degree of impulsivity (Gottlieb 2006). While it is certainly possible that "opposites attract," when it comes to romance, we tend toward people more like ourselves.

VARIATIONS IN FAMILY LIFE AND INTIMATE RELATIONSHIPS

Within the United States, social class, race, and ethnicity create variations in family life. Studying these variations will give us a more sophisticated understanding of contemporary family styles in our country. The desire to avoid having to negotiate such differences also helps to explain why people often practice homogamy.

Social Class Differences Social class differences matter when it comes to parenting. Historically, poor and working-class families were more authoritarian, and

SOCthink

> > > How important are factors such as age, education, race, ethnicity, social class, gender, and religion in whom you might choose for a serious relationship? To what extent are you conscious of such influences when you pick someone to date?

middle-class families were more permissive and less likely to use physical punishment. Starting in the 1950s, exposure to common child-rearing advice in books, magazines, and on television reduced the extremes by creating a shared understanding of appropriate parenting techniques, but recent research shows that parenting practices still differ. For example, middle-class parents provide more structure through participation in organized activities, and working-class parents allow their children greater freedom so long as they don't overstep disciplinary bounds. The material, social, and cultural resources children inherit from their parents (whether in the form of money, connections, language, tastes, attitudes, or experience) help to reproduce social class across generations (Kronstadt and Favreault 2008; Lareau 2003).

sharing goods and services. In addition to these strong kinship bonds, Black family life has emphasized deep religious commitment and high aspirations for achievement (F. Furstenberg 2007; Stack 1974).

Like African Americans, Native Americans draw on family ties to cushion many of the hardships they face. On the Navajo reservation, for example, teenage parenthood is not regarded as the crisis that it is elsewhere in the United States. The Navajo trace their descent matrilineally. Traditionally, couples reside with the wife's family after marriage, allowing the grandparents to help with the child rearing. While the Navajo do not approve of teenage parenthood, the deep emotional commitment of their extended families provides a warm home environment for fatherless children (Dalla and Gamble 2001).

The goal in marriage is not to think alike, but to think together.

Robert C. Dodds

Among the poor, women often play a significant role in the economic support of the family. Men may earn low wages, may be unemployed, or may be entirely absent from the family. In 2007, 28 percent of all families headed by women with no husband present were below the official poverty line. The rate for married couples was only 4.9 percent (DeNavas-Walt et al. 2008:15). Racial and class factors are often closely related. In examining family life among racial and ethnic minorities, keep in mind that certain patterns may result from class as well as cultural factors.

Racial and Ethnic Differences The subordinate status of racial and ethnic minorities in the United States profoundly affects their family lives. For example, the lower incomes of African Americans, Native Americans, most Hispanic groups, and selected Asian American groups make creating and maintaining successful marital unions a difficult task. The economic restructuring of the past 50 years, described by sociologist William Julius Wilson (1996) and others, in which blue-collar jobs disappeared from urban areas as companies moved production facilities abroad, has especially affected people living in inner cities and desolate rural areas. Furthermore, the immigration policy of the United States has complicated the successful relocation of intact families from Asia and Latin America.

The African American family suffers from many negative and inaccurate stereotypes. It is true that in a significantly higher proportion of Black than White families, no husband is present in the home. Yet Black single mothers often belong to stable, functioning kin networks, which mitigate the pressures of sexism and racism. Members of these networks—predominantly female kin such as mothers, grandmothers, and aunts—ease financial strains by

Sociologists also have taken note of differences in family patterns among other racial and ethnic groups. For example, although Mexican American men have been described as exhibiting a sense of virility, personal worth, and pride in their maleness that is called **machismo,** Mexican Americans are also described as being more familistic than many other subcultures. **Familism** refers to pride in the extended family, expressed through the maintenance of close ties and strong obligations to kinfolk outside the immediate family. Traditionally, Mexican Americans have placed proximity to their extended families above other needs and desires.

> **homogamy** The conscious or unconscious tendency to select a mate with personal characteristics and interests similar to one's own.
>
> **machismo** A sense of virility, personal worth, and pride in one's maleness.
>
> **familism** Pride in the extended family, expressed through the maintenance of close ties and strong obligations to kinfolk outside the immediate family.

These family patterns are changing, however, in response to changes in Latinos' social class standing, educational achievements, and occupations. Like other Americans, career-oriented Latinos in search of a mate but short on spare time are turning to the Internet. As Latinos and other groups assimilate into the dominant culture of the United States, their family lives take on both the positive and the negative characteristics associated with White households (Landale and Orapesa 2007).

CHILD-REARING PATTERNS

Caring for children is a universal function of the family, yet the ways in which different societies assign this function to family members can vary significantly. The Nayars of southern India acknowledge the biological role of fathers, but the mother's eldest brother is responsible for her children. In contrast, uncles play only a peripheral role in child care in the United States. Even within the United States, child-rearing patterns are varied. Just as our conception of families has changed, so also has our practice of child rearing.

adoption In a legal sense, a process that allows for the transfer of the legal rights, responsibilities, and privileges of parenthood to a new legal parent or parents.

Parenthood and Grandparenthood The socialization of children is essential to the maintenance of any culture. Consequently, parenthood is one of the most important (and most demanding) social roles in the United States. Sociologist Alice Rossi (1968, 1984) has identified four factors that complicate the transition to parenthood and the role of socialization. First, there is little anticipatory socialization for the social role of caregiver. The nor-

POPSOC

Parenthood has been a frequent source of entertainment in the movies. Examples of such films include *Mr. Mom, Parenthood, Finding Nemo, Freaky Friday, Cheaper by the Dozen, Daddy's Little Girls, Juno, Baby Mama,* and even *Alvin and the Chipmunks.* They all convey messages of what it means to be a parent. What lessons might we learn from an analysis of how mothers and fathers are portrayed in such films? What recurring images and themes occur? How common is the bungling dad or the career mom who wonders if she is making the right choices? What are the consequences of such films for how we practice parenting?

mal school curriculum gives scant attention to the subjects most relevant to successful family life, such as child care and home maintenance. Second, only limited learning occurs during the period of pregnancy itself. Third, the transition to parenthood is quite abrupt. Unlike adolescence, it is not prolonged; unlike the transition to work, the duties of caregiving cannot be taken on gradually. Finally, in Rossi's view, our society lacks clear and helpful guidelines for successful parenthood. There is little consensus on how parents can produce happy and well-adjusted offspring— or even on what it means to be well adjusted. For these reasons, socialization for parenthood involves difficult challenges for most men and women in the United States.

One recent development in family life in the United States has been the extension of parenthood, as adult children continue to live at home or return home after college. In 2008, 56 percent of men and 48 percent of women ages 18–24 lived with their parents (U.S. Census Bureau 2009a: Table AD-1). Some of these adult children were still pursuing an education, but in many instances, financial difficulties underlay these living arrangements. While rents and real estate prices have skyrocketed, salaries for younger workers have not kept pace, and many find themselves unable to afford their own homes. Moreover, with many marriages now ending in divorce, divorced sons and daughters often return to live with their parents, sometimes with their own children.

Given that the dominant cultural expectation in the United States remains some form of the nuclear family, in which children are expected to set up households on their own once they reach adulthood, such arrangements present challenges for everybody involved. Social scientists have just begun to examine the phenomenon, sometimes called the "boomerang generation" or the "full-nest syndrome." One survey in Virginia showed that neither the parents nor their adult children were happy about continuing to live together. The children often felt resentful and isolated, but the parents suffered too. Learning to live without children in the home is an essential stage of adult life and may even be a significant turning point for a marriage (Casey 2004; Rouvalis 2008; Scott 2008).

In some homes, the full nest holds grandchildren. In 2004, 6.5 million children, or 9 percent of all children in the United States, lived in a household with a grandparent (Kreider 2008). In about a third of these homes, no parent was present to assume responsibility for the youngsters. Special difficulties are inherent in such relationships, including legal custodial concerns, financial issues, and emotional problems for adults and youths alike. Perhaps not surprisingly, support groups such as Grandparents as Parents have emerged to provide assistance.

Adoption In a legal sense, **adoption** is a "process that allows for the transfer of the legal rights, responsibilities, and privileges of parenthood" to a new legal parent or parents (E. Cole 1985:638). In many cases, these rights are transferred from a biological parent or parents (often called birth parents) to an adoptive parent or parents.

Hollywood stars Angelina Jolie and Brad Pitt and several of their children, many from overseas adoptions.

About 4 percent of all people in the United States are adopted, and about 2 percent by persons not related to them at birth. There are two legal methods of adopting an unrelated person: (1) the adoption may be arranged through a licensed agency, or (2) in some states it may be arranged through a private agreement sanctioned by the courts. Adopted children may come from the United States or from abroad. In 2006, more than 20,000 children entered the United States as the adopted children of U.S. citizens. While the number of international adoptions remains substantial, it has declined in recent years. China, the source for about one-third of overseas adoptions, recently began to tighten the rules for foreigners. Applicants who are single, obese, or older than 50 may now be disqualified automatically (Carr 2007; Gross 2007).

In the United States, one of the limitations historically was that only married couples could adopt. In 1995, an important court decision in New York held that a couple does not have to be married to adopt a child. Under this ruling, unmarried heterosexual couples, lesbian couples, and gay couples can all legally adopt children in New York. Writing for the majority, Chief Justice Judith Kaye argued that by expanding the boundaries of who can be legally recognized as parents, the state may be able to assist more children in securing "the best possible home." With this ruling, New York became the third state (after Vermont and Massachusetts) to recognize the right of unmarried couples to adopt children (Dao 1995; Human Rights Campaign 2009).

For every child who is adopted, many more remain the wards of state-sponsored child protective services. At any given time, about half a million children in the United States are living in foster care. Approximately 130,000 of these children are waiting for adoption (Administration for Children and Families 2008).

Dual-Income Families The idea of a family consisting of a wage-earning husband and a stay-at-home wife has largely given way to the dual-income household. Among married couples with children under 6, 59 percent have both husband and wife in the labor force (U.S. Census Bureau 2008b:Table 580).

SOCthink

> > > What are the advantages and disadvantages of the dual-income model for women, for men, for children, and for society as a whole?

Both opportunity and need have driven the rise in the number of dual-income couples. Women now have the chance to pursue opportunities in a way that previously had been closed due to cultural expectations regarding gender. This has resulted in increased education levels for women and increased participation in occupational fields that had been largely closed. At the same time, however, couples find it harder to make it on a single income. Evidence of this trend can be found in the rise of married couples living apart for reasons other than marital discord. The 3.6 million couples who now live apart represent 1 out of every 33 marriages. More than half live farther than 100 miles apart, and half of those live 1000 or more miles apart. Of course, couples living apart are nothing new; men have worked at transient jobs for generations as soldiers, truck drivers, or traveling salesmen. The existence of such household arrangements re-

Did You Know?

. . . Until 1978 it was legal in the United States to fire a woman for being pregnant. The Supreme Court upheld that principle in key cases in 1974 and 1976. Two years later, in response to these rulings, Congress passed the Pregnancy Discrimination Act, which prohibited denying benefits to, firing, or refusing to hire someone for being pregnant.

flects an acceptance of the egalitarian family type (L. Cullen 2007; Holmes 2006).

Single-Parent Families The 2004 *American Idol* winner Fantasia Barrino's song "Baby Mama" offers a tribute to young single mothers—a subject she knows about. Barrino was 17 when she became pregnant with her daughter. Though critics charged that the song sends the wrong message to teenage girls, Barrino says it is not about encouraging teens to have sex. Rather, she sees the song as an anthem for young mothers courageously trying to raise their children alone (Cherlin 2006).

In recent decades, the stigma attached to unwed mothers and other single parents has significantly diminished. **Single-parent families,** in which only one parent is present to care for the children, can hardly be viewed as a rarity in the United States. In 2004, a single parent headed about 20 percent of White families with children under age 18, 29 percent of Hispanic families, 59 percent of African American families, and 11 percent of Asian/Pacific Islander families (as we can see in the figure on page 153).

The life of single parents and their children is not inevitably more difficult than that of a traditional nuclear family. It is as inaccurate to assume that a single-parent family is necessarily deprived as it is to assume that a two-parent

Comedians Tina Fey and Amy Poehler starred in the 2008 film Baby Mama, in which Fey played a would-be single mother.

> What greater thing is there for human souls than to feel that they are joined for life— to be with each other in silent unspeakable memories.

George Eliot

family is always secure and happy. Nevertheless, to the extent that such families have to rely on a single income or a sole caregiver, life in the single-parent family can be extremely stressful. A family headed by a single mother faces especially difficult problems when the mother is a teenager, especially when she lacks access to significant social and economic resources (Sawhill 2006).

Why might low-income teenage women wish to have children and face the obvious financial difficulties of motherhood? Some theorists argue that these women tend to have low self-esteem and limited options; a child may provide a sense of motivation and purpose for the teenager whose economic worth in our society is limited at best. Given the barriers that many young women face because of their gender, race, ethnicity, and class, many teenagers may believe they have little to lose and much to gain by having a child.

Although 88 percent of single parents in the United States are mothers, the number of households headed by single fathers more than quadrupled between 1980 and 2000. Single mothers often develop social networks, but single fathers are typically more isolated. In addition, they must deal with schools and social service agencies that are more accustomed to women as custodial parents (Kreider 2008).

Stepfamilies Approximately 45 percent of all people in the United States will marry, divorce, and then remarry. The rising rates of divorce and remarriage have led to a

Rise of Single–Parent Families in the United States, 1970–2004

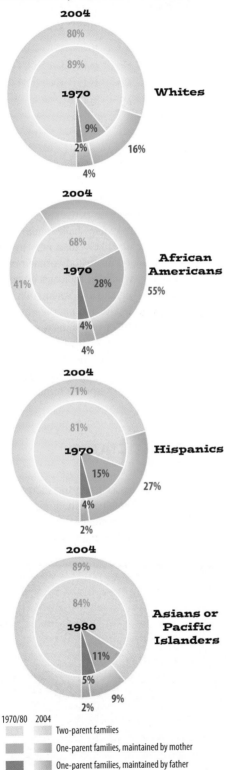

Whites
- 2004
- 80%
- 89%
- 1970
- 9%
- 2%
- 16%
- 4%

African Americans
- 2004
- 68%
- 1970
- 41%
- 28%
- 55%
- 4%
- 4%

Hispanics
- 2004
- 71%
- 81%
- 1970
- 15%
- 27%
- 4%
- 2%

Asians or Pacific Islanders
- 2004
- 89%
- 84%
- 1980
- 11%
- 5%
- 9%
- 2%

1970/80 2004
- Two-parent families
- One-parent families, maintained by mother
- One-parent families, maintained by father

Note: "Children" refers to children under 18. Early data for Asian Americans are for 1980. Hispanics can be of any race. Not included are unrelated people living together with no children present. All data exclude the 4 percent of children in nonparental households.

Source: Bureau of the Census 1994:63; Kreider 2008.

noticeable increase in stepfamily relationships. The exact nature of blended families has social significance for adults and children alike.

Family members in stepfamilies must deal with resocialization issues when an adult becomes a stepparent or a child becomes a stepchild and stepsibling. In evaluating these stepfamilies, some observers have assumed that children would benefit from remarriage because they would be gaining a second custodial parent and would potentially enjoy greater economic security. However, after reviewing many studies of stepfamilies, sociologist Andrew J. Cherlin (2008b:800) concluded that "the well-being of children in stepfamilies is no better, on average, than the well-being of children in divorced, single-parent households."

> **single-parent family** A family in which only one parent is present to care for the children.

Stepparents can and do play valuable and unique roles in their stepchildren's lives, but their involvement does not guarantee an improvement in family life. In fact, standards may decline. Studies suggest that children raised in families with stepmothers are likely to have less health care, education, and money spent on their food than children raised by biological mothers. The measures are also negative for children raised by stepfathers, but only half as negative as in the case of stepmothers. This may be due to the stepmother holding back out of concern for seeming too intrusive or relying on the biological father to carry out parental duties (Schmeeckle 2007; Schmeeckle et al. 2006).

>> Divorce

"Do you promise to love, honor, and cherish . . . until death do you part?" Every year, people of all social classes and racial and ethnic groups make this legally binding agreement. Yet a significant number of these promises shatter prior to divorce.

STATISTICAL TRENDS IN DIVORCE

Just how common is divorce? Surprisingly, this is not a simple question to answer; divorce statistics are difficult to in-

Cartoon by Signe Wilkerson, Cartoon Arts International. Reprinted with the permission of Signe Wilkerson, Cartoonists & Writers Syndicate, www.cartoonweb.com.

Percentage of Marriages to Reach Milestones*

Men, year of first marriage	Anniversary (percentage still married)*							
	5th	10th	15th	20th	25th	30th	35th	40th
1955–59	96.4	88.3	80.3	73.8	70.4	67.3	64.7	61.4
1960–64	95.1	85.0	75.2	69.7	65.0	62.4	59.7	52.5
1965–69	90.5	76.9	67.4	62.3	58.6	55.5	48.2	
1970–74	88.5	74.4	64.6	58.1	53.8	46.2		
1975–79	88.1	73.0	65.2	59.6	49.5			
1980–84	88.7	73.7	65.3	53.8				
1985–89	89.3	76.4	60.6					
1990–94	89.4	70.0						

Women, year of first marriage	Anniversary (percentage still married)*							
	5th	10th	15th	20th	25th	30th	35th	40th
1955–59	94.0	86.8	79.4	72.4	67.2	63.5	58.9	54.7
1960–64	92.8	82.3	72.7	66.5	60.4	56.1	52.7	44.9
1965–69	89.5	74.9	65.7	60.0	55.1	51.3	43.8	
1970–74	87.1	71.6	61.4	55.4	50.6	42.1		
1975–79	85.3	70.0	61.4	55.7	46.4			
1980–84	86.5	70.7	63.1	52.4				
1985–89	85.7	73.0	56.9					
1990–94	87.2	69.2						

*Counts marriages ended by divorce, separation, and death

Source: U.S. Census Bureau 2004:Table 2.

terpret. The media frequently report that one out of every two marriages ends in divorce. But that figure is misleading in that many marriages last for decades. It is based on a comparison of all divorces that occur in a single year (regardless of when the couples were married) with the number of new marriages in that same year. We get a somewhat more complete picture by looking at marital milestones people reach based on the year they first married (as shown in the table above). These data include marriages that end due to the death of the partner; given that life expectancy has increased, it does provide a sense of shifting patterns. Following either the rows or the columns provides insight into both the generational effect and the impact of changing attitudes and practices over time.

In the United States and many other countries, overall divorce rates began to increase in the late 1960s but then leveled off; since the late 1980s, the divorce rate has declined by 30 percent. This trend is due partly to the aging of the baby boomer generation and the corresponding decline in the proportion of people of marriageable age. But it also indicates an increase in marital stability in recent years (Coontz 2006).

Getting divorced obviously does not sour people on marriage. About 63 percent of all divorced people in the United States have remarried. However, women are less likely than men to remarry because many retain custody of their children after a divorce, which complicates a new adult relationship (Bianchi and Spain 1996; Saad 2004).

Some people regard the nation's high rate of remarriage as an endorsement of the institution of marriage, but it does lead to the new challenges of a kin network characterized by both current and prior marital relationships. Such networks can be particularly complex if children are involved or if an ex-spouse remarries.

FACTORS ASSOCIATED WITH DIVORCE

One of the major factors shaping the increase in divorce over the past 100 years has been the greater social acceptance of divorce. It is no longer considered necessary to endure an unhappy marriage. Even major religious groups

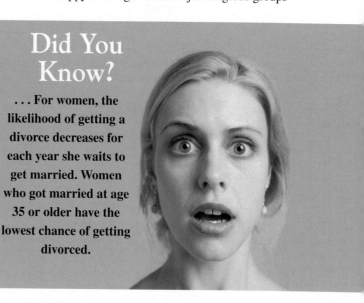

Did You Know?

. . . For women, the likelihood of getting a divorce decreases for each year she waits to get married. Women who got married at age 35 or older have the lowest chance of getting divorced.

Trends in Marriage and Divorce in the United States, 1920–2006

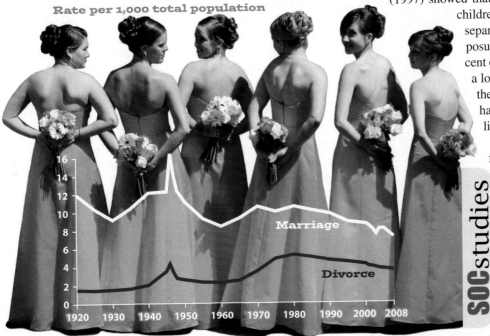

Rate per 1,000 total population

Marriage

Divorce

1920 1930 1940 1950 1960 1970 1980 1990 2000 2008

Sources: Bureau of the Census 1975:64; *National Vital Statistics Reports* 2009.

SOCstudies

ents divorce each year. Of course, for some of these children, divorce signals the welcome end to a highly dysfunctional relationship. A national sample conducted by sociologists Paul R. Amato and Alan Booth (1997) showed that in about a third of divorces, the children actually benefited from parental separation because it lessened their exposure to conflict. But in about 70 percent of divorces, the parents engaged in a low level of conflict; in those cases, the realities of divorce appeared to be harder for the children to bear than living with the marital unhappiness.

Other researchers, using differing definitions of conflict, have found greater unhappiness for children living in homes with marital differences. Still, it would be simplistic to assume that children are automatically better off following the breakup of their parents' marriage. The interests of the parents do not necessarily serve children well (Cherlin 2009; Sun and Li 2008).

have relaxed what were often negative attitudes toward divorce, commonly having treated it as a sin.

The growing acceptance of divorce is a worldwide phenomenon. Only a decade ago, Sunoo, South Korea's foremost matchmaking service, had no divorced clients. Few Koreans divorced, and those who did felt social pressure to resign themselves to the single life. In one recent seven-year period, South Korea's divorce rate doubled. Today, 15 percent of Sunoo's membership is divorced (Onishi 2003).

In the United States, a variety of factors have contributed to the growing social acceptance of divorce. For instance, most states have adopted less restrictive divorce laws in the past three decades. No-fault divorce laws, which allow a couple to end their marriage without assigning blame (by specifying adultery, for instance), accounted for an initial surge in the divorce rate after they were introduced in the 1970s, though these laws appear to have had little effect beyond that. Additionally, a general increase in family incomes, coupled with the availability of free legal aid to some poor people, has meant that more couples can afford costly divorce proceedings. Also, as society provides greater opportunities for women, more and more wives are becoming less dependent on their husbands, both economically and emotionally. They may feel more able to leave a marriage if it seems hopeless.

IMPACT OF DIVORCE ON CHILDREN

Divorce is traumatic for all involved, but it has special meaning for the more than 1 million children whose par-

>> Diverse Lifestyles

Marriage is no longer the presumed route from adolescence to adulthood. In fact, it has lost much of its social significance as a rite of passage. Now, establishing oneself through education and a career has taken precedence (Cherlin 2004, 2009). The nation's marriage rate has declined since 1970 because people are postponing marriage until later in life and because more couples, including same-sex couples, are deciding to form partnerships without marriage.

COHABITATION

In the United States, testing the marital waters by living together before making a commitment is a common practice among marriage-wary 20- and 30-somethings. The tremendous increase in the number of male–female couples who choose to live together without marrying, a practice called **cohabitation,** is one of the most dramatic social trends of recent years.

> **cohabitation** The practice of living together as a male–female couple without marrying.

About half of all currently married couples in the United States say that they lived together prior to marriage. And this percentage is likely to increase. The number of unmarried-couple households in the United States rose sixfold in the 1960s and increased another 72 percent between 1990 and 2000. Presently, over 8 percent of opposite-sex couples are unmarried. Cohabitation is more common among African Americans and American

Indians than among other racial and ethnic groups; it is least common among Asian Americans. The figure below shows how cohabitation varies by region (Peterson 2003; T. Simmons and O'Connell 2003).

In much of Europe, cohabitation is so common that the general sentiment seems to be "Love, yes; marriage, maybe." In Iceland, 62 percent of all children are born to single mothers; in France, Great Britain, and Norway, the proportion is about 40 percent. Government policies in these countries make few legal distinctions between married and unmarried couples or households (Lyall 2002; M. Moore 2006).

People commonly associate cohabitation only with younger couples, but according to a study done in Los Angeles, working couples are almost twice as likely to cohabit as college students. And census data show that in 2003, 45 percent of unmarried couples had one or more children present in the household. These cohabitants are more like spouses than dating partners. Moreover, in contrast to the common perception that people who cohabit have never been married, researchers report that about half of all people involved in cohabitation in the United States have been previously married. Cohabitation serves as a temporary or permanent alternative to matrimony for many men and women who have experienced their own or their parents' divorces (Fields 2004; Popenoe and Whitehead 1999).

REMAINING SINGLE

More and more people in the United States are postponing entry into a first marriage. The trend toward maintaining a single lifestyle for a longer period is related to the growing economic independence of young people. This trend is especially significant for women. Freed from financial needs, women don't necessarily need to marry to enjoy a satisfying life. Divorce, late marriage, and longevity also figure into this trend. Even so, fewer than 4 percent of women and men in the United States are likely to remain single throughout their lives (Bureau of the Census 2007a:Table 56).

There are many reasons a person may choose not to marry. Some singles do not want to limit their sexual intimacy to one lifetime partner. Some men and women do not want to become highly dependent on any one person—and do not want anyone depending heavily on them. In a society that values individuality and self-fulfillment, the single lifestyle can offer certain freedoms that marriage may not.

Remaining single represents a clear departure from societal expectations and can feel targeted in a society that presumes marriage. A single adult must confront the inaccurate view that he or she

Unmarried-Couple Households by State, 2000

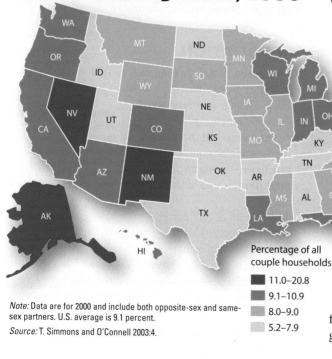

Note: Data are for 2000 and include both opposite-sex and same-sex partners. U.S. average is 9.1 percent.

Source: T. Simmons and O'Connell 2003:4.

Percentage of all couple households

- 11.0–20.8
- 9.1–10.9
- 8.0–9.0
- 5.2–7.9

is always lonely, is a workaholic, or is immature. These stereotypes help to support the traditional assumption in the United States and most other societies that to be truly happy and fulfilled, a person must get married and raise a family. To counter these societal expectations, singles have formed numerous support groups (Hertz 2006; Lundquist 2006).

MARRIAGE WITHOUT CHILDREN

There has been a significant increase in childlessness in the United States. According to census data, about 16 to 17 percent of women will now complete their childbearing years without having borne any children, compared to 10 percent in 1980. As many as 20 percent of women in their 30s expect to remain childless (Clausen 2002).

Childlessness within marriage has generally been viewed as a problem that can be solved through such means as adoption and artificial insemination. More and more couples today, however, choose not to have children and regard themselves as child-free rather than childless. They do not believe that having children automatically follows from marriage, nor do they feel that reproduction is the duty of all married couples. Childless couples have formed support groups (with names like No Kidding) and set up websites (K. Park 2005; Terry 2000).

Economic considerations have contributed to this shift in attitudes; having children has become quite expensive. According to a government estimate made for 2007, the average middle-class family will spend $204,060 to feed, clothe, and shelter a child from birth to age 18. If the child attends college, that amount could double, depending on the college chosen. Aware of the financial pressures, some couples are having fewer children than they otherwise might, and others are weighing the advantages of a child-free marriage (Lino 2008).

LESBIAN AND GAY RELATIONSHIPS

One of the more active political debates about families in recent years has involved marriage of same-sex couples. Such couples highlight the difficulty of defining families in too narrow terms. If we stick with a narrow, substantive definition, such relationships have not counted as families.

Same-Sex Marriage Laws, 2009

States that define marriage as a male-female union

States that do *not* define marriage as a male-female union

States that issue marriage licenses to same-sex couples

Note: Current as of June 2009.

Source: Human Rights Campaign 2009.

When we define families in terms of what they do—what functions they perform—however, we find a growing acceptance that such relationships do constitute families.

The lifestyles of lesbians and gays are varied, just like those of heterosexuals. Some live in long-term, monogamous relationships; others live alone or with roommates. Some remain in "empty shell" heterosexual marriages and do not publicly acknowledge their homosexuality; others live with children from a former marriage or with adopted children. Based on 2008 election exit polls, researchers found that 4 percent of the adult voting population identify themselves as either gay or lesbian. An analysis of 2006 U.S. Census data shows a minimum of at least 700,000 gay households and a gay and lesbian adult population approaching 10 million (CNN 2008; O'Connell and Lofquist 2009).

Gay and lesbian couples face discrimination on both a personal and a legal level. Their inability to marry in most states denies them many rights that married couples take for granted, from the ability to make decisions for an incapacitated partner to the right to receive government benefits to dependents, such as Social Security payments (see the figures above and on page 158). Though gay couples consider themselves families, legally they are usually treated as if they are not. Precisely because of such inequities, many gay and lesbian couples are now demanding the right to marry.

> Call it a clan, call it a network, call it a tribe, call it a family. Whatever you call it, whoever you are, you need one.
>
> Jane Howard

Forty states still have laws that define marriage as between a man and a woman, but recent changes in state laws have expanded legal rights for gay and lesbian couples. In 1999, Vermont provided legal rights through civil unions but stopped short of calling such relationships marriage. Then, in 2003, Massachusetts became the first state to legalize same-sex marriage when its Supreme Court ruled 4–3 that under the state's constitution, gay couples have the right to marry—a ruling the U.S. Supreme Court has refused to review. In 2008, Connecticut's Supreme Court reached the same conclusion, as did Iowa's in 2009. Vermont then became the first state to pass a law that legalized same-sex marriage; Maine and New Hampshire followed shortly thereafter. As a result, six states have provided gay and lesbian couples the same right to marry as guaranteed to heterosexual couples as of June 2009.

In the United States, many local jurisdictions have proactively passed legislation allowing for the registration of domestic partnerships and have extended employee benefits to those relationships. Under such policies, a **domestic partnership** may be defined as two unrelated adults who share a mutually caring relationship, reside together, and agree to be jointly responsible for their dependents, basic living expenses, and other common necessities. Domestic partnership benefits can apply to couples' inheritance, parenting, pensions, taxation, housing, immigration, workplace fringe benefits, and health care. Even though the most passionate support for domestic partnership legislation has come from lesbian and gay activists,

Attitudes Toward Gay Rights Depend on Who You Know

the majority of those eligible for such benefits would be cohabiting heterosexual couples.

Recently, national surveys of attitudes toward gay marriage in the United States have shown an even split among the public. In 2007, 46 percent of those surveyed felt that marriages between same-sex couples should be considered valid, while 53 percent felt that they should not be recognized. These results reflect the gradual shift in the level of acceptance of gay marriage since 1982, when 34 percent of respondents felt that it should be legal (Gallup 2008b).

The debates surrounding same-sex families highlight many of the issues sociologists seek to address in their investigation of family life. What families are, what they do, how they do it, and what obstacles they face are issues relevant for all families. In our modern, pluralistic world, the singular traditions of the past can no longer be taken for granted, as Tevye and Golde discovered in *The Fiddler on the Roof*. People come from many different cultures with multiple taken-for-granted assumptions. Sociology investigates such complexity, providing us with tools so that we might better understand how we think and act in the context of families.

Gay couples should be able to adopt — 28% / 50%

Gay partners should have Social Security benefits — 43% / 60%

Gay and lesbian people should serve openly in the military — 48% / 63%

Hate-crime laws should include violence committed against gay and lesbian people — 54% / 69%

Gay partners should have inheritance rights — 50% / 73%

Gay and lesbian people should have equal rights in employment — 77% / 90%

Doesn't know someone gay or lesbian
Knows someone gay or lesbian

Source: www/hrc.org. October 4, 2006.

domestic partnership Two unrelated adults who share a mutually caring relationship, reside together, and agree to be jointly responsible for their dependents, basic living expenses, and other common necessities.

get involved!

Volunteer! There are numerous organizations designed to assist children in situations of need, including Big Brothers and Big Sisters, CASA (Court Appointed Special Advocates), and school tutoring programs. Such programs can fulfill some of the functions of families. Seek out one of these organizations, and find out ways that you can help.

Couple getting married in San Francisco after a state Supreme Court ruling to allow same-sex marriage and before Proposition 8, a state constitutional amendment, banned the practice.

For REVIEW

I. **What is the family?**
- Sociologists define the family in terms of both what a family is, with an emphasis on blood and law, and what families do or what functions they perform, including reproduction, socialization, protection, regulation of sexual behavior, affection and companionship, and provision of social status.

II. **How do people pick partners?**
- Social factors shape the pool of potential partners from which individuals select. People balance selection, favoring someone who is from within their group (endogamy) but not too close (exogamy). People tend to pick people with similar social characteristics (homogamy), including age, education, class, race, and ethnicity.

III. **How do families vary?**
- There is significant variation in terms of proximity (extended versus nuclear), authority (patriarchal, matriarchal, and egalitarian), duration (divorce), and structure (dual-income, single-parent, stepfamilies, cohabitation, singlehood, child-free, and same-sex).

Pop Quiz

1. Which definition of the family focuses on the importance of blood and law?
   a. functionalist
   b. matrilineal
   c. substantive
   d. extended

2. Which system of descent is followed in the United States?
   a. matrilineal
   b. patrilineal
   c. bilateral
   d. unilateral

3. Alice, age seven, lives at home with her parents, her grandmother, and her aunt. Alice's family is an example of a(n)
   a. nuclear family.
   b. patrilineal family.
   c. extended family.
   d. polygynous family.

4. In which form of marriage may a person have several spouses in his or her lifetime but only one spouse at a time?
   a. serial monogamy
   b. monogamy
   c. polygamy
   d. polyandry

5. The marriage of a woman to more than one man at the same time is referred to as
   a. polygyny.
   b. monogamy.
   c. serial monogamy.
   d. polyandry.

6. In what type of societies do women dominate in family decision making?
   a. polygyny
   b. egalitarian
   c. patriarchy
   d. matriarchy

7. Which norm requires mate selection outside certain groups, usually one's own family or certain kinfolk?
   a. exogamy
   b. endogamy
   c. matriarchy
   d. patriarchy

8. The principle that prohibits sexual relationships between certain culturally specified relatives is known as
   a. monogamy.
   b. the incest taboo.
   c. polygamy.
   d. endogamy.

9. Overall, the divorce rate in the United States in the past 30 years
   a. has risen dramatically.
   b. has risen slowly but steadily.
   c. has declined after having risen significantly in the 1960s and 1970s.
   d. shows no clear pattern.

10. How many states guaranteed gay and lesbian couples the right to marry as of mid-2009?
    a. 0
    b. 6
    c. 23
    d. 41

1. (c); 2. (c); 3. (c); 4. (a); 5. (d); 6. (d); 7. (a); 8. (b); 9. (c); 10. (b)

8

EDUCATION&R

FAITH AND LEARNING

Patrick Henry College, located near Washington, D.C., was founded in 2000 with the explicit intention of competing with Ivy League schools. The elite students it pursues, however, come from a particular niche: Approximately 80 percent of them were homeschooled, and they all share a strong commitment to evangelical Christian faith.

In keeping with the school's expectation of a high level of religious commitment, students must sign a "Statement of Faith" that sets out a series of Christian beliefs, including the virgin birth of Jesus Christ, the existence of Satan, and eternal punishment in hell for non-Christians. Students are required to abide by a strict dress code, attend daily chapel, and abstain from alcohol, smoking, and premarital sex.

The students by and large take these commitments quite seriously. As journalist Hannah Rosin (2007) recounts in her book on Patrick Henry College entitled *God's Harvard,* "To them, a 'Christian' keeps a running conversation with God in his or her head . . . and believes that at any moment God might in some palpable way step in and show He either cares or disapproves" (p. 5).

Student Elisa Muench was something of a trailblazer at Patrick Henry College. She was the first woman to run for a leadership position in student government, in the face of disapproval by students who thought it inappropriate that a woman should serve in such an office. As a junior, she had an internship in the White House. Yet she found herself fearing that what counted as success in the eyes of the dominant society, including a professional career, might conflict with success in the eyes of God (Rosin 2007:85). Elisa struggled to be true to both her educational and religious teachings.

It is within such educational and religious communities that we learn what to believe and how to act. All of us are, in some respects, like Elisa, seeking to balance the sometimes conflicting demands of the various spheres of our lives, including family, education, religion, work, and politics. In this chapter, we focus on the roles education and religion play both for individuals and for society as a whole.

ELIGION

As You READ

>>

• How does education help to maintain social order?

• How does education support the existing system of inequality?

• How do sociologists define religion?

>> Education in Society

Historically, we counted on families to be significant agents of socialization, teaching us the basic knowledge, values, and norms we needed to survive. As societies became more diverse and the division of labor increased, however, our educational needs expanded, and we placed a greater emphasis on more formal socialization. To do so we turned to **education,** the formal process of instruction in which some people consciously teach while others adopt the social role of learner.

education A formal process of instruction in which some people consciously teach while others adopt the social role of learner.

As a society, we invest a significant amount of time and money in education because we believe the individual and collective benefits are worth it. On the one hand, we value education as a path to knowledge and understanding. We investigate the deeper mysteries of life—truth, beauty, wisdom—so that we might have a better understanding of ourselves and our world. As sociologist W.E.B. Du Bois ([1903] 1994) put it, "The true college will ever have one goal,—not to earn meat, but to know the end and aim of that life which meat nourishes" (p. 51). On the other hand, we see education as a means of ensuring fairness and opportunity; we count on schools to provide us all with the knowledge and the tools we need to achieve better circumstances in life, including good jobs.

SOCthink

> > > Who most influenced you to go to college? Considering people you know who did not go to college, what influenced them to make that choice? How powerful are socialization and social networks in making such decisions?

Did You Know?

. . . In 2007, 69 percent of high school seniors enrolled in college in the fall semester following their graduation. During the 1970s, the average was about 50 percent.

In the United States, this commitment to education goes back to a belief that our outcomes should not be determined by birth, but by ability and effort. According to this value, being born to aristocratic parents should not ensure economic and social privilege any more than being born to parents with limited means should consign one to a life of poverty. Early American political leaders such as Benjamin Franklin and Thomas Jefferson advocated public education as an essential component of democratic societies because it provides individuals with opportunities and society with informed citizens. Horace Mann, "the father of public education," wrote in 1848, "Education, beyond all other devices of human origin, is the great equalizer of the conditions of men" ([1848] 1957). Mann hoped that public education would ensure that children without means would share classrooms, curriculum, and experiences with children of the well-off, and thus have a chance to get ahead in society.

The history of education in the United States is one of expansion and institutionalization. Initially, public schools were open only to White males. Over time, due in part to the efforts of sociologists like Du Bois and Jane Addams, public education expanded to include everyone regardless of race, ethnicity, sex, or national origin. Ex-

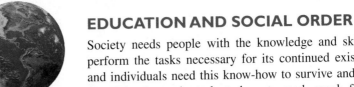

Going GLOBAL

Percentage of Young Adults with University Degrees*

Country	Percentage
Iceland	63%
Australia	59%
Poland	47%
United Kingdom	39%
Japan	39%
OECD average	37%
United States	36%
Canada	35%
Spain	33%
Czech Republic	29%
Germany	21%
Turkey	15%

* Note: Young adult typically means age 22–25, but different countries report data for slightly different ranges. University degree is the equivalent of a BA or BS. The Organization for Economic Cooperation and Development (OECD) is an international organization composed of 30 democratic nations.

Source: OECD 2008:Table A3.2.

pansion is further reflected in the growing percentage of Americans staying in school longer. From 1940 to 2008, the proportion of people with a high school diploma increased from 25 to 87 percent, and the number with a college degree rose from 5 to 29 percent (U.S. Census Bureau 2009b:Table A-2). This growth has resulted in greater institutionalization as education has become more formalized—and a distinct part of the public sphere. Educational organizations have become more professional and bureaucratic in their attempt to provide services efficiently to the whole population.

>> Sociological Perspectives on Education

Sociologists have closely examined the degree to which education actually succeeds in providing social order and individual opportunity. They have found that while it does offer opportunity and helps to establish social order, it also perpetuates inequality. Fulfilling the hopes of Jefferson, Franklin, and Mann, it has produced an educated citizenry equipped to take on the challenges of modern life. At the same time, however, it reinforces existing beliefs, values, and norms that justify the status quo and its inequalities. Sociologists seek to understand how education can do both at the same time.

EDUCATION AND SOCIAL ORDER

Society needs people with the knowledge and skills to perform the tasks necessary for its continued existence, and individuals need this know-how to survive and prosper. Schools teach students how to read, speak foreign languages, repair automobiles, and much more. Sociologists have identified four positive functions that education serves for both individuals and society.

Transmitting Culture As a social institution, education preserves and transmits the dominant culture. In schools each generation of young people learns the existing beliefs, norms, and values of their culture. In the United States, students learn respect for existing values and norms and reverence for established institutions, such as the economy, the family, and the presidency. Of course, this is true of many other cultures as well. While schoolchildren in the United States are hearing about the accomplishments of George Washington and Abraham Lincoln, British children are hearing about the distinctive contributions of Queen Elizabeth I and Winston Churchill.

In Great Britain, the transmission of the dominant culture through schools goes beyond traditional content such as learning about monarchs, prime ministers, and generals. In 1996 the government's chief curriculum advisor—noting the need to fill a void left by the diminishing authority of the Church of England—proposed that British schools socialize students into a set of core values. The set included honesty, respect for others, politeness, a sense of fair play, forgiveness, punctuality, nonviolent behavior, patience, faithfulness, and self-discipline

POPSOC

Schools have been a source of entertainment in popular culture for a long time. We see examples of this in films like *High School Musical, School of Rock, Rushmore, Legally Blonde, Ferris Bueller's Day Off, The Breakfast Club,* and *Freedom Writers,* and in television programs such as *Saved by the Bell* and *Freaks and Geeks.*

(Charter and Sherman 1996). Similar programs have been established in the United States, such as the Character Counts program, which highlights the Six Pillars of Character: trustworthiness, respect, responsibility, fairness, caring, and citizenship.

SOCthink

> > > Why do you think there has been a move toward character education in schools? What changes in society might contribute to that perceived need?

Sometimes nations reassess the ways in which they transmit culture to students. Recently, the Chinese government revised the nation's history curriculum. Students are now taught that the Chinese Communist Party, not the United States, played a central role in defeating Japan in World War II. No mention is made of the estimated 30 million Chinese who died from famine because of party founder Mao Zedong's disastrous Great Leap Forward (1958–1962), a failed effort to transform China's agrarian economy into an industrial powerhouse. In urban, Western-oriented areas such as Shanghai, textbooks acknowledge the technological advances made in Western industrial countries but avoid any criticism of past policies of the Chinese government (French 2004; Kahn 2006).

Hot or Not?

Does offering bilingual education to accommodate non-English-speaking students undermine social integration in the U.S.?

Promoting Social Integration Schools also seek to bring students together to provide a shared sense of identity. Many colleges and universities require first- and second-year students to live on campus for just this reason. Such programs become more important when students come from diverse backgrounds with different cultural expectations. The goal is to provide experiences that will unify a population composed of diverse racial, ethnic, and religious groups into a community whose members share— to some extent—a common identity. Historically, schools at all levels in the United States have played an important role in socializing the children of immigrants into the norms, values, and beliefs of the dominant culture. The common identity and social integration fostered by education contributes to societal stability and consensus (Durkheim [1925] 1961).

In the past, the integrative function of education was most obvious in its emphasis on promoting a common language. Immigrant children were expected to learn English. In some instances, they were even forbidden to speak their native language on school grounds. More recently, bilingualism has been defended both for its educational value and as a means of encouraging cultural diversity. However, critics argue that bilingualism undermines the social and political integration that education traditionally has promoted.

Training and Social Control Schools teach students how to behave. In the early grades in particular, significant time and effort is spent getting students to do what the teacher wants them to do, when and how the teacher wants them to do it. Through the exercise of social control, schools teach students various skills and values essential to their future positions in society. Norms provide us with the order and stability we need to make our individual and collective lives predictable. Schools teach us what is expected of us. Students learn manners, punctuality, creativity, disci-

Education Pays

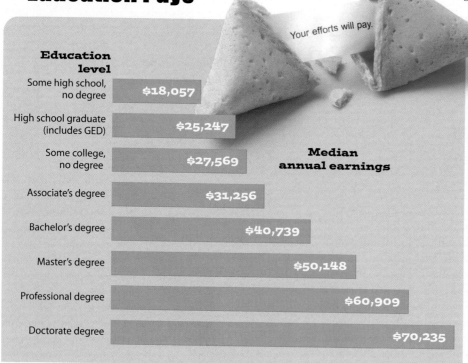

Your efforts will pay.

Education level	Median annual earnings
Some high school, no degree	$18,057
High school graduate (includes GED)	$25,247
Some college, no degree	$27,569
Associate's degree	$31,256
Bachelor's degree	$40,739
Master's degree	$50,148
Professional degree	$60,909
Doctorate degree	$70,235

* Includes full-time, full-year wage and salary for workers ages 25–34.
Source: U.S. Census Bureau 2008c.

Government policies at the national, state, and local levels all influence public education in the United States.

pline, and responsibility, skills and abilities we need well beyond the classroom. In effect, schools serve as a transitional agent of social control, bridging the gap between childhood and entry into the labor force and wider society.

In a society with a complex division of labor, we especially count on schools to select and train students so that they can become effective workers in specialized jobs. We expect schools to choose those with the most ability to pursue degrees in fields that demand the greatest skill. For example, we want students with aptitude in math and science to become engineers. We use grades as an indicator of such ability and provide degrees to certify that the graduate has sufficient training to perform the job well. We hold out the promise of higher pay to reward those who make the sacrifices that higher education calls for in terms of time and money. As we will see below, however, many people are concerned about the degree to which this ideal is achieved.

Stimulating Cultural Innovation While schools do preserve and transmit existing culture, education can also stimulate social change. In response to the soaring pregnancy rate among teenagers, for example, public schools began to offer sex education classes. Many schools endorse affirmative action in admissions—giving priority to females or minorities—as a means of countering discrimination based on race or sex. Project Head Start, an early-childhood program that serves more than 908,000 children annually, has sought to compensate for the disadvantages in school readiness experienced by children from low-income families (U.S. Census Bureau 2008b:Table 555). To ensure school readiness, it provides classes for preschool children from families below a certain income level, working with them on letter recognition, vocabulary, nutrition, and other basic skills.

Colleges and universities are particularly committed to cultural innovation. Faculty members, especially at large universities, must pursue research and publish articles and books. In so doing, they produce new technology, techniques, knowledge, and practices. Cultural innovation on

campuses goes beyond such concrete results, however, because college provides a context within which we can challenge existing ideas and try out new practices. Such experimentation sometimes leads people to accuse professors, especially those with innovative or unpopular ideas, of being out of touch or out of line, but we need people to experiment with new ideas so that our culture does not stagnate.

Campuses also provide an environment in which students from around the world with widely divergent ideas and experiences can interact. In 2007–2008, U.S. campuses hosted just over 624,000 international students. Such exposure provides opportunities for cultural innovation as people from various cultures are exposed to and experiment with new and different cultural norms and values (Planty et al. 2009).

EDUCATION AND INEQUALITY

Although education does promote social order and provide individual opportunity, there are significant inequalities in the educational opportunities available to different groups. For example, wide disparities exist in funding and facilities between urban and suburban schools. Jonathan Kozol (2005:321), who has studied educational inequality for decades, reports that, in the same year, Chicago public schools spent $8482 per student while the wealthy northern suburban Highland Park and Deerfield school district spent $17,291. This is just one example among many. Schools in well-off areas have the funding to offer programs and facilities that poor districts cannot hope to match, including high-tech labs, athletic facilities, and elective classes in art, music, and languages. As a former New York City principal, in an interview with Kozol, puts it, "I'll believe money doesn't count the day the rich stop spending so much on their own children" (Kozol 2005:59). In this section, we look at a number of such ways that the experience of and outcomes from education are not equal for everyone.

© 1993 Kirk Anderson. Reprinted with the permission of Kirk Anderson, www.kirktoons.com.

SOCthink

> > > Only about 9 percent of funding for public schools comes from the federal government. In most states, a significant percentage of funding comes from local property taxes. What are the consequences of this model for equitable funding of education? Why might some districts resist changing this model?

The Hidden Curriculum One of the ways that schools reinforce the existing system of inequality is through the teaching of what sociologists call the **hidden curriculum**—standards of behavior that society deems proper and that teachers subtly communicate to students (Langhout and Mitchell 2008; Thornberg 2008). It prepares students to submit to authority. For example, children learn not to speak until the teacher calls on them, and they learn to regulate their activities according to the clock or bells. A classroom environment that is overly focused on obedience rewards students for pleasing the teacher and remaining compliant rather than for creative thought and academic learning. In this way, schools socialize students to submit to authority figures, including bosses and political leaders.

hidden curriculum Standards of behavior that are deemed proper by society and are taught subtly in schools.

teacher-expectancy effect The impact that a teacher's expectations about a student's performance may have on the student's actual achievements.

Teacher Expectancy Student outcomes can also become a self-fulfilling prophecy based on how teachers perceive students. Psychologist Robert Rosenthal and school principal Lenore Jacobson (1968) documented what they referred to as a **teacher-expectancy effect**—the impact that a teacher's expectations about a student's performance may have on the student's actual achievements. They conducted experiments to document this effect.

Rosenthal and Jacobson informed teachers that they were administering a verbal and reasoning pretest to children in a San Francisco elementary school. After administering the tests, the researchers told the teachers that some of the students were "spurters"—children who showed particular academic potential. However, rather than using the actual test scores to make this determination, the research-

PRINCIPAL

From Me to You

My daughters Emily and Eleanor make me proud. They get good grades and their scores on the standardized exams are sky high. But as a sociologist, I know that they benefit from the fact that their parents are college graduates. As parents, Lori and I provide Em and El with economic, social, and cultural resources in the form of books, activities, and even vacations to historic locations. Kids from such families tend to do better in school than children who lack such opportunities. It's almost as if they are cheating. They did nothing to deserve such advantages, and yet, as a society, we act as if educational outcomes—good or bad—are solely based on merit.

UNEARNED ADVANTAGES

ers randomly selected the 20 percent of the students they identified as spurters. When the students were later retested, the spurters scored not only significantly higher than they had in previous tests but also significantly higher than their peers. Moreover, teachers evaluated the spurters as more interesting, more curious, and better adjusted than their classmates. This is a classic case of a self-fulfilling prophecy at work. Teachers expected some students to do well, and so they did. Such effects are of particular concern if factors such as race, ethnicity, class, or gender shape teachers' perceptions.

Bestowal of Status As we saw above, part of the public school ideal was that education would contribute to the creation of opportunity and the establishment of a more open society. In a classic sociology study, Kingsley Davis and Wilbert E. Moore (1945) argued that all societies have positions that are more important for the society's survival or that require greater skill

The Influence of Parents' Education on Test Performance

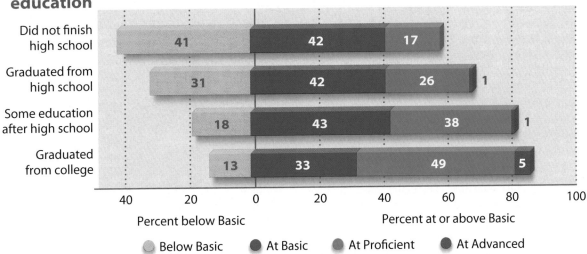

Parental education

Note: Percentage distribution of 12th-grade students across NAEP economics achievement levels, by highest level of parental education, 2006.
Source: Planty et al. 2008:25.

or knowledge to perform. Ideally, the institution of education selects those with ability and trains them for such positions. We reward people in such positions with social prestige and high pay, Davis and Moore claim, because we value such skills and respect the fact that these individuals sacrificed the time and energy necessary to acquire those skills. For example, not everyone has the skill necessary to become a medical doctor, and in order to encourage people who do have the potential to pursue that path, we promise them sufficient social and economic compensation.

The problem with this model is that, in practice, factors other than potential and ability shape outcomes such as social class, race, ethnicity, and gender. Although the educational system helps certain poor children to move into middle-class professional positions, it denies most disadvantaged children the same educational opportunities afforded to children of the affluent. In this way, schools tend to preserve social class inequalities in each new generation (Giroux 1988; Pinkerton 2003).

Did You Know?

... Harvard University accepted only 7 percent of the 29,112 high school graduates who applied for admission in 2008. Not even a perfect score on their SAT was a guarantee of acceptance.

One way schools reinforce class differences is by putting students in tracks. The term **tracking** refers to the practice of placing students in specific curriculum groups on the basis of their test scores and other criteria. Tracking begins very early, often in first-grade reading groups. The practice can reinforce the disadvantages that children from less affluent families may face if they haven't been exposed to reading materials, computers, and other forms of educational stimulation during their early-childhood years. In the guise of providing opportunity, such programs reinforce racial, ethnic, and class differences that students bring with them on their first day of kindergarten (Oakes 2008).

> **tracking** The practice of placing students in specific curriculum groups on the basis of their test scores and other criteria.

SOCthink

> > > What experiences have you had with tracking? To what extent do you believe it was effective both for high-track and low-track students? What are its limitations in terms of equal opportunity?

Most recent research on tracking raises questions about its effectiveness, especially for low-ability students. In one study of low-income schools in California, researchers discovered a staggering difference between students who were tracked and those who were not. At one school, all interested students were allowed to enroll in advanced placement (AP) courses, not just those who were selected by the administration. Half the open-enrollment students scored high enough to qualify for college credit—a much higher proportion than in selective programs, in which only 17 percent of students qualified for college credit. Tracking programs do not necessarily identify those students with the potential to succeed (B. Ellison 2008; Sacks 2007).

Sociologists Samuel Bowles and Herbert Gintis (1976) have argued that the educational inequalities produced by tracking are designed to meet the needs of modern capitalist societies. They claim that capitalism requires a skilled, disciplined labor force and that the educational system of the United States is structured with that objective in mind. Citing numerous studies, they offer support for what they call the **correspondence principle.** According to this approach, schools promote the values expected of individuals in each social class and perpetuate social class divisions from one generation to the next. Thus, working-class children, assumed to be destined for subordinate positions, are likely to be placed in high school vocational and general tracks, which emphasize close supervision and compliance with authority. In contrast, young people from more affluent families are likely to be directed to college preparatory tracks, which stress leadership and decision making—the skills they are expected to need as adults.

Credentialism Students today also face elevated expectations. When it comes to educational attainment, they now have to go farther just to stay in the same place. Fifty years ago, a high school diploma was enough to get a good job. Today, a college diploma is virtually the bare minimum. This change reflects the process of **credentialism**—a term used to describe an increase in the lowest level of education needed to enter a field.

One of the driving factors in the rise of credentialism has been the expansion of occupations considered to be professions. Employers and occupational associations typically contend that reclassifying jobs is a logical response to the increasing complexity of many jobs. However, in many cases, employers raise the degree requirements for a position simply because all applicants have achieved the existing minimum credential (D. Brown 2001; G. Brown 2006).

One potential effect of credentialism is to reinforce social inequality. Applicants from poor

correspondence principle The tendency of schools to promote the values expected of individuals in each social class and to prepare students for the types of jobs typically held by members of their class.
credentialism An increase in the lowest level of education required to enter a field.

and minority backgrounds are especially likely to suffer from the escalation of qualifications, since they may lack the financial resources needed to obtain degree after degree.

In addition, upgrading of credentials serves the self-interest of the two groups most responsible for this trend. First, educational institutions profit because people must spend more time and money on schooling. Moreover, current jobholders have a stake in raising occupational requirements because credentialism can increase the status of an occupation and demands for higher pay. Max Weber anticipated this possibility as early as 1916, concluding that the "universal clamor for the creation of educational certificates in all fields makes for the formation of a privileged stratum in businesses and in offices" (Gerth and Mills 1958:240–41).

Gender The educational system of the United States, like many other social institutions, has long been characterized by discriminatory treatment of women. It took until 1833 for Oberlin College to become the first institution of higher learn-

5 Movies on EDUCATION

Saved!
A pregnant girl at a Christian high school.

Dead Poets Society
An unorthodox English professor teaches at a conservative prep school.

Stand and Deliver
A new teacher in East Los Angeles.

Igby Goes Down
A rebellious teenager struggles with a life of privilege.

Election
Dark comedy about a high school election.

ing to admit female students—some 200 years after the founding of Harvard, the first men's college in the United States. Even so, Oberlin believed that women should aspire to become wives and mothers, not lawyers and intellectuals. In addition to attending classes, female students washed men's clothing, cared for their rooms, and served them meals.

In the 20th century, sexism in education showed up in many ways—in textbooks with negative stereotypes of women, in counselors' pressure on female students to prepare for "women's work," and in unequal funding for women's and men's athletic programs. In fact, throughout most of the century, only about one-third of college students were women. During that time they sat in class-

rooms staffed predominantly by male professors, as just about one-quarter of college faculty members were female (Snyder et al. 2009:Table 187).

Today women have much greater educational opportunity, largely as a result of women's movements that worked for social change. Title IX of the Education Amendments of 1972 played a pivotal role in expanding access. It states, "No person in the United States shall, on the basis of sex, be excluded from participation in, be denied the benefits of, or be subjected to discrimination under any education program or activity receiving Federal financial assistance." While Title IX is most commonly associated with equal opportunity for women in athletics, among other things, it also eliminated sex-segregated classes and prohibited sex discrimination in admissions. And women have made the most of this opportunity (Corbett et al. 2008). Starting in the late 1960s, the percentage of women earning college degrees began rising dramatically. In 1980 women earned 49 percent of degrees conferred, and the current rate is 57 percent. Women students are also more likely to be taught by women professors, who now comprise 45 percent of total faculty (Snyder et al. 2009:Table 187).

SOCthink

> > > Women's participation in college athletics has increased over 500 percent since 1972, from 31,852 then to 178,084 in 2007–2008. And high school rates have risen almost 1000 percent, with 3.06 million participants in 2008. To what extent would we have seen such an increase had it not been for a law that mandated increased opportunity? How might increased opportunity for women in athletics have an impact on increased opportunity in other areas?

Education does establish social order and provide opportunities for individuals to get ahead. At the same time, in preserving the existing order, it reproduces practices of inequality. Sociology allows us to better understand how these seemingly contradictory goals can be accomplished through education. As the experience with Title IX demonstrates, positive social change is possible. Having a bet-

> Good schools, like good societies and good families, celebrate and cherish diversity.
>
> Deborah Meier

ter appreciation of how education functions enables us to more effectively work toward realizing the initial goal of education: to provide opportunity and a more open society.

>> Schools as Formal Organizations

The early advocates of public education would be amazed at the scale of the education system in the United States in the 21st century. For example, California's public school system, the largest in the nation, currently enrolls as many children as there were in secondary schools nationwide in 1950 (Bureau of the Census 1975:368; 2004).

In many respects, today's schools, when viewed as an example of a formal organization, are similar to factories, hospitals, and business firms. Instead of producing cars, patients, or profits, they pump out millions of students per year. In doing so, schools must be responsive to the various constituencies outside of the student body, including parents, employers, neighborhoods, and politicians. To handle their complex mission, schools have had to become increasingly institutionalized. The parallels between schools and other types of formal organizations will become more apparent as we examine the bureaucratic nature of schools, teaching as an occupation, and the student subculture.

THE BUREAUCRATIZATION OF SCHOOLS

It simply is not possible for a single teacher to transmit all the necessary culture and skills to children who will enter many diverse occupations. The growing number of students being served by school systems and the greater degree of specialization required within a technologically complex society have combined to bureaucratize schools.

In many respects, schools put into practice all of Max Weber's principles of bureaucracy that we considered in Chapter 5. When it comes to the division of labor, teachers specialize in particular age levels and specific subjects. Schools are hierarchically organized, with teachers reporting to principals, who are themselves answerable to the superintendent of schools and the board of education. In terms of written rules and regulations, teachers must submit written lesson plans, and students, teachers, and administrators must all adhere to established policies and procedures or face sanctions for not doing so. As schools grow, they become increasingly impersonal, and teachers are expected to treat all students in the same way, regardless of their distinctive personalities and learning needs. Finally, hiring and promotion—and even grading—are based on technical qualifications alone, and standards are established and rubrics created in an effort to ensure this practice (Vanderstraeter 2007).

The trend toward more centralized education particularly affects disadvantaged people, for whom education promises to be a path to opportunity. The standardization of educational curricula, including textbooks, generally reflects the values, interests, and lifestyles of the most powerful groups in our society, and may ignore those of racial and ethnic minorities. In addition, in comparison to the affluent, the resource poor often lack the time, financial resources, and knowledge necessary to sort through complex educational bureaucracies and to organize effective lobbying groups. As a result, low-income and minority parents

Teacher Turnover, 2003–2004

21% High-poverty

Leavers

| 11% | 2% | 3% | 1% | 3% | 1% |

15% Low-poverty

Leavers

| 6% | 3% | 4% | 1% | 0.5% | 0.5% |

- Transferred to another school
- Retired
- Took other job
- Pursued further education
- Left for family reasons
- Other

Note: Percentage of public K–12 teachers who did not teach in the same school the following year, by poverty level of school and the reason teachers left.
Source: Planty et al. 2008:51.

will have even less influence over citywide and statewide educational administrators than they have over local school officials (Kozol 2005).

TEACHING AS A PROFESSION

As schools become more bureaucratic, teachers increasingly encounter the conflicts inherent in serving as a professional within the context of a bureaucracy. Teachers must work within the system, submitting to its hierarchical structure and abiding by its established rules. At the same time, teachers want to practice their craft as professionals with some degree of autonomy and respect for their judgment. Conflicts arise from having to serve simultaneously as instructor, disciplinarian, administrator, and employee of a school district.

As professionals, teachers feel pressure from a number of directions. First, the level of formal schooling required for teaching remains high, and the public has begun to call for new competency examinations. Second, teachers' salaries are significantly lower than those of many comparably educated professionals and skilled workers. Finally, the overall prestige of the teaching profession has declined over the past decade.

Average Salaries for Teachers, 2007

- Over $50,000
- $43,000–49,999
- $39,100–42,999
- Under $39,100

Source: American Federation of Teachers, 2007.

Many teachers, disappointed and frustrated, have left the educational world for careers in other professions. In fact, between a quarter and a third of new teachers quit within their first three years, and as many as half leave poor urban schools within their first five years (Wallis 2008). Even within a single year, teacher turnover is significant; in high-poverty areas, over 20 percent of teachers did not teach in the same school the following year.

STUDENT SUBCULTURES

Schools also provide an arena for students' social and recreational needs. Education helps toddlers and young children develop interpersonal skills that are essential during adolescence and adulthood. In their high school and college years, students may meet future spouses and establish life-long friendships.

School leaders often seek to develop a sense of school spirit and collective identity, but student subcultures are actually complex and diverse. High school cliques and social groups may crop up according to race, social class, physical attractiveness, academic placement, athletic ability, and leadership roles in the school and community. In his classic community study of "Elmtown," August B. Hollingshead (1975) found some 259 distinct cliques in a single high school. The cliques, whose average size was five, were centered on the school itself, on recreational activities, and on religious and community groups.

Amid these close-knit and often rigidly segregated cliques, some students get left out. Historically, gay and lesbian students have been particularly vulnerable to such exclusion. Many have organized to establish their own stronger sense of collective identity, including through the establishment of gay–straight alliances (GSAs)—school-sponsored support groups that bring gay teens together with sympathetic straight peers. Begun in Los Angeles in 1984, these programs numbered over 4000 nationwide in 2009.

We can find a similar diversity of student groups at the college level. Burton Clark and Martin Trow (1966) and, more recently, Helen Lefkowitz Horowitz (1987) have identified four distinctive subcultures among college students:

- The *collegiate* subculture focuses on having fun and socializing. These students define what constitutes a "reasonable" amount of academic work (and what amount of work is "excessive" and leads to being labeled as a "grind"). Members of the collegiate subculture have little commitment to academic pursuits. Athletes often fit into this subculture.

- The *academic* subculture identifies with the intellectual concerns of the faculty and values knowledge for its own sake.

- The *vocational* subculture is interested primarily in career prospects and views college as a means of obtaining degrees that are essential for advancement.

- The *nonconformist* subculture is hostile to the college environment and seeks out ideas that may or may not relate to academic studies. This group may find outlets through campus publications or issue-oriented groups.

Each college student is eventually exposed to these competing subcultures and must determine which (if any) seems most in line with his or her feelings and interests.

The typology used by the researchers reminds us that the school is a complex social organization—almost like a community with different neighborhoods. Of course, these four subcultures are not the only ones evident on college campuses in the United States. For example, one might find subcultures of Iraq war veterans or former full-time homemakers, or students may gather together on the basis of race, ethnicity, or nationality.

Public High School Graduates by Race and Ethnicity, 2019 (projected)

Note: Percentages do not add to 100 due to rounding error.

Source: Western Interstate Commission for Higher Education 2008.

Black, non-Hispanic **14.9%**

Asian/Pacific Islander **6.9%**

American Indian/ Alaska Native **1.3%**

Hispanic **27.2%**

White, non-Hispanic **49.8%**

COMMUNITY COLLEGES

Community colleges exist as a testament to the ideals put forth by Jefferson, Franklin, and Mann. The GI bill in the 1940s and Pell Grants in the 1960s provided significant college financial aid for those with limited means, opening wide the doors to college. However, availability of financial aid, especially in the form of grants, has declined significantly in recent years. Community colleges continue to give students a chance to prove themselves, however, and their relatively low cost and open enrollment lower the barriers to success. As a result, an increasing number of students have turned to community colleges, including a surge in fall 2009 enrollments due to a weak economy.

There are now more than 6 million community college students in the United States, making up 35 percent of all postsecondary students. This represents an almost 750 percent increase in students since 1963. These students are more likely to be older, female, Black, Hispanic, low-income, and part-time, compared to their peers at four-year schools. In fact, the more income and education a student's parents have, the less likely she or he is to attend a community college. This highlights the role these schools play in providing opportunity for those with limited resources. Enrollment at community colleges raises the aspirations of students. Whether they initially expected to take only a few courses or to finish with a two-year degree, almost one-half of these students later aspired to more education, including a four-year degree or beyond (Provasnik and Planty 2008).

One of the concerns raised about community colleges is persistence—the degree to which students pursue an education. The rate at which such students leave community college without completing a degree or certificate program (45 percent) is significantly higher than that for students at four-year schools (16 to 17 percent). Even those who had initially enrolled intending to pursue a four-year degree left school early at a rate of 39 percent. Such high rates led some theorists to suggest that community colleges serve a "cooling out" function. They argue that the limited number of good jobs in society is a given, so not everyone can succeed in obtaining one. Because community colleges appear to provide opportunities for anyone to succeed, failure to do so is perceived to be the individual's responsibility alone. As such, students are more likely to blame themselves than to develop a critique of the social structure that shaped their likely outcomes. In other words, community colleges do provide opportunity for some, but they also help to justify the existing system of inequality (Bahr 2008; Clark 1960, 1980).

HOMESCHOOLING

Some view formal schooling as a path to opportunity; others have decided to opt out altogether. More than 1.5 million students are now being educated at home—about 2.9 percent of the K-12 school population. Homeschooled families are more likely to be White, have two parents in the household with only one in the labor force, have parents with a bachelor's degree, and have three or more children (Planty et al. 2009).

In a sense this represents a return to the pre–public school days of American education, in which the primary responsibility for teaching rested with parents. When asked to identify the most important reason for choosing this path, 36 percent of parents said they were motivated by a desire to provide religious or moral instruction (the most common response), and 83 percent overall identified that as an important factor. A concern about the environment of schools—safety, drugs, and negative peer pressure—was most important to 21 percent, and 17 percent attributed their decision primarily to dissatisfaction with the school's academic instruction (Planty et al. 2009). In addition, some immigrants choose homeschooling as a way to ease their children's transition to a new society. For example, increasing numbers of the nation's growing Arab American population have joined the movement toward homeschooling (Cooper and Sureau 2007; MacFarquhar 2008). Other parents see it as a good alternative for children who suffer from attention deficit hyperactivity disorder (ADHD) and learning disorders (LDs). A study by the Home School Legal Defense Association (2005), a home-school advocacy organization, found that homeschooled students score higher than others on standardized exams in every subject and in every grade.

The rise in homeschooling points toward a growing dissatisfaction with the institutionalized practice of education. Early public school advocates argued for the importance of a common curriculum rooted in a shared sense of values. Homeschooling, on the other hand, points toward pluralism and the desire to retain the unique subcultural values of a community. Although new forms of schooling may meet the individual needs of diverse groups in today's society, they also undermine the historical commitment to public education as a means of fostering unity within society.

SOCthink

> > > What do you think are the advantages and disadvantages of being homeschooled? How might it contribute to a stronger sense of identity? How might it threaten the social order?

>> Defining Religion

Education plays a major role in socializing members of society into shared values and norms, and religion helps to cement those beliefs and practices into people's hearts and minds. Religion contributes to social order, provides a sense of shared identity, and offers believers meaning and purpose. Though levels of religious participation vary from place to place, religion continues to be a major force both on the world stage and in the lives of individuals. To fully understand its various forms, sociologists take two basic approaches to defining religion. The first focuses on what religion is, and the second focuses on what it does.

SUBSTANCE: WHAT RELIGION IS

According to a **substantive definition of religion,** religion has a unique content or substance that separates it from other forms of knowledge and belief. Most commonly, this unique focus involves some conception of a supernatural realm, such as heaven, but it does not have to be outside the physical world. The key is that religion centers around something that goes above and beyond the mundane realities of our everyday existence, that points to something larger, and that calls for some response from us in terms of how we think and act. Sociologist Peter Berger (1969) provided a substantive definition of religion as "the human enterprise by which a sacred cosmos is established" (p. 25). The sacred here refers to that extraordinary realm that becomes the focus of religious faith and practice. It provides believers with meaning, order, and coherence. In describing that sacred realm, people might touch on concepts such as gods and goddess, angels and demons, heaven and hell, nirvana, or other beings or realms. A society with broad agreement about the nature and importance of this sacred realm is, by definition, more religious.

substantive definition of religion The idea that religion has a unique content or substance relating to the sacred that separates it from other forms of knowledge and belief.

Sociologists that follow a substantive approach focus on the ways in which religious groups rally around what they define to be sacred. The **sacred** encompasses elements beyond everyday life that inspire respect, awe, and even fear. People interact with the sacred realm through ritual practices, such as prayer or sacrifice. Because believers have faith in the sacred, they accept what they cannot understand. The sacred realm exists in contrast to the **profane,** which includes the ordinary and commonplace.

Different religious groups define their understanding of the sacred or profane in different ways. For example, who or what constitutes "god" varies between Muslims, Christians, and Hindus. Even within a group, different believers may treat the same object as sacred or profane, depending on whether it connects them to the sacred realm. Ordinarily, a piece of bread is profane, but it becomes sacred during the Christian practice of communion because through it believers enter into connection with God. Similarly, a candelabrum becomes sacred to Jews if it is a menorah. For Confucians and Taoists, incense sticks are not mere decorative items, but highly valued offerings to the gods in religious ceremonies that mark the new and full moons.

sacred Elements beyond everyday life that inspire respect, awe, and even fear.

profane The ordinary and commonplace elements of life, as distinguished from the sacred.

functionalist definition of religion The idea that religion unifies believers into a community through shared practices and a common set of beliefs relative to sacred things.

Hot or Not?

Is it appropriate for religious leaders, such as pastors, priests, rabbis, or imams, to discuss political issues during religious services?

FUNCTION: WHAT RELIGIONS DO

A functionalist approach focuses less on what religion is than on what religions do, with a particular emphasis on how religions contribute to social order. According to a **functionalist definition of religion,** religion unifies believers into a community through shared practices and a common set of beliefs relative to sacred things. The emphasis here is on the unifying dimension of religion rather than on the substance of that which unifies. For functionalists, the supernatural or something like it is not an essential part of religion. Religion need not have gods or goddesses, an afterlife, or other such conventional elements. In fact, any social practices that strongly unite us, such as being a sports fan, can function like religion for the individual and for society.

The functional approach to defining religion has roots in the work of Émile Durkheim. He defined religion as "a unified system of beliefs and practices relative to sacred things, that is to say things set apart and forbidden—beliefs and practices which unite into a single moral community, called a 'church,' all those who adhere to them" ([1887] 1972:224). This definition points to three aspects sociologists focus on when studying religion: a unified system of beliefs and practices, involving sacred things, in the context of community.

The first element of Durkheim's functional approach is the unified system of beliefs and practices. What those beliefs and practices are matters less than the fact that they are shared. Terms historically used to describe religious beliefs include *doctrine, dogma, creeds,* and *scripture,* all representing principles believers share through faith. Practices refer to shared rituals such as attendance at services, prayer, meditation, and fasting. Because beliefs and practices are central to religion, we look at them in more detail below.

Unlike the substantive approach, Durkheim's emphasis on sacred things focuses less on the objects themselves than on the believers' attitude toward those objects. Sacred objects and sacred places convey a sense of awe, and religion calls upon believers to treat them with reverence and care. Roman Catholics, for example, treat the bread and wine of communion with respect because they believe that the sacrament transforms those elements into the body and blood of Christ. For Muslims, the Qur'an is a sacred object, and the Kaaba in Mecca is a sacred place. In the functional approach to religion, however, sacredness is in the eyes of the beholders. Any object can be sacred so long as people define it as such and treat it accordingly.

The most important component of Durkheim's definition is this third part: community. It is not the church,

From Me to You

I confess to being a Green Bay Packers fan. I follow them religiously. Even though I know better, I practice superstitions in the hope that they will help, including wearing a lucky shirt, not talking on the phone during the game, and though I am embarrassed to admit it, doing a "touchdown dance" around the dining room table after the Packers score, with high-fives for everyone including the dog. I was fortunate enough to be at "the frozen tundra of Lambeau Field" to see Brett Favre play his last game with the Packers, and I have tucked the ticket stub away, preserving it as if it were a sacred object. And each new season I believe that they will take us to the promised land of the Super Bowl.

mosque, or temple as a building that matters, but the unification of a body of believers into a shared community. What they believe, what they practice, or what they view as sacred is less important than that they have these beliefs, practices, and shared sacred things in common.

SOCthink

> > > What other things function like religion for us? How about followers of bands, TV shows, or politics? To what extent might consumerism or even work function like religion?

As suggested above, according to this approach, religion need not look like what we conventionally think of as religion. Anything that does what Durkheim's three elements do can function as religion. Just as our understanding of what families are has expanded to include people who are "like family" to us, so also has the definition of religion expanded to include things that function like religion. Sports provides a classic example. When it comes to beliefs and practices, sports fans—short for *fanatics,* a term that historically had religious connotations—share beliefs about the superiority of their team and regularly practice rituals in hopes that it will help their team win. They may wear the same jersey to watch the game, sit in the same chair, or do a touchdown dance after their team scores, all out of superstitious fear that failure to do so will make them lose. In terms of sacred things, there are autographs, jerseys, balls; and the stadium where the team plays, often referred to by fans as a shrine, represents a sacred space. Finally, fans are united into a community with other fans of the team. Being a fan of the team becomes part of their identity. It provides them with joy, satisfaction, and even a sense of purpose. In a personal essay recounting his obsession with soccer, Michael Elliott (2005) put it this way: "What does being a fan mean? It means you will never walk alone" (p. 76).

>> Components of Religion

In studying religion, regardless of which definitional approach they take, sociologists investigate components of religion that are common to most groups. Their goal is to gain a more complete picture of the role religion plays for both individuals and groups. Sociologists using both approaches focus on how religious groups organize beliefs, rituals, experience, and community. We will look at some examples of what they learn about religion by focusing on each in turn.

BELIEFS

Some people believe in life after death, in supreme beings with unlimited powers, or in supernatural forces. **Religious beliefs** are statements to which members of a particular religion adhere. The focus can vary dramatically from religion to religion.

In the late 1960s, a significant shift occurred in the nature of religious belief in the United States. Denominations that held to relatively liberal interpretations of religious scripture (such as the Presbyterians, Methodists, and Lutherans) declined in membership, while those that held to more conservative interpretations and sought a return to the fundamentals of the faith grew in numbers. The term **fundamentalism** refers to a rigid adherence to core religious doctrines. Often, fundamentalism is accompanied by a literal application of scripture or historical beliefs to today's world. Fundamentalism grows out of a sense that the world is falling apart due to a decline in true religious belief and practice. Fundamentalists see themselves as presenting a positive vision for the future through a return to the purity of the original religious message.

religious belief A statement to which members of a particular religion adhere.
fundamentalism Rigid adherence to core religious doctrines, often accompanied by a literal application of scripture or historical beliefs to today's world.

The phrase "religious fundamentalism" was first applied to Protestants in the United States who took a literal interpretation of the Bible, but fundamentalism is found worldwide among most major religious groups, including Roman Catholicism, Islam, and Judaism. Fundamentalists vary immensely in their beliefs and behavior. Some stress the need to be strict in their own personal faith but take little interest in broad social issues. Others are watchful of societal actions, such as government policies, that they see as conflicting with fundamentalist doctrine (Emerson et al. 2006).

Christian fundamentalists in the United States have fought against the teaching of evolution in public schools because they believe not only that it represents a threat to their beliefs but also that it is itself a type of religious faith in naturalism (as opposed to the supernaturalism of God). The first, and most famous, court case over the teaching of evolution in public schools occurred in 1925 and is often referred to as the "Scopes Monkey Trial." In that trial, high school biology teacher John T. Scopes was convicted of violating a Tennessee law that made it a crime to teach the scientific theory of evolution in public schools (Larson 2006). Since that time there have been numerous other court challenges. The most recent major case, known as the "Dover Case," occurred in Pennsylvania in 2005. Those opposed to the teaching of evolution sought to force schools to teach the "science" of intelligent design—the idea that life is so complex that there had to be some form of intelligence behind its creation. The judge ruled that intelligent design was a variation on creationism, the teaching of which in a public school would violate the separation of church and state (Padian 2007).

RITUALS

Religious rituals are practices required or expected of members of a faith. Rituals usually honor the divine power (or powers) worshiped by believers; they also remind adherents of their religious duties and responsibilities. Rituals and beliefs can be interdependent; rituals generally affirm beliefs, as in a public or private statement confessing a sin. Like any social institution, religion develops distinctive norms to structure people's behavior. Moreover, sanctions are attached to religious rituals, in the form of either rewards (such as bar mitzvah gifts) or penalties (such as expulsion from a religious institution for violation of norms).

Rituals may be very simple, such as saying grace at a meal or observing a moment of silence to commemorate someone's death. Other rituals, such as the process of canonizing a saint, are quite elaborate. Most religious rituals in the United States focus on services conducted at houses of worship. Attendance at a service, silent and spoken prayers, communion, and the singing of hymns and chants are common forms of ritual behavior that generally take place in group settings. These rituals serve as important face-to-face encounters in which people reinforce their religious beliefs and their commitment to their faith. Religious participation varies widely from country to country.

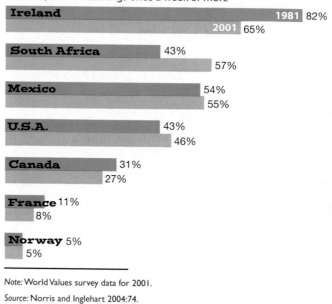

Going **GLOBAL**

Religious Participation in Selected Countries, 1981 and 2001

Percentage attending religious services other than weddings, funerals, and christenings once a week or more

Country	1981	2001
Ireland	82%	65%
South Africa	43%	57%
Mexico	54%	55%
U.S.A.	43%	46%
Canada	31%	27%
France	11%	8%
Norway	5%	5%

Note: World Values survey data for 2001.

Source: Norris and Inglehart 2004:74.

For Muslims, a very important ritual is the *hajj*—a pilgrimage to the Grand Mosque in Mecca, Saudi Arabia. Every Muslim who is physically and financially able is expected to make this trip at least once. Each year 2 million pilgrims go to Mecca during the one-week period indicated by the Islamic lunar calendar. Muslims from all over the world make the *hajj,* including those in the United States, where many tours are arranged to facilitate the trip.

EXPERIENCE

In the sociological study of religion, the term **religious experience** refers to the feeling or perception of being in direct contact with the ultimate reality, such as a divine

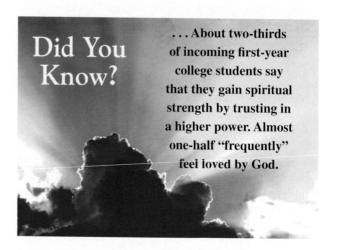

Did You Know?

...About two-thirds of incoming first-year college students say that they gain spiritual strength by trusting in a higher power. Almost one-half "frequently" feel loved by God.

being, or of being overcome with religious emotion. A religious experience may be rather slight, such as the feeling of exaltation a person might receive from hearing a choir sing Handel's "Hallelujah Chorus." Many religious experiences, however, are more profound, such as a Muslim's experience on a *hajj*. In his autobiography, the late African American activist Malcolm X (1964:338) wrote of his *hajj* and how deeply moved he was by the way that Muslims in Mecca came together across racial and color lines. For Malcolm X, the color blindness of the Muslim world "proved to me the power of the One God."

Another profound religious experience for many Christians is being "born again," which involves making a personal commitment to Jesus Christ, marking a major turning point in one's life. According to a 2008 national survey, 34 percent of people in the United States claim they have had a born-again Christian experience at some time in their lives (Kasmin and Keyser 2009). Another survey found that 81 percent of Assembly of God attendees reported having had such experiences, with Baptists coming in at 67 percent. In contrast, only 25 percent of Catholics responded that they had been born again (Barna Group 2001).

The collective nature of religion, as emphasized by Durkheim, is evident in these statistics. The beliefs and rituals of a particular faith can create an atmosphere either friendly toward or less conducive to this type of religious experience. Thus, an Assembly member would be encouraged to "come forward" to make such a commitment and then to share her or his experience with others. A Roman Catholic who claimed to have been born again, on the other hand, would receive much less attention within his or her church (Gallup 2008c; Gallup Opinion Index 1978).

COMMUNITY

Religious communities organize themselves in varieties of ways. Specific structures such as churches and synagogues have been constructed for religious worship; individuals have been trained for occupational roles within various fields. These developments make it possible to distinguish clearly between the sacred and secular parts of one's life—a distinction that could not be made easily in earlier times, when religion was largely a family activity carried out in the home.

Sociologists find it useful to distinguish between four basic forms of organization: the ecclesia, the denomination, the sect, and the new religious movement, or cult. We can see differences among these four forms of organization in their size, power, degree of commitment expected from members, and historical ties to other faiths (Dawson 2009).

Ecclesiae When studying how groups organize their communities, sociologists have used the term **ecclesia** (plural, *ecclesiae*) to describe a religious organization that claims to include most or all members of a society and is recognized as the national or official religion. Since virtually everyone belongs to the faith, membership is by birth rather than conscious decision. The classic example in sociology was the Roman Catholic Church in medieval Europe. Contemporary examples of ecclesiae include Islam in Saudi Arabia and Buddhism in Thailand. However, significant differences exist within this category. In Saudi Arabia's Islamic regime, leaders of the ecclesia hold vast power over actions of the state. In contrast, the historical state church in Sweden, Lutheranism, holds no such power over the Riksdag (parliament) or the prime minister.

Generally, ecclesiae are conservative, in that they do not challenge the leaders of a secular government. In a society with an ecclesia, the political and religious institutions often act in harmony and reinforce each other's power in their relative spheres of influence. In the modern world, ecclesiae are declining in power.

Denominations A denomination is a large, organized religion that is not officially linked to the state or government. Like an ecclesia, it tends to have an explicit set of beliefs, a defined system of authority, and a generally respected position in society. Denominations often claim large segments of a population as members. Generally, children accept the denomination of their parents and give little thought to membership in other faiths. Although considered respectable and not viewed as a challenge to the secular government, unlike ecclesia, denominations lack

> **religious ritual** A practice required or expected of members of a faith.
> **religious experience** The feeling or perception of being in direct contact with the ultimate reality, such as a divine being, or of being overcome with religious emotion.
> **ecclesia** A religious organization that claims to include most or all members of a society and is recognized as the national or official religion.
> **denomination** A large, organized religion that is not officially linked to the state or government.

Major Religious Traditions in the United States

Roman Catholics, Episcopalians, and Lutherans, are the outgrowth of ecclesiae established in Europe. New Christian denominations also emerged, including the Mormons and Christian Scientists. Within the last generation, immigrants have increased the number of Muslims, Hindus, and Buddhists living in the United States.

Although by far the largest single denomination in the United States is Roman Catholicism, at least 24 other Christian faiths have 1 million or more members. Protestants collectively account for about 51.3 percent of the nation's adult population, compared to 23.9 percent for Roman Catholics and 1.7 percent for Jews. Muslims account for approximately 0.6 percent, Buddhists about 0.7 percent, and Hindus about 0.4 percent. Self-described atheists and agnostics make up about 4 percent of the population (Pew Research Center 2008).

Protestant 51.3%

Mainline Protestant churches **18.1%**

Evangelical Protestant churches **26.3%**

Christian 78.4%

Historically Black, Protestant churches **6.9%**

Don't Know/ Refused **0.8%**

Religious unaffiliated **5.8%**

Unaffiliated 16.1%

Other Religions 4.7%

Secular unaffiliated **6.3%**

Catholic **23.9%**

Agnostic **2.4%**

Atheist **1.6%**

Other faiths **1.2%**
Unitarians and other liberal faiths **0.7%**
New Age **0.4%**
Native American religion **<0.3%**

Other world religions **<0.3%**

Hindu **0.4%**

Muslim **0.6%**
Sunni **0.3%**
Shia **<0.3%**
Other **<0.3%**

Buddhist **0.7%**
Zen Buddhist **<0.3%**
Theravada Buddhist **<0.3%**
Tibetan Buddhist **<0.3%**
Other **0.3%**

Mormon **1.7%**

Jehovah's Witness **0.7%**

Orthodox
Greek Orthodox **<0.3%**
Russsian Orthodox **<0.3%**
Other **<0.3%**

Other Christian **0.3%**

Jewish **1.7%**
Reform **0.7%**
Conservative **0.5%**
Orthodox **<0.3%**
Other **0.3%**

Notes: Due to rounding, figures may not add to 100 and nested figures may not add to the subtotal indicated.

Source: Pew Research Center 2008.

Sects

A **sect** can be defined as a relatively small religious group that has broken away from some other religious organization to renew what it considers the original vision of the faith. Many sects, such as that led by Martin Luther during the Reformation in the 1500s, claim to be the "true church" because they seek to cleanse the established faith of what they regard as extraneous beliefs and rituals. Max Weber ([1916] 1958b:114) termed the sect a "believer's church" because affiliation is based on conscious acceptance of a specific religious dogma.

Sects are at odds with the dominant society and do not seek to become established national religions. Unlike ecclesiae and denominations, they require intensive commitments and demonstrations of belief by members. Partly owing to their outsider status, sects frequently exhibit a higher degree of religious fervor and loyalty than more established religious groups. They actively recruit adults as new members, and acceptance comes through conversion.

Sects are often short-lived. Those that are able to survive may become less antagonistic to society over time and

the official recognition and power held by an ecclesia (Doress and Porter 1977).

The United States is home to a large number of denominations. This diversity is largely the result of the nation's immigrant heritage. Many settlers brought with them the religious commitments native to their homelands. Some Christian denominations in the United States, such as the

begin to resemble denominations. In a few instances, sects have been able to endure over several generations while remaining fairly separate from society. Sociologist J. Milton Yinger (1970:226–73) uses the term **established sect** to describe a religious group that is the outgrowth of a sect, yet remains isolated from society. The Hutterites, Jehovah's Witnesses, Seventh-Day Adventists, and Amish are contemporary examples of established sects in the United States.

Throughout the world, including the United States, Muslims are divided into a variety of sects, such as Sunni and Shia (or Shiite). The great majority of Muslims in the United States are Sunni Muslims—literally, those who follow the *Sunnah,* or way of the Prophet. Compared to other Muslims, Sunnis tend to be more moderate in their religious orthodoxy. The Shia, who come primarily from Iraq and Iran, are the second-largest group. Shia Muslims are more attentive to guidance from accepted Islamic scholars than are Sunnis. About two-thirds of Muslims in the United States are native-born citizens.

Cults or New Religious Movements
Historically, sociologists have used the term *cult* to describe alternative religious groups with unconventional religious beliefs. Partly as a result of the notoriety generated by some of these more extreme groups—such as the Heaven's Gate cult members who committed mass suicide in 1997 so that their spirits might be freed to catch a ride on the spaceship hidden behind the Hale-Bopp comet—many sociologists have abandoned the use of the term. In its place they have adopted the expression "new religious movement."

A **new religious movement (NRM)** or **cult** is generally a small, alternative religious group that represents either a new faith community or a major innovation in an existing faith. NRMs are similar to sects in that they tend to be small and are often viewed as less respectable than more established faiths. Unlike sects, however, NRMs normally do not result from schisms or breaks with established ecclesiae or denominations. Some cults, such as those focused on UFO sightings, may be totally unrelated to existing faiths. Even when a cult does accept certain fundamental tenets of a dominant faith—such as a belief in Jesus as divine or in Mohammad as a messenger of God—it will offer new revelations or insights to justify its claim to being a more advanced religion (Stark and Bainbridge 1979, 1985).

sect A relatively small religious group that has broken away from some other religious organization to renew what it considers the original vision of the faith.
established sect A religious group that is the outgrowth of a sect, yet remains isolated from society.
new religious movement (NRM) or **cult** A small, alternative faith community that represents either a new religion or a major innovation in an existing faith.

Like sects, NRMs may be transformed over time into other types of religious organization. An example is the Christian Science Church, which began as a new religious movement under the leadership of Mary Baker Eddy. Today, this church exhibits the characteristics of a denomination. In fact, most major religions, including Christianity, began as cults. NRMs may be in the early stages of developing into a denomination or new religion, or they may just as easily fade away through the loss of members or weak leadership (Schaefer and Zellner 2007).

Comparing Forms of Religious Organization How can we determine whether a particular religious group falls into the sociological category of ecclesia, denomination, sect, or NRM? As we have seen, these types of religious organization have somewhat different relationships to society. Ecclesiae are recognized as national churches; denominations, although not officially approved by the state, are generally widely respected. In contrast, sects and NRMs are much more likely to be at odds with the larger culture.

Still, ecclesiae, denominations, and sects are best viewed as types along a continuum in terms of their level of accommodation with the larger society. With ecclesiae, church and state merge together as one. On the other end, however, sects find themselves at odds with the dominant society. Denominations fall between the two. Because they offer an alternative to the mainstream, NRMs might fall close to sects. But NRMs could be said to lie outside the continuum because they define themselves in terms of a new view of life rather than in terms of existing religious faiths. Since the United States has no ecclesiae, sociologists studying this country's religions have focused on denominations, sects, and NRMs.

secularization Religion's diminishing influence in the public sphere, especially in politics and the economy.

>> World Religions

Early sociologists predicted that modern societies would experience widespread **secularization,** which involves religion's diminishing influence in the public sphere, especially in politics and the economy. In the United States today, those who are nonreligious account for about 10–14 percent of the population; in 1900, however, they constituted a mere 1.3 percent of all Americans. In 2006, 19 percent of incoming U.S. college students had no religious preference compared to 10 percent of their mothers (Hout and Fischer 2002; Pryor et al. 2006; Winseman 2005). Though the percentage of those who opt out of organized religion continues to rise, tremendous diversity exists worldwide in religious beliefs and practices. Overall, about 85 percent of the world's population adheres to some religion; only about 15 percent is nonreligious. Major religions continue to exert a significant influence both collectively and individually.

Christianity is the largest single faith in the world; the second largest is Islam (see the table on page 184). Although global news events often suggest an inherent conflict between Christians and Muslims, the two faiths are similar in many ways. Both are monotheistic (that is, based on a single deity), and both include a belief in prophets, an afterlife, and a judgment day. In fact, Islam recognizes Jesus as a prophet, though not as the son of God.

Going **GLOBAL**

Religions of the World

Religious adherence is one of the defining social characteristics of a culture.

Source: Allen 2008.

Both faiths impose a moral code on believers, which varies from fairly rigid proscriptions for fundamentalists to relatively relaxed guidelines for liberals.

The followers of Islam, called Muslims, believe that the prophet Muhammad received Islam's holy scriptures from Allah (God) nearly 1400 years ago. They see Muhammad as the last in a long line of prophets, preceded by Adam, Abraham, Moses, and Jesus. Islam is more communal in its expression than Christianity, particularly the more individualistic Protestant denominations. Consequently, in countries that are predominantly Muslim, the separation of religion and the state is not considered necessary or even desirable. In fact, Muslim governments often reinforce Islamic practices through their laws. Muslims do vary sharply in their interpretation of several traditions, some of which—such as the wearing of veils by women—are more cultural than religious in origin.

Like Christianity and Islam, Judaism is monotheistic. Jews believe that God's true nature is revealed in the Torah, which Christians know as the first five books of the Old Testament. According to these scriptures, God formed a covenant, or pact, with Abraham and Sarah, the ancestors of the twelve tribes of Israel. Even today, religious Jews believe, this covenant holds them accountable to God's will. If they follow both the letter and the spirit of the Torah, a long-awaited Messiah will one day bring paradise to earth. Although Judaism has a relatively small following compared to other major faiths, it forms the historical foundation for both Christianity and Islam. That is why Jews revere many of the same sacred Middle Eastern sites as Christians and Muslims.

Two other major faiths developed in a different part of the world—India. The earliest, Hinduism, originated around 1500 B.C. Hinduism differs from Judaism, Christianity, and Islam in that it embraces a number of gods and minor gods, although most worshipers are devoted primarily to a single deity, such as Shiva or Vishnu. Hinduism is also distinguished by a belief in reincarnation, or the perpetual rebirth of the soul after death. Unlike Judaism, Christianity, and Islam, which are based largely on sacred texts, Hindu beliefs have been preserved mostly through oral tradition.

Buddhism developed in the sixth century B.C. as a reaction against Hinduism. This faith is founded on the teachings of Siddhartha (later called Buddha, or "The Enlightened One"). Through meditation, followers of Buddhism strive to overcome selfish cravings for physical or material pleasures, with the goal of reaching a state of enlightenment, or nirvana. Buddhists created the first monastic orders, which are thought to be the models for monastic orders in other religions, including Christianity. Though Buddhism emerged in India, its followers were eventually driven out of that country by the Hindus. It is now found primarily in other parts of Asia.

Although the differences among religions are striking, they are exceeded by variations within faiths. Consider the differences within Christianity, from relatively liberal de-

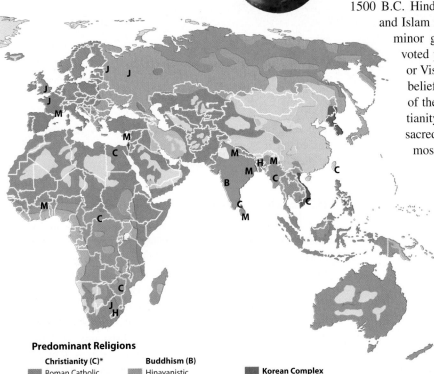

Predominant Religions

Christianity (C)*
Roman Catholic
Protestant
Mormon (LDS)
Eastern Churches
Mixed Sects

Islam (M)
Sunni
Shia

Buddhism (B)
Hinayanistic
Lamaistic

Hinduism (H)
Judaism (J)
Sikhism
Animism (Tribal)
Chinese Complex
(Confucianism, Taoism, and Buddhism)

Korean Complex
(Buddhism, Confucianism, Christianity, and Chondogyo)
Japanese Complex
(Shinto and Buddhism)
Vietnamese Complex
(Buddhism, Taoism, Confucianism, and Cao Dai)
Unpopulated Regions

* Capital letters indicate the presence of locally important minority adherents of nonpredominant faiths.

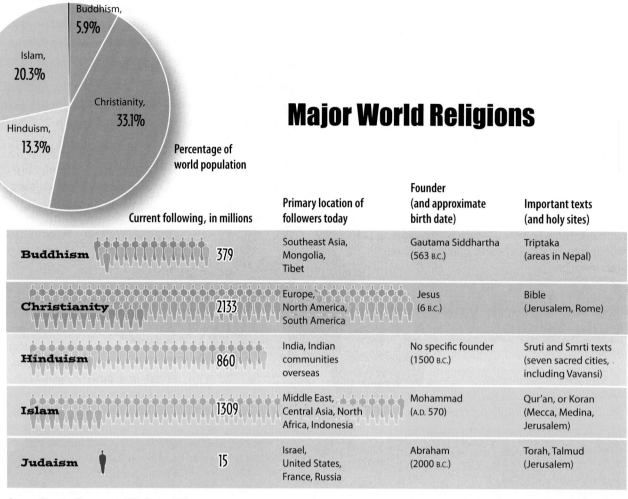

Major World Religions

	Current following, in millions	Primary location of followers today	Founder (and approximate birth date)	Important texts (and holy sites)
Buddhism	379	Southeast Asia, Mongolia, Tibet	Gautama Siddhartha (563 B.C.)	Triptaka (areas in Nepal)
Christianity	2133	Europe, North America, South America	Jesus (6 B.C.)	Bible (Jerusalem, Rome)
Hinduism	860	India, Indian communities overseas	No specific founder (1500 B.C.)	Sruti and Smrti texts (seven sacred cities, including Vavansi)
Islam	1309	Middle East, Central Asia, North Africa, Indonesia	Mohammad (A.D. 570)	Qur'an, or Koran (Mecca, Medina, Jerusalem)
Judaism	15	Israel, United States, France, Russia	Abraham (2000 B.C.)	Torah, Talmud (Jerusalem)

Sources: Based on Barrett et al. 2006; Swatos 1998.

nominations such as Presbyterians or Episcopalians to the more conservative Mormons and Greek Orthodox Catholics. Similar divisions exist within Hinduism, Islam, and other world religions (Barrett et al. 2006; Swatos 1998).

>> Sociological Perspectives on Religion

Sociology emerged as a discipline in the 19th century in the context of significant intellectual, political, and economic upheaval. Intellectuals at the time felt that the religious teachings that had guided society in times of crisis in the past were failing. Auguste Comte and other early sociologists sought to provide a science of society that would tap the ways of knowing built into the scientific method and apply them to the study of society. They recognized the significant role that religion had played in maintaining social order in the past and believed it essential to understand how it had accomplished this, so the study of religion became a significant topic in early sociology. Among classical theorists, for example, Émile Durkheim concluded

that religion promoted social order; Max Weber maintained that it helped generate social change; and Karl Marx argued that it reinforced the interests of the powerful.

INTEGRATION

Durkheim viewed religion as an integrative force in human society. He sought to answer a perplexing question: "How can human societies be held together when they are generally composed of individuals and social groups with diverse interests and aspirations?" In his view, religious bonds often transcend these personal and divisive forces.

How does religion provide this "societal glue"? Religion, whether it be Buddhism, Islam, Christianity, or Judaism, gives meaning and purpose to people's lives. It offers ultimate values and ends to hold in common. Although they are subjective and not always fully accepted, these values and ends help society to function as an integrated social system. For example, funerals, weddings, bar and bat mitzvahs, and confirmations serve to integrate people into larger communities by reaffirming shared beliefs and values related to the ultimate questions of life.

Religion also serves to bind people together in times of crisis and confusion. Immediately after the terrorist attacks of September 11, 2001, on New York City and Washington, D.C., attendance at worship services in the United States increased dramatically. Muslim, Jewish, and Christian clerics made joint appearances to honor the dead and to urge citizens not to retaliate against those who looked, dressed, or sounded different from others. A year later, however, attendance levels had returned to normal (D. Moore 2002).

The integrative power of religion can be seen, too, in the role that churches, synagogues, and mosques have traditionally played and continue to play for immigrant groups in the United States. For example, Roman Catholic immigrants may settle near a parish church that offers services in their native language, such as Polish or Spanish. Similarly, Korean immigrants may join a Presbyterian church that has many Korean American members and follows religious practices similar to those of churches in Korea. Like other religious organizations, these Roman Catholic and Presbyterian churches help to integrate immigrants into their new homeland (Warner 2007).

Religion also strengthens feelings of social integration within specific faiths and denominations. In many faiths, members share certain characteristics that help to bind them together, including their race, ethnicity, and social class.

Such integration, while unifying believers, can come at the expense of outsiders. In this sense, religion can contribute to tension and even conflict between groups or nations. During the Second World War, Nazi Germany attempted to exterminate the Jewish people; approximately 6 million European Jews were killed. In modern times, nations such as Lebanon (Muslims versus Christians), Israel (Jews versus Muslims, as well as Orthodox versus secular Jews), Northern Ireland (Roman Catholics versus Protestants), and India (Hindus versus Muslims and, more recently, Sikhs) have been torn by clashes that are in large part based on religion. Such conflicts often do, however, have the effect of drawing the believers closer together.

SOCIAL CHANGE

Max Weber sought to understand how religion, which so often seems conservative in that it works to maintain order, might also contribute to social change. To do so, he focused on the relationship between religious faith and the rise of capitalism. Weber's findings appeared in his sociology classic, *The Protestant Ethic and the Spirit of Capitalism* ([1904] 2009).

The Weberian Thesis Weber noted that in European nations with both Protestant and Catholic citizens, an overwhelming number of business leaders, owners of capital, and skilled workers were Protestant. In his view, this was no mere coincidence. Weber explained it as a consequence of what he called the **Protestant ethic**—a disciplined commitment to worldly labor driven by a desire to

Income and Education Levels, Selected Denominations

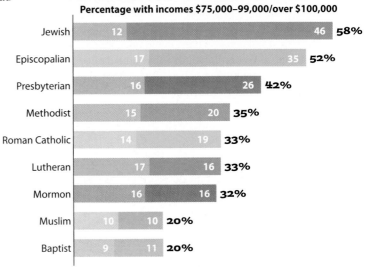

Percentage with incomes $75,000–99,000/over $100,000

Denomination			Total
Jewish	12	46	58%
Episcopalian	17	35	52%
Presbyterian	16	26	42%
Methodist	15	20	35%
Roman Catholic	14	19	33%
Lutheran	17	16	33%
Mormon	16	16	32%
Muslim	10	10	20%
Baptist	9	11	20%

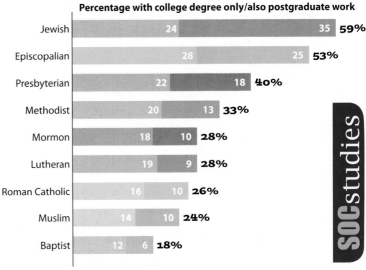

Percentage with college degree only/also postgraduate work

Denomination			Total
Jewish	24	35	59%
Episcopalian	28	25	53%
Presbyterian	22	18	40%
Methodist	20	13	33%
Mormon	18	10	28%
Lutheran	19	9	28%
Roman Catholic	16	10	26%
Muslim	14	10	24%
Baptist	12	6	18%

Source: Pew Research Center, 2008.

SOCstudies

bring glory to God that was shared by followers of Martin Luther and John Calvin. Weber argued that this emphasis on hard work and self-denial provided capitalism with an approach toward labor that was essential to capitalism's development.

To explain the impact of the Protestant ethic on the rise of capitalism, Weber highlights three keys: Luther's concept of a calling, Calvin's concept of predestination, and Protestant believers' resulting experience of "salvation panic." According to Protestant reformer Martin Luther (1483–1546), God called believers to their position in life, and they had to work hard in that calling so as to bring glory to God, regardless of whether they were rich or poor. Protestant Reformer John Calvin (1509–1564) added to this the concept of predestination, according to which

> **protestant ethic** Max Weber's term for the disciplined commitment to worldly labor driven by a desire to bring glory to God, shared by followers of Martin Luther and John Calvin.

God, before the beginning of time, picked who would go to heaven and who would go to hell, and there was nothing anyone could do to change their fate. It was impossible to earn salvation through good works; salvation was totally dependent upon the grace of God. Complicating this was the fact that no individual could ever know for sure that he or she was saved because none could presume to know the mind of God. Weber concluded that this created a sense of salvation panic among believers who wanted assurance that they were going to heaven.

SOCthink

> > > To what extent do you think religion can be a force for social change? What examples have you seen in your lifetime?

Weber theorized that believers would seek to resolve this uncertainty by leading the kinds of lives they thought God would expect godly people to lead. This meant hard work, humility, and self-denial, not for the sake of salvation or individual gain, but for the sake of God. Although doing so would not earn them salvation, to do otherwise would be an almost certain sign that they were not among the chosen. But they could never fully be sure, so they could never let up in their commitment to do God's will. Thus they worked hard not because they had to (either for subsistence or because they were forced) but because they wanted to in response to the salvation they hoped would come from God. It was precisely this kind of worker, internally motivated to work hard and willing to show up every day even after getting paid, that capitalism needed if it was to engage in rationally planned production. This "spirit of capitalism," to use Weber's phrase, contrasted with the moderate work hours, leisurely work habits, and lack of ambition that Weber saw as typical of traditional labor.

In this way, religion contributed, through the Protestant Reformation, to one of the most significant examples of social change, in the form of the rise of capitalism and its effects, in human history. Weber's argument has been hailed as one of the most important theoretical works in the field and as an excellent example of macrolevel analysis. Like Durkheim, Weber demonstrated that religion is not solely a matter of intimate personal beliefs. He stressed that the collective nature of religion has consequences for society as a whole.

liberation theology Use of a church, primarily Roman Catholicism, in a political effort to eliminate poverty, discrimination, and other forms of injustice from a secular society.

Liberation Theology A more contemporary example of religion serving as a force for social change came through liberation theology, in which the clergy were at the forefront. Many religious activists, especially in the Roman Catholic Church in Latin America, support **liberation theology**—the use of a church in a political effort to eliminate poverty, discrimination, and other forms of injustice from a secular society. Advocates of this religious movement sometimes sympathize with Marxism. Many believe that radical change, rather than economic development in itself, is the only acceptable solution to the desperation of the masses in impoverished developing countries. Activists associated with liberation theology believe that organized religion has a moral responsibility to take a strong public stand against the oppression of the poor, racial and ethnic minorities, and women (Bell 2001; Rowland 2007).

The term *liberation theology* dates back to the publication in 1973 of the English translation of *A Theology of Liberation*. The book was written by a Peruvian priest, Gustavo Gutiérrez, who lived in a slum area of Lima in the early 1960s. After years of exposure to the vast poverty around him, Gutiérrez concluded that "in order to serve the poor, one had to move into political action" (R. M. Brown 1980:23; Gutiérrez 1990). Eventually, politically committed Latin American theologians came under the influence of social scientists who viewed the domination of capitalist multinational

5 Movies on RELIGION

The Apostle
A Pentecostal preacher in the South.

The Believer
The story of Danny Balint, a young New York Jew who becomes a neo-Nazi.

Dogma
Satire on traditional Catholicism.

A Jihad for Love
Documentary about the intersection of Islam and homosexuality.

Jonestown: The Life and Death of People's Temple
Documentary about American cult leader Jim Jones.

corporations as central to the hemisphere's problems. One result was a new approach to theology that built on the cultural and religious traditions of Latin America rather than on models developed in Europe and the United States.

SOCIAL CONTROL

Liberation theology is a relatively recent phenomenon that marks a break with the traditional role of churches. It was this traditional role that Karl Marx opposed. In his view,

religion inhibited social change by encouraging oppressed people to focus on otherworldly concerns rather than on their immediate poverty or exploitation.

Marx on Religion Marx described religion as an "opiate" that was particularly harmful to oppressed peoples. He felt that religion often, in essence, drugged the masses into submission by offering a consolation for their harsh lives on earth: the hope of salvation in an ideal afterlife. For example, during the period of slavery in the United States, White masters forbade Blacks to practice native African religions. Instead, they encouraged slaves to adopt Christianity, which taught that obedience would lead to salvation and eternal happiness in the hereafter. Viewed from this perspective, Christianity may have pacified certain slaves and blunted the rage that often fuels rebellion.

For Marx, religion plays an important role in propping up the existing social structure. The values of religion, as already noted, tend to reinforce other social institutions and the social order as a whole. From Marx's perspective, however, religion's promotion of social stability only helps to perpetuate patterns of social inequality. According to Marx, the dominant religion reinforces the interests of those in power.

From a Marxist perspective, religion keeps people from seeing their lives and societal conditions in political terms—for example, by obscuring the overriding significance of conflicting economic interests. Marxists suggest that by inducing a "false consciousness" among the disadvantaged, religion lessens the possibility of collective political action that could end capitalist oppression and transform society. Sociological analysis in this tradition seeks to reveal the ways in which religion serves the interests of the powerful at the expense of others.

Gender and Religion Drawing on the feminist approach, researchers and theorists point to the fundamental role women play in religious socialization. Women play a critical role in the functioning of religious organizations, yet when it comes to positions of leadership, women generally take a subordinate role in religious governance. Indeed, most faiths have a long tradition of exclusively male spiritual leadership. Furthermore, because most religions are patriarchal, religious beliefs tend to reinforce men's dominance in secular as well as spiritual matters. Women do play a vital role as volunteers, staff, and religious educators, but even today, religious decision making and leadership typically fall to the men. Exceptions to this rule, such as the Shakers and Christian Scientists, as well as Hinduism with its long goddess heritage, are rare (Schaefer and Zellner 2007).

> But the poor person does not exist as an inescapable fact of destiny.... The poor are a by-product of the system in which we live and for which we are responsible.

Liberation Theologian Gustavo Gutierrez

In the United States, women compose 12.8 percent of the clergy, even though they account for 51 percent of students enrolled in theological institutions. Female clerics typically have shorter careers than men and are often relegated to fields that do not involve congregational leadership, such as counseling. In faiths that restrict leadership positions to men, women still serve unofficially. For example, about 4 percent of Roman Catholic congregations are led by women who hold nonordained pastoral positions—a necessity in a church that faces a shortage of male priests (Adams 2007; Banerjee 2006; Bureau of the Census 2007a:Table 598).

In this chapter, we have looked at both education and religion. In both cases we find institutions that play a powerful role in shaping how we think and act. Each provides opportunity and reinforces the status quo, including its system of inequality. Sociologists believe that by having a better appreciation for both the opportunities and constraints such institutions present, we can better act both individually and collectively to bring about positive social change.

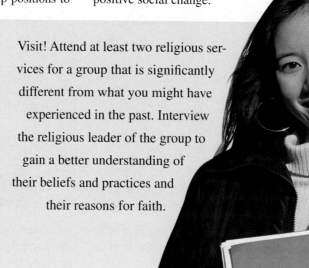

get involved!

Visit! Attend at least two religious services for a group that is significantly different from what you might have experienced in the past. Interview the religious leader of the group to gain a better understanding of their beliefs and practices and their reasons for faith.

For REVIEW

I. **How does education help to maintain social order?**
- Education transmits culture, promotes social integration, provides training and social control, and contributes to cultural innovation.

II. **How does education support the existing system of inequality?**
- Education reinforces the status quo, and therefore its existing inequalities, through the hidden curriculum, teacher expectancy, bestowal of status, and credentialism.

III. **How do sociologists define religion?**
- One approach focuses on the substance of what religion is, defining religion as knowledge and beliefs relating to the sacred realm. The other approach looks at what religions do for society in terms of social order and integration. Both approaches analyze common components including belief, ritual, experience, and community.

Pop Quiz

1. Horace Mann, often referred to as the "father of public education," refers to education as
   a. the great equalizer.
   b. the opiate of the masses.
   c. an instrument for social control.
   d. an opportunity engine.

2. One of the ways education contributes to social order is by providing an environment within which we can challenge existing ideas and experiment with new norms and values. This is known as
   a. transmitting culture.
   b. promoting social integration.
   c. training and social control.
   d. cultural innovation.

1. (a); 2. (d),

3. Samuel Bowles and Herbert Gintis have argued that capitalism requires a skilled, disciplined labor force and that the educational system of the United States is structured with that objective in mind. Citing numerous studies, they offer support for what they call

   a. tracking.
   b. credentialism.
   c. the correspondence principle.
   d. the teacher-expectancy effect.

4. Fifty years ago, a high school diploma was the minimum requirement for entry into the paid labor force of the United States. Today, a college diploma is virtually the bare minimum. This change reflects the process of

   a. tracking.
   b. credentialism.
   c. the hidden curriculum.
   d. the correspondence principle.

5. The college student subculture that focuses on having fun and socializing and doesn't take its studies too seriously is the

   a. collegiate subculture.
   b. academic subculture.
   c. vocational subculture.
   d. nonconformist subculture.

6. The approach to defining religion that emphasizes the significance of the sacred, most often supernatural, realm is known as the

   a. functionalist approach.
   b. component approach.
   c. substantive approach.
   d. ecclesiae approach.

7. Religious rituals are

   a. statements to which members of a particular religion adhere.
   b. the feelings or perceptions of being in direct contact with the ultimate reality, such as a divine being.
   c. the religious structures through which faith communities organize themselves.
   d. practices required or expected of members of a faith.

8. Looking at world religions, the religion with the most followers around the world is

   a. Buddhism.
   b. Islam.
   c. Judaism.
   d. Christianity.

9. Sociologist Max Weber pointed out that the followers of John Calvin emphasized a disciplined work ethic, worldly concerns, and a rational orientation to life. Collectively, this point of view has been referred to as

   a. capitalism.
   b. the Protestant ethic.
   c. the sacred.
   d. the profane.

10. The use of a church, primarily Roman Catholic, in a political effort to eliminate poverty, discrimination, and other forms of injustice evident in a secular society is referred to as

    a. creationism.
    b. ritualism.
    c. religious experience.
    d. liberation theology.

3. (c); 4. (b); 5. (a); 6. (c); 7. (d); 8. (d); 9. (b); 10. (d)

9

LENDER FOREC

REDC
REAL ESTATE DISPOSITION CORPORATION

PUBLIC H

AUCT

OPEN HOUSE: 4
1-800-89

www.USHome

USHome

GOVERNI

ADAPTING AND SURVIVING IN A MULTINATIONAL WORLD

In 2002, Jim Wier headed to Wal-Mart's corporate headquarters in Bentonville, Arkansas, to tell their executives that he would no longer be selling his company's Snapper lawn mowers in Wal-Mart stores. This was highly unusual for a Wal-Mart supplier. Most would go to great lengths to get their products on Wal-Mart shelves because, with 127 million U.S. customers per week, the possibilities for high-volume sales are immense. In fact, when they pulled their mowers from Wal-Mart, Snapper's sales dropped 20 percent (Fishman 2006).

Wal-Mart began as a single store in 1962, and there are now 3656 U.S. stores and 3615 abroad. In fact, Wal-Mart is the largest corporation in the world, with a total of $401 billion in revenues in fiscal year 2009. It is also the world's largest private employer, with 1.4 million U.S. workers and a total of 2.1 million worldwide.

Wier understood the appeal of gaining access to all those Wal-Mart customers, but as he put it, "Once you get hooked on the volume, it's like getting hooked on cocaine" (Fishman 2006:117). The need to maintain volume, he argued, would change the character of the company, requiring it to cut corners and change operating procedures. He opted instead to sell to a different kind of customer, one who wants quality, durability, and service more than up-front savings.

Ironically, to compete with Wal-Mart, Snapper had to adopt similar business techniques. To maximize efficiency, Wal-Mart measures everything. Snapper, too, now tracks every step of the production process to increase efficiency. Their productivity is three times what it was a decade ago with a workforce half the size. Though they continue to thrive, Snapper still faces an uphill fight.

Companies and workers have no choice but to adapt to compete with huge multinational corporations such as Wal-Mart and with firms and workers globally. When a company's revenues are greater than the gross national income for the majority of the world's nations—Wal-Mart would rank 21st out of 209 nations—it cannot help but have economic and political consequences (World Bank 2008). In this chapter we look at both the economy and politics to better understand how both shape our lives.

- How is economic and political power organized?
- How does power operate?
- How has the economy changed over time?

>> Power and Authority

On January 20, 2009, Barack Obama was sworn in as the 44th president of the United States of America. It was a historic event. All 43 presidents before him had been White men, so his election as the first African American was widely hailed as a milestone signaling greater opportunity for all.

Sociologists have always been interested in how power, presidential or otherwise, is achieved and maintained. In the midst of major political and economic shifts, early sociologists developed theories of power intended to be sufficiently broad to explain the rise of democracy or the expansion of market-based capitalism, yet sufficiently narrow to explain who gets their way within interpersonal relationships.

POWER

According to Max Weber, **power** is the ability to exercise one's will over others, even if they resist. To put it another way, if you can make people do what you want them to do—whether that is to go to war, coordinate a business meeting, clean their room, or even take an exam—you have power. Power relations can involve large organizations, small groups, or even people in intimate relationships.

There are three basic sources of power within any political system: force, influence, and authority. **Force** is the actual or threatened use of coercion to impose one's will on others. When leaders imprison or even execute political dissidents, they are applying force; so, too, are terrorists when they seize or bomb an embassy or assassinate a political leader. **Influence,** on the other hand, refers to the exercise of power through a process of persuasion. A citizen may change his or her view of a Supreme Court nominee because of a newspaper editorial, the expert testimony of a law school dean before the Senate Judiciary Committee, or a stirring speech by a political activist at a rally. In each case, sociologists would view such efforts to persuade people as examples of influence.

TYPES OF AUTHORITY

Authority, the third source of power, refers to institutionalized power that is recognized by the people over whom it is exercised. Sociologists commonly use the term in connection with those who hold legitimate power through elected or publicly acknowledged positions. A person's authority is often limited by her or his position. Thus, a referee has the authority to decide whether a penalty should be called during a football game but has no authority over the price of tickets to the game.

Max Weber ([1913] 1947) developed a classification system for authority that has become one of the most useful and frequently cited contributions of early sociology.

From Me to You

My daughters, Emily and Eleanor, mostly do what I ask, accepting my authority as legitimate. The fact that I am their father is usually enough to get them to obey. As they grew, however, they sometimes disobeyed, creating a power struggle. In such instances, they faced the prospect of "sitting in the green chair" until I said they could get out. Just the threat of being sent there usually did the trick. It was not much of a punishment, really. Our green rocking chair sits in the living room, in full view of the television, and is not isolated from the rest of the family. But having to just sit there had the desired effect of reinforcing my traditional authority as a parent.

SOCthink

> > > Which of these three forms of power do parents, bosses, or professors most rely on? Are there times when each of those groups use each of the three types of power?

He identified three ideal types of authority: traditional, rational-legal, and charismatic. Weber did not insist that only one type applies to a given society or organization. All can be present, but their relative importance will vary. Sociologists have found Weber's typology valuable in understanding different manifestations of legitimate power within a society.

Traditional Authority Until the middle of the 20th century, Japan was ruled by a revered emperor whose absolute power was passed down from generation to genera-

tion. In a political system based on **traditional authority,** legitimate power is conferred by custom and accepted practice. The past is a justification of the present. A king or queen is accepted as ruler of a nation simply by virtue of inheriting the crown; a tribal chief rules because that is the accepted practice. The ruler may be loved or hated, competent or destructive; in terms of legitimacy, that does not matter. For the traditional leader, authority rests in custom, not in personal characteristics, technical competence, or even written law. People accept the ruler's authority because that is how things have always been done. Traditional authority is absolute when the ruler has the ability to determine laws and policies.

power The ability to exercise one's will over others even if they resist.

force The actual or threatened use of coercion to impose one's will on others.

influence The exercise of power through a process of persuasion.

authority Institutionalized power that is recognized by the people over whom it is exercised.

traditional authority Legitimate power conferred by custom and accepted practice.

rational-legal authority Authority based on formally agreed-upon and accepted rules, principles, and procedures of conduct that are established in order to accomplish goals in the most efficient manner possible.

charismatic authority Power made legitimate by a leader's exceptional personal or emotional appeal to his or her followers.

Rational-Legal Authority The U.S. Constitution gives Congress and the president the authority to make and enforce laws and policies. Power made legitimate by law is a form of rational-legal authority. **Rational-legal authority** involves formally agreed-upon and accepted rules, principles, and procedures of conduct that are established in order to accomplish goals in the most efficient manner possible. Such authority extends beyond governments to include any organization. Bureaucracies are the purest form of rational-legal authority. Generally, in societies based on rational-legal authority, leaders are thought to have specific areas of competence and authority, but are not thought to be endowed with divine inspiration, as in certain societies with traditional forms of authority.

Charismatic Authority Joan of Arc was a simple peasant girl in medieval France, yet she was able to rally the French people and lead them into major battles against English invaders despite having no formally recognized position of power. How was this possible? As Weber observed, power can be legitimized by the charisma of an individual. **Charismatic authority** refers to power made legitimate by a leader's exceptional personal or emotional appeal to his or her followers.

Charisma lets a person such as Joan of Arc lead or inspire without relying on set rules or traditions. In fact, charismatic authority is derived more from the beliefs of followers than from the actual qualities of leaders. So long as people perceive a charismatic leader such as Jesus, Joan of Arc, Gandhi, Malcolm X, or Martin Luther King Jr. as having qualities that set him or her apart from ordinary citizens, that leader's authority will remain secure and often unquestioned (Adair-Toteff 2005; Potts 2009). That unfortunately is also the case with malevolent figures such as Adolf Hitler, whose charismatic appeal turned people toward violent and destructive ends in Nazi Germany.

Political leaders increasingly depend on television, radio, and the Internet to establish and maintain charismatic authority. This practice took hold with President Franklin D. Roosevelt's use of fireside chats over the radio to calm a nation that faced the Great Depression and World War II. News coverage of Barack Obama's presidency frequently mentions his capacity to charm; early approval ratings reflect significant faith in his leadership (Bligh and Kohles 2009). Public opinion can shift, however, as President George W. Bush learned. His approval ratings after the September 11, 2001, terrorist attacks soared to 85 percent, but by the end of his second term they hovered around 25 percent (among the lowest recorded for a president), making it difficult for him to advance his legislative agenda.

>> Economic Systems

industrial society A society that depends on mechanization to produce its goods and services.
economic system The social institution through which goods and services are produced, distributed, and consumed.
capitalism An economic system in which the means of production are held largely in private hands and the main incentive for economic activity is the accumulation of profits.

Out of the Industrial Revolution grew a new kind of political and economic structure known as the **industrial society,** a society that depends on mechanization to produce its goods and services. People left their rural agricultural communities and migrated to the cities to work in factories. Chicago saw explosive growth as a result of this revolution. The city had a population of about 300 when it was founded in 1833. By 1850 it had grown to about 30,000; in 1890 it broke the 1-million barrier; and by 1900 it was the fifth-largest city in the world, with a population of 1.7 million. Such changes, driven by economic

transformations and opportunities, had radical impacts on the lives of its residents. In fact, we cannot fully understand what happens in the context of families or education without taking into account such economic change.

This new, more global economy of the industrial age called for large-scale systems of power and authority. The term **economic system** refers to the social institution through which goods and services are produced, distributed, and consumed. Two basic types of economic systems distinguish contemporary industrial societies: capitalism and socialism. Capitalism and socialism, as described below, serve as ideal types of economic systems. In practice, no nation fully embodies either model. Instead, the economy of each individual state represents a mixture of capitalism and socialism.

CAPITALISM

In preindustrial societies based on an agricultural economy, land functioned as the source of virtually all wealth. The Industrial Revolution changed all that. It required that certain individuals and institutions be willing to take substantial monetary risks in order to finance new inventions, machinery, and business enterprises. Eventually, bankers, industrialists, and other holders of large sums of money replaced landowners as the most powerful economic force. These people invested their funds in the hope of realizing even greater profits and thereby became owners of property and business firms.

The transition to private ownership of business was accompanied by the emergence of **capitalism**—an economic system in which the means of production are held largely in private hands and the main incentive for economic activity is the accumulation of profits. In practice, capitalist systems vary in the degree to which the government regulates private ownership and economic activity (Fulcher 2004).

Immediately following the Industrial Revolution, the prevailing form of capitalism was what is termed **laissez-faire** ("let them do [as they choose]"). Under the principle of laissez-faire, as expounded and endorsed by British economist Adam Smith (1723–1790), people could compete freely, with minimal government intervention, in the economy. Business retained the right to regulate itself and

Did
You Know?

. . . The average
annual sales
for Wal-
Mart equal
$2060.36 per
household in
the United
States.

operated essentially without fear of government interference (A. Smith [1776] 2003).

In principle, through competition in the free market, capitalist economies should reach a natural balance between what consumers demand and what producers supply. In practice, capitalism produces monopolistic conditions. A **monopoly** exists when a single business firm controls the market. Domination of an industry allows the firm to effectively control a commodity by dictating pricing, quality standards, and availability. Buyers have little choice but to yield to the firm's decisions; there is no other place to purchase the product or service. Monopolistic practices violate the ideal of free competition cherished by Adam Smith and other supporters of laissez-faire capitalism.

SOCthink

> > > Why is competition essential to capitalism? Why might capitalists seek to establish monopolies?

Some capitalistic nations, in an effort to preserve competition, outlaw monopolies through antitrust legislation. Such laws prevent any business from taking over so much of the competition in an industry that it controls the market. The U.S. federal government allows monopolies to exist only in certain exceptional cases, such as the utility and transportation industries. Even then, regulatory agencies scrutinize these officially approved monopolies to protect the public. The protracted legal battle between the Justice Department and Microsoft, owner of the dominant operating system for personal computers, illustrates the uneasy relationship between the government and private monopolies in capitalistic countries.

Globalization and the rise of multinational corporations have spread the capitalistic pursuit of profits around the world. Especially in developing countries, governments are not always prepared to deal with the sudden influx of foreign capital and its effects on their economies. One particularly striking example of how unfettered capitalism can harm developing nations is found in the Democratic Republic of Congo (formerly Zaire). The Congo has significant deposits of the metal columbite-tantalite—coltan, for short—which is used in the production of electronic circuit boards. Until the market for cell phones, pagers, and laptop computers heated up recently, U.S. manufacturers obtained most of their coltan from Australia. But at the height of consumer demand, they turned to miners in the Congo to increase their supply.

Predictably, the escalating price of the metal—as much as $400 per kilogram at one point, or more than three times the average Congolese worker's yearly wages—attracted undesirable attention. Soon the neighboring countries of Rwanda, Uganda, and Burundi, at war with one another and desperate for resources to finance the conflict, were raiding the Congo's national parks, slashing and burning to expose the coltan underneath the forest floor. Indirectly, the sudden increase in the demand for coltan was financing war and the rape of the environment. U.S. manufacturers have since cut off their sources in the Congo in an effort to avoid abetting the destruction. However, their action has only penalized legitimate miners in the impoverished country (Lasker 2008; Lovgren 2006).

SOCIALISM

In their writings, Karl Marx and Friedrich Engels developed and refined socialist theory. They were disturbed by the exploitation of the working class during the Industrial Revolution. In their view, capitalism forced large numbers of people to exchange their labor for low wages. Marx and Engels argued that the owners of industry profit from the labor of workers primarily by paying workers less than the value of the goods produced.

> **laissez-faire** A form of capitalism under which people compete freely, with minimal government intervention, in the economy.
> **monopoly** Control of a market by a single business firm.

munist economic systems. However, this usage represents an incorrect application of a term with sensitive political connotations. All nations known as communist in the 20th century actually fell far short of the ideal type.

By the early 1990s, Communist parties were no longer ruling the nations of Eastern Europe. As of 2007, however, China, Cuba, Laos, and Vietnam remained socialist societies ruled by Communist parties. Even in those countries, however, capitalism has begun to make inroads. By 2000, fully 25 percent of China's production originated in the private business sector.

THE MIXED ECONOMY

In practice, national economic systems combine elements of both capitalism and socialism. A **mixed economy** features elements of more than one economic system. Starting from a socialist ideal and moving toward a mixed economy (China serves as a prime example) involves opening up some aspects of the state-controlled economy to competition and the free market. Conversely, moving from a capitalist ideal toward a mixed economy removes some goods and services from the competitive free market and provides them for all or subsidizes them to assure broader access. In the United States, we are provided with goods and services such as police and fire protection, roads, and public schools. Most agree that we should all have access to such public goods without regard for our ability to pay. There is currently a debate under way about whether health care should be considered a similar public good.

There has long been a debate in the United States about the degree to which the government should be involved

In principle, a socialist economic system attempts to eliminate such economic exploitation. Under **socialism,** the means of production and distribution in a society are collectively rather than privately owned. Marx predicted that technological advances would make it possible for society to produce enough for everyone, and a socialist system would ensure that everyone got enough. Socialists reject the laissez-faire philosophy that free competition benefits the general public. Instead, they believe that the central government, acting as the representative of the people, should make basic economic decisions. Therefore, government ownership of all major industries—including steel production, automobile manufacturing, and agriculture—is a primary feature of socialism as an ideal type.

socialism An economic system under which the means of production and distribution are collectively owned.

communism As an ideal type, an economic system under which all property is communally owned and no social distinctions are made on the basis of people's ability to produce.

Marx believed further that socialist states would eventually "wither away" and evolve into communist societies. In principle, **communism** is an economic system under which all property is communally owned and no social distinctions are made on the basis of people's ability to produce. In recent decades, the former Soviet Union, the People's Republic of China, Vietnam, Cuba, and the nations of Eastern Europe were popularly thought of as examples of com-

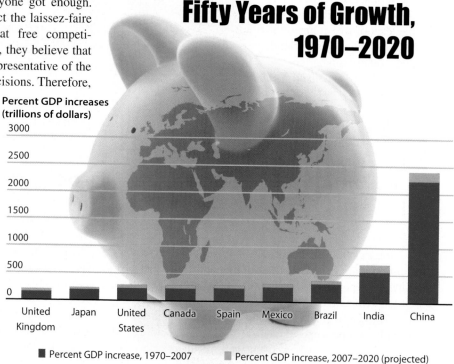

Fifty Years of Growth, 1970–2020

Percent GDP increases (trillions of dollars)

Chart showing Percent GDP increases for: United Kingdom, Japan, United States, Canada, Spain, Mexico, Brazil, India, China. Y-axis ranges from 0 to 3000 (in increments of 500).

■ Percent GDP increase, 1970–2007   ■ Percent GDP increase, 2007–2020 (projected)

Source: U.S. Department of Agriculture 2007.

in the economy, but with the severe economic downturn starting in late 2008, the U.S. government took a more active role. The situation looked grim. The housing market bubble burst, major banking and investment companies failed, and the stock market plummeted 40 percent from October 1, 2008, to March 9, 2009. Retail sales fell, production levels dropped, and unemployment rates spiked. Comparisons were being drawn to events leading up to the Great Depression, and elected officials moved toward a more mixed economy in hopes of avoiding an even greater collapse.

Government officials decided that some companies were "too big to fail," meaning that the domino effect of their failure would be greater than the cost of violating the laissez-faire ideal. The Bush administration, itself a strong proponent of free market principles, took the first steps toward this recent government intervention in the economy. In September 2008, they pushed the Troubled Assets Relief Program (TARP) through Congress to provide up to $700 billion to buy mortgage-backed securities and to prop up the financial sector. The Obama administration continued along the same lines. For example, in an effort to kick-start the U.S. economy, Congress passed the American Recovery and Reinvestment Act in February 2009, providing almost $800 billion for infrastructure projects, education and health care funding, and tax cuts. And in June 2009, General Motors, which for years was the world's largest company, went bankrupt. The U.S. government became its majority stock holder, owning 60 percent of its shares.

Though critics charged that presidents Bush and Obama were moving the nation toward socialism, most people were willing to accept such actions in hopes that they would minimize the negative impacts the economic downturn had on their lives. Families were already feeling the pinch: one-quarter had a member of their household lose a job within the past year, and almost half saw 20 percent or more of a retirement account or other investments disappear. One-fifth struggled to meet mortgage or rent payments, and the national average for credit card debt rose to $5729 per user (Morin and Taylor 2009). In hopes of hanging onto jobs and keeping the economy functioning, the majority accepted these huge government expenditures as a means to save capitalism from its own excesses.

THE INFORMAL ECONOMY

An informal economy operates within the confines of the dominant macroeconomic system in many countries, whether capitalist or socialist. In this **informal economy,** transfers of money, goods, or services take place but are not reported to the government. Examples of the informal economy include bartering in which people trade goods and services with someone (say, exchanging a haircut for a computer lesson), selling goods on the street, and engaging in illegal transactions, such as gambling or drug deals. Participants in this type of economy avoid taxes and government regulations.

> **mixed economy** An economic system that combines elements of both capitalism and socialism.
> **informal economy** Transfers of money, goods, or services that are not reported to the government.

In the developing world, governments often create burdensome business regulations that overworked bureaucrats must administer. When requests for licenses and permits pile up, delaying business projects, legitimate entrepreneurs find that they need to "go underground" to get anything done. Despite its apparent efficiency, this type of informal economy is dysfunctional for a country's overall political and economic well-being. Since informal firms typically operate in remote locales to avoid detection, they cannot easily expand when they become profitable. And given the limited protection for their property and contractual rights, participants in the informal economy are less likely than others to save and invest their income.

Informal economies can also be dysfunctional for workers. Working conditions in these businesses are often unsafe or dangerous, and the jobs rarely provide any benefits to those who become ill or cannot continue to work. Perhaps more significant, the longer a worker remains in the informal economy, the less likely he or she is to make the transition to the regular economy. No matter how efficient or productive a worker may be, employers expect to see experience in the formal economy on a job application. Experience as a successful street vendor or self-employed cleaning person does not carry much weight with interviewers (Venkatesh 2006).

Hot or Not?

Should the U.S. government let companies fail regardless of apparent economic consequences?

SOCthink

> > > When doing jobs in the informal economy such as babysitting, lawn mowing, house cleaning, or construction, it can be nice to get cash under the table without having to pay taxes, Social Security, and so on. What are the long-term disadvantages of doing so for the individual? What about for society? Why might someone opt to do so anyway?

>> Changing Economies

As recent economic upheaval demonstrates, economies are not static. Just as they changed due to the impact of the Industrial Revolution, economies continue to adapt to new contexts. The current changes are part of an ongoing shift in the workplace. Technological innovation and globalization have reduced the number of traditional blue-collar jobs through deindustrialization. Microfinancing has opened up opportunities for poor people, especially women, around the world.

deindustrialization The systematic, widespread withdrawal of investment in basic aspects of productivity, such as factories and plants.

THE CHANGING FACE OF THE WORKFORCE

The workforce in the United States constantly adapts to circumstances. During World War II, when men were mobilized to fight abroad, women entered the workforce in large numbers. With the coming of the civil rights movement in the 1960s, minorities found numerous job oppor-

Workforce Diversity: Past, Present, and Future

Percentage of the workforce

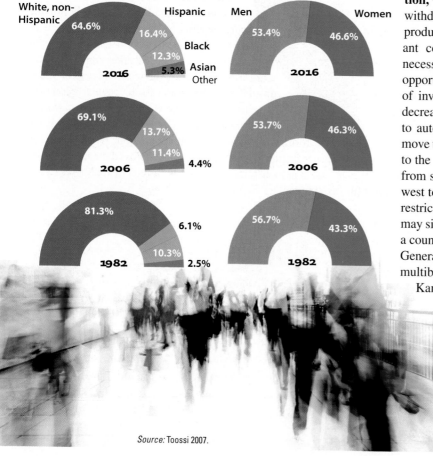

White, non-Hispanic
Hispanic
Black
Asian
Other

64.6% 16.4% 12.3% 5.3% **2016**

69.1% 13.7% 11.4% 4.4% **2006**

81.3% 6.1% 10.3% 2.5% **1982**

Men Women

53.4% 46.6% **2016**

53.7% 46.3% **2006**

56.7% 43.3% **1982**

Source: Toossi 2007.

tunities opening to them. While predictions are not always reliable, sociologists and labor specialists foresee a workforce increasingly composed of women and racial and ethnic minorities. In 1960 there were twice as many men in the labor force as women. As of March 2009, the labor force was 49.7 percent female, due in part to the fact that men have received 80 percent of recent layoffs (Boushey 2009). The dynamics for minority group workers are even more dramatic, as the number of Black, Latino, and Asian American workers continues to increase at a faster rate than the number of White workers.

More and more, then, the workforce reflects the diversity of the population, as ethnic minorities enter the labor force and immigrants and their children move from marginal jobs or employment in the informal economy to positions of greater visibility and responsibility. A sociological study of workplace programs designed to increase managerial diversity found that 39 percent of employers had diversity training programs. Researchers discovered that relying solely on education programs designed to reduce managerial bias was not particularly effective. The most successful approach is to have a point person, task force, or affirmative action plan that holds people responsible for change (Kalev, Dobbin, and Kelly 2006).

DEINDUSTRIALIZATION

In recent decades, the U.S. economy has moved away from its industrial base through the process of **deindustrialization,** which refers to the systematic, widespread withdrawal of investment in basic aspects of productivity, such as factories and plants. Giant corporations that deindustrialize are not necessarily refusing to invest in new economic opportunities. Rather, the targets and locations of investment change, and the need for labor decreases as advances in technology continue to automate production. First, companies may move their plants from the nation's central cities to the suburbs. The next step may be relocation from suburban areas of the Northeast and Midwest to the South, where labor laws place more restrictions on unions. Finally, a corporation may simply relocate outside the United States to a country with a lower rate of prevailing wages. General Motors, for example, decided to build a multibillion-dollar plant in China rather than in Kansas City or even in Mexico (Lynn 2003).

Although deindustrialization often involves relocation, it can also take the form of corporate restructuring known as **downsizing,** which involves reducing the size of a company's workforce. The goal is to increase efficiency and reduce costs in the face of growing worldwide competition. When such restructuring occurs, the impact on the bureaucratic hierarchy

The effects of the economic downturn have been wide spread. Recent college graduates have found a difficult job market. Many people have expressed frustration that large corporations have received billions while individual workers struggle.

SOCthink

> > > If you were the CEO of an American manufacturing company that was facing declining profits due to international competition, and Wal-Mart insisted that you reduce the price of your products another 5 percent this year, what would you do? To what extent does the system within which companies operate shape the choices that are available to them?

of formal organizations can be significant. A large corporation may choose to sell off or entirely abandon less productive divisions and to eliminate layers of management it views as unnecessary. Wages and salaries may be frozen and fringe benefits cut—all in the name of restructuring. Increasing reliance on automation also spells the end of work as we have known it.

> Majority rule only works if you're also considering individual rights. Because you can't have five wolves and one sheep voting on what to have for supper.
>
> **Larry Flynt**

U.S. firms have been outsourcing certain types of work for generations. For example, moderate-sized businesses such as furniture stores and commercial laundries have long relied on outside trucking firms to make deliveries to their customers. The more recent trend toward **offshoring** carries this practice one step further by transferring other types of work to foreign contractors. Now, even large companies are turning to overseas firms, many of them located in developing countries. Offshoring has become the latest tactic in the time-worn business strategy of raising profits by reducing costs.

Offshoring began when U.S. companies started transferring manufacturing jobs to foreign factories, where wage rates were much lower. But the transfer of work from one country to another is no longer limited to manufacturing. Office and professional jobs are being exported, too, thanks to advanced telecommunications and the growth of skilled, English-speaking labor forces in developing nations with relatively low wage scales. The trend includes even those jobs that require considerable training, such as accounting and financial analysis, computer programming, claims adjustment, telemarketing, and hotel and airline reservations. Today, when you call a toll-free num-

> **downsizing** Reductions in a company's workforce as part of deindustrialization.
> **offshoring** The transfer of work to foreign contractors.

Reprinted with the permission of Mike Thompson and Creators Syndicate.

ber to reach a customer service representative, chances are that the person who answers the phone will not be speaking from the United States.

The social costs of deindustrialization and downsizing cannot be overemphasized. Plant closings lead to substantial unemployment in a community, which can have a devastating impact on both the micro and macro levels. On the micro level, the unemployed person and his or her family must adjust to a loss of spending power. Painting or re-siding the house, buying health insurance or saving for retirement, even thinking about having another child—all must be put aside. Both marital happiness and family cohesion may suffer as a result. Although many dismissed workers eventually reenter the paid labor force, they often must accept less desirable positions with lower salaries and fewer benefits. Unemployment and underemployment are tied to many of the social problems discussed throughout this textbook, among them the need for child care and the controversy over welfare.

Alan S. Blinder (2006), former vice chair of the Federal Reserve, predicts that offshoring will become the "third Industrial Revolution"—a life-altering shift in the way goods and services are produced and consumed. Blinder says we have barely seen the "tip of the offshoring iceberg." While offshoring may not lead to large-scale unemployment, it will likely produce a shift in Western labor markets. Jobs that are easily outsourced, like accounting and computer programming, will migrate to developing countries, leaving those that must be done on site, like nursing and construction, at home.

politics In Harold Lasswell's words, "who gets what, when, and how."
political system The social institution that is founded on a recognized set of procedures for implementing and achieving society's goals.

While this shift has brought jobs and technology to nations such as India, there is a downside to offshoring for foreign workers as well. Although outsourcing is a significant source of employment for India's upper middle class, hundreds of millions of other Indians have benefited little if at all from the trend. Most households in India do not possess any form of high technology: only about 20 percent have phones and 7 percent have Internet access. Instead of improving these people's lives, the new business centers have siphoned water and electricity away from those who are most in need. Even the high-tech workers are experiencing negative consequences. Many suffer from stress disorders such as stomach problems and difficulty sleeping; more than half quit their jobs before the end of a year (International Telecommunications Union 2009; Waldman 2004a, 2004b, 2004c).

MICROFINANCING

Economic development can, however, have a significant positive impact on people's lives around the globe. Microfinancing, for example, involves lending small sums of money to the poor so that they can work their way out of poverty. Borrowers use the money to get small businesses off the ground—to buy the tools, equipment, and bamboo to make stools, the yarn to weave into cloth, or cows to produce milk. They then sell the products they produce in local shops. The typical microloan is less than $100, and often as little as $12. The recipients are people who ordinarily would not be able to qualify for banking services.

Sometimes referred to as "banking the unbanked," microfinancing was the brainchild of Bangladeshi economist Muhammad Yunus. In 1976, in the midst of a devastating famine in Bangladesh, Yunus founded the Grameen (meaning "village") Bank. The idea came to him when he reached into his pocket to lend $27 to a group of villagers who had asked him for help. Working through local halls or meeting places, the Grameen Bank has now extended credit to nearly 8 million people. The idea has spread, and microloans have even been underwritten by multinational organizations such as the International Monetary Fund and for-profit banks like Citigroup. Estimates suggest that by 2009 microfinancing had reached 133 million people (Gardner 2008).

Microfinancing works well in countries that have experienced economic devastation. For example, in 2002, after decades of conflict and military occupation, Afghanistan did not have a single functioning bank. Five years later, with the help of the World Bank and other donors, Afghans could get microloans and other financial services in 22 of the country's 34 provinces. The new microlenders are the first evidence of a formal financial sector that Afghanistan has seen in years. Their funds have helped to start businesses and allowed farmers to convert from opium growing to other crops.

Because an estimated 90 percent of the recipients of microcredit are women, feminist theorists are especially interested in the growth of microfinancing. Women's economic status has been found to be critical to the well-being of their children, and the key to a healthy household environment. In developing countries, where women often are not treated as well as men, being entrusted with credit is particularly empowering to them. In recognition of these social and economic benefits of microfinancing, the United Nations proclaimed 2005 the International Year of Microcredit (Dugger 2006; Flynn 2007).

>> Types of Government

Just as new economic systems developed in response to broader historical changes, political systems also adapted. In all societies, someone or some group—whether it be a tribal chief, a dictator, a council, or a parliament—makes important decisions about how to use resources and allocate goods. Inevitably, the struggle for power and authority involves **politics,** which political scientist Harold Lasswell (1936) tersely defined as "who gets what, when, and how." Politics takes place within the context of a **political system,** which is the social institution that is founded on a recognized set of procedures for implementing and achieving society's goals, such as the allocation of valued resources.

Government represents an institutionalized form of authority. Given the scope of international relations and the globalization of national economies, these formal systems of authority make a significant number of critical political decisions. Such systems take a variety of forms, including monarchy, oligarchy, dictatorship, totalitarianism, and democracy.

MONARCHY

A **monarchy** is a form of government headed by a single member of a royal family, usually a king, queen, or some other hereditary ruler. In earlier times, many monarchs claimed that God had granted them a divine right to rule. Typically, they governed on the basis of traditional forms of authority, sometimes accompanied by the use of force. By the beginning of the 21st century, however, monarchs held genuine governmental power in only a few nations, such as Monaco. Most monarchs, such as Queen Elizabeth II in England, now have little practical power; they serve primarily ceremonial roles.

monarchy A form of government headed by a single member of a royal family, usually a king, queen, or some other hereditary ruler.
oligarchy A form of government in which a few individuals rule.

OLIGARCHY

An **oligarchy** is a form of government in which a few individuals rule. A venerable method of governing that flourished in ancient Greece and Egypt, oligarchy now often takes

Did You Know?

. . . One of Queen Elizabeth's official duties is to appoint the prime minister. Given that political power rests with Parliament, however, this too has become largely a ceremonial duty.

the form of military rule. In developing nations in Africa, Asia, and Latin America, small factions of military officers may forcibly seize power, either from legally elected regimes or from other military cliques (Michels [1915] 1949).

Strictly speaking, the term *oligarchy* is reserved for governments that are run by a few selected individuals. However, the People's Republic of China can be classified as an oligarchy if we stretch the meaning of the term. In China, power rests in the hands of a large but exclusive ruling *group,* the Communist Party. In a similar vein, we might argue that many industrialized nations of the West should be considered oligarchies (rather than democracies), because only a powerful few—leaders of big business, government, and the military—actually rule. Later in this chapter, we will examine the "elite model" of the U.S. political system in greater detail.

dictatorship A government in which one person has nearly total power to make and enforce laws.

totalitarianism Virtually complete government control and surveillance over all aspects of a society's social and political life.

democracy In a literal sense, government by the people.

representative democracy A form of government in which certain individuals are selected to speak for the people.

DICTATORSHIP AND TOTALITARIANISM

A **dictatorship** is a government in which one person has nearly total power to make and enforce laws. Dictators rule primarily through the use of coercion, which often includes imprisonment, torture, and executions. Typically, they *seize* power rather than being freely elected (as in a democracy) or inheriting power (as in a monarchy). Some dictators are quite charismatic and manage to achieve a certain popularity, although their supporters' enthusiasm is almost certainly tinged with fear. Other dictators rely on force and are often bitterly hated by their people.

Frequently, dictators develop such overwhelming control over people's lives that their governments are called

SOC think

> > > In 2001, expressing a sentiment shared by many past presidents, George W. Bush joked that, when it came to working with Congress, "a dictatorship would be a heck of a lot easier." In what ways is the U.S. system of government intentionally inefficient? Why might that be on purpose?

totalitarian. (Monarchies and oligarchies may also achieve this type of dominance.) **Totalitarianism** involves virtually complete government control and surveillance over all aspects of a society's social and political life. Germany during Hitler's reign, the Soviet Union under Stalin in the 1930s, and North Korea today are classified as totalitarian states.

DEMOCRACY

In a literal sense, **democracy** means government by the people. The word comes from two Greek roots— *demos,* meaning "the populace" or "the common people," and *kratia,* meaning "rule." Of course, in large, populous nations such as the United States, government by the people is impractical at the national level. Americans cannot vote on every important issue. Consequently, popular rule is generally maintained through **representative democracy,** a form of government in which certain individuals are selected to speak for the people.

SOC think

> > > The United States is commonly classified as a representative democracy, because the elected members of Congress and state legislatures make our laws. However, critics have questioned how representative our democracy really is. Do Congress and the state legislatures genuinely represent the masses? Are the people of the United States legitimately self-governing, or has our government become a forum for powerful elites?

Going GLOBAL

Voter Turnout Worldwide

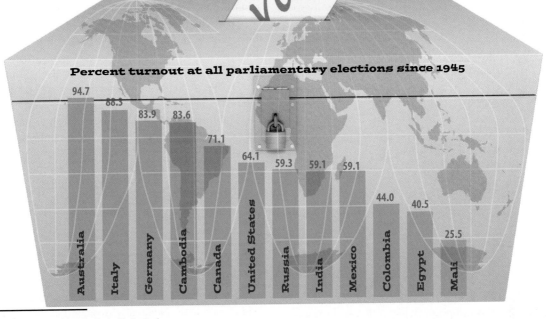

Percent turnout at all parliamentary elections since 1945

- Australia: 94.7
- Italy: 88.3
- Germany: 83.9
- Cambodia: 83.6
- Canada: 71.1
- United States: 64.1
- Russia: 59.3
- India: 59.1
- Mexico: 59.1
- Colombia: 44.0
- Egypt: 40.5
- Mali: 25.5

Note: Includes national elections to the legislative body.

Source: International Institute for Democracy and Electoral Assistance 2009.

>> Political Behavior in the United States

Citizens of the United States take for granted many aspects of their political system. They are accustomed to living in a nation with a Bill of Rights, two major political parties, voting by secret ballot, an elected president, state and local governments distinct from the national government, and so forth. Because it is, in principle, a representative democracy, the system depends upon all individuals having equal access to and input into the political process in order to be fully responsive. In practice, two particular concerns—voter participation and race and gender representation—raise questions about the degree to which this is happening.

VOTER PARTICIPATION

In a democratic system, voters have the right to select their political leaders. They are free to vote for whom they choose, and political parties seek to persuade voters to support their positions. In 2009, 35 percent of registered voters in the United States saw themselves as Democrats, 23 percent as Republicans, and 36 percent as independents. This represented a swing away from the Republican Party, though most who switched declared themselves to be independents.

Historically, voter participation rates in the United States were highest from 1848–1896, during which an average of about 80 percent of eligible voters participated in presidential elections. The rate declined steadily until it reached 48.9 percent in 1928. It fluctuated throughout the rest of the 20th century, rising to over 60 percent in 1940 and 1960 and falling to around 50 percent in 1948, 1988, and 1996. Concerns about voter apathy were expressed going into the 21st century, so the increases in the new millennium were greeted as a welcome trend.

In 2008, voter turnout hit a 40-year high, representing the third straight presidential election with an increase in voter participation. In the battle between Barack Obama and John McCain, 61.7 percent of eligible voters participated. Compare this to 60.1 percent in the race between George W. Bush and John Kerry in 2004 and 54.2 percent in the 2000 election, which pitted George W. Bush against Al Gore (McDonald 2009).

While a few nations still command high voter turnout, it is increasingly common to hear national leaders of other countries complain of voter apathy. Still, among the 166 countries that have held parliamentary elections since 1945, the United States

Did You Know?

... Young voters were much more likely to vote for Obama in 2008 than any other age group. Of voters aged 18–29, 66 percent voted for Obama. This compares to 52 percent among 30–44 year-olds and 50 percent for those aged 45–64. People 65 and older preferred McCain; only 45 percent of that age group chose Obama.

ranked only 147th in voter turnout in 2006 and 109th in 2008 (International Institute for Democracy and Electoral Assistance 2009).

Political participation makes government accountable to the voters. If participation declines, government operates with less of a sense of accountability to society. This issue is most serious for the least powerful individuals and groups in the United States. Historically, voter turnout has been particularly low among members of racial and ethnic minorities, although in the 2008 presidential election participation rates increased 9 percent among African Americans and 5 percent among Hispanics (Lopez and Taylor 2009). The poor—whose focus understandably is on survival—are also traditionally underrepresented among voters. The low turnout found among these groups is due at least in part to their common feeling of powerlessness. By the same token, by declining to vote, they encourage political power brokers to continue to ignore the interests of the less affluent and the nation's minorities. The segment of the voting population that has shown the most voter apathy is the young (Holder 2006).

RACE AND GENDER IN POLITICS

Because politics is synonymous with power and authority, we should not be surprised that marginalized groups lack political strength. Nationally, women did not get the vote until 1920. Most Chinese Americans were turned away from the polls until 1926. American Indians did not win the right to vote until 1954. And African Americans were disenfranchised until 1965, when national voting rights legislation was passed. Predictably, it has taken these groups some

Reasons for Not Voting, 18- to 24-Year-Olds

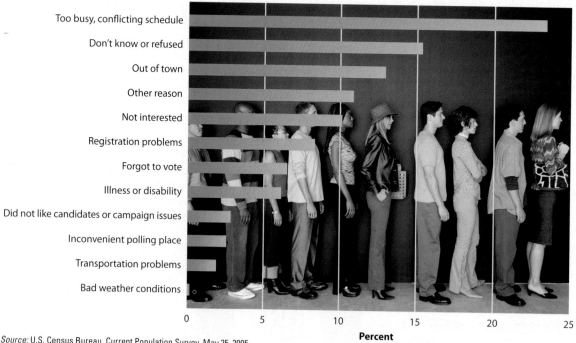

Source: U.S. Census Bureau, Current Population Survey, May 25, 2005.

Going GLOBAL

Women in National Legislatures, Selected Countries, 2009

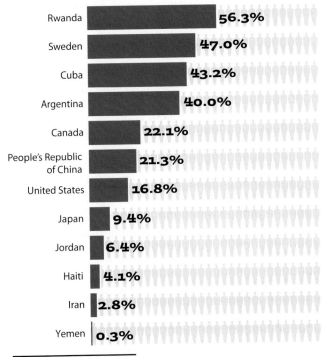

Country	Percent
Rwanda	56.3%
Sweden	47.0%
Cuba	43.2%
Argentina	40.0%
Canada	22.1%
People's Republic of China	21.3%
United States	16.8%
Japan	9.4%
Jordan	6.4%
Haiti	4.1%
Iran	2.8%
Yemen	0.3%

Note: Data are for lower legislative houses only, as of April 30, 2009; data on upper houses, such as the U.S. Senate or the U.K. House of Lords, are not included.

Source: Inter-Parliamentary Union 2009.

time to develop their political power and begin to exercise it effectively.

Progress toward the inclusion of minority groups in government has been slow as well. As of mid-2009, only 17 out of 100 U.S. senators were women. One senator was an African American, 3 were Latinos, and 2 were Asian Americans, leaving 77 White non-Hispanic men. Among the 435 members of the U.S. House of Representatives, 310 were White non-Hispanic men. Seventy-three were women, 39 were African Americans (including 12 women), 28 were Latinos (including 6 Latinas), 7 were Asian Americans, and 1 was an American Indian. These numbers, though low, represent a high-water mark for these groups.

(Under) Representation in Congress Compared to Overall Population

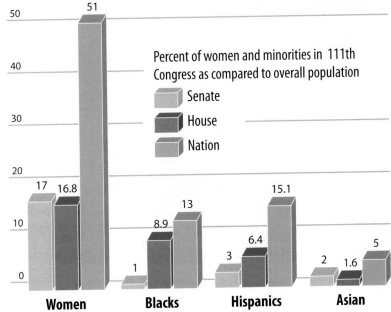

Percent of women and minorities in 111th Congress as compared to overall population

- Senate
- House
- Nation

Women: 17, 16.8, 51
Blacks: 1, 8.9, 13
Hispanics: 3, 6.4, 15.1
Asian: 2, 1.6, 5

Source: Amer and Manning 2008.

Many critics within minority communities decry what they term "fiesta politics." This refers to the tendency of White power brokers to visit racial and ethnic minority communities only when they need electoral support, making a quick appearance on a national or ethnic holiday to get their picture taken and then vanishing. When the election is over, they too often forget to consult the residents who supported them about community needs and concerns.

Female politicians may be enjoying more electoral success now than in the past, but there is evidence that the media cover them differently than male politicians. A content analysis of newspaper coverage of gubernatorial races showed that reporters wrote more often about a female candidate's personal life, appearance, or personality than a male candidate's, and less often about her political viewpoints and voting record. Furthermore, when political issues were raised in newspaper articles, reporters were more likely to illustrate them with statements made by male candidates than by female candidates (Devitt 1999; Jost 2008; Paxton et al. 2007).

While the proportion of women in national legislatures has increased in the United States and many other nations, women account for at least half the members of the national legislature in only one country. The African Republic of Rwanda ranks the highest, with 56.3 percent of its legislative seats held by women. Overall, the United States ranked 82nd among 187 nations in the proportion of women serving as national legislators in 2009 (Inter-Parliamentary Union 2009).

elite model A view of society as being ruled by a small group of individuals who share a common set of political and economic interests.

power elite A small group of military, industrial, and government leaders who control the fate of the United States.

To remedy this situation, many countries have adopted quotas for female representatives. In some, the government sets aside a certain percentage of seats for women, usually 10–30 percent. In others, political parties have decided that 20–40 percent of their candidates should be women. Thirty-two countries now have some kind of quota system (Vasagar 2005).

>> The Power Structure in the United States

The issue of power extends beyond just politics and the people who occupy formally recognized offices. Over the years, sociologists repeatedly have sought to discover who really holds power in the United States. Do "we the people" genuinely run the country through our elected representatives? Or does a small elite behind the scenes control both the government and the economic system? It is difficult to determine the location of power in a society as complex as the United States. In exploring this critical question, social scientists have developed two basic views of our nation's power structure: the power elite and the pluralist models.

POWER ELITE MODELS

Karl Marx believed that 19th-century representative democracy was essentially a sham. He argued that industrial societies were dominated by relatively small numbers of people who owned the factories and controlled natural resources. In Marx's view, government officials and military leaders were essentially servants of this capitalist class and followed their wishes. Therefore, any key decisions made by politicians inevitably reflected the interests of the dominant business owners. Like others who hold an **elite model** of power relations, Marx believed that society is ruled by a small group of individuals who share political and economic interests.

Mills' Model Sociologist C. Wright Mills, who developed the concept of the sociological imagination that we looked at in Chapter 1, put forth a model similar to Marx's in his pioneering work *The Power Elite* ([1956] 2000). Mills described a small group of military, industrial, and government leaders who controlled the fate of the United States—the **power elite.** Power rested in the hands of a few, both inside and outside government.

A pyramid illustrates the power structure of the United States in Mills' model. The power elite rests at the top and includes the corporate rich, leaders of the executive branch of government, and heads of the military (whom Mills called the "warlords"). Directly below are local opinion leaders, members of the legislative branch of government, and leaders of special-interest groups. Mills contended that these individuals and groups basically follow the wishes of the dom-

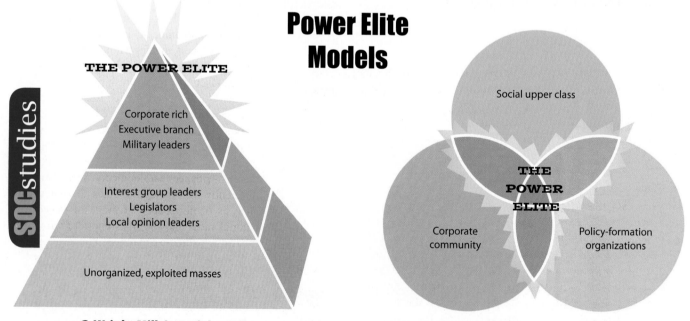

Power Elite Models

THE POWER ELITE

Corporate rich
Executive branch
Military leaders

Interest group leaders
Legislators
Local opinion leaders

Unorganized, exploited masses

SOCstudies

C. Wright Mills's model, 1956

Social upper class

THE POWER ELITE

Corporate community

Policy-formation organizations

G. William Domhoff's model, 2006

Source: Left, based on C. W. Mills (1956) 2000; right, Domhoff 2006:105.

Which Interests Are Best Represented?

Percentage of all Lobbying Expenditures by Organization

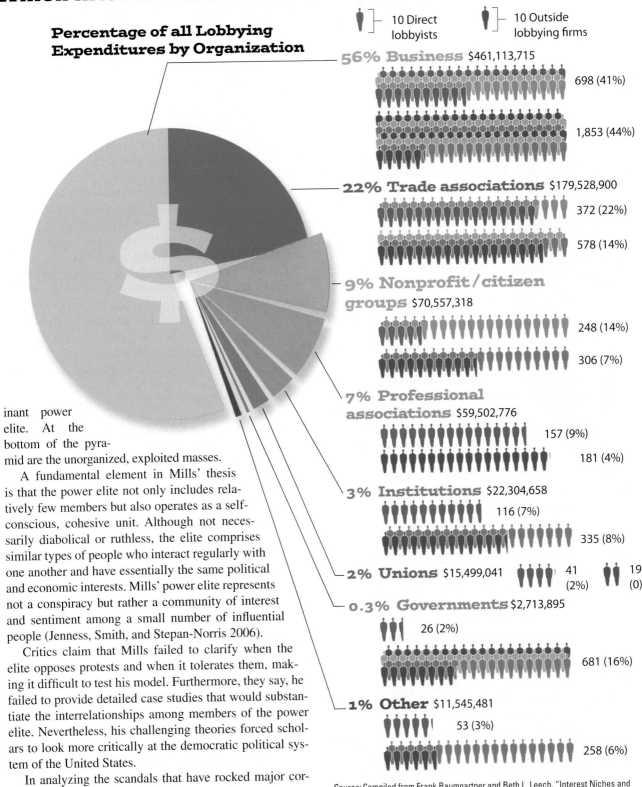

	10 Direct lobbyists	10 Outside lobbying firms

56% Business $461,113,715
698 (41%)
1,853 (44%)

22% Trade associations $179,528,900
372 (22%)
578 (14%)

9% Nonprofit / citizen groups $70,557,318
248 (14%)
306 (7%)

7% Professional associations $59,502,776
157 (9%)
181 (4%)

3% Institutions $22,304,658
116 (7%)
335 (8%)

2% Unions $15,499,041   41 (2%)   19 (0)

0.3% Governments $2,713,895
26 (2%)
681 (16%)

1% Other $11,545,481
53 (3%)
258 (6%)

Source: Compiled from Frank Baumgartner and Beth L. Leech, "Interest Niches and Policy Bandwagons: Patterns of Interest Group Involvement in National Politics," *Journal of Politics* 63 (4) 2001, Table 1, p. 1195, and Table 3, p. 1197.

inant power elite. At the bottom of the pyramid are the unorganized, exploited masses.

A fundamental element in Mills' thesis is that the power elite not only includes relatively few members but also operates as a self-conscious, cohesive unit. Although not necessarily diabolical or ruthless, the elite comprises similar types of people who interact regularly with one another and have essentially the same political and economic interests. Mills' power elite represents not a conspiracy but rather a community of interest and sentiment among a small number of influential people (Jenness, Smith, and Stepan-Norris 2006).

Critics claim that Mills failed to clarify when the elite opposes protests and when it tolerates them, making it difficult to test his model. Furthermore, they say, he failed to provide detailed case studies that would substantiate the interrelationships among members of the power elite. Nevertheless, his challenging theories forced scholars to look more critically at the democratic political system of the United States.

In analyzing the scandals that have rocked major corporations such as Enron and Arthur Andersen over the past decade, observers have noted that members of the business elite are closely interrelated. In a study of the members of the boards of directors of Fortune 1000 corporations, researchers found that each director can reach *every* other board of directors in just 3.7 steps. That is, by consulting acquaintances of acquaintances, each director can quickly reach someone who sits on each of the other 999 boards. Furthermore, the face-to-face contact directors regularly have in their board meetings makes them a highly cohesive elite. Finally, the corporate elite not only is wealthy, powerful, and cohesive but also is overwhelmingly White and male (G. Davis 2003, 2004; Kentor and Jang 2004; Mizruchi 1996; Strauss 2002).

Domhoff's Model Sociologist G. William Domhoff (2006, 2009) agrees with Mills that a powerful elite runs the United States. Domhoff stresses the role played by elites from within networks of organizations including the corporate community; policy formation organizations such as think tanks, chambers of commerce, and labor unions; and the social upper class. Membership in these groups overlaps, and members with connections in more than one of these spheres have more power and influence. Domhoff finds that those in this latter group are still largely White, male, and upper class, but he notes the presence of a small number of women and minority men in key positions—groups that were excluded from Mills' top echelon and are still underrepresented today (Zweigenhaft and Domhoff 2006).

Although the three groups in Domhoff's power elite model do overlap, they do not necessarily agree on specific policies. Domhoff notes that in politics, two different coalitions have exercised influence. A corporate-conservative coalition has played a large role in both political parties, generating support for particular candidates through direct-mail appeals. A liberal-labor coalition is based in unions, local environmental organizations, a segment of the minority group community, liberal churches, and the university and arts communities (Zweigenhaft and Domhoff 2006). This suggests that the interests of members of the power elite are not always singular or uniform but that overall they do work together to advance their larger interests.

THE PLURALIST MODEL

Other theorists argue that power in the United States is shared more widely, that there is no core group at the top who are able to advance their common interests. In their view, a pluralist model more accurately describes the nation's power structure. According to the **pluralist model,** many competing groups within the community have access to government, so that no single group is dominant.

The pluralist model suggests that a variety of groups play a significant role in decision making. Typically, pluralists make use of intensive case studies or community studies based on observation research. One of the most famous—an investiga-

tion of decision making in New Haven, Connecticut—was reported by Robert Dahl (1961). Dahl found that, although the number of people involved in any important decision was rather small, community power was nonetheless diffuse. Few political actors exercised decision-making power on all issues, and no one group got its way all the time. One individual or group might be influential in a battle over urban renewal but have little impact on educational policy.

The pluralist model, too, has its critics. Domhoff (1978, 2006) reexamined Dahl's study of decision making in New Haven and argued that Dahl and other pluralists had failed to trace how local elites who were prominent in decision making belonged to a larger national ruling class. In addition, studies of community power, such as Dahl's work in New Haven, can examine decision making only on issues that become part of the political agenda. They fail to address the potential power of elites to keep certain matters entirely out of the realm of political debate.

Dianne Pinderhughes (1987) has criticized the pluralist model for failing to account for the exclusion of African Americans from the political process. Drawing on her studies of Chicago politics, Pinderhughes points out that the residential and occupational segregation of Blacks and their long political disenfranchisement violate the logic of pluralism—which would hold that such a substantial minority should always have been influential in community decision making. This critique applies to many cities across the United States, where other large racial and ethnic minorities, among them Asian Americans, Puerto Ricans, and Mexican Americans, are relatively powerless.

Historically, pluralists have stressed ways in which large numbers of people can participate in or influence governmental decision making. New communications technologies like the Internet are increasing the opportunity to be heard, not just in countries like the United States but in developing countries the world over. The ability to communicate with political leaders via email, for example, increases the opportunity for the average citizen to have a voice in politics.

>> War and Peace

When it comes to political power, perhaps no decision is as weighty as the decision to go to war. Conflict is a central aspect of social relations. Sociologists Theodore Caplow and Louis Hicks (2002:3) have defined **war** as conflict between organizations that possess trained combat forces equipped with deadly weapons. This meaning is broader than the legal definition, which typically requires a formal declaration of hostilities.

WAR

Sociologists approach war in three different ways. Those who take a global view study how and why two or more nations

Hot or Not?

Is there a relatively small and unified group of powerful people in the United States who, in effect, rule the country through their power and influence?

U.S. Public Opinion on the Necessity of War, 1971–2007

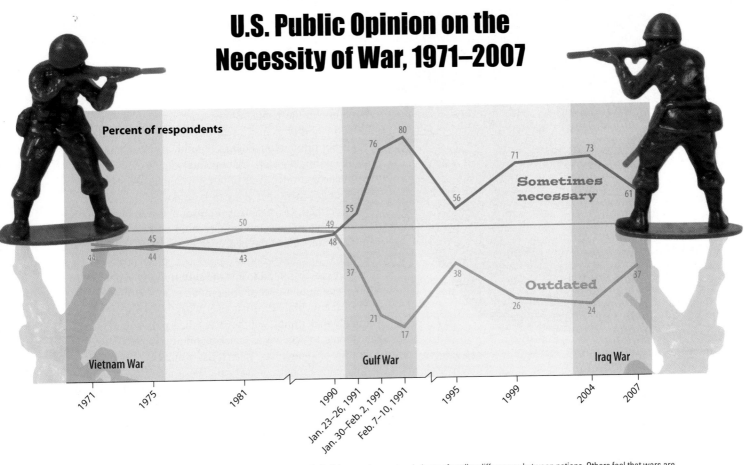

Percent of respondents

Sometimes necessary: 44, 45, 50, 49, 55, 76, 80, 56, 71, 73, 61

Outdated: 44, 43, 48, 37, 21, 17, 38, 26, 24, 37

Vietnam War   Gulf War   Iraq War

1971 1975 1981 1990 Jan. 23–26, 1991 Jan. 30–Feb. 2, 1991 Feb. 7–10, 1991 1995 1999 2004 2007

Note: Respondents replied to the following question: "Some people feel that war is an outmoded way of settling differences between nations. Others feel that wars are sometimes necessary to settle differences. With which point of view do you agree?"

Source: Gallup 2009.

become engaged in military conflict. Those who take a nation-state view stress the interaction of internal political, socioeconomic, and cultural forces. And those who take a micro view focus on the social impact of war on individuals and the groups to which they belong.

Analysis at the global level focuses on macro issues such as the distribution of resources, struggles over political philosophies, and debates about boundaries. Often it involves nations with competing political and economic systems, as was the case in World War I, World War II, and the Cold War. Some have argued that the conflict in Iraq is about bringing freedom and democracy to the Middle East, and others argue it was motivated by oil and profits.

Sociologists have devoted much effort to studying the internal decision-making process that leads to war. During the Vietnam War, Presidents Johnson and Nixon both misled Congress, painting a falsely optimistic picture of the likely outcome. Based on their intentional distortions, Congress appropriated the military funds the two administrations requested. However, in 1971, *The New York Times* published a set of classified documents now known as "The Pentagon Papers," which revealed that many members of both administrations had knowingly distorted the real prospects for the war. Two years later—over Nixon's veto—Congress passed the War Powers Act, which requires the president to notify Congress of the reasons for committing combat troops to a hostile situation (Patterson 2003).

Even though government leaders make the decision to go to war, public opinion plays a significant role in its execution. By 1971, the number of U.S. soldiers killed in Vietnam had surpassed 50,000, and antiwar sentiment was strong. Surveys done at that time showed that the public was split roughly equally on the question of whether war was an appropriate way to settle differences between nations (see the figure above). This division in public opinion continued until the United States led the charge in the Gulf War following Iraq's invasion of Kuwait in 1990. Since then, however, support for war has declined.

pluralist model A view of society in which many competing groups within the community have access to government, so that no single group is dominant.
war Conflict between organizations that possess trained combat forces equipped with deadly weapons.

A major change relating to the conduct of war involves the composition of the U.S. military. Women represent a growing presence among the troops. Almost 200,000 women, or about 20 percent of U.S. military forces, are now in uniform, serving not just as support personnel but as an integral part of combat units. The first casualty of the war in Iraq, in fact, was Private First Class Lori Piestewa, a member of the Hopi tribe and a descendant of Mexican

During World War II, the U.S. government sponsored films to garner support for the war effort, boost people's morale, and even demonize the enemy. From cartoons featuring Mickey Mouse and Donald Duck to films including *This Is the Army* (which starred Ronald Reagan), Hollywood cooperated in getting the message out in the 1940s. In more recent years, antiwar films have also raised difficult questions that governments would sometimes rather not be aired. During the Cold War, *Dr. Strangelove* called into question the insanity of the nuclear standoff; in 1970, the film version of *M*A*S*H*, though set in Korea, raised questions about the conflict in Vietnam. More recently, there have been numerous films about the war in Iraq, including Michael Moore's *Fahrenheit 9/11, No End in Sight, Stop-Loss,* and *War, Inc.*

mentary film about the experiment to train military interrogators to avoid mistreatment of prisoners (Zarembo 2004).

TERRORISM

As people in the United States learned on September 11, 2001, the ability to instill fear through large-scale violent acts is not limited to recognized political states, and it can involve political groups that operate outside the bounds of legitimate authority. Acts of terror, whether perpetrated by a few or by many people, can be a powerful force. Formally defined, **terrorism** is the use or threat of violence against random or symbolic targets in pursuit of political aims. For terrorists, the end justifies the means. They believe that the status quo is oppressive and that desperate measures are essential to end the suffering of the deprived.

An essential aspect of contemporary terrorism involves use of the media. Terrorists may wish to keep secret their individual identities, but they want their political messages and goals to receive as much publicity as possible. The purpose of many acts of terrorist violence is more symbolic than strategic or tactical. These attacks represent a statement made by people who feel that the world has gone awry, that accepted political paths to problem resolution are ineffective or blocked, and that there is a larger or cosmic struggle going on, raising the stakes and so justifying the means (Juergensmeyer 2003). Whether through calls to the media, anonymous manifestos, or other means, terrorists typically admit responsibility for and defend their violent acts.

Terrorism is a global concern. Since September 11, 2001, governments around the world have renewed their efforts to fight terrorism. Even though the public generally regards increased surveillance and social control as

Aftermath of a 2009 suicide blast attack of a five-star hotel in Pakistan.

settlers in the Southwest (Bureau of the Census 2007a: Table 503).

At the level of interpersonal interaction, war can bring out the worst as well as the best in people. In 2004, graphic images of the abuse of Iraqi prisoners by U.S. soldiers at Iraq's Abu Ghraib prison shocked the world. For social scientists, the deterioration of the guards' behavior brought to mind Philip Zimbardo's mock prison experiment, in which volunteer guards in a simulated prison acted sadistically toward volunteer prisoneers. In July 2004, the U.S. military began using a docu-

a necessary evil, these measures have nonetheless raised governance issues. For example, some citizens in the United States and elsewhere have expressed concern that measures such as the USA PATRIOT Act of 2001 threaten civil liberties. Citizens also complain about the heightened anxiety created by the vague "terror alerts" the federal government issues from time to time. Worldwide, immigration and the processing of refugees have slowed to a crawl, separating families and preventing employers from filling job openings. As these efforts to combat political violence illustrate, the term *terrorism* is an apt one (R. Howard and Sawyer 2003).

PEACE

Sociologists have considered **peace** both as the absence of war and as a proactive effort to develop cooperative relations among nations. It is impor-

tant to note, however, that armed conflict involves more than just warring nations. From 1945 to the end of the 20th century, the 25 major wars that occurred between countries killed a total of 3.3 million people. While this is significant, the 127 civil wars that occurred in the same time period resulted in 16 million deaths. In other words, five times as many people died as a result of conflicts *within* nations than died in wars *between* nations (Fearon and Laitin 2003).

> **terrorism** The use or threat of violence against random or symbolic targets in pursuit of political aims.
> **peace** The absence of war, or more broadly, a proactive effort to develop cooperative relations among nations.

Sociologists and other social scientists who draw on sociological theory and research have tried to identify conditions that deter war. One of their findings is that international trade may act as a deterrent to armed conflict. As countries exchange goods, people, and then cultures, they become more integrated and less likely to threaten each other's security. Viewed from this perspective, not just trade but also immigration and foreign exchange programs have a beneficial effect on international relations.

Another means of fostering peace is the activity of international charities and activist groups, or nongovernmental

Going GLOBAL

The Global Reach of Terrorism

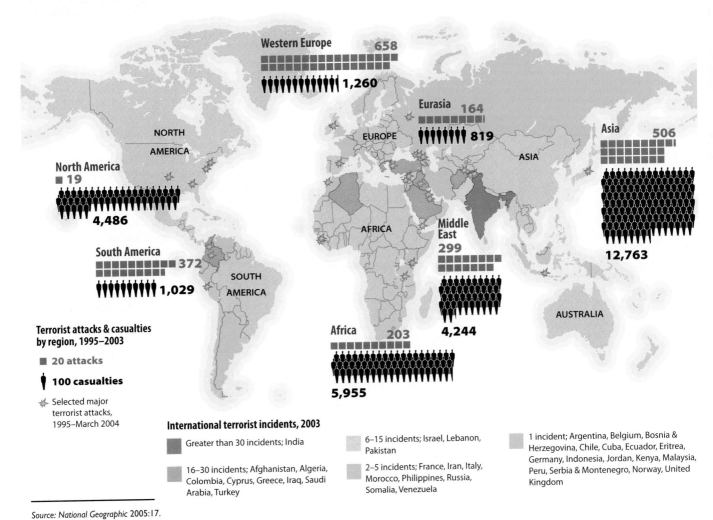

Terrorist attacks & casualties by region, 1995–2003

■ 20 attacks

♦ 100 casualties

⚝ Selected major terrorist attacks, 1995–March 2004

North America ■ 19 / 4,486
South America 372 / 1,029
Western Europe 658 / 1,260
Eurasia 164 / 819
Asia 506 / 12,763
Africa 203 / 5,955
Middle East 299 / 4,244

International terrorist incidents, 2003

▮ Greater than 30 incidents; India

▮ 16–30 incidents; Afghanistan, Algeria, Colombia, Cyprus, Greece, Iraq, Saudi Arabia, Turkey

▮ 6–15 incidents; Israel, Lebanon, Pakistan

▮ 2–5 incidents; France, Iran, Italy, Morocco, Philippines, Russia, Somalia, Venezuela

▮ 1 incident; Argentina, Belgium, Bosnia & Herzegovina, Chile, Cuba, Ecuador, Eritrea, Germany, Indonesia, Jordan, Kenya, Malaysia, Peru, Serbia & Montenegro, Norway, United Kingdom

Source: National Geographic 2005:17.

organizations (NGOs). The Red Cross and Red Crescent, Doctors Without Borders, and Amnesty International donate their services wherever they are needed, without regard to nationality. In the past decade or so, these NGOs have been expanding in number, size, and scope. By sharing news of local conditions and clarifying local issues, they often prevent conflicts from escalating into violence and war. Some NGOs have initiated cease-fires, reached settlements, and even ended warfare between former adversaries.

Finally, many analysts stress that nations cannot maintain their security by threatening violence. Peace, they contend, can best be maintained by developing strong mutual security agreements among potential adversaries (Etzioni 1965; Shostak 2002). Following this path involves active diplomacy and, to the extent that it involves negotiations with countries viewed as enemies, can be controversial.

From Snapper mowers to microloans to peace movements, stories such as these provide hope. Even though large-scale economic trends can have negative impacts on companies, communities, and individuals, as well as shaping political outcomes, positive social change is possible. Sociological analysis helps us to see the underlying processes at work in the economy and politics, and in so doing can assist us in recognizing places in those systems where opportunities for bringing about such change exist.

get involved!

Investigate! Who contributed and how much to the senators and representatives in your state? What interests do those contributors represent? OpenSecrets.org provides an easily searchable database to track down who gives what to whom.

For REVIEW

I. **How is economic and political power organized?**

- The two major economic systems are capitalism and socialism, though in practice most economies are some mix of the two. Political systems of government include monarchy, oligarchy, dictatorship, totalitarianism, and democracy. A debate exists when looking at formal power in the United States about the degree to which there is a small, cohesive group of power elites who effectively rule or if leadership is more diverse and pluralistic, operating through democratic processes.

II. **How does power operate?**

- Power involves the capacity to get others to do what you want, which can involve force, influence, and authority. In the case of authority, followers accept your power as legitimate, whether based on a traditional, rational-legal, or charismatic foundation.

III. **How has the economy changed over time?**

- The rise of a global economy has brought with it a changing composition of the national and international workforce, deindustrialization, and in the form of microfinancing, economic opportunities for people who are poor.

Pop Quiz

1. Which source of power depends primarily on persuasion to achieve its goals?
   a. oligarchy
   b. influence
   c. force
   d. authority

2. Which of the following is *not* part of the classification system of authority developed by Max Weber?
   a. traditional authority
   b. pluralist authority
   c. legal-rational authority
   d. charismatic authority

3. Under capitalism, laissez-faire means that
   a. the means of production and distribution in a society are collectively held.
   b. people should compete freely, with minimal government intervention in the economy.
   c. a single business firm controls the market.
   d. society depends on mechanization to produce its goods and services.

4. Transfers of money, goods, and services that take place but are not reported to the government are best described as
   a. globalization.
   b. the mixed economy.
   c. laissez-faire capitalism.
   d. the informal economy.

5. The systematic, widespread withdrawal of investment in basic aspects of productivity such as factories and plants is called
   a. deindustrialization.
   b. downsizing.
   c. postindustrialization.
   d. gentrification.

6. Political scientist Harold Lasswell defined *politics* as
   a. the struggle for power and authority.
   b. the allocation of valued resources.
   c. who gets what, when, and how.
   d. a cultural universal.

7. The type of government in which a few individuals rule is known as
   a. a monarchy.
   b. a democracy.
   c. a dictatorship.
   d. an oligarchy.

8. Comparing voter turnout in the United States to that of other nations, the United States ranks
   a. first with the highest level of turnout.
   b. in the top 10 internationally.
   c. in about the top third of all nations.
   d. in the bottom half of all nations.

9. According to C. Wright Mills, power rests in the hands of the
   a. people.
   b. power elite.
   c. aristocracy.
   d. representative democracy.

10. The use or threat of violence against random or symbolic targets in pursuit of political aims is referred to as
    a. politics.
    b. power.
    c. terrorism.
    d. authority.

1. (b); 2. (b); 3. (b); 4. (d); 5. (a); 6. (c); 7. (d); 8. (d); 9. (b); 10. (c)

10

SOCIAL C

LIVING THE GOOD LIFE— OR NOT

Grayer is four years old. He takes lessons in French, Latin, music, swimming, ice skating, karate, and physical education—in addition to attending preschool. When he failed to get into the elite kindergarten of her choice, his mother hired a grief counselor for him. He lives on Park Avenue in Manhattan with his mother and father, but the person with whom he spends most of his time is his nanny.

Grayer's fictional character was drawn from the real-life experiences of Emma McLaughlin and Nicola Kraus (2002), who worked as nannies to help pay their way through college. They told their stories in the book *The Nanny Diaries,* which later became a film (2007). They depict a world in which, like ours, social class matters.

Sima, one of the nannies in the novel, was an engineer in her home country of El Salvador. She came to the United States with her husband and children, but when he was unable to obtain a green card her husband went back to El Salvador with the kids. Nan, the main nanny character in the book, refers to Sima as "a woman who has a higher degree than I will ever receive, in a subject I couldn't get a passing grade in, and who has been home [to see her husband and children] less than one month in the last twenty-four" (p. 173).

In her book, *Just Like Family,* Tasha Blaine (2009), found that the story of immigrant women leaving their own families for months or years at a time to raise the children of others is hardly unique. After interviewing more than 100 nannies, she found that women like Sima often felt guilty about leaving their children behind but did so in hopes of providing a better life for them. She also found that nannies often are caught between being treated as an employee and "like family," increasing the possibility that nannies will be taken advantage of in the workplace. In this chapter we see how the social class positions we occupy, from corporate executive to nanny, shape our hopes, dreams, and likely outcomes.

LASS

As You READ >>

- What is social class?
- How does social class operate?
- What are the consequences of social class?

>> Understanding Stratification

Social class was among the earliest interests of sociologists and remains of interest to this day. Marx, Weber, and Durkheim all highlighted the significance of class differences and sought to understand both their causes and consequences. Du Bois and Addams carried this a step further, actually working to ameliorate the excesses of social stratification.

In the United States, however, social class has long been a touchy subject (DeMott 1990). When the topic of social class does come up here, many people's first response is to deny that it exists. Some even angrily argue that opportunity is open to everyone and that individual effort alone determines one's life outcome. From a sociological perspective, however, we must understand the consequences of social class differences if we are to understand why we think and act the way we do. This is especially true in capitalist societies, in which the significance of economic position is heightened. To provide context, we begin by considering the varieties of ways in which societies are stratified.

SYSTEMS OF STRATIFICATION

Ever since people first began to speculate about the nature of human society, they have focused on the differences between individuals and groups within society. The term **social inequality** describes a condition in which members of society have different amounts of wealth, prestige, or power. Some degree of social inequality characterizes every society. Sociologists refer to social inequality that

is built into the structure of society as **stratification**—the structured ranking of entire groups of people that perpetuates unequal economic rewards and power in a society.

Stratification shapes individual opportunity based on the level that one occupies in the system. Certain groups of people stand higher in social rankings, control scarce resources, wield power, and receive special treatment. Unequal rewards include income and wealth, but they are also related to the power conveyed by social networks (who you know) and knowledge (what you know). Control over such resources enables one generation to pass on social advantages to the next, producing groups of people arranged in rank order, from low to high.

Sociologists focus on four major systems of stratification: slavery, caste, estate, and class. To understand these systems better, it is helpful to recall the distinction between achieved status and ascribed status from Chapter 5. **Ascribed status** is a social position assigned to a person by society without regard for his or her unique talents or characteristics. In contrast, **achieved status** is a social position that a person attains largely through his or her own efforts. The nation's most affluent families generally inherit wealth and status, while many members of racial and ethnic minorities inherit disadvantaged status. Age and gender are additional ascribed statuses that influence a person's wealth and social position.

Slavery The most extreme form of legalized social inequality for individuals and groups is **slavery.** Enslaved individuals are the property of other people, who have the right to treat them as they please, as if they were tools or draft animals.

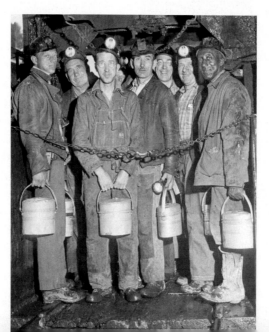

Did You Know?

...There are approximately 12 million people worldwide who are enslaved today. About 80 percent of them are female, and half are children, according to the International Labour Organization.

The practice of slavery has varied over different times and places. Most of the slaves in ancient Greece were prisoners of war or individuals captured and sold by pirates. Although succeeding generations could inherit slave status, it was not necessarily permanent. A person's status might change, depending on which city-state happened to triumph in a military conflict. In effect, all citizens had the potential to become slaves or gain freedom, depending on the historical circumstances. By contrast, slavery in the United States and Latin America was an ascribed status, and slaves faced racial and legal barriers to freedom.

Today, the Universal Declaration of Human Rights, which is binding on all members of the United Nations, prohibits slavery in all its forms. Yet around the world, millions of people still live as slaves. In many developing countries, bonded laborers are imprisoned in virtual lifetime employment; in some countries, human beings are owned outright. Though slavery is outlawed in the United States and Europe, guest workers and illegal immigrants have been forced to labor for years under terrible conditions, either to pay off debts or to avoid being turned over to immigration authorities. In 2007 a wealthy couple from New York was convicted of holding two Indonesian women as slaves in their home for four years (Eltman 2007; Greenhouse 2007).

Castes Castes are hereditary ranks, usually dictated by religion, that tend to be fixed and immobile. The caste system is generally associated with Hinduism in India and other countries. In India there are four major castes, or *varnas*: priests (*Brahman*), warriors (*Kshatriya*), merchants (*Vaishya*), and artisans/farmers (*Shudra*). A fifth category of outcastes, referred to as the *dalit,* or untouchables, is considered to be so lowly and unclean as to have no place within this system of stratification. There are also many minor castes. Caste membership is an ascribed status (at birth, children automatically assume the same position as their parents). Each caste is quite sharply defined, and members are expected to marry within that caste.

In 1950, after gaining independence from Great Britain, India adopted a new constitution that formally outlawed

> **social inequality** A condition in which members of society have different amounts of wealth, prestige, or power.
> **stratification** A structured ranking of entire groups of people that perpetuates unequal economic rewards and power in a society.
> **ascribed status** A social position assigned to a person by society without regard for the person's unique talents or characteristics.
> **achieved status** A social position that a person attains largely through his or her own efforts.
> **slavery** A system of enforced servitude in which some people are owned by others as property.
> **caste** A hereditary rank, usually religiously dictated, that tends to be fixed and immobile.

the caste system. Over the past decade or two, however, urbanization and technological advances have brought more change to India's caste system than the government has in more than half a century. The anonymity of city life tends to blur caste boundaries, allowing the *dalit* to pass unrecognized in temples, schools, and workplaces. The globalization of high technology also has opened up India's social order, bringing new opportunities to those who possess the skills and ability to capitalize on them, regardless of caste.

Estates A third type of stratification system developed within the feudal societies of medieval Europe. Under the **estate system,** or feudalism, nobles owned the land, which they leased to peasants who worked it and lived on it. The peasants turned over a portion of what they produced to the landowner, who in return offered the peasants military protection against bandits and rival nobles. The basis for the system was the nobles' ownership of land, which was critical to their superior and privileged status. As in systems based on slavery and caste, inheritance of one's position largely defined the estate system. The nobles inherited their titles and property; the peasants were born into a subservient position within an agrarian society.

As the estate system developed, it became more differentiated. Nobles began to achieve varying degrees of authority. By the 12th century, a priesthood had emerged in most of Europe, along with classes of merchants and artisans. For the first time, there were groups of people whose wealth did not depend on land ownership or agriculture. This economic change had profound social consequences as the estate system ended and a class system of stratification came into existence.

Social Classes A **class system** is a social ranking based primarily on economic position in which achieved characteristics can influence social mobility. In contrast to slavery and caste systems, in a class system the boundaries between classes are imprecisely defined, and one can move from one stratum, or level, of society to another. Even so, class systems maintain stable stratification hierarchies and patterns of class divisions, and they, too, are marked by an unequal distribution of wealth and power. Class standing, though it can be achieved, is heavily dependent on family and on ascribed factors such as race and ethnicity.

Sociologists commonly use a five-class model to describe the class system in the United States: upper, upper-middle, lower-middle, working, and lower class (Beeghley 2007; Rossides 1997). Although the lines separating social classes are not as sharp as the divisions between castes, there are differences between the five classes in terms of key resources. Among these are income, occupation, bureaucratic authority, educational attainment, social networks, and political connections.

The upper class, or capitalist class, is the smallest and most exclusive, including 1–2 percent of the U.S. population. Members are wealthy, well respected, and politically powerful. On the other end of the spectrum is the lower class, also known as the underclass, or the poor. This class, 15–20 percent of the population, has limited access to the paid labor force, lacks wealth, and is too weak politically to exert significant power. It consists of a disproportionate number of Blacks, Hispanics, single mothers with dependent children, and recent immigrants.

Sandwiched between these two classes are the upper-middle, lower-middle, and working classes. The upper-

SOCthink

> > > People with incomes well above average often prefer to identify themselves as middle class. Why might they do this? How might this tendency be an outgrowth of the dominant American values of equality and democracy?

middle class is composed of business executives and upper-level management (a subset called the corporate class), doctors, lawyers, architects, and other professionals. Comprising about 15 percent of the population, they participate extensively in politics and take leadership roles in voluntary associations. The lower-middle class, sometimes simply referred to as the middle class, includes less affluent professionals (such as elementary school teachers and nurses), owners of small businesses, and a sizable number of clerical workers. Although not all members of this varied class hold a college degree, they typically hope to send their children to college. They make up 30–35 percent of the population.

Members of the working class, who make up the remaining 30–35 percent of population, usually hold jobs that involve manual labor. Some blue-collar members of this class, such as electricians, may have higher incomes than people in the middle class. Yet even if they have achieved some degree of economic security, they tend to identify with manual workers and have a long history of involvement in the labor movement. Of the five classes, the working class faces the greatest declines in the United States as jobs that once required physical labor are taken over by machines, or sent abroad where labor is cheaper.

SOCthink

> > > Into which class would you place most of the people in your community? Are there relatively clear boundaries between class neighborhoods there?

SOCIAL MOBILITY

A key component of each of these systems of stratification is **social mobility**—the degree to which one

can change the social stratum into which one is born. The ascent of a person from a poor background to a position of prestige, power, or financial reward—such as in the movie *Maid in Manhattan*—is an example of social mobility. In the film, Jennifer Lopez plays a chambermaid in a big-city hotel who rises to become a company supervisor and the girlfriend of a well-to-do politician. While stories in which the commoner marries the prince truly were fairy tales in the era of the estate system, today they are metaphors for the seeming permeability of modern class boundaries.

Open Versus Closed Stratification Systems

Sociologists distinguish between stratification systems that are open versus closed to indicate the degree of social mobility in a society. An **open system** implies that a person's achieved status influences his or her social position. Such a system encourages competition among members of society. The United States has sought to move toward this ideal by removing once-legal barriers faced by women, racial and ethnic minorities, and people born in lower social classes.

At the other extreme is the **closed system,** which allows little or no possibility of individual social mobility. Caste systems are examples of closed systems. In such societies, social placement is based on ascribed statuses, such as race or family background, which cannot be changed.

Types of Social Mobility Sociologists also distinguish between mobility within a strata versus movement between levels. For example, a bus driver who becomes a hotel clerk moves from one social position to another of approximately the same rank. Sociologists call this kind of movement

estate system A system of stratification under which peasants were required to work land leased to them by nobles in exchange for military protection and other services. Also known as feudalism.
class system A social ranking based primarily on economic position in which achieved characteristics can influence social mobility.
social mobility Movement of individuals or groups from one position in a society's stratification system to another.
open system A social system in which the position of each individual is influenced by his or her achieved status.
closed system A social system in which there is little or no possibility of individual social mobility.

horizontal mobility The movement of an individual from one social position to another of the same rank.

vertical mobility The movement of an individual from one social position to another of a different rank.

intergenerational mobility Changes in the social position of children relative to their parents.

intragenerational mobility Changes in social position within a person's adult life.

capitalism An economic system in which the means of production are held largely in private hands and the main incentive for economic activity is the accumulation of profits.

horizontal mobility. However, if the bus driver were to become a lawyer, he or she would experience **vertical mobility**—the movement of an individual from one social position to another of a different rank (Sorokin [1927] 1959). Vertical mobility can also involve moving downward in a society's stratification system, as would be the case if the lawyer became a bus driver.

Sociologists also consider the differences between intergenerational and intragenerational mobility when evaluating mobility. **Intergenerational mobility** involves changes in the social position of children relative to their parents. Thus, a plumber whose father was a physician provides an example of downward intergenerational mobility. A film star whose parents were both factory workers illustrates upward intergenerational mobility. Because education contributes significantly to upward mobility, any barrier to the pursuit of advanced degrees can definitely limit intergenerational mobility (Isaacs et al. 2008).

Intragenerational mobility, on the other hand, involves changes in social position within a person's adult life. Thus, a woman who enters the paid labor force as a teacher's aide and eventually becomes superintendent of the school district experiences upward intragenerational mobility. A man who becomes a cab driver after his accounting firm goes bankrupt undergoes downward intragenerational mobility.

SOCthink

> > > What is the story of social mobility in your family? To what extent have there been shifts both across and within generations? What factors, such as family connections or historical events, contributed to the social mobility that occurred?

In the United States, one way to define the "American Dream" is as upward vertical mobility that is intragenerational. In other words, a person could experience a significant shift in social class position over the course of her or his career, from a relatively low-level position to one of significant wealth and power. While this does happen, as we will see below, the "American reality" is that we tend to end up in positions relatively close to where we began.

SOCIOLOGICAL PERSPECTIVES ON STRATIFICATION

Sociologists have examined the relative significance of key resources that shape social stratification. Early in the development of sociology, Karl Marx argued that material resources were most important, especially ownership of the means of production. Max Weber, who sought to extend Marx's model and make it more broadly applicable, argued that three primary resources shape social position: class, status, and party. More recently, Pierre Bourdieu has highlighted the significance of culture as an additional resource. We will look at each of their models in turn.

Marx on Class Karl Marx has been aptly described as both a revolutionary and a social scientist. Marx was concerned with stratification in all types of human societies, beginning with primitive agricultural tribes and continuing into feudalism. But his main focus was on the effects of economic inequality on all aspects of his own society—19th-century Europe. The plight of the working class made him feel that it was imperative to strive for changes in the class structure of society.

In Marx's view, social relations during any period of history depend on who controls the

5 Movies on SOCIAL CLASS

Bread and Roses
Poorly paid janitors struggle to unionize in Los Angeles.

The Breakfast Club
Teenagers from five different high school cliques spend a day in detention.

The Pursuit of Happyness
Striving to move up in American society.

Trouble the Water
Two street hustlers become heroes in the aftermath of Hurricane Katrina.

Pride and Prejudice
Social class dictates young women's lives in 19th-century English society.

primary mode of economic production, such as land or factories. Differential access to scarce resources shapes the relationship between groups. Under the feudal estate system, most production was agricultural, and the nobility owned the land. Peasants had little choice but to work according to terms dictated by the landowners.

Using this type of analysis, Marx examined social relations within **capitalism**—the economic system in which private individuals control the means of production and the main incentive for economic activity is the accumulation of

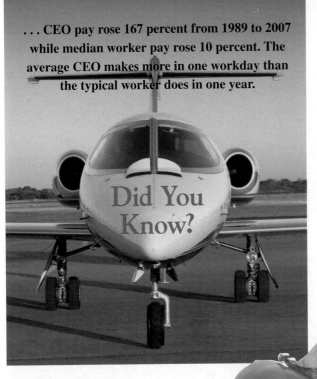

Hot or Not?

Is a classless society possible?

profits. Marx focused on the two classes that began to emerge as the feudal estate system declined: the bourgeoisie and the proletariat. The **bourgeoisie,** or capitalist class, owns the means of production, such as factories and machinery; the **proletariat** is the working class. In capitalist societies, the members of the bourgeoisie maximize profit in competition with other firms. To keep profits up, they seek to drive wages down. They do so by simplifying labor through machine production, thus reducing the skills workers need to do their jobs. Because less skill is required, the pool of potential workers expands, making workers more interchangeable. This undercuts existing workers' ability to insist on higher wages.

According to Marx, exploitation of the proletariat would inevitably lead to the destruction of the capitalist system, because the workers would revolt. Two keys help us to understand why: the problem of scarcity and the capitalist system of social relations. Marx believed that humans had to produce in order to survive, but as we saw in Chapter 1, how we do so is not narrowly determined by our genes. Our natural creative capacity, Marx believed, would lead to technological innovation that would make it possible for us to produce enough food, clothes, shelter, and other goods so eventually everyone would have more than enough. Capitalism actually encourages such technological innovation in the context of the competitive marketplace.

Once this technological obstacle to providing for all our needs was solved, Marx felt that the only obstacle to an equitable society would be the capitalist system of social relations. Its emphasis on private property enabled the few at the top, the bourgeoisie, to own and control much more than they could ever hope to need or want while the majority at the bottom, the proletariat, struggled. Eventually, Marx argued, the proletariat would see that they had no real interest in the existing set of social relations. They would develop **class consciousness**—a subjective awareness of common vested interests and the need for collective political action to bring about social change. This would lead to the overthrow of capitalism in favor of a system of more equitable distribution in the form of socialism and then communism.

A question that often arises in response to Marx's work is this: Why hasn't that revolution happened? One answer is that Marx thought capitalists would work against the development of such class consciousness by shaping society's accepted values and norms. The term **dominant ideology** describes a set of cultural beliefs and practices that helps to maintain powerful social, economic, and political interests. Private property is a core principle of this ideology, but our failure to recognize the collective efforts that go into the production of any products and services contributes as well. For Marx, the bourgeoisie controlled not only material resources but also the means of producing beliefs about reality through religion, education, and the media (Abercrombie et al. 1980, 1990; Marx [1845] 2000). As a result, workers had to overcome what Marx termed **false consciousness**—an attitude held by members of a class that does not accurately reflect their objective position. A worker with false consciousness may adopt an individualistic viewpoint toward capitalist exploitation ("*I* am being exploited by *my* boss"). In contrast, the class-conscious worker realizes that all workers are being exploited by the bourgeoisie and have a common stake in revolution.

Weber's Multidimensional Model

Unlike Marx, Max Weber insisted that class does not totally define a person's position within the stratification system. Instead, writing in 1916, he identified three distinct components of stratification: class, status, and party (Weber [1916] 1958a). These three point to the importance of material, social, and organizational resources in shaping how much power people have.

Weber used the term **class** to refer to a group of people who have a similar level of economic resources. He agreed with Marx

> **bourgeoisie** Karl Marx's term for the capitalist class, comprising the owners of the means of production.
> **proletariat** Karl Marx's term for the working class in a capitalist society.
> **class consciousness** In Karl Marx's view, a subjective awareness held by members of a class regarding their common vested interests and need for collective political action to bring about social change.
> **dominant ideology** A set of cultural beliefs and practices that helps to maintain powerful social, economic, and political interests.
> **false consciousness** A term used by Karl Marx to describe an attitude held by members of a class that does not accurately reflect their objective position.
> **class** A group of people who have a similar level of economic resources.

that this includes ownership of the means of production, but he went further than Marx, adding income, wealth, and skill knowledge to the equation. Regarding such knowledge, Marx thought that mechanization and extreme division of labor would make skill less significant under capitalism. But Weber argued that skill would continue to be a valuable commodity in the labor market and that by developing our skill knowledge—for example, by going to college—we could enhance our class position. For Weber, people who shared similar economic positions, such as workers in minimum-wage jobs, were in the same class. Although Weber agreed with Marx on the importance of this economic dimension of stratification, he argued that social power cannot be understood solely in economic terms.

Class represents an economic resource, whereas status is a social resource. We gain or lose power as a consequence of the social groups to which we belong. Weber used the term **status group** to refer to people who have the same prestige or lifestyle. Membership in a highly regarded group (e.g., MDs or Supreme Court justices) "has its privileges," but being part of other groups (e.g., hotel clerks or janitors) can convey disadvantage. Furthermore, participation in such groups often limits our social interactions with others whom the group sees as outsiders. Such memberships are often associated with a particular lifestyle, including the kind of car you drive or vacations you take, but status is not the same as economic class standing. In our culture, a successful pickpocket may belong to the same income class as a college professor. Yet the thief is widely regarded as a member of a low-status group, whereas the professor holds high status.

For Weber, the third major component of stratification involved organizational resources. **Party** refers to the capacity to organize to accomplish some particular goal. This is what we mean when we talk of a political party, but such organization extends beyond politics to all spheres of life. As we have seen before with Weber, bureaucracies represent the ideal form of this resource because they are organized explicitly to maximize available resources and to accomplish their goals in the most efficient manner possible. For Weber, party was a potential resource, available to any individuals or groups who would seize it. The civil rights movement in the United States provides a classic example. With minimal class or status resources as defined by the larger society, organization was critical to the success of this movement.

SOCthink

> > > How might a group coordinate their class, status, and party resources to accomplish their goals? Pick a group on campus or in your community that is seeking to bring about social change, and imagine how you might advise them using Weber's principles.

Weber maintained that, in practice, these three resources work together to shape individual and group power. Each factor influences the other two, and in fact the rankings on these three dimensions often tend to coincide. For example, John F. Kennedy came from an extremely wealthy family, attended exclusive preparatory schools, graduated

From Me to You

As a professor, I have seen that grades are shaped by more than just effort and intellectual ability. Students with more cultural capital, including significant background educational resources, simply do not have to work as hard. Seniors in my introductory course, for example, know the rules of the game. In comparison, first-year students often have a hard time distinguishing what is essential versus what is secondary. Over time, however, most learn how to study effectively. This same principle is at work before students even arrive on campus. Students who come to college with the kinds of cultural capital that professors reward have advantages over those who lack such resources.

"middle-brow" or below. People draw distinctions, for example, between watching *Masterpiece* on PBS versus *I Survived a Japanese Game Show* and listening to Pavarotti versus Celine Dion. Such judgments are based on a certain level of cultural elitism in which those at the top are able to define their preferences as apparently superior to those of the masses (Wilson 2007). The cultural capital of people who are working class, often disparaged as redneck or ghetto, is valued least of all—until it is claimed by others as their own, as was the case with jazz, blues, rock and roll, and rap (Gans 1971).

> **status group** People who have the same prestige or lifestyle, independent of their class positions.
> **party** The capacity to organize to accomplish some particular goal.
> **cultural capital** Our tastes, knowledge, attitudes, language, and ways of thinking that we exchange in interaction with others.

When we interact with others, we draw on the cultural capital resources we possess. Such interaction is fairly easy with others who share the same basic set of resources. When interaction occurs with others who possess a different stock of cultural capital, however, it becomes more complex. We see these kinds of difficulties when executives try to interact casually with workers on the factory floor or when we find ourselves dining in a place where we aren't quite sure what the rules are. If this were only a matter of social difference between various subcultures, it might not be a big deal. But the cultural capital of the elite is also tied to their control over economic and social resources. As a result, cultural capital can be used as a

from Harvard University, and went on to become president of the United States. Like Kennedy, many people from affluent backgrounds achieve high status and demonstrate impressive political organization.

Bourdieu and Cultural Capital Marx emphasized material resources, and Weber highlighted the significance of social resources in the form of both status and party. Sociologist Pierre Bourdieu added to these the significance of cultural resources. Bourdieu introduced the concept of **cultural capital,** by which he meant our tastes, knowledge, attitudes, language, and ways of thinking that we exchange in interaction with others. Often associated with artistic or literary preferences, cultural capital goes much deeper than this as it is rooted in our perception of reality itself. For Bourdieu, because culture is hierarchically valued, it is a form of power.

Bourdieu argued that people in different social class positions possess different types of cultural capital. From NASCAR to Mozart, for example, the tastes of the working class differ from those of the upper class. Symphonic concerts, operas, and foreign films, for instance, are considered "high culture," whereas "pop culture," including popular movies, TV shows, and music CDs, is considered

Whether it is the rags-to-riches dreams of *American Idol,* the glitz and glamour of *Dancing with the Stars,* the upper-middle-class aspirations of *The Apprentice,* or the conspicuous consumption of *Pimp My Ride,* TV shows have found social class lifestyle differences a tempting topic. Perhaps no program uses the contrast between class preferences as effectively, however, as does *Wife Swap* on ABC. In this show, two wives/mothers switch families for two weeks, frequently pitting families from different social classes against each other. The tension between their cultural capital resources is on display, highlighting the contrast between the two family environments.

form of exclusion from jobs, organizations, and opportunities. For example, a qualified applicant may lose out on a job during the interview due to inappropriate syntax or inadequate familiarity with cultural references, such as current news events or the latest in the world of golf. Employers tend to hire people they feel comfortable with, and cultural capital plays a significant role in that process (Kanter 1993).

Compounding this problem of cultural inequality is the fact that our preferences and perceptions often pass down from parent to child in the same way that material capital is inherited. Parents teach their children linguistic patterns and cultural tastes, from the use of double negatives to the appreciation of literature. Cultural capital is also reproduced in the next generation in the context of schools, where class distinctions within the community shape the curriculum and patterns of discipline. Jonathan Kozol (2005), for example, in his most recent study on how education perpetuates inequality, told the story of an inner-city high school student who wanted to take an AP class in preparation for college but was placed in a sewing class instead. As a friend of hers put it, the factory owners need workers, and it won't be their kids: "You're ghetto—so you sew!" (p. 180). Such transmission increases the likelihood that social advantage will be passed from one generation to the next.

Social mobility from this perspective involves more than just acquiring more money and better social connections. Winning the lottery, for example, does not transform a person at the bottom of the hierarchy into one at the top, or, as Bourdieu put it, "having a million does not in itself make one able to live like a millionaire" (1984:374). Such movement requires a social and cultural transformation as well. For mobility to happen, the individual must earn and learn a different set of knowledge and skills, as well as a whole new lifestyle: new tastes, attitudes, language, and thoughts. The same goes for someone who would drop from a higher rank into a lower one.

Material, Social, and Cultural Resources Considering these perspectives together we can point to three critical categories of resources that shape the positions we occupy and influence our likelihood for social mobility. Material resources refer to economic resources that we own or control, including money, property, and land. Social resources include prestige based on the position we occupy and connections based on the social networks we are a part of. It turns out that the old saying "It's not what you know; it's who you know" has some truth to it. Position and connections make it possible for us to increase the likelihood of accomplishing our goals. Finally, cultural resources include our tastes, language, and way of looking at the world. They represent our knowledge of cognitive, normative, and material elements of culture that we can draw on when acting to accomplish our goals. A simple but classic example involves knowing which fork to use for the various courses of a formal dinner. But it also includes knowing how to respond when we are put on the spot, whether in a business meeting, at a rock concert, or in class. Viewing social class in terms of material, social, and cultural resources makes social class a much more useful concept when trying to map our social lives or figure out why we think and act as we do.

All societies have some degree of stratification, and tracking these three resources helps us to better understand how stratification works. As we saw in Chapter 8 on education, Davis and Moore (1945) suggested that, especially in societies with a complex division of labor, some positions are more important or require more skill. Perhaps we need to hold out the promise of high pay and prestige as a reward so that those with the necessary skill and determination take the time and money required to develop their talents. Even if we accept the principle that a certain degree of inequality is inevitable, however, questions remain about the extent of inequality that is practiced. In addition, if inequality is to be tied to ability and effort, we need to investigate the degree to which positions are earned versus inherited. We turn next to an analysis of the degree of inequality that exists in the United States.

> Anyone who has ever struggled with poverty knows how extremely expensive it is to be poor.
>
> **James A. Baldwin**

>> Social Class in the United States

Social class dividing lines in the United States are not as clear-cut or firm as they were historically in, say, England. When we take a step back, however, we see that social class differences do impact our everyday lives. We may not label them as such, and we might want to dismiss their significance. Nevertheless, when we look through the lens of class as highlighted by these three resources, we bring to the surface differences that we already recognize as important.

CULTURAL CAPITAL

In some ways it is easiest to look first at cultural resources because, while we recognize that such differences exist, we may feel that they are not such a big deal. If one person likes Chopin while another likes Kenny Chesney, what difference does that make? As indicated above, however, such tastes do not exist in isolation; rather, they are tied to social and material resources as well and can serve as a means of exclusion (Halle 1993; Wilson 2007). Looking at just a few examples, we can appreciate the degree to which we already see class, even if we don't usually identify it as such.

We can recognize class in the clothes we wear, and even in the terms we use to describe them, such as "business casual" or "blue collar." Some people would not be caught dead wearing a suit and tie (or maybe that's the only way they will wear them), while others are incapable of being comfortable in blue jeans and a T-shirt. And brands can matter, whether it's Lilly Pulitzer, Sean Jean, J. McLaughlin, Gap, Rocawear, H&M, Free People, Baby Phat, Juicy Couture, Wrangler, Calypso, Abercrombie & Fitch, Coach, or Gucci. Even the fabrics clothes are made of suggest class differences, with higher classes more likely to wear clothes made out of organic materials (such as wool, silk, or cotton) and lower classes more likely to wear synthetic fabrics (including nylon, rayon, and orlon). This is likely driven not only by the initial cost differences for such materials but also by the long-term care costs for dry-cleaning.

SOCthink

> > > Paul Fussell (1992), in his book *Class: A Guide Through the American Status System,* argued that the writing on our clothes says a lot about our social class. What story do the logos, brands, and writing on your clothes tell about you? How might your clothing choices have differed had you been in a different class position?

We also see class differences when it comes to houses. Just driving through neighborhoods we recognize class indicators of houses: the distance they are located from the street; the composition of a driveway, if there is one; the fastidiousness of lawn care; the existence of flamingoes, gnomes, or gazing balls; and the presence of pillars or fountains. When it comes to where we live, expressions such as "the wrong side of the tracks," "snob hill," and "McMansion" point to our recognition that class matters.

Similarly, class makes a difference when it comes to vacations. Elites might head to Martha's Vineyard or the Hamptons, or they might "summer" in Nepal or Istanbul. Middle-class people are more likely to head to Disney World or perhaps go on a cruise, though either dream vacation may be possible only after having saved for some time or going into debt. Because money and vacation time are often limited, working-class families are more likely to go on a one-week trip, probably not too far from home, to which they are more likely to drive, and it might involve camping.

We could look at other areas too, including what we eat (fast food versus haute cuisine), what we drink (Bud Light versus fine wine), and what sports we watch (NASCAR and professional wrestling versus tennis and America's Cup yachting). In all kinds of ways, our preferences are shaped by our social class positions. Yet we seldom take seriously the source of such preferences or their effect on the choices we make and the doors that these choices may open or close to us.

prestige The respect and admiration that an occupation holds in a society.
esteem The reputation that a specific person has earned within an occupation.

STATUS AND PRESTIGE

We have a sense of where people fit relative to each other. Some we see as higher, while others we see as lower. We have seen as much already with regard to cultural preferences, but when it comes to status, it is not just what people like that we rank, but who they are. Sociologists seek to describe those systems of ranking and the advantages and disadvantages they convey.

Occupational Prestige One way sociologists describe the relative social class positions people occupy is by focusing on their occupational prestige. The term **prestige** refers to the respect and admiration that an occupation holds in a society. Fairly or not, "my daughter, the physicist" connotes something very different from "my daughter, the waitress." Prestige is independent of the particular individual who occupies a job, a characteristic that distinguishes it from esteem. **Esteem** refers to the reputation that a specific person has earned within an occupation. Therefore, we can say that the position of president of the United States has high prestige even though it has been occupied by people with varying degrees of esteem. A hairdresser may have the esteem of his clients, but he lacks the prestige of a corporate executive.

Using the results from a series of national surveys, sociologists have identified prestige rankings for about 500 occupations. They created a scale with 0 as the lowest possible score and 100 as the highest, and ranked the occupations based on the results of their surveys. Surgeon, physician, lawyer, dentist, and college professor were among the most highly regarded occupations, while bartender, farmworker, janitor, newspaper vendor, prostitute, and

Did You Know?

...According to Harris polls, the status of teachers has risen more than any other occupational category they have tracked over the past 30 years. In 2007, 54 percent of respondents identified teachers as having "very great prestige" compared with 29 percent in 1977.

Prestige Rankings of Occupations

Occupation	Score	Occupation	Score
Surgeon	87	Farmer	40
Physician	86	Correctional officer	40
Lawyer	75	Receptionist	39
Dentist	74	Carpenter	39
College professor	74	Barber	36
Architect	73	Child care worker	35
Psychiatrist	72	Hotel clerk	32
Clergy	69	Bus driver	32
Pharmacist	68	Auto body repairer	31
Registered nurse	66	Truck driver	30
High school teacher	66	Salesworker (shoes)	28
Accountant	65	Garbage collector	28
Optician	65	Waiter and waitress	28
Elementary school teacher	64	Cook in a pizza shop	27
Banker	63	Bartender	25
Veterinarian	62	Farm worker	23
Legislator	61	Janitor	22
Airline pilot	60	Newspaper vendor	19
Police officer or detective	60	Prostitute	14
Prekindergarten teacher	55	Panhandler	11
Librarian	54		
Firefighter	53		
Social worker	52		
Dental hygienist	52		
Electrician	51		
Funeral director	49		
Farm manager	48		
Mail carrier	47		
Secretary	46		
Insurance agent	45		
Bank teller	43		
Nurse's aide	42		

Note: 100 is the highest and 0 the lowest possible prestige score.

Source: J. Davis et al. 2007; see also Nakao and Treas 1994.

individual characteristics, whereas the reverse is true for someone from a lower position.

Socioeconomic Status As a single variable, occupation provides us with a sense of where people stand, but status involves more than just occupational prestige. In their research, sociologists add variables to the mix to gain a more complete picture of social class standing. These include such things as the value of homes, sources of income, assets, years in present occupations, neighborhoods, and considerations regarding dual careers. Adding these variables will not necessarily paint an alternative picture of class differentiation in the United States, but it does allow sociologists to measure class in a more complex and multidimensional way. When researchers use multiple measures, they typically speak of **socioeconomic status (SES),** a measure of social class that is based on income, education, occupation, and related variables.

One of the lessons we learn from SES research is that society often undervalues, in terms of prestige and pay, work that is essential for our individual and collective survival. In an effort to make the value of women's contribution to the economy more visible, for example, the International Women Count Network, a global grassroots feminist organization, has sought to give a monetary value to women's unpaid work. Besides providing symbolic recognition of women's contributions to society, they propose that this value also be used to calculate pension and other benefits that are based on wages received. The United Nations has placed an $11-*trillion* price tag on unpaid labor by women, largely in child care, housework, and agriculture. In March 2009, in order to ensure the full integration of women into the formal economy and to have their economic contributions considered in policy making, the United Nation's Commission on the Status of Women called on governments to incorporate the value of unpaid work in the household into policies and budgets.

panhandler were at the bottom. Sociologists have found a significant amount of stability in such rankings from 1925 to the present (Nakao and Treas 1994:11; J. Davis et al. 2007). This suggests that we do confer status to people based on the positions they occupy. Someone with a higher status is more likely to get the benefit of the doubt because of the position she or he occupies, regardless of her or his

We gain additional insight into this inequality by looking at the relative placement of households from bottom to top. One of the most common ways to present income dispersion is to line up all income-earning households from low to high and then break them into quintiles, or blocks of 20 percent. There are approximately 117 million households in the United States, so each quintile would include an equal number of about 23.4 million households. Doing so allows us to get a sense of what the average income is within each of these quintiles, along with the percentage of the total income pie that each quintile earns.

> **socioeconomic status (SES)** A measure of class that is based on income, education, occupation, and related variables.
> **income** Wages and salaries measured over some period, such as per hour or year.
> **wealth** The total of all a person's material assets, including savings, land, stocks, and other types of property, minus his or her debt at a single point in time.

INCOME AND WEALTH

Cultural capital and status provide a clearer picture of how we perceive social class, but income and wealth serve as its material foundation. **Income** refers to wages and salaries measured over some period, such as per hour or year. **Wealth** encompasses all of a person's material assets, including savings, land, stocks, and other types of property, minus his or her debts at a single point in time. If you were to sell everything you own and pay off all your debts, what you had left would be the value of your wealth. These material resources make our class-based lifestyles possible (Bourdieu 1986). As such, if we are to understand social class in the United States, we need a clear picture of their distribution.

Income Income inequality is a basic characteristic of a class system. In 2007, the median household income in the United States was $50,233. In other words, half of all households had higher incomes in that year, and half had lower incomes. But this fact does not fully convey the income disparities in our society. We get some sense of income inequality by contrasting the median (middle) score with the mean (arithmetic average), which in 2007 was $67,609. The mean is so much higher because some people make a lot more money than others, which draws the mean up, making it a less useful statistic for describing "average" or typical income (DeNavas-Walt, Proctor and Smith 2008).

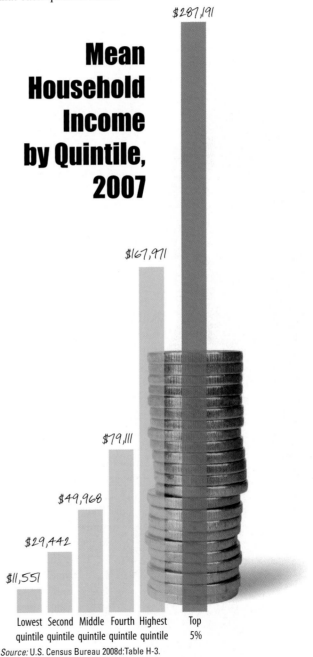

Mean Household Income by Quintile, 2007

$287,191

$167,971

$79,111

$49,968

$29,442

$11,551

Lowest quintile | Second quintile | Middle quintile | Fourth quintile | Highest quintile | Top 5%

Source: U.S. Census Bureau 2008d: Table H-3.

The Income Pie: Percent Share of Total Income, 2007

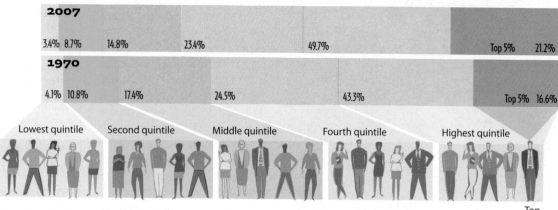

2007

3.4% | 8.7% | 14.8% | 23.4% | 49.7% | Top 5% | 21.2%

1970

4.1% | 10.8% | 17.4% | 24.5% | 43.3% | Top 5% | 16.6%

Lowest quintile | Second quintile | Middle quintile | Fourth quintile | Highest quintile

Top 5%

Source: U.S. Census Bureau 2008d:Table H-2.

As we can see in the accompanying graphs, looking at the population in this way shows a significant degree of income inequality. Focusing on the extremes, the mean income for households in the lowest quintile is $11,551, while households in the top quintile average $167,971. Those households in the top 5 percent, the ones most responsible for bringing up the arithmetic mean, average $287,191. Those in the bottom quintile earn just 3.4 percent of the nation's total income, while those in the top quintile earn 49.7 percent. In fact, the top 5 percent earns a significantly greater percent of total income than the bottom 40 percent combined (DeNavas-Walt et al. 2008).

By all measures, income in the United States is distributed unevenly. The 14,835 families in the top 0.01 percent had average incomes of $30 million, and the top 400 taxpayers averaged $263 million. At the same time, almost 29 million households reported incomes under $15,000 (Internal Revenue Service 2009; Pinketty and Saez 2008). Nobel Prize–winning economist Paul Samuelson has described the situation in the following way: "If we made an income pyramid out of building blocks, with each layer por-

traying $500 of income, the peak would be far higher than Mount Everest, but most people would be within a few feet of the ground" (Samuelson and Nordhaus 2005:383).

Income inequality has increased steadily since 1970. Former Federal Reserve Board Chair Alan Greenspan was referring to this trend when he told Congress that the rising gap between the rich and the poor in the United States was a "very disturbing trend" that threatens democratic society (Greenspan 2005). Just how dramatic has this growth in inequality been? As the "Income Pie" chart above shows, the share earned by each of the bottom quintiles has decreased since 1970, while the top quintile now earns almost one-half of total income. This represents the greatest degree of income inequality since before the Great Depression.

Americans do not appear to be seriously concerned about income and wealth inequality in the United States. In a comparison of opinions about social inequality in 27 different countries, respondents in the United States were less aware than those in other countries of the extent of inequality of the income distribution. Americans would prefer to "level down" the top of the nation's earning distribution, but compared to people in other countries, they are less concerned about reducing income differentials at the bottom of the distribution (Osberg and Smeeding 2006).

SOCthink

> > > Why do you think that most Americans do not seem to be aware of or concerned about the degree of income inequality in the United States? To what extent might it be due to the power of the American Dream, the influence of the media, or the working of the dominant ideology?

Wealth Wealth in the United States is much more unevenly distributed than income. The median wealth for families in 2007 was $120,300. Contrast this with the mean of $556,300 and, just as with income, we see significant inequality. Comparing the top end to the bottom, we get a sense of the scale of difference. On the low end, the bottom 25 percent of wealth-holding families had a median wealth of $1200 and mean wealth of –$2300, meaning that, on average, they owed more than they owned. The top 10 percent, on the other hand, had a median wealth of $1.9 million and a mean wealth of $4.0 million (Bucks et al. 2009:A11).

Percentage of Wealth Owned, by Percentile

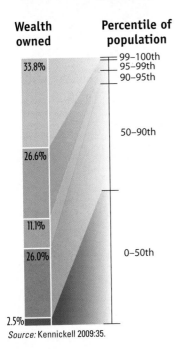

Wealth owned / **Percentile of population**

- 33.8% — 99–100th / 95–99th / 90–95th
- 26.6% — 50–90th
- 11.1%
- 26.0% — 0–50th
- 2.5%

Source: Kennickell 2009:35.

We can get a better sense of the degree of difference by looking at how total wealth is distributed. As the accompanying chart shows, the top 1 percent owns 33.8 percent of all wealth in the United States. By contrast, the bottom 50 percent owns just 2.5 percent. In fact, the top 1 percent owns more than the bottom 90 percent combined. The concentration of ownership is even more extreme when it comes to stocks, with the top 1 percent owning 51.9 percent of their total value, and business assets, of which they own 62.7 percent. In fact, the only place where the bottom 50 percent comes close to matching its share of wealth relative to its portion of the population is with debt. The bottom 50 percent owes 52.8 percent of all installment debt and 43.1 percent of outstanding credit card debt (Kennickell 2009).

The Shrinking Middle Class The cherished belief that the poor can rise to middle-class status has long been central to the United States' reputation as a land of opportunity. However, according to economics professor Lester C. Thurow, the American middle class is shrinking. Using a common definition of a middle-class household as one whose income falls between 75 and 125 percent of the nation's median household income (that is, between $37,675 and $62,791), only about 22 percent of American households qualified as middle class in 2007, compared to 28 percent in 1967 (DeNavas-Walt et al. 2008; Witte 2005).

Of those who relinquished their middle-class standing during this period, about half rose to a higher ranking in the social class system and half dropped to a lower posi-

tion. These data suggest that the United States is moving toward a bipolar income distribution. That is, a broadly based middle class is slowly being replaced by two growing groups of rich and poor (Greenblatt 2005).

Sociologists and other scholars have identified several factors that have contributed to the shrinking size of the middle class:

- *Disappearing opportunities for those with little education.* Today, increasing numbers of jobs require formal schooling, yet fewer than a third of adults ages 25–29 have a college degree.

- *Global competition and rapid advances in technology.* These two trends, which began several decades ago, have rendered workers more replaceable than they once were. Increasingly, these trends are affecting the more complex jobs that were once the bread and butter of middle-class life. Experts disagree on whether they represent a permanent setback to the workforce or the foundation for new industries that will someday generate millions of new jobs. In the meantime, however, U.S. households are struggling.

- *Growing dependence on the temporary workforce.* Some workers depend on temporary jobs for a second income to maintain their middle-class lifestyle. For those workers who have no other job, these positions are tenuous at best, because they rarely offer health care coverage or retirement benefits.

- *The rise of new-growth industries and nonunion workplaces.* In the past, workers in heavy industry were able to achieve middle-class incomes through the efforts of strong labor unions. But today, the growth areas in the economy are fast-food restaurants and large retail outlets. Though these industries have added employment opportunities, they are at the lower end of the wage scale.

Did You Know?

...According to the Consumer Price Index, overall prices rose about 30 percent from 1996 to 2006, but the cost of preschool care rose 60 percent, the cost of college rose 80 percent, and the cost of both a median-priced home and health insurance premiums doubled.

In response to these concerns, observers note that living standards in the United States are improving. Middle-class families want large homes, college degrees for their children, and high-quality health care—the cost of which has been rising faster than inflation. Accomplishing these goals, however, has often meant becoming a dual-income family, working longer hours, or taking multiple jobs (Leonhardt 2007; Massey 2007).

POVERTY

In 2007, 37.3 million people in the United States—12.5 percent of the population—were living in poverty. The problem of insufficient income, however, affects more people than these official numbers indicate. A recent Bureau of the Census report showed that one in five households has trouble meeting basic needs, from paying the utility bills to buying food (DeNavas-Walt et al. 2008).

Defining Poverty The efforts of sociologists and other social scientists to better understand poverty are complicated by the difficulty of defining it. This problem is evident even in government programs that conceive of poverty in either absolute or relative terms.

Absolute poverty refers to a minimum level of subsistence that no family should be expected to live below. One commonly used measure of absolute poverty is the federal government's poverty line. This is a money income figure that the government adjusts annually to reflect the consumption requirements of families based on their size and composition. It serves as an official definition of who is poor. In 2007, a family consisting of two adults and two children with a combined income of $21,027 or less

Going **GLOBAL**

The Poverty Rate in Households with Children, Selected Countries

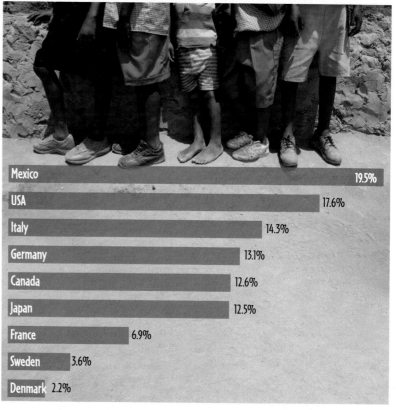

Mexico	19.5%
USA	17.6%
Italy	14.3%
Germany	13.1%
Canada	12.6%
Japan	12.5%
France	6.9%
Sweden	3.6%
Denmark	2.2%

Source: OECD 2009: Table EQ3.2.

fell below the poverty line. By contrast, a single person under the age of 65 must earn less than $10,787 to be con-

to those above them. Someone who would be considered poor by U.S. standards would be well off by global stan-

> **Civilization is unbearable, but it is less unbearable at the top.**
>
> Timothy Leary

sidered officially poor (DeNavas-Walt et al. 2008). These cutoffs determine which individuals and families will be eligible for certain government benefits.

Although by absolute standards, poverty has declined in the United States—for example, it was 22.4 percent in 1959—it remains higher than in many other industrial nations. As we can see in the accompanying graph, a comparatively high proportion of U.S. households are poor, meaning that they are unable to purchase basic consumer goods. If anything, this cross-national comparison understates the extent of poverty in the United States because U.S. residents are likely to pay more for housing, health care, child care, and education than residents of other countries, where such expenses are often subsidized.

In contrast, **relative poverty** is a floating standard of deprivation by which people at the bottom of a society, whatever their lifestyles, are judged to be disadvantaged in comparison with the nation as a whole. Therefore, even if the poor today are better off in absolute terms than the poor of the 1930s or 1960s, they are still seen as poor relative

dards of poverty; hunger and starvation are daily realities in many regions of the world.

Since the 1990s, debate has grown over the adequacy of the federal government's measure of poverty. If non-cash benefits such as Medicare, Medicaid, food stamps, public housing, and health care and other employer-provided fringe benefits were included, the reported poverty rate would be lower. On the other hand, if out-of-pocket medical expenses and mandatory work expenses for transportation and child care were included, the poverty rate would be higher. The Census Bureau estimates that on balance, if both these recommendations were followed, the official poverty rate would be 2.5 percent higher, and 5 million more people would fall below the poverty line (Bernasek 2006; U.S. Census Bureau 2009c).

absolute poverty A minimum level of subsistence that no family should be expected to live below.

relative poverty A floating standard of deprivation by which people at the bottom of a society, whatever their lifestyles, are judged to be disadvantaged in comparison with the nation as a whole.

Who Are the Poor in the United States?

	Percentage of the population of the United States	Percentage of the poor of the United States
Age		
Under 18 years old	25	36
18 to 64 years old	63	55
65 years and older	12	10
Race/Ethnicity		
Whites (non-Hispanic)	66	43
Blacks	13	25
Hispanics	15	27
Asians and Pacific Islanders	4	4
Families		
Married couples	75	37
Female householder, no husband present	17	53
Male householder, no wife present	7	9

Note: Data for 2007, as reported by the Bureau of the Census in 2008e.

Source: DeNavas-Walt et al. 2008.

Who Are the Poor? One of the lessons that we learn by analyzing those who fall below the poverty line is that our stereotypes about poverty are flawed. For example, many people in the United States believe that the vast majority of the poor are able to work but will not. Yet of the 37.3 million people in poverty, 16.9 million are either under age 18 or 65 years old or older. Many working-age adults who are poor do work outside the home, although often in part-time positions. In 2007, about 30 percent of all poor adults worked full-time, compared to 69 percent of all adults. Of those poor adults who do not work, most are ill or disabled, or are occupied in maintaining a home. As we can see in the accompanying table, the likelihood of being in poverty is also shaped by factors such as age, race, ethnicity, and family type (DeNavas-Walt et al. 2008).

underclass The long-term poor who lack training and skills.

Since World War II, an increasing proportion of the poor people of the United States have been women, many of whom are divorced or never-married mothers. In 1959, female householders accounted for 26 percent of the nation's poor; by 2006, that figure had risen to 53 percent. This alarming trend, known as the feminization of poverty, is evident not just in the United States but around the world.

About half of all women living in poverty in the United States are in transition, coping with an economic crisis caused by the departure, disability, or death of a husband. The other half tend to be economically dependent either on the welfare system or on friends and relatives living nearby. A major factor in the feminization of poverty has been the increase in families with women as single heads of household. In 2007, 28.3 percent of families headed by single mothers lived in poverty, compared to 13.6 percent for single-father households and 4.9 percent for married couples. Contributing to such rates are factors such as the difficulty in finding affordable child care and sex discrimination in the labor market (DeNavas-Walt et al. 2008).

In 2007, 43 percent of poor people in the United States were living in big cities. These urban residents are the focus of most governmental efforts to alleviate poverty. Yet according to many observers, the plight of the urban poor is growing worse, owing to the devastating interplay of inadequate education and limited employment prospects. Traditional employment opportunities in the industrial sector are largely closed to the unskilled poor. Past and present discrimination heightens these problems for those low-income urban residents who are Black and Hispanic (DeNavas-Walt et al. 2008).

Along with other social scientists, sociologist William Julius Wilson (1980, 1987, 1989, 1996), and his colleagues (2004) have used the term **underclass** to describe the long-term poor who lack training and skills. According to an analysis of Census 2000 data, 7.9 million people live in high-poverty neighborhoods. About 30 percent of the population in these neighborhoods is Black, 29 percent Hispanic, and 24 percent White. In central cities, about 49 percent of the underclass is African American, 29 percent Hispanic, 17 percent White, and 5 percent "other" (Jargowsky and Yang 2006).

Analyses of the poor in general reveal that they are, however, not a static social class. The overall composition of the poor changes continually; some individuals and families move above the poverty level after a year or two, while others slip below it. Still, hundreds of thousands of people remain in poverty for many years at a time. African Americans and Latinos are more likely than Whites to be persistently poor. Over a 21-year period, 15 percent of African Americans and 10 percent of Latinos were persistently poor, compared to only 3 percent of Whites. Both Latinos and Blacks are less likely than Whites to leave the welfare rolls as a result of recent welfare reform (Mangum et al. 2003).

In late 1996, in a historic shift in federal policy, Congress passed the Personal Responsibility and Work Opportunity Reconciliation Act, ending the longstanding federal guarantee of assistance to every poor family that meets eligibility requirements. The law sets a lifetime limit of five years of welfare benefits and requires all able-bodied adults to work after receiving two years of benefits (although hardship exceptions are allowed). The federal government gives block grants to the states to use as they wish in assisting poor and needy residents, and it permits states to experiment with ways to move people off welfare.

Other countries vary widely in their commitment to social service programs. But most industrialized nations devote higher proportions of their expenditures to housing, social security, welfare, health care, and unemployment compensation than the United States does. Data available in 2004 indicated that in Great Britain, 86 percent of health care expenditures were paid for by the government; in Sweden, 85 percent; in Canada, 70 percent; but in the United States, only 45 percent (World Bank 2007a:92–94).

The issue of poverty is ultimately about more than just money. It is also tied to social and cultural resources. Poor people often lack the social network connections to help them get good

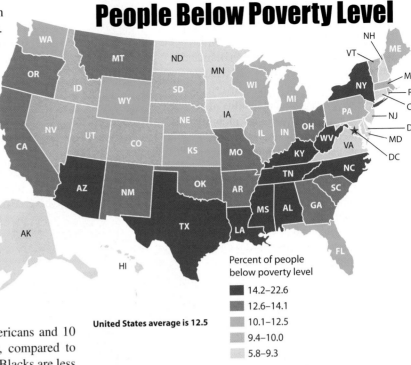

People Below Poverty Level

United States average is 12.5

Percent of people below poverty level

- 14.2–22.6
- 12.6–14.1
- 10.1–12.5
- 9.4–10.0
- 5.8–9.3

Source: U.S. Census Bureau 2008e:Table Pov46.

Hot or Not?

Should welfare recipients be required to work? If so, what should happen to their children while they are at work?

jobs, not to mention having to overcome the negative prestige associated with being poor. When it comes to cultural capital, they also often lack the same kind of educational credentials that can serve as a valuable cultural resource. Journalist David Shipler (2004), in his in-depth study titled *The Working Poor: Invisible in America,* referred to the combination of factors that poor people must overcome as the "interlocking deficits of poverty." As Shipler put it, "Breaking away and moving a comfortable distance from poverty seems to require a perfect lineup of favorable conditions. A set of skills, a good starting wage, and a job with the likelihood of promotion are prerequisites. But so are clarity of purpose, courageous self-esteem, a lack of substantial debt, freedom from mental illness or addiction, a functional family, a network of upstanding friends, and the right help from private or governmental agencies" (2004:4–5). To deal with poverty as a social problem, we must address all three of the major resource areas because mobility out of poverty is a difficult task. The truth is, however, most of us end up near where we start.

SOCIAL MOBILITY

The belief in upward mobility is an important value in the United States. As we saw above, social class systems are more open than other stratification systems, but this does not mean that the principle of opportunity necessarily matches the practice of mobility. For such mobility to be possible, ascribed statuses and inherited positions, along with the resources to which they provide access, should not play a significant role in shaping outcomes.

Occupational Mobility Two classic sociological studies conducted a decade apart offered insight into the degree of mobility in the nation's occupational structure (Blau and Duncan 1967; Featherman and Hauser 1978). Taken together, these investigations lead to several noteworthy conclusions. First, occupational mobility (both intergenerational and intragenerational) has been common among males. Approximately 60–70 percent of sons are employed in higher-ranked occupations than their fathers. Second, although there is a great deal of mobility in the United States, much of it is minor. That is, people who reach an occupational level above or below that of their parents usually advance or fall back only one or two out of a possible eight occupational levels. Thus, the child of a laborer may become an artisan or a technician, but he or she is less likely to become a manager or professional. The odds of reaching the top are extremely low unless one begins from a relatively privileged position.

Income and Wealth More recent studies focusing on income and wealth mobility show much the same results. Mobility does occur, but most people do not move very far. In comparing father's and son's income, researchers found that sons of low-income fathers have almost a 60 percent chance of rising above the lowest quintile, but only a 22.5 percent chance of reaching the median and a 4.5 percent chance of breaking into the top quintile (Mishel, Bernstein, and Shierholz 2009). Similarly, as we can see in the accompanying graph, when looking at wealth,

36 percent of children with parents in the lowest quintile end up there themselves while only 7 percent make it to the top quintile. On the other end of the scale, 36 percent of children with parents in the top wealth quintile stay there while only 11 percent drop down into the bottom quintile (Haskins 2008:8). In fact, the likelihood of ending up in the same position as your parents has been rising since about 1980 (Aaronson and Mazumder 2007).

Education Studies also conclude that education plays a critical role in mobility. The impact of formal schooling on adult status is even greater than that of family background (although, as we have seen, family background influences the likelihood that one will receive higher education). Furthermore, education represents an important means of intergenerational mobility. A person who was born into a poor family but who graduates from college has a one in five chance of entering the top quintile of all income earners as an adult (Isaacs et al. 2008).

Education is a critical factor in the development of cultural capital. As such, access to higher education plays an important role in social mobility. In 2004, 40 percent of first-year students at major state universities came from families with incomes of more than $100,000 a year. In other words, close to half of all students came from high-income families. This statistic should not be surprising, given the high cost of tuition and room and board at state universities. For students from families with the lowest incomes, the cost can be prohibitive. Only 11 percent of children from the poorest families in the United States have earned college degrees, compared to 53 percent of children from the top fifth of the population. Those moderate-income students who do graduate, and even those who fail to complete their degrees, are often saddled with heavy postgraduate debt (Isaacs et al. 2008).

Did You Know?

... **Although 67 percent of families make more money than their parents, only half of those earn enough to jump them into the next income quintile.**

SOCthink

> > > The percentage of financial aid in the form of grants has gone down while the percentage of loan aid has increased. Why do you think that has occurred? What are the consequences of such a shift for social mobility?

The impact of education on mobility has diminished somewhat over the past decade. An undergraduate degree—a BA or BS—serves less as a guarantee of upward mobility now than it did in the past, simply because more and more entrants into the job market hold such a degree.

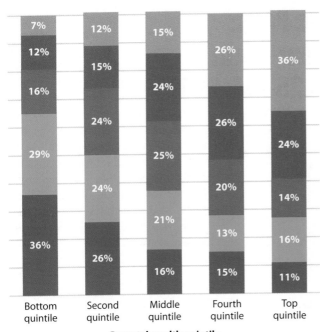

Wealth Mobility: Percentage of Children in Each Wealth Quintile Compared to Parental Wealth Quintile

Child wealth quintile

- Top
- Fourth
- Middle
- Second
- Bottom

Source: Haskins 2008.

Chart data (Parental wealth quintile):

Child wealth quintile	Bottom quintile	Second quintile	Middle quintile	Fourth quintile	Top quintile
Top	7%	12%	15%	26%	36%
Fourth	12%	15%	24%	26%	24%
Middle	16%	24%	25%	20%	14%
Second	29%	24%	21%	13%	16%
Bottom	36%	26%	16%	15%	11%

Parental wealth quintile

Moreover, intergenerational mobility is declining because there is no longer such a stark difference between generations. In earlier decades, many high school–educated parents managed to send their children to college, but today's college students are increasingly likely to have college-educated parents (Economic Mobility Project 2007).

Race and Ethnicity Sociologists have long documented the fact that the class system is more rigid for African Americans than it is for members of other racial groups. Black men who have good jobs, for example, are less likely than White men to see their adult children attain the same status. The cumulative disadvantage of discrimi-

nation plays a significant role in the disparity between the two groups' experiences. Compared to White households, the relatively modest wealth of African American households means that adult Black children are less likely than adult White children to receive financial support from their parents. Indeed, young Black couples are much more likely than young White couples to be assisting their parents—a sacrifice that hampers their social mobility.

The African American middle class has grown over the past few decades due to economic expansion and the benefits of the civil rights movement of the 1960s. Yet many of these middle-class households have little savings, a fact that puts them in danger during times of crisis. Studies have consistently shown that downward mobility is significantly higher for Blacks than it is for Whites (Isaacs 2007c; Oliver and Shapiro 1995).

The Latino population is not doing much better. The typical Hispanic has less than 10 percent of the wealth that a White person enjoys. A 2004 study suggests that in recent years Latinos have even lost ground. Their continuing immigration accounts for part of the disparity: Most of the

new arrivals are destitute. But even the wealthiest 5 percent of Latino households have only a third as much net worth as the top 5 percent of White households (Bucks et al. 2009; Kochhar 2004).

Gender Studies of mobility, even more than those of class, have traditionally ignored the significance of gender, but some research findings are now available that explore the relationship between gender and mobility. Women's employment opportunities are much more limited than men's. Moreover, according to recent research, women whose skills far exceed the jobs offered them are more likely than men to withdraw entirely from the paid labor force. Their withdrawal violates an assumption common to traditional mobility studies: that most people will aspire to upward mobility and seek to make the most of their opportunities.

In contrast to men, women have a rather large range of clerical occupations open to them. But the modest salary ranges and limited prospects for advancement in many of these positions reduce the possibility of upward mobility. Self-employment as shopkeepers, entrepreneurs, independent professionals, and the like—an important road to upward mobility for men—is more difficult for women, who find it harder to secure the necessary financing. Although sons commonly follow in the footsteps of their fathers, women are less likely to move into their fathers' positions. Consequently, gender remains an important factor in shaping social mobility. Women in the United States (and in other parts of the world) are especially likely to be trapped in poverty, unable to rise out of their low-income status (Heilman 2001).

Education Pays: Full-Time, Year-Round Workers, Ages 25–64, 2007

Education level	Median annual earnings
Professional degree	$100,000
Doctorate degree	$85,837
Master's degree	$62,920
Bachelor's degree	$53,141
Associate's degree	$41,837
Some college, no degree	$38,728
High school grad (includes GED)	$32,462
Some high school, no degree	$25,802

Source: U.S. Census Bureau 2008c.

On the positive side, although today's women lag behind men in employment, their earnings have increased faster than their mothers' did at a comparable age, so that their incomes are substantially higher. The one glaring exception to this trend involves the daughters of low-income parents. Because these women typically care for children—many as single parents—and sometimes for other relatives as well, their mobility is severely restricted (Isaacs 2007b).

>> Life Chances

One of the lessons we learn from sociology is that class matters. Max Weber saw class as being closely related to people's **life chances**—that is, their opportunities to provide themselves with material goods, positive living conditions, and favorable life experiences (Weber [1916] 1958a). Life chances are reflected in measures such as housing, education, and health. Occupying a higher position in a society improves individuals' life chances and brings greater access to social rewards. In contrast, people in the lower social classes are forced to devote a larger proportion of their limited resources to the necessities of life.

In fact, our very survival can be at stake. When the supposedly unsinkable British ocean liner *Titanic* hit an iceberg in 1912, it was not carrying enough lifeboats to accommodate all passengers. Plans had been made to evacuate only first- and second-class passengers. About 62 percent of the first-class passengers survived the disaster. Despite a rule that women and children would go first, about a third of those passengers were male. In contrast, only 25

percent of the passengers in third class survived. The first attempt to alert them to the need to abandon ship came well after other passengers had been notified (D. A. Butler 1998; Crouse 1999).

SOCthink

> > > What factors have shaped your life chances? What kinds of resources have you inherited from others? What resources might you have lacked access to?

Class position also affects people's vulnerability to natural disasters. When Hurricane Katrina hit the Gulf Coast of the United States in 2005, affluent and poor people alike became its victims. However, poor people who did not own automobiles (100,000 of them in New Orleans alone) were less able than others to evacuate in advance of the storm. Those who survived its fury had no nest egg to draw on, and thus were more likely than others to accept relocation wherever social service agencies could place them—sometimes hundreds or even thousands of miles from home (Department of Homeland Security 2006; Fussell 2006).

Some people have hoped that the Internet revolution would help to level the playing field by making information and markets uniformly available. Unfortunately, however, not everyone can get onto the information superhighway, so yet another aspect of social inequality has emerged—the **digital divide.** The poor, minorities, and those who live in rural communities and inner cities are not getting connected at home or at work. For example, 55 percent of households in the United States have broadband Internet access from home, but Internet access varies signifi-

cantly by income. Only 25 percent of households making $20,000 or less have broadband access, compared to 85 percent of those with incomes over $100,000. Among the 10 percent of households still using dial-up, 29 percent make less than $30,000 per year; cost was cited as the most significant reason for not upgrading to broadband. And, finally, people who identified themselves as non–Internet users were much more likely to be from low-income households (Horrigan 2008).

> **life chances** The opportunities people have to provide themselves with material goods, positive living conditions, and favorable life experiences.
> **digital divide** The relative lack of access to the latest technologies among low-income groups, racial and ethnic minorities, rural residents, and the citizens of developing countries.

Wealth, status, and power may not ensure happiness, but they certainly provide additional ways of coping with problems and disappointments. For this reason, the opportunity for advancement—for social mobility—is of special significance to those at the bottom of society. These people want the chance to attain the rewards and privileges that are granted to high-ranking members of a culture.

If we are to better understand why we think and act the way we do, we must consider the impact of social class. The positions we occupy shape our access to material, social, and cultural resources, which in turn shapes our future positions. In the United States, part of the American Dream is that anyone who is willing to work hard can get ahead. The principle of meritocracy—that we earn our positions—is at the heart of that faith, which represents a rejection of aristocracy in which positions are inherited. Class patterns in the United States call into question the degree to which principle and practice meet.

. . . Researchers found that, by the age of three, children whose parents have professional jobs have heard 500,000 instances of praise and 80,000 of disapproval. In families receiving welfare, the ratio reverses; children have been praised 75,000 times and reprimanded 200,000 times.

Did You Know?

Calculate! Figure out what it takes to get by in your community using the Basic Family Budget Calculator at the Economic Policy Institute website: www.epi.org/content.cfm/datazone_ fambud_budget. Contrast that amount with the official poverty line. Compare your results with those from other communities.

get involved!

For REVIEW

I. What is social class?

- Like slavery, caste, and estate, it is a stratification system in which people and groups are ranked, but it places them based primarily on economic position.

II. How does social class operate?

- Three categories of resources are key: material, including income and wealth; social, including social networks and prestige; and, cultural, including tastes, education, and knowledge. Power is based on access to and control over these resources.

III. What are the consequences of social class?

- While class-based systems are more open than the others, our life chances are shaped by our inherited class position and the material, social, and cultural resources that go with it. For most people, the social mobility that does occur, whether in terms of occupation, income, or wealth, is of a relatively short distance.

Pop Quiz

1. Social inequality refers to
   a. the structured ranking of entire groups of people that perpetuates unequal economic rewards and power in a society.
   b. social ranking based primarily on economic position.
   c. the positive or negative reputation an individual has in the eyes of others.
   d. a condition in which members of society have different amounts of wealth, prestige, or power.

2. The stratification system in which hereditary ranks are usually religiously dictated is the
   a. class system.
   b. estate system.
   c. caste system.
   d. slave system.

3. A plumber whose father was a physician is an example of
   a. downward intergenerational mobility.
   b. upward intergenerational mobility.
   c. downward intragenerational mobility.
   d. upward intragenerational mobility.

4. According to Karl Marx, the class that owns the means of production is the
   a. nobility.
   b. proletariat.
   c. Brahman.
   d. bourgeoisie.

5. Which of the following were viewed by Max Weber as distinct components of stratification?
   a. conformity, deviance, and social control
   b. class, status, and party
   c. class, caste, and age
   d. class, prestige, and esteem

6. According to Pierre Bourdieu, our tastes, our education, the way we talk, and the things we like all represent forms of
   a. social capital.
   b. esteem.
   c. cultural capital.
   d. intelligence.

7. The respect or admiration that an occupation holds in a society is referred to as
   a. status.
   b. esteem.
   c. prestige.
   d. ranking.

1. (d); 2. (c); 3. (a); 4. (d); 5. (b); 6. (c); 7. (c);

8. Approximately how much wealth does the top 1 percent of families own in the United States?

   a. 20 percent

   b. 33 percent

   c. 50 percent

   d. 80 percent

9. Approximately what percentage of the U.S. population lived in poverty in 2007?

   a. 2.1 percent

   b. 8.6 percent

   c. 12.5 percent

   d. 19.4 percent

10. What term do sociologists use to describe the opportunities people have to provide themselves with material goods, positive living conditions, and favorable life experiences?

   a. esteem

   b. wealth

   c. social mobility

   d. life chances

11

GLOBAL INEQ

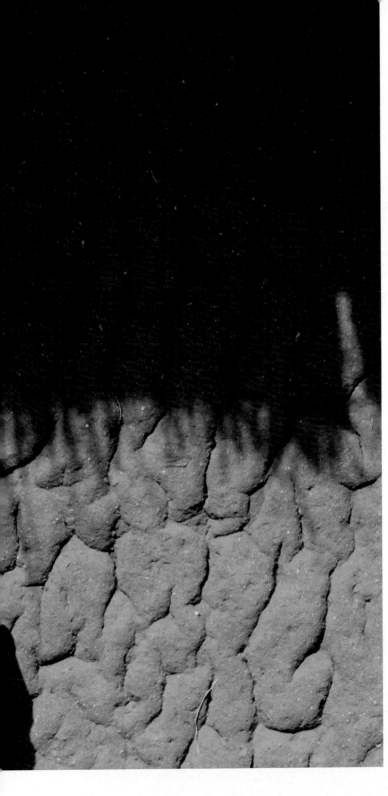

STRUGGLING TO SURVIVE IN A WORLD OF PLENTY

In spring of 2008, riots broke out in countries around the world in response to a global food crisis. From sub-Saharan African nations to countries including Egypt, India, and Yemen, people took to the streets in response to skyrocketing prices and food shortages. Hit hardest by the effects of this crisis were people in the poorest countries, where the margin between survival and starvation is razor-thin.

In Haiti, where three-quarters of the population live on less than $2 a day, price increases have been devastating. Georges Jean Wesner gets up every day at 4:00 A.M. to walk two hours to get two small pails of rice and beans from a charity food kitchen—the only source of food he and his family have had for weeks. "I'm 52 years old, I have lots of energy and I want to work," he says, "but I can't work because there is no work" (Williams 2008). People are turning to patties made of mud, oil, and sugar, about which Olwich Louis Jeune, 24, says, "It's salty and it has butter, and you don't know you're eating dirt. . . . It makes your stomach quiet down" (Lacey 2008).

In the Darfur region of Sudan, Khamisa Tafaela worried because her 10-month-old son was vomiting and suffering from diarrhea. She had already lost one son who had the same symptoms. She, along with her husband and their five children, had been living in a camp in West Darfur for over four years with thousands of others forced from their homes in Sudan. For the second month in a row, she had been living on halved food rations, not because there was insufficient food, but because it was too dangerous to get the food from the warehouses to the camps (*Sudan Tribune* 2008).

We see in this Darfur story that the food crisis may be due not only to insufficient food but also to insufficient access to food. Dominique Strauss-Kahn, the Managing Director of the International Monetary Fund, says, "There is enough food to feed the world . . . the problem is that prices have risen and many people cannot afford food. So we need to get food—or the money to buy food—to those most in need" (IMF 2008). In other words, we produce enough globally so that everyone can have enough, but we do not allocate resources in such a way that people now facing starvation can gain access to the food they need to survive.

UALITY

As You READ >>

- How did the global divide develop?
- How significant is global stratification?
- Why did the global movement for universal human rights develop?

>> The Global Divide

When it comes to resources, the global divide is immense. Millions of people struggle on the very edge of survival even as others around the world lead lives of relative comfort and leisure. A few centuries ago, most people were poor. There was a significant divide between the few who were extremely wealthy and the many who lacked significant resources, with little concept of a middle class between the nobility and the peasants. In much of Europe, life was as difficult as it was in Asia or South America. This was true until the Industrial Revolution and increased agricultural productivity resulted in explosive economic growth. However, the ensuing rise in living standards was not evenly distributed across the world.

We get a glimpse of the relative share of resources, and their consequences, by looking at splits between developing and industrial nations. For example, the likelihood of dealing with the death of a child or the burden of disease is much greater for those in developing nations. At the same time, the industrial nations of the world, with a much smaller share of the total population, have much higher incomes and many more exports than the developing nations. People in industrial nations also receive better health care and have greater security due to what those nations spend on health care and the military (Sachs 2005a; Sutcliffe 2002). As we will see, the divide within countries in terms of income, wealth, poverty, and social mobility is also significant.

Average income varies significantly across the nations of the world along a continuum from those that are the richest in natural resources to those that are the poorest. The contrast between those at the top and those at the bottom is stark. For example, in 2007, per capita gross national income (the

> ### Before you finish eating breakfast in the morning, you've depended on more than half of the world.
>
> Martin Luther King Jr.

Gross National Income per Capita, 2007

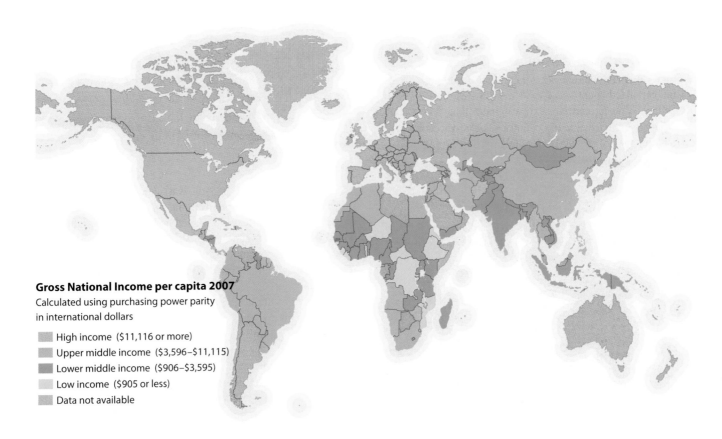

Gross National Income per capita 2007
Calculated using purchasing power parity
in international dollars

- High income ($11,116 or more)
- Upper middle income ($3,596–$11,115)
- Lower middle income ($906–$3,595)
- Low income ($905 or less)
- Data not available

Going GLOBAL

Fundamental Global Inequality

	Developing nations	Industrial nations
Deaths of children	99%	1%
Rural population	94%	6%
Total births	94%	6%
The burden of disease	93%	7%
TOTAL POPULATION	85%	15%
Cultivated land	74%	26%
Urban population	73%	27%
Income	46%	54%
CO₂ emissions	36%	64%
Health spending	24%	76%
Exports	22%	78%
Military spending	12%	88%

Note: In this comparison, industrial nations include the United States and Canada, Japan, western Europe, and Australasia. Developing nations include Africa, Asia (except Japan), Latin America, eastern Europe, the Caribbean, and the Pacific.

Source: Adapted from Sutcliffe 2002:18.

total value of goods and services produced per citizen) in the industrialized countries of the United States, Canada, Switzerland, France, and Norway was more than $35,000. By comparison, over a dozen countries had a per capita gross national income of $900 or less (World Bank 2009a).

>> Perspectives on Global Stratification

Theorists have taken a step back to look at this global system from a top-down, macro perspective. In so doing, they provide us with insights into how the world system developed and how the various parts fit together. We will focus on three areas of analysis: the rise of modernization, the legacy of colonialism, and the growth of multinational corporations.

THE RISE OF MODERNIZATION

Early sociologists often assumed that society was progressing toward some common positive future. We certainly get that sense from both Karl Marx and Émile Durkheim, who believed that societies would all inevitably evolve along a similar path, ending up in some shared version of the good society. For Durkheim this meant a natural balance between interdependence and individual freedom; for Marx it meant some form of socialism. For his part, though his vision was not as hopeful, Max Weber also believed that all societies would move toward a rational-legal form of authority.

SOCthink

> > > Early sociologists were optimistic that positive social change was inevitable. To what extent do you think people today share this vision of the inevitable rise of the good society? How might cynicism about the possibility for change contribute to the maintenance of the status quo?

This notion that the present was superior to the past, with its petty tyrannies and irrational superstitions, and that the future would unite us all shaped how people viewed the world throughout much of the 20th century. Many people supposed that, through **modernization,** nations would move from traditional forms of social organization toward forms characteristic of post–Industrial Revolution societies. Features of the latter include a complex division of labor in which work is specialized; the separation of institutions including family, economy, government, education, and religion into specialized spheres, each with their own experts; the decline of the local and the rise of a societal or global orientation; the rise of rational decision making in the public sphere and a corresponding decline in public religious authority; and the spread of both cultural diver-

THE PROGRESS OF THE CENTURY.

THE LIGHTNING STEAM PRESS.   THE ELECTRIC TELEGRAPH.   THE LOCOMOTIVE.   THE STEAMBOAT.

PUBLISHED BY CURRIER & IVES   Copyright, 1876 by Currier & Ives, N.Y.   125 NASSAU ST. NEW YORK

sity, as more peoples from different backgrounds come into contact with each other, and a corresponding growth in egalitarianism as a value that embraces such diversity (Bruce 2000).

From this modernization perspective, countries such as China and India are in the process of becoming modern societies. Even if the transition from traditional to mod-

ern is difficult for many, the presupposition is that their people will benefit in the long term. According to these theorists, just as many people in the United States and Europe experienced displacement and poverty in the early years of the Industrial Revolution, only later to lead more comfortable lives, the same future awaits people in developing nations.

> **modernization** The far-reaching process by which nations pass from traditional forms of social organization toward those characteristic of post–Industrial Revolution societies.

Many sociologists today are quick to note that terms such as *modernization* and even *development* contain an ethnocentric bias. There is an implicit sense in this model that people in such nations are more "primitive" and that modern Western culture is more advanced, more "civilized." The unstated assumption is that what "they" (people living in developing countries) really want is to become more like "us" (people in modern industrialized nations). According to this vision, they want both our economic development and our cultural values including democracy, freedom, and consumerism. Such modernization, then, represents a form of cultural imperialism. Many groups around the world reject this path, viewing such "development" as an attack on their way of life including their core values and norms.

When it comes to U.S. media portrayals of people from around the world, we frequently see negative stereotypes reinforced, perpetuating a sense of U.S. cultural superiority. In an analysis of over 1000 films, communications professor Jack Shaheen (2006, 2009) found that only 5 percent of Arab and Muslim characters were presented in a positive light. Arabs were repeatedly caricatured as villains, buffoons, lechers, incompetents, and terrorists. For example, Shaheen argues that Disney's *Aladdin* recycles Arab stereotypes, describing the fictional city of Agrabah as barbaric but home. The good news, he said, is that positive representations have risen to about 30 percent, thanks to films such as *Syriana* and *Babel*.

THE LEGACY OF COLONIALISM

An alternative perspective to modernization focuses on colonialism as a model for better understanding the expansion of our interconnected world. **Colonialism** occurs when a foreign power maintains political, social, economic, and cultural domination over a people for an extended period. In simple terms, it is rule by outsiders. The long reign of the British Empire over much of North America, parts of Africa, and India is an example of colonial domination. The same can be said of French rule over Algeria, Tunisia, and other parts of North Africa. Relations between the colonial nation and the colonized people are similar to those between the dominant capitalist class and the proletariat, as described by Marx.

By the 1980s, such global political empires had largely disappeared. Most of the nations that were colonies prior to World War I had achieved political independence and established their own governments. However, for many of these countries, the transition to genuine self-rule was not yet complete. Colonial domination had established patterns of economic exploitation that continued even after nationhood was achieved—in part because the

colonialism The maintenance of political, social, economic, and cultural dominance over a people by a foreign power for an extended period.

neocolonialism Continuing dependence of former colonies on foreign countries.

world systems analysis A view of the global economic system as one divided between certain industrialized nations that control wealth and developing countries that are controlled and exploited.

former colonies were unable to develop their own industry and technology. Their dependence on more industrialized nations, including their former colonial masters, for managerial and technical expertise, investment capital, and manufactured goods kept the former colonies in a subservient position. Such continuing dependence and foreign domination are referred to as **neocolonialism.**

Sociologist Immanuel Wallerstein (2000, 2004) views the global economic system as being divided between nations that control wealth and nations from which resources are taken. Through his **world systems analysis,** Wallerstein has described the unequal economic and political relationships in which certain industrialized nations (among them the United States, Japan, and Germany) and their global corporations dominate the core of this system. At the semiperiphery of the system are countries with marginal economic status, such as Israel, Ireland, and South Korea. Wallerstein suggests that the poor developing countries of Asia, Africa, and Latin America are on the periphery of the world economic system. The key to Wallerstein's analysis is the exploitative relationship of core nations toward noncore nations. Core nations and their corporations control and exploit noncore nations' economies. Unlike other nations, they are relatively independent of outside control (Chase-Dunn and Grimes 1995).

The division between core and periphery nations is both significant and remarkably stable. A study by the International Monetary Fund (2000) found little change over the past century for the 42 economies studied. The only changes were Japan's movement up into the group of core nations and China's movement down toward the margins of the semiperiphery nations. Yet Wallerstein (2000) speculates that the world system as we currently understand it may soon undergo unpredictable changes. The world is

World Systems Analysis at the Beginning of the 21st Century

Core	Semiperiphery	Periphery
Canada	China	Afghanistan
France	India	Bolivia
Germany	Ireland	Chad
Japan	Mexico	Dominican Republic
United Kingdom	Pakistan	Egypt
United States	Panama	Haiti
		Philippines
		Vietnam

Note: Figure shows only a partial listing of countries.

Did You Know?

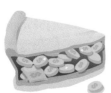

. . . Jamaica spends 27.9 percent of its government budget on debt relief and 16.1 percent on health and education. Such ratios are not uncommon in developing nations, although Lebanon spends 52.1 percent on debt service.

becoming increasingly urbanized, a trend that is gradually eliminating the large pools of low-cost workers in rural areas. In the future, core nations will have to find other ways to reduce their labor costs. The exhaustion of land and water resources through clear-cutting and pollution is also driving up the costs of production.

Wallerstein's world systems analysis is the most widely used version of **dependency theory.** According to this theory, even as developing countries make economic advances, they remain weak and subservient to core nations and corporations in an increasingly intertwined global economy. This interdependency allows industrialized nations to continue to exploit developing countries for their own gain.

According to world systems analysis and dependency theory, a growing share of the human and natural resources of developing countries is being redistributed to the core industrialized nations. This redistribution happens in part because developing countries owe huge sums of money to industrialized nations as a result of foreign aid, loans, and trade deficits. The global debt crisis has intensified the Third World dependency rooted in colonialism, neocolonialism, and multinational investment. International financial institutions are pressuring indebted countries to take severe measures to meet their interest payments. The result is that developing nations may be forced to devalue their currencies, freeze workers' wages, increase privatization of industry, and reduce government services and employment.

Closely related to these problems is **globalization**—the worldwide integration of government policies, cultures, social movements, and financial markets through trade and the exchange of ideas. Because the forces of world financial markets transcend governance by conventional nation-states, international organizations such as the World Bank and the International Monetary Fund have emerged as major players in the global economy. The function of these institutions, which are heavily funded and influenced by core nations, is to encourage trade and development and to ensure the smooth operation of international financial markets. As such, they are seen as promoters of globalization

and defenders primarily of the interests of core nations. Critics call attention to a variety of related issues, including violations of workers' rights, the destruction of the environment, the loss of cultural identity, and discrimination against minority groups in periphery nations.

THE GROWTH OF MULTINATIONAL CORPORATIONS

Worldwide, corporate giants have played a key role in the rise of globalization. The term **multinational corporations** refers to commercial organizations that are headquartered in one country but do business around the world. Such private trade and lending relationships are not new; merchants have conducted business abroad for hundreds of years, trading gems, spices, garments, and other goods. Today's multinational giants are not merely buying and selling overseas; they are also producing goods all over the world (Wallerstein 1974, 2004). Through deindustrialization, corporate executives also have relocated production jobs around the globe.

Increasingly, it is not just production jobs that are being relocated. Today's global factories may now have the "global office" alongside them. Multinationals based in core nations are beginning to establish reservation services and centers for processing data and insurance claims in the periphery nations. As service industries become a more important part of the international marketplace, many companies are concluding that the low costs of overseas operations more than offset the expense of transmitting information around the world.

> **dependency theory** An approach contending that industrialized nations continue to exploit developing countries for their own gain.
> **globalization** The worldwide integration of government policies, cultures, social movements, and financial markets through trade and the exchange of ideas.
> **multinational corporation** A commercial organization that is headquartered in one country but does business throughout the world.

SOCthink

> > > How has the rise of multinational corporations and the trend toward globalization affected you, your family, and your community, both positively and negatively?

These multinational corporations are huge, with total revenues on a par with the total value of goods and services exchanged in entire nations. Foreign sales represent an important source of profit for multinational corporations, encouraging them to expand into other countries (in

Going GLOBAL

Multinational Corporations Compared to Nations

Rank	Corporate revenue	Gross domestic product

Millions of dollars

Rank		
1	$378.8 **Wal-Mart** (USA)	381.7 Saudi Arabia
2	$372.8 **Exxon Mobil** (USA)	373.2 Austria
3	$355.8 **Royal Dutch Petroleum** (Britain/Netherlands)	313.3 Greece
4	$291.4 **BP British Petroleum** (Britain)	286.1 Iran
5	$230.2 **Toyota Motor** (Japan)	228.1 Venezuela
6	$210.8 **Chevron** (USA)	207.8 Colombia
7	$201.5 **ING Group** (Netherlands)	207.2 Hong Kong
8	$187.3 **Total** (France)	186.7 Malaysia
9	$182.4 **General Motors** (USA)	175.0 Czech Republic
10	$178.6 **Conoco Philips** (USA)	166.0 Romania

Note: Total is an oil, petroleum, and chemical company.

Sources: For corporate data, *Fortune* 2008; for GDP data, World Bank 2009b.

SOCthink

> > > Multinational corporations have become so big that they have more economic resources than do some nations. What consequences arise from the fact that they can relocate their headquarters, offices, and production facilities anywhere in the world? How might this affect a nation's political power?

---

many cases, the developing nations). The U.S. economy is heavily dependent on foreign commerce, much of which is conducted by multinationals. Over one-fourth of all goods and services in the United States involve either the export of goods to foreign countries or the import of goods from abroad (U.S. Trade Representative 2003).

Modernization

Consistent with the modernization approach, some analysts believe that the relationship between the corporation and the developing country is mutually beneficial. Multinational corporations can help the developing nations of the world by bringing industries and jobs to areas where subsistence agriculture once served as the only means of survival. Multinationals also promote rapid development through the diffusion of inventions and innovations from industrial nations. The combination of skilled technology and management provided by multinationals and the relatively cheap labor available in developing nations benefits the corporation. Multinationals can take maximum advantage of technology while reducing costs and boosting profits. Through their international ties, multinationals also make the nations of the world more interdependent. These ties may prevent certain disputes from reaching the point of serious conflict. A country cannot afford to sever diplomatic relations or engage in warfare with a nation that is the headquarters for its main business suppliers or a key market for its exports.

Dependency Critics of multinational expansion challenge this favorable evaluation of the impact of corporations. They argue that multinationals exploit local workers to maximize profits. For example, Starbucks—the international coffee retailer based in Seattle—gets some of its coffee beans from farms in Ethiopia. They sell their "Black Apron Exclusives" coffee in a fancy black box for $26 per pound, but they paid Ethiopian workers who picked the beans 66 cents per day (Knudson 2007).

The pool of cheap labor in the developing world prompts multinationals to move factories out of core countries. Workers in these developing countries do not have the same kinds of legal protections and also lack unions to fight on their behalf. In industrialized countries, organized labor insists on decent wages and humane working conditions, but governments seeking to attract or keep multinationals may develop a "climate for investment," including repressive antilabor laws that restrict union activity and collective bargaining. If labor's demands become too threatening, the multinational firm will simply move its plant elsewhere, leaving a trail of unemployment behind. Nike, for example, has moved its factories from the United States to Korea to Indonesia to Vietnam in search of the lowest labor costs.

Workers in the United States and other core countries are beginning to recognize that their own interests are served by helping to organize workers in developing nations. As long as multinationals can exploit cheap labor abroad, they will be in a strong position to reduce wages and benefits in industrialized countries. With this in mind, in the 1990s, labor unions, religious organizations, campus groups, and other activists began to mount public relations campaigns to pressure companies such as Nike, Starbucks, Reebok, Gap, and Wal-Mart to improve wages and working conditions in their overseas operations (Global Alliance for Workers and Communities 2003; Gonzalez 2003).

Sociologists studying the effects of foreign investment by multinationals have found that, although it initially may contribute to a host nation's wealth, such investment eventually increases economic inequality within developing nations. This finding holds for both income and ownership. The upper and middle classes ben-

efit most from economic expansion; the lower classes are less likely to benefit. And because multinationals invest in limited economic sectors and restricted regions of a nation, only some sectors benefit. The expansion of such sectors of the host nation's economy, such as hotels and high-end restaurants, appears to retard growth in agriculture and other economic sectors. Moreover, multinational corporations often buy out or force out local entrepreneurs and companies, thereby increasing economic and cultural dependence (Kerbo 2009; Wallerstein 1979b, 2004).

Hot or Not?

Do CEOs owe anything to local communities, either here or abroad, when they make the decision to move jobs overseas?

>> Stratification Around the World

As these economic investments by multinationals suggest, at the same time that the gap between rich and poor nations is widening, so too is the gap between rich and poor citizens within nations. As discussed earlier, stratification in developing nations is closely related to their relatively weak and dependent position in the global economy. Local elites work hand in hand with multinational corporations and prosper from such alliances. At the same time, the economic system creates and perpetuates the exploitation of industrial and agricultural workers.

INCOME AND WEALTH

Global inequality is staggering, as these two graphs suggest. In at least 18 nations around the world, the most affluent 10 percent of the population receives at least 40 percent of all income. Among these countries are the African nation of Namibia (the leader, at 65 percent of all income) as well as Colombia, Brazil, Honduras, and South Africa (World Bank 2008).

Percent Shares of Global Household Wealth

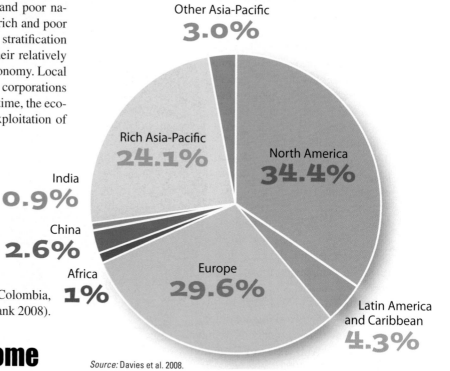

Other Asia-Pacific **3.0%**

Rich Asia-Pacific **24.1%**

North America **34.4%**

India **0.9%**

China **2.6%**

Africa **1%**

Europe **29.6%**

Latin America and Caribbean **4.3%**

Source: Davies et al. 2008.

Distribution of Income in Nine Nations

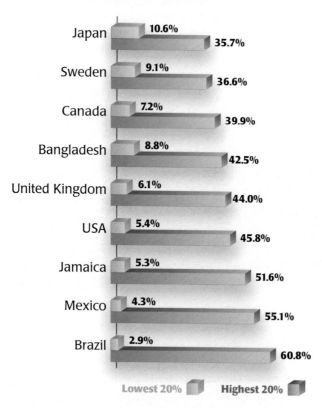

Japan 10.6% / 35.7%
Sweden 9.1% / 36.6%
Canada 7.2% / 39.9%
Bangladesh 8.8% / 42.5%
United Kingdom 6.1% / 44.0%
USA 5.4% / 45.8%
Jamaica 5.3% / 51.6%
Mexico 4.3% / 55.1%
Brazil 2.9% / 60.8%

Lowest 20%   Highest 20%

Note: Data are considered comparable although based on statistics covering 1993 to 2001.

Source: World Bank 2008:Table 2.8.

When it comes to wealth, the top 10 percent of the world's population own 85 percent of global household wealth, and the top 1 percent own 40 percent. On the other end of the spectrum, the bottom 50 percent of the world's population combined own 1 percent of global wealth. Median household wealth globally is estimated to be $2138 per adult. To make it into the top 1 percent takes $510,000. Analyzing the distribution globally, the bulk of the wealth is held by countries in North America, Europe, and the rich Asia-Pacific nations. The United States has 4.7 percent of the world's population but owns 25.4 percent of global household wealth. Africa, by contrast, has 13.4 percent of the population but only 2.6 percent of wealth (Davies et al. 2007, 2008).

Looking in more detail at the world's top 10 percent of wealth holders, 25 percent come from the United States, 20 percent come from Japan, and Germany, Italy, Britain, France, and Spain combine for 29 percent. Within nations, the amount of wealth held by the top 10 percent varies. Denmark demonstrates the most significant amount of wealth inequality, with the top 10 percent of wealth holders there owning 76.4 percent of household wealth—significantly more than Japan, where the top 10 percent hold 39.3 percent of the wealth (Davies et al. 2008).

Women in developing countries often face significant obstacles, making it difficult for them to attain economic assets. Karuna Chanana Ahmed, an anthropologist from India who has studied women in developing nations, calls women the most exploited of oppressed people. Begin-

Amount of Wealth Held by the Top 10 Percent

Source: Davies et al. 2008.

Top 10% | Bottom 90%

Denmark — 76.4% / 23.6%

United States — 69.8% / 30.2%

Indonesia — 65.4% / 34.6%

United Kingdom — 56% / 44%

Canada — 53% / 47%

India — 52.9% / 47.1%

Australia — 45% / 55%

South Korea — 43.1% / 56.9%

Ireland — 42.3% / 57.7%

Spain — 41.9% / 58.1%

China — 41.4% / 58.6%

Japan — 39.3% / 60.7%

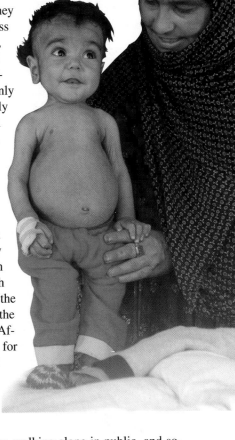

ning at birth, women face sex discrimination. They are commonly fed less than male children, are denied educational opportunities, and often are hospitalized only when they are critically ill. In countries with advanced economies, women made up 60 percent of employment growth from 1990 to 2005, but in other countries they made up less than a third of growth. Nearly 80 percent of women in the Middle East, North Africa, and Asia and the Pacific are not part of the paid labor force. In Afghanistan, it is illegal for a wife to step out of the house without her husband's permission. In Saudi Arabia, women are prohibited from driving, walking alone in public, and socializing with men other than their families (International Labour Organization 2008).

Poverty Worldwide

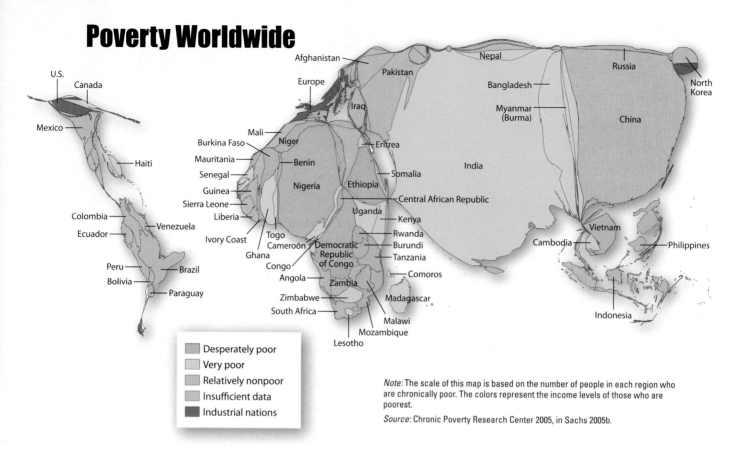

Desperately poor
Very poor
Relatively nonpoor
Insufficient data
Industrial nations

Note: The scale of this map is based on the number of people in each region who are chronically poor. The colors represent the income levels of those who are poorest.

Source: Chronic Poverty Research Center 2005, in Sachs 2005b.

POVERTY

In developing countries, any deterioration in the economic well-being of the least well-off threatens their very survival. Using the global poverty line established by the World Bank of $1.25 per day, 1.4 billion people in the world are considered poor, and 2.6 billion people consume less than $2 a day. In fact, 80 percent of the world's population lives on less than $10 a day (Chen and Ravallion 2008; Shah 2009).

Though poverty is a worldwide problem affecting billions of people, it is distributed unequally. As the world map above demonstrates, if we drew each country to scale based on its number of poor people, Africa and Asia would appear huge. The relatively affluent areas of North America and Europe would be quite small.

In an effort to reduce global poverty, the United Nations passed the Millennium Declaration

Millennium Project Goals by 2015

Source: www.unmillenniumproject.org.

SOCthink

> > > What are the major obstacles to accomplishing the Millennium Project's goals? To what extent are they economic, social, and/or cultural? Is it simply a matter of will?

Eradicate extreme poverty and hunger

Achieve universal primary education

Promote gender equality and empower women

Reduce child mortality

Improve maternal health

Combat HIV/AIDS, malaria, and other diseases

Ensure environmental sustainability

Develop a global partnership for development

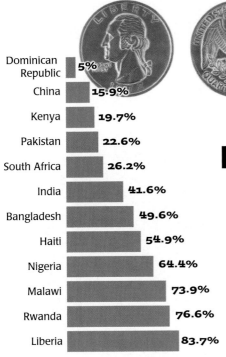

Dominican Republic	5%
China	15.9%
Kenya	19.7%
Pakistan	22.6%
South Africa	26.2%
India	41.6%
Bangladesh	49.6%
Haiti	54.9%
Nigeria	64.4%
Malawi	73.9%
Rwanda	76.6%
Liberia	83.7%

Percent of Population Living on Less than $1.25 a Day

Source: United Nations Development Programme 2008, Table 3.

in 2000, promising to "spare no effort to free our fellow men, women, and children from the abject and dehumanizing conditions of extreme poverty." They established 2015 as the target date for reaching specific, measurable goals to alleviate hunger and improve education, gender equality, and child mortality.

Significant progress on reaching these goals has already been made. The percentage of the

continue to fall. In fact, the goal of cutting the developing world's poverty rate in half is on track. This was driven primarily by the reduction of extreme poverty in East Asia, which saw its rate fall from almost 80 percent in 1981 to 18 percent by 2005. In China alone there are 600 million fewer people living below the global poverty line. Over that same period, rates in Africa have changed less dramatically, though there was a decline from 58 to 50 percent between 2000 and 2005 (Chen and Ravallion 2008, 2009; United Nations 2008).

To accomplish the project's goals, planners estimate that industrial nations must set aside 0.7 percent of their **gross national income (GNI)**—the total value of a nation's goods and services—for aid to developing nations. In 2008, only five countries were giving at least that much: Denmark, Luxembourg, the Netherlands, Norway, and Sweden. The average level of official development assistance from developed countries was 0.47 percent, with the United States contributing 0.18 percent. Although the U.S. government delivers far more total aid dollars than any other nation, the rate of GNI it contributes puts it in last place (tied with Japan) among 22 industrialized nations including the United Kingdom, France, and Germany (OECD 2009a: Table 1).

> **gross national income (GNI)** The total value of a nation's goods and services.

SOCIAL MOBILITY

Although there is significant global inequality, perhaps sufficient social mobility exists to provide hope for those born without significant access to resources. As we saw in the previous chapter, mobility can and does happen in the United States, though the majority of such movement is over only short distances. Here we will look at the possibility for mobility in both industrial nations and developing nations, as well as consider the impact gender has on mobility.

Intergenerational Mobility Across Nations

Intergenerational mobility varies across countries; for example, the amount of income advantage passed from fathers to sons is significantly higher in the United Kingdom, the United States, and France than in Denmark, Norway, or Finland (Corak 2006). What this means, in contrast to the classic vision of the American Dream, is that

5 Movies on GLOBAL INEQUALITY

Babel
Four stories on hardship from around the globe.

Slumdog Millionaire
A boy from the slums of Mumbai is accused of cheating on a game show.

Life and Debt
The IMF exploits Jamaica.

Maria Full of Grace
A factory worker is forced to transport heroin to the United States.

The Girl in the Cafe
An unlikely couple meets in the midst of a G8 summit.

population in developing countries living on $1.25 per day fell from 52 percent to 26 percent between 1981 and 2005. Though the global economic downturn is expected to slow the pace of progress, the global poverty rate is expected to

there is less chance for intergenerational mobility in the United States than in those Scandinavian countries.

In developing nations, macrolevel social and economic changes often overshadow microlevel movement from one occupation to another. For example, there is typically a substantial wage differential between rural and urban areas, which leads to high levels of migration to the cities. Yet the urban industrial sectors of developing countries generally cannot provide sufficient employment for all those seeking work.

In large developing nations, the most socially significant mobility is the movement out of poverty. This type of mobility is difficult to measure and confirm, however, because economic trends can differ from

Foreign Aid per Capita in Eight Countries

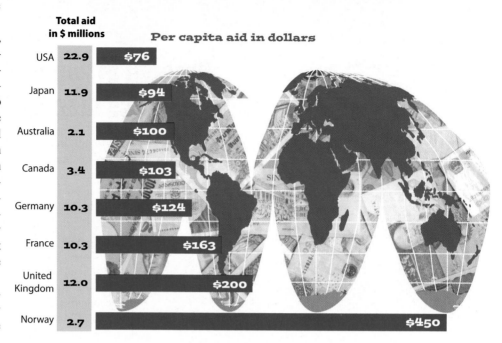

Country	Total aid in $ millions	Per capita aid in dollars
USA	22.9	$76
Japan	11.9	$94
Australia	2.1	$100
Canada	3.4	$103
Germany	10.3	$124
France	10.3	$163
United Kingdom	12.0	$200
Norway	2.7	$450

Note: Data for bilateral aid in 2006 released by World Bank in 2008.
Source: World Bank 2008, Table 6.12.

Intergenerational Earnings Mobility by Country

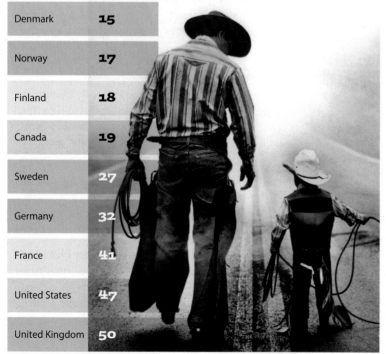

Country	Percentage of earning advantage passed from fathers to sons
Denmark	15
Norway	17
Finland	18
Canada	19
Sweden	27
Germany	32
France	41
United States	47
United Kingdom	50

Source: Corak 2006.

one area of a country to another. For instance, China's rapid income growth has been accompanied by a growing disparity in income between urban and rural areas and among different regions. Similarly, in India during the economic development of the 1990s, poverty declined in urban areas but may have remained static at best in rural areas. Around the world, social mobility is also dramatically influenced by catastrophes such as crop failure and warfare (World Bank 2006c).

Gender Differences and Mobility
Only recently have researchers begun to investigate the impact of gender on the mobility patterns of developing nations. Many aspects of the development process—especially modernization in rural areas and the rural-to-urban migration just described—may result in modification or abandonment of traditional cultural practices and even marital systems. The effects on women's social standing and mobility are not necessarily positive. As a country develops and modernizes, women's vital role in food production deteriorates, jeopardizing both their autonomy and their material well-being. Moreover, the movement of families to the cities weakens women's ties to relatives who can provide food, financial assistance, and social support.

In the Philippines, however, women have moved to the forefront of the indigenous

peoples' struggle to protect their ancestral land from exploitation by outsiders. Having established their right to its rich minerals and forests, members of indigenous groups had begun to feud among themselves over the way in which the land's resources should be developed. Aided by the United Nations Partners in Development Programme, women volunteers established the Pan-Cordillera Women's Network for Peace and Development, a coalition of women's groups dedicated to resolving local disputes. The women mapped boundaries, prepared development plans, and negotiated more than 2000 peace pacts among community members. They have also run in elections, campaigned on issues related to social problems, and organized residents to work together for the common good (United Nations Development Programme 2000:87).

SOCIAL STRATIFICATION IN MEXICO

To get a more complete picture of these global stratification issues, it helps to look at a particular case. Here we will focus on the dynamics of stratification in Mexico, a country of 111 million people.

In May 2003, on a stretch of highway in southern Arizona, the open doors of an abandoned tractor trailer revealed the dead bodies of 19 Mexicans. The truck had been carrying a group of about 75 men, women, and children across the Sonoran Desert illegally into the United States when the people hidden inside began to suffer from the intense desert heat. Their story is not unusual. In recent years, as many as 500 people per year have died trying to cross the U.S.–Mexican border. From October 2008 through April 2009, according to border patrol officials in Arizona, 72 died in the Tucson sector alone (McCombs 2009).

Why do Mexicans risk their lives crossing the dangerous desert that lies between the two countries? The answer to this question can be found primarily in the income

disparity between the two nations—one an industrial giant and the other a partially developed country still recovering from a history of colonialism and neocolonialism. Since the early 20th century, there has been a close cultural, economic, and political relationship between Mexico and the United States, one in which the United States is the dominant party. According to Immanuel Wallerstein's analysis, the United States is at the core while neighboring Mexico is still on the semiperiphery of the world economic system.

Mexico's Economy If we compare Mexico's economy to that of the United States, differences in the standard of living and in life chances are quite dramatic, even though Mexico is considered a semiperiphery nation. Gross national income is a commonly used measure of an average resident's economic well-being. In 2007, the gross national income per person in the United States came to $45,850; in Mexico, it was a mere $12,580. About 87 percent of adults in the United States have a high school education, compared to only 32 percent of those in Mexico. And fewer than 7 of every 1000 infants in the United States die in the first year of life, compared to about 19 per 1000 in Mexico (Bureau of the Census 2007a:Table 1312; Population Reference Bureau 2008; Snyder et al. 2009).

Not only is Mexico unquestionably a poor country, but the gap between its richest and poorest citizens is one of the widest in the world. The top quintile earns 55.1 percent of total income while the bottom earns just 4.3 per-

cent. The World Bank reports that, in 2006, 5 percent of Mexico's population survived on just $2 per day. At the same time, the wealthiest 10 percent of Mexico's people accounted for 39 percent of the nation's income. According to a *Forbes* magazine portrait of the world's wealthiest individuals, that year Mexico ranked 11th in terms of the number of residents who were among the world's wealthiest people (Kroll and Fass 2006; World Bank 2008).

Political scientist Jorge Castañeda (1995:71), who later served as Mexico's Foreign Minister, called Mexico a "polarized society with enormous gaps between rich and poor, town and country, north and south, white and brown (or *criollos* and *mestizos*)." He added that the country is also divided along lines of class, race, religion, gender, and age. To better understand the nature of the stratification within Mexico, we will examine race relations and the plight of Mexican Indians, the status of Mexican women, and immigration to the United States and its impact on the U.S.–Mexican borderlands.

> **borderlands** The area of common culture along the border between Mexico and the United States.

Race Relations in Mexico: The Color Hierarchy

Mexico's indigenous Indians account for an estimated 14 percent of the nation's population. According to a United Nations report, more than 90 percent of Mexico's indigenous people (the ethnic group historically native to a region) live in extreme poverty. The literacy rate in Mexico as a whole is 92 percent, but it hovers around 50 percent among the indigenous population (Cevallos 2009; Minority Rights Group International 2007; United Nations Development Programme 2008).

The subordinate status of Mexico's Indians is but one reflection of the nation's color hierarchy, which links social class status to the appearance of racial purity. At the top of this hierarchy are the *criollos*, the 10 percent of the population who are typically White, well-educated members of the business and intellectual elites, with familial roots in Spain. In the middle is the large, impoverished *mestizo* majority, most of whom have brown skin and a mixed racial lineage as a result of intermarriage. At the bottom of the color hierarchy are the destitute, full-blooded Mexican Indian minority and a small number of Blacks, some descended from 200,000 African slaves brought to Mexico. This color hierarchy is an important part of day-to-day life—enough so that some Mexicans in the cities use hair dyes, skin lighteners, and blue or green contact lenses to appear more White and European. Ironically, however, nearly all Mexicans are considered part Indian because of centuries of intermarriage (Castañeda 1995; Standish and Standish 2009).

Many observers take note of widespread denial of prejudice and discrimination against people of color in Mexico. Schoolchildren are taught that the election of Benito Juárez, a Zapotec Indian, as president of Mexico in the 19th century proves that all Mexicans are equal. Yet there has been a marked growth in the past decade of formal organizations and voluntary associations representing indigenous Indians (Escárcega 2008; Stavenhagen 1994; Utne 2003).

The Status of Women in Mexico

Though the United Nations convened the first international conference on the status of women in Mexico in 1975, and opportunities there have improved, women still face significant obstacles. Women now constitute 45 percent of the labor force—an increase from 31 percent in 1980. Unfortunately, Mexican women are even more mired in the lowest-paying jobs than their counterparts in industrial nations, on average earning 42 percent less than men. Men are still typically viewed as heads of the household, making it difficult for women to obtain credit and technical assistance in many parts of the country and to inherit land in rural areas. As for education, the literacy rate for women in Chiapas (71 percent) and Oaxaca (73 percent), states with high levels of indigenous populations, is well below the national average (INEGI 2009; United Nations Development Programme 2008).

In the political arena, though they rarely occupy top decision-making positions, women have significantly increased their representation in the national legislature to 23 percent. Mexico now ranks 39th among 189 nations in female representation. In spite of this, the struggle for enforcement of legal rights continues. In February 2007, Mexico passed the General Law on Women's Access to a Life Free from Violence. States have not followed through with implementation of the law's basic requirements, such as establishing protocols to follow when claims of abuse are filed or constructing shelters for domestic violence victims. In fact, there are only 60 such shelters in all of Mexico (Amnesty International 2009a; Inter-Parliamentary Union 2007).

In recent decades, Mexican women have organized to address an array of economic, political, and health issues. For example, as far back as 1973, women in Monterrey—the nation's third-largest city—protested the continuing disruptions of the city's water supply. Through coordinated efforts, including delegations of politicians, rallies, and public demonstrations, they succeeded in improving Monterrey's water service, a major concern in developing nations. After being denied the opportunity to run for mayor in her hometown in 2007, Eufrosina Cruz organized QUIEGO (Queremos Unir Integrando por Equidad y Género en Oaxaca, meaning "we want to come together for equity and gender in Oaxaca") to raise awareness about political rights for women in her home state and ultimately

SOCthink

> > > How might racial categories in Mexico differ from those in the United States? Why might such differences arise?

From Me to You

Central College, where I teach, started its first international program in 1965. It was a leader in establishing study abroad programs for students. It now operates programs around the world in places such as Merida in Mexico, Bangor in Wales, and Hangzhou in China. Central instituted these programs to provide students with a prolonged experience in another country in hopes that such exposure would enable them to go beyond being just a tourist and achieve a deeper understanding of another culture. I always encourage my students to go abroad because I find that those who do come back changed. They return to campus with a deeper understanding, not only of the world but of themselves.

throughout Mexico (Bennett, Dávila-Poblete, and Rico 2005; Cevallos 2009).

The Borderlands Growing recognition of the borderlands reflects the increasingly close and complex relationship between Mexico and the United States. The term **borderlands** refers to the area of common culture along the border between Mexico and the United States. Legal and illegal emigration from Mexico to the United States, day laborers crossing the border regularly to go to work in the United States, the implementation of the North American Free Trade Agreement (NAFTA), the exchange of media across the border—all make the notion of separate Mexican and U.S. cultures obsolete in the borderlands.

The economic position of the borderlands is rather complicated, as demonstrated by the emergence of *maquiladoras*. These are foreign-owned factories, often located just across the border in Mexico, that are allowed to import parts and materials without tariffs. Typical jobs include manufacturing electronics, transportation equipment, electrical machinery, and textiles and apparel, as well as service jobs in call centers and coupon processing operations. The chief appeal for U.S. companies is less expensive labor. As of 2006, hourly compensation costs (including salary and benefits) for maquiladora manufacturing production workers was $2.64. This compares to $29.98 per hour in the United States (Bureau of Labor Statistics 2009a, 2009b; Cañas and Gilmer 2009).

Maquiladoras now employ over 1.2 million workers. They account for about 40 percent of all Mexico's exports. Overall, 80 percent of Mexico's exports go to the United States. This makes Mexico's economy more sensitive to

The Borderlands

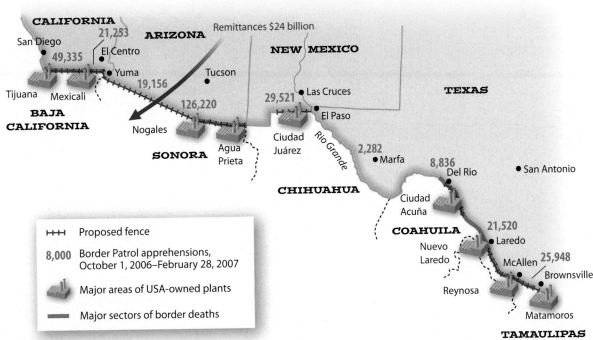

Source: Prepared by Schaefer 2009 based on Marosi 2007; Romano and Ramirez 2007; G. Thompson 2001a.

U.S. fluctuations, a significant problem with the recent economic downturn. Maquiladoras estimate a job loss of 163,000 for 2009, a rate two to four times higher than in other Mexican firms (Black 2009; Bogan et al. 2008).

Though the maquiladora program was established in 1965, it really took off after the North American Free Trade Agreement (NAFTA) was implemented in 1994, removing most barriers to trade between Mexico, the United States, and Canada. Things changed, however, with China's entry into the World Trade Organization in 2001. Labor costs were even lower there. As a result, jobs that had moved from the United States to Mexico, especially those requiring minimal skills, are now being transferred to China (Cañas and Gilmer 2009; Sargent and Matthews 2009).

Emigration to the United States From the Mexican point of view, the United States too often regards Mexico simply as a reserve pool of cheap labor, encouraging Mexicans to cross the border when workers are needed but discouraging and cracking down on them when they are not. Some people, then, see immigration more as a labor market issue than a law enforcement issue. Viewed from the perspective of Wallerstein's world systems analysis and dependency theory, it is yet another example of a core industrialized nation exploiting a developing country.

SOCthink

> > > How do U.S. consumers benefit from the buildup of factories along the U.S.–Mexican border? What impact might they have on U.S. workers?

Mass grave site in Srebrenica, Bosnia-Herzegovina.

The social impact of immigration to the United States is felt throughout Mexico. According to sociological research, the earliest emigrants were typically married men of working age from the middle of the stratification system. They had sufficient financial resources to afford the costs and risks of immigration, yet were experiencing enough financial strain that entering the United States was attractive to them. Over time, kinship ties to emigrants multiplied, and immigration became less class-selective, with entire families making the trek to the United States (Massey 1998, 2008).

Many Mexicans who have come to the United States send a portion of their earnings back across the border to family members in Mexico. This substantial flow of money, referred to as **remittances** (or *remesas*), amounted to $25 billion in 2008. It is second only to oil as a source of foreign revenue for Mexico. After years of growth, remittances sent to Mexico fell 3.6 percent in 2008, due to the economic downturn in the United States. The decline was more dramatic in 2009, falling 19 percent in April 2009. Though remittances still totaled $1.8 billion, it meant a loss of $300 million to the Mexican economy for that month alone. As a result of the weak economy, more Mexicans left the United States to head back to Mexico than entered the United States in the first quarter of 2009, a dramatic reversal of events (Barta and Millman 2009; Booth 2009; Wilkinson 2009).

>> Universal Human Rights

As globalization has spread, affecting more and more peoples around the world, a movement toward ensuring universal human rights has arisen. Recognizing the harm-

Ongoing violence in East Timor has driven children like these to seek safety in refugee camps in the country.

ful effects of such global expansion, activists in this movement fight to preserve and protect the interests of people who lack significant power or access to resources. The sheer size and economic might of multinational corporations, along with their freedom to move jobs and plants around the world without regard for the impact on national populations, encouraged the establishment of universal human rights as a countervailing source of power. The goal of human rights activists is to establish a nonnegotiable and inviolable foundation of rights that applies no matter where people are or which governments or multinational corporations are involved.

DEFINING HUMAN RIGHTS

The term **human rights** refers to universal moral rights that all people possess by virtue of being human. The most important elaboration of human rights appears in the Universal Declaration of Human Rights, adopted by the United Nations in 1948. This declaration prohibits slavery, torture, and degrading punishment; grants everyone the right to a nationality and its culture; affirms freedom of religion and the right to vote; proclaims the right to seek asylum in other countries to escape persecution; and prohibits arbitrary interference with one's privacy and the arbitrary seizure of a person's property. It also emphasizes that mothers and children are entitled to special care and assistance.

At first, the United States opposed a binding obligation to the Universal Declaration of Human Rights. The government feared loss of national sovereignty—the right to rule over its people without external interference. This concern was driven in part by the existence of racial segregation laws that were still common at the time the UN issued the Universal Declaration and that violated the human rights principles. By the early 1960s, however, the United States had begun to use the declaration to promote democracy abroad (Forsythe 1990).

In the 1990s, concerns about human rights brought the term *ethnic cleansing* into the world's vocabulary as a euphemism for forcible expulsion and murder. In the former Yugoslavia, Serbs initiated a policy intended to "cleanse" Muslims from parts of Bosnia-Herzegovina and ethnic Albanians from the province of Kosovo. Hundreds of thousands of people were killed in fighting there, while many others were uprooted from their homes. Moreover, reports surfaced of Serbian soldiers raping substantial numbers of Muslim, Croatian, and Kosovar women. Regrettably, ethnic cleansing has since spread to other parts of the world, including East Timor, Iraq, Kenya, and Sudan.

remittances The monies that immigrants return to their families of origin. Also called *remesas*.

human rights Universal moral rights possessed by all people because they are human.

An ongoing human rights concern is the transnational crime of trafficking in humans. Each year an estimated 600,000–800,000 men, women, and children are transported across international borders for slavery or sexual exploitation, In 2000, Congress passed the Trafficking Victims Protection Act, which established minimum standards

Human Trafficking Report

Tier 1 Full Compliance	Tier 2 Significant Effort	Tier 2 Watch Some Effort, but Trafficking Remains a Concern	Tier 3 Noncompliant, No Effort
Australia	Afghanistan	Armenia	Algeria
Canada	Azerbaijan	Bahrain	Burma
Columbia	Brazil	Cambodia	Cuba
Denmark	Greece	China	Iran
France	Israel	Dominican Republic	Kuwait
Germany	Japan	Egypt	Malaysia
Hong Kong	Nicaragua	Honduras	North Korea
Italy	Nigeria	India	Qatar
Morocco	Philippines	Mexico	Saudi Arabia
Norway	Romania	Mozambique	Sudan
Poland	Turkey	Russia	Syria
South Korea	Vietnam	South Africa	Uzbekistan
Spain	Yemen	Ukraine	Venezuela

Note: Table is incomplete; each tier lists only sample nations.
Source: Ribando 2008:22 for the Department of State.

for the elimination of human trafficking. The act requires the State Department to monitor other countries' efforts to vigorously investigate, prosecute, and convict individuals who participate in trafficking—including government officials. Each year the department reports its findings, dividing countries into three groups, or tiers, depending upon their level of compliance. Tier-1 countries are thought to be largely in compliance with the act. Tier-2 nations are making a significant effort to comply, while tier-2 "watch" nations are making efforts to comply, though trafficking remains a real concern. Tier-3 countries are not compliant (Kapstein 2006; Kempadoo and Doezema 1998; Ribando 2008).

PRINCIPLE AND PRACTICE

When it comes to human rights, the balance between principle and practice can be problematic. In the wake of the terrorist attacks of September 11, 2001, increased police personnel and surveillance at U.S. airports and border crossings caused some observers to wonder whether human rights were not being jeopardized in the name of security. At the same time, thousands of noncitizens of Arab and south Asian descent were questioned for no other reason than their ethnic and religious backgrounds. A few were placed in custody, sometimes without access to legal assistance. And as the war on terror moved overseas, human rights concerns escalated. In 2005, then Secretary-General Kofi Annan of the UN criticized the United States and Britain for equating people who were resisting the presence of foreign troops in Afghanistan and Iraq with terrorists (Parker 2004; Steele 2005).

SOCthink

> > > To what extent do you think violations of human rights are excusable in a time of war? At such times, how might our perception of the balance between rights and security alter what we think of as universal?

What this points to is the significance of perspective even when it comes to something that appears to be a fundamental principle. Cultural insiders and outsiders can disagree about what constitutes a violation. For example, was India's caste system an inherent violation of human rights? What about the many cultures of the world that view the subordinate status of women as an essential element in their traditions? Should human rights be interpreted differently in different parts of the world?

We can consider, as an example, female genital mutilation, a practice that is common in more than 30 countries around the world but that has been condemned in Western nations as a human rights abuse. This controversial practice often involves removal of the clitoris, in the belief that its excision will inhibit a young woman's sex drive, making her chaste and thus more desirable to her future husband. Though some countries have passed laws against the practice, they have gone largely unenforced. Emigrants from countries where genital mutilation is common often insist that their daughters undergo the procedure, to protect them from Western cultural norms that allow premarital sex (Religious Tolerance 2008). To what extent should outside nations have the power to dictate such internal laws? In this sense, the movement for universal human rights also represents a form of cultural imperialism.

SOCthink

> > > How active should the U.S. government be in addressing violations of human rights in other countries? At what point, if any, does concern for human rights turn into ethnocentrism through failure to respect the distinctive norms, values, and customs of another culture?

In 1993, the United States opted for an absolute definition of human rights, insisting that the Universal Declaration of Human Rights set a single standard for acceptable behavior around the world. In practice, however, interpretation still plays a role. Some have argued that the United States practices selective enforcement of human rights. Critics contend, for example, that officials in the United States are more likely to become concerned about human rights abuses when oil is at stake, as in the Middle East, or when military alliances come into play, as in Europe.

HUMAN RIGHTS ACTIVISM

Efforts to protect and ensure human rights seldom come from inside governments but arise out of social movements that organize to generate economic, social, and political pressure in an effort to force change. For example, in June 2008, Human Rights Watch (www.hrw.org), a premier international human rights organization, called for other African nations to impose sanctions on Zimbabwe after what they called the sham reelection of President Robert Mugabe. They monitor human rights abuses around the world, including calling upon U.S. officials to end abuses against prisoners in the Guantanamo Bay detention camps.

In Sudan, the Save Darfur Coalition (www .savedarfur.org) fights for justice and relief for refugees who were attacked, driven off their land and out of the country, and often killed by the Janjaweed, a group of armed gunmen backed by the Sudanese government. Their cause was helped significantly with the release of the film *The Devil Came on Horseback*—translated from the Janjaweed—in which ex-marine Brian Steidle, who was hired as a human rights

observer by the African Union, documented genocide in Darfur with photos and video. He ultimately testified before Congress and at the UN, providing his documentation to support the genocide claims. In addition to numerous other organizational efforts, the Save Darfur Coalition also coordinated an agreement on May 28, 2008, in which presidential candidates Barack Obama, John McCain, and Hillary Clinton issued a joint statement demanding an end to the violence in Darfur.

Médecins sans Frontières (Doctors Without Borders), the world's largest independent emergency medical aid organization, won the 1999 Nobel Peace Prize for its work in countries worldwide. Founded in 1971 and based in Paris, the organization has 5000 doctors and nurses working in 80 countries. "Our intention is to highlight current upheavals, to bear witness to foreign tragedies and reflect on the principles of humanitarian aid," explains Dr. Rony Brauman, the organization's president (Bortolotti 2006).

In recent years, awareness has been growing of lesbian and gay rights as an aspect of universal human rights. In 1994, Amnesty International (1994:2) published a pioneering report in which it acknowledged that "homosexuals in many parts of the world live in constant fear of government persecution." The report examined abuses in Brazil, Greece, Mexico, Iran, the United States, and other countries, including cases of torture, imprisonment, and extrajudicial execution. Later in 1994, the United States issued an order that would allow lesbians and gay men to seek political asylum in the United States if they could prove they had suffered government persecution in their home countries solely because of their sexual orientation (Amnesty International 2009b; Johnston 1994).

One of the things we learn from sociology is that we are embedded in larger networks in which decisions and events that happen far away, and about which we may know little or nothing, shape our daily life experiences.

Hot or Not?

Should outside nations, including the UN, have the power to force the United States to change its laws to comply with human rights principles?

There can be no peace as long as there is grinding poverty, social injustice, inequality, oppression, environmental degradation, and as long as the weak and small continue to be trodden by the mighty and powerful.

the Dalai Lama

Ethnic cleansing in the former Yugoslavia, human rights violations in Iraq and Afghanistan, increased surveillance in the name of counterterrorism, violence against women inside and outside the family, governmental torture of lesbians and gay men—all these are vivid reminders that social inequality can have life-and-death consequences. In each case, people recognized the consequences of global inequality, and individuals, groups, and nations took steps to address the problems. By developing a more fully formed sociological imagination, we can more readily see such issues and take necessary steps toward addressing them.

For REVIEW

I. **How did the global divide develop?**

- Theorists emphasizing modernization argue that it is part of the natural evolution of societies as they pass through the effects of the Industrial Revolution and beyond. Dependency theorists argue that it is due to a fundamental power struggle between wealthy nations at the core and developing nations at the periphery.

II. **How significant is global stratification?**

- Analyses of wealth, income, poverty, and social mobility demonstrate a wide gap both within and between nations.

III. **Why did the global movement for universal human rights develop?**

- As global inequality became more apparent, activists worked to establish a foundational set of human rights that would protect people regardless of who or where they were.

Pop Quiz

1. Which of the following terms is used by contemporary social scientists to describe the far-reaching process by which nations pass from traditional forms of social organization toward those characteristic of post–Industrial Revolution societies?
   a. dependency
   b. globalization
   c. industrialization
   d. modernization

2. The maintenance of political, social, economic, and cultural domination over a people by a foreign power for an extended period of time is referred to as
   a. globalization.
   b. government-imposed stratification.
   c. colonialism.
   d. dependency.

3. Immanuel Wallerstein's world systems analysis focuses on
   a. the unequal access to and control of resources between core and periphery nations.
   b. the natural evolutionary development of all societies toward the modern ideal.
   c. the rise of multinational corporations.
   d. the global pattern of inequality faced by women.

4. Companies that are headquartered in one country but do business throughout the world are known as
   a. global corporations.
   b. multinational corporations.
   c. *maquiladoras.*
   d. international agencies.

1. (d); 2. (c); 3. (a); 4. (b);

5. Approximately how much of global household wealth is owned by households in North America?

   a. about one-tenth

   b. about one-quarter

   c. about one-third

   d. about one-half

6. Globally, approximately how many people subsist on less than $1.25 per day?

   a. 500 million

   b. 1.4 billion

   c. 3.2 billion

   d. 5 billion

7. How much of total global wealth do the bottom 50 percent of the world's population own?

   a. 1 percent

   b. 6 percent

   c. 23 percent

   d. 47 percent

8. Karuna Chanana Ahmed, an anthropologist from India who has studied developing nations, calls which group the most exploited of oppressed people?

   a. children

   b. women

   c. the elderly

   d. the poor

9. Which of the following terms refers to the foreign-owned factories established just across the border in Mexico, where the companies that own them don't have to pay taxes or high wages, or provide insurance or benefits for their workers?

   a. maquiladoras

   b. hombres

   c. mujeres

   d. remesas

10. What year did the United Nations adopt the Universal Declaration of Human Rights?

   a. 1865

   b. 1919

   c. 1948

   d. 1993

5. (c); 6. (b); 7. (a); 8. (b); 9. (a); 10. (c)

GENDER &

RAISING WOMEN'S CONSCIOUSNESS

Betty Friedan was living the American Dream. She came from a solid middle-class background and graduated from Smith College, a prestigious liberal arts college. Friedan worked as a journalist before marrying and settling into life as a 1950s suburban housewife and mother. However, she continued to work as a freelance journalist, writing articles for magazines such as *Redbook* and *Cosmopolitan.*

Fifteen years after her college graduation, Friedan surveyed her college classmates about their lives for a story she planned to write. During her research, she heard a consistent message from well-educated, middle-class suburban housewives: They shared a sense of nameless, aching dissatisfaction that she famously labeled "the problem that has no name." The message they received from educators, psychologists, and the mass media was of one voice: They should be happy. And yet, something was missing. They mostly blamed themselves for this feeling of emptiness or incompleteness, and when they sought help, doctors and psychiatrists would prescribe charity work, community activities, or perhaps tranquilizers.

In her best-selling classic *The Feminine Mystique,* Friedan argued that the problem was not with women as individuals but with the position they occupied in American society at the time. Friedan's realization that this was not a private trouble but a public issue represents a classic case of using the sociological imagination (Mills [1959] 2000). Women were cut off from the public sphere, and their lack of access to valued economic, social, and cultural resources—including money and power in the workplace—was the real problem. (Friedan herself attributed part of her relative happiness to the fact that she retained dual status as both journalist and housewife.) In order to challenge this structural problem, women had to challenge the cultural assumption that the primary and most "natural" goal for women was to be a wife and mother in the private sphere. As Friedan put it, "We can no longer ignore that voice within women that says: 'I want something more than my husband and my children and my home'" ([1963] 1983: 32).

AGE

As You READ

>>

- How has opportunity for women in the United States changed over time?
- To what extent does gender still shape access to resources?
- How do sociologists approach the study of aging?

>> The Social Construction of Gender

We tend to take for granted that differences between men and women must be "natural." Historically, however, things that we took for granted as natural often turned out not to be so. Unfortunately, in the meantime, such differences may have been used to justify unequal opportunity in education, employment, politics, and more. Members of groups defined as inferior in some way, including women but also racial and ethnic minorities and the elderly, have consistently had to fight against such characterizations in order to pursue equal opportunity.

sex The biological differences between males and females.

It was once thought, for example, that women were incapable of succeeding at college because their biological makeup limited them. At the Jefferson Medical College in Philadelphia in 1847, Professor Charles Meigs, in a famous speech delivered to an all-male class of gynecology students, said of women, "She has a head almost too small for intellect and just big enough for love . . . She reigns in the heart . . . the household altar is her place of worship and service" (quoted in Collins 2003:89–90). In 1874, at Harvard University, Dr. Edward Clarke, a member of their board of overseers, wrote that women were too delicate to handle the rigors of college education. The increased effort needed for thinking would sap energy from a woman's uterus and ovaries, leading these reproductive organs to shrink (Clarke 1874). In

fact, Harvard did not formally admit women to its undergraduate program until the early 1970s.

When they were given the opportunity, however, women excelled in college. They now have a higher overall grade point average and outnumber men among college graduates. Just as Friedan found with the feminine mystique, our cultural presuppositions are more often rooted in our social constructions of what is natural than in biological limitations themselves. In this chapter, we examine how such constructions develop and what their consequences are in terms of opportunity. We will then do the same for the issue of age.

SEX AND GENDER

To better understand the nature of social realities for men and women, sociologists typically make a distinction between sex and gender. **Sex** refers to biological differences between males and females. **Gender** involves the social and cultural significance that we attach to those presumed biological differences.

Sex includes variation that occurs at the cellular level (chromosomes and sex-specific genes), the hormonal level (estrogen and testosterone), and the anatomical level (genitals and secondary sexual characteristics). In the taken-for-granted biological model of sex, females have XX chromosome patterns, estrogen hormones, ovaries, and a vagina; males have XY chromosome patterns, androgen hormones, testicles, and a penis. This definition of sex assumes a simple, two-sex, or "dimorphic," model in which the line between females and males is distinct and absolute. In fact, however, there is no absolute biological dividing line; we find a range of

... Anne Fausto-Sterling, a geneticist, argues that, when it comes to biology, there are three intersexual categories between male and female. They include hermaphrodites, who have one testis and one ovary; male pseudohermaphrodites, with testes and what appear to be female genitalia; and female pseudohermaphrodites, who have ovaries and male genitalia. She estimates that 5.1 million Americans are born intersexual in some way.

Did You Know?

these characteristics throughout the population (Fausto-Sterling 2000).

Gender, on the other hand, varies across time and place. We construct gender by attaching social and cultural significance to the presumed biological differences between the sexes. Sex refers to who we are as males and females; gender refers to what we become as men and women. This process of becoming occurs through socialization, in which we learn the appropriate cognitive, normative, and material culture information assumed to be natural in our social worlds.

GENDER ROLES IN THE UNITED STATES

In studying gender, sociologists are interested in the gender-role socialization that leads females and males to behave differently. In Chapter 4 on socialization, we defined gender roles as expectations regarding the proper behavior, attitudes, and activities of males and females. The application of dominant gender roles leads to many forms of differentiation between women and men. Both sexes are physically capable of learning to cook and sew, yet in most Western societies, women predominantly perform

those tasks. Both men and women are capable of learning to weld and to fly airplanes, but men generally fill those jobs. We learn such expectations through our interactions with others.

Gender-Role Socialization We reinforce male–female differences through our actions. Male babies get blue blankets; females get pink ones. Boys are expected to play with trucks, blocks, and toy soldiers; girls receive dolls and kitchen goods. Boys must be masculine—active, aggressive, tough, daring, and dominant—but girls must be feminine—soft, emotional, sweet, and submissive. These traditional gender-role patterns have been influential in the socialization of children in the United States.

> **gender** The social and cultural significance that we attach to the biological differences of sex.
> **heterosexism** The systematic reinforcement of male–female sexual and marital relationships as normative.

Children learn these preferences primarily from adults, who play a critical role in guiding them into those gender roles that a society deems appropriate. Parents are normally the first and most crucial agents of socialization. However, other adults, along with older siblings, the mass media, and religious and educational institutions, also exert an important influence on gender-role socialization, in the United States and elsewhere.

The prevalence of **heterosexism**—the systematic reinforcement of male–female sexual and marital relationships as normative—provides a sense of the importance attached to maintaining clear lines between masculinity and femininity in the United States. Heterosexism presupposes an absolute or binary separation between the sexes. Those who deviate from such expectations, falling into the gray area between these two categories—whether gay, lesbian, bisexual, or transgendered—are stigmatized and face discrimination. Men and women who deviate from traditional expectations about gender roles are often presumed to be gay. Despite the advances made by the gay liberation movement, the continuing stigma attached to homosexuality in the United States becomes a mechanism for reinforc-

ing narrow "masculine" and "feminine" characteristics for men and women (Herek 2004, 2007; Pascoe 2007).

It is not hard to test how rigid gender-role socialization can be. Just try transgressing some gender norm—say, by smoking a cigar in public if you are female, or by carrying a purse if you are male. That was exactly the assignment given to sociology students at the University of Colorado and at Luther College in Iowa. Professors asked students to behave in ways that they thought violated the norms of how a man or woman should act. The students had no trouble coming up with gender-norm transgressions, and they kept careful notes on others' reactions to their behavior, ranging from amusement to disgust (Nielsen et al. 2000).

Women's Gender Roles Parents, schools, friends, and the mass media all socialize us to internalize dominant gender norms. The positive and negative sanctions that we experience during such interactions shape the thoughts, actions, and appearances we accept as appropriate. Women, for example, continue to face pressure to be thin, beautiful, submissive, sexy, and maternal.

In 2004, Dove launched a series of ads in what they called the Campaign for Real Beauty (www.campaignforrealbeauty.com). In preparation for this campaign, they conducted a for-

From Me to You

When they were little, our refrigerator was covered with pictures of our family drawn by Emily and Eleanor. In the pictures, the girls wore dresses while I wore pants. They had long eyelashes and I did not. They had long hair and I had what looked like a plate on my head. I asked Eleanor, "What about the women we know with short hair and the men we know with long hair?" She replied, "Yeah, but women have long hair and men have short hair." She knew there were people who didn't fit her hair theory, but she had already come to accept an image in which the line between men and women was obvious, important, and inevitable.

DRAWING DISTINCTIONS

mal research project in which they hired academic researchers to conduct surveys of women from 10 countries around the world, including the United States. They found that only 2 percent of women around the world feel comfortable describing themselves as beautiful. This was in spite of the fact that these women distinguished between beauty (which they maintain involves happiness, confidence, dignity, and humor) and physical attractiveness (which involves how a person looks). Regarding their weight and body shape, overall, just 13 percent of women said they were very satisfied.

In the survey, 68 percent strongly agreed that "the media and advertising set an unrealistic standard of beauty that most women can't ever achieve." Dove set out to address this through an advertising campaign that featured a wide range of body types and highlighted an expanded definition of beauty.

While television consistently portrays youth, thinness, and beauty as essential to this ideal, it is far from alone in stereotyping women. Stud-

An Experiment in Gender Norm Violation by College Students

SOCstudies

Norm Violations by Men

Wear fingernail polish
Needlepoint in public
Throw Tupperware party
Cry in public
Have pedicure
Apply to baby-sit
Shave body hair

Norm Violations by Women

Send men flowers
Spit in public
Use men's bathroom
Buy jockstrap
Talk knowledgeably about cars
Buy/chew tobacco
Open doors for men

Source: Nielsen et al. 2000:287.

ies of children's books published in the United States in the 1940s, 1950s, and 1960s found that females were significantly underrepresented in central roles and in illustrations. The books portrayed virtually all female characters as helpless, passive, incompetent, and in need of a strong male caretaker. Starting in the 1970s, publishers made explicit attempts to provide more balanced representations of gender roles for both women and men. However, recent research continues to find sex-based stereotypes at work. Authors still show females primarily in traditional roles, such as mother, grandmother, or volunteer—even if they also hold nontraditional roles, such as working professional. A study of children's picture books found that fathers were significantly less likely to touch, hug, kiss, talk to, or feed children (Anderson and Hamilton 2005; Etaugh 2003; Hamilton et al. 2006).

The pervasiveness of these traditional gender roles extends even to unpaid labor as volunteers. Researchers found that men and women are equally likely to volunteer, but male volunteers from high-prestige occupations are much more likely than women to serve on boards and committees. An exception to this was men who work in traditionally "feminine" fields such as education and the fine arts. Female volunteers, in contrast, are disproportionately involved in direct charitable service as caregivers, nurturers, and food preparers. A significant exception is involvement in political campaigns, where gender roles are not pronounced among volunteers (Rotolo and Wilson 2007).

Men's Gender Roles How about stay-at-home fathers? Until recent decades, such an idea was unthinkable. Yet, in a nationwide survey, 69 percent of respondents said that if one parent stays home with the children, it makes no difference whether that parent is the mother or the father. Only 30 percent thought that the mother should be the one to stay home. Although people's conceptions of gender roles are obviously changing, the fact is that men who stay home to care for their children are still an unusual phenomenon. For every stay-at-home dad, there are 38 stay-at-home moms (Robison 2002; U.S. Census Bureau 2009a:Table FG8).

While attitudes toward parenting may be changing, studies show little change in the traditional male gender role. Men's roles are

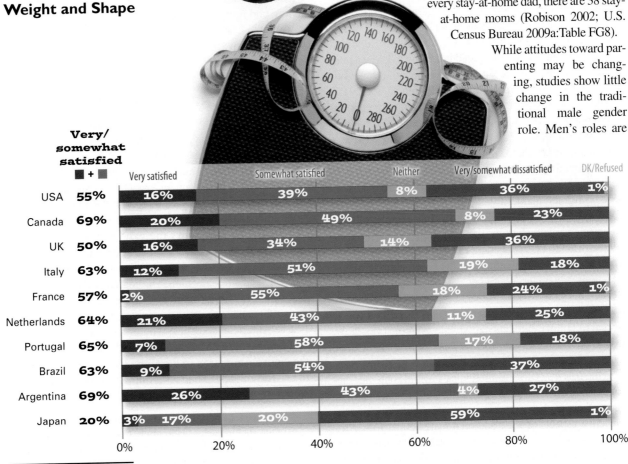

Going GLOBAL

Satisfaction with Body Weight and Shape

	Very/somewhat satisfied ■ + ■	Very satisfied	Somewhat satisfied	Neither	Very/somewhat dissatisfied	DK/Refused
USA	55%	16%	39%	8%	36%	1%
Canada	69%	20%	49%	8%	23%	
UK	50%	16%	34%	14%	36%	
Italy	63%	12%	51%	19%	18%	
France	57%	2%	55%	18%	24%	1%
Netherlands	64%	21%	43%	11%	25%	
Portugal	65%	7%	58%	17%	18%	
Brazil	63%	9%	54%		37%	
Argentina	69%	26%	43%	4%	27%	
Japan	20%	3% 17%	20%		59%	1%

0%   20%   40%   60%   80%   100%

Source: Etcoff et al. 2004.

socially constructed in much the same way as women's. Family, peers, and the media all influence how a boy or man comes to view his appropriate role in society. The male gender role includes proving one's masculinity at work and in sports—often by using force in dealing with others—as well as initiating and controlling sexual relations (Kimmel 2008).

Males who do not conform to the socially constructed gender role often face criticism and even humiliation. Boys who deviate from expected patterns of masculinity risk being called a "chicken," "sissy," or "fag" even by fathers or brothers (Katz 1999; Pascoe 2007). And grown men who pursue nontraditional occupations, such as preschool teaching or nursing, must constantly deal with others' misgivings and strange looks. In one study, interviewers found that such men frequently had to alter their behavior in order to minimize others' negative reactions. One 35-year-old nurse reported that he had to claim he was "a carpenter or something like that" when he "went clubbing," because women weren't interested in getting to know a male nurse. The subjects made similar accommodations in casual exchanges with other men (Cross and Bagilhole 2002:215).

There may be a price to pay for such narrow conceptions of manhood. Boys who successfully adapt to cultural standards of masculinity may grow up to be inexpressive men who cannot share their feelings with others. They remain forceful and tough, but they are also closed and isolated. In fact, a small but growing body of scholarship suggests that these traditional gender roles may be putting men at a disadvantage. Today girls outdo boys in high school, grabbing a disproportionate share of the leadership positions, from valedictorian to class president to yearbook editor—everything, in short, except captain of the boys' athletic teams. And their advantage continues after high school. In the 1980s, girls in the United States became more likely than boys to go to college. By 2007, women accounted for 57 percent of college students nationwide. And in 2006–2007, for the first time, more women than men in the United States earned doctoral degrees (Planty et al. 2008).

In the past 40 years, inspired in part by the contemporary women's movement that Betty Friedan helped start, increasing numbers of men in the United States have criticized the restrictive aspects of the traditional male gender role. Australian sociologist R. W. Connell (2002, 2005) has written about **multiple masculinities,** meaning that men learn and play a range of gender roles. These may include a nurturing-

caring role, an effeminate-gay role, or their more traditional role. Sociologist Michael Kimmel gave voice to this broader conception of what it means to be a man when he was sitting with his newborn son in the park. When a woman came up to him and said that he was expressing his "feminine side," he responded, "I'm not expressing anything of the sort, ma'am.

I'm being tender and loving and nurturing toward my child. As far as I can tell, I'm expressing my *masculinity*" (Kimmel 2004:290–91).

GENDER ACROSS CULTURES

Though socialization into gender roles can narrow what we come to think of as appropriate behavior, examples such as Kimmel's suggest that what we define as appropriate does change over time. Gender expectations also differ across cultures. The fact that gender expectations and performance vary across time and place suggests that masculinity and femininity are not strictly determined by our genes.

Some cultures assume the existence of three or four gender categories. Judith Lorber (1994) notes that "male women," biological males who live for the most part as women, and "female men," biological females who live for the most part as men, can be found in various societies. "Female men" can be found in some African and Native American societies, where they take on male work and family roles. "Male women" include the *berdaches* of the Native Americans of the Great Plains and *hijras* of India (Reddy 2005). Michael Kimmel (2004) describes the *xanith* of Oman in the Middle East:

They work as skilled domestic servants, dress in men's tunics (but in pastel shades more associated with feminine colors), and sell themselves in passive homosexual relationships. They are permitted to speak with women on the street (other men are prohibited). At sex-segregated public events, they sit with the women. However, they can change their minds. (p. 65)

These gender categories are a well-accepted part of their social lives. Individuals who fill them are not simply tolerated or viewed as deviant. The *berdache*, for example, have high status because they are thought to have special powers (Kimmel, 2004).

Beginning with the path-breaking work of Margaret Mead ([1935] 2001) and continuing through contemporary fieldwork, scholars have shown that gender roles can vary greatly from one physical environment, economy, and political system to the next. Peggy Reeves Sanday's (2002, 2008) work in West Sumatra, Indonesia, for example, describes the 4-million-member Minangkabau society as one in which men and women are not competitors but partners for the common good. This society is characterized by a nurturing approach to the environment, blended with Islamic religious ethics. Women control the land through inheritance; in the event of a divorce, the ex-husband leaves with only his clothes. The larger community may be governed by men, women, or both men and women working together. Sanday's findings, together with Mead's, confirm the influential role of culture and socialization in gender-role differentiation.

SOCthink

> > > Given that our understandings of gender vary across time and place, why are we so committed to the notion that gender differences are narrowly determined by biology?

>> Gender and Inequality

Although the work of early sociologists such as Harriet Martineau, Charlotte Perkins Gilman, and Ida B. Wells-Barnett highlighted the significance of gender inequality, in the 1950s sociologists Talcott Parson and Robert Bales (1955) argued that families needed both an instrumental and an expressive leader. The **instrumental leader** is the person in the family who bears responsibility for completion of tasks, focuses on more distant goals, and manages the external relationship between the family and other social institutions. The **expressive leader** is the person in the family who bears responsibility for the maintenance of harmony and internal emotional affairs. According to their theory, women's interest in expressive goals frees men for instrumental tasks, and vice versa. Women become naturally anchored in the family as wives, mothers, and household man-

agers; men become anchored in the occupational world outside the home.

As a result of insights from feminist theorists and findings from further research, sociologists now argue that such separate abilities are not innate but are instead social constructs. The key sociological task is to analyze how gender expectations are created and maintained—for example, through gender-role socialization—and then to investigate the consequences of such constructs. We turn next to how resources are distributed based on gender.

multiple masculinities The idea that men learn and play a full range of gender roles.
instrumental leader The person in the family who bears responsibility for the completion of tasks, focuses on more distant goals, and manages the external relationship between one's family and other social institutions.
expressive leader The person in the family who bears responsibility for the maintenance of harmony and internal emotional affairs.

WOMEN IN THE UNITED STATES

More than 30 years ago, the U.S. Commission on Civil Rights (1976) concluded that the phrase in the Declaration of Independence proclaiming that "all men are created equal" had been taken literally for too long. They found that women in the United States experienced a consistent pattern of inequality. Looking at the workplace, income, housework, politics, and more, we can see that their concern is still valid.

Labor Force Participation The labor market has opened up significantly since Betty Friedan published *The Feminine Mystique* in 1963. Today, millions of women—married or single, with or without children, pregnant or recently having given birth—are in the labor force. Overall, 57 percent of adult women in the United States were in the labor force in 2007, compared to 41 percent in 1970. By contrast, in 2007, 70 percent of adult men in the United States were in the labor force, compared to 76 percent in 1970. Presently, 67 percent of women who are pregnant with their first child work full-time, compared to 44 percent in the early 1960s. Among married mothers, 41 per-

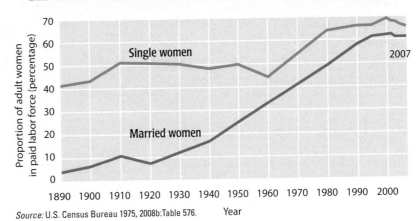

Trends in U.S. Women's Participation in the Paid Labor Force, 1890–2007

Source: U.S. Census Bureau 1975, 2008b:Table 576.

cent of those with children under age 6 were in the labor force in 2007, compared to 30 percent in 1970 (T. Johnson 2008; U.S. Census Bureau 2008b:Table 569).

Still, women entering the job market find their options restricted in important ways. Particularly damaging is occupational segregation, or confinement to sex-typed "women's jobs." For example, in 2007, women accounted for 99 percent of all dental hygienists and 83 percent of all librarians. Entering such sex-typed occupations often places women in "service" roles that parallel the traditional gender-role standard (U.S. Census Bureau 2008b).

Women are underrepresented in occupations historically defined as "men's jobs," which often offer much greater financial rewards and prestige than women's jobs. For example, in 2007, women accounted for approximately 46 percent of the paid labor force of the United States, yet they constituted only 12 percent of civil engineers, 28 percent of all dentists, 25 percent of all computer programmers, and 30 percent of physicians.

When it comes to getting promotions, women sometimes encounter attitudinal or organizational bias that prevents them from reaching their full potential. The term **glass ceiling** refers to an invisible barrier that blocks the promotion of a qualified individual in a work environment because of the individual's gender, race, or ethnicity. A

2007 study showed that women held less than 15 percent of the seats on the boards of directors of the 500 largest corporations in the United States. Furthermore, only 11 of those corporations had a female CEO while 489 had a male in that post (Catalyst 2007; Guerrera and Ward 2007).

Income Today we claim to value "equal pay for equal work," meaning that someone's sex (race, ethnicity, or age) shouldn't matter in determining what the person earns; the only characteristic that should matter is job performance. But in practice, women do not earn as much on average as men, even in the same occupations. When comparing individuals who worked full time, year-round in 2007, the median income for men was $45,113, and the median for women was $35,102 (DeNavas-Walt et al. 2008). In other words, women earned 78 cents for every dollar that men earned overall.

Taking occupational segregation into account does not explain away the wage gap. Although women are often more concentrated in occupations with lower average wages than men (child care worker or receptionist versus physician or civil engineer), a detailed analysis by researchers at the Census Bureau found only 9 out of 509 occupational categories within which women earned at least 95 percent of men's earnings (Weinberg 2004).

Significant wage gaps exist within occupations across the board (Bureau of Labor Statistics 2008b). For example, wage gaps persist in the three occupations for which women receive the highest average pay: pharmacist (85 percent of men's earnings), lawyer (78 percent), and soft-

U.S. Women in Selected Occupations, 2007: Women as a Percentage of All Workers in the Occupation

Underrepresented		Overrepresented	
Aircraft pilots	4.2	High school teachers	56.9
Firefighters	5.3	Cashiers	75.6
Civil engineers	11.5	Elementary teachers	80.9
Police officers	13.7	File clerks	82.0
Clergy	15.1	Social workers	82.0
Printers	17.2	Librarians	83.2
Chefs and head cooks	20.6	Tellers	87.5
Computer systems analysts	27.1	Word processors and typists	89.6
Dentists	28.2	Registered nurses	91.7
Physicians	30.0	Receptionists	93.0
Lawyers	32.6	Child care workers	94.6
Mail carriers	36.9	Dental hygienists	99.2

Note: Women constitute 45 percent of the entire labor force.

Source: Data for 2007 reported in U.S. Census Bureau 2008b:Table 596.

ware engineer (87 percent). Of course, in some occupations the gap is significantly wider, including insurance agent (68 percent), retail sales (64 percent), and physician/surgeon (59 percent).

Even in occupations where women are more likely to be concentrated, they still earn less on average than do men in the same field. Examples include cashier (84 percent), elementary or middle school teacher (90 percent), and registered nurse (89 percent). Observers of the labor force have termed this advantage for men in female-dominated occupations the "glass escalator," in contrast to the glass ceiling (Cognard-Black 2004).

What accounts for these wage gaps between men and women in the same occupation? The Census Bureau studied the following characteristics of men and women in the same occupation:

- Age and degree of formal education
- Marital status and the presence of children at home
- Specialization within the occupation (for example, family practice versus surgical practice)
- Years of work experience
- Hours worked per year

Taking all these factors into consideration reduced the pay gap between men and women by only 2 cents. Even taking such factors into account, women still earned 80 cents for every dollar earned by men, though more recent research

Actual and Projected Wage Gaps Between Male and Female Earnings

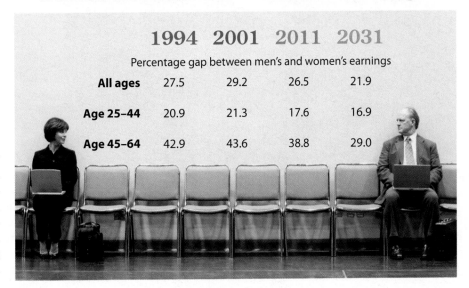

	1994	2001	2011	2031
Percentage gap between men's and women's earnings				
All ages	27.5	29.2	26.5	21.9
Age 25–44	20.9	21.3	17.6	16.9
Age 45–64	42.9	43.6	38.8	29.0

Source: Kelly Rathie, "Male Versus Female Earnings—Is the Gender Gap Converging?" *Economist Ltd.,* Spring 2002, vol. 7, no. 1.

found mothers face a significant wage penalty. In sum, the disparity in pay between men and women cannot be explained by pointing to women's career choices (Correll, Bernard, and Paik 2007; Government Accountability Office 2003; Weinberg 2007).

Home and Work Today, many women face the challenge of trying to juggle work and family. Who does the housework when women become productive wage earners? In households where both work full time, wives do on average 28 hours of housework while husbands do 16. This approximate 2:1 ratio holds across social class levels. Even

Did You Know?

. . . Married mothers spend about twice as much time per week on child care and housework as married fathers. Mothers spend about 13 hours per week on child care and 19 hours on housework compared to 7 and 10, respectively, for fathers.

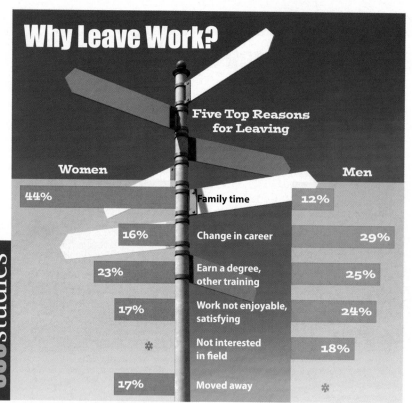

Why Leave Work?

Five Top Reasons for Leaving

Women		Men
44%	Family time	12%
16%	Change in career	29%
23%	Earn a degree, other training	25%
17%	Work not enjoyable, satisfying	24%
*	Not interested in field	18%
17%	Moved away	*

* Not one of top 5 reasons

Note: Based on a representative Harris interactive survey of "highly qualified" workers, defined as those with a graduate degree, a professional degree, or a high honors undergraduate degree.

Source: Figure adapted from Sylvia Ann Hewlett and Carolyn Buck Luce, "Off-Ramps and On-Ramps: Keeping Talented Women on the Road to Success," *Harvard Business Review,* March 2005. Copyright © 2005 by the Harvard Business School Publishing Corporation, all rights reserved. Reprinted by permission of Harvard Business Review.

in households where she works and he does not, wives still do more housework (Belkin 2008).

Sociologist Arlie Hochschild (1989, 1990, 2005) has used the phrase **second shift** to describe the double burden—work outside the home followed by child care and housework—that many women face and few men share equitably. On the basis of interviews with and observations of 52 couples over an eight-year period, Hochschild reported that the wives (and not their husbands) drive home from the office while planning domestic schedules and play dates for children—and then begin their second shift. Drawing on national studies, she concluded that women spend 15 fewer hours each week in leisure activities than their husbands. In a year, these women work an extra month of 24-hour days because of the second shift; over a dozen years, they work an extra year of 24-hour days. Hochschild found that the married couples she studied were fraying at the edges, and so were their careers and their marriages. With such reports in mind, many feminists have advocated greater governmental and corporate support for child care, more flexible family leave policies, and other reforms designed to ease the burden on the nation's families (Moen and Roehling 2005).

Politics Turning to political involvement, after years of struggle, women won the right to vote with the passage of the 19th Amendment in 1920. Looking at voter participation rates we can see that they have taken advantage of that opportunity. In fact, a higher percentage of women turn out to vote than do men. This has been true in every presidential election since 1980. In 2008, for example, 65.7 percent of voting-age women reported having voted, compared with 61.5 percent of men (Lopez and Taylor 2009).

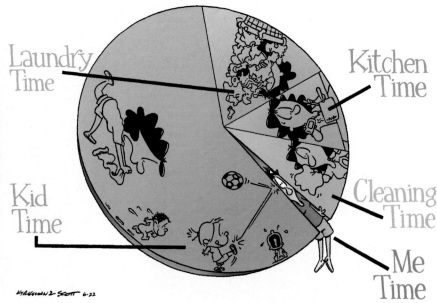

Young Women and Men Voters (18–29) in Presidential Elections

	Women	Men
1992	54%	50%
1996	43%	36%
2000	43%	38%
2004	52%	46%
2008	55%	47%

Source: Kirby and Kawashima-Ginsberg 2009.

When it comes to holding elected office, however, we find the same kind of underrepresentation in positions of power by women as is evident in the workplace. Even though women make up slightly more than half of the population, they make up a significantly smaller proportion of elected officials. As of mid-2009, for example, only 6 of the nation's 50 states had a female governor (Arizona, Connecticut, Hawaii, Michigan, North Carolina, and Washington).

Women have made slow but steady progress in certain political arenas. In 1981, out of 535 members of Congress, only 21 were women: 19 in the House of Representatives and 2 in the Senate. In contrast, the Congress that held office in mid-2009 had 90 women: 73 in the House and 17 in the Senate. Yet even with the election of Nancy Pelosi as Speaker of the House—the first woman ever to serve in that role —the membership and leadership of Congress remain overwhelmingly male. Since 1789, 11,648 men have served as members of Congress compared to only 255 women—a mere 2 percent of the total (Center for American Women and Politics 2009).

At the Supreme Court, Sandra Day O'Connor became the nation's first female justice in 1981 (and retired in 2006). She was joined by Ruth Bader Ginsberg in 1993. In May 2009, President Barack Obama nominated Sonia Sotomayor who, if confirmed, would become the third woman and first Hispanic on the court. In the executive branch, no woman has ever been elected either vice president or president of the United States, although Hillary Clinton and Sarah Palin challenged that barrier in 2008.

WOMEN AROUND THE WORLD

Opportunities for women vary significantly around the world. In an attempt to quantify the degree of gender inequality, the World Economic Forum releases an annual global gender gap index. It ranks 130 nations in four categories, including economic participation and opportunity, educational attainment, health and survival, and political empowerment. Researchers then combine these rankings into a single value intended to measure the inequality gap that exists between men and women in each country, with a score of 100 percent indicating equality. In 2008, only three countries—Norway, Finland, and Sweden—scored above 80 percent. The United States ranked 27th, with a score of 72 percent, behind nations such as the Philippines, the United Kingdom, South Africa, and Cuba. The bottom 10 nations, which include Ethiopia, Turkey, Pakistan, and Chad, had scores below 60 percent (Hausmann, Tyson, and Zahidi 2008).

> **second shift** The double burden—work outside the home followed by child care and housework—that many women face and few men share equitably.

When it comes to the economy, it is estimated that women grow half the world's food, but they rarely own land. They constitute one-third of the world's paid labor force but are generally found in the lowest-paying jobs. Women perform much of the exploited labor in developing nations, especially in the nonindustrial sector. Female workers typically toil long hours for low pay, but they still contribute significantly to their families' incomes (Quisumbing, Meinzen-Dick, and Bassett 2008; UNCTAD 2009). Single-parent households headed by women, which appear to be on the rise in many nations, are typically

Somalian-born author Ayaan Hirsi Ali, now a Dutch feminist and activist, and named by TIME magazine in 2005 as one of the 100 most influential people in the world.

Going GLOBAL

Gender Inequality in Industrial Nations

Striking differences exist in women's empowerment—that is, the percentage of women in leadership positions—from one country to the next (right). Yet there is much less difference in the division of housework, even in the same countries (left).

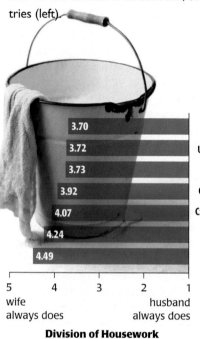

	Division of Housework	Empowerment
Canada	3.70	0.81
United States	3.72	0.68
Norway	3.73	1.00
Great Britain	3.92	0.46
Czech Republic	4.07	0.28
Italy	4.24	0.26
Japan	4.49	0.13

```
5      4      3      2      1
wife                    husband
always does        always does
```

```
0    0.20   0.40   0.60   0.80   1.00
least                           most
equality                    equality
```

Division of Housework
(includes laundry, grocery shopping, dinner preparation, and care for sick family members)

Empowerment
(includes the proportions of women in parliament, in management, and in professional/technical positions)

Source: Adapted from Fuwa 2004:757.

---

they can do." The goal was not complete equity for women, but 40 percent representation by 2008. The percentage in Norway now stands at 36—much higher than Europe's average of 21 percent (Inter Parliamentary Union 2009; Norwegian Ministry of Children and Equality 2009).

Women in other industrial nations also struggle with the balance between home and work, especially regarding housework. According to one survey, 30 percent of the couples in U.S. households share most of the housework, compared to 4 percent in Japan, 25 percent in Great Britain, 27 percent in Sweden, and 32 percent in Canada (C. Geist 2005). Sociologist Makiko Fuwa (2004) analyzed gender inequality in 22 industrial countries using data from the International Social Survey Programme. Fuwa compared how couples divided their housework to society-wide measures of women's presence in high-status occupations, as well as their wages relative to men's. A pattern emerged in which those countries that placed greater emphasis on empowerment for women tended to have more balanced housework loads between men and women.

SEXISM AND DISCRIMINATION

Both in the United States and around the world, this systematic pattern of inequality in income, occupation, housework, and politics points to the existence of institutional sexism. **Sexism** is the ideology that claims one sex is superior to the other. The term generally refers to male prejudice and discrimination against women. It is not enough, however, to understand gender inequality only by looking at the attitudes and practices of individuals, such as sexist remarks and acts of aggression. We must analyze it as a characteristic of the social system itself. Sociologists refer to such patterns of treatment that, as part of a society's normal operations, systematically deny a group access to resources and opportunities as **institutional discrimination.**

All the major institutions of our society—including the government, the armed forces, large corporations, the media, uni-

---

found in the poorest sections of the population. The feminization of poverty has become a global phenomenon.

As is the case in the United States, women in other industrialized nations also experience occupational segregation. In Great Britain, for example, only 29 percent of computer analysts are women, while 81 percent of cashiers and 90 percent of nurses are women (Cross and Bagilhole 2002; Women and Work Commission 2006). Worldwide, women hold less than 1 percent of corporate managerial positions.

In recognition of the underrepresentation of women on boards of directors, the Norwegian legislature established minimum quotas for the number of female board members. As the architects of the plan put it, "Instead of assuming what people *can't* do at work, provide opportunities for employees to prove what

sexism The ideology that one sex is superior to the other.
institutional discrimination A pattern of treatment that systematically denies a group access to resources and opportunities as part of society's normal operations.
feminism The belief in social, economic, and political equality for women.

versities, and the medical establishment—are controlled by men. These institutions, in their normal, day-to-day routines, often discriminate against women and perpetuate sexism. For example, if the central office of a nationwide bank sets a policy that single women are a bad risk for loans—regardless of their incomes and investments—that bank will discriminate against women in state after state. It will do so even at branches where loan officers hold no personal biases toward women but are merely obeying company policy.

>> Working for Change: Women's Movements

One of the lessons we learn from research on gender is that change is possible. As we saw with college education for women, past norms need not determine future practices. Change, however, seldom comes without conflict. People have fought against existing cultural assumptions about what is natural in order to advance opportunity for women in politics, the economy, and other spheres of public and private life. **Feminism** is the term for this belief in social, economic, and political equality for women.

THE FIRST WAVE

The feminist movement in the United States was born in upstate New York, in the town of Seneca Falls, in the summer of 1848. On July 19, the first women's rights convention began, attended by Elizabeth Cady Stanton, Lucretia Mott, and other pioneers in the struggle for women's rights. This first wave of feminists, as they are currently known, faced ridicule and scorn as they fought for legal and political equality for women. They were not afraid to risk controversy on behalf of their cause; in 1872, Susan B. Anthony was arrested for attempting to vote in that year's presidential election.

Ultimately, the early feminists won many victories. As indicated above, among them was the passage and ratification of the 19th Amendment to the Constitution, which granted women the right to vote in national elections beginning in 1920. However, suffrage did not lead to other reforms related to women's social and economic position, and in the early and mid-20th century, the women's movement became a much less powerful force for social change.

THE SECOND WAVE

The second wave of feminism in the United States emerged in the 1960s and came into full force in the 1970s. Betty

> Gender equality is more than a goal in itself. It is a precondition for meeting the challenge of reducing poverty, promoting sustainable development and building good governance.
>
> **Kofi Annan**

... When the 19th Amendment finally passed in 1920, it did so by a single vote. Having passed the House and Senate in 1919, it still needed to win approval in 36 state legislatures. It reached this milestone when Tennessee legislator Harry T. Burn switched his vote and broke the tie after receiving a letter from his mother that said, "Don't forget to be a good boy and help Mrs. [Carrie Chapman] Catt put the 'Rat' in ratification."

Did You Know?

Friedan's book *The Feminine Mystique* played a crucial part, as did two other pioneering books that argued for women's rights: Simone de Beauvoir's *The Second Sex* (1952) and Kate Millett's *Sexual Politics* (1970). In addition, the general political activism of the 1960s led women—many of whom were working for Black civil rights or against the war in Vietnam—to reexamine their own powerlessness. The sexism they often found within allegedly progressive and radical political circles convinced many women that they needed to establish their own movement for women's liberation (MacLean 2009; Rosen 2007).

In 1966, Friedan helped found the National Organization for Women (NOW) in order to fight for equality for women; she served as its president until 1970. In addition to political and legal battles, one of the organization's tools was "consciousness-raising groups." Among other things, these groups sought to elevate awareness among women of the degree to which they shared "the problem that has no name." This shared consciousness could then lead to collective action and the development of a new structure with enhanced opportunities. Choice was a core value at the center of these efforts. NOW contended that women should be able to choose their own paths and should not be cut off from opportunity in society simply because they are women.

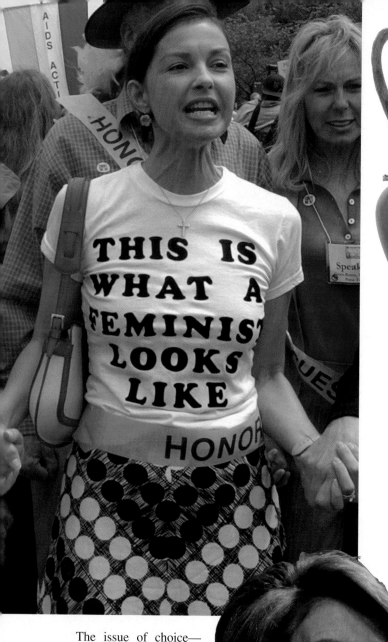

under any circumstances. These findings have held fairly steady for the past 35 years (Gallup 2008a).

As more and more women became aware of sexist attitudes and practices—including attitudes they themselves had accepted through socialization into traditional gender roles—they began to challenge male dominance. A sense of sisterhood, much like the class consciousness that Marx hoped would emerge in the proletariat, became evident. Individual women identified their interests with women as a whole, and they rejected the principle that their happiness depended upon their acceptance of submissive and subordinate roles.

Hot or Not?

What does it mean to be a feminist?

FEMINISM TODAY

Current national surveys show that while women generally endorse feminist positions, they do not necessarily accept the label "feminist." In 1987, 57 percent of U.S. women considered themselves feminists; the proportion dropped to about 25 percent by 2001, but by 2006 was back at 53 percent. Both women and men prefer to express their views on complex issues such as abortion, sexual harassment, pornography, and welfare individually rather than under the banner of feminism. Still, feminism is very much alive in the growing acceptance of women in nontraditional roles and even the basic acknowledgment that a married mother not only can work outside the home but perhaps belongs in the labor force. A majority of women say that, given the choice, they would prefer to work outside the home rather than stay home and take care of a house and family, and about one-quarter of women prefer "Ms." to "Miss" or "Mrs." (McCabe 2005; *Ms* 2006; Robison 2002).

While women still face inequality, much has changed. In 2008, for example, Senator Hillary Clinton came extremely close to securing the Democratic nomination for president and Sarah Palin was selected as John McCain's running mate. While there are still people who believe that women are not suited to such positions of power, they are in the minority. Our dominant cultural values now suggest that we believe women

The issue of choice—the question of whether women should have control over their reproductive rights and their bodies—has also been at the heart of the battle over abortion. In the United States, most people support a woman's right to a legal abortion, but with reservations. According to a 2007 national survey, 18 percent oppose a woman's right to a legal abortion under all circumstances. However, 26 percent feel that abortion should be legal

Nancy Pelosi, Democrat from California, and the first female Speaker of the U.S. House of Representatives.

should not be denied opportunity based on their gender. The only way for these values to be realized in practice is if people continue to fight to make them a reality.

>> Aging and Society

In addition to *The Feminine Mystique,* Betty Friedan wrote another book later in life in which she addressed many of the stereotypes about aging. In *The Fountain of Age* (1993), she argued that, just as was the case with gender, cultural presuppositions related to aging were limiting people's opportunity. In so doing, she contributed to the movement to change our cultural perceptions about what it means to be elderly and opened up more opportunities for older citizens.

Like gender stratification, age stratification varies from culture to culture. One society may treat older people with reverence, whereas another sees them as unproductive and "difficult." The Sherpas—a Tibetan-speaking Buddhist people in Nepal—live in a culture that idealizes old age. Almost all elderly members of the Sherpa culture own their homes, and most are in relatively good physical condition. Typically, older Sherpas value their

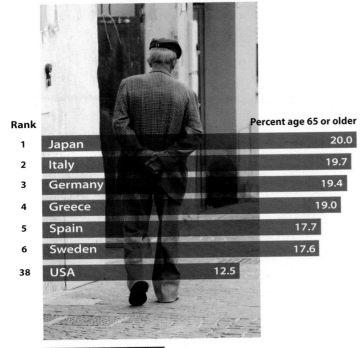

Going GLOBAL

World's "Oldest" Countries Versus the United States, 2006

Rank		Percent age 65 or older
1	Japan	20.0
2	Italy	19.7
3	Germany	19.4
4	Greece	19.0
5	Spain	17.7
6	Sweden	17.6
38	USA	12.5

Source: Bureau of the Census 2005d (projected).

independence and prefer not to live with their children. Among the Fulani of Africa, however, older men and women move to the edge of the family homestead. Since that is where people are buried, the elderly sleep over their own graves, for they are viewed socially as already dead (Goldstein and Beall 1981; Stenning 1958; Tonkinson 1978).

Understandably, all societies have some system of age stratification that associates certain social roles with distinct periods in life. Some of this age differentiation seems inevitable; it would make little sense to send young children off to war or to expect older citizens to handle physically demanding tasks, such as loading freight at shipyards. However, as is the case with stratification by gender, in the United States, age stratification goes far beyond the physical constraints on human beings at different ages.

"Being old" is a master status that commonly overshadows all others in the United States. Once people have been labeled "old," the designation has a major impact on how others perceive them, and even on how they view themselves. Negative stereotypes of the elderly contribute to their position as a minority group subject to discrimination. There is one crucial difference between older people and other subordinate groups, such as racial and ethnic minorities or women: All of us who live long enough will eventually assume the ascribed status of elderly.

Around the world, there are more than 469 million people age 65 and over, representing about 7 percent of the world's population. By 2050, one in three people will be over 65. In an important sense, the aging of the world's population represents a major success story that unfolded during the latter 20th century. Through the efforts of both national governments and international agencies, many societies have drastically reduced the incidence of disease and the rate of death. Consequently, these nations—especially the industrialized countries of Europe and North America—now have increasingly higher proportions of older members (Kinsella and Phillips 2005; Population Reference Bureau 2008; Vidal 2004).

>> Perspectives on Aging

Aging is one important aspect of socialization throughout the life course—the lifelong process through which an individual learns the cultural norms and values of a particular society. There are no clear-cut definitions for different periods of the aging cycle in the United States. In the recent past, old age has been regarded as beginning at 65, which corresponds to the retirement age for many workers, but not everyone in the United States accepts that definition. With increases in life expectancy, writers are beginning to refer to people in their 60s as the "young old," to distinguish them from those in their 80s and beyond—the "old old."

gerontology The study of the sociological and psychological aspects of aging and the problems of the aged.

The particular problems of the elderly have become the focus of a specialized field of research and inquiry known as **gerontology**—the study of the sociological and psychological aspects of aging and the problems of the aged. It originated in the 1930s, as an increasing number of social scientists became aware of the plight of the elderly.

Gerontologists rely heavily on sociological principles and theories to explain the impact of aging on the individual and society. They also draw on psychology, anthropology, physical education, counseling, and medicine in their study of the aging process. Three perspectives on aging—disengagement theory, activity theory, and age discrimination—arise out of these studies.

SOCthink

> > > What do you think about getting old? Can you picture yourself at age 65? What might your life look like?

DISENGAGEMENT THEORY

After studying elderly people in good health and relatively comfortable economic circumstances, Elaine Cumming

and William Henry (1961) introduced their **disengagement theory,** which implicitly suggests that society and the aging individual mutually sever many of their relationships. Highlighting the significance of social order in society, disengagement theory emphasizes that passing social roles on from one generation to another ensures social stability.

According to this theory, the approach of death forces people to drop most of their social roles—including those of worker, volunteer, spouse, hobby enthusiast, and even reader. Younger members of society then take on these functions. The aging person, it is held, withdraws into an increasing state of inactivity while preparing for death. At the same time, society withdraws from the elderly by segregating them residentially (in retirement homes and communities), educationally (in programs designed solely for senior citizens), and recreationally (in senior citizens' centers). Implicit in disengagement theory is the view that society should help older people to withdraw from their accustomed social roles.

Since it was first outlined more than four decades ago, disengagement theory has generated considerable controversy. Some gerontologists have objected to the implication that older people want to be ignored and put away—and even more to the idea that they should be encouraged to withdraw from meaningful social roles. Critics of disengagement theory insist that society forces the elderly into an involuntary and painful withdrawal from the paid labor force and from meaningful social relationships. Rather than voluntarily seeking to disengage, older employees find themselves pushed out of their jobs—in many instances, even before they are entitled to maximum retirement benefits (Boaz 1987).

People who are elderly have been fighting that trend, and postretirement employment has been increasing in recent decades. In the United States, fewer than half of all employees actually stop working when they retire from their career jobs. Instead, most move into a "bridge job"—employment that spans the period between the end of their career and their retirement. Unfortunately, the elderly can easily be victimized in such bridge jobs. Psychologist Kathleen Christensen (1990), warning of "bridges over troubled water," emphasizes that older employees do not want to end their working days as minimum-wage jobholders engaged in activities unrelated to their careers (Doeringer 1990; Giandrea, Cahill, and Quinn 2007).

SOCthink

> > > Consider people over the age of 65 that you have known well, such as grandparents or great-grandparents. How did their lifestyle change after they crossed that age barrier? To what extent did they remain connected in close-knit social networks?

ACTIVITY THEORY

When asked if she would like to trade her custom lamp-shade business in New York City for a condo in Flor-

ida, Ruth Vitow always gave a quick response: "Deadly! I'd hate it." Vitow, in her 90s, vowed to give up her business "when it gives me up." James Russell Wiggins worked at a weekly newspaper in Maine starting in 1922. At age 95, he still worked as an editor. Vitow and Wiggins are examples of the 9 percent of men and 3 percent of women age 75 years or older who continue participating in the nation's labor force (Himes 2001).

How important is it for older people to stay actively involved, whether at a job or in other pursuits? A tragic disaster in Chicago in 1995 showed that it can be a matter of life and death. An intense heat wave lasting more than a week—with a heat index exceeding 115 degrees on two consecutive days—resulted in 733 heat-related deaths. About three-fourths of the deceased were 65 or older. Subsequent analysis showed that older people who lived alone had the highest risk of dying, suggesting that support networks for the elderly literally help to save lives. Older Hispanics and Asian Americans had lower death rates from the heat wave than other racial and ethnic groups. Their stronger social networks probably resulted in more regular contact with family members and friends (Klinenberg 2002; Schaefer 1998a).

Often seen as the opposite of disengagement theory, **activity theory** suggests that those elderly people who remain active and socially involved will be best adjusted. Proponents of this perspective acknowledge that a 70-year-old person may not have the ability or desire to perform various social roles that he or she had at age 40. Yet they contend that old people have essentially the same need for social interaction as any other group.

The improved health of older people—sometimes overlooked by social scientists—has strengthened the arguments of activity theorists. Illness and chronic disease are no longer quite the scourge of the elderly that they once were. The recent emphasis on fitness, the availability of better medical care, greater control

disengagement theory A theory of aging that suggests that society and the aging individual mutually sever many of their relationships.

activity theory A theory of aging that suggests that those elderly people who remain active and socially involved will be best adjusted.

of infectious diseases, and the reduction in the number of fatal strokes and heart attacks have combined to reduce the traumas of growing old.

Accumulating medical research also points to the importance of remaining socially involved. Among those who decline in their mental capacities later in life, deterioration is most rapid in those who withdraw from social relationships and activities. Fortunately, the aged are finding new ways to remain socially engaged, as evidenced by their increasing use of the Internet, especially to keep in touch with family and friends (Korczyk 2002).

Admittedly, many activities open to the elderly involve unpaid labor, for which younger adults may receive salaries. Unpaid elderly workers include hospital volunteers (versus aides and orderlies), drivers for charities such as the Red Cross (versus chauffeurs), tutors (as opposed to teachers), and craftspeople for charity bazaars (as opposed to carpenters and dressmakers). However, some companies have recently begun programs to hire retirees for full- or part-time work.

Though disengagement theory suggests that older people find satisfaction in withdrawal from society, con-

POPSOC

In 2002, the Senate Special Committee on Aging convened a panel on the media's portrayal of older people and sharply criticized media and marketing executives for bombarding audiences with negative images of the aged. How many characters on top TV shows today can you think of who are over 65? How does that compare to the number of characters you can think of who are under 30?

veniently receding into the background and allowing the next generation to take over, proponents of activity theory view such withdrawal as harmful to both the elderly and society. Activity theorists focus on the potential contributions of older people to the maintenance of society. In their opinion, aging citizens will feel satisfied only when they can be useful and productive in society's terms—primarily by working for wages (Civic Ventures 1999; Crosnoe and Elder 2002; Quadagno 2005).

AGEISM AND DISCRIMINATION

Physician Robert Butler (1990) became concerned 30 years ago when he learned that a housing development near his home in metropolitan Washington, D.C., barred the elderly. Butler coined the term **ageism** to refer to prejudice and discrimination based on a person's age. For example, we may choose to assume that someone cannot handle a rigorous job because he is "too old," or we may refuse to give someone a job with authority because she is "too young."

In order to more fully understand issues regarding aging, it is important to also consider the impact of social structure on patterns of aging. Critics argue that neither disengagement nor activity theory answers the question of *why* social interaction must change or decrease in old age. The low status of older people is seen in prejudice and discrimination against them, in age segregation, and in unfair job practices—none of which are directly addressed by either disengagement or activity theory. In addition, these theories often ignore the impact of social class on the lives of the elderly.

The privileged upper class generally enjoys better health and vigor and has less likelihood of dependency in old age. Affluence cannot forestall aging indefinitely, but it can soften the economic hardships people face in later years. Although pension plans, retirement packages, and insurance benefits may be developed to assist older people, those whose wealth allows them access to investment funds can generate the greatest income for their later years.

In contrast, the working class often faces greater health hazards and a greater risk of disability; aging is particularly difficult for those who suffer job-related injuries or illnesses. Working-class people also depend more heavily on Social Security benefits and private pension programs. And during inflationary times, their relatively fixed incomes from these sources barely keep pace with the escalating costs of food, housing, utilities, and other necessities (Atchley and Barusch 2004; Cherkas et al. 2006).

>> Aging in the United States

Just as women face institutional discrimination because they are female, people who are elderly face discrimination because they are old. While these trends may change as the average age of the population increases, we still see a pattern of unequal treatment.

THE GRAYING OF AMERICA

At age 82, Lenore Schaefer decided to bring her dancing shoes out of retirement and enter the world of competitive ballroom dancing. Having been a successful dancer in her youth, she decided it was time. She competed for the rest of her life, winning over 200 awards. When she was 101, she won a dance competition, leading to her appearance on the *Tonight Show with Jay Leno*. Stories such as Lenore's are becoming less uncommon in our society. Today, people over 100 constitute, proportionately, the country's fastest-growing age group (Hull 2007; Rimer 1998).

In 1900, men and women age 65 or older constituted only 4.1 percent of the nation's population, but that age group grew to 12.6 percent in 2007. According to current projections, the over-65 segment will continue to increase throughout this century. As the decades pass, the population of "old old" (people who are 85 or older) will increase at an ever-faster rate (Frey 2007).

In 2007, 15.4 percent of non-Hispanic Whites were older than 65, compared to 8.3 percent of African Americans, 9.2

"Good news, honey—seventy is the new fifty."

Actual and Projected Growth of the Elderly Population of the United States

Proportion of population

- ■ 65–84 years
- ■ 85 years and older

Year	85 years and older	65–84 years
1900	0.2%	3.9%
1930	0.2%	5.1%
1980	1.0%	10.3%
2010	2.0%	11.1%
2050 (projection)	4.3%	15.8%

Source: He et al. 2005:9; U.S. Census Bureau 2008f:Table 1.

percent of Asian Americans, and 5.5 percent of Hispanics. In part, these differences reflect the shorter life spans of the latter groups. They also stem from immigration patterns among Asians and Hispanics, who tend to be young when they enter the country (U.S. Census Bureau 2008b:Table 8).

The highest proportions of older people are found in Florida, Pennsylvania, Rhode Island, Iowa, West Virginia, and Arkansas. However, that will soon change. In 2000, Florida was the state most populated by the elderly, with 17.6 percent of the population over age 65. In another 25 years or so, more than half the states will have an even greater proportion of elderly than Florida does now. The graying of the United States is a phenomenon that can no longer be ignored, either by social scientists or by government policy makers. Advocates for the elderly have spoken out on a wide range of issues. Politicians court the votes of older people because they are the age group most likely to register and vote. For example, in the 2008 U.S. presidential race, the 18–29 age group was the only cohort to increase their turnout, but their voter participation rate of 51 percent was still significantly smaller than the 70 percent rate for those 65 years and older (Kirby and Kawashima-Ginsberg 2009).

ageism Prejudice and discrimination based on a person's age.

On a local scale, one of the more recent residential patterns we find among senior citizens has been the tendency to congregate together. Many do not reside in nursing homes or planned retirement communities. Instead, they congregate in areas that gradually become informal centers for senior citizens. Social scientists have dubbed such areas "naturally occurring retirement communities" (NORCs). NORCs can be as small as a single apartment building or as large as a neighborhood in a big city. The larger they are, the more likely they are to attract business establishments that cater to the elderly, such as pharmacies, medical supply outlets, and small restaurants, making them even more attractive to older citizens.

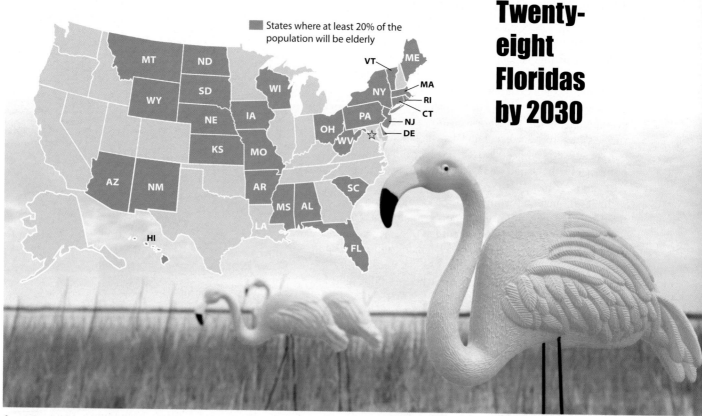

States where at least 20% of the population will be elderly

Twenty-eight Floridas by 2030

Source: Bureau of the Census 2005c.

The largest known NORC in the United States is Co-op City, a high-rise apartment complex in the Bronx, north of Manhattan. Built in the 1960s, the huge community was meant to house low-income workers and their families in apartments that were relatively spacious by New York City's standards. More than three decades later, many of the buildings' first residents are still there, "aging in place," as the social workers say. Today, roughly 8300 of Co-op City's 55,000 residents are 65 or older (Brenner 2008; A. Feuer 2002).

WEALTH AND INCOME

There is significant variation in wealth among the nation's older people. Some individuals and couples find themselves poor in part because of fixed pensions and skyrocketing health care costs. Nevertheless, as a group, older people in the United States are neither homogeneous nor poor. The typical elderly person enjoys a standard of living that is much higher now than at any point in the nation's past. Class differences among the elderly remain evident but tend to narrow somewhat. Those older people who enjoyed middle-class incomes while younger tend to remain better off after retirement, but less so than before (Smith 2003).

To some extent, older people owe their overall improved standard of living to a greater accumulation of wealth—in the form of home ownership, private pensions, and other financial assets. But much of the improvement is due to more generous Social Security benefits. While modest when compared with other countries' pension programs, Social Security nevertheless provides 37 percent of

all income received by older people in the United States. Still, in 2007, 9.7 percent of people age 65 or older lived below the poverty line (DeNavas-Walt 2008; Social Security Administration 2008).

Members of groups who face a greater likelihood of income inequality earlier in their lives, including women and members of racial and ethnic minorities, continue to do so when they are older. For women age 65 or older, the poverty rate is 12.0 percent compared to the rate for elderly men of 6.6 percent. Considering race and ethnicity, in 2007, 17.1 percent of Latinos age 65 or older had incomes below the poverty level, which was more than twice the rate of 7.4 percent for non-Hispanic Whites. The 23.2 percent poverty rate for elderly African Americans was more than three times as high (DeNavas-Walt et al. 2008; U.S. Census Bureau 2008e:Table Pov01).

COMPETITION IN THE LABOR FORCE

Participation in paid work is not typical after the age of 65, but that is changing. In 2007, 34 percent of men ages 65–69 participated in the paid labor force, as did 26 percent of women of the same age. This represents a 28 percent increase for men and a 44 percent increase for women since 1994. While some people view these workers as experienced contributors to the labor force, others see them as "job stealers," a biased judgment similar to that directed against undocumented immigrants. This mistaken belief not only intensifies age conflict but leads to age discrimination (Gendell 2008).

Rising Labor Force Participation Rates Among the Elderly

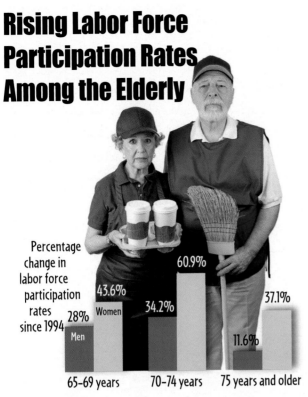

Percentage change in labor force participation rates since 1994

	65-69 years	70-74 years	75 years and older
Men	28%	60.9%	11.6%
Women	43.6%	34.2%	37.1%

Source: Gendell 2008:47.

Although firing people simply because they are old violates federal law, courts have upheld the right to lay off older workers for economic reasons. Critics contend that, later, the same firms hire young, cheaper workers to replace experienced older workers. When economic growth slows and companies cut back on their workforces, the number of complaints of age bias rises sharply as older workers begin to suspect they were bearing a disproportionate share of the layoffs. According to the Equal Employment Opportunity

around the United States. In situations for which positions were actually available, the younger applicant received a favorable response 43 percent of the time. By contrast, the older applicant received favorable responses only 17 percent of the time. One Fortune 500 corporation asked the younger applicant for more information while informing the older applicant that no appropriate positions were open (Bendick et al. 1993; Neumark 2008).

Perhaps in part due to the rising numbers of people who continue to work, more companies have come to realize that older workers can be an asset. One study found that older workers can be retrained in new technologies, have lower rates of absenteeism than younger employees, and are often more effective salespeople. The study focused on two corporations based in the United States (the hotel chain Days Inns of America and the holding company Travelers Corporation of Hartford) and a British retail chain—all of which have long-term experience in hiring workers age 50 or over. More and more U.S. corporations, from Borders to Home Depot, are actively trying to recruit retired people, recognizing their comparatively lower turnover rates and often superior work performance (Freudenheim 2005; Telsch 1991).

DEATH AND DYING

In the film *The Bucket List,* Morgan Freeman and Jack Nicholson play the two main characters, who are diagnosed with terminal cancer and have less than one year to live. They make a list of all the things they would like to do before they "kick the bucket." On the list are things they had never dared to do, such as traveling the world and sky-diving, but it also includes reconciling broken relationships.

Until recently, death was a taboo topic in the United States. Death represents a fundamental disruption that cannot be undone, so we often find it easier to live with a sense

> First you are young; then you are middle-aged; then you are old; then you are wonderful.
>
> **Lady Diana Cooper**

Commission, between 1999 and 2007, complaints of age discrimination rose more than 35 percent. However, evidence of a countertrend has emerged. To hang onto experienced workers, some firms have been giving larger raises to older workers, to encourage their retirement at the higher salary—a tactic that prompts younger workers to complain of age discrimination (EEOC 2008; Novelli 2004; Uchitelle 2003).

A controlled experiment conducted by the AARP (formerly known as the American Association of Retired Persons) confirmed that older people often face discrimination when applying for jobs. Comparable résumés for two applicants—one 57 years old and the other 32 years old—were sent to 775 large firms and employment agencies

of denial about our mortality. In the words of sociologist Peter Berger, "Death presents society with a formidable problem . . . because it threatens the basic assumptions of order on which society rests" (1969:23). However, psychologist Elisabeth Kübler-Ross (1969), through her pioneering book *On Death and Dying,* greatly encouraged open discussion of the process of dying. Drawing on her work with 200 cancer patients, Kübler-Ross identified five stages of the experience: denial, anger, bargaining, depression, and finally acceptance.

While we may still be uncomfortable with the topic, *The Bucket List*'s portrayal of a "good death" represents one of the ways we have become more open about it. Gerontologist Richard Kalish (1985) laid out some of the issues people must face in order to prepare for a "good death." These included completing unfinished business, such as settling insurance and inheritance matters; restoring harmony to social relationships and saying farewell to friends and family; dealing with medical needs; and making funeral plans and other arrangements for survivors. In accomplishing these tasks, the dying person actively contributes to smooth intergenerational transitions, role continuity, compliance with medical procedures, and minimal disruption of the social system, despite the loss of a loved one.

hospice care Treatment of the terminally ill in their own homes, or in special hospital units or other facilities, with the goal of helping them to die comfortably, without pain.

We have also begun to create institutions to facilitate our wishes for a good death. The practice of **hospice care,** introduced in England in the 1960s, is devoted to easing this final transition. Hospice workers seek to improve the quality of a dying person's last days by offering comfort and by helping the person to remain at home, or in a homelike setting at a hospital or other special facility, until the end. Currently, there are more than 3200 hospice programs serving almost 1 million people a year.

Recent studies in the United States suggest additional ways in which people have broken through the historical taboos about death. For example, bereavement practices—once highly structured—are becoming increasingly varied and therapeutic. More and more people are actively addressing the inevitability of death by making wills, establishing "living wills" (health care proxies that explain their feelings about the use of life support equipment), donating organs, and providing instructions for family members about funerals, cremations, and burials. Given medical and technological advances and increasingly open discussion and negotiation regarding death and dying, it is possible that good deaths may become a social norm in the United States (Pew Research Center 2006).

get involved!

Resist! There are growing resources out there that encourage new ways to attain healthier body images for women and men. The website of the organization About-Face (www.about-face.org) brings public awareness to negative stereotypes of women in the media. Visit the site and explore the lists of "winners" and "offenders" in the media.

Sociology often confronts us with things that can make us uncomfortable. Whether that is gender inequality, age inequality, or even death, the point of doing so is a more complete understanding of what we do and why we do it. Such knowledge can lead us to new and better practices that provide greater understanding, fairness, equality, and opportunity. Through practicing the sociological imagination, as Betty Friedan did in the case of gender and age, we can make the world a better place.

For REVIEW

I. **How has opportunity for women in the United States changed over time?**

- In the 1950s, women's primary roles were wife and mother. Since that time, largely due to the efforts of the second wave of the women's movement, their labor force participation and income have risen significantly.

II. **To what extent does gender still shape access to resources?**

- Women continue to be paid less than men in the same occupations, tend to be segregated into a narrower range of female-dominated occupations, bear greater responsibility for housework, and are underrepresented as elected officials.

III. **How do sociologists approach the study of aging?**

- There is a debate about the degree to which old age represents a stage during which elderly people are expected to fade away, making way for the next generation, versus a stage when they are denied opportunities and face discrimination. Increased willingness to talk about death shows that we are becoming more open about discussing aging and its consequences.

Pop Quiz

1. What term do sociologists use to describe the biological differences between males and females?
   a. gender
   b. sexism
   c. anatomy
   d. sex

2. When college students conducted an experiment in which they violated expected gender norms, they demonstrated the power of
   a. gender-role socialization.
   b. biological determinism.
   c. instrumental leadership.
   d. the glass ceiling.

3. What is the expression used when claiming that gender for men is not narrowly limited to traditional conceptions of masculinity?
   a. disengagement
   b. gender modification
   c. sex
   d. multiple masculinities

4. According to early sociologists Talcott Parsons and Robert Bales, which type of leader bears responsibility for completion of tasks, focuses on more distant goals, and manages the external relationship between the family and other social institutions?
   a. expressive
   b. charismatic
   c. instrumental
   d. traditional

5. As of 2007, what percentage of adult women were in the labor force?
   a. 28 percent
   b. 41 percent
   c. 57 percent
   d. 76 percent

6. Overall, when comparing full-time, year-round workers, how much do women earn compared to every dollar men earn?
   a. 42 cents
   b. 63 cents
   c. 78 cents
   d. 92 cents

7. The expression "second shift" refers to
   a. doing the emotional work of maintaining family relationships.
   b. maintaining the household including housework in addition to a job outside the home.
   c. having a work shift ranging approximately between 4:00 P.M. and midnight.
   d. doing paid labor at the workplace.

8. The primary accomplishment of the first wave of the women's movement was
   a. making women citizens.
   b. gaining the right to an abortion.
   c. earning the right to nondiscrimination in the workplace.
   d. winning the right to vote.

9. Which theory argues that elderly people have essentially the same need for social interaction as any other group and that those who remain active and socially involved will be best adjusted?
   a. disengagement theory
   b. institutional discrimination theory
   c. activity theory
   d. ageism theory

10. In recent years, labor force participation rates for people over age 65 have
    a. gone down for both men and women.
    b. gone up for both men and women.
    c. gone down for men but up for women.
    d. stayed about the same for both men and women.

1. (d); 2. (a); 3. (d); 4. (c); 5. (c); 6. (c); 7. (b); 8. (d); 9. (c); 10. (b)

13

RACE AND ETH

COMING TO AMERICA

On May 12, 2008, Santiago Cordero was on a high school field trip when he got an urgent text message. The Immigration and Customs Enforcement agency (ICE) had raided the meat processing plant where his mother worked. ICE had arrested 389 people, and his mother was one of them (Fuson 2008).

The raid occurred at Agriprocessors, Inc., in Postville, a rural Iowa town with a population of about 2500. It was the largest such raid in U.S. history. The plant employed 968 people, and ICE agents had warrants for the arrest of 697 of them.

Santiago's immigration story is not uncommon. His dad was the first in the family to come from Mexico. He gained legal work documentation and now serves as a custodian in the local school district. Santiago arrived a year later, and his mom and siblings arrived after that. They had no such papers.

In high school, Santiago served as an interpreter for student–teacher conferences, started on the varsity football team, and organized the school's first soccer team, which included 28 students from five nationalities. As a senior he won the class volunteer award and received two scholarships. He graduated on May 25 and faced the possibility of arrest and deportation as soon as he walked across the stage to receive his diploma (Fuson 2008).

The Postville workers represented the latest in a long line of immigration stories. Earlier immigrants arrived from Germany, Italy, Poland, Lithuania, China, Vietnam, or Laos, but the obstacles and opposition they faced were similar. A decade before, the Postville workers would have likely been from Mexico or Bosnia. Now many of those workers had moved on to better jobs. Of the 389 workers arrested, 295 were from Guatemala. Other processing plants were employing increasing numbers of immigrants from Somalia and Sudan. People immigrate because conditions in their homelands are so poor. Like every other immigration stream in U.S. history, they were looking for opportunity (Leys 2008).

Postville represents a microcosm of the United States. It has a diverse population from around the world, both rich and poor. In a small community like this, face-to-face interaction with people from other cultures is inevitable. Such contact can break down some barriers and lead to greater understanding on all sides. As Postville's school superintendent, David Strudthoff, put it, "It's harder than hell to hate people when you get to know them" (Fuson 2008).

NICITY

As You READ

>>

- How do sociologists define race and ethnicity?
- What are prejudice and discrimination, and how do they operate?
- What are the consequences of race and ethnicity for opportunity?

>> Racial and Ethnic Groups

The election of Barack Obama as president marked a watershed moment in American history. Every president who served before him was a White, non-Hispanic male. From all over the country, there were reports of children from various racial and ethnic backgrounds, both boys and girls, saying that anyone could grow up to be president. Once he took office, what

minority group A subordinate group whose members, even if they represent a numeric majority, have significantly less control or power over their own lives than the members of a dominant or majority group have over theirs.

had seemed unthinkable only a generation ago gave way to a new sense of possibility, opening the door for greater opportunity for all throughout the nation.

Since European colonists established their first settlement in Jamestown in 1607 with the help of the native Powhatan tribe, intergroup relations based on ethnic and racial background have played a powerful role in shaping both interaction and opportunity. One of the factors shaping opportunity was access to valued material, social, and cultural resources, a factor strongly influenced by the

Racial and Ethnic Groups in the United States, 2007

Classification	Number in Thousands	Percentage of Total Population
Racial Groups		
Whites (non-Hispanic)	198,553	65.8%
Blacks/African Americans	37,334	12.2
Native Americans, Alaskan Native	2,365	0.7
Asian American	13,234	4.3
Chinese	3,046	1.0
Asian Indians	2,570	0.9
Filipinos	2,412	0.8
Vietnamese	1,508	0.5
Koreans	1,344	0.4
Japanese	803	0.3
Pacific Islanders and other	435	0.1
Ethnic Groups		
White ancestry (single or mixed, non-Hispanic)		
Germans	50,754	16.8
Irish	36,496	12.0
English	28,177	9.3
Italians	17,844	5.9
Scottish and Scotch-Irish	11,333	3.8
Poles	9,976	3.3
French	9,616	3.2
Jews	6,444	2.2
Hispanic (or Latinos)	45,427	15.1
Mexican Americans	29,167	9.7
Puerto Ricans	4,120	1.4
Cubans	1,611	0.5
Salvadorans	1,474	0.5
Dominicans	1,208	0.4
Other Hispanics	7,846	2.6
Total (all groups)	**301,621**	

Note: Percentages do not total 100 and subtotals do not add up to totals in major categories because of overlap between groups (for example, Polish American Jews or people of mixed ancestry, such as Irish and Italian).

Source: U.S. Census Bureau 2008g:Tables B03001, DP-2, DP-5.

social status of the group to which one belonged. A **minority group** is a subordinate group whose members have significantly less control or power over their own lives than the members of the dominant or majority group have over theirs. Sociologists consider groups that lack power to be minority groups even if they represent a numeric majority of the population in a society.

Race and ethnicity historically have served as markers of minority group status. The term **racial group** describes a group that is set apart from others because of physical differences that have taken on social significance. Whites, African Americans, and Asian Americans are all considered racial groups in the United States. Although the construct of race emphasizes the significance of external physical differences, it is the culture of a particular society that identifies and attaches social significance to those differences. An **ethnic group** is one that is set apart from others primarily because of its national origin or distinctive cultural patterns. In the United States, Puerto Ricans, Jews, and Polish Americans are all categorized as ethnic groups. As a nation comprised primarily of immigrants and their descendants, the United States has a significant amount of racial and ethnic diversity.

> **racial group** A group that is set apart from others because of physical differences that have taken on social significance.
>
> **ethnic group** A group that is set apart from others primarily because of its national origin or distinctive cultural patterns.

RACE

We tend to think of race as strictly a biological category, but researchers for the Human Genome Project (HGP), who mapped the entire genetic code, concluded that race as we understand it does not exist. Craig Venter (2000), one of the project's lead scientists, declared in his presentation of the HGP results that "the concept of race has no genetic or scientific basis," and in a later interview, he said, "Race is a social concept, not a scientific one" (Angier 2000). The researchers found that all humans share the same basic genetic material, and physical manifestations such as skin color represent different combinations, in greater or lesser degrees, of the same shared genes.

When it comes to genetic variation, the biological differences within what we think of as racial groups are actually greater than the differences between those groups. Genetic researchers Luca Cavalli-Sforza, Paolo Menozzi, and Alberto Piazza (1994), for example, point out that people from northeast China are genetically closer to Europeans, Eskimos, and North American Indians than they are to people from south China (p. 78). In fact, the overall degree of human genetic variation is quite small when compared with genetic variation among other large mammals—due primarily to the fact that communities of human beings have always interacted, even across great distances (MacEachern 2003:20).

Social Construction of Race The racial categories that we typically take for granted grow out of sociocultural traditions and historical experiences that are specific to various groups. If we look cross-culturally, we see that different groups define racial categories in different ways at different times. Each society defines which differences are important while ignoring other characteristics that could serve as a basis for social differentiation. In the United States, we see differences in both skin color and hair color. Yet people learn informally that differences in skin color have a dramatic social and political meaning whereas differences in hair color do not.

racial formation A sociohistorical process in which racial categories are created, inhibited, transformed, and destroyed.

stereotype An unreliable generalization about all members of a group that does not recognize individual differences within the group.

When observing skin color, many people in the United States tend to lump others rather casually into the traditional categories of "Black," "White," and "Asian." More subtle differences in skin color often go unnoticed. In many nations of Central America and South America, by contrast, people recognize color gradients on a continuum from light to dark skin color. Brazil has approximately 40 color groupings, and in other countries people may be described as "Mestizo Honduran," "Mulatto Colombian," or "African Panamanian." What we see as "obvious" differences, then, are subject to each society's social definitions.

Racial definitions are crystalized through what Michael Omi and Howard Winant (1994) have called **racial formation**—a sociohistorical process in which racial categories are created, inhibited, transformed, and destroyed. In

this process, those who have power define groups of people according to a racist social structure. The creation of a reservation system for Native Americans in the late 1800s is one example of racial formation. Federal officials combined what were distinctive tribes into a single racial group, which we refer to today as Native Americans. The extent to which and frequency with which peoples are subject to racial formation is such that no one escapes it.

Another example of racial formation from the 1800s involves what was known as the "one-drop rule." If a person had even a single drop of "Black blood"—that is, if any of his or her ancestors, no matter how remote, were Black—society defined and viewed that person as Black, even if he or she appeared to be White. Clearly, race had social significance, enough so that White legislators established official standards about who was "Black" and who was "White."

The one-drop rule was a vivid example of the social construction of race—the process by which people come to define a group as a race based in part on physical characteristics, but also on historical, cultural, and economic factors. For example, in the 1800s, immigrant groups such as Italian Americans and Irish Americans were seen not as "White" but as members of another race who were not necessarily trustworthy (Ignatiev 1995). The social construction of race is an ongoing process that is subject to debate, especially in a diverse society such as the United States, where each year

Like many Americans, champion golfer Tiger Woods is of mixed racial heritage. His father's ancestry was African American, Chinese, and Native American, and his mother is of Thai, Chinese, and Dutch descent. Woods is shown here with his wife, Swedish model Elin Nordgegren.

increasing numbers of children are born to parents of different racial backgrounds.

Even though these differences are socially constructed, their consequences are no less real. Race is often used to justify unequal access to economic, social, and cultural resources based on the assumption that such inequality is somehow "natural." This can happen through the use of **stereotypes,** for example, which are unreliable generalizations about all members of a group that do not recognize individual differences within the group. Anthropologist Ashley Montagu (1997), who was at the forefront of the movement to use scientific evidence to demonstrate the socially constructed nature of race, suggested that "the very word (*race*) is racist; that the idea of 'race,' implying the existence of significant biologically determined mental differences rendering some populations inferior to others, is wholly false" (p. 31).

SOCthink

> > > To what extent does the race you belong to shape opportunities you face? How conscious are you of your race and its impact?

Multiple Identities In recognition of the growing diversity of the nation's population, the 2000 census gave people the option of identifying themselves with multiple racial categories for the first time. With the addition of this multirace option, 63 total race combinations are possible. Over 7 million people in the United States (or about 2.6 percent of the population) reported that they were of two or more races. Half the people classified as multiracial were under age 18, suggesting that this segment of the population will grow in the years to come. People who claimed both White and American Indian ancestry were the largest group of multiracial residents (Bonilla-Silva 2004; N. Jones 2005). Racial categories used by the Census Bureau have themselves varied over time, providing additional support for the notion that our definition of race is not so much determined by biology as it is subject to historical and cultural forces.

The historical approach to racial classification of including only a handful of choices is part of a long history that dictates single-race identities. This move by the Census Bureau to expand choice points toward a growing awareness of population diversity. It also reflects the struggle by many individuals, especially young adults, against social pressure to choose a single identity, and instead openly embrace multiple heritages. The classic case is Tiger Woods, the world's best-known golfer. Woods created his own racial category, referring to himself as "Cablinasian," a combination of his Caucasian, Black, American Indian, and Asian (Chinese and Thai) ancestry.

U.S. Race Categories, 1790–2000

Year	Race Categories
1790	Free White males Free White females All other free persons Slaves
1890	White Black Mulatto Chinese Indian
1940	White Negro Indian Chinese, Japanese, Filipino, Hindu, Korean Other
1990	White Black or Negro American Indian Eskimo Aleut Asian or Pacific Islander, Chinese, Filipino, Hawaiian, Korean, Vietnamese, Japanese, Asian Indian, Samoan, Guamanian, other Asian or Pacific Islander Other race
2000	White Black, African American, or Negro American Indian or Alaskan Native (print name of tribe) Asian: Asian Indian, Chinese, Filipino, Japanese, Korean, Vietnamese, other Asian Native Hawaiian, Guamanian or Chamorro, Samoan, or other Pacific Islander Some other race (print race)

Source: Nobles 2000: 1739.

ETHNICITY

An ethnic group is set apart from others explicitly because of its national origin or cultural patterns. Distinctive characteristics can include language, diet, sports, and religious beliefs, along with various traditions, norms, and values.

Puerto Rican Day Parade, New York City.

or not she would technically be the first Hispanic on the court, or whether that honor should fall retroactively to Justice Benjamin Cardozo, who served during the 1930s (Passel and Taylor 2009). Despite sometimes unclear boundaries, sociologists maintain that membership in a racial or ethnic group has a powerful impact.

Although we will look at various ethnic and racial groups in more detail later in the chapter, it is important to understand the significance such categories have in society. As we have already seen, often they are used to justify exclusion from critical resources. This exclusion is rooted in both values and norms, that is, in how we think and how we act. When it comes to race and ethnicity, the terms that describe such practices are *prejudice* and *discrimination*.

Among the ethnic groups in the United States are peoples with a Spanish-speaking background, referred to collectively as Latinos or Hispanics, such as Puerto Ricans, Mexican Americans, and Cuban Americans. Other ethnic groups in this country include Jewish, Irish, Italian, and Norwegian Americans.

The distinction between racial and ethnic minorities is not always clear-cut. For example, the U.S. census categorizes Hispanic as an ethnicity rather than a race, which causes confusion from some respondents who think of it as the latter. And when Sonia Sotomayor was nominated to the Supreme Court, there was a brief debate over whether

>> Prejudice and Discrimination

In recent years, college campuses across the United States have been the scene of bias-related incidents. Student-run newspapers and radio stations have ridiculed racial and ethnic minorities; threatening literature has been stuffed under the doors of minority students; and graffiti endorsing the views of White supremacist organizations such as the Ku Klux Klan have been scrawled on university walls. In some cases, there have even been violent clashes between groups of White and Black students (Schmidt 2008). Such acts grow out of attitudes people have about other groups.

Did You Know?

... Of the Muslims in the United States, 65 percent are foreign born. Of those who were born here, about one-half are African American. Approximately one-fourth of all U.S. Muslims are third generation.

PREJUDICE

Prejudice is a negative attitude toward an entire category of people, often an ethnic or racial minority. If you resent your roommate because he or she is sloppy, you are not necessarily guilty of prejudice. However, if you immediately stereotype your roommate on the basis of such characteristics as race, ethnicity, or religion, that is a form of prejudice. Prejudice tends to perpetuate false definitions of individuals and groups.

Sometimes prejudice results from **ethnocentrism**—the tendency to assume that one's own culture and way of life represent the norm or are superior to all others. Ethnocentric people judge other cultures by the standards of their own group without taking into account the perspectives and experiences of others. This leads quite easily to prejudice against cultures they view as inferior.

One important and widespread ideology that reinforces prejudice is **racism**—the belief that one race is supreme and all others are innately inferior. When racism prevails in a society, members of subordinate groups generally experience prejudice, discrimination, and exploitation. In 1990, as concern mounted about racist attacks in the United States, Congress passed the Hate Crimes Statistics Act. A **hate crime** is a criminal offense committed because of

Before passage of the Civil Rights Act in 1964, segregation of public accommodations was the norm throughout the South.

Categorization of Reported Hate Crimes

16.6%
Sexual orientation

18.4%
Religion

13.2%
Ethnicity

Disability
1.0%

Race
50.8%

Source: U.S. Department of Justice 2008a.

the offender's bias against an individual based on race, religion, ethnicity, national origin, or sexual orientation. In 2007 alone, more than 7600 hate crimes were reported to authorities. More than 60 percent of those crimes against persons involved racial or ethnic bias.

Over the past three generations, nationwide surveys have consistently shown growing support among Whites for integration, interracial dating, and the election of minority group members to public office—including even the presidency of the United States. Nevertheless, there are persistent patterns of unequal treatment. People claim not to be prejudiced, affirming principles such as equal opportunity, yet many fail to put these ideals into practice.

Some suggest that **color-blind racism,** which uses the principle of race neutrality to perpetuate a racially unequal status quo, is at work. In such cases, commitment to the principle of equality actually serves to perpetuate inequality. In a system where inequality based on race and ethnicity is built into the structure of society, unwillingness to address these issues explicitly in those terms serves to perpetuate the status quo. Although it might seem counter to the principle of

prejudice A negative attitude toward an entire category of people, often an ethnic or racial minority.

ethnocentrism The tendency to assume that one's own culture and way of life represent the norm or are superior to all others.

racism The belief that one race is supreme and all others are innately inferior.

hate crime A criminal offense committed because of the offender's bias against an individual based on race, religion, ethnicity, national origin, or sexual orientation.

color-blind racism The use of race-neutral principles to perpetuate a racially unequal status quo.

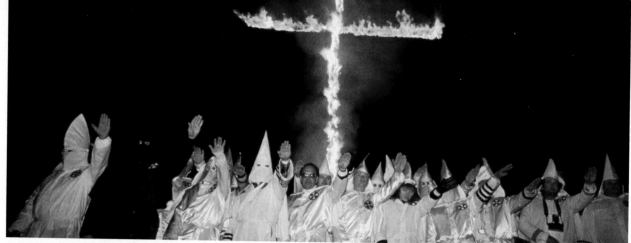

Members of the Ku Klux Klan, masked in white robes and hoods, used nighttime cross-burnings to instill terror.

equality, some nations have established quotas in political representation and hiring to force the social structure to provide greater opportunity, a practice that is controversial in the United States.

DISCRIMINATION

Prejudice often leads to **discrimination**—the denial of opportunities and equal rights to individuals and groups because of prejudice or other arbitrary reasons. While prejudice is a way of thinking, discrimination involves action. Imagine that a White corporate president with a prejudice against Asian Americans has to fill an executive position, and the most qualified candidate for the job is a Vietnamese American. If the president refuses to hire this candidate and instead selects an inferior White candidate, he or she is engaging in an act of racial discrimination.

Discriminatory Behavior Prejudiced attitudes should not be equated with discriminatory behavior. Although the two are generally related, they are not identical; either condition can be present without the other. A prejudiced person does not always act on his or her biases. The White president, for example, might choose—despite his or her prejudices—to hire the Vietnamese American because that person is the most qualified. That would be prejudice without discrimination. On the other hand, a White corporate president with a completely respectful view of Vietnamese Americans might refuse to hire them for executive posts out of fear that biased clients would take their business else-

Federal troops were needed to support the Supreme Court decision that led to the integration of schools in the 1950s.

where. In that case, the president's action would constitute discrimination without prejudice.

Sometimes racial and ethnic discrimination is overt. Internet forums like Craigslist.org or Roommate.com feature classified ads that state "African Americans and Arabians tend to clash with me" or "Clean, Godly Christian men only." While antidiscrimination laws prevent such notices from being published in the newspapers, existing law has not caught up with online bigotry in hiring and renting (Liptak 2006).

In sociologist Devah Pager's 2003 experiment investigating racial discrimination in hiring (see Chapter 2), a White job applicant with a prison record received slightly more callbacks than a Black applicant with no criminal record. Over time, the cumulative impact of such differential behavior contributes to significant differences in access to critical resources. For example, income varies significantly based on race and ethnicity in the United States (Pager and Shepherd 2008).

The Glass Ceiling Discrimination persists even for the most educated and qualified minority group members

U.S. Median Income by Race, Ethnicity, and Gender

Median income (thousands of dollars)

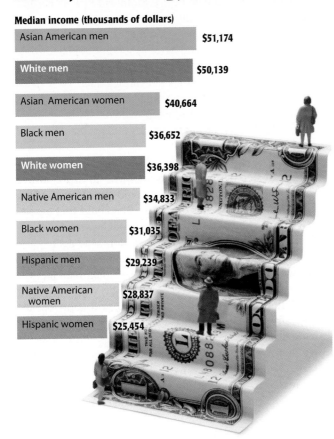

Asian American men	$51,174
White men	$50,139
Asian American women	$40,664
Black men	$36,652
White women	$36,398
Native American men	$34,833
Black women	$31,035
Hispanic men	$29,239
Native American women	$28,837
Hispanic women	$25,454

Note: Includes only people working full-time, year-round, 16 years and older. White refers to non-Hispanic Whites.

Source: Bishaw and Semega 2008.

from the best family backgrounds. Despite their talent and experience, they sometimes encounter attitudinal or organizational bias that prevents them from reaching their full potential. Recall that the term *glass ceiling* refers to an invisible barrier that blocks the promotion of a qualified individual in a work environment because of the individual's gender, race, or ethnicity (Jackson and O'Callaghan 2009; Schaefer 2006).

In early 1995, the federal Glass Ceiling Commission issued the first comprehensive study of barriers to promotion in the United States. The commission found that glass ceilings continue to block women and minority group men from top management positions in the nation's industries. For example, in 2006, 72 percent of the members on the boards of directors for Fortune 100 companies were White men, compared to 13 percent White women, 11 percent minority males, and 4 percent minority females (Catalyst 2008). In fact, the glass ceiling appears to harm firms. Researchers have found that having more diversity increases performance in groups; firms with more diverse boards also are more profitable than those that are more homogenous (Phillips, Liljenquist, and Neale 2009; Virtcom 2009).

Racial Profiling Another form of discrimination involves **racial profiling,** which is any arbitrary action initiated by an authority based on race, ethnicity, or national origin rather than on a person's behavior. Generally, racial profiling occurs when law enforcement officers, including customs officials, airport security, and police, assume that people who fit a certain description are likely to engage in illegal activities. With the emergence of crack cocaine in the 1980s, skin color became a key characteristic in racial profiling. This practice is often based on very explicit stereotypes. For example, one federal antidrug initiative encouraged officers to look specifically for people with dreadlocks and for Latino men traveling together.

> **discrimination** The denial of opportunities and equal rights to individuals and groups because of prejudice or other arbitrary reasons.
> **racial profiling** Any police-initiated action based on race, ethnicity, or national origin rather than on a person's behavior.

Today, authorities continue to rely on racial profiling despite overwhelming evidence that race is not a valid predictor of criminal behavior. A recent study showed that African Americans are still more likely than Whites to be frisked and handled with force when they are stopped. Yet Whites are more likely than Blacks to possess weapons, illegal drugs, and stolen property (Ridgeway 2007).

Research on the ineffectiveness of racial profiling, coupled with complaints by minority communities about the stigmatization it fosters, has led to growing demands to end the practice. However, these efforts came to an abrupt halt after the September 11, 2001, terrorist attacks on the United States, in the face of widespread suspicion toward Muslim and Arab immigrants. Federal authorities

Did You Know?

... Blacks and Whites have significantly different perceptions of local law enforcement. In a 2007 survey, when asked how much confidence they had in local police, 42 percent of Whites and 14 percent of Blacks had a "great deal," while 31 percent of Blacks and 10 percent of Whites had "very little."

other social scientists are becoming increasingly interested in what it means to be "White," for White privilege is the other side of the proverbial coin of racial discrimination.

The feminist scholar Peggy McIntosh (1988) became interested in White privilege after noticing that most men would not acknowledge the privileges attached to being male—even if they would agree that being female had its disadvantages. She wondered whether White people suffer from a similar blind spot regarding their own racial privilege. Intrigued, McIntosh began to list all the ways in which she benefited from her Whiteness. She soon realized that the list of unspoken advantages was long and significant.

McIntosh found that as a White person, she rarely needed to step out of her comfort zone, no matter where she went. If she wished to, she could spend most of her time with people of her own race. She could find a good place to live in a pleasant neighborhood, buy the foods she liked to eat from almost any grocery store, and get her hair styled in almost any salon. She could attend a public meeting without feeling that she did not belong, that she was different from everyone else.

McIntosh discovered, too, that her skin color opened doors for her. She could cash checks and use credit cards without suspicion, and she could browse through stores without being shadowed by security guards. She could be seated without difficulty in a restaurant. If she asked to see the manager, she could assume he or she would be of her own race. If she needed help from a doctor or a lawyer, she could get it.

> ## Whites of course have the privilege of not caring, of being colorblind. Nobody else does.
>
> **Ursula K. LeGuin**

subjected foreign students from Arab countries to special questioning, and they scrutinized legal immigrants identified as Arab or Muslim for possible illegal activity. They also prosecuted Arab and Muslim detainees for violations that were routinely ignored among immigrants of other ethnicities and faiths (Withrow 2006).

THE PRIVILEGES OF THE DOMINANT

One often-overlooked aspect of discrimination is the privileges that dominant groups enjoy at the expense of others. For instance, we tend to focus more on the difficulty women have balancing career and family than on the ease with which men avoid household chores and advance in the workplace. Similarly, we concentrate more on discrimination against racial and ethnic minorities than on the advantages members of the White majority enjoy. Indeed, most White people rarely think about their "Whiteness," taking their status for granted. However, sociologists and

McIntosh also realized that her Whiteness made the job of parenting easier. She did not need to worry about protecting her children from people who didn't like them due to their race. She could be sure that their books would show pictures of people who looked like them and that their history texts would describe White people's achievements. She knew that the television programs they watched would include White characters.

Finally, McIntosh had to admit that others did not constantly evaluate her in racial terms. When she appeared in public, she didn't need to worry that her clothing or behavior might reflect poorly on White people. If she was recognized for an achievement, it was seen as her own accomplishment, not that of an entire race. And no one ever assumed that the personal opinions she voiced should be those of all White people. Because McIntosh blended in with the people around her, she wasn't always onstage.

These are not all the privileges White people take for granted as a result of their membership in the dominant racial group in the United States. As Devah Pager's study showed, White job seekers enjoy a tremendous advantage over equally well-qualified—even better-qualified—Blacks. Whiteness *does* carry privileges—to a much greater extent than most White people realize.

INSTITUTIONAL DISCRIMINATION

Such persistent patterns of inequality suggest that discrimination is practiced not only by individuals in one-to-one encounters but also by institutions in their daily operations. Social scientists are particularly concerned with the ways in which structural factors such as employment, housing, health care, and government operations maintain the social significance of race and ethnicity. **Institutional discrimination** refers to the denial of opportunities and equal rights to individuals and groups that results from the normal operations of a society. This kind of discrimination consistently affects certain racial and ethnic groups more than others.

A recent example of institutional discrimination occurred in the wake of the September 11, 2001, terrorist attacks on the United States. Under pressure to prevent terrorist takeovers of commercial airplanes, Congress passed the Aviation and Transportation Security Act, which was intended to strengthen airport screening procedures. The law stipulated that all airport screeners must be U.S. citizens. Nationally, 28 percent of all airport screeners were legal residents but not citizens of the United States; as a group, they were disproportionately Latino, Black, and Asian. Many observers noted that other airport and airline workers, including pilots, cabin attendants, and even armed National Guardsmen stationed at airports, need not be citizens. Currently, the constitutionality of the act is being challenged. Even well-meant legal measures can have disastrous consequences for racial and ethnic minorities (H. Weinstein 2002).

In some cases, even ostensibly neutral institutional standards can have discriminatory effects. African American students at a midwestern state university protested a policy under which fraternities and sororities that wished to use campus facilities for a dance were required to post a $150 security deposit to cover possible damages. The Black students complained that the policy had a discriminatory impact on minority student organizations. Campus police countered that the university's policy applied to all student groups interested in using the facilities. However, since the overwhelmingly White fraternities and sororities at the school had their own houses, which they used for dances, the policy indeed affected only African American and other minority organizations.

> **institutional discrimination** The denial of opportunities and equal rights to individuals and groups that results from the normal operations of a society.

Attempts have been made to eradicate or compensate for discrimination in the United States. The 1960s saw the passage of many pioneering civil rights laws, including the landmark 1964 Civil Rights Act, which prohibits discrimination in public accommodations and publicly owned facilities on the basis of race, color, creed, national origin, and gender. In two important rulings in 1987, the Supreme Court held that federal

prohibitions against racial discrimination protect members of all ethnic minorities—including Hispanics, Jews, and Arab Americans—even though they may be considered White.

For more than 40 years, government, schools, and industry have instituted affirmative action programs to overcome past discrimination. **Affirmative action** refers to positive efforts to recruit minority group members or women for jobs, promotions, and educational opportunities. Many people resent these programs, arguing that advancing one group's cause merely shifts the discrimination to another group. By giving priority to African Americans in admissions, for example, schools may deny more academically qualified White candidates. In many parts of the country and many sectors of the economy, affirmative action is being rolled back, even though it was never fully implemented.

Discriminatory practices continue to pervade nearly all areas of life in the United States. In part, that is because various individuals and groups actually benefit from racial and ethnic discrimination in terms of money, status, and influence. Discrimination permits members of the majority to enhance their wealth, power, and prestige at the expense of others. Less qualified people get jobs and promotions simply because they are members of the

affirmative action Positive efforts to recruit minority group members or women for jobs, promotions, and educational opportunities.

exploitation theory A belief that views racial subordination in the United States as a manifestation of the class system inherent in capitalism.

dominant group. Such individuals and groups will not surrender these advantages easily.

>> Sociological Perspectives on Race and Ethnicity

Sociologists seek to understand and explain why prejudice and discrimination develop and persist and what might be done to address them. As we have seen, often such negative characteristics exist because they serve certain interests. Here we look at how prejudice and discrimination contribute to the maintenance of the existing social order by reinforcing the dominant culture.

SOCIAL ORDER AND INEQUALITY

One of the ways we see such beliefs and practices perpetuated is through acceptance of the dominant ideology that supports them. Prejudice and discrimination are rooted in fundamental beliefs about the natural order of the world. Such values provide a moral justification for maintaining an unequal society that routinely deprives minority groups of their rights and privileges. Southern Whites, for example, justified slavery by asserting that Africans were physically and spiritually subhuman and devoid of souls. It is easy in retrospect to find such beliefs appalling, but they became part of what people assumed was natural and were therefore difficult to challenge.

This does not mean, however, that certain groups do not intentionally promote such beliefs at the expense of others. Prejudice and discrimination help to preserve the existing system of inequality. **Exploitation theory,** for example, argues that such practices are a basic part of the capitalist economic system (Blauner 1972; Cox 1948; Hunter 2000). Racism keeps minorities in low-paying jobs, thereby supplying the capitalist ruling class with a pool of cheap labor. Moreover, by forcing racial minorities to accept low wages, capitalists can restrict the wages of all members of the proletariat. Business owners can always replace workers from the dominant group who demand higher wages with minorities who have no choice but to accept low-paying jobs. This increases the likelihood that working-class members of the majority group will develop racist attitudes toward working-class members of minority groups, whom they view as threats to their jobs. As a result, they direct their hostilities not toward the capitalists but toward other workers, thereby not challenging the structure of the existing system.

Hot or Not?

Should companies establish hiring quotas based on race, ethnicity, or gender to ensure greater opportunity?

Perceptions of Discrimination

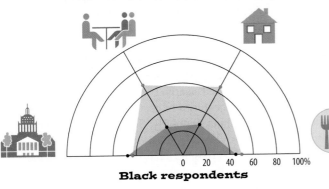

Black respondents

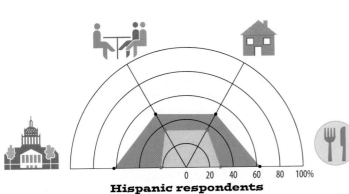

Hispanic respondents

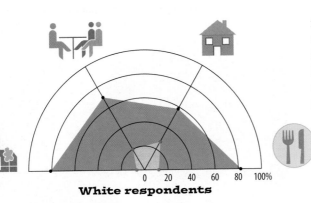

White respondents

How often do Blacks face discrimination when . . . ?

Applying to a college or university

Renting an apartment or buying a house

Applying for a job

Eating at a restaurant or shopping in a retail store

Almost always/frequently

Not often/hardly ever

Source: Pew Research Center 2007:30.

SOCstudies

Maintaining these practices, however, comes at significant cost to society. For example, a society that practices discrimination fails to use the resources of all individuals. Discrimination limits the search for talent and leadership to the dominant group. Advocates for the children whose parents were caught up in the Postville immigration raid, for example, bemoaned the loss of creativity and talent that those kids would take with them when they left the country

with their deported parents. Discrimination also aggravates social problems such as poverty, delinquency, and crime. Such effects require the investment of a good deal of time and money in which the primary goal is to maintain barriers to the full participation of all members (Rose 1951).

Challenging prejudice and discrimination, however, involves questioning taken-for-granted views of the world in which people have invested their faith and trust. Women in the 1950s in the United States had to do just that. They challenged the idea that it was "natural" for women to stay at home and have babies rather than get an education and enter the paid labor force. At the same time, workers in the civil rights movement faced a similar challenge in confronting social attitudes that represented barriers to the full participation of African Americans in U.S. society.

THE CONTACT HYPOTHESIS

At its heart, racism is about division, separating the human population into us versus them. As society becomes more global and pluralistic, more people from diverse cultural backgrounds have increased opportunities to interact with others unlike themselves on a daily basis. This is precisely what the school superintendent from Postville gave voice to. When people interact with others as people, rather than as stereotypes or distant others, the possibility arises for prejudice and discrimination to decrease.

Take, for example, a Hispanic woman who is transferred from a job on one part of an assembly line to a similar position working next to a White man. At first, the White man is patronizing, assuming that she must be incompetent. For her part, the Latina is cold and resentful; even when she needs assistance, she refuses to admit it. After a week, the growing tension between the two leads to a bitter quarrel. Yet over time, each slowly comes to appreciate the other's strengths and talents. A year after they begin working together, these two workers become respectful friends. This story is an example of the contact hypothesis in action.

Civil rights activist Rosa Parks being fingerprinted upon her arrest in 1955 for her act of civil disobedience in refusing to give up her seat on a bus to a White man.

The **contact hypothesis** states that in cooperative circumstances, interracial contact between people of equal status will cause them to become less prejudiced and to abandon old stereotypes. People begin to see one another as individuals and to discard the broad generalizations characteristic of stereotyping. Note the phrases "equal status" and "cooperative circumstances." In our assembly line example, if the two workers had been competing for one vacancy as a supervisor, the racial hostility between them might have worsened, highlighting the significance of power and position when it comes to the issue of racism (Allport 1979; Fine 2008).

contact hypothesis The theory that in cooperative circumstances interracial contact between people of equal status will reduce prejudice.
genocide The deliberate, systematic killing of an entire people or nation.
expulsion The systematic removal of a group of people from society.
amalgamation The process through which a majority group and a minority group combine to form a new group.
assimilation The process through which a person forsakes his or her own cultural tradition to become part of a different culture.

As Latinos and other minorities slowly gain access to better-paying and higher-responsibility jobs, the contact hypothesis may take on even greater significance. The trend in our society is toward increasing contact between individuals from dominant and subordinate groups. That may be one way of eliminating—or at least reducing—racial and ethnic stereotyping and prejudice. Another may be the establishment of interracial coalitions, an idea suggested by sociologist William Julius Wilson (1999). To work, such coalitions would obviously need to provide an equal role for all members.

PATTERNS OF INTERGROUP RELATIONS

The possibility of equal status, however, is shaped by how societies handle racial and ethnic differences. Some societies are more open to diverse groups maintaining their cultural traditions. Others pressure groups to abandon their beliefs and practices in favor of those of the dominant society. We will focus on six characteristic patterns of intergroup relations: genocide, expulsion, amalgamation, assimilation, segregation, and pluralism. Each pattern defines the dominant group's actions and the minority group's responses. The first two are relatively rare, though their consequences are extreme; the final four are more common.

Genocide The most devastating pattern of intergroup relations is **genocide**—the deliberate, systematic killing of an entire people or nation. This is precisely what happened when Turkish authorities killed 1 million Armenians beginning in 1915. The term is most commonly associated with Nazi Germany's extermination of 6 million European Jews, along with gays, lesbians, and the Romani people ("Gypsies"), during World War II. The term also describes the United States' policies toward Native Americans in the 19th century. In 1800, the Native American (or American Indian) population of the United States was about 600,000; by 1850, warfare with the U.S. cavalry, disease, and forced relocation to inhospitable environments had reduced it to 250,000.

Expulsion Another extreme response is **expulsion**—the systematic removal of a group of people from society. In 1979, Vietnam expelled nearly 1 million ethnic Chinese, partly as a result of centuries of hostility between Vietnam and neighboring China. Similarly, Serbian forces began a program of "ethnic cleansing" in 1991, in the newly independent states of Bosnia and Herzegovina. Throughout the former Yugoslavia, the Serbs drove more than 1 million Croats and Muslims from their homes. Some they tortured and killed; others they abused and terrorized, in an attempt to "purify" the land (Cigar 1995; Petrovic 1994). More recently, the government of Sudan has pushed people off their land and out of the country in Darfur (Steidle 2007).

Amalgamation When a majority group and a minority group combine to form a new group, **amalgamation** results. This often occurs through intermarriage over several generations. This pattern can be expressed as A + B + C → D, where A, B, and C represent different groups in a society, and D signifies the end result, a unique cultural-racial group unlike any of the initial groups (Newman 1973).

The belief in the United States as a "melting pot" became compelling in the early 20th century, particularly since that image suggested that the nation had an almost divine mission to amalgamate various groups into one peo-

POPSOC

In a survey about media portrayals of African Americans, the majority of Whites and Hispanics felt that the way Blacks are portrayed in television and films is better today than it was 10 years ago. Among African Americans, however, only 43 percent agreed. Blacks were also more likely than the other groups to say that negative portrayals have a negative impact on society's views of Blacks. Both Blacks and Whites agreed, at almost identical levels, that hip-hop and rap have a bad influence on society today.

ple. In actuality, however, many residents were not willing to include Native Americans, Jews, Blacks, Asians, and Irish Roman Catholics in the melting pot. Therefore, this pattern does not adequately describe dominant-subordinate relations in the United States.

Assimilation In India, many Hindus complain about Indian citizens who emulate the traditions and customs of the British. In France, people of Arab and African origin, many of them Muslim, complain they are treated as second-class citizens—a charge that provoked riots in 2005. In Australia, Aborigines who have become part of the dominant society refuse to acknowledge their darker-skinned grandparents on the street. All of these cases are examples of the effects of **assimilation**—the process through which a person forsakes his or her own cultural tradition to become part of a different culture. Generally, it is practiced by minority group members who want to conform to the standards of the dominant group. Assimilation can be described as a pattern in which A + B + C → A. The majority, A, dominates in such a way that members of minorities B and C imitate it and attempt to become indistinguishable from it (Newman 1973).

Assimilation can strike at the very roots of a person's identity. In the United States, some immigrants have changed their ethnic-sounding family names to names that better fit into the dominant White Protestant culture. Jennifer Anastassakis, for example, changed her name to Jennifer Aniston, Ralph Lipschitz became Ralph Lauren, Natalie Portman switched from Natalie Hershlag, and the Academy Award–winning British actress Helen Mirren gave up her birth name of Ilyena Vasilievna Mironova. Name changes, switches in religious affiliation, and the dropping of native languages can obscure one's roots and

heritage. Especially across generations, assimilation can lead to the virtual death of a culture in that family's history. It is not uncommon for grandchildren of immigrants who have not learned the language or the cultural traditions of their ancestors to regret this loss.

Segregation Separate schools, separate seating on buses and in restaurants, separate washrooms, even separate drinking fountains—these were all part of the lives of African Americans in the South when segregation ruled early in the 20th century. **Segregation** refers to the physical separation of two groups of people in terms of residence, workplace, and social events. Generally, a dominant group imposes this pattern on a minority group. Segregation is rarely complete, however. Intergroup contact inevitably occurs, even in the most segregated societies.

From 1948 (when it received its independence) to 1990, the Republic of South Africa severely restricted the movement of Blacks and other non-Whites by means of a wide-ranging system of segregation known as **apartheid.** Apartheid even included the creation of separate homelands where Blacks were expected to live. However, decades of local resistance to apartheid, combined with international pressure, led to marked political changes in the 1990s. In 1994, a prominent Black activist, Nelson Mandela, became South Africa's president

> **segregation** The physical separation of two groups of people in terms of residence, workplace, and social events; often imposed on a minority group by a dominant group.
> **apartheid** A former policy of the South African government, designed to maintain the separation of Blacks and other non-Whites from the dominant Whites.

Former South African President Nelson Mandela oversaw that country's transition from a segregated society.

Composition of Neighborhoods by Racial and Ethnic Groups June 6–25, 2005			
	% of non-Hispanic Whites who say there are "many" of each group in area	% of Blacks who say there are "many" of each group in area	% of Hispanics who say there are "many" of each group in area
Whites	86%	45%	52%
Blacks	28%	66%	32%
Hispanics	32%	26%	61%
Asians	12%	6%	13%
Recent immigrants	14%	18%	30%

Source: *Who Are the People in Your Neighborhood?* Gallup Organization July 12, 2005.

spite federal laws that forbid housing discrimination, residential segregation is still the norm. Across the nation, neighborhoods remain divided along both racial and ethnic lines. The average White person lives in an area that is at least 83 percent White, while the average African American lives in a neighborhood that is mostly Black. The typical Latino lives in an area that is 42 percent Hispanic. Overall, segregation flourishes at the community and neighborhood levels, despite the increasing diversity of the nation as a whole (Lewis Mumford Center 2001).

Whatever the country, residential segregation directly limits people's economic opportunity. Sociologists Douglas Massey and Nancy Denton (1993), in a book aptly titled *American Apartheid,* noted that segregation separates poor people of color from job opportunities and isolates them from successful role models. This pattern repeats itself the world over, from South Central Los Angeles to Oldham, England, and Soweto, South Africa.

in the first election in which Blacks (the majority of the nation's population) were allowed to vote. Mandela had spent almost 28 years in South African prisons for his anti-apartheid activities. His election was widely viewed as the final blow to South Africa's oppressive policy of segregation.

Long-entrenched social patterns are difficult to change, however. A recent analysis of living patterns in U.S. metropolitan areas shows that, de-

pluralism Mutual respect for one another's cultures among the various groups in a society, which allows minorities to express their own cultures without experiencing prejudice.

Pluralism In a pluralistic society, a subordinate group does not have to forsake its lifestyle and traditions. **Pluralism** is based on mutual respect for one another's cultures among the various groups in a society. This pattern allows a minority group to express its own culture and still participate without prejudice in the larger society. Earlier, we described amalgamation as A + B + C → D, and assimilation as A + B + C → A. Using this same approach, we can conceive of pluralism as A + B + C → A + B + C; that is, all the groups coexist in the same society (Newman 1973).

In the United States, pluralism is more of an ideal than a reality. There are distinct instances of pluralism—the ethnic neighborhoods in major cities, such as Koreatown, Little Tokyo, Andersonville (Swedish Americans), and Spanish Harlem—yet there are also limits to cultural freedom. To survive, a society must promote a certain consensus among its members regarding basic ideals, values, and beliefs. Thus, if a Romanian immigrant to the United States wants to move up the occupational ladder, he or she cannot avoid learning English.

Switzerland exemplifies the modern pluralistic state. There the absence of both a national language and a dominant religious faith leads to a tolerance for cultural diversity. In addition, various political devices safeguard the interests of ethnic groups in a way that has no parallel in the United States. By contrast, Great Britain has had difficulty achieving cultural pluralism in a multiracial society. East Indians, Pakistanis, and Blacks from the Caribbean and Africa experience prejudice and discrimination within the dominant White society there. Some British advocate cutting off all Asian and Black immigration, and a few even call for expulsion of those non-Whites currently living in Britain.

>> Race and Ethnicity in the United States

Few societies have a more diverse population than the United States; the nation is truly a multiracial, multiethnic society. Of course, this has not always been the case. The population of what is now the United States has changed dramatically since the arrival of European settlers in the 1600s. Immigration, colonialism, and, in the case of Blacks, slavery determined the racial and ethnic makeup of our present-day society.

RACIAL GROUPS

The largest racial minorities in the United States are African Americans, Native Americans, and Asian Americans.

African Americans "I am an invisible man," wrote Black author Ralph Ellison in his novel *Invisible Man* (1952:3). "I am a man of substance, of flesh and bone, fiber and liquids—and I might even be said to possess a mind. I am invisible, understand, simply because people refuse to see me."

Over five decades later, many African Americans still feel invisible. Despite their large numbers, they have long been treated as second-class citizens. As of 2007, according to official government statistics, 24.5 percent of African Americans were in poverty compared to 8.2 percent for non-Hispanic Whites (DeNavas-Walt 2008).

Contemporary institutional discrimination and individual prejudice against African Americans are rooted in the

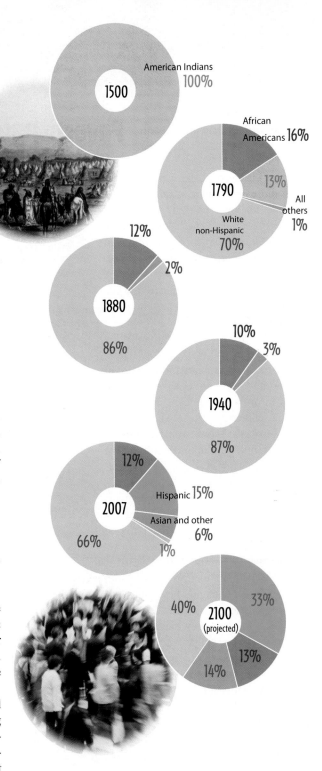

Racial and Ethnic Groups in the United States, 1500–2100 (Projected)

Source: Author's estimate; American Community Survey 2006 in Bureau of the Census 2004a; U.S. Census Bureau 2008g. Data for 2007 and 2100, African Americans and Asian and other are for non-Hispanics.

history of slavery in the United States. Many other subordinate groups had little wealth and income, but as sociologist W.E.B. Du Bois (1909) and others have noted, enslaved Blacks were in an even more oppressive situation because they could not own property legally and could not pass on the benefits of their labor to their children. In spite of generations of slavery with its long-term economic consequences, African Americans never received slave reparations to compensate for the historical injustices of forced servitude (Williams and Collins 2004).

The end of the Civil War did not bring genuine freedom and equality for Blacks. Whites were able to maintain their dominance formally through legalized segregation and informally by means of vigilante terror and violence. The southern states passed "Jim Crow" laws to enforce official segregation, and the Supreme Court in the case of *Plessy v. Ferguson* upheld them as constitutional in 1896. In addition, Blacks faced the danger of lynching campaigns, often led by the Ku Klux Klan, during the late 1800s and early 1900s (Franklin and Moss 2000).

During the 1950s and 1960s, a vast civil rights movement emerged, with many competing factions and strategies for change. The Southern Christian Leadership Conference (SCLC), founded by Dr. Martin Luther King Jr., used nonviolent civil disobedience to oppose segregation. The National Association for the Advancement of Colored People (NAACP) favored use of the courts to press for equality for African Americans. Many younger Black leaders, most notably Malcolm X, turned toward an ideology of Black power. Proponents of **Black power** rejected the goal of assimilation into White middle-class society. They defended the beauty and dignity of Black and African cultures and supported the creation of Black-controlled politi-

cal and economic institutions (Ture and Hamilton 1992).

Despite numerous courageous actions to achieve Black civil rights, Black and White citizens are still separate, still unequal. The median household income for African American households is $33,916, compared to $54,920 for Whites. The majority of Black children from middle-income families end up earning less than their parents, whereas 68 percent of children in middle-income White families earn more. And due in part to unequal access to health care, the life expectancy of African Americans is shorter than that for Whites (DeNavas-Walt 2008; Isaacs 2008).

Some African Americans—especially middle-class men and women—have made economic gains over the past 50 years. For example, data compiled by the Department of Labor show that the number of African Americans in management increased nationally from 2.4 percent of the total in 1958 to 7.5 percent in 2007. Yet Blacks still represent only 6 percent or less of all physicians, civil engineers, scientists, lawyers, chief execu-

Poverty Rates by Race and Ethnicity, 2007

21.5% Hispanic, any race

10.2% Asian

24.5% Black

8.2% White, non-Hispanic

Source: DeNavas-Walt 2008:Table 3.

Life Expectancy by Race and Sex, 1950–2005

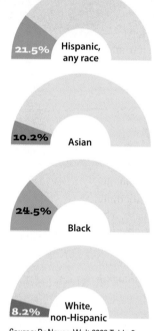

Life expectancy at birth

White male — White female
Black male — Black female

Year

Source: National Center for Health Statistics 2007:175.

tives, and financial analysts. In another occupation important to developing role models, African Americans and Hispanics together account for less than 9 percent of all reporters in the United States (U.S. Census Bureau 2008b:Table 596).

In many respects, the civil rights movement of the 1960s left institutionalized discrimination against African Americans untouched. Consequently, in the 1970s and 1980s, Black leaders worked to mobilize African American political power as a force for social change. Between 1969 and 2009, the number of African Americans in Congress rose from 6 to 40. While the election of Barack Obama as president represents a major breakthrough in the glass ceiling, Blacks remain significantly underrepresented. Such lack of progress is especially distressing in view of sociologist W.E.B. Du Bois' observation over a century ago that Blacks could not expect to achieve equal social and economic opportunity without first gaining political rights (Amer 2008b).

Native Americans Today about 2.2 million Native Americans represent a diverse array of cultures distinguishable by language, family organization, religion, and livelihood. The outsiders who came to the United States—European settlers and their descendants—came to know these native peoples' forebears as "American Indians." By the time the Bureau of Indian Affairs (BIA) was organized as part of the War Department in 1824, Indian–White relations had featured three centuries of hostility that had led to the virtual elimination of native peoples. During the 19th century, many bloody wars wiped out a significant part of the nation's Indian population. By the end of the century, schools for Indians—operated by the BIA or by church missions—prohibited the practice of Native American cultures. Yet at the same time, such schools did little to make the children effective competitors in White society (U.S. Census Bureau 2008g:Table C02005).

Today, life remains difficult for members of the 562 tribal groups in the United States, whether they live in urban areas or on reservations. For example, one Native American teenager in six has attempted suicide—a rate four times higher than the rate for other teenagers. Over time, some Native Americans have chosen to assimilate and abandon all vestiges of their tribal cultures to escape certain forms of prejudice. However, by the 1990s, an increasing number of people in the United States were openly claiming a Native American identity. Since 1960, the federal government's count of Native Americans has tripled. According to the 2000 census, the Native American population increased 26 percent during the 1990s. Demographers believe that more and more Native Americans who previously concealed their identity are no longer trying to pass as White (Grieco and Cassidy 2001).

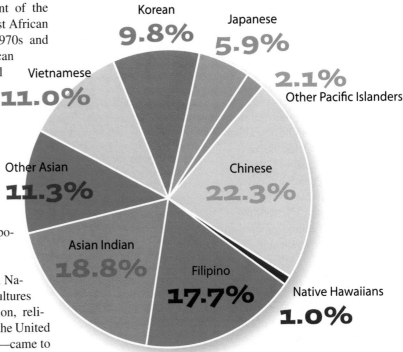

Major Asian American Groups in the United States, 2007

Source: U.S. Census Bureau 2008g:Table DP-5.

The introduction of gambling on Indian reservations has transformed the lives of some Native Americans. Native Americans got into the gaming industry in 1988, when Congress passed the Indian Gambling Regulatory Act. The law stipulates that states must negotiate agreements with tribes interested in commercial gaming; they cannot prevent tribes from engaging in gambling operations even if state law prohibits such ventures. The income from these lucrative operations is not evenly distributed, however. About two-thirds of recognized Indian tribes are not involved in gambling ventures. And those tribes that earn substantial revenues from gambling constitute only a small fraction of Native Americans (J. Taylor and Kalt 2005).

> **black power** A political philosophy, promoted by many younger Blacks in the 1960s, that supported the creation of Black-controlled political and economic institutions.

Asian Americans Asian Americans are a diverse group, one of the fastest-growing segments of the U.S.

Did You Know?

... **With the release of *The Princess and the Frog* in December 2009, Princess Tiana became Disney's first African American princess in a feature film. At the same time, Disney has been criticized for drawing on racial stereotypes of 1920s New Orleans in the film.**

population. Among the many groups of Americans of Asian descent are Vietnamese Americans, Chinese Americans, Japanese Americans, and Korean Americans.

Asian Americans are often held up as a **model** or **ideal minority** group, supposedly because they have succeeded economically, socially, and educationally despite past prejudices and discrimination. Yet this picture minimizes the degree of diversity among Asian Americans. There are rich and poor Japanese Americans, rich and poor Filipino Americans, and so on. In fact, Southeast Asians living in the United States have the highest rate of welfare dependency of any racial or ethnic group. Even though Asian Americans have substantially more schooling than other ethnic groups, their median income is only slightly higher than that of Whites, and their poverty rate is higher as well. In 2006, for every Asian American family with an annual income of $100,000 or more, there was another earning less than $35,000 a year (DeNavas-Walt et al. 2007:33).

The fact that as a group Asian Americans work in the same occupations as Whites suggests that they have been successful—and many have. However, there are some differences between the two groups. Asian immigrants, like other minorities and immigrants, are found disproportionately in low-paying service occupations. At the same time, better-educated Asian Americans are concentrated near the top in professional and managerial positions, although they rarely reach the pinnacle. Instead, they hit the glass ceiling, or try to "climb a broken ladder," as some put it. In 2007, only 1.5 percent of the 5563 people who served on the boards of the nation's 500 largest corporations were Asian American (Young and Young 2007).

model or *ideal minority*
A subordinate group whose members supposedly have succeeded economically, socially, and educationally despite past prejudice and discrimination.

> One day our descendants will think it incredible that we paid so much attention to things like the amount of melanin in our skin or the shape of our eyes or our gender instead of the unique identities of each of us as complex human beings.
>
> **Franklin Thomas**

Vietnamese Americans Each Asian American group has its own history and culture. Vietnamese Americans, for instance, came to the United States primarily during and after the Vietnam War—especially after the U.S. withdrawal from the region in 1975—and currently number 1.5 million. Assisted by local agencies, refugees from communist Vietnam settled throughout the United States, tens of thousands of them in small towns. Over time, Vietnamese Americans have gravitated toward the larger urban areas, establishing ethnic enclaves featuring Vietnamese restaurants and grocery stores.

In 1995, the United States resumed normal diplomatic relations with Vietnam. Gradually, the *Viet Kieu,* or Viet-namese living abroad, began to return to their old country to visit, but usually not to take up permanent residence. Today, more than 30 years after the end of the Vietnam War, sharp differences of opinion remain among Vietnamese Americans, especially the older ones, concerning the war and the present government of Vietnam (Pfeifer 2008).

Chinese Americans Unlike African slaves and Native Americans, the Chinese were initially encouraged to immigrate to the United States. From 1850 to 1880, thousands of Chinese immigrated to this country, lured by job opportunities created by the discovery of gold. However, as employment possibilities decreased and competition for mining jobs grew, the Chinese became the target of a bitter campaign to limit their numbers and restrict their rights. Chinese laborers were exploited, then discarded.

In 1882, Congress enacted the Chinese Exclusion Act, which prevented Chinese immigration and even forbade Chinese in the United States to send for their families. As a result, the Chinese population declined steadily until after World War II. More recently, the descendants of the 19th-century immigrants have been joined by a new influx from Hong Kong and Taiwan. These groups may contrast sharply in their degree of assimilation, desire to live in Chinatowns, and feelings about this country's relations with the communist People's Republic of China.

Currently, about 3 million Chinese Americans live in the United States. Some Chinese Americans have entered lucrative occupations, yet many immigrants struggle to survive under living and working conditions that belie the model minority stereotype. New York City's Chinatown district is filled with illegal sweatshops in which recent immigrants—many of them Chinese women—work for minimal wages. Even in legal factories in the garment industry, hours are long and rewards are limited. A seamstress typically works 11 hours per day, 6 days a week, and earns $10,000–15,000 a year (Greenhouse 2008; Louie 2001; Shipler 2004).

Japanese Americans Approximately 800,000 Japanese Americans live in the United States. As a people, they are relatively recent arrivals. In 1880, only 148 Japanese lived in the United States, but by 1920, there were more than 110,000. Japanese immigrants—called the *Issei,* or first generation—were usually males seeking employment opportunities. Many Whites saw them (along with Chinese immigrants) as a "yellow peril" and subjected them to prejudice and discrimination.

Census 2000: The Image of Diversity

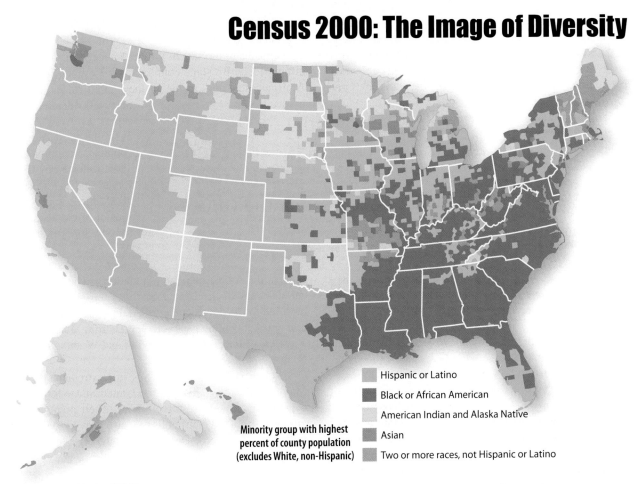

Minority group with highest percent of county population (excludes White, non-Hispanic)

- Hispanic or Latino
- Black or African American
- American Indian and Alaska Native
- Asian
- Two or more races, not Hispanic or Latino

Source: Brewer and Suchan 2001:20.

In 1941, the attack on Hawaii's Pearl Harbor by Japan had severe repercussions for Japanese Americans. The federal government decreed that all Japanese Americans on the West Coast had to leave their homes and report to "evacuation camps." Japanese Americans became, in effect, scapegoats for the anger that other people in the United States felt concerning Japan's role in World War II. By August 1943, 113,000 Japanese Americans had been forced into hastily built camps. In striking contrast, only a few German Americans and Italian Americans were sent to such camps (Neiwert 2005).

This mass detention was costly for Japanese Americans. The Federal Reserve Board estimates their total income and property losses at nearly half a billion dollars. Moreover, the psychological effect on these citizens—including the humiliation of being labeled "disloyal"—was immeasurable. Eventually, children born in the United States to the *Issei,* called *Nisei,* were allowed to enlist in the army and serve in Europe in a segregated combat unit. Others resettled in the East and Midwest to work in factories.

In 1983, a federal commission recommended government payments to all surviving Japanese Americans who had been held in detention camps. The commission reported that the detention was motivated by "race prejudice, war hysteria, and a failure of political leadership." It added that "no documented acts of espionage, sabotage, or fifth-column activity were shown to have been committed" by Japanese Americans. In 1988, President Ronald Reagan signed the Civil Liberties Act, which required the federal government to issue individual apologies for all violations of Japanese Americans' constitutional rights and established a $1.25 billion trust fund to pay reparations to the approximately 77,500 surviving Japanese Americans who had been detained (U.S. Department of Justice 2000).

SOCthink

> > > There is significant variation among numerous Asian nations and the billions of people they represent. Why do you think there is a tendency to lump people of Asian descent into a single category? How might factors such as geographical region and immigration history influence this perception?

Korean Americans At 1.3 million, the population of Korean Americans now exceeds that of Japanese Americans. Yet Korean Americans are often overshadowed by other groups from Asia. Today's Korean American community is the result of three waves of immigration. The initial wave arrived between 1903 and 1910, when Korean laborers migrated to Hawaii. The second wave followed the end of the Korean War in 1953; most of those immigrants were wives of U.S. servicemen and war orphans. The third wave, continuing to the present, has reflected the admissions priorities established by the 1965 Immigration Act. These well-educated immigrants arrive in the United States with professional skills, though they often must settle, at least initially, for positions of lower responsibility than those they held in Korea.

In the early 1990s, the apparent friction between Korean Americans and another subordinate racial group, African Americans, attracted nationwide attention. In New York City, Los Angeles, and Chicago, Korean American merchants confronted Blacks who were allegedly threatening them or robbing their stores. Black neighborhoods responded with hostility to what they perceived as the disrespect and arrogance of Korean American entrepreneurs. In South Central Los Angeles, the only places to buy groceries, liquor, and gas were owned by Korean immigrants, who had largely replaced White businesspeople. African Americans were well aware of the dominant role that Korean Americans played in their local retail markets. During the 1992 riots in South Central, small businesses owned by Koreans were a particular target. More than 1800 Korean businesses were looted or burned during the riots (Kim 1999).

Conflict between the two groups was dramatized in Spike Lee's 1989 movie *Do the Right Thing*. The situation stems from Korean Americans' position as the latest immigrant group to cater to the needs of inner-city populations abandoned by those who have moved up the economic ladder. This type of friction is not new; generations of Jewish, Italian, and Arab merchants have encountered similar hostility from another oppressed minority that to outsiders might seem an unlikely source.

Arab Americans Arab Americans are immigrants and their descendants who hail from the 22 nations of the Arab world. As defined by the League of Arab States, these are the nations of North Africa and what is commonly known as the Middle East. Not all residents of those countries are Arab; for example, the Kurds of northern Iraq are not Arab. And some Arab Americans may have immigrated to the United States from non-Arab countries such as Great Britain or France, where their families have lived for generations.

The Arabic language is the single most unifying force among Arabs, although not all Arabs, and certainly not all Arab Americans, can read and speak Arabic. Moreover, the language has evolved over the centuries so that people in different parts of the Arab world speak different dialects. The fact that the Muslim holy book the Qur'an (or Koran) was originally written in Arabic gives the language special importance to Muslims.

Estimates of the size of the Arab American community differ widely. By some counts, up to 3 million people of Arab ancestry now reside in the United States. Among those who identify themselves as Arab Americans, the most common country of origin is Lebanon, followed by Syria, Egypt, and Palestine. In 2000, these four countries of origin accounted for two-thirds of all Arab Americans. As with other racial and ethnic groups, the Arab American population is concentrated in certain areas of the United States. Their rising numbers have led to the development of Arab retail centers in several cities, including Dearborn and Detroit, Michigan; Los Angeles; Chicago; New York City; and Washington, D.C. (David 2008).

As a group, Arab Americans are extremely diverse. Many families have lived in the United States for several generations; others are foreign born. Their points of origin range from the metropolis of Cairo, Egypt, to the rural villages of Morocco. Despite the stereotype, most Arab Americans are *not* Muslim, and not all practice religion.

> A fully functional multiracial society cannot be achieved without a sense of history and open, honest dialogue.
>
> **Cornel West**

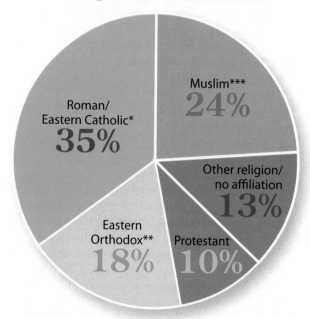

Arab American Religious Affiliation

Roman/ Eastern Catholic* **35%**

Muslim*** **24%**

Other religion/ no affiliation **13%**

Eastern Orthodox** **18%**

Protestant **10%**

*Catholic includes Roman Catholic, Maronite, and Melkite (Greek Catholic).

**Orthodox includes Antiochian, Syrian, Greek, and Coptic.

***Muslim includes Sunni, Shi'a, and Druze.

Source: Arab American Institute 2008.

The majority of Arab Americans are Christian. Nor can Arab Americans be characterized as having a specific family type, gender role, or occupational pattern (David 2004).

For years, airport personnel and law enforcement authorities used appearance and ethnic-sounding names to identify Arab Americans and search their belongings. After the terrorist attacks of September 2001, criticism of this practice declined as concern for the public's safety mounted.

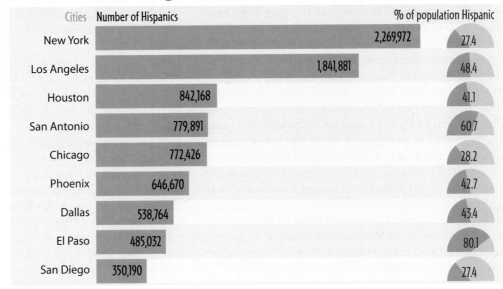

Cities with Large Numbers of Hispanics, 2007

Cities	Number of Hispanics	% of population Hispanic
New York	2,269,972	27.4
Los Angeles	1,841,881	48.4
Houston	842,168	41.1
San Antonio	779,891	60.7
Chicago	772,426	28.2
Phoenix	646,670	42.7
Dallas	538,764	43.4
El Paso	485,032	80.1
San Diego	350,190	27.4

Source: U.S. Census Bureau 2008g.

ETHNIC GROUPS

Unlike racial minorities, members of subordinate ethnic groups may not be hindered by physical differences from assimilating into the dominant culture of the United States. However, members of ethnic minority groups still face many forms of prejudice and discrimination. Take, for instance, the country's largest ethnic groups—Latinos, Jews, and White ethnics.

Latinos Together, the various groups included under the general category Latinos represent the largest minority in the United States. In 2007, there were more than 45 million Hispanics in this country, including 29 million Mexican Americans, over 4 million Puerto Ricans, 1.6 million Cuban Americans, and a smaller number of people of Central and South American origin. The latter group represents the fastest-growing and most diverse segment of the Hispanic community.

According to Census Bureau data, the Latino population now outnumbers the African American population in 6 of the 10 largest cities of the United States: Los Angeles, Houston, Phoenix, San Diego, Dallas, and San Antonio. Hispanics are now the majority of residents in cities such as Miami, Florida; El Paso, Texas; and Santa Ana, California. The rise in the Hispanic population of the United States—fueled by comparatively high birthrates and levels of immigration—has intensified debates over public policy issues such as bilingualism and immigration.

The various Latino groups share a heritage of Spanish language and culture, which can cause serious problems in their assimilation. An intelligent student whose first language is Spanish may be presumed to be slow or even unruly by English-speaking schoolchildren, and frequently by English-speaking teachers as well. The labeling of Latino children as underachievers, as learning disabled, or as emotionally disturbed can act as a self-fulfilling prophecy for some children. Bilingual education aims at easing the educational difficulties experienced by Hispanic children and others whose first language is not English.

The educational challenges facing Latinos is reflected in the fact that 68 percent of Hispanics ages 25–29 have completed high school, compared to 88 percent for non-Hispanic Whites. At the college level, 37 percent of Whites have a bachelor's degree, whereas only 12.4 percent of Hispanics have the same. The average income for Hispanic households is $38,679, 70 percent as much as non-Hispanic White households. In terms of wealth, 49 percent of Hispanics own their own home, compared to 75 percent for Whites (DeNavas-Walt 2008; Kochhar, Gonzalez-Barrera, and Docktorman 2009; Planty et al. 2009).

Mexican Americans The largest Latino population is Mexican American (see the graph on page 312). There were 12.7 million Mexican immigrants living in the United States in 2008, 17 times as many as the 760,000 in 1970. Approximately 55 percent of them are unauthorized immigrants. The opportunity for a Mexican to earn in one hour what it would take an entire day to earn in Mexico has pushed millions of immigrants, legal and illegal, north.

Aside from the family, the most important social institution in the Mexican American community is the church—specifically, the Roman Catholic Church. This strong identification with the Catholic faith has reinforced the already formidable barriers between Mexican Americans and their predominantly White and Protestant neighbors in the Southwest. At the same time, the Catholic Church helps many immigrants to develop a sense of identity and assists their assimilation into the dominant culture of the United

States. The complexity of the Mexican American community is underscored by the fact that Protestant churches—especially those that endorse expressive, open worship—have attracted increasing numbers of Mexican Americans.

Puerto Ricans The second-largest segment of Latinos in the United States is Puerto Ricans. Since 1917, residents of Puerto Rico have held the status of American citizens; many have migrated to New York and other eastern cities. Puerto Ricans have experienced serious poverty both in the United States and on the island. Those who live in the continental United States earn barely half the family income of Whites. As a result, a reverse migration began in the 1970s, with more Puerto Ricans leaving for the island than coming to the mainland (Torres 2008).

Politically, Puerto Ricans in the United States have not been as successful as Mexican Americans in organizing for their rights. For many mainland Puerto Ricans—as for many residents of the island—the paramount political issue is the destiny of Puerto Rico itself. Should it continue in its present commonwealth status, petition for admission to the United States as the 51st state, or attempt to become an independent nation? This question has divided Puerto Rico for decades and remains a central issue in Puerto Rican elections. In a 1998 referendum, for example, voters supported a "none of the above" option, effectively favoring continuation of the commonwealth status over statehood or independence.

Cuban Americans Cuban immigration to the United States dates back as far as 1831, but it began in earnest following Fidel Castro's seizure of power in the Cuban revolution of 1959. The first wave of 200,000 Cubans included many professionals with relatively high levels of schooling; these men and women were largely welcomed as refugees from communist tyranny. However, more recent waves of immigrants have aroused growing concern, partly because they were less likely to be skilled professionals. After Castro's revolution, the United States severed formal relations with Cuba, preventing all trade and banning travel. In recent years there has been some softening of that relationship, and in April 2009, President Obama signed a bill easing both economic and travel restrictions.

Jewish Americans
Jews constitute about 2.2 percent of the population of the United States. They play a prominent role in the worldwide Jewish community because the United States has the world's largest concentration of Jews. Like the Japanese, many Jewish immigrants came to this country and became white-collar professionals in spite of prejudice and discrimination.

Anti-Semitism—that is, anti-Jewish prejudice—has often been vicious in the United States, although rarely so widespread and never so formalized as in Europe. In many cases, Jews have been used as scapegoats for other people's failures. Given such attitudes, Jews continue to face discrimination. Despite high levels of education and professional training, they are still conspicuously absent from the top management of large corporations (except for the few firms founded by Jews). Until the late 1960s, many prestigious universities maintained restrictive quotas that limited Jewish enrollment. Private social clubs and fraternal groups frequently limit membership to gentiles (non-Jews), a practice upheld by the Supreme Court in the 1964 case *Bell v. Maryland.*

The Anti-Defamation League (ADL) of B'nai B'rith funds an annual tally of reported anti-Semitic incidents. Although the number has fluctuated, the 1994 tabulation reached the highest level in the 19 years the ADL had been recording them. In 2007, the total reported incidents of harassment, threats, vandalism, and assaults came to 1337. Some incidents were inspired and carried out by neo-Nazi skinheads—groups of young people who champion racist and anti-Semitic ideologies. Such threatening behavior only intensifies the fears of many Jewish Americans, who remember the Holocaust—the extermination of 6 million Jews by

Major Hispanic Groups in the United States, 2007

Other Hispanic
7.2%

Other Central and South American
10.0%

Dominican **2.7%**

Salvadoran **3.2%**

Cuban **3.5%**

Mexican
64.2%

Puerto Rican **9.1%**

Source: U.S. Census Bureau 2008g:Table B03001.

selected anti-Semitism (American Jewish Committee 2001; Sheskin and Dushefky 2007).

White Ethnics A significant segment of the population of the United States is made up of White ethnics whose ancestors arrived from Europe within the past century. The nation's White ethnic population includes about 51 million people who claim at least partial German ancestry, 36 million Irish Americans, 18 million Italian Americans, and 10 million Polish Americans, as well as immigrants from other European nations. Some of these people continue to live in close-knit ethnic neighborhoods, while others have largely assimilated and left the "old ways" behind (U.S. Census Bureau 2008g:Table DP-2).

> **anti-Semitism** Anti-Jewish prejudice.
> **symbolic ethnicity** An ethnic identity that emphasizes concerns such as ethnic food or political issues rather than deeper ties to one's ethnic heritage.

Many White ethnics today identify only sporadically with their heritage. **Symbolic ethnicity** refers to an emphasis on concerns such as ethnic food or political issues rather than on deeper ties to one's ethnic heritage. It is reflected in the occasional family trip to an ethnic bakery, the celebration of a ceremonial event such as St. Joseph's Day among Italian Americans, or concern about the future of Northern Ireland among Irish Americans. Except in cases in which new immigration reinforces old traditions, symbolic ethnicity tends to decline with each passing generation (Anangnostou 2009a, 2009b; Gans 2009; Waters 2009).

White ethnics and racial minorities have often been antagonistic to one another because of economic competition. As Blacks, Latinos, and Native Americans emerge from the lower class, they must compete with working-class Whites for jobs, housing, and educational opportunities. In times of high unemployment or inflation, any such competition can easily generate intense intergroup conflict.

In many respects, the plight of White ethnics involves the same basic issues as that of other subordinate people

CELEBRATING ETHNICITY

From Me to You

I live in Pella, Iowa, a small town in Iowa with a strong Dutch heritage. The first weekend in May, Pella holds its annual Tulip Time festival (www.pellatuliptime.com). Hundreds of thousands of tourists come to the three-day celebration to watch the parades, eat the food, and see people scrub streets in their Dutch costumes. Even though I have no Dutch ancestors, I regularly put on my costume and take part. I have carved wooden shoes in the historical museum, peddled the Jaarsma Bakery cart in the two daily parades, and more. Like other ethnic celebrations in other communities, Tulip Time plays a significant role in fostering a sense of community solidarity.

Nazi Germany during World War II (Anti-Defamation League 2008).

As is true for other minorities in the United States, Jewish Americans face the choice of maintaining ties to their long religious and cultural heritage or becoming as indistinguishable as possible from gentiles. Many Jews have tended to assimilate, as is evident from the rise in the rate of marriages between Jews and Christians. A study of 50

> ### Race hate isn't human nature; race hate is the abandonment of human nature.
> Orson Welles

Jewish communities in the United States found a median intermarriage rate of 33 percent. Many people in the Jewish community worry that intermarriage will lead to a rapid decline in those who identify themselves as "Jewish." Yet when asked which was the greater threat to Jewish life in the United States—intermarriage or anti-Semitism—only 41 percent of respondents chose intermarriage; 50 percent

in the United States. How ethnic can people be—how much can they deviate from an essentially White, Anglo-Saxon, Protestant norm—before society responds to their desire to be different? The United States does seem to reward people for assimilating. Yet, as we have seen, assimilation is no easy process. In the years to come, more and more people will face the challenge of fitting in, not only in the United States but around the world, as the flow of immigrants from one country to another continues to increase.

>> Immigration

According to a United Nations report, there are 191 million international immigrants in the world, or 3 percent of the global population. This includes 38.4 million in the United States. Of these, 54 percent are from Latin America, 27 percent from Asia, 13 percent from Europe, and 4 percent from Africa (United Nations 2009; U.S. Census Bureau 2008g:Table DP-2). The constantly increasing numbers of immigrants and the pressure they put on employment opportunities and welfare capabilities in the countries they enter raise troubling questions for many of the world's economic powers. Who should be allowed in? At what point should immigration be curtailed (Schmidley and Robinson 2003; Stalker 2000)?

IMMIGRATION TRENDS

The migration of people is not uniform across time or space. At certain times, war or famine may precipitate large movements of people, either temporarily or permanently. Temporary dislocations occur when people wait until it is safe to return to their home areas. However, more and more migrants who cannot eke out an ad-

equate living in their home nations are making permanent moves to developed nations. The major migration streams flow into North America, the oil-rich areas of the Middle East, and the industrial economies of western Europe and Asia. Currently, seven of the world's wealthiest nations (including Germany, France, the United Kingdom, and the United States) shelter about one-third of the world's migrant population but less than one-fifth of the world's total population. As long as disparities in job opportunities exist among countries, there is little reason to expect this international trend to reverse.

Even though the sending nation loses a significant source of labor and talent due to emigration, the process does contribute to its economy. For example, it reduces the size of the population that an economy with limited resources has a difficult time supporting, and it leads to an economic infusion in the form of remittances—monies that immigrants send back to their home nations. Worldwide, immigrants send more than $300 billion a year back home to their relatives—an amount that represents a major source of income for developing nations. In Guatemala, for example, the home country of the majority of workers at the Postville meat packing plant, $3.6 billion was sent back home in 2006, representing 9 percent of Guatemala's economy (DeParle 2007; Leys 2008).

Immigrants continue to face obstacles due to their relative lack of resources. Immigrant women, for example, face all the challenges that immigrant men do, plus some additional ones. Typically, they bear the responsibility for obtaining services for their families, particularly their children. Women are often left to navigate the bureaucratic tangle of schools, city services, and health care, as well as the unfamiliar stores and markets they must shop at to feed their families. Women who need special medical services

Going **GLOBAL**

World Immigration Since 1500

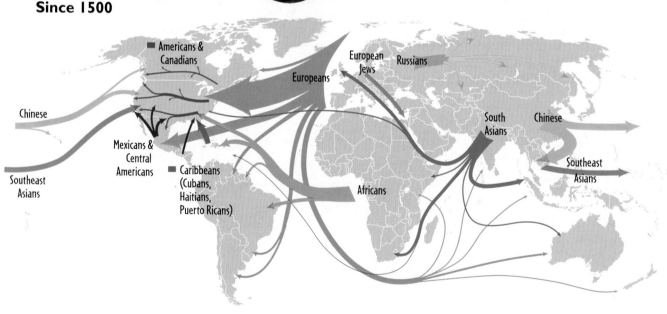

Source: J. Allen 2008.

or are victims of domestic violence are often reluctant to seek outside help. Finally, because many new immigrants view the United States as a dangerous place to raise a family, women must be especially watchful over their children's lives (Hondagneu-Sotelo 2003).

One consequence of global immigration has been the emergence of transnationals—people or families who move across borders multiple times in search of better jobs and education. The industrial tycoons of the early 20th century, whose power outmatched that of many nation-states, were among the world's first transnationals. Today, however, millions of people, many of very modest means, move back and forth between countries much as commuters do between city and suburbs. More and more of these people have dual citizenship. Rather than being shaped by allegiance to one country, their identity is rooted in their struggle to survive—and in some instances prosper—by transcending international borders (Croucher 2004; Sassen 2005).

IMMIGRATION POLICIES

Countries that have long been a destination for immigrants, such as the United States, usually have policies to determine who has preference to enter. Often, clear racial and ethnic biases are built into these policies. In the 1920s, U.S. policy gave preference to people from western Europe while making it difficult for residents of southern and eastern Europe, Asia, and Africa to enter the country. During the late 1930s and early 1940s, the federal government refused to loosen restrictive immigration quotas in order to allow Jewish refugees to escape the terror of Nazi Germany. In line with this policy, the SS *St. Louis,* with more than 900 Jewish refugees on board, was denied permission to dock in the United States in 1939. The ship was forced to sail back to Europe, where at least a few hundred of its passengers later died at the hands of the Nazis (Morse 1967; G. Thomas and Witts 1974).

Since the 1960s, U.S. policy has encouraged the immigration of relatives of U.S. residents and of people who have desirable skills. This policy has significantly altered the pattern of sending nations. Previously, Europeans dominated, but for the past 40 years, immigrants have come primarily from Latin America and Asia. Thus, an ever-growing proportion of the U.S. population will be Asian or Hispanic. To a large degree, fear and resentment of racial and ethnic diversity is a key factor in opposition to immigration. In many nations, people are concerned that the new arrivals do not reflect and will not embrace their own cultural and racial heritage.

The long border with Mexico provides ample opportunity for illegal immigration into the United States. Throughout the 1980s, the public perception grew that the United States had lost control of its borders. Feeling pressure to control immigration, Congress ended a decade of debate by approving the Immigration Reform and

Going GLOBAL

Legal Migration to the United States, 1820–2010

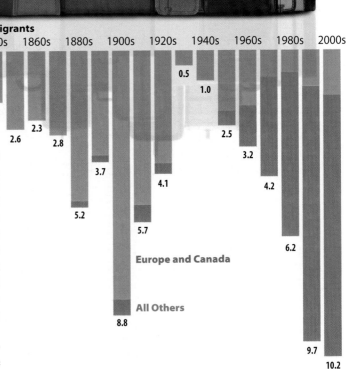

Millions of immigrants

1820s	1840s	1860s	1880s	1900s	1920s	1940s	1960s	1980s	2000s
0.1	0.6	1.7	2.8	3.7	4.1	0.5	2.5	4.2	10.2
	2.6	2.3	5.2		5.7	1.0	3.2	6.2	9.7
					8.8				

Europe and Canada

All Others

Source: Author's estimates for the period 2000–2010; Office of Immigration Statistics, 2007.

Control Act of 1986. The act marked a historic change in the nation's immigration policy. For the first time, the hiring of illegal aliens was outlawed, and employers caught violating the law became subject to fines and even prison. Just as significant a change was the extension of amnesty and legal status to many illegal immigrants already living in the United States. Over 20 years later, however, the act appears to have had mixed results. Substantial numbers of unauthorized immigrants continue to enter the country each year, with an estimated 12 million present now at any given time—a marked increase since 2000 (Passel and Cohn 2009).

Recently, immigrants have staged massive marches to pressure Congress to speed the naturalization process and develop ways for illegal immigrants to gain legal residency. Opponents of illegal immigration have called for more resources with which to track down and deport illegal immigrants and close up the U.S.–Mexican border. Despite this widespread public dissatisfaction with the nation's immigration policy, little progress has been made. Congress has had difficulty reaching a bipartisan compromise that pleases both sides.

In the wake of the September 11, 2001, attacks on the World Trade Center and the Pentagon, immigration procedures were complicated by the need to detect potential terrorists. Illegal immi-

grants especially, but even legal immigrants, have faced increased scrutiny by government officials around the world. For would-be immigrants to many nations, the wait to receive the right to enter a country—even to join relatives—has increased substantially, as immigration officials scrutinize what were once routine applications more closely.

The intense debate over immigration reflects deep value conflicts in the cultures of many nations. One strand of our culture, for example, has traditionally emphasized egalitarian principles and a desire to help people in time of need. At the same time, hostility to potential immigrants and refugees—whether the Chinese in the 1880s, European Jews in the 1930s and 1940s, or Mexicans, Haitians, and Arabs today—reflects not only racial, ethnic, and religious prejudice but a desire to maintain the dominant culture of the in-group by excluding those viewed as outsiders.

get involved!

Investigate! Most immigrant groups have museums dedicated to preserving their heritage. Find one in your area and learn the local immigrant story. If a local museum is not available, take advantage of online museums that preserve that history.

For REVIEW

I. **How do sociologists define race and ethnicity?**

- Race is shaped by biological differences but is defined by the social significance that groups attach to external physical characteristics. Ethnicity is rooted in cultural and national traditions that define a population. Sociologists emphasize the significance of culture and its consequences for both.

II. **What are prejudice and discrimination, and how do they operate?**

- Prejudice involves attitudes and beliefs while discrimination involves actions. In both cases, they represent a negative response to a group of people that denies them full equality as persons. Institutional discrimination is built in to the structure of society itself, systematically denying some groups access to key resources.

III. **What are the consequences of race and ethnicity for opportunity?**

- Racial and ethnic groups in the United States—including African Americans, Native Americans, Asian Americans, Latino Americans, Jewish Americans, and White ethnic Americans—face differing levels of opportunity based on their relative position in society. Groups within each of these categories continue to face significant structural inequality.

Pop Quiz

1. A group that is set apart because of its national origin or distinctive cultural patterns is a(n)
   a. assimilated group.
   b. ethnic group.
   c. minority group.
   d. racial group.

2. According to the findings of the Human Genome Project, race
   a. determines intellectual ability.
   b. is a biological, not a social, concept.
   c. explains significant social outcomes.
   d. has no genetic or scientific basis.

3. Starting with the 2000 census, there were a total of _____ possible race combinations you could choose from to identify yourself.
   a. 3
   b. 6
   c. 27
   d. 63

4. Suppose that a White employer refuses to hire a Vietnamese American and selects an inferior White applicant. This decision is an act of
   a. prejudice.
   b. ethnocentrism.
   c. discrimination.
   d. stigmatization.

5. The term that Peggy McIntosh uses to describe the unearned advantages that those in the majority take for granted is
   a. privilege.
   b. discrimination.
   c. racism.
   d. institutional discrimination.

6. Working together as computer programmers for an electronics firm, a Hispanic woman and a Jewish man overcome their initial prejudices and come to appreciate each other's strengths and talents. This scenario is an example of
   a. the contact hypothesis.
   b. a self-fulfilling prophecy.
   c. amalgamation.
   d. reverse discrimination.

7. Intermarriage over several generations, resulting in various groups combining to form a new group, would be an example of
   a. pluralism.
   b. assimilation.
   c. segregation.
   d. amalgamation.

8. Jennifer Anastassakis changed her name to Jennifer Aniston. Her action was an example of
   a. expulsion.
   b. assimilation.
   c. segregation.
   d. pluralism.

9. The largest racial minority group in the United States is
   a. Asian Americans.
   b. African Americans.
   c. Native Americans.
   d. Jewish Americans.

10. Which of the following is the largest overall minority group in the United States?
    a. African Americans
    b. Asian Americans
    c. Latinos
    d. Arab Americans

1. (b); 2. (d); 3. (d); 4. (c); 5. (a); 6. (a); 7. (d); 8. (b); 9. (b); 10. (c)

HEALTH, MED ENVI

ICINE, AND RONMENT

LIVING ON MOTHER EARTH

Earth is alive. At least it functions as if it is. So claims scientist James Lovelock, the originator of Gaia theory, which analyzes the planet and its interdependent parts as if it were a single, living organism. Today, Lovelock claims, humans are in danger of pushing this living system out of balance.

Gaia (pronounced "GUY-uh") is the ancient Greek earth goddess. Lovelock chose this name for his theory to emphasize that all living things represent a single interdependent system. He believes that we must develop an integrated vision of life to better understand the environment and our relationship with it.

Lovelock argues that Gaia maintains conditions on earth suitable for life through feedback loops. The oxygen cycle, in which humans and other animals breathe in oxygen and exhale carbon dioxide while plants do the reverse, is one simple example. Lovelock and his colleagues demonstrate that temperature, the salinity of oceans, and oxygen and methane levels are regulated by similar systems. Balance is maintained through natural evolution in which life responds to environmental conditions in ways that perpetuate its survival. If things get out of balance, organisms respond in ways that seek a return to balance.

Like all living things, however, Gaia can become sick and potentially even die. Lovelock has already played a significant role in averting an environmental crisis. In 1957, Lovelock invented the electron capture detector (ECD), which measures minute traces of particles. The ECD provided marine biologist Rachel Carson with data she used in her book *Silent Spring* (1962), which helped give birth to the modern environmental movement. Carson found that cancer-causing pesticides, such as DDT, were distributed around the world far from their sources of origin. She argued that our local actions have global consequences.

Gaia theory tells us we are globally interconnected. By looking at the planet as if it were a single organism, we can recognize how the various parts affect each other. Such a perspective is akin to that of the sociologist who looks at society and the way its various parts work together. We ignore such interdependent processes, and any cues that they may be out of balance, at our peril.

- What does sociology contribute to something as seemingly biological as health?
- What is social epidemiology?
- What environmental lessons do we learn from sociology?

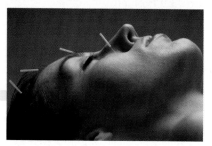

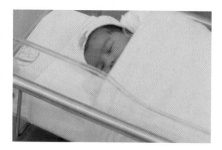

>> Culture, Society, and Health

When it comes to health and illness, we must take seriously the interdependent connections that shape our likely outcomes. To understand health, we cannot focus on biology alone. We must consider relationships, contexts, and the significance and impact of culture and society. The communities in which we live shape how we think about health and the body, as do our access to health care and our exposure to health risks.

health As defined by the World Health Organization, a state of complete physical, mental, and social well-being, and not merely the absence of disease and infirmity.

We can begin, however, with a general definition of health from the preamble to the 1946 constitution of the World Health Organization (WHO). They defined **health** as a "state of complete physical, mental, and social well-being, and not merely the absence of disease and infirmity" (Leavell and Clark 1965:14). This absolute standard provides an ideal type of what constitutes health, although in practice most people fall somewhere along a continuum between this ideal on one extreme and death on the other.

Our culture influences where we place ourselves along that continuum. Different places present us with differing levels of health risk. The type of health care available and our access to it also influences what we come to count as essential care, as do the risks we face. In rural areas, for example, residents must travel many miles to see a doctor. On the other hand, people who live in the country may escape many of the stresses and strains, along with environmental risks, that plague people who live in cities. Similarly, in Japan, organ transplants are rare. The Japanese do not generally favor harvesting organs from brain-dead donors. As a result, they forgo the health benefits that such transplants provide.

Researchers have shown that diseases, too, are rooted in the shared meanings of particular cultures. The term **culture-bound syndrome** refers to a disease or illness that cannot be understood apart from some specific social context. This means that there is something particular about the culture—how it is organized, what it believes, what is expected of members—that contributes to that malady (Buckle et al. 2007; Nicholas et al. 2006; U.S. Surgeon General 1999).

Anorexia is not a new disease, though it is discussed much more openly today. Seventies rock star Karen Carpenter died from anorexia in 1983.

three times that of the general U.S. population (Alvord and Van Pelt 1999:12; Heron et al. 2009).

>> Sociological Perspectives on Health and Illness

Whether we are considered "healthy" or "ill" is not our decision alone to make. Family, friends, co-workers, physicians, and others all shape how we perceive the state of our own and others' health. To fully understand the scope of health and illness in society, we have to consider how society defines illness, what the consequences of such definitions are, and how social position and access to resources shape health outcomes.

> **culture-bound syndrome** A disease or illness that cannot be understood apart from some specific social context.

ILLNESS AND SOCIAL ORDER

Illness represents a threat to the social order. If too many people are sick at the same time, it not only presents a problem for those who are ill but also undercuts our collective ability to perform tasks necessary for the continued operation of society. This can result in debates over what constitutes being "sick enough" to be considered truly ill. At what point, for example, do we stay home from school or work due to illness, and who gets to decide? All of us have likely faced this dilemma, sometimes dragging ourselves out of bed and going anyway because we felt we needed to be there, whether for the sake of ourselves or for others.

Did You Know?

. . . The average American woman is 5 feet 4 inches tall, weighs 155 pounds, and wears a size 14 dress, while the average model is 5 feet 9 inches tall, weighs 110 pounds, and wears a size 0 or 2.

In the United States, a culture-bound syndrome known as anorexia nervosa has received increasing attention in recent decades. First described in England in the 1860s, this condition is characterized by an intense fear of becoming obese and a distorted image of one's body. Those who suffer from anorexia nervosa (primarily young women in their teens or 20s) lose weight drastically through self-induced semistarvation. Anorexia nervosa is best understood in the context of Western culture, which typically views the slim, youthful individual as healthy and beautiful, and the fat person as ugly and lacking in self-discipline.

Until recently, U.S. researchers dealt with the concept of culture-bound syndromes only in cross-cultural studies. However, recent increases in immigration, along with efforts by the medical establishment to reach out to immigrant communities, have led to a belated recognition that not everyone views medicine in the same way. Medical practitioners are now being trained to recognize cultural beliefs that are related to medicine. For example, people from Central America may consider pain a consequence of the imbalance of nature, and Muslim women are particularly concerned about personal modesty. Health care professionals are increasingly incorporating such knowledge into their practices.

Culture can also influence the relative incidence of a disease or disorder. In her book *The Scalpel and the Silver Bear*, Dr. Lori Arviso Alvord, the first Navajo woman to become a surgeon, writes of the depression and alcoholism that attend life on the reservation. These diseases, she says, are born from "historical grief": "Navajo children are told of the capture and murder of their forefathers and mothers, and then they too must share in the legacy." Not just for the Navajo, Alvord writes, but for African Americans as well, the weight of centuries of suffering, injustice, and loss too often manifests itself in despair and addiction. The rate of alcoholism mortality among Native Americans is over

When people cross the line into illness, they take on what sociologists call the **sick role,** a term that refers to societal expectations about the attitudes and behavior of a person labeled as ill (Parsons 1951, 1975). Fit members of society exempt the sick from normal, day-to-day responsibilities and generally do not blame them for their condition. Yet the sick are obligated to attempt recovery, which includes seeking competent professional care. This obligation arises from the sense of responsibility we have to perform our normal roles in society, whether as student, worker, parent, or more. It also is motivated by the reality that we may well face sanctions from others for failing to return to those normal roles quickly. In fact, especially in the context of competitive work environments, we often look down on those who seem to get sick too easily or frequently, suspecting that they are either lazy or weak. Such attitudes present significant difficulties for those facing chronic health problems.

SOCthink

> > > What factors shape your likelihood of doing all you can to avoid "being sick"? How might the power others have over you influence your actions? What positions do they occupy relative to you?

Physicians and nurses have the power to label people as healthy or sick and, thus, to function as gatekeepers for the sick role. For example, instructors often require students to get a note from a health care professional to verify a claim of illness as a legitimate excuse for missing a paper or an exam. The ill person becomes dependent on the doctor or nurse, because the latter control the resources the patient needs, whether it be a note for a professor or a prescription for medication. We look to such professionals to solve our health care needs, trusting that they have sufficient expertise and experience to diagnose and treat our problems.

Factors such as gender, age, social class, and ethnic group all influence patients' judgments regarding their own state of health. Younger people may fail to detect the warning signs of a dangerous illness, and the elderly may focus too much on the slightest physical malady. Whether one is employed also seems to affect one's willingness to assume the sick role—as does the impact of socialization into a particular occupation or activity. For example, from an early age, athletes learn to define certain ailments as "sports injuries" and so do not regard themselves as "sick" when suffering from such maladies.

POWER, RESOURCES, AND HEALTH

The faith we place in physicians to heal what ails us has helped them attain significant levels of prestige and power.

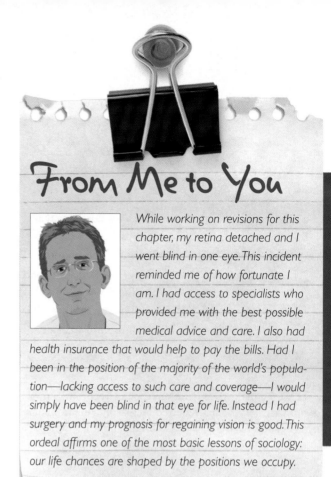

From Me to You

While working on revisions for this chapter, my retina detached and I went blind in one eye. This incident reminded me of how fortunate I am. I had access to specialists who provided me with the best possible medical advice and care. I also had health insurance that would help to pay the bills. Had I been in the position of the majority of the world's population—lacking access to such care and coverage—I would simply have been blind in that eye for life. Instead I had surgery and my prognosis for regaining vision is good. This ordeal affirms one of the most basic lessons of sociology: our life chances are shaped by the positions we occupy.

Sociologist Eliot Freidson (1970:5) has likened the status of medicine today to that of state religions in the past—it has an officially approved monopoly on the right to define health and to treat illness. Theorists use the phrase "medicalization of society" to refer to the growing role of medicine as a major institution of social control (Conrad 2007; Zola 1972, 1983).

The Medicalization of Society Social control involves techniques and strategies for regulating behavior in order to enforce the distinctive norms and values of a culture. How does medicine manifest its social control? First, medicine has greatly expanded its domain of expertise in recent decades. Physicians now examine a wide range of issues in addition to basic health, among them sexuality, old age, anxiety, obesity, child development, alcoholism, and drug addiction. We tolerate this expansion of the boundaries of medicine because we hope that these experts can provide factual and effective cures to complex human problems, as they have to various infectious diseases.

The social significance of this expanding medicalization is that once a problem is viewed from a medical model framework—once medical experts become influential in proposing and assessing relevant public policies—it becomes more difficult for common people to join the discussion and exert influence on decision making. It also becomes more difficult to view these issues as being shaped by social, cultural, or psychological factors rather than simply by physical or medical factors (Caplan 1989; Davis 2006; Starr 1982).

A second way that medicine serves as an agent of social control is by retaining absolute jurisdiction over many health care procedures. The medical industry has even attempted to guard its jurisdiction by placing health care professionals such as chiropractors and nurse-midwives outside the realm of acceptable medicine. Despite the fact that midwives first brought professionalism to child delivery, they have been portrayed as having invaded the "legitimate" field of obstetrics, in both the United States and Mexico. Nurse-midwives have sought licensing as a way to achieve professional respectability, but physicians continue to exert power to ensure that midwifery remains a subordinate occupation (Scharnberg 2007).

Inequities in Health Care Another serious concern regarding power and resources in the context of contemporary medicine involves the glaring inequities that exist in health care. Around the world, poor areas tend to be underserved because medical services concentrate where the wealth is. The United States, for example, has about 26 physicians per 10,000 people, whereas African nations have less than 2 per 10,000 (World Health Organization 2009).

The supply of health care in poorer countries is further reduced by what is referred to as **brain drain**—the immigration to the United States and other industrialized nations of skilled workers, professionals, and technicians who are desperately needed in their home countries. As part of this brain drain, physicians, nurses, and other health care

professionals have come to the United States from developing countries such as India, Pakistan, and various African states. Their emigration out of the Third World represents yet another way in which the world's core industrialized nations enhance their quality of life at the expense of developing countries (List 2009).

Such inequities in health care have clear life-and-death consequences. For example, there are dramatic differences in infant mortality rates between developing countries such as Afghanistan, Sierra Leone, and Pakistan and industrial nations like Iceland, Japan, and Australia. The **infant mortality rate** is the number of deaths of infants under one year old per 1000 live births in a given year. This measure is an important indicator of a society's level of health care; it reflects prenatal nutrition, delivery procedures, and infant screening measures. Such differences in infant mortality reflect unequal distribution of health care resources based on the wealth or poverty of various nations. Surprisingly, despite our national wealth and the huge amounts spent on health care in the United States, at least 45 nations have lower infant mortality rates. An additional way that developing countries suffer the consequences of health care inequality is in reduced life expectancy. In Africa as a whole, life expectancy at birth averages 54 years with a low of 33 in Swaziland, whereas in the United States it is 78 years (Population Reference Bureau 2008).

> **sick role** Societal expectations about the attitudes and behavior of a person viewed as being ill.
> **brain drain** The immigration to the United States and other industrialized nations of skilled workers, professionals, and technicians who are desperately needed in their home countries.
> **infant mortality rate** The number of deaths of infants under one year old per 1000 live births in a given year.

Labeling and Power Sometimes the power to label and the power to oppress go hand in hand. A historical example illustrates perhaps the ultimate extreme in labeling social behavior as a sickness. As enslavement of Africans in the United States came

5 Movies on HEALTH AND MEDICINE

The Diving Bell and the Butterfly
A man suddenly becomes completely paralyzed.

My Sister's Keeper
Cancer puts a strain on family relationships.

Philadelphia
One man's battle with AIDS and the society that shuns him.

Sicko
A documentary criticizing the U.S. health care system.

One Flew over the Cuckoo's Nest
Doctor–patient dynamics go haywire at a mental institution.

Going GLOBAL

Infant Mortality Rates in Selected Countries

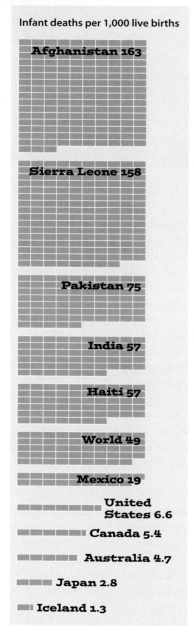

Infant deaths per 1,000 live births

Afghanistan	163
Sierra Leone	158
Pakistan	75
India	57
Haiti	57
World	49
Mexico	19
United States	6.6
Canada	5.4
Australia	4.7
Japan	2.8
Iceland	1.3

Source: Population Reference Bureau 2008.

and Surgical Journal suggested that the remedy for this "disease" was to treat slaves kindly, as one might treat children. Apparently, these medical authorities would not entertain the view that it was healthy and sane to flee slavery or join in a slave revolt (Szasz 1971).

By the late 1980s, the power of one particular label—"person with AIDS"—had become quite evident. This label often functions as a master status that overshadows all other aspects of a person's life. Once someone is told that he or she has tested positive for HIV, the virus associated with AIDS, that person is forced to confront immediate and difficult questions: Should I tell my family members? My sex partners? My friends? My co-workers? My employer? How will these people respond? People's intense fear of the disease has led to prejudice and discrimination—even social ostracism—against those who have (or are suspected of having) AIDS. A person who has AIDS must deal not only with the serious medical consequences of the disease but also with the distressing social consequences associated with the label.

AIDS caught major social institutions—particularly the government, the health care system, and the economy—by surprise when it was first noticed by medical practitioners in the 1970s. It has since spread around the world, with the first U.S. cases of AIDS reported in 1981. Rather than being a distinct disease, AIDS is actually a predisposition to various diseases that is caused by a virus, the human immunodeficiency virus (HIV). The virus gradually destroys

under increasing attack in the 19th century, medical authorities provided new rationalizations for the oppressive practice. Noted physicians published articles stating that the skin color of Africans deviated from "healthy" white skin coloring because Africans suffered from congenital leprosy. Moreover, physicians classified the continuing efforts of enslaved Africans to escape from their White masters as an example of the "disease" of drapetomania (or "crazy runaways"). The prestigious *New Orleans Medical*

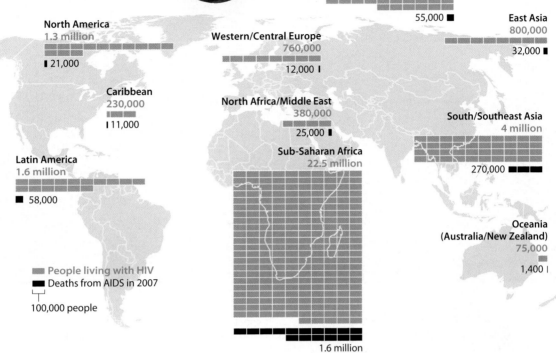

Going GLOBAL

HIV/AIDS Cases, 2007

Eastern Europe/Central Asia
1.6 million
55,000 ■

East Asia
800,000
32,000 ■

North America
1.3 million
■ 21,000

Western/Central Europe
760,000
12,000 I

Caribbean
230,000
I 11,000

North Africa/Middle East
380,000
25,000 ■

South/Southeast Asia
4 million
270,000 ■■■

Latin America
1.6 million
■ 58,000

Sub-Saharan Africa
22.5 million
1.6 million

Oceania
(Australia/New Zealand)
75,000
1,400 I

■■ People living with HIV
■ Deaths from AIDS in 2007
└┘
100,000 people

Sources: Centers for Disease Control and Prevention 2007a; UNAIDS 2007.

Note: Midpoint estimates for December 2007. Total number of adults and children living with HIV, 33.2 million; total number of estimated adult and child deaths during 2007, 2.1 million.

the body's immune system, leaving the carrier vulnerable to infections such as pneumonia that those with healthy immune systems generally can resist.

While the numbers of new cases and deaths have recently shown some evidence of decline, more than a million people in the United States were living with AIDS or HIV as of December 2007. Globally, an estimated 33.2 million people are now infected; however, the disease is not evenly distributed. Those areas least equipped to deal with it—the developing nations of sub-Saharan Africa—face the greatest challenge (Centers for Disease Control and Prevention 2007c).

Because those in high-risk groups—gay men and IV drug users—were comparatively powerless, and labeled as such, policy makers were slow to respond to the AIDS crisis in the United States. Over time, however, the response has improved, and today people with HIV or AIDS who receive appropriate medical treatment are living longer than they did in the past. The high cost of drug treatment programs has generated intensive worldwide pressure on the major pharmaceutical companies to lower the prices to patients in developing nations, especially in sub-Saharan Africa. Bowing to this pressure, several of the companies have agreed to make the combination therapies available at

cost. As a result, the accessibility of HIV treatment has increased steadily, though inequalities remain. By the beginning of 2008, only 11 percent of mothers who need therapy to prevent transmission of the virus to their babies were receiving it (R. Wolf 2008).

According to labeling theorists, we can view a variety of life experiences as illnesses or not. Recently, the medical community has recognized premenstrual syndrome, posttraumatic disorders, and hyperactivity as medical disorders. Probably the most noteworthy medical example of labeling is the case of homosexuality. For years, psychiatrists classified being gay or lesbian not as a lifestyle but as a mental disorder subject to treatment. This official sanction by the psychiatry profession became an early target of the growing gay and lesbian rights movement in the United States. In 1974, members of the American Psychiatric Association voted to drop homosexuality from the standard manual on mental disorders (Conrad 2007).

NEGOTIATING CURES

In practice, we seek to strike a balance between the authority of the physician and the agency of the patient. Physicians use cues to reinforce their prestige and power. According to medical sociologist Brenda Beagan (2001), the technical language students learn in medical school becomes the basis for the script they follow as novice physicians. The familiar white coat and stethoscope is their costume—one that helps them to appear confident

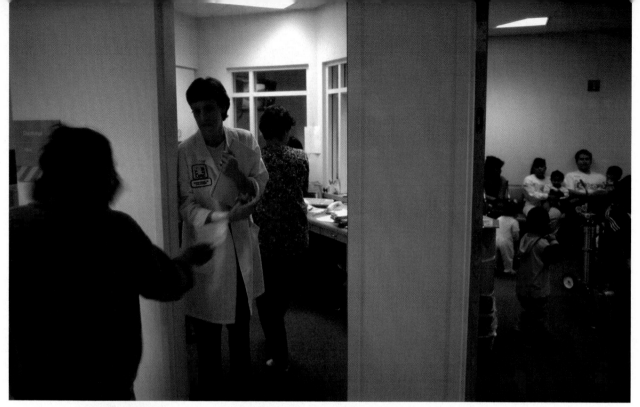

but over time most become accustomed to expecting respect and deference.

Patients, on the other hand, are not passive. Sometimes patients play an active role in health care by failing to follow a physician's advice. For example, some patients stop taking medications long before they should. Some take an incorrect dosage on purpose, and others never even fill their prescriptions. Such noncompliance results in part from the prevalence of self-medication in our society; many people are accustomed to self-diagnosis and self-treatment.

Patients' active involvement in their health care can have very positive consequences. Some patients consult books, magazines, and websites about preventive health care techniques, attempt to maintain a healthful and nutritious diet, carefully monitor any side effects of medication, and adjust the dosage based on perceived side effects. Recognizing this change, pharmaceutical firms are advertising their prescription drugs directly to potential customers. For their part, medical professionals are understandably suspicious of these new sources of information. Studies, including one published in the *Journal of the American Medical Association,* found that health information on the Internet is often incomplete and inaccurate, even on the best sites. Nevertheless, there is little doubt that Internet research is transforming patient–physician encounters (Adams and de Bont 2007; Arora et al. 2008; Berland 2001).

>> Social Epidemiology

By looking at patterns of health and illness throughout society, we can better understand which factors are at work in shaping health outcomes. **Social epidemiology** is the study of disease distribution, impairment, and general health status across a population. Initially, epidemiology

and professional at the same time that it identifies them as doctors to patients and other staff members. Beagan found that many medical students struggle to project the appearance of competence they think their role demands,

concentrated on the scientific study of epidemics, focusing on how they started and spread. Contemporary social epidemiology is much broader in scope, concerned not only with epidemics but also with nonepidemic diseases, injuries, drug addiction and alcoholism, suicide, and mental illness. Recently, epidemiologists took on the new role of tracking bioterrorism. In 2001, they mobilized to trace an anthrax outbreak and prepare for any terrorist use of smallpox or other lethal microbes. Epidemiologists draw on the work of a wide variety of scientists and researchers, among them physicians, sociologists, public health officials, biologists, veterinarians, demographers, anthropologists, psychologists, and meteorologists.

Researchers in social epidemiology commonly use two concepts: incidence and prevalence. **Incidence** refers to the number of new cases of a specific disorder that occur within a given population during a stated period, usually a year. For example, the incidence of AIDS in the United States in 2007 was 37,041 cases. In contrast, **prevalence** refers to the total number of cases of a specific disorder that exist at a given time. The prevalence of AIDS in the United States through 2007 was about 460,000 cases (Department of Health and Human Services 2007).

When disease incidence figures are presented as rates—for example, the number of reports per 100,000 people—they are called **morbidity rates.** This is distinct from the **mortality rate,** which refers to the incidence of death in a given population. Sociologists find morbidity rates useful because they can reveal whether a specific disease occurs more frequently among one segment of a population than another. As we shall see, social class, race, ethnicity, gender, and age can all affect a population's morbidity rates (Barr 2008).

SOCIAL CLASS

Social class is clearly associated with differences in morbidity and mortality rates. Studies in the United States and

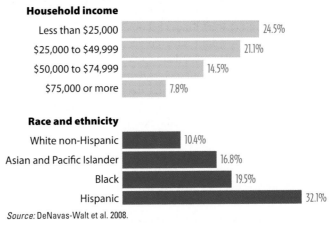

Percentage of People Without Health Insurance, 2007

Household income

Less than $25,000	24.5%
$25,000 to $49,999	21.1%
$50,000 to $74,999	14.5%
$75,000 or more	7.8%

Race and ethnicity

White non-Hispanic	10.4%
Asian and Pacific Islander	16.8%
Black	19.5%
Hispanic	32.1%

Source: DeNavas-Walt et al. 2008.

instances, poor education may lead to a lack of awareness of measures necessary to maintain good health. Financial strains are certainly a major factor in the health problems of less affluent people.

People who are poor—many of whom belong to racial and ethnic minorities—are less able than others to afford quality medical care (see the accompanying graph). Not surprisingly, those with high incomes are significantly more likely to have health insurance, either because they can afford it or because they have jobs that provide it. The middle class has been particularly hard hit by the decision of companies to eliminate employer-provided coverage (the most common form of health insurance). Such rates

> **social epidemiology** The study of the distribution of disease, impairment, and general health status across a population.
> **incidence** The number of new cases of a specific disorder that occur within a given population during a stated period.
> **prevalence** The total number of cases of a specific disorder that exist at a given time.
> **morbidity rate** The incidence of disease in a given population.
> **mortality rate** The incidence of death in a given population.

It is a lot harder to keep people well than it is to just get them over a sickness.

DeForest Clinton Jarvis

other countries have consistently shown that people in the lower classes have higher rates of mortality and disability than others. One study concluded that Americans with 12 years or less of schooling could expect to die seven years sooner than those with more than 12 years of schooling (Meara, Richards and Cutler 2008; Pear 2008).

A number of factors appear to influence the effect class has on health. Crowded living conditions, substandard housing, poor diet, and stress all contribute to the ill health of many low-income people in the United States. In certain

declined steadily from 2000 to 2007 (DeNavas-Walt et al. 2008; E. Gould 2008).

The ultimate price to pay for a lack of health insurance is the increased risk of early death. Uninsured women who develop breast cancer tend to be diagnosed later—when treatment is less effective—than insured women. Uninsured men who develop high blood pressure are more likely than others to forgo screenings and medication, a decision that jeopardizes their health. According to estimates, 22,000 deaths among the uninsured could have been prevented in 2006 (Dorn 2008).

What is particularly troubling about social class differences is that they appear to be cumulative. Little or no health care in childhood or young adulthood is likely to mean more illness later in life. The longer that low income presents a barrier to adequate health care, the more chronic and difficult to treat illness becomes (Prus 2007).

Karl Marx would have argued, and some contemporary sociologists agree, that capitalist societies such as the United States care more about maximizing profits than they do about the health and safety of industrial workers. As a result, government agencies do not take forceful action to regulate conditions in the workplace, and workers suffer many preventable job-related injuries and illnesses. As we will see later in this chapter, research also shows that the lower classes are more vulnerable to environmental pollution, another consequence of capitalist production, than are the affluent, not only where they work but where they live.

curanderismo Latino folk medicine, a form of holistic health care and healing.

RACE AND ETHNICITY

The health profiles of many racial and ethnic minorities reflect the social inequality evident in U.S. society. The poor economic and environmental conditions of groups such as African Americans, Hispanics, and Native Americans are manifested in high morbidity and mortality rates for these groups. It is true that some afflictions, such as sickle-cell anemia among Blacks, are influenced by genetics, but in most instances, environmental factors contribute to the differential rates of disease and death.

As noted earlier, infant mortality is regarded as a primary indicator of health care. There is a significant gap in the United States between the infant mortality rates of African Americans and Whites. On average, the rate of infant death is more than twice as high among Blacks. African Americans account for 15 percent of all live births in the nation but 29 percent of infant deaths. Puerto Ricans and Native Americans have infant mortality rates that are lower than African Americans' but higher than Whites' (Mac-Dorman et al. 2005).

Considering mortality rates, Blacks have higher death rates from heart disease, pneumonia, diabetes, and cancer than do Whites. The death rate from stroke is twice as high among African Americans. Such epidemiological findings are related to the social class effects noted previously—the fact that average income for African Americans is lower than that for Whites. The effect of these factors can be seen in terms of life expectancy. The U.S. life expectancy for Whites is 78.2 years compared to 73.2 years for Blacks. This five-year gap is the lowest recorded difference, down from a high of 7.1 years in 1989 (Heron et al. 2009).

The medical establishment is not exempt from institutional discrimination. There is evidence that minorities receive inferior care even when they are insured. Despite having access to care, Blacks, Latinos, and American Indians are treated unequally as a result of differences in the quality of various health care plans. Furthermore, national clinical studies have shown that even allowing for differences in income and insurance coverage, racial and ethnic minorities are less likely than other groups to receive both standard health care and life-saving treatment (Dressler et al. 2005; A. Green et al. 2007).

Numerous examples in the history of African American health care demonstrate that such institutional discrimination has been around for a long time. For example, in the notorious Tuskegee syphilis study, begun by the federal government in 1932, doctors knowingly infected Black men from Alabama with syphilis in order to observe the disease's progression. Another study, conducted from 1992 to 1997, was designed to determine whether there is a biological or genetic basis for violent behavior. Researchers misled the parents of young subjects, all of whom were Black males, by telling them that the children would undergo a series of tests and questions. In fact, the boys were given potentially risky doses of the same drug found in the now-banned Fen-phen weight-loss pill, which causes heart irregularities.

Infant Motality Rates in the United States, 2003–2005

Race/Ethnicity	Infant deaths per 1000 live births
Black, non-Hispanic	13.6
American Indian or Alaska Native	8.4
White, non-Hispanic	5.7
Hispanic	5.6
Asian or Pacific Islander	4.8

Source: National Center for Health Statistics 2008:Table 18.

SOCthink

> > > Studies such as the Tuskegee syphilis experiment seem to clearly violate ethical principles of research. How do you think that researchers justify studies involving race that appear to violate the ethical guidelines they are bound to follow?

Having to deal with the effects of racism may itself contribute to the medical problems of Blacks (Waitzkin 1986).

The stress that results from racial prejudice and discrimination helps to explain the higher rates of hypertension found among African Americans (and Hispanics) compared to Whites. Hypertension—twice as common in Blacks as in Whites—is believed to be a critical factor in Blacks' high mortality rates from heart disease, kidney disease, and stroke (Fiscella and Holt 2008).

Mexican Americans and many other Latinos adhere to cultural beliefs that make them less likely to use the established medical system. They may interpret their illnesses according to traditional Latino folk medicine, or *curanderismo*—a form of holistic health care and healing. *Curanderismo* influences how one approaches health care and even how one defines illness. Although most Hispanics use folk healers, or *curanderos,* infrequently, perhaps 20 percent rely on home remedies. Some define such illnesses as *susto* (fright sickness) and *atague* (fighting attack) according to folk beliefs. Because these complaints often have biological bases, sensitive medical practitioners need to deal with them carefully in order to diagnose

and treat illnesses accurately (Tafur, Crowe and Torres 2009).

Also affecting Latino morbidity rates is the fact that Latinos are much more likely to wait to seek treatment. Due in part to a lack of health insurance, they seek treatment for pressing medical problems at clinics and emergency rooms rather than receiving regular preventive care through a family physician. Such delays in treatments increase the severity of the consequences of illness and disease (Durden and Hummer 2006).

GENDER

A large body of research indicates that compared with men, women experience a higher prevalence of many illnesses, although they do have a longer life expectancy. There are some variations—for example, men are more likely to have parasitic diseases, whereas women are more likely to become diabetic—but as a group, women appear to be in poorer health than men.

The apparent inconsistency between the ill health of women and their greater longevity appears to be tied to lifestyle differences between men and women that grow out of gendered norms. Women's lower rate of cigarette smoking (reducing their risk of heart disease, lung cancer, and emphysema), lower consumption of alcohol (reducing the risk of auto accidents and cirrhosis of the liver), and lower rate of employment in dangerous occupations explain about one-third of their greater longevity than men. Researchers argue that women are much more likely than men to seek treatment, to be diagnosed as having a disease, and thus to have their illnesses reflected in the data examined by epidemiologists.

With everything from birth to beauty being treated in an increasingly medical context, women have been particularly vulnerable to the medicalization of society. Ironically, even given the increased power of the medical establishment in women's lives, medical researchers have often excluded them from clinical studies. Female physicians and researchers charge that sexism lies at the heart of such research practices and insist there is a desperate need for studies of female subjects (Pinnow et al. 2009; Rieker and Bird 2000).

Smoking Rates by Gender, 1965–2006

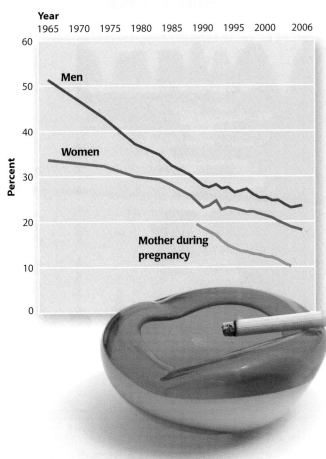

Year
1965 1970 1975 1980 1985 1990 1995 2000 2006

Men

Women

Mother during pregnancy

Percent

Source: National Center for Health Statistics 2008:Table 63.

AGE

Health is the overriding concern of the elderly. Most older people in the United States report having at least one chronic illness, but only some of those conditions are potentially life threatening or require medical care. The quality of life among older people is of particular concern in the face of potentially escalating health problems. Almost half of older people in the United States are troubled by arthritis, and many have visual or hearing impairments that can interfere with the performance of everyday tasks.

Older people are also especially vulnerable to certain mental health problems. Alzheimer's disease, the leading cause of dementia in the United States, afflicts an estimated 5.1 million older people. While some individuals with Alzheimer's exhibit only mild symptoms, the risk of severe problems resulting from this disease rises substantially with age (Alzheimer's Association 2009:10).

Due to their increased health risks, the rate at which older people in the United States (age 75 or older) use health services is more than three times greater than that for younger people (ages 15–24). This heightened use level is tied to health insurance coverage, with people over age 65 the most likely to be covered (see the graph below). The disproportionate use of the U.S. health care system by older people is a critical factor in all discussions about the cost of health care and possible reforms of the health care system (U.S. Census Bureau 2008:Table 159).

A person's odds of good health are shaped by her or his class, race and ethnicity, gender, and age. Even geography matters, as there are significant differences in the number of physicians from one state to the next. Health care professionals and program advisors need to take such differential effects into account when considering what constitutes equitable health care coverage. Any attempts to do so, however, are constrained by the cost of health care.

Availability of Physicians by State, 2006

Source: U.S. Census Bureau 2008:Table 156.

Physicians per 100,000
National average 267

- 315 and over
- 314–267
- 266–217
- Under 216

Total Health Care Expenditures in the United States, 1970–2018 (projected)

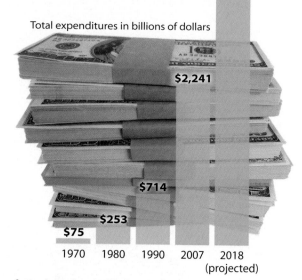

Total expenditures in billions of dollars

$4,353

$2,241

$714

$253

$75

1970   1980   1990   2007   2018 (projected)

Source: Centers for Medicare and Medicaid Services 2009a:Table 1; 2009b:Table 1.

Health Insurance Rates by Age, 2007

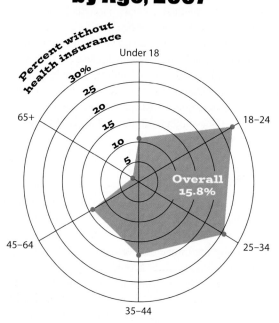

Percent without health insurance

Under 18

18–24

25–34

35–44

45–64

65+

30%
25
20
15
10
5

Overall 15.8%

Source: DeNavas-Walt et al. 2008:Table 6.

>> Health Care in the United States

The costs of health care have skyrocketed in the past 40 years. In 1997, total expenditures for health care in the United States crossed the trillion-dollar threshold—more than four times the 1980 figure. In 2000, the amount spent on health care equaled what we spent on education, defense, prisons, farm subsidies, food stamps, and foreign aid combined. By the year 2018, total expenditures for health care in the United States are expected to exceed $4.4 trillion or $13,100 per person. The United States currently devotes a greater proportion of its spending (15.3 percent of GDP) to health care than do all other OECD (Organization for Economic Cooperation and Development) nations, including France (11.0 percent), Canada (10.0 percent), the United Kingdom (8.4 percent) and Japan (8.1 percent). Over time health care in the United States has evolved to become a big business (Center for Medicare and Medicaid Services 2009a, 2009b; Kaiser Family Foundation 2009).

A HISTORICAL VIEW

Today, state licensing and medical degrees confer a widely recognized level of authority on medical professionals. This was not always the case. The "popular health movement" of the 1830s and 1840s emphasized preventive care and what is termed "self-help." It voiced strong criticism of "doctoring" as a paid occupation. New medical philosophies or sects established their own medical schools and challenged the authority and methods of more traditional doctors. By the 1840s, most states had repealed medical licensing laws, and the health care field was largely unregulated.

In response, through the leadership of the American Medical Association (AMA), founded in 1848, "regular" doctors marginalized lay practitioners, sectarian doctors, and female physicians in general. They institutionalized their authority through standardized programs of education and licensing. Only those who successfully completed AMA programs gained legitimate authority as medical practitioners. The authority of the physician no longer depended on lay attitudes or on the person occupying the sick role; increasingly, it was built into the structure of the medical profession and the health care system.

As the institutionalization of health care proceeded, the medical profession gained control over both the market for its services and the various organizational hierarchies that govern medical practice, financing, and policy making. By the 1920s, physicians controlled hospital technology, the division of labor of health personnel, and indirectly, other professional practices such as nursing and pharmaceutical services (Coser 1984).

THE ROLE OF GOVERNMENT

Not until the 20th century did health care receive federal aid in conjunction with the expansion of medicine as a social institution. The first significant government involvement was the 1946 Hill-Burton Act, which provided subsidies for building and improving hospitals, especially in rural areas. An even more important development was the enactment in 1965 of two wide-ranging government assistance programs: Medicare, which is essentially a compulsory health insurance plan for the elderly, and Medicaid, which is a noncontributory federal and state insurance plan for the poor. These programs greatly expanded federal involvement in health care financing for needy men, women, and children.

While health care costs were rising, a growing portion of the U.S. population (46 million by 2009) remained uninsured. An inability to afford coverage was a major factor. In 1993, the Clinton administration proposed health care reform designed to provide universal coverage, but the legislation failed to pass. Throughout the George W. Bush administration, the United States remained the only wealthy, industrialized nation that did not provide some form of universal coverage.

By 2009 there was widespread political agreement that the existing system, with its projected escalating costs, was not sustainable. From 1999 to 2008, for example, the cost of health insurance premiums rose 119 percent, while wages rose only 34 percent (Kaiser Family Foundation 2009). The Obama administration pledged to enact reform

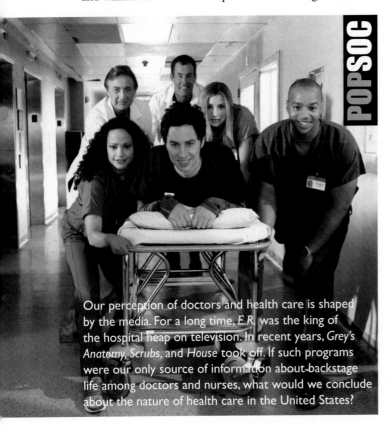

POPSOC

Our perception of doctors and health care is shaped by the media. For a long time, *E.R.* was the king of the hospital heap on television. In recent years, *Grey's Anatomy*, *Scrubs*, and *House* took off. If such programs were our only source of information about backstage life among doctors and nurses, what would we conclude about the nature of health care in the United States?

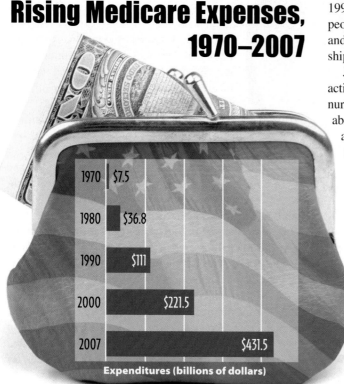

Rising Medicare Expenses, 1970–2007

Year	Expenditures (billions of dollars)
1970	$7.5
1980	$36.8
1990	$111
2000	$221.5
2007	$431.5

Expenditures (billions of dollars)

Source: National Center for Health Statistics 2008:Table 142.

that would both contain costs and expand coverage. Though there was general consensus regarding these aims, there were significant disagreements on how best to accomplish them. Some supported a single-payer system in which the government is the primary source of health care funding. Others continued to support market-based reforms that minimize government involvement. A significant intervening position focused on whether or not the government should provide a "public option," allowing people to choose a government-funded plan among many private company plans. President Obama (2009) proposed this as part of establishing a Health Insurance Exchange, which he described as "a market where Americans can one-stop shop for a health care plan, compare benefits and prices, and choose the plan that's best for them, in the same way that Members of Congress and their families can."

PHYSICIANS, NURSES, AND PATIENTS

The power of medicine and the prestige of doctors have risen together. As the occupation became more professional and training more standardized, some of the depersonalizing effects of working in a bureaucratic organization came to influence role performance. For example, when reflecting on the medical school training she received, Dr. Lori Arviso Alvord commented, "I had been trained by a group of physicians who placed much more emphasis on their technical abilities and clinical skills than on their abilities to be caring and sensitive" (Alvord and Van Pelt

1999:13). Though doctors were taught to treat patients like people, bureaucratic demands, including patient overload and cost-cutting by hospitals, tended to undercut relationship building.

Just as physicians maintain dominance in their interactions with patients, they often control interactions with nurses. Even when nurses may have more information about a patient, nurses must still defer to the physician's authority. Psychiatrist Leonard Stein (1967) referred to this process as the "doctor–nurse game." In this game, the nurse should never openly disagree with the physician. When nurses have recommendations concerning a patient's care, they must communicate them indirectly, in a deferential tone. For example, if asked by a doctor, "What sleeping medication has been helpful to Mrs. Brown in the past?" (an indirect request for a recommendation), the nurse will respond with a disguised recommendation, such as "Pentobarbital 100 mg was quite effective night before last." This careful response allows the physician to authoritatively restate the same prescription as if it were his idea.

Traditionally, this power relationship between doctors and nurses has paralleled the male dominance of the United States. Like other women in subordinate roles, the nurses (mostly female) were expected to perform their duties without challenging the authority of the doctors (mostly male). More recently, however, increasing numbers of women are becoming physicians. In 2008, 48 percent of all new medical school students in the United States were female, up from 31 percent in 1982. In nursing, however, the overwhelming majority continues to be female (AAMC 2009).

A study of male and female medical residents suggests that the increasing number of women physicians may alter the traditional doctor–patient relationship. The study found male residents to be more focused on the intellectual challenges of medicine and the prestige associated with certain medical specialties. In contrast, female residents were more likely to express a commitment to caring for patients and devoting time to them. As women continue to enter and move higher in the hierarchies of the medical profession, sociological studies will surely be done to see whether these apparent gender differences persist.

Hot or Not?

Is the way doctors act due more to the fact that they are mostly male or to their level of prestige and power?

ALTERNATIVES TO TRADITIONAL HEALTH CARE

In modern forms of health care, people rely on physicians and hospitals for the treatment of illness. Yet a significant proportion of adults in the

United States attempt to maintain good health or respond to illness through the use of alternative health care techniques. For example, in recent decades, interest has been growing in holistic medical principles, first developed in China. **Holistic medicine** refers to therapies in which the health care practitioner considers the person's physical, mental, emotional, and spiritual characteristics. The individual is regarded as a totality rather than a collection of interrelated organ systems. Treatment methods include massage, chiropractic medicine, acupuncture, respiratory exercises, and the use of herbs as remedies. Nutrition, exercise, and visualization may also be used to treat ailments (Stratton and McGivern-Snofsky 2008).

SOCthink

> > > What do you think about alternative medicine? Would you be willing to get assistance from a holistic healer? What background factors, such as age, race and ethnicity, or gender, might play a role in your willingness or unwillingness to do so?

Practitioners of holistic medicine do not necessarily function totally outside the traditional health care system. Some have medical degrees and rely on X-rays and EKG machines for diagnostic assistance. Others who staff holistic clinics, often referred to as wellness clinics, reject the use of medical technology. The recent resurgence of holistic medicine comes amid widespread recognition of the value of nutrition and the dangers of overreliance on prescription drugs (especially those used to reduce stress, such as Valium).

The medical establishment—professional organizations, research hospitals, and medical schools—contin-

Complementary and Alternative Medicine Use

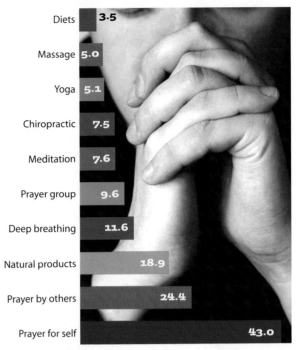

Diets	3.5
Massage	5.0
Yoga	5.1
Chiropractic	7.5
Meditation	7.6
Prayer group	9.6
Deep breathing	11.6
Natural products	18.9
Prayer by others	24.4
Prayer for self	43.0

Source: Barnes et al. 2004.

ues to zealously protect its authority. However, a major breakthrough occurred in 1992 when the federal government's National Institutes of Health (NIH)—the nation's major funding source for biomedical research—opened an Office of Alternative Medicine and empowered it to accept grant requests. A 2002 NIH-sponsored national study found that 36 percent of adults in the United States had used some form of "complementary and alternative medicine" within the previous year. Examples included practices such as acupuncture, folk medicine, meditation, yoga, homeopathic treatment, megavitamin therapy, and chiropractic treatment. When prayer was included as an alternative form of medicine, the number rose to 62.1 percent (Baer and Coulter 2008; Barnes et al. 2004).

> **holistic medicine** Therapies in which the health care practitioner considers the person's physical, mental, emotional, and spiritual characteristics.

On the international level, the World Health Organization (WHO) has begun to monitor the use of alternative medicine around the world. According to the WHO, 80 percent of people who live in the poorest countries in the world use alternative medicine, from herbal treatments to the services of a faith healer. In most countries, these treatments are largely unregulated, even though some of them can be fatal. For example, Kava Kava, an herbal tea used in the Pacific Islands to relieve anxiety, can be toxic to the liver in concentrated form. Other alternative treatments have been found to be effective in the treatment of serious diseases, such as malaria and sickle-cell anemia. The WHO's goal is to compile a list of such practices, as well

as to encourage the development of universal training programs and ethical standards for practitioners of alternative medicine. To date, the organization has published findings on about 100 of the 5000 plants believed to be used as herbal remedies (World Health Organization 2005).

Sociological analysis of health and illness suggests that if we are to understand sickness we must look beyond biology. Society and culture, family and friends, the medical profession, and social position all help shape medical outcomes. Given the increasing costs of health care, and the fact that different groups experience different outcomes, this issue becomes one of equality and fairness. To what extent, for example, are we willing to accept that a child will live or die due to his or her income, race, or ethnicity? Or that one's life expectancy is shaped by such factors? It is precisely such concerns that drive debates about the expansion of health care coverage as a social right.

>> Sociological Perspectives on the Environment

We have seen that the environment people live in has a noticeable affect on their health. Those who live in stressful, overcrowded places suffer more from disease than those who do not. Likewise, people have a noticeable effect on their environment. Around the world, increases in population, together with the economic development that accompanies them, have had serious environmental consequences. We can see signs of despoliation almost everywhere: our air, our water, and our land are being polluted, whether we live in St. Louis; Mexico City; or Lagos, Nigeria. Although environmental problems may be easy to identify, devising socially and politically acceptable solutions to them is much more difficult. Sociologists provide us with some models to better understand the issues we must consider (Sutton 2007).

HUMAN ECOLOGY

Human ecology is an area of study that is concerned with interrelationships between people and their environment. As the environmentalist Barry Commoner (1971:39) put it, "Everything is connected to everything else." Human ecologists focus on how the physical environment shapes people's lives and on how people influence the surrounding environment.

In an application of the human ecological perspective, sociologists and environmentalists have identified several relationships between

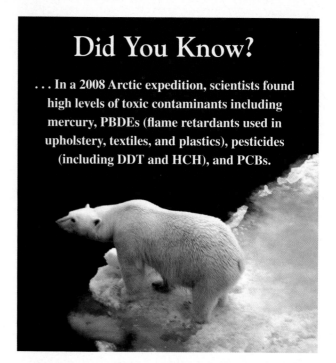

Did You Know?

. . . In a 2008 Arctic expedition, scientists found high levels of toxic contaminants including mercury, PBDEs (flame retardants used in upholstery, textiles, and plastics), pesticides (including DDT and HCH), and PCBs.

the environment and people. Among them are the following:

- *The environment provides the resources essential for life.* These include air, water, and materials used to create shelter, transportation, and needed products. If human societies exhaust these resources—for example, by polluting the water supply or cutting down rain forests—the consequences could be dire.

- *The environment serves as a waste repository.* More so than other living species, humans produce a huge quantity and variety of waste products—bottles, cans, boxes, paper, sewage, garbage, and so on. Various types of pollution have become more common because human societies are generating more wastes than the environment can safely absorb.

- *The environment "houses" our species.* It is our home, our living space, the place where we reside, work, and play. At times we take this truism for granted, but not when day-to-day living conditions become unpleasant and problematic. If our air is "heavy," if our tap water turns brown, or if toxic chemicals seep into our neighborhood, we remember why it is vital to live in a healthful environment.

There is no shortage of illustrations of the interconnectedness of humans and the environment. For example, scientific research has linked pollutants in the environment to people's health and behavior. The increasing prevalence of asthma, lead poisoning, and cancer has been tied to human alterations to the environment. Similarly, the rise in melanoma (skin can-

cer) diagnoses has been linked to global warming. And ecological changes in our food and diet have been related to early obesity and diabetes.

With its view that "everything is connected to everything else," human ecology stresses the trade-offs inherent in every decision that alters the environment. In facing the environmental challenges of the 21st century, government policy makers and environmentalists must determine how they can fulfill humans' pressing needs for food, clothing, and shelter while preserving the environment as a source of resources, a waste repository, and a home.

POWER, RESOURCES, AND THE ENVIRONMENT

Analyzing environmental issues from a world systems approach allows us to better understand the global consequences of differential access to resources. This approach highlights the difference in relative power between core nations, which control wealth and so dominate the global economy, and developing countries, which lack control and whose resources are exploited. This process only intensifies the destruction of natural resources in poorer regions of the world. Less affluent nations are being forced to exploit their mineral deposits, forests, and fisheries in order to meet their debt obligations. People in developing nations often end up turning to the only means of survival available to them, including plowing mountain slopes, burning sections of tropical forests, and overgrazing grasslands (Palm et al. 2005).

Brazil exemplifies this interplay between economic troubles and environmental destruction. Each year more than 5.7 million acres of rain forest are cleared for crops and livestock. The elimination of the rain forest affects worldwide weather patterns, heightening the gradual warming of the earth. These socioeconomic patterns, with their harmful environmental consequences, are evident not only in Central and South America but in many regions of Africa and Asia.

> **human ecology** The area of study concerned with the interrelationships between people and their environment.

Although destruction of the rain forest has long been a concern, only in the past few years have policy makers begun to listen to the indigenous peoples who live in these areas. Preservation of the rain forests may make sense at the global level, but for many local peoples, it limits their ability to cultivate crops or graze cattle. Even though it harms the global environment, they feel they have no choice but to take advantage of their available resources. In 2008, native peoples from Brazil to the Congo to Indonesia convened to make the case that wealthier countries should compensate them for conservation of the tropical rain forests (Barrionuevo 2008).

There is, in fact, a certain amount of ethnocentrism involved when people in industrialized countries insist that those developing nations change their practices to save the planet. In calling for the poverty-stricken and "food-hungry" populations of the world to sacrifice, they should also consider the lifestyle consequences for the "energy-hungry" nations. The industrialized nations of North America and Europe account for only 12 percent of the world's population but are responsible for 60 percent of worldwide consumption. The money their residents spend on ocean cruises each year could provide clean drinking water for everyone on the planet. Ice cream expenditures in Europe alone could be used to immunize every child in the world. The global consumer represents a serious environmental threat, but it is often difficult to look in the mirror and blame ourselves because our individual contribution to the problem seems so small. Collectively, however, the choices we

along racial and social class lines. In general, poor people and people of color are much more likely than others to be victimized by the everyday consequences of economic development, including air pollution from expressways and incinerators (Sandler and Pezzullo 2007).

Sociologists Paul Mohai and Robin Saha (2007) examined over 600 hazardous waste treatment, storage, and disposal facilities in the United States. They found that

> # Suburbia is where the developer bulldozes out the trees, then names the streets after them.
>
> Bill Vaughn

make have a significant global impact (Gardner, Assadourian, and Sarin 2004).

The rise in global consumption is tied to a capitalist system that depends upon growth for its survival. Capitalism creates a "treadmill of production" (Baer 2008; Schnaiberg 1994). Cutting back on consumption means cutting back on purchases, which leads to reduced production and the loss of profits and jobs. This treadmill necessitates creating an increasing demand for products, obtaining natural resources at minimal cost, and manufacturing products as quickly and cheaply as possible—no matter what the long-term environmental consequences.

ENVIRONMENTAL JUSTICE

In autumn 1982, nearly 500 African Americans participated in a six-week protest against a hazardous waste landfill containing cancer-causing chemicals in Warren County, North Carolina. Their protests and legal actions continued until 2002, when decontamination of the site finally began. This 20-year battle can be seen as yet another "not-in-my-backyard" (NIMBY) event in which people desire the benefits of growth but want someone else to pay for its negative effects. In any event, the Warren County struggle is viewed as a transformative moment in contemporary environmentalism: the beginning of the environmental justice movement (Bullard 2000; McGurty 2007; North Carolina Department of Environment and Natural Resources 2008).

environmental justice A legal strategy based on claims that racial minorities are subjected disproportionately to environmental hazards.

Environmental justice is a legal strategy based on claims that racial minorities are subjected disproportionately to environmental hazards. Some observers have heralded environmental justice as the "new civil rights of the 21st century" (Kokmen 2008:42). Since the advent of the environmental justice movement, activists and scholars have identified other environmental disparities that break

non-Whites and Latinos make up 43 percent of the people who live within one mile of these dangerous sites. There are two possible explanations for this finding. One is that racial and ethnic minorities possess less power than others, so that they cannot prevent toxic sites from being located in their backyards. The other is that they end up settling near the sites after they are constructed, because economics and the forces of discrimination push them into the least desirable living areas.

Following reports from the Environmental Protection Agency (EPA) and other organizations documenting the discriminatory location of hazardous waste sites, President Bill Clinton issued an executive order in 1994 requiring all federal agencies to ensure that low-income and minority communities have access to better information about their environment, as well as an opportunity to participate in shaping government policies that affect their health. Initial efforts to implement the policy, along with increased activity by the environmental justice movement, aroused widespread opposition because of the delays the policy imposes in establishing new industrial sites. Some observers question the wisdom of an order that slows economic development in areas that are in dire need of employment opportunities. Others counter that such businesses employ few unskilled or less skilled workers and only make the environment less livable (Stretesky 2006; D. Taylor 2000).

Meanwhile, the poor and oppressed continue to bear the brunt of environmental pollution. In the 1990s, the federal government, unable to find a disposal site for spent

SOCthink

> > > It took 20 years for the Warren County protest to succeed. Why do you think it took so long? How might access to resources shape the length of such struggles?

nuclear fuel, turned to tribal reservations. Agents eventually persuaded a tiny band of Goshute Indians in Skull Valley, Utah, to accept more than 44,000 barrels of the highly radioactive substance, which will remain dangerous for an estimated 10,000 years. The government dropped the plan only after opposition from surrounding towns and

tain Power Project, which generates coal-fired e1ectrical power for consumers in California (Eureka County 2006; Foy 2006).

In considering environmental issues, sociologists have emphasized the interconnectedness of humans and the environment, as well as the divisiveness of race and social class. Scientific findings can also play a role in our understanding of the nature and scope of environmental concerns. Of course, when such findings affect government policy and economic regulations, they become highly politicized. Such struggles are inevitable when core values and differential access to resources are at stake.

5 Movies on THE ENVIRONMENT

The Happening
Nature fights back.

An Inconvenient Truth
The truth about global warming.

Encounters at the End of the World
A documentary about the people living and working in Antarctica.

The Day After Tomorrow
Man against nature.

WALL-E
A robot in the year 2700 discovers his destiny.

>> Environmental Problems

Unfortunately, as we have already seen, the environmental problems caused by development have effects far beyond the places where they are created. Witness Muhammad Ali, a Bangladeshi man who has had to flee floodwaters five times in the last decade. Scientists believe that global warming is to blame both for worsening monsoons and for the raging waters of the Iamuna River, swollen by abnormally high glacier melt from the Himalayas. Every time the river floods, Ali tears down his house, made of tin and bamboo, and moves to higher ground. But he is running out of land to move to. "Where we are standing, in five days it will be gone," he says. "Our future thinking is that if this problem is not taken care of, we will be swept away" (Goering 2007).

cities, whose residents objected to the movement of the material through their communities. This was not the first time the government had attempted to persuade the impoverished tribe to accept environmentally objectionable installations. The military's nerve gas storage facility resides on or near the reservation, along with the Intermoun-

Increasingly, people are recognizing the need to address such challenges to the environment. In recent surveys, 69

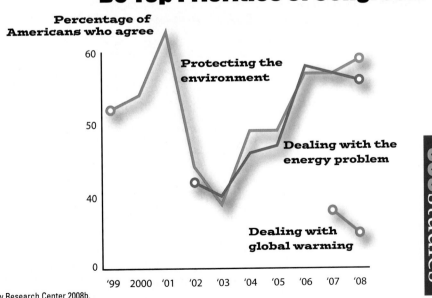

Should Environmental Issues Be Top Priorities of Congress?

Percentage of Americans who agree

Protecting the environment

Dealing with the energy problem

Dealing with global warming

'99 2000 '01 '02 '03 '04 '05 '06 '07 '08

SOCstudies

Source: Pew Research Center 2008b.

percent agreed that global warming was already happening. Though 44 percent expressed concern that actions to reduce global warming would lead to more government regulation, 92 percent agreed that the nation should act to reduce global warming, even if it has economic consequences (Gallup 2008d; Jacobe 2008; Leiserowitz, Maibach, and Roser-Renouf 2009). Three environmental areas are of particular concern: air pollution, water pollution, and global warming.

AIR POLLUTION

Worldwide, more than 1 billion people are exposed to potentially health-damaging levels of air pollution. Unfortunately, in cities around the world, residents have come to accept smog and polluted air as normal. Urban air pollution is caused primarily by emissions from automobiles and secondarily by emissions from electric power plants and heavy industries. Smog not only limits visibility but can lead to health problems as uncomfortable as eye irritation and as deadly as lung cancer. Such problems are especially severe in developing countries. The WHO estimates that up to 600,000 premature deaths per year could be prevented if pollutants were brought down to safer levels (World Health Organization 2002).

People are capable of changing their behavior, but they are also often unwilling to make such changes permanent. During the 1984 Olympics in Los Angeles, authorities asked residents to carpool and stagger their work hours to relieve traffic congestion and improve the quality of the air athletes would breathe. These changes resulted in a remarkable 12 percent drop in ozone levels. After the Olympics ended, however, people reverted to their normal behavior, and the ozone levels climbed once again. Similarly, China took drastic action to ensure that Beijing's high lev-

els of air pollution did not mar the 2008 Olympic Games. Construction work in the city ceased, polluting factories and power plants closed down, and workers swept roads and sprayed them with water several times a day. This temporary solution, however, has not solved China's ongoing pollution problem (*The Economist* 2008b).

WATER POLLUTION

Throughout the United States, waste materials dumped by industries and local governments have polluted streams, rivers, and lakes. Consequently, many bodies of water have become unsafe for fishing and swimming, let alone drinking. Around the world, pollution of the oceans is an issue of growing concern. Such pollution results regularly from waste dumping and is made worse by fuel leaks from shipping and occasional oil spills. When the oil tanker *Exxon Valdez* ran aground in Prince William Sound, Alaska, in 1989, its cargo of 11 million gallons of crude oil spilled into the sound and washed onto the shore, contaminating 1285 miles of shoreline. Altogether, about 11,000 people joined in a massive cleanup effort that cost over $2 billion. Globally, oil spills occur regularly. In 2002, the oil tanker *Prestige* spilled twice as much fuel as the *Valdez*, greatly damaging coastal areas in Spain and France (ITOPF 2006).

Less dramatic than large-scale accidents or disasters, but more common in many parts of the world, are problems with the basic water supply. Worldwide, over 884 million

people lack safe and adequate drinking water, and 2.5 billion lack access to improved sanitation facilities—a problem that further threatens the quality of water supplies. The health costs of unsafe water are enormous (UNICEF and World Health Organization 2008).

Given such water shortages, it should not come as a surprise that water is now a highly contested commodity in many parts of the world. In the United States, competition over water is intense, especially in booming Las Vegas and the Southwest. In the Middle East, the immense political challenges posed by ethnic and religious conflict are often complicated by battles over water. There, competing nations accuse each other of taking unfair advantage of existing water supplies, and water tanks are a likely target for both military forces and terrorists (Carmichael 2007).

GLOBAL WARMING

The scientific evidence for global warming is clear, consistent, and compelling, yet we continue to struggle with how seriously we should take it. "Global warming" refers to the significant rise in the earth's surface temperatures that occurs when industrial gases like carbon dioxide turn the planet's atmosphere into a virtual greenhouse. Even one additional degree of warmth in the globe's average surface temperature can increase the likelihood of wildfires, shrinkage of rivers and lakes, expansion of deserts, and torrential downpours, including typhoons and hurricanes. Scientists now track carbon dioxide emissions around the world and can map the current and projected CO_2 contribution each country makes. Such analyses show the sizable and growing contribution of the United States to the problem (Lymas 2008).

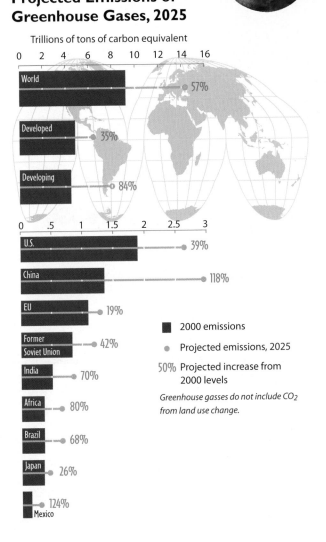

Going **GLOBAL**

Projected Emissions of Greenhouse Gases, 2025

In 2000, the United States was the largest emitter of CO_2 from fossil fuels. China is expected to take the lead by 2025.

Source: Baumert 2005.

Reprinted with the permission of Mike Luckovich and Creators Syndicate.

Although scientific concern over global warming has heated up, climate change remains low on policy makers' list of concerns. For some politicians, the problem seems too abstract and distant. Others recognize that effective solutions demand a difficult-to-manage multinational response, and they fear that their nation may bear too much of the cost. The Kyoto Protocol was intended to provide a unified response in which the nations of the world would take collective responsibility to reduce global emissions of greenhouse gases. To date, 184 countries have signed the accord, but the United States, which produces 21 percent of the world's carbon dioxide, has failed to ratify it. Opponents of the protocol argue that doing so would place the nation at a disadvantage in the global marketplace (Energy Information Administration 2008).

We can again draw on world systems analysis when it comes to seeing who pays the highest price for global warming. Historically, core nations have been the major emitters of greenhouse gases. Today, much manufacturing has moved to semiperiphery and periphery nations, where greenhouse gas emissions are escalating. Ironically, many of those who are now calling for a reduction in the human activity that contributes to global warming are located in core nations, which have contributed disproportionately to the problem. We want our hamburgers, but we decry the destruction of the rain forests to create grazing land for cattle. We want inexpensive clothes and toys, but we condemn developing countries for depending on coal-fired power plants, the number of which are expected to in-

Estimated Time for Each Successive Increase of 1 Billion People in World Population

Population Level	Time taken to reach new population level	Year of Attainment
First billion	Human history before 1800	1804
Second billion	123 years	1927
Third billion	32 years	1959
Fourth billion	15 years	1974
Fifth billion	13 years	1987
Sixth billion	12 years	1999
Seventh billion	13 years	2012
Eighth billion	14 years	2026
Ninth billion	17 years	2043

Source: Bureau of the Census 2008b.

crease 46 percent by 2030. The challenge of global warming, then, is closely tied to global inequality (M. Jenkins 2008; J. Roberts et al. 2003).

One of the primary factors causing this global environmental crisis is the rise in global population. As of July

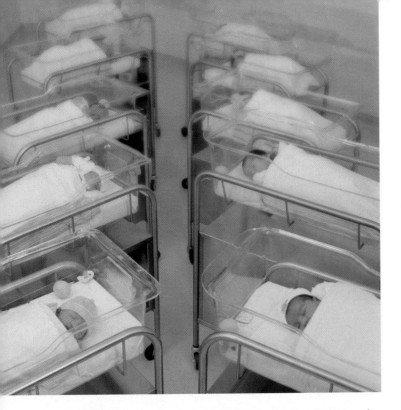

2009, there were 6.8 billion people on the planet, an increase of 1.7 billion since 1987. To put this in terms of the human ecology model, the more people there are on the planet, the more resources we need to use to sustain them, the more waste they produce that we must process, and the more strain we place on our capacity to house us all (Ehrlich 1968; Ehrlich and Ehrlich 1990; Ehrlich and Ellison 2002).

Technological advances also contribute to increased environmental concerns. At least since the Industrial Revolution and the invention of the steam engine, the automobile, coal-burning power plants, and more, the environmental effects of technological innovation have been extreme. Biologist Barry Commoner argues that additional contributors to the probem include plastics, detergents, synthetic fibers, pesticides, herbicides, and chemical fertilizers. We appreciate the lifestyles that such innovations allow us to experience, but we pay a significant price for their benefits (Commoner 1971, 1990).

THE GLOBAL RESPONSE

Globalization can be both good and bad for the environment. On the negative side, it can create a race to the bottom as polluting companies relocate to countries with less stringent environmental standards. Also of concern is that globalization allows multinationals to exploit the resources of developing countries for short-term profit. From Mexico to China, the industrialization that often accompanies globalization has increased pollution of all types.

Yet globalization can have a positive impact as well. As barriers to the international movement of goods, services, and people fall, multinational corporations have an incentive to carefully consider the cost of natural resources. As the establishment of the Kyoto protocols demonstrated,

Percentage of People Citing Pollution and Environmental Problems as a Top Global Threat

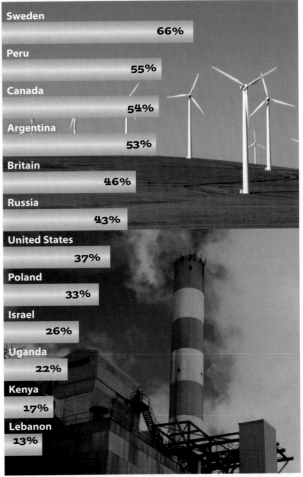

Country	Percentage
Sweden	66%
Peru	55%
Canada	54%
Argentina	53%
Britain	46%
Russia	43%
United States	37%
Poland	33%
Israel	26%
Uganda	22%
Kenya	17%
Lebanon	13%

Source: Pew Research Center 2007b.

countries around the world can come together on a global level to take action that makes a significant difference. For example, the industrialized nations that agreed to the Kyoto Accord are on track to meet the 2010 emission reduction targets. And in December 2009, nations around the world will again come together, this time in Copenhagen, to commit themselves to a new set of global environmental targets under a new global climate change treaty (Netherlands Environmental Assessment Agency 2007). Overusing or wasting resources makes little sense, especially when they are in danger of depletion (Kwong 2005). Perhaps, as Émile Durkheim might have argued long ago, by recognizing the negative effects of our global expansion, along with our mutual interdependence, we will take the steps necessary to bring about positive social change.

There are signs that individuals, countries, and corporations are beginning to understand and appreciate our interdependence. In response, individuals are taking greater responsibility for their global impact by recycling and switching to fluorescent light bulbs. Increasing numbers of corporations are "going green" and even finding profits in doing so. Sociology helps us to better see the ways we are interconnected by highlighting the significance of the system as a whole, as well as raising awareness about the inequalities that are a consequence of the global system we have constructed. Such analysis can prepare us to more effectively respond to the global challenges we face.

get involved!

Investigate! Research the air and water quality in your community. Talk with local environmental officials about the extent to which current quality levels have improved or deteriorated in the past few years. How adequate are the indicators of quality they utilize? What evidence do leaders cite regarding the extent to which national, state, or local policies have affected water and air quality? What changes in policy may be necessary to meet desired quality goals?

For REVIEW

I. **What does sociology contribute to something as seemingly biological as health?**

- Our understanding of what counts as health and illness is shaped by the society to which we belong. Similarly, control over resources shapes our likelihood of exposure to illness and our access to health care.

II. **What is social epidemiology?**

- Social epidemiology involves the study of factors that shape the health status of various groups within a population. In the United States and elsewhere, social class, race and ethnicity, gender, and age all have an impact.

III. **What environmental lessons do we learn from sociology?**

- The natural environment represents our human home, within which all social interaction occurs, and the way we organize our social relations shapes the impact we have on the environment. Countries that control a larger amount of resources have a bigger impact and therefore bear a greater responsibility for those effects.

Pop Quiz

1. A disease that cannot be understood apart from its specific social context is an example of
   a. human ecology.
   b. culture-bound syndrome.
   c. the sick role.
   d. holistic medicine.

2. The expansion of medicine's domain of expertise and its assertion of absolute jurisdiction over many health care procedures are examples of
   a. labeling and power.
   b. social epidemiology.
   c. the medicalization of society.
   d. human ecology.

3. Which one of the following nations has the lowest infant mortality rate?
   a. the United States
   b. Sierra Leone
   c. Canada
   d. Japan

4. Compared with Whites, Blacks have higher death rates from
   a. heart disease.
   b. diabetes.
   c. cancer.
   d. all of the above.

5. The age group that is most likely to be covered by some form of health insurance is
   a. under 18.
   b. 18–34.
   c. 35–64.
   d. 65 and older.

6. Which program is essentially a compulsory health insurance plan for the elderly?
   a. Medicaid
   b. Blue Cross
   c. Medicare
   d. holistic medicine

7. Not counting prayer, what percentage of Americans reported using some form of complementary or alternative medicine in a 2002 survey?
   a. 17
   b. 36
   c. 62
   d. 84

8. The sociological perspective that emphasizes the interrelationships between people and their environment is known as
   a. human ecology.
   b. resource allocation.
   c. environmental justice.
   d. labeling theory.

9. The industrialized nations of North America and Europe account for 12 percent of the world's population. What percentage of worldwide consumption are they responsible for?
   a. 15 percent
   b. 30 percent
   c. 45 percent
   d. 60 percent

10. What is the international treaty that sought to reduce global emissions of greenhouse gases?
    a. Valdez Treaty
    b. Kyoto Protocol
    c. Port Huron Statement
    d. Gore Accord

1. (b); 2. (c); 3. (d); 4. (d); 5. (d); 6. (c); 7. (b); 8. (a); 9. (d); 10. (b)

15

END THE KILL
IN DARFU

SOCIAL CH

CHANGING THE WORLD ONE CAMPUS AT A TIME

In the summer of 1964, college students traveled to Mississippi to change the world. As volunteers in Freedom Summer, their goal was to make a difference in the lives of African Americans who had been systematically denied the right to vote, quality education, and legal and political representation. The volunteers—mostly upper-middle-class White students from northern colleges—registered Black voters, established Freedom Schools, and provided legal advice and medical assistance. By the end of the summer, they had registered 17,000 voters and taught 3000 children. In 1964, 6.7 percent of voting age African Americans in Mississippi were registered, but by 1967, 66.5 percent were (Colby 1986; McAdam 1988).

From April 18 to May 8, 2001, students at Harvard University occupied Massachusetts Hall, the location of the president's and provost's offices, as part of their Living Wage Campaign. The city of Cambridge, where Harvard is located, had passed a living wage ordinance ensuring a minimum wage of $10 per hour, adjustable for inflation. Students argued that a school with a multi-billion-dollar endowment could do better than the $6.50 many employees were receiving. After numerous attempts at negotiation, students decided to make a statement. During the sit-in, students organized daily pickets and rallies involving thousands of people. After three weeks, the administration agreed to establish a committee to implement living wage principles (Progressive Student Labor Movement 2008).

In January 2007, students at Middlebury College in Vermont convinced their board of trustees to invest in an $11 million biomass power plant and pushed officials to attain net carbon neutrality on campus. Catherine McEachern, who is involved in a similar student movement at Cornell University in New York, says, "Global warming has been neglected by the previous generation, and we see it as an injustice that needs to be changed" (James 2008).

College students continue to fight for and bring about significant change on campuses around the world. Max Weber argued that all of us have the potential power to change our world. In fact, change will happen whether we like it or not. A key question is this: Will we be active agents seeking the change we desire or passive recipients who accept the change enacted by others?

As You READ >>

- How and why does social change happen?
- What factors shape the success of a social movement?
- What does it mean to practice sociology?

>> Global Social Change

We are at a truly dramatic era in history in terms of global social change. Within the past two decades, we have witnessed the computer revolution and the explosion of Internet connectivity; the collapse of communism; major regime changes and severe economic disruptions in Africa, the Middle East, and Eastern Europe; the spread of AIDS; the first verification of the cloning of a complex animal, Dolly the sheep; and the first major terrorist attack on U.S. soil. Today we continue to face global challenges including international terrorism, a global economic meltdown, and climate change, along with other threats.

social change Significant alteration over time in behavior patterns and culture, including norms and values.

The transformation of society has been a fundamental concern of sociologists from the very beginning. At the time of sociology's birth, social life was undergoing dramatic change. The taken-for-granted norms and values that made sense in a traditional agricultural society no longer fit with the lived experience of most people. The Indus-

trial Revolution, the rise of capitalism, and the transformation from aristocratic to democratic rule all challenged traditional practices and beliefs. Sociological theory and research provide us with tools that allow us to make sense of where we are now and where we are headed.

The collapse of communist regimes in the former Soviet Union and the nations of Eastern Europe in the late 1980s and early 1990s, for example, took many people by surprise. Yet prior to the collapse, sociologist Randall Collins (1986, 1995) had observed a crucial sequence of events that most observers missed. Long before it happened, Collins had argued that Soviet expansionism had resulted in an overextension of resources, including disproportionate spending on the military. Such overextension strains a regime's stability. Moreover, geopolitical theory suggests that nations in the middle of a geographic region, such as the Soviet Union, tend to fragment into smaller units over time. Collins correctly predicted that the confluence of social crises on several frontiers would precipitate the collapse of the Soviet Union.

Political systems often seek to control how changes such as transfers of power happen to minimize such disruptions. In the United States, for example, political change is built into the system and arises out of the normal operation of existing practices. Barack Obama's inauguration as president occurred as a peaceful transfer of power, in spite of the fact that it represented a major shift in terms of policy and personnel. At other times, change seems more spontaneous, as was the case with the June 2009 protests in Iran. Here, too, there was a presidential election, but the results were seen as illegitimate by tens of thousands of citizens. Protesters took to the streets to voice their opposition, leading to a bloody confrontation with

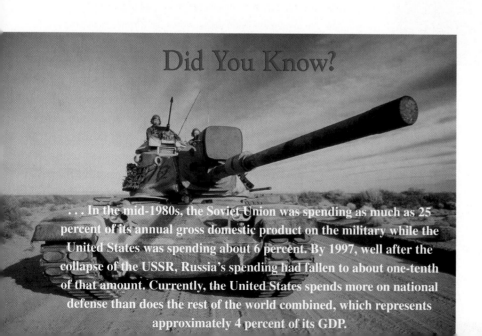
Did You Know?
...In the mid-1980s, the Soviet Union was spending as much as 25 percent of its annual gross domestic product on the military while the United States was spending about 6 percent. By 1997, well after the collapse of the USSR, Russia's spending had fallen to about one-tenth of that amount. Currently, the United States spends more on national defense than does the rest of the world combined, which represents approximately 4 percent of its GDP.

the existing government. However, even when seemingly impromptu challenges to the existing system of authority arise, it is possible to identify the social factors that gave rise to the protest.

Sociology helps us to understand such shifts by paying attention both to large-scale, or macro, shifts that alter the basic landscape of society and the relationships among groups, and to the small-scale, or micro, changes in social interaction within which decisions are made that can alter the course of history. We construct society through our everyday actions. As such, we have the power to change society by altering the choices we make. Of course, some people, due to their control over valued resources, have more power than do others. Sociology can better focus our attention so that we might understand which direction change might follow.

>> Sociological Perspectives on Social Change

As humans, we are creative beings. We continually innovate and experiment, developing new technologies, ideas, and ways of doing things. Each of these represents an example of **social change,** which involves significant alteration over time in behavior patterns and culture. Social change can occur so slowly as to be almost undetectable to those it affects, but it can also happen with breathtaking rapidity. In the past century or so, for example, the U.S. population has more than doubled, the percentage of people finishing high school and attending college has skyrocketed, women have entered the paid labor force in significant numbers, life ex-

The United States: A Changing Nation

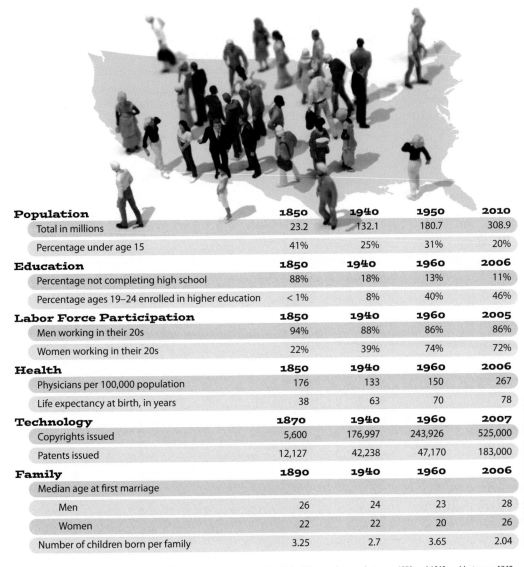

Population	1850	1940	1950	2010
Total in millions	23.2	132.1	180.7	308.9
Percentage under age 15	41%	25%	31%	20%
Education	**1850**	**1940**	**1960**	**2006**
Percentage not completing high school	88%	18%	13%	11%
Percentage ages 19–24 enrolled in higher education	< 1%	8%	40%	46%
Labor Force Participation	**1850**	**1940**	**1960**	**2005**
Men working in their 20s	94%	88%	86%	86%
Women working in their 20s	22%	39%	74%	72%
Health	**1850**	**1940**	**1960**	**2006**
Physicians per 100,000 population	176	133	150	267
Life expectancy at birth, in years	38	63	70	78
Technology	**1870**	**1940**	**1960**	**2007**
Copyrights issued	5,600	176,997	243,926	525,000
Patents issued	12,127	42,238	47,170	183,000
Family	**1890**	**1940**	**1960**	**2006**
Median age at first marriage				
Men	26	24	23	28
Women	22	22	20	26
Number of children born per family	3.25	2.7	3.65	2.04

Note: Data are comparable, although definitions vary. Definition of the United States changes between 1850 and 1940 and between 1940 and 1960. Earliest date for children born per family is 1905.

Source: U.S. Census Bureau 2008b.

SOCstudies

pectancy has risen, technological innovation has exploded, men and women have been marrying later, and family size has shrunk. In our global, interdependent world, there is no reason to suspect that such changes will cease, and many future changes will be difficult to predict.

Explaining social change is clearly a challenge in the diverse and complex world we inhabit. Nevertheless, theo-

simple to more complex forms of social organization. Both believed that by gaining an understanding of the principles of order and change in such societies, we would be able to more effectively shape the direction our modern, more complex societies would take.

Since that time, we have learned that the idea that societies will follow a singular path from simple to complex,

> **All change is not growth,**
> **as all movement is not forward.**
>
> Ellen Glasgow

rists from several disciplines have sought to analyze social change. In some instances, they have examined historical events to arrive at a better understanding of contemporary changes. We will look at change from three perspectives so that we might better identify issues we should include when considering how and why change happens.

THE EVOLUTION OF SOCIETIES

One approach to understanding how societies change draws upon the principle of evolution. It was inspired, in part, by Charles Darwin's (1809–1882) work on the biological evolution of species. Darwin's approach stresses a continuing progression of successive generations of life forms as they adapt to their environment. For example, human beings came at a later stage of evolution than reptiles and represent a more complex form of life. Social theorists seeking an analogy to this biological model proposed **evolutionary theory,** in which society is viewed as moving in a definite direction. Early evolutionary theorists generally agreed that society was progressing from the simple to the complex, which they assumed was superior.

Early sociologists and anthropologists believed it was possible to study what they referred to at that time as simple or "primitive" societies for clues about the essential building blocks that serve as the foundation for all societies. August Comte (1798–1857), a founder of sociology, was an evolutionary theorist of change. He saw human societies as moving forward in their thinking, from mythology to the scientific method. Similarly, Émile Durkheim ([1893]1933) maintained that society progressed from

from primitive to modern, is flawed. The notion that traditional societies are simple or primitive has proven to be both incorrect and ethnocentric. Such societies demonstrate significant levels of sophistication and innovation, in terms of both social relations and technological adaptation to their environments. In addition, there is no single path of social evolution that all societies must pass through. Social change can impact one area of social life, such as politics, while leaving other areas of life relatively unchanged, such as work and the economy. For example, a society might move toward a democratic form of government, but the traditional nature of work, primarily small-scale and agricultural, might stay the same.

Though there are limits to the evolutionary model of social change, it does provide a helpful metaphor when thinking about how change happens. For example, we can look to past practices to better understand where new ways of thinking and acting come from. In addition, it highlights the role that context or environment plays in shaping change. In biology, when the environment changes, mutations in species can occur, making them more fit to survive in that new context than were past generations. For Darwin, however, this did not mean that the new was superior to the old; it was simply more likely that the new would survive given changed environmental circumstances. The danger when applying this analogy to society is to assume that those who adapt to changed circumstances are superior. The truth is that all societies must adapt to change. Sometimes it comes fast and is thus easier to recognize, and other times it is gradual. Sometimes that change comes from within, and other times it is a product of environmental forces, whether social or natural.

SOCthink

> > > Why would early theorists have thought of traditional societies as "primitive"? How is this a reflection of the evolutionary theoretical paradigm they adopted?

EQUILIBRIUM AND SOCIAL ORDER

Another approach to understanding social change is rooted in the principle that societies naturally seek to attain stability or balance. Any social change that occurs represents necessary adjustments as society seeks to return to that state of equilibrium. For example, sociologist Talcott Parsons (1902–1979), an advocate of this approach, viewed even prolonged labor strikes or civilian riots as temporary disruptions in the status quo rather than as significant alterations in the social structure. According to his **equilibrium model,** as changes occur in one part of society, adjustments must be made in other parts. If not, society's equilibrium will be threatened, and strains will occur.

Parsons (1966) maintained that four processes of social change are inevitable. The first, differentiation, refers to the increasing complexity of social organization. We see this in the form of job specialization as is evident in more bureaucratic systems. The transition from a healer—a

5 Movies on SOCIAL MOVEMENTS AND SOCIAL CHANGE

Ghandi
His story.

Erin Brockovich
How one person can affect big business.

Norma Rae
Union! Union!

Milk
The story of the first openly gay elected official, Harvey Milk.

Miracle
How a game of hockey brought about the symbolic end of the Cold War.

single person who handles all your health care needs—to a series of positions, including physician, anesthetist, nurse, and pharmacist, is an illustration of differentiation in the field of medicine. This process is accompanied by adaptive upgrading, in which social institutions become more specialized in their purposes. The division of physicians into obstetricians, internists, surgeons, and so forth is an example of adaptive upgrading.

The third process Parsons identified is the inclusion of groups that were previously excluded because of their gender, race, ethnicity, and social class. Recently, medical schools have practiced inclusion by admitting increasing numbers of women and African Americans. Finally, Parsons contended that societies experience value generalization—the development of new values that legitimate a broader range of activities. The acceptance of preventive and alternative medicine is an example of value generalization: Society has broadened its view of health care. All four processes identified by Parsons stress consensus—societal agreement on the nature of social organization and values (Gerhardt 2002).

SOCthink

> > > Why might the equilibrium model have a difficult time addressing issues such as inequality and poverty as social problems to be solved?

One of the sources of potential strain that can lead to such social adaptation involves technological innovation. As we saw in Chapter 3, sociologist William F. Ogburn (1922) distinguished between material and nonmaterial aspects of culture. Material culture includes inventions, artifacts, and technology; nonmaterial culture encompasses ideas, norms, communications, and social organization. Ogburn pointed out that technology often changes faster than do the ideas and values with which we make sense of such change. Thus, the nonmaterial culture typically must respond to changes in the material culture. Ogburn introduced the term **culture lag** to refer to the period of adjustment when the nonmaterial culture is still struggling to adapt to new material conditions. One example is the Internet. Its rapid uncontrolled growth raises questions about whether to regulate it, and if so, how much.

In certain cases, the changes in the material culture can strain the relationships between social institutions. For example, new means of birth control have been developed in recent decades. Large families are no longer economically necessary, nor are they commonly endorsed by social norms. But certain religious faiths, among them Roman Catholicism, continue to extol large families and to disapprove methods of limiting family size, such as contraception and abortion. This issue represents a lag between aspects of the material culture (technology) and nonmaterial culture (religious beliefs). Conflicts may also emerge between religion and other social institutions, such as government and the educational system, over the dissemination of birth control and family-planning information (Allen 2008; Tentler 2004).

From Parsons's point of view, such tensions represent little more than normal adjustments needed to maintain the inevitable balance that is the natural state of all societies. Though his approach explicitly incorporates the evolutionary notion of continuing progress, the dominant theme in this model is stability. Society may change, but it remains stable through new forms of integration. For example, in place of the kinship ties that provided social cohesion in the past, people develop laws, judicial processes, and new values and belief systems. Parsons and

evolutionary theory A theory of social change that holds that society is moving in a definite direction.

equilibrium model The view that society tends toward a state of stability or balance.

culture lag A period of adjustment when the nonmaterial culture is still struggling to adapt to new material conditions.

other theorists would argue that those parts of society that persist, even including crime, terrorism, and poverty, do so because they contribute to social stability. Critics note, however, that his approach virtually disregards the use of coercion by the powerful to maintain the illusion of a stable, well-integrated society (Gouldner 1960).

RESOURCES, POWER, AND CHANGE

Such theories are helpful, but it is not enough to look at change as part of the natural evolution or equilibrium of societies. Some groups in society, because they control valued resources, are able either to inhibit or to facilitate social change more effectively than are others. Although Karl Marx, for example, accepted the evolutionary argument that societies develop along a particular path, he did not view each successive stage as an inevitable improvement over the previous one. History, according to Marx, proceeds through a series of stages, and within each stage, those who control the means of production exploit an entire class of people.

vested interests Those people or groups who will suffer in the event of social change and who have a stake in maintaining the status quo.

technology Cultural information about how to use the material resources of the environment to satisfy human needs and desires.

Thus, ancient society exploited slaves, the estate system of feudalism exploited serfs, and modern capitalist society exploits the working class. Ultimately, through a socialist revolution led by the proletariat, human society would move toward the final stage of development: a classless communist society, or "community of free individuals," as Marx described it in 1867 in *Das Kapital* (McLellan 2000).

Marx argued that conflict is a normal and desirable aspect of social change. In fact, change must be encouraged as a means of eliminating social inequality. In his view, people are not restricted to a passive role in responding to inevitable cycles or changes in the material culture. Rather, Marxist theory offers a tool for those who wish to seize control of the historical process and gain their freedom from injustice. Efforts to promote social change are, however, likely to meet with resistance.

Certain individuals and groups have a stake in maintaining the existing state of affairs. Social economist Thorstein

Veblen (1857–1929) coined the term **vested interests** to refer to those people or groups who will suffer in the event of social change. For example, the American Medical Association (AMA) has taken strong stands against national health insurance and the professionalization of midwifery. National health insurance could lead to limits on physicians' income, and a rise in the status of midwives could threaten the preeminent position of doctors as deliverers of babies. In general, those with a disproportionate share of society's wealth, status, and power, such as members of the AMA, have a vested interest in preserving the status quo (Furedi 2006; Scelfo 2008; Veblen 1919).

Economic factors play an important role in resistance to social change. For example, it can be expensive for manufacturers to meet mandated standards for the safety of products and workers and for the protection of the environment. In the pursuit of both profit and survival, many firms seek to avoid the costs of meeting strict safety and environmental standards. If they have sufficient power in society, they can effectively pass the costs of such practices on to others who must bear the consequences. To battle against such influence requires a countervailing source of power. Government regulations, for example, force all companies to bear the common burden of such costs, and labor unions can present the unified power of workers as a group.

Communities, too, protect their vested interests, often in the name of "protecting property values." The abbreviation NIMBY stands for "not in my backyard," a cry often heard when people protest landfills, prisons, nuclear power facilities, and even bike trails and group homes for people with developmental disabilities. The targeted community may not challenge the need for the facility, but may simply insist that it be located elsewhere. The NIMBY attitude has become so common that it is almost impossible for policy makers to find acceptable locations for facilities such as hazardous waste dumps. Unfortunately, it is often those

with the fewest resources who end up on the losing end of such battles (Lambert 2009; Schelly and Stretesky 2009).

In today's world, change is inevitable. From sociology we learn that we need to watch for the ways in which change evolves out of existing practices. We also must be aware of the ways in which societies perpetuate existing social order by seeking an acceptable level of balance between stability and change. Finally, we recognize the role that power and control over resources plays in shaping what changes do or do not occur. In all these cases, because of the ways it both enables and constrains, we must be aware of the role that technology plays in affecting the nature and direction of social change.

>> Technology and the Future

Technology is cultural information about how to use the material resources of the environment to satisfy human needs and desires. Technological advances—the telephone, the automobile, the airplane, the television, the atomic bomb, and more recently, the computer, digital media, and the cellular phone—have brought striking changes to our culture, our patterns of socialization, our social institutions, and our day-to-day social interactions. Technological innovations are, in fact, emerging and being accepted with remarkable speed.

In the past generation alone, industrial countries have seen a major shift in consumer technologies. We no longer buy electronic devices to last for 10 years. Increasingly, we buy them with the expectation that within three years or less, we will need to upgrade to an entirely new technology, whether it be a handheld device or a home computer. These technologies have both positive and negative

consequences. They enable us to maintain contacts with friends and family around the world, but they can cut us off from the person right next to us. Take, for example, the iPod-wearing, cell-phone-talking person we encounter who barely seems to notice we exist.

Adopting Technology

Omnivores: 8% of American adults constitute the most active participants in the information society, consuming information goods and services at a high rate and using them as a platform for participation and self-expression.

The Connectors: 7% of the adult population surround themselves with technology and use it to connect with people and digital content. They get a lot out of their mobile devices and participate actively in online life.

Lackluster Veterans: 8% of American adults make up a group who are not at all passionate about their abundance of modern information and communication technologies (ICTs). Few like the intrusiveness their gadgets add to their lives and not many see ICTs adding to their personal productivity.

Productivity Enhancers: 9% of American adults happily get a lot of things done with information technology, both at home and at work.

Mobile Centrics: 10% of the general population are strongly attached to their cell phones and take advantage of a range of mobile applications.

Connected but Hassled: 9% of American adults fit into this group. They have invested in a lot of technology, but the connectivity is a hassle for them.

Inexperienced Experimenters: 8% of adults have less ICT on hand than others. They feel competent in dealing with technology, and might do more with it if they had more.

Light but Satisfied: 15% of adults have the basics of information technology, use it infrequently, and it does not register as an important part of their lives.

Indifferents: 11% of adults have a fair amount of technology on hand, but it does not play a central role in their daily lives.

Off the Net: 15% of the population, mainly older Americans, are off the modern information network.

Note: From a Pew Internet and American Life Project Survey conducted in April 2006.

Source: Horrigan 2007:vii.

COMPUTER TECHNOLOGY

In the past decade, computer access has gone global, and Internet access along with it. While the revolutions in transportation and communication have brought us together since the Industrial Revolution, the Internet provides a potential for immediate global connection that previously was virtually and physically impossible. In 2009, the Internet reached 1.6 billion users, or 24 percent of the world's population.

The Internet evolved from a computer system built in 1962 by the U.S. Defense Department to enable scholars and military researchers to continue their government work, even if part of the nation's communications system were destroyed by nuclear attack. Until recently, it was difficult to gain access to the Internet without holding a position at a university or a government research laboratory. Today, however, virtually anyone with sufficient resources can reach the Internet with a phone line, a computer, and a modem. People buy and sell cars, trade stocks, auction off items, research new medical remedies, vote, and track down long-lost friends online, to mention just a few of the thousands of possibilities (Reddick and King 2000).

If we look at global Internet use, the regions with the greatest number of users are Asia and Europe. Asia alone represents over 650 million users. However, a larger proportion of the population in North America—about 75 percent—has access to the Internet than in any other continent. Even though Asia has the greatest number of users, only about 17 percent of the population there has Internet access. Another sign of the global nature of this expansion has been the increase in languages used on the Internet. While English continues to lead, Chinese usage increased 900 percent between 2000 and 2009 compared to only 227 percent for English (Internet World Stats 2009a, 2009b).

Unfortunately, a digital divide persists, and not everyone can get onto the information highway, especially not the less affluent. Moreover, this pattern of inequality is global. In Africa, for example, only 5.6 percent of the population has access to the Internet. The core nations that Immanuel Wallerstein described in his world systems analysis have a virtual monopoly on information technology; the peripheral nations of Asia, Africa, and Latin America depend on the core nations both for technology and for the information it provides. For example, North America, Europe, and a few industrialized nations in other regions

Internet Use and Penetration by World Region

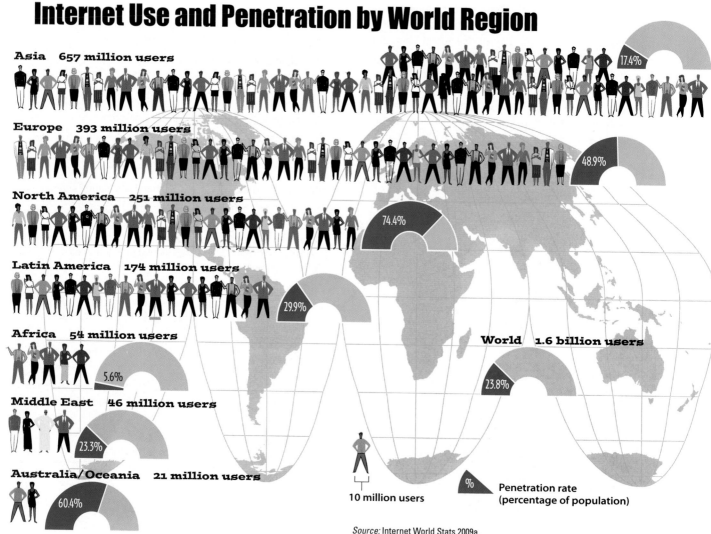

Asia 657 million users — 17.4%

Europe 393 million users — 48.9%

North America 251 million users — 74.4%

Latin America 174 million users — 29.9%

Africa 54 million users — 5.6%

Middle East 46 million users — 23.3%

Australia/Oceania 21 million users — 60.4%

World 1.6 billion users — 23.8%

10 million users

% Penetration rate (percentage of population)

Source: Internet World Stats 2009a.

possess almost all the world's Internet hosts—computers that are connected directly to the worldwide network.

One way to address this divide is to provide computing technology to those people who do not have it. The "One Laptop per Child" (OLPC) campaign seeks to do just that (http://laptop.org). In January 2005, Nicholas Negroponte of the Massachusetts Institute of Technology announced his revolutionary idea for just such a giveaway. For several years, he had been trying to develop a low-cost computer, called the XO, for the 1.2 billion children of the developing world. Negroponte's goal was to sell the laptop for $100, complete with a wireless hookup and a battery with a five-year life span. His intention was to persuade foundations and the governments of industrial countries to fund the distribution, so that the laptop would be available to the children for free. As of June 2009, OLPC had distributed over 800,000 computers around the world to children in Peru, Haiti, Cambodia, Mexico, Rwanda, Iraq, and more.

SOCthink

> > > From a purely business point of view, what would be the pros and cons of giving a free XO to every needy child in the developing world? Would the social benefits of doing so outweigh the business costs and benefits?

PRIVACY AND CENSORSHIP IN A GLOBAL VILLAGE

In addition to the digital divide, sociologists have also raised concerns about threats to privacy and the possibility of censorship. Recent advances have made it increasingly easy for business firms, government agencies, and even criminals to retrieve and store information about everything from our buying habits to our Web-surfing patterns.

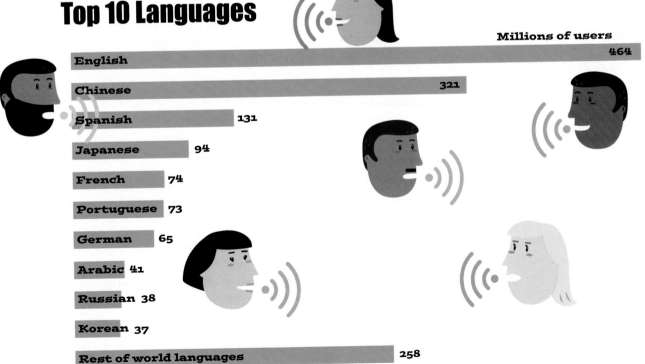

Internet Top 10 Languages

Millions of users

Language	Users
English	464
Chinese	321
Spanish	131
Japanese	94
French	74
Portuguese	73
German	65
Arabic	41
Russian	38
Korean	37
Rest of world languages	258

Source: Internet World Stats 2009b.

In public places, at work, and on the Internet, surveillance devices now track our every move, be it a keystroke or an ATM withdrawal. As technology spreads, so does the exposure to risk. In 2006, for example, the theft of a laptop computer from the home of an employee of the Veterans' Administration compromised the names, Social Security numbers, and dates of birth of up to 26.5 million veterans.

At the same time that these innovations have increased others' power to monitor our behavior, they have raised fears that they might be misused for undemocratic purposes. In short, new technologies threaten not just our privacy but our freedom from surveillance and censorship (O'Harrow 2005). There is, for example, the danger that the most powerful groups in a society will use technology to violate the privacy of the less powerful. Indeed, officials in the People's Republic of China have attempted to censor online discussion groups and web postings that criticize the government. Civil liberties advocates remind us that the same abuses can occur in the United States if citizens are not vigilant in protecting their right to privacy (Magnier 2004).

In the United States, legislation regulating the surveillance of electronic communications has not always upheld citizens' right to privacy. In 1986, the federal government passed the Electronic Communications Privacy Act, which outlawed the surveillance of telephone calls except with the permission of both the U.S. attorney general and a federal judge. Telegrams, faxes, and email did not receive the same degree of protection, however. In 2001, one month after the terrorist attacks of September 11, Congress passed the USA PATRIOT Act, which relaxed existing legal checks on surveillance by law enforcement officers. Federal agencies are now freer to gather data electronically, including credit card receipts and banking records (Etzioni 2007; Singel 2008; Zetter 2009).

In the early days of Internet expansion, many people were quite concerned about sharing any personal information online for fear that someone might use it against them. Now, with the advent of Facebook, Flickr, Twitter, and a whole host of other social networking sites, many Internet users see no such risk. People regularly share their thoughts, feelings, and actions with others, including total strangers. But some have learned the hard way that schools and employers can use this information to make decisions about discipline and hiring (Finder 2006; Relerford et al. 2008; Solove 2008).

BIOTECHNOLOGY AND THE GENE POOL

Another field in which technological advances have spurred global social change is biotechnology. Sex selection of fetuses, genetically engineered organisms, the cloning of animals—these have been among the significant yet controversial scientific advances in the field of biotechnology in recent years. No phase of life now seems exempt from therapeutic or medical intervention. In fact, sociologists view many aspects of biotechnology as as an extension of the recent trend toward the medicalization of society. Through genetic manipulation, the medical profession is expanding its turf still further (Clarke et al. 2003).

One area of genetic modification that has raised concern involves genetically modified (GM) food. This issue arose in Europe but has since spread to other parts of the world, including the United States. The idea behind the technology is to increase food production and make agriculture more efficient and economical. But critics use the term *frankenfood* (as in Frankenstein) to refer to everything from breakfast cereals

Cloning Milestones

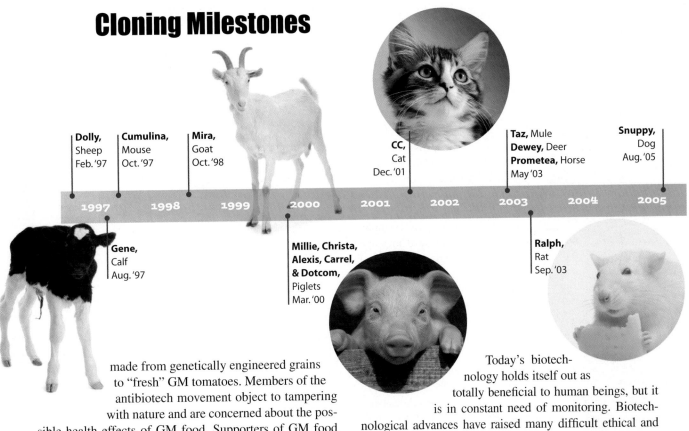

Dolly,
Sheep
Feb. '97

Cumulina,
Mouse
Oct. '97

Mira,
Goat
Oct. '98

CC,
Cat
Dec. '01

Taz, Mule
Dewey, Deer
Prometea, Horse
May '03

Snuppy,
Dog
Aug. '05

1997   1998   1999   2000   2001   2002   2003   2004   2005

Gene,
Calf
Aug. '97

**Millie, Christa,
Alexis, Carrel,
& Dotcom,**
Piglets
Mar. '00

Ralph,
Rat
Sep. '03

made from genetically engineered grains to "fresh" GM tomatoes. Members of the antibiotech movement object to tampering with nature and are concerned about the possible health effects of GM food. Supporters of GM food include not just biotech companies but those who see the technology as a way to help feed the growing populations of Africa and Asia (Golden 1999; Schurman 2004).

Even as the genetic modification of plants continues to be a concern, the debate about the genetic manipulation of animals escalated in 1997 when scientists in Scotland announced that they had cloned a sheep, which they named Dolly. After many unsuccessful attempts, they were finally able to replace the genetic material of a sheep's egg with DNA from an adult sheep, creating a lamb that was a clone of the adult. Shortly thereafter, Japanese researchers successfully cloned cows. Since then many other species have been successfully cloned (see the timeline above), and it is now even possible to get your pet cat or dog cloned. Such accomplishments point to the possibility that in the near future, scientists may be able to clone human beings.

Manipulation that goes even further than cloning involves potentially altering species through genetic engineering. Fish and plant genes have already been mixed to create frost-resistant potato and tomato crops. More recently, human genes have been implanted in pigs to provide humanlike kidneys for organ transplants. Geneticists working with mouse fetuses have managed to disable genes that carry an undesirable trait and replace them with genes carrying a desirable trait. Such advances raise staggering possibilities for altering animal and human life forms (Avise 2004). But they also raise ethical concerns related to applying such engineering to humans to eliminate disease or infirmities or to enhance physical abilities such as sight or strength.

Today's biotechnology holds itself out as totally beneficial to human beings, but it is in constant need of monitoring. Biotechnological advances have raised many difficult ethical and political questions. Among them is the desirability of tinkering with the gene pool, which could alter our environment and ourselves in unexpected and unwanted ways (McKib-

ben 2003). William F. Ogburn probably could not have anticipated such scientific developments when he wrote about culture lag 70 years ago.

RESISTANCE TO TECHNOLOGY

Given such consequences, it should come as no surprise that, through the ages, there have been those who questioned whether such technological innovation equals progress. Inventions that grew out of the Industrial Revolution, for example, led to strong resistance in some countries. In England, beginning in 1811, masked craft workers took extreme measures: They mounted nighttime raids on factories and destroyed some of the new machinery. The government hunted these rebels, known as **Luddites,** and ultimately banished or hanged them. In a similar effort in France, angry workers threw their wooden shoes (sabots) into factory machinery to destroy it, giving rise to the term *sabotage*. Although the resistance of the Luddites and the French workers was short-lived and unsuccessful, they have come to symbolize resistance to technology.

It would be a mistake, however, to simply dismiss their actions as antitechnology or irrational. Their primary concern was with the impact such technology had on their employment, their communities, and their way of life. They recognized that it would undercut taken-for-granted norms and values and fought against such threats. Today we often uncritically adopt the latest technologies without

From Me to You

I confess to having mixed emotions about technology. I love my iPhone but worry about the consequences such technologies have on community and on the environment. One of the first sociologists who had a significant influence on me was Jacques Ellul. In college I read his book The Technological Society, which raised questions not so much about technology itself, but about the way technological approaches to nature, objects, and each other—what he referred to as "technique"—shaped how we thought and what we did. Technology can enhance communication, but might it be that our quest for efficiency and productivity undercuts community and relationships?

taking time to step back and ask what consequences they have for social order and meaning.

Just as the Luddites resisted the Industrial Revolution, people in many countries today continue to resist postindustrial technological changes. The term *neo-Luddites* refers to those who are wary of technological innovations and who question the incessant expansion of industrialization, the increasing destruction of the natural and agrarian world, and the "throw-it-away" mentality of contemporary capitalism with its resulting pollution of the environment. Whether it is TiVo, the iPhone, or even the latest microwave oven or digital camera, many consumers are critical of these so-called must-have items. Neo-Luddites insist that whatever the presumed benefits of industrial and postindustrial technology, such technology has distinctive social costs and may represent a danger to the future of both the human species and the planet (Jones 2006; Postman 1999; Sale 1996).

Hot or Not?

If you could modify your children's genes to protect them from genetic diseases, would you do it? How about enhance abilities such as eyesight, strength, or intelligence?

Five Questions to Ask When Adopting New Technology

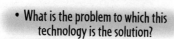

- What is the problem to which this technology is the solution?
- Whose problem is it?
- What new problems might be created because we solve the problem?
- Which people and institutions might be most seriously harmed?
- Which people and institutions might acquire special economic and political power?

Source: Postman 1988.

>> Social Movements

We do have the power to resist change even when it seems inevitable. More than that, we also have the power to bring about positive social change. Although factors such as the physical environment, population, technology, and social inequality serve as sources of change, it is the collective effort of individuals organized in social movements that ultimately leads to change. Sociologists use the term **social movements** to refer to organized collective activities to bring about or resist fundamental change in an existing group or society. Herbert Blumer (1955:19) recognized the special importance of social movements when he defined them as "collective enterprises to establish a new order of life."

In many nations, including the United States, social movements have had a dramatic impact on the course of history and the evolution of the social structure. Consider the actions of abolitionists, suffragists, civil rights workers, and anti–Vietnam War activists. Members of each social movement stepped outside traditional channels for bringing about social change, yet they had a noticeable influence on public policy. In Eastern Europe, equally dramatic collective efforts helped to topple communist regimes in a largely peaceful manner, in nations that many observers had thought were "immune" to such social change (Marples 2004).

Social movements change how we think and act. Even if they initially fail to accomplish their explicit goals, social movements can influence cultural attitudes and expectations in ways that open people up to future change. Initially, people viewed the ideas of Margaret Sanger and other early advocates of birth control as radical, yet contraceptives are now widely available in the United States. Similarly, protests—whether against the practices of multinational corporations, same-sex marriage, the unethical treatment of animals, environmental destruction, or war—challenge us to question our taken-for-granted understandings of what is happening and why. This holds true even if we never formally participate ourselves or do not fully subscribe to all the beliefs and practices of the protesters.

At least since the work of Karl Marx, sociologists have studied how and why social movements emerge. Obviously, one factor is that people become discontented with the way things are. To explain how this develops and is transformed into action, sociologists rely on two primary explanations: relative deprivation and resource mobilization.

RELATIVE DEPRIVATION

Those members of a society who feel most frustrated with and disgruntled by social and economic conditions are not necessarily the worst off in an objective sense. Social scientists have long recognized that what is most significant is how people perceive their situation. As Marx pointed out, although the misery of the workers was important to their perception of their oppressed state, so was their position in relation to the capitalist ruling class (McLellan 2000).

The term **relative deprivation** refers to the conscious feeling of a negative discrepancy between legitimate expectations and present actualities. In other words, things aren't as good as one hoped they would be. Such a state may be characterized by scarcity rather than a complete lack of necessities. A relatively deprived person is dissatisfied because he or she feels downtrodden relative to some appropriate reference group. Thus, blue-collar workers who live in two-family houses on small plots of land—though hardly destitute—may nevertheless feel deprived in comparison to corporate managers and professionals who live in lavish homes in exclusive suburbs (Stewart 2006).

In addition to the feeling of relative deprivation, however, two other elements must be present before discontent will be channeled into a social movement. First, people must feel that they have a right to their goals, that they deserve better than what they have. For example, the struggle against European colonialism in Africa intensified when growing numbers of Africans decided that it was legitimate for them to have political and economic independence. Second, the disadvantaged group must perceive that its goals cannot be attained through conventional means. This belief may or may not be correct. In any case, the group will not mobilize into a social movement unless there is a shared perception that members can end their relative deprivation only through collective action (Walker and Smith 2002).

Critics of this approach have noted that people don't need to feel deprived to be moved to act. In addition, this approach fails to explain why certain feelings of deprivation are transformed into social movements, whereas in other, similar situations, no collective effort is made to

Did You Know?

. . . In 1916, Margaret Sanger opened a family planning and birth control clinic. Nine days later, it was raided by police, and she served 30 days in jail as a result. She was undeterred and continued working to dispense birth control information.

Luddites Rebellious craft workers in 19th-century England who destroyed new factory machinery as part of their resistance to the Industrial Revolution.

social movement An organized collective activity to bring about or resist fundamental change in an existing group or society.

relative deprivation The conscious feeling of a negative discrepancy between legitimate expectations and present actualities.

reshape society. Consequently, in recent years, sociologists have paid increasing attention to the forces needed to bring about the emergence of social movements (Finkel and Rule 1987; Ratner 2004).

SOCthink

> > > Are there any issues on your campus or in your community that people persistently complain about? What factors might inhibit them from organizing to bring about social change?

RESOURCE MOBILIZATION APPROACH

It takes more than desire to start a social movement. It helps to have money, political influence, access to the media, and personnel. The term **resource mobilization** refers to the ways in which a social movement utilizes such resources. The success of a movement for change will depend in good part on what resources it has and how effectively it mobilizes them (Balch 2006; J. Jenkins 2004; Ling 2006).

Sociologist Anthony Oberschall (1973:199) has argued that to sustain social protest or resistance, there must be an "organizational base and continuity of leadership." As people become part of a social movement, norms develop to guide their behavior. Members of the movement may be expected to attend regular meetings of organizations, pay dues, recruit new adherents, and boycott "enemy" products or speakers. In forming a distinct identity, an emerging social movement may give rise to special language or new words for familiar terms. In recent years, social movements have been responsible for new terms of self-reference such as *Blacks* and *African Americans* (to replace *Negroes*), *senior citizens* (to replace *old folks*), *gays* (to replace *homosexuals*), and *people with disabilities* (to replace the *handicapped*).

Leadership is a central factor in the mobilization of the discontented into social movements. Often, a movement will be led by a charismatic figure, such as occurred in the civil rights movement with Dr. Martin Luther King Jr. Charisma alone, however, may not be enough. If a group is to succeed, coordinated action is essential. As they grow, such organizations may find they need to take advantage of the efficiency that bureaucratic structures provide. This can result in their taking on some of the characteristics of the groups they were organized to protest. For example, leaders might dominate the decision-making process with-

out directly consulting followers. The bureaucratization of social movements is not inevitable, however. More radical movements that advocate major structural change in society and embrace mass actions tend not to be hierarchical or bureaucratic (Fitzgerald and Rodgers 2000; Michels [1915] 1949).

One of the tasks such movements face is to raise consciousness among those who would be inclined to support the movement but who may lack the language or the sense of solidarity with others to mount a systematic critique of the existing system. Marx, for example, recognized the importance of recruitment when he called on workers to become aware of their oppressed status and to develop a class consciousness. Like theorists of the resource mobilization approach, Marx held that a social movement would require leaders to sharpen the awareness of the oppressed. They would need to help workers to overcome feelings of **false consciousness**—attitudes that do not reflect workers' objective position—in order to organize a revolutionary movement.

GENDER AND SOCIAL MOVEMENTS

Betty Friedan's publication of *The Feminine Mystique* in 1963 gave voice to a sense that many women had at the time that something was wrong, but they did not know that others felt the same way. The book alone, however, was not enough. One of the challenges faced by women's liberation activists of the late 1960s and early 1970s was to convince women that they were being deprived of their rights and of socially valued resources. Consciousness-raising groups represented a critical tool used by women's liberation activists in the 1960s and 1970s. In these groups, women gathered to discuss topics relevant to their experience in the home, at work, in politics, and more. This helped to create a popular base that contributed to significant political and social change (Morgan 2009; Sarachild 1978).

Sociologists point out that gender continues to be an important element in understanding social movements. In our male-dominated society, women continue to find themselves cut off from leadership positions in social movement organizations. Though women often serve disproportionately as volunteers in these movements, their contributions are not always recognized, nor are their voices as easily heard as men's. Gender bias causes the real extent of their influence to be overlooked. Indeed, traditional examination of the sociopolitical system tends to focus on such male-dominated corridors of power as legislatures and corporate boardrooms, to the neglect of more female-dominated domains such as households, community-based groups, and faith-based networks. But efforts

> I cannot say whether things will get better if we change; what I can say is they must change if they are to get better.

George Christoph Lichtenberg

NEW SOCIAL MOVEMENTS

Beginning in the late 1960s, European social scientists observed a change in both the composition and the targets of emerging social movements. Previously, traditional social movements had focused on economic issues, often led by labor unions or by people who shared the same occupation.

However, many social movements that have become active in recent decades—including the contemporary women's movement, the peace movement, and the environmental movement—do not have the social class roots typical of the labor movements in the United States and Europe over the past century (Carty and Onyett 2006).

> **resource mobilization** The ways in which a social movement utilizes such resources as money, political influence, access to the media, and personnel.
> **false consciousness** A term used by Karl Marx to describe an attitude held by members of a class that does not accurately reflect their objective position.
> **new social movement** An organized collective activity that addresses values and social identities, as well as improvements in the quality of life.

The term **new social movements** refers to organized collective activities that address values and social identities, as well as improvements in the quality of life. These movements may be involved in developing collective identities. Many have complex agendas that go beyond a single issue and even cross national boundaries. Educated, middle-class people are significantly represented in some of these new social movements, such as the women's movement and the movement for lesbian and gay rights (Tilly 1993, 2004).

New social movements generally do not view government as their ally in the struggle for a better society. They typically do not seek to overthrow the government, but they may criticize, protest, or harass public officials. Researchers have found that members of new social movements call into question the legitimacy of arguments made by established authorities. Even scientific or technical claims, they argue, do not simply represent objective facts, but

to influence family values, child rearing, relationships between parents and schools, and spiritual values are clearly significant to a culture and society (Ferree and Merrill 2000; Kuumba 2001; V. Taylor 1999, 2004).

Prior to the June 2009 presidential election in Iran, women's social movement organizations foresaw an opportunity for change and organized to take advantage of it. Almost 40 equal-rights groups combined to form an organization called the "Coalition of Women's Movements to Advocate Electoral Demands." Noushin Ahmadi Khorasani (2009), a key leader of the women's rights movement in Iran, described the opportunity this way, "We could grasp this relatively short and transient moment with both hands, with hope and motivation (and looking forward to tomorrow) in order to voice our demands." During the government crackdown on the protests that followed the election, women continued to fight for change. Perhaps the most visible symbol of their fight was Neda Agha-Soltan, a protester who was shot and bled to death in the street. The violent image was caught on video and quickly spread around the world (Gheytanchi 2009; Ravitz 2009).

often serve specific interests. This characteristic is especially evident in the environmental and anti–nuclear power movements, whose activists present their own experts to counter those of government or big business (Clammer 2009; Jamison 2006; Rootes 2007).

The environmental movement is one of many new social movements with a worldwide focus. In their efforts to reduce air and water pollution, curtail global warming, and protect endangered animal species, environmental activists have realized that strong regulatory measures within a single country are not sufficient. Similarly, labor union leaders and human rights advocates cannot adequately address exploitative sweatshop conditions in a developing country if a multinational corporation can simply move the factory to another country, where workers earn even less. Whereas traditional views of social movements tended to emphasize resource mobilization on a local level, new social movement theory offers a broader, global perspective on social and political activism (Obach 2004).

COMMUNICATION AND THE GLOBALIZATION OF SOCIAL MOVEMENTS

Although technological advances have contributed to some of the problems people in social movements have raised, new technologies also facilitate activism and social movement formation. Using social networking technologies, social activists can reach a large number of people around the world almost instantaneously, with relatively little effort and expense. For example, Facebook and Twitter allow organizers of social movements to enlist like-minded people without face-to-face contact or simultaneous interaction. In fact, significant social action can occur without the participants ever having met in person (Kavada 2005; Shirky 2008).

The potential power of new communication technologies was made apparent during Iran's postelection protests in June 2009. A majority of Iran's population is under 30 and technologically well connected. Before the election, young people used their online social networking skills to coordinate campaign events and raise support for candidates. After President Ahmadinejad's re-election was declared, technologies such as Twitter, Facebook, and SMS texting became critical tools for sharing information, coordinating actions, and documenting abuses by government forces. It was possible to organize rallies without revealing their location until the last minute, making it more difficult for the government to have troops in place to disperse the crowd.

Equally significant, these networking tools also were used to send stories, pictures, and video to the wider world, revealing the brutality of the government's crackdown. The result was an outpouring of global sympathy for the protesters. Iranian authorities sought to shut down wireless phone service and restrict Internet access, including blocking sites such as YouTube and Facebook. In spite of this, people were able to use various technological hacks to get around such restrictions and spread the word (Bray 2009; Quirk 2009; Stelter and Stone 2009).

>> Sociology Is a Verb

Ultimately, social change happens because we begin to act in new ways. It involves our stepping off expected paths and, in doing so, creating new sets of norms. Although external changes in our technological and environmental contexts do influence social change, it still takes people willing to do things differently to bring about such shifts.

Sociology is a tool that helps open up new pathways for us. By enabling us to see things we might have missed before, it helps us to view ourselves and the world around us differently. Sociology allows us to recognize how the dis-

POPSOC

Stephen Colbert worked for several years as a sarcastic correspondent on *The Daily Show* on Comedy Central, but he became famous doing his cynical spoof of a TV talking head on his show *The Colbert Report.* He was quite serious, however, when he gave advice in a 2006 commencement speech at Knox College. He challenged students not to give in to cynicism, telling them, "Cynicism masquerades as wisdom, but it is the farthest thing from it. Because cynics don't learn anything. Because cynicism is a self-imposed blindness, a rejection of the world because we are afraid it will hurt us or disappoint us. Cynics always say 'no.' But saying 'yes' begins things. Saying 'yes' is how things grow. Saying 'yes' leads to knowledge. 'Yes' is for young people. So for as long as you have the strength to, say 'yes.'"

tribution of social, cultural, and material resources gives advantage to some and disadvantage to others. It helps us to understand whether the things we do are consistent with what we claim to believe. It can inform our conversation of whether we are headed where we want to go. It does these things by getting us to pay attention to the world around us in a new way.

We need to move from thinking of sociology as only something we learn about to thinking of sociology as something we *do.* In our daily lives, sociology can help us to better understand our own individual actions and the actions of those around us. In the context of our larger society and the world, it also enables us to better appreciate the forces at work shaping outcomes—knowledge that we can

then use to act in ways that make the world a better place. In both our personal and public lives, we need to practice sociology in the same way that doctors practice medicine.

PERSONAL SOCIOLOGY

Sociology should be something we use in the present, in our everyday lives, to understand our beliefs and actions and to make more informed choices. We learn from sociology that we are in society and society is in us. Self and society are not two separate things. Being an individual necessitates understanding the importance of place, of position, of connection, and of interaction. Theoretically, any choice is available to us; but in reality, only limited paths are open to us.

Practicing sociology means asking uncomfortable questions and not settling for easy answers. It means considering the significance of both the individual and society, of both action and structure, of both freedom and constraint. It means recognizing the significance of power and the impact that access to material, social, and cultural resources has on the choices available to us. In short, doing **personal sociology** means recognizing the impact our individual position has on who we are and how we think and act, and taking responsibility for the impacts our actions have on others.

From the beginning, sociologists wanted to understand our constraints so that we might be able to change them. As Pierre Bourdieu put it, "To those who always tax the sociologist with determinism and pessimism, I will only say that if people became fully aware of them, conscious action aimed at controlling the structural mechanisms that engender moral failure would be possible" (1998b:56). In other words, we need to be honest with ourselves about the degree to which society limits our choices so that we might be empowered to make choices that are more informed and therefore more effective in helping us to attain our goals.

> **personal sociology** The process of recognizing the impact our individual position has on who we are and how we think and act, and of taking responsibility for the impacts our actions have on others.

As individuals, we need to see the degree to which we follow visible and invisible rules. We need to ask whether our current paths represent the values, norms, and goals that we really want to follow. As we have seen, the shows we watch, the things we buy, our likelihood for suicide, our chances of facing a wage gap, our perception of reality, our very selves—all are shaped by the positions we occupy. Understanding these influences empowers us to change.

PUBLIC SOCIOLOGY: TOOLS FOR CHANGE

Beyond providing a more informed understanding of why we as individuals act and think the way we do, sociology calls on us to look beyond ourselves to the world around us and ask, What might we do to make the world a better place? Sociologists since the very beginning have sought

Citizen Activities in a Democratic Society

PRIVATE LIFE		CIVIC LIFE	
Individual activity	**Civic engagement activities**		
	Nonpolitical activities	Political participation	
Family School Work	Recycling Fellowship meetings Service activities	Voting Attending political meetings Political campaigning	
Functions Cultivates personal relationships, serves individual needs—e.g., getting an education, earning a living	Provides community services and acts as a training ground for political participation	Fulfills demands of democratic citizenship	

to understand and explain social processes for the purpose of shaping the future of society. **Public sociology** involves bringing the insights gained through sociological observation and analysis into the public sphere, thereby seeking to bring about positive social change. As Michael Burawoy, former president of the American Sociological Association, put it, public sociology seeks to speak to a wide audience, aiming to "enrich public debate about moral and political issues by infusing them with sociological theory and research" (Burawoy 2004:1603).

Because we construct the existing social structures through our collective and recurring actions, we bear responsibility for their consequences. Existing systems—the structure and culture we create—are not inevitable. We can choose to change them; we can act differently, as the accompanying table suggests. It can be difficult to step off the "paths of least resistance" that support the existing system (Johnson, 1997), and the consequences for action and belief that run counter to the status quo can be severe. But we can do so.

> **public sociology** The process of bringing the insights gained through sociological observation and analysis into the public sphere, thereby seeking to bring about positive social change.

What we cannot do is absolve ourselves of responsibility for the systems we end up with. In fact, to not act differently is to support the existing system of inequality. As sociologist Scott Schaffer (2004) points out, we can no longer ignore practices that violate our basic beliefs, trying to wash our hands of responsibility:

> Our hands are already dirty; the question I leave here is whether our hands will be dirtied through action intended to bring concrete, actual, enacted freedom into the world, or through our choice to preserve ourselves at the cost of all others in the here and now and in the future. (pp. 271–272)

Our cynicism and resignation only reinforce systems of oppression and violence. To not act to bring about positive change still represents a choice, and our hands are dirty either way.

By helping us to see why we think and act as we do, by helping us to clarify the relationship between belief and practice, and by helping us to better understand the con-

sequences of difference, personal and public sociology can encourage discussion that can lead to a better future. We can use the tools of sociology to allow ourselves to enter into conversations in which we share our stories with others (both positive and negative), clarifying places where we agree and disagree, and opening ourselves up to our blind spots. We often want to avoid uncomfortable conflict, opting instead for polite discourse, but to fail to be more genuinely engaged in our cultural and structural differences virtually ensures a lack of progress toward implementing our core principles (Schaffer, 2004).

PRACTICING SOCIOLOGY

Change comes because people continue not only to believe that it is possible but also to act on their hopes and dreams (see the figure on page 363). As ethnographer Studs Terkel put it, "In all epochs, there were at first doubts and the fear of stepping forth and speaking out, but the attribute that spurred the warriors on was hope. And the *act*" (2003:xviii). We can change the world for the better. We can do so by becoming more informed about ourselves and others, and then acting on that knowledge. Here are some possibilities for action:

- *Practice personal sociology.* Become more conscious of the factors that shape your beliefs and actions.

- *Become more aware of privilege.* Identify the advantages you have, especially relative to the rest of the world; you likely have sufficient food, clothes, and shelter; you can read this; you can plan for the future; and so on.

- *Become more informed.* We have access to more information about our world now than ever. Seek it out; find out what's going on.

- *Interpret what you learn.* Analyze the information you receive. Remember that data never speak for themselves; they aren't just facts but are embedded in networks and systems that have their own interests.

- *Vote.* Elected leaders in a democracy, whether local, state, or national, are chosen by voters. It may not seem like your individual vote is significant, but the simple fact is that all those votes still add up to a winner. And even if your candidate cannot win, you can still make a statement; for example, if you don't think any of the candidates would make a good choice, write in someone who would.

- *Participate in local politics.* Think of politics as a contact sport: Go to rallies, protests, school board meetings, city council meetings, and more. You might be surprised how much of a difference a single voice can make, especially on the local level.

- *Run for office.* Don't assume that such positions of leadership are only for others who are somehow better or more informed than you. We need more people to believe that they can lead so that we get more diversity in our leaders.

- *Volunteer.* There are local organizations in every community seeking to bring about positive social change. You might contact a local school to see if you can read to kids, work at a homeless shelter, or help build houses with Habitat for Humanity.

- *Join.* There are many organizations that provide long-term outreach opportunities, such as AmeriCorps, the Peace Corps, and the American Red Cross, in which you provide assistance to people with varieties of needs, in communities near and far.

- *Organize.* Work to bring about the world you envision; there are undoubtedly others out there who share your views. Find them and work with them, both inside and outside existing institutions, to bring about change.

- *Fight for change.* Regardless of where you are, whether in your relationships, your family, your work-place, your community, or elsewhere, work to bring about positive social change. We have the power to change the world; we can't do so in a vacuum, but if sociologists are at all correct about the social construction of reality, things could be otherwise.

As Comte wrote at sociology's very founding, "Science leads to foresight, and foresight leads to action" (quoted in Bourdieu 1998b:55). It is only by seeing those things that limit us that we can move toward freedom.

We learn a lesson from sociology that is reminiscent of the one Ebenezer Scrooge learns in Charles Dickens' *A Christmas Carol,* written in 1843. Scrooge, a miserly businessman, thinks only of himself, caring little if anything for others, including his employee, his family, and the poor. But on Christmas Eve, he is visited by three ghosts: the Ghost of Christmas Past, the Ghost of Christmas Present, and the Ghost of Christmas Yet to Come. After each of these spirits shows him visions of their time, Scrooge repents, promising to live "an altered life" in which he will reaffirm relationships and reconnect to those around him. What is particularly interesting sociologically is the way he phrases that promise: "I will live in the Past, the Present, and the Future! The Spirits of all Three shall strive within me."

Do You Believe You Can Effect Political Change?

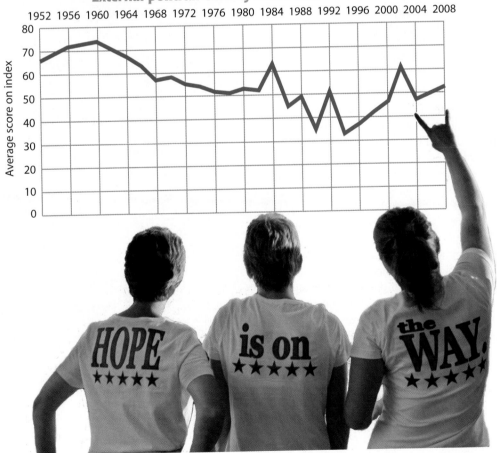

External political efficacy index 1952–2008

Note: 2008 is preliminary data.

Source: The American National Election Studies, 2009.

future together in our minds, we can act to make the world a better place to live.

Sociology is more than just a noun. Sociology is a verb. It is something we do, not something we possess. Our overreliance on individualistic models, and our failure to appreciate the impact of social forces, presents a distorted picture of our freedom. An appreciation of the relationship between self and society and of the consequences of difference allows us to make more informed choices and to shape the future. It allows us to provide answers to the questions Why do we think the way we think? and Why do we act the way we act? Sociology shouldn't be something confined to college classrooms. It shouldn't be left only to professionals. We are all sociologists now, and there is work to be done.

Investigate. Learn. Vote. Organize. Run for office. Fight for change. Practice sociology. Make a difference.

get involved!

At its core, Scrooge's resolution represents what we are called to do by the sociological imagination. Just as history and biography intersect, so also do we need to understand that the past, created by the actions of ourselves and those who came before us, has shaped who we are now. As American novelist and essayist James Baldwin wrote, "The great force of history comes from the fact that we carry it within us, are unconsciously controlled by it in many ways, and history is literally *present* in all that we do" ([1965] 1985:410). Further, our present actions shape the future directions of both our lives and the lives of others in the worlds around us and of those yet to come. Like Scrooge, we can reject the myth of the isolated individual and affirm the significance of relationships and companionship (to return to one of the root word meanings of sociology). By simultaneously holding the past, present, and

For REVIEW

I. How and why does social change happen?
   - Social change evolves out of past social practices; it represents a response by those in society to maintain social order by seeking an acceptable level of balance between stability and change; and it is influenced by the distribution of power and control over resources, which shapes what changes do or do not occur. Technological innovation has played a powerful role causing social change.

II. What factors shape the success of a social movement?
   - There needs to be a sense of relative deprivation in which people have a sense that injustice exists that can and should be challenged. In addition, people must have the capacity to mobilize resources to bring about the change they seek.

III. What does it mean to practice sociology?
   - Personal sociology involves better understanding the influence social factors have on our thoughts and actions and using this information to our advantage. Public sociology means taking responsibility for the collective impacts our individual actions have in shaping society and opportunity and working for positive social change.

Pop Quiz

1. According to the definition, what is social change?
   a. tumultuous, revolutionary alterations that lead to changes in leadership
   b. a significant alteration over time in behavior patterns and culture
   c. regular alterations in a consistent social frame of reference
   d. subtle alterations in any social system

2. Nineteenth-century theories of social change reflect the pioneering work in biological evolution done by
   a. Albert Einstein.
   b. Harriet Martineau.
   c. James Audubon.
   d. Charles Darwin.

3. According to Talcott Parsons's equilibrium model, during which process do social institutions become more specialized in their purposes?
   a. differentiation
   b. adaptive upgrading
   c. inclusion
   d. value generalization

4. Which of the following did William F. Ogburn use to describe the period of maladjustment during which the nonmaterial culture is still struggling to adapt to new material conditions?
   a. economic shift
   b. political turmoil
   c. social change
   d. culture lag

5. The One Laptop per Child campaign was designed to overcome the problem of
   a. relative deprivation.
   b. social change.
   c. the digital divide.
   d. vested interests.

6. You are a student and do not own a car. All your close friends who are attending your college or university have vehicles of their own. You feel downtrodden and dissatisfied. You are experiencing
   a. relative deprivation.
   b. resource mobilization.
   c. false consciousness.
   d. depression.

1. (b); 2. (d); 3. (b); 4. (d); 5. (c); 6. (a);

7. It takes more than desire to start a social movement; it helps to have money, political influence, access to the media, and workers. The ways in which a social movement uses such things are referred to collectively as

   a. relative deprivation.

   b. false consciousness.

   c. resource mobilization.

   d. economic independence.

8. Karl Marx held that leaders of social movements must help workers overcome feelings of

   a. class consciousness.

   b. false consciousness.

   c. socialist consciousness.

   d. surplus value.

9. Organized collective activities that promote autonomy and self-determination, as well as improvements in the quality of life, are referred to as

   a. new social movements.

   b. social revolutions.

   c. resource mobilizations.

   d. crazes.

10. Recognizing the impact our individual position has on who we are and how we think and act, and taking responsibility for the impacts our actions have on others is known as

   a. resource mobilization.

   b. false consciousness.

   c. public sociology.

   d. personal sociology

7. (c); 8. (b); 9. (a); 10. (d)

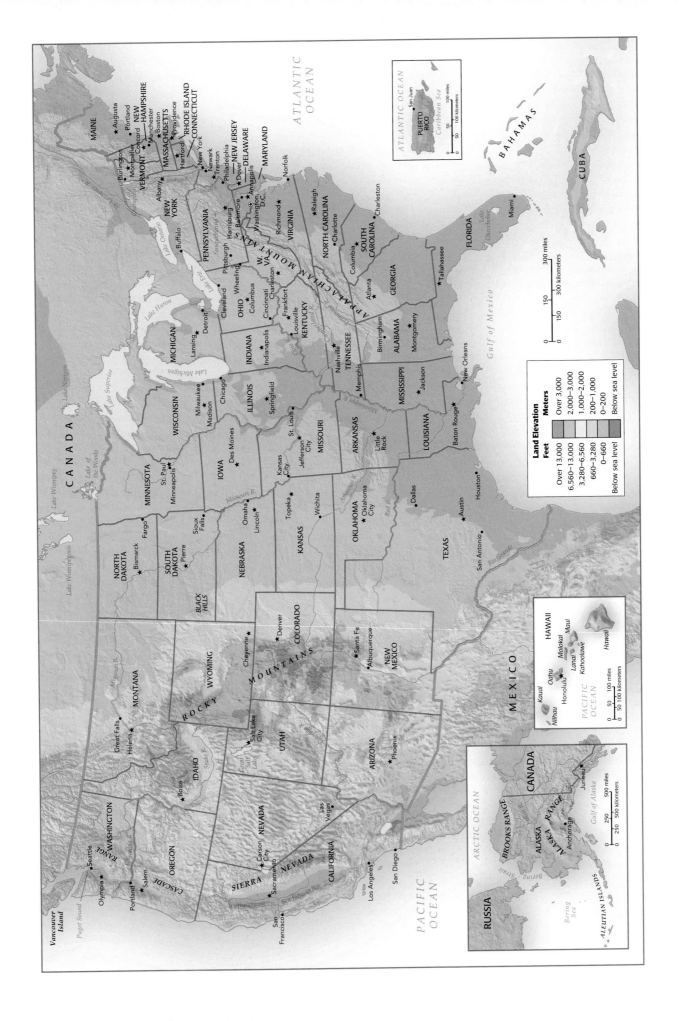

Vancouver
Island

PACIFIC
OCEAN

Puget Sound

WASHINGTON
Seattle ★
Olympia ★
Portland ★ Salem
Columbia R.

OREGON

CASCADE RANGE

San
Francisco •

Sacramento ★
Carson City ★

NEVADA

SIERRA NEVADA

CALIFORNIA
Los Angeles •

San Diego •

Boise ★
IDAHO

Snake R.

Great
Salt Lake
Salt Lake City ★
UTAH

Great Falls •
Helena ★
MONTANA

WYOMING
Cheyenne ★

ROCKY MOUNTAINS

Las
Vegas •

ARIZONA

Phoenix ★

Santa Fe ★
Albuquerque •
NEW
MEXICO

Colorado R.

Denver ★
COLORADO

MEXICO

Rio Grande

Missouri R.

CANADA

Lake Winnipeg

Lake of
the Woods

Lake Winnipegosis

NORTH
DAKOTA
Bismarck ★

Fargo •

SOUTH
DAKOTA
Pierre ★

BLACK
HILLS

Sioux
Falls •
Omaha •
Lincoln ★
NEBRASKA

Des Moines ★
IOWA

St. Paul ★
Minneapolis •
MINNESOTA

Missouri R.

Topeka ★
Wichita •
KANSAS

OKLAHOMA
Oklahoma
City ★

Arkansas R.

Red R.

TEXAS

Dallas •

Austin ★
San Antonio •

Houston •

Jefferson
City ★
Kansas
City •
MISSOURI

St. Louis •
Springfield ★
ILLINOIS
Chicago •

WISCONSIN
Madison ★
Milwaukee •

Lake Michigan

Lake Superior

MICHIGAN
Lansing ★
Detroit •

Lake Huron

Lake Erie

Lake Ontario

Buffalo •

Mississippi R.

Little
Rock ★
ARKANSAS

LOUISIANA
Baton Rouge ★
New Orleans •

Gulf of Mexico

Indianapolis ★
INDIANA

Cincinnati •
Frankfort ★
Louisville •
KENTUCKY

Nashville ★
TENNESSEE
Memphis •

Ohio R.

Tennessee R.

Cumberland R.

MISSISSIPPI
Jackson ★

Birmingham •
ALABAMA
Montgomery ★

Columbus ★
OHIO
Columbus
Cleveland •
Wheeling •
W. VA.
Charleston ★

Pittsburgh •
PENNSYLVANIA
Harrisburg ★

NEW
YORK
Albany ★

MAINE
Augusta ★
Portland •
NEW
HAMPSHIRE
Montpelier ★ Concord ★ Manchester •
Burlington • Boston •
VERMONT MASSACHUSETTS
Providence ★
RHODE ISLAND
Hartford ★ CONNECTICUT
Newark • New York
Trenton ★ NEW JERSEY
Philadelphia •
Dover ★ DELAWARE
Annapolis ★ MARYLAND
Washington, D.C.
Baltimore •
Norfolk •

Hudson R.

Delaware R.

Susquehanna R.

APPALACHIAN MOUNTAINS

Richmond ★
VIRGINIA
★Raleigh
NORTH CAROLINA
Charlotte •

Charleston •

SOUTH
CAROLINA
Columbia ★

GEORGIA
Atlanta ★

ATLANTIC
OCEAN

Charleston •

Tallahassee ★

FLORIDA
Lake
Okeechobee

Miami •

CUBA

BAHAMAS

Land Elevation
Feet   Meters
Over 13,000   Over 3,000
6,560–13,000   2,000–3,000
3,280–6,560   1,000–2,000
660–3,280   200–1,000
0–660   0–200
Below sea level Below sea level

| 0 | 150 | 300 miles |
| 0 | 150 | 300 kilometers |

ATLANTIC OCEAN

San Juan •
PUERTO
RICO
Caribbean Sea

| 0 | 50 | 100 miles |
| 0 | 50 | 100 kilometers |

HAWAII

Kauai
Niihau
Oahu
Honolulu •
Molokai
Lanai Maui
Kahoolawe
Hawaii

PACIFIC
OCEAN

| 0 | 50 | 100 miles |
| 0 | 50 | 100 kilometers |

ARCTIC OCEAN

RUSSIA

Bering
Sea

Bering Strait

ALASKA
BROOKS RANGE
ALASKA RANGE
Juneau ★
Anchorage •
CANADA
Gulf of Alaska

ALEUTIAN ISLANDS

| 0 | 250 | 500 miles |
| 0 | 250 | 500 kilometers |

RUSSIA

GREENLAND

CANADA

NORTH AMERICA

UNITED STATES

ATLANTIC OCEAN

Hawaiian Islands

MEXICO

BAHAMAS

CUBA

JAMAICA

BELIZE

DOMINICAN REPUBLIC

~ Puerto Rico (to US)

GUATEMALA

HONDURAS

HAITI

EL SALVADOR

NICARAGUA

Lesser Antilles

CAPE VERDE

COSTA RICA

TRINIDAD AND TOBAGO

VENEZUELA

GUYANA

SURINAME

PACIFIC OCEAN

PANAMA

COLOMBIA

FRENCH GUIANA

Galapagos Is. ›

ECUADOR

SOUTH AMERICA

PERU

BRAZIL

BOLIVIA

PARAGUAY

CHILE

URUGUAY

ARGENTINA

Falkland Is.

Abbreviations

ALB.	ALBANIA
AZERB.	AZERBAIJAN
BELG.	BELGIUM
BOS.	BOSNIA-HERZEGOVINA
BULG.	BULGARIA
CRO.	CROATIA
CZECH.	CZECH REPUBLIC
EST.	ESTONIA
HUNG.	HUNGARY
LITH.	LITHUANIA
LUX.	LUXEMBOURG
MACE.	MACEDONIA
MONT.	MONTENEGRO
NETH.	NETHERLANDS
ROM.	ROMANIA
RUSS.	RUSSIA
SERB.	SERBIA
SLOVAK.	SLOVAKIA
SLOVN.	SLOVENIA
SWITZ.	SWITZERLAND
U.A.E.	UNITED ARAB EMIRATES

ICELAND

NORWAY

GREAT BRITAIN

SWEDEN

FINLAND

RUSSIA

UNITED
KINGDOM

IRELAND

DENMARK

EST.

LATVIA

LITH.

RUSS.

BELARUS

NETH.
BELG.
LUX.

GERMANY

POLAND

EUROPE

FRANCE

CZECH

SLOVAK.

UKRAINE

KAZAKHSTAN

MONGOLIA

SWITZ.

AUSTRIA

HUNG.

MOLDOVA

SLOV.

CRO.

ROM.

ASIA

N. KOREA

ITALY

BOS.

SERB.

KOSOVO

BULG.

GEORGIA

UZBEKISTAN

KYRGYZSTAN

MONT.

SPAIN

ALB.

MACE.

TURKEY

ARM.

TURKMENISTAN

TAJIKISTAN

CHINA

S. KOREA

JAPAN

PORTUGAL

GREECE

AZERB.

SYRIA

IRAN

LEBANON

ISRAEL

IRAQ

AFGHANISTAN

TUNISIA

PAKISTAN

NEPAL

BHUTAN

TAIWAN

Canary Is.

MOROCCO

JORDAN

KUWAIT

ALGERIA

LIBYA

EGYPT

SAUDI
ARABIA

U.A.E.

QATAR

INDIA

MYANMAR

HONG KONG

PACIFIC OCEAN

WESTERN
SAHARA

OMAN

LAOS

MAURITANIA

MALI

NIGER

CHAD

SUDAN

ERITREA

YEMEN

BANGLADESH

THAILAND

VIETNAM

SENEGAL

BURKINA
FASO

DJIBOUTI

CAMBODIA

PHILIPPINES

GAMBIA

NIGERIA

GUINEA-
BISSAU

GUINEA

CENTRAL
AFRICAN REP.

ETHIOPIA

SRI LANKA

SIERRA LEONE

IVORY
COAST

GHANA

BENIN

LIBERIA

TOGO

EQUATORIAL GUINEA

CAMEROON

SOMALIA

BRUNEI

SAO TOME AND PRINCIPE

GABON

CONGO

UGANDA

MALAYSIA

DEMOCRATIC
REPUBLIC
OF THE
CONGO

KENYA

RWANDA

SEYCHELLES

INDONESIA

PAPUA
NEW
GUINEA

Solomon
Islands

AFRICA

BURUNDI

TANZANIA

EAST TIMOR

TUVALU

ANGOLA

ZAMBIA

MALAWI

MADAGASCAR

VANUATU

FIJI

NAMIBIA

ZIMBABWE

MOZAMBIQUE

MAURITIUS

New Caledonia
(Fr.)

BOTSWANA

RÉUNION

AUSTRALIA

SWAZILAND

SOUTH
AFRICA

LESOTHO

INDIAN OCEAN

Tasmania

NEW ZEALAND

Absolute poverty   A minimum level of subsistence that no family should be expected to live below.

Achieved status   A social position that a person attains largely through his or her own efforts.

Activity theory   A theory of aging that suggests that those elderly people who remain active and socially involved will be best adjusted.

Adoption   In a legal sense, a process that allows for the transfer of the legal rights, responsibilities, and privileges of parenthood to a new legal parent or parents.

Affirmative action   Positive efforts to recruit minority group members or women for jobs, promotions, and educational opportunities.

Ageism   Prejudice and discrimination based on a person's age.

Agency   The freedom individuals have to choose and to act.

Agrarian society   The most technologically advanced form of preindustrial society. Members are engaged primarily in the production of food, but they increase their crop yields through technological innovations such as the plow.

Alienation   Loss of control over our creative human capacity to produce, separation from the products we make, and isolation from our fellow producers.

Amalgamation   The process through which a majority group and a minority group combine to form a new group.

Anomie   Durkheim's term for the loss of direction felt in a society when social control of individual behavior has become ineffective.

Anomie theory of deviance   Robert Merton's theory of deviance as an adaptation of socially prescribed goals or of the means governing their attainment, or both.

Anticipatory socialization   Processes of socialization in which a person "rehearses" for future positions, occupations, and social relationships.

Anti-Semitism   Anti-Jewish prejudice.

Apartheid   A former policy of the South African government, designed to maintain the separation of Blacks and other non-Whites from the dominant Whites.

Applied sociology   The use of the discipline of sociology with the specific intent of yielding practical applications for human behavior and organizations.

Argot   Specialized language used by members of a group or subculture.

Ascribed status   A social position assigned to a person by society without regard for the person's unique talents or characteristics.

Assimilation   The process through which a person forsakes his or her own cultural tradition to become part of a different culture.

Authority   Institutionalized power that is recognized by the people over whom it is exercised.

Avatar   A person's online representation as a character, whether in the form of a 2-D or 3-D image or simply through text.

Bilateral descent   A kinship system in which both sides of a person's family are regarded as equally important.

Black power   A political philosophy, promoted by many younger Blacks in the 1960s, that supported the creation of Black-controlled political and economic institutions.

Borderlands   The area of common culture along the border between Mexico and the United States.

Bourgeoisie   Karl Marx's term for the capitalist class, comprising the owners of the means of production.

Brain drain   The immigration to the United States and other industrialized nations of skilled workers, professionals, and technicians who are desperately needed in their home countries.

Bureaucracy   A component of formal organization that uses rules and hierarchical ranking to achieve efficiency.

Bureaucratization   The process by which a group, organization, or social movement increasingly relies on technical-rational decision making in the pursuit of efficiency.

Capitalism   An economic system in which the means of production are held largely in private hands and the main incentive for economic activity is the accumulation of profits.

Caste   A hereditary rank, usually religiously dictated, that tends to be fixed and immobile.

Causal logic   The relationship between a condition or variable and a particular consequence, with one event leading to the other.

Charismatic authority   Power made legitimate by a leader's exceptional personal or emotional appeal to his or her followers.

Class   A group of people who have a similar level of economic resources.

Class consciousness   In Karl Marx's view, a subjective awareness held by members of a class regarding their common vested interests and need for collective political action to bring about social change.

Class system   A social ranking based primarily on economic position in which achieved characteristics can influence social mobility.

Classical theory   An approach to the study of formal organizations that views workers as being motivated almost entirely by economic rewards.

Clinical sociology   The use of the discipline of sociology with the specific intent of altering social relationships or restructuring social institutions.

Closed system   A social system in which there is little or no possibility of individual social mobility.

Coalition   A temporary or permanent alliance geared toward a common goal.

Code of ethics   The standards of acceptable behavior developed by and for members of a profession.

Cognitive theory of development   The theory that children's thought progresses through four stages of development.

Cohabitation   The practice of living together as a male–female couple without marrying.

Colonialism   The maintenance of political, social, economic, and cultural dominance over a people by a foreign power for an extended period.

Color-blind racism   The use of race-neutral principles to perpetuate a racially unequal status quo.

Communism   As an ideal type, an economic system under which all property is communally owned and no social distinctions are made on the basis of people's ability to produce.

Conflict perspective   A sociological approach that assumes that social behavior is best understood in terms of tension between groups over power or the allocation of resources, including housing, money, access to services, and political representation.

Conformity   The act of going along with peers—individuals of our own status who have no special right to direct our behavior.

Contact hypothesis   The theory that in cooperative circumstances interracial contact between people of equal status will reduce prejudice.

Content analysis   The systematic coding and objective recording of data, guided by some rationale.

Control group   The subjects in an experiment who are not introduced to the independent variable by the researcher.

Control theory   A view of conformity and deviance that suggests that our connection to members of society leads us to systematically conform to society's norms.

Control variable   A factor that is held constant to test the relative impact of an independent variable.

Correlation   A relationship between two variables in which a change in one coincides with a change in the other.

Correspondence principle   The tendency of schools to promote the values expected of individuals in each social class and to prepare students for the types of jobs typically held by members of their class.

Counterculture   A subculture that deliberately opposes certain aspects of the larger culture.

Credentialism   An increase in the lowest level of education required to enter a field.

Crime   A violation of criminal law for which some governmental authority applies formal penalties.

Cross-tabulation   A table that shows the relationship between two or more variables.

Cultural capital   Our tastes, knowledge, attitudes, language, and ways of thinking that we exchange in interaction with others.

Cultural relativism   The viewing of people's behavior from the perspective of their own culture.

Cultural transmission   A school of criminology that argues that criminal behavior is learned through social interactions.

Cultural universal   A common practice or belief shared by all societies.

Culture lag   A period of adjustment when the nonmaterial culture is still struggling to adapt to new material conditions.

Culture shock   The feelings of disorientation, uncertainty, and even fear that people experience when they encounter unfamiliar cultural practices.

Culture   The totality of our shared language, knowledge, material objects, and behavior.

Culture-bound syndrome   A disease or illness that cannot be understood apart from some specific social context.

Curanderismo   Latino folk medicine, a form of holistic health care and healing.

Death rate   The number of deaths per 1000 population in a given year. Also known as the *crude death rate.*

Degradation ceremony   An aspect of the socialization process within some total institutions, in which people are subjected to humiliating rituals.

Deindustrialization   The systematic, widespread withdrawal of investment in basic aspects of productivity, such as factories and plants.

Democracy   In a literal sense, government by the people.

Denomination   A large, organized religion that is not officially linked to the state or government.

Dependency theory   An approach that contends that industrialized nations continue to exploit developing countries for their own gain.

Dependent variable   The variable in a causal relationship that is subject to the influence of another variable.

Deviance   Behavior that violates the standards of conduct or expectations of a group or society.

Dictatorship   A government in which one person has nearly total power to make and enforce laws.

Differential association   A theory of deviance that holds that violation of rules results from exposure to attitudes favorable to criminal acts.

Differential justice   Differences in the way social control is exercised over different groups.

Diffusion   The process by which a cultural item spreads from group to group or society to society.

Digital divide   The relative lack of access to the latest technologies among low-income groups, racial and ethnic minorities, rural residents, and the citizens of developing countries.

Discovery   The process of making known or sharing the existence of an aspect of reality.

Discrimination   The denial of opportunities and equal rights to individuals and groups because of prejudice or other arbitrary reasons.

Disengagement theory   A theory of aging that suggests that society and the aging individual mutually sever many of their relationships.

Domestic partnership   Two unrelated adults who share a mutually caring relationship, reside together, and agree to be jointly responsible for their dependents, basic living expenses, and other common necessities.

Dominant ideology   A set of cultural beliefs and practices that helps to maintain powerful social, economic, and political interests.

Downsizing   Reductions in a company's workforce as part of deindustrialization.

Dramaturgical approach   A view of social interaction in which people are seen as theatrical performers.

Ecclesia   A religious organization that claims to include most or all members of a society and is recognized as the national or official religion.

Economic system   The social institution through which goods and services are produced, distributed, and consumed.

Education   A formal process of instruction in which some people consciously teach while others adopt the social role of learner.

Egalitarian family   An authority pattern in which spouses are regarded as equals.

Elite model   A view of society as being ruled by a small group of individuals who share a common set of political and economic interests.

Endogamy   The restriction of mate selection to people within the same group.

Environmental justice   A legal strategy based on claims that racial minorities are subjected disproportionately to environmental hazards.

Equilibrium model   The view that society tends toward a state of stability or balance.

Established sect   A religious group that is the outgrowth of a sect, yet remains isolated from society.

Estate system   A system of stratification under which peasants were required to work land leased to them by nobles in exchange for military protection and other services. Also known as feudalism.

Esteem   The reputation that a specific person has earned within an occupation.

Ethnic group   A group that is set apart from others primarily because of its national origin or distinctive cultural patterns.

Ethnocentrism   The tendency to assume that one's own culture and way of life represent what's normal or are superior to all others.

Ethnography   The study of an entire social setting through extended systematic observation.

Evolutionary theory   A theory of social change that holds that society is moving in a definite direction.

Exogamy   The requirement that people select a mate outside certain groups.

Experiment   An artificially created situation that allows a researcher to manipulate variables.

Experimental group   The subjects in an experiment who are exposed to an independent variable introduced by a researcher.

Exploitation theory   A belief that views racial subordination in the United States as a manifestation of the class system inherent in capitalism.

Expressive leader   The person in the family who bears responsibility for the maintenance of harmony and internal emotional affairs.

Expulsion   The systematic removal of a group of people from society.

Extended family   A family in which relatives—such as grandparents, aunts, or uncles—live in the same household as parents and their children.

Face-work   The efforts people make to maintain a proper image and avoid public embarrassment.

False consciousness   A term used by Karl Marx to describe an attitude held by members of a class that does not accurately reflect their objective position.

Familism   Pride in the extended family, expressed through the maintenance of close ties and strong obligations to kinfolk outside the immediate family.

Feminism   The belief in social, economic, and political equality for women.

Folkway   Norms governing everyday behavior, whose violation raises comparatively little concern.

Force   The actual or threatened use of coercion to impose one's will on others.

Formal norm   A norm that generally has been written down and that specifies strict punishments for violators.

Formal organization   A group designed for a special purpose and structured for maximum efficiency.

Formal social control   Social control that is carried out by authorized agents, such as police officers, judges, school administrators, and employers.

Functionalist definition of families   A definition of families that focuses on what families do for society and for their members.

Functionalist definition of religion   The idea that religion unifies believers into a community through shared practices and a common set of beliefs relative to sacred things.

Functionalist perspective   A sociological approach that emphasizes the way in which the parts of a society are structured to maintain its stability.

Fundamentalism   Rigid adherence to core religious doctrines, often accompanied by a literal application of scripture or historical beliefs to today's world.

Gemeinschaft   A close-knit community, often found in rural areas, in which strong personal bonds unite members.

Gender role   Expectations regarding the proper behavior, attitudes, and activities of males or females.

Gender   The social and cultural significance that we attach to the biological differences of sex.

Generalized other   The attitudes, viewpoints, and expectations of society as a whole that a child takes into account in his or her behavior.

Genocide   The deliberate, systematic killing of an entire people or nation.

Gerontology   The study of the sociological and psychological aspects of aging and the problems of the aged.

Gesellschaft   A community, often urban, that is large and impersonal, with little commitment to the group or consensus on values.

Glass ceiling   An invisible barrier that blocks the promotion of a qualified individual in a work environment because of the individual's gender, race, or ethnicity.

Globalization   The worldwide integration of government policies, cultures, social movements, and financial markets through trade and the exchange of ideas.

Goal displacement   Overzealous conformity to official regulations of a bureaucracy.

Gross national income (GNI)   The total value of a nation's goods and services.

Group   Any number of people with shared norms, values, and goals who interact with one another on a regular basis.

Hate crime   A criminal offense committed because of the offender's bias against an individual based on race, religion, ethnicity, national origin, or sexual orientation.

Hawthorne effect   The unintended influence that observers of experiments can have on their subjects.

Health   As defined by the World Health Organization, a state of complete physical, mental, and social well-being, and not merely the absence of disease and infirmity.

Heterosexism   The systematic reinforcement of male–female sexual and marital relationships as normative.

Hidden curriculum   Standards of behavior that are deemed proper by society and are taught subtly in schools.

Holistic medicine   Therapies in which the health care practitioner considers the person's physical, mental, emotional, and spiritual characteristics.

Homogamy   The conscious or unconscious tendency to select a mate with personal characteristics and interests similar to one's own.

Horizontal mobility   The movement of an individual from one social position to another of the same rank.

Horticultural society   A preindustrial society in which people plant seeds and crops rather than merely subsist on available foods.

Hospice care   Treatment of the terminally ill in their own homes, or in special hospital units or other facilities, with the goal of helping them to die comfortably, without pain.

Human ecology   The area of study concerned with the interrelationships between people and their environment.

Human relations approach   An approach to the study of formal organizations that emphasizes the role of people, communication, and participation in a bureaucracy and tends to focus on the informal structure of the organization.

Human rights   Universal moral rights possessed by all people because they are human.

Hunting-and-gathering society   A preindustrial society in which people rely on whatever foods and fibers are readily available in order to survive.

Hypothesis   A testable statement about the relationship between two or more variables.

I   The acting self that exists in relation to the Me.

Ideal type   An abstract model of the essential characteristics of a phenomenon.

Impression management   The altering of the presentation of the self in order to create distinctive appearances and satisfy particular audiences.

Incest taboo   The prohibition of sexual relationships between certain culturally specified relatives.

Incidence   The number of new cases of a specific disorder that occur within a given population during a stated period.

Income   Wages and salaries measured over some period of time, such as per hour or year.

Independent variable   The variable in a causal relationship that causes or influences a change in a second variable.

Index crimes   The eight types of crime reported annually by the FBI in the *Uniform Crime Reports:* murder, forcible rape, robbery, aggravated assault, burglary, larceny-theft, motor vehicle theft, and arson.

Industrial society   A society that depends on mechanization to produce its goods and services.

Infant mortality rate   The number of deaths of infants under one year old per 1000 live births in a given year.

Influence   The exercise of power through a process of persuasion.

Informal economy   Transfers of money, goods, or services that are not reported to the government.

Informal norm   A norm that is generally understood but not precisely recorded.

Informal social control   Social control that is carried out casually by ordinary people through such means as laughter, smiles, and ridicule.

In-group   Any group or category to which people feel they belong.

Innovation   The process of introducing a new idea or object to a culture through discovery or invention.

Institutional discrimination   The denial of opportunities and equal rights to individuals and groups that results from the normal operations of a society.

Instrumental leader   The person in the family who bears responsibility for the completion of tasks, focuses on more distant goals, and manages the external relationship between one's family and other social institutions.

Interactionist perspective   A sociological approach that generalizes about everyday forms of social interaction in order to explain society as a whole.

Intergenerational mobility   Changes in the social position of children relative to their parents.

Interview   A face-to-face or telephone questioning of a respondent to obtain desired information.

Intragenerational mobility   Changes in social position within a person's adult life.

Invention   The combination of existing cultural items into a form that did not exist before.

Iron law of oligarchy   The principle that all organizations, even democratic ones, tend to develop into bureaucracies ruled by an elite few.

Kinship   The state of being related to others.

Labeling theory   An approach to deviance that attempts to explain why certain people are viewed as deviants while others engaged in the same behavior are not.

Laissez-faire   A form of capitalism under which people compete freely, with minimal government intervention in the economy.

Language   A system of shared symbols; it includes speech, written characters, numerals, symbols, and nonverbal gestures and expressions.

Law   Formal norms enforced by the state.

Liberation theology   Use of a church, primarily Roman Catholicism, in a political effort to eliminate poverty, discrimination, and other forms of injustice from a secular society.

Life chances   The opportunities people have to provide themselves with material goods, positive living conditions, and favorable life experiences.

Life course approach   A research orientation in which sociologists and other social scientists look closely at the social factors that influence people throughout their lives, from birth to death.

Looking-glass self   A theory that we become who we are based on how we think others see us.

Luddites   Rebellious craft workers in 19th-century England who destroyed new factory machinery as part of their resistance to the Industrial Revolution.

Machismo   A sense of virility, personal worth, and pride in one's maleness.

Macrosociology   Sociological investigation that concentrates on large-scale phenomena or entire civilizations.

Master status   A status that dominates others and thereby determines a person's general position in society.

Material culture   The physical or technological aspects of our daily lives.

Matriarchy   A society in which women dominate in family decision making.

Matrilineal descent   A kinship system in which only the mother's relatives are significant.

McDonaldization   The process by which the principles of efficiency, calculability, predictability, and control shape organization and decision making, in the United States and around the world.

Me   The socialized self that plans actions and judges performances based on the standards we have learned from others.

Mean   A number calculated by adding a series of values and then dividing by the number of values.

Mechanical solidarity   Social cohesion based on shared experiences, knowledge, and skills in which things function more or less the way they always have, with minimal change.

Median   The midpoint, or number that divides a series of values into two groups of equal numbers of values.

Microsociology   Sociological investigation that stresses the study of small groups and the analysis of our everyday experiences and interactions.

Midlife crisis   A stressful period of self-evaluation that begins at about age 40.

Minority group   A subordinate group whose members, even if they represent a numeric majority, have significantly less control or power over their own lives than the members of a dominant or majority group have over theirs.

Mixed economy   An economic system that combines elements of both capitalism and socialism.

Mode   The single most common value in a series of scores.

Model or ideal minority   A subordinate group whose members supposedly have succeeded economically, socially, and educationally despite past prejudice and discrimination.

Modernization   The far-reaching process by which nations pass from traditional forms of social organization toward those characteristic of post-Industrial Revolution societies.

Monarchy   A form of government headed by a single member of a royal family, usually a king, queen, or some other hereditary ruler.

Monogamy A form of marriage in which one woman and one man are married only to each other.

Monopoly Control of a market by a single business firm.

Morbidity rate The incidence of disease in a given population.

Mores Norms deemed highly necessary to the welfare of a society.

Mortality rate The incidence of death in a given population.

Multinational corporation A commercial organization that is headquartered in one country but does business throughout the world.

Multiple masculinities The idea that men learn and play a full range of gender roles.

Natural science The study of the physical features of nature and the ways in which they interact and change.

Neocolonialism Continuing dependence of former colonies on foreign countries.

New religious movement (NRM) or cult A small, alternative faith community that represents either a new religion or a major innovation in an existing faith.

New social movement An organized collective activity that addresses values and social identities, as well as improvements in the quality of life.

Nonmaterial culture Ways of using material objects, as well as customs, ideas, expressions, beliefs, knowledge, philosophies, governments, and patterns of communication.

Nonverbal communication The use of gestures, facial expressions, and other visual images to communicate.

Norm An established standard of behavior maintained by a society.

Nuclear family A married couple and their unmarried children living together.

Obedience Compliance with higher authorities in a hierarchical structure.

Observation A research technique in which an investigator collects information through direct participation and/or by closely watching a group or community.

Offshoring The transfer of work to foreign contractors.

Oligarchy A form of government in which a few individuals rule.

Open system A social system in which the position of each individual is influenced by his or her achieved status.

Operational definition Transformation of an abstract concept into indicators that are observable and measurable.

Organic solidarity A collective consciousness that rests on mutual interdependence, characteristic of societies with a complex division of labor.

Organized crime The work of a group that regulates relations among criminal enterprises involved in illegal activities, including prostitution, gambling, and the smuggling and sale of illegal drugs.

Out-group A group or category to which people feel they do not belong.

Party The capacity to organize to accomplish some particular goal.

Patriarchy A society in which men dominate in family decision making.

Patrilineal descent A kinship system in which only the father's relatives are significant.

Peace The absence of war, or more broadly, a proactive effort to develop cooperative relations among nations.

Personal sociology The process of recognizing the impact our individual position has on who we are and how we think and act, and of taking responsibility for the impacts our actions have on others.

Peter principle A principle of organizational life according to which every employee within a hierarchy tends to rise to his or her level of incompetence.

Pluralism Mutual respect for one another's cultures among the various groups in a society, which allows minorities to express their own cultures without experiencing prejudice.

Pluralist model A view of society in which many competing groups within the community have access to government, so that no single group is dominant.

Political system The social institution that is founded on a recognized set of procedures for implementing and achieving society's goals.

Politics In Harold Lasswell's words, "who gets what, when, and how."

Polyandry A form of polygamy in which a woman may have more than one husband at the same time.

Polygamy A form of marriage in which an individual may have several husbands or wives simultaneously.

Polygyny A form of polygamy in which a man may have more than one wife at the same time.

Postindustrial society A society whose economic system is engaged primarily in the processing and control of information.

Postmodern society A technologically sophisticated, pluralistic, interconnected, globalized society.

Power elite A small group of military, industrial, and government leaders who control the fate of the United States.

Power The ability to exercise one's will over others even if they resist.

Prejudice A negative attitude toward an entire category of people, often an ethnic or racial minority.

Prestige The respect and admiration that an occupation holds in a society.

Prevalence The total number of cases of a specific disorder that exist at a given time.

Primary group   A small group characterized by intimate, face-to-face association and cooperation.

Private troubles   Obstacles that individuals face as individuals rather than as a consequence of their social position.

Profane   The ordinary and commonplace elements of life, as distinguished from the sacred.

Proletariat   Karl Marx's term for the working class in a capitalist society.

Protestant ethic   Max Weber's term for the disciplined commitment to worldly labor driven by a desire to bring glory to God, shared by followers of Martin Luther and John Calvin.

Public issues   Obstacles that individuals in similar positions face; also referred to by sociologists as "social problems."

Public sociology   The process of bringing the insights gained through sociological observation and analysis into the public sphere, thereby seeking to bring about positive social change.

Qualitative research   Research that relies on what is seen in field or naturalistic settings more than on statistical data.

Quantitative research   Research that collects and reports data primarily in numerical form.

Questionnaire   A printed or written form used to obtain information from a respondent.

Racial formation   A sociohistorical process in which racial categories are created, inhibited, transformed, and destroyed.

Racial group   A group that is set apart from others because of physical differences that have taken on social significance.

Racial profiling   Any police-initiated action based on race, ethnicity, or national origin rather than on a person's behavior.

Racism   The belief that one race is supreme and all others are innately inferior.

Random sample   A sample for which every member of an entire population has the same chance of being selected.

Rational-legal authority   Authority based on formally agreed upon and accepted rules, principles, and procedures of conduct that are established in order to accomplish goals in the most efficient manner possible.

Reference group   Any group that individuals use as a standard for evaluating themselves and their own behavior.

Relative deprivation   The conscious feeling of a negative discrepancy between legitimate expectations and present actualities.

Relative poverty   A floating standard of deprivation by which people at the bottom of a society, whatever their lifestyles, are judged to be disadvantaged in comparison with the nation as a whole.

Reliability   The extent to which a measure produces consistent results.

Religious belief   A statement to which members of a particular religion adhere.

Religious experience   The feeling or perception of being in direct contact with the ultimate reality, such as a divine being, or of being overcome with religious emotion.

Religious ritual   A practice required or expected of members of a faith.

Remittances   The monies that immigrants return to their families of origin; also called *remesas*.

Representative democracy   A form of government in which certain individuals are selected to speak for the people.

Research design   A detailed plan or method for obtaining data scientifically.

Resocialization   The process of discarding former behavior patterns and accepting new ones as part of a transition in one's life.

Resource mobilization   The ways in which a social movement utilizes such resources as money, political influence, access to the media, and personnel.

Rite of passage   A ritual marking the symbolic transition from one social position to another.

Role conflict   The situation that occurs when incompatible expectations arise from two or more social statuses held by the same person.

Role exit   The process of disengagement from a role that is central to one's self-identity in order to establish a new role and identity.

Role strain   The difficulty that arises when the same social status imposes conflicting demands and expectations.

Role taking   The process of mentally assuming the perspective of another and responding from that imagined viewpoint.

Sacred   Elements beyond everyday life that inspire respect, awe, and even fear.

Sample   A selection from a larger population that is statistically representative of that population.

Sanction   A penalty or reward for conduct concerning a social norm.

Sandwich generation   The generation of adults who simultaneously try to meet the competing needs of their parents and their children.

Sapir-Whorf hypothesis   The idea that the language a person uses shapes his or her perception of reality and therefore his or her thoughts and actions.

Science   The body of knowledge obtained by methods based on systematic observation.

Scientific management approach   Another name for the classical theory of formal organizations.

Scientific method   A systematic, organized series of steps that ensures maximum objectivity and consistency in researching a problem.

Second shift The double burden—work outside the home followed by child care and housework—that many women face and few men share equitably.

Secondary analysis A variety of research techniques that make use of previously collected and publicly accessible information and data.

Secondary group A formal, impersonal group in which there is little social intimacy or mutual understanding.

Sect A relatively small religious group that has broken away from some other religious organization to renew what it considers the original vision of the faith.

Secularization Religion's diminishing influence in the public sphere, especially in politics and the economy.

Segregation The physical separation of two groups of people in terms of residence, workplace, and social events; often imposed on a minority group by a dominant group.

Self A distinct identity that sets us apart from others.

Serial monogamy A form of marriage in which a person may have several spouses in his or her lifetime, but only one spouse at a time.

Sex The biological differences between males and females.

Sexism The ideology that one sex is superior to the other.

Sick role Societal expectations about the attitudes and behavior of a person viewed as being ill.

Significant other An individual who is most important in the development of the self, such as a parent, friend, or teacher.

Single-parent family A family in which only one parent is present to care for the children.

Slavery A system of enforced servitude in which some people are owned by others as property.

Social change Significant alteration over time in behavior patterns and culture, including norms and values.

Social control The techniques and strategies for preventing deviant human behavior in any society.

Social disorganization theory The theory that attributes increases in crime and deviance to the absence or breakdown of communal relationships and social institutions, such as the family, school, church, and local government.

Social epidemiology The study of the distribution of disease, impairment, and general health status across a population.

Social inequality A condition in which members of society have different amounts of wealth, prestige, or power.

Social institution An organized pattern of beliefs and behavior centered on basic social needs.

Social interaction The shared experiences through which people relate to one another.

Social mobility Movement of individuals or groups from one position in a society's stratification system to another.

Social movement An organized collective activity to bring about or resist fundamental change in an existing group or society.

Social network A series of social relationships that links individuals directly to others, and through them indirectly to still more people.

Social role A set of expectations for people who occupy a given social position or status.

Social science The study of the social features of humans and the ways in which they interact and change.

Social structure The way in which a society is organized into predictable relationships.

Socialism An economic system under which the means of production and distribution are collectively owned.

Socialization The lifelong process through which people learn the attitudes, values, and behaviors appropriate for members of a particular culture.

Societal-reaction approach Another name for *labeling theory.*

Society The structure of relationships within which culture is created and shared through regularized patterns of social interaction.

Sociobiology The systematic study of how biology affects human social behavior.

Socioeconomic status (SES) A measure of class that is based on income, education, occupation, and related variables.

Sociological imagination An awareness of the relationship between who we are as individuals and the social forces that shape our lives.

Sociology The systematic study of the relationship between the individual and society and of the consequences of difference.

Status The social positions we occupy relative to others.

Status group People who have the same prestige or lifestyle, independent of their class positions.

Stereotype An unreliable generalization about all members of a group that does not recognize individual differences within the group.

Stigma A label used to devalue members of certain social groups.

Stratification A structured ranking of entire groups of people that perpetuates unequal economic rewards and power in a society.

Subculture A segment of society that shares a distinctive pattern of mores, folkways, and values that differs from the pattern of the larger society.

Substantive definition of religion The idea that religion has a unique content or substance relating to the sacred that separates it from other forms of knowledge and belief.

Substantive definition of the family A definition of the family based on blood, meaning shared genetic heritage, and law, meaning social recognition and affirmation of the bond including both marriage and adoption.

Survey   A study, generally in the form of an interview or questionnaire, that provides researchers with information about how people think and act.

Symbol   A gesture, object, or word that forms the basis of human communication.

Symbolic ethnicity   An ethnic identity that emphasizes concerns such as ethnic food or political issues rather than deeper ties to one's ethnic heritage.

Teacher-expectancy effect   The impact that a teacher's expectations about a student's performance may have on the student's actual achievements.

Technology   "Cultural information about how to use the material resources of the environment to satisfy human needs and desires."

Terrorism   The use or threat of violence against random or symbolic targets in pursuit of political aims.

Theory   In sociology a set of statements that seeks to explain problems, actions, or behavior.

Total institution   An institution that regulates all aspects of a person's life under a single authority, such as a prison, the military, a mental hospital, or a convent.

Totalitarianism   Virtually complete government control and surveillance over all aspects of a society's social and political life.

Tracking   The practice of placing students in specific curriculum groups on the basis of their test scores and other criteria.

Traditional authority   Legitimate power conferred by custom and accepted practice.

Trained incapacity   The tendency of workers in a bureaucracy to become so specialized that they develop blind spots and fail to notice potential problems.

Transnational crime   Crime that occurs across multiple national borders.

Underclass   The long-term poor who lack training and skills.

Validity   The degree to which a measure or scale truly reflects the phenomenon under study.

Value   A collective conception of what is considered good, desirable, and proper—or bad, undesirable, and improper—in a culture.

Value neutrality   Max Weber's term for objectivity of sociologists in the interpretation of data.

Variable   A measurable trait or characteristic that is subject to change under different conditions.

Vertical mobility   The movement of an individual from one social position to another of a different rank.

Vested interests   Those people or groups who will suffer in the event of social change and who have a stake in maintaining the status quo.

Victimization survey   A questionnaire or interview given to a sample of the population to determine whether people have been victims of crime.

Victimless crime   A term used by sociologists to describe the willing exchange among adults of widely desired, but illegal, goods and services.

War   Conflict between organizations that possess trained combat forces equipped with deadly weapons.

Wealth   The total of all a person's material assets, including savings, land, stocks, and other types of property, minus their debt at a single point in time.

White-collar crime   Illegal acts committed by affluent, "respectable" individuals in the course of business activities.

World systems analysis   A view of the global economic system as one divided between certain industrialized nations that control wealth and developing countries that are controlled and exploited.

A

AAMC. 2009. "Facts: Applicants, Matriculants, Graduates, and Residency Applicants." Association of American Medical Colleges, Washington, DC. Accessed June 27, 2009 (www.aamc.org/data/facts).

Aaronson, Daniel, and Bhashkar Mazumder. 2007. "Intergenerational Economic Mobility in the U.S., 1940 to 2000." FRB Chicago Working Paper No. WP 2005-12, revised February, 2007. Federal Reserve Bank of Chicago. Accessed June 21, 2008 (http://ssrn.com/abstract=869435).

AARP. 2004. "Baby Boomers Envision Retirement II: Survey of Baby Boomers' Expectations for Retirement." Prepared for AARP Environmental Analysis by Roper ASW. Washington, DC: AARP. Accessed May 13, 2008 (http://assets.aarp.org/rgcenter/econ/boomers_envision.pdf).

Abercrombie, Nicholas, Stephen Hill, and Bryan S. Turner. 1980. *The Dominant Ideology Thesis.* London: George Allen and Unwin.

———. 1990. *Dominant Ideologies.* Cambridge, MA: Unwin Hyman.

———. 2006. *The Penguin Dictionary of Sociology,* 5th ed. New York: Penguin Books.

Aberle, David E., A. K. Cohen, A. K. Davis, M. J. Leng Jr., and F. N. Sutton. 1950. "The Functional Prerequisites of a Society." *Ethics* 60 (January): 100–111.

Adair-Toteff, Christopher. 2005. "Max Weber's Charisma." *Journal of Classical Sociology* 5 (2): 189–204.

Adams, Jimi. 2007. "Stained Glass Makes the Ceiling Visible: Organizational Opposition to Women in Congregational Leadership." *Gender and Society* 21 (February): 80–115.

Adams, Samantha, and Antoinette de Bont. 2007. "Information Rx: Prescribing Good Consumerism and Responsible Citizenship." *Health Care Analysis* 15 (4): 273–290.

Addams, Jane. 1910. *Twenty Years at Hull-House.* New York: Macmillan.

———. 1930. *The Second Twenty Years at Hull-House.* New York: Macmillan.

Adler, Patricia A., and Peter Adler. 1985. "From Idealism to Pragmatic Detachment: The Academic Performance of College Athletes." *Sociology of Education* 58 (October): 241–250.

——— 1996. "Preadolescent Clique Stratification and the Hierarchy of Identity." *Sociological Inquiry* 66 (2): 111–142.

——— 2004. *Paradise Laborers: Hotel Work in the Global Economy.* Ithaca, NY: Cornell University Press.

——— 2007. "The Demedicalization of Self-Injury: From Psychopathology to Sociological Deviance." *Journal of Contemporary Ethnography* 36 (October):537–570.

Adler, Patricia A., Peter Adler, and John M. Johnson. 1992. "Street Corner Society Revisited." *Journal of Contemporary Ethnography* 21 (April): 3–10.

Adler, Patricia A., Steve J. Kless, and Peter Adler. 1992. "Socialization to Gender Roles: Popularity Among Elementary School Boys and Girls." *Sociology of Education* 65 (July): 169–187.

Administration for Children and Families. 2008. "Trends in Foster Care and Adoption—FY 2002-FY 2007." Department of Health and Human Services, Washington, DC. Accessed May 27, 2009 (http://www.acf.hhs.gov/programs/cb/stats_research/afcars/trends.htm).

Allen, John L., Jr. 2008. "The Pope vs. the Pill." *New York Times,* July 27. Accessed June 30, 2009 (www.nytimes.com/2008/07/27/opinion/27allen.html).

Allen, John L. 2008. *Student Atlas of World Politics,* 8th ed. New York: McGraw-Hill.

Allport, Gordon W. 1979. *The Nature of Prejudice,* 25th anniversary ed. Reading, MA: Addison-Wesley.

Alter, Alexandria. 2007. "Is This Man Cheating on His Wife?" *The Wall Street Journal,* August 10, p. W1. Accessed June 3, 2008 (http://online.wsj.com/article/SB118670164592393622.html).

Alvord, Lori Arviso, and Elizabeth Cohen Van Pelt. 1999. *The Scalpel and the Silver Bear.* New York: Bantam.

Alzheimer's Association. 2009. *2009 Alzheimer's Disease Facts and Figures.* Chicago: Alzheimer's Assocation. Accessed June 26, 2009 (www.alz.org/national/documents/report_alzfactsfigures2009.pdf).

Amato, Paul R. and Alan Booth. 1997. *A Generation at Risk.* Cambridge, MA: Harvard University Press.

Amer, Mildred L. 2008b. "African American Members of the United States Congress: 1870–2008." CRS Report for Congress, Congressional Research Service, Washington, DC. Accessed June 21, 2009 (www.senate.gov/reference/resources/pdf/RL30378.pdf).

Amer, Mildred, and Jennifer E. Manning. 2008. "Membership of the 111th Congress: A Profile." CRS Report for Congress, Congressional Research Service, Washington, DC. Accessed June 3, 2009 (http://assets.opencrs.com/rpts/R40086_20081231.pdf).

American Academy of Cosmetic Surgery. 2009. "American Academy of Cosmetic Surgery 2008 Procedural Census." Accessed May 19, 2009 (http://www.cosmeticsurgery.org/media/2008_procedural_survey_results.pdf).

American Bar Association. 2009. "Death Penalty Moratorium Implementation Project." ABA Section of Individual Rights and Responsibilities. Accessed May 20, 2009 (http://www.abanet.org/moratorium/home.html).

American Federation of Teachers. 2007. *Survey and Analysis of Teacher Salary Trends 2005.* Washington, DC: AFT.

American Lung Association. 2003. "Scenesmoking." Accessed December 19 (www.scenesmoking.org).

American National Election Studies. 2009. "The ANES Guide to Public Opinion and Electoral Behavior." Accessed June 30, 2009 (www.electionstudies.org/nesguide/nesguide.htm).

American Sociological Association. 1997. *Code of Ethics.* Washington, DC: American Sociological Association (www.asanet.org/members/ecoderev.html).

———. 2006a. *Careers in Sociology with an Undergraduate Degree in Sociology,* 7th ed. Washington, DC: ASA.

———. 2006b. "What Can I Do with a Bachelor's Degree in Sociology." *A National Survey of Seniors Majoring in Sociology: First Glances: What Do They Know and Where Are They Going?* Washington DC: American Sociological Association. Accessed August 2, 2008 (http://www.asanet.org/galleries/default-file/b&b_first_report_final.pdf).

Amnesty International. 1994. *Breaking the Silence: Human Rights Violations Based on Sexual Orientation.* New York: Amnesty International.

———. 2009a. "Mexico: Two Years On: The Law to Protect Women Has Had No Impact at State Level." Accessed June 15, 2009 (www.amnesty.org/en/for-media/press-releases/mexico-two-years-law-protect-women-has-had-no-impact-state-level-2009012).

———. 2009b. "Sexual Orientation and Gender Identity." Accessed June 15, 2009 (www.amnesty.org/en/sexual-orientation-and-gender-identity).

Anagnostou, Yiorgos. 2009a. "A Critique of Symbolic Ethnicity: The Ideology of Choice?" *Ethnicities* 9(1): 94–122.

———. 2009b. "About Facts and Fictions: Reply to Herbert Gans and Mary Waters." *Ethnicities* 9(1):.

Anderson, David and Mykol C. Hamilton. 2005. "Gender Role Stereotyping of Parents in Children's Picture Books: The Invisible Father." *Sex Roles* 52: 145–151.

Anderson, Elijah. 1990. *Streetwise: Race, Class, and Change in an Urban Community.* Chicago: University of Chicago Press.

Anderson, Terry H. 2007. *The Sixties,* 3d ed. Englewood Cliffs, NJ: Prentice Hall.

Angier, Natalie. 2000. "Do Races Differ? Not Really, Genes Show." *New York Times,* August 22, p. F6. Accessed June 30, 2008 (http://query.nytimes.com/gst/fullpage.html?res=9E07E7DF1E3EF931A1575BC0A9669C8B63&scp=2&sq=natalie+angier&st=nyt).

Anti-Defamation League. 2008. "Anti-Semitic Incidents Decline for Third Straight Year in U.S., According to Annual ADL Audit." Accessed March 5 (www.adl.org).

Arab American Institute. 2008. "Arab Americans: Demographics." Accessed July 1, 2008 (http://www.aaiusa.org/arab-americans/22/demographics).

Arora, Neeraj K., Bradford W. Hesse, Barbara K. Rimer, K. Viswanath, Marla L. Clayman, and Robert T. Croyle. 2008. "Frustrated and Confused: The American Public Rates Its Cancer-Related Information-Seeking Experiences." *Journal of General Internal Medicine* 23 (3): 223–228.

Astin, Alexander, Sarah A. Parrott, William S. Korn, and Linda J. Sax. 1994. *The American Freshman: Thirty Year Trends.* Los Angeles: Higher Education Research Institute.

Atchley, Robert C. 1976. *The Sociology of Retirement.* New York: Wiley.

Atchley, Robert C., and Amanda S. Barusch. 2004. *Social Forces and Agency: An Introduction to Social Gerontology,* 10th ed. Belmont, CA: Thompson.

Avise, John C. 2004. *The Hope, Hype, and Reality of Genetic Engineering: Remarkable Stories from Agriculture, Industry, Medicine, and the Environment.* New York: Oxford University Press.

B

Baby Name Wizard. 2009. "NameVoyager." Accessed August 2, 2009 (www.babynamewizard.com).

Baby Name Wizard. 2009. "NameVoyager." Accessed April 27, 2009 (www.babynamewizard.com).

Baer, Hans. 2008. "Global Warming as a By-product of the Capitalist Treadmill of Production and Consumption—The Need for an Alternative Global System." *The Australian Journal of Anthropology* 19 (1): 58–62.

Baer, Hans, and Ian Coulter. 2008. "Introduction—Taking Stock of Integrative Medicine: Broadening Biomedicine or Co-Option of Complementary and Alternative Medicine?" *Health Sociology Review* 17 (4): 331–341.

Bahr, Peter Riley. 2008. "*Cooling Out* in the Community College: What Is the Effect of Academic Advising on Students' Chances of Success?" *Research in Higher Education* 49: 704–732.

Bainbridge, William Sims. 2007. "The Scientific Research Potential of Virtual Worlds." *Science* 317 (July 27): 472–476.

Balch, Robert W. 2006. "The Rise and Fall of Aryan Nations: A Resource Mobilization Perspective." *Journal of Political & Military Sociology* 34 (1): 81–113.

Baldwin, James. [1965] 1985. "White Man's Guilt." Pp. 409–414 in *The Price of the Ticket: Collected Non-Fiction, 1948–1985.* New York: St. Martin's Press.

Banerjee, Neela. 2006. "Clergywomen Find Hard Path to Bigger Pulpit." *New York Times,* August 26, pp. A1, A11.

Barna Group. 2001. "Religious Beliefs Vary Widely by Denomination." Ventura, CA: The Barna Group, Ltd. Accessed June 1, 2009 (http://www.barna.org/barna-update/article/5-barna-update/53-religious-beliefs-vary-widely-by-denomination).

Barnes, Patricia M., Eve Powell-Griner, Kim McFann, and Richard L. Nahin. 2004. *Complimentary and Alternative Medicine Use Among Adults, United States, 2002.* Advance Data from Vital and Health Statistics, No. 343. Hyattsville, MD: National Center for Health Statistics. Accessed July 5, 2008 (http://nccam.nih.gov/news/camsurvey_fs1.htm).

Barr, Donald A. 2008. *Health Disparities in the United States: Social Class, Race, Ethnicity, and Health.* Baltimore: Johns Hopkins University Press.

Barrett, David B., Todd M. Johnson, and Peter F. Crossing. 2006. "The 2005 Annual Megacensus of Religions." Pp. 282–283 in 2006 *Book of the Year.* Chicago: Encyclopedia Britannica.

Barrionuevo, Alexei. 2008. "Amazon's 'Forest Peoples' Seek a Role in Striking Global Climate Agreements." *New York Times,* April 6, p. 6.

Barta, Patrick, and Joel Millman. 2009. "The Great U-Turn." *The Wall Street Journal,* June 6. Accessed June 15, 2009 (http://online.wsj.com/article_email/SB124424701106590613-lMyQjAxMDI5NDA0NzIwNDc3Wj.html).

Basso, Keith H. 1972. "Ice and Travel Among the Fort Norman Slave: Folk Taxonomies and Cultural Rules." *Language in Society* 1 (March): 31–49.

Baudrillard, Jean. [1981] 1994. *Simulacra and Simulation.* Ann Arbor: The University of Michigan Press.

Baumert, Kevin, Timothy Herzog, and Jonathan Pershing. 2005. *Navigating the Numbers: Greenhouse Gas Data and International Climate Policy.* Washington, DC: World Resources Institute. Accessed August 6, 2009 (http://pdf.wri.org/navigating_numbers.pdf).

BBC News. 2005a. "Indonesian Village Report: January 12, 2005." Accessed January 19 (www.theworld.org).

BBC. 2006. "Madrid Bans Waifs from Catwalks." September 13. Accessed June 7, 2008 (http://news.bbc.co.uk/2/hi/europe/5341202.stm).

Beagan, Brenda L. 2001. " 'Even If I Don't Know What I'm Doing I Can Make It Look Like I Know What I'm Doing': Becoming a Doctor in the 1990s." *Canadian Review of Sociology and Anthropology* 38: 275–292.

Bearman, Peter S., James Moody, and Katherine Stovel. 2004. "Chains of Affection: The Structure of Adolescent Romantic and Sexual Networks." *American Journal of Sociology* 110 (July): 44–91.

Beauvoir, Simone de. 1952. *The Second Sex.* New York: Knopf.

Becker, Howard S. 1952. "Social Class Variations in the Teacher–Pupil Relationship." *Journal of Educational Sociology* 25 (April): 451–465.

———. 1963. *The Outsiders: Studies in the Sociology of Deviance.* New York: Free Press.

———, ed. 1964. *The Other Side: Perspectives on Deviance.* New York: Free Press.

———. 1973. *The Outsiders: Studies in the Sociology of Deviance,* rev. ed. New York: Free Press.

Beeghley, Leonard. 2007. *The Structure of Social Stratification in the United States,* 5th ed. Boston: Allyn & Bacon.

Belkin, Lisa. 2008. "When Mom and Dad Share It All." *New York Times* June 15. Accessed June 17, 2009 (www.nytimes.com/2008/06/15/magazine/15parenting-t.html).

Bell, Daniel. 1953. "Crime as an American Way of Life." *Antioch Review* 13 (Summer): 131–154.

———. 1999. *The Coming of Post-Industrial Society: A Venture in Social Forecasting.* With new foreword. New York: Basic Books.

———. 2001. *Liberation Theology After the End of History: The Refusal to Cease Suffering.* New York: Routledge.

Bendick, Marc, Jr., Charles W. Jackson, and J. Horacio Romero. 1993. *Employment Discrimination Against Older Workers: An Experimental Study of Hiring Practices.* Washington, DC: Fair Employment Council of Greater Washington.

Benhorin, Shira, and Susan D. McMahon. 2008. "Exposure to Violence and Aggression: Protective Roles of Social Support Among Urban African American Youth." *Journal of Community Psychology* 36 (6): 723–743.

Bennett, V., S. Dávila-Poblete, and M.N. Rico, eds. 2005. *Opposing Currents: The Politics of Water and Gender in Latin America.* Pittsburgh, PA: University of Pittsburgh Press.

Benschop, Yvonne. 2009. "The Micro-Politics of Gendering in Networking." *Gender, Work & Organization* 16 (2): 217–237.

Berenson, Alex, and Diana B. Henriques. 2008. "Look at Wall St. Wizard Finds Magic Had Skeptics." *New York Times,* December 12. Accessed May 21, 2009 (http://www.nytimes.com/2008/12/13/business/13fraud.html).

Bergen, Raquel Kennedy. 2006. *Marital Rape: New Research and Directions.* Harrisburg, PA: VAW Net.

Berger, Peter, and Thomas Luckmann. 1966. *The Social Construction of Reality.* New York: Doubleday.

Berger, Peter. 1969. *The Sacred Canopy: Elements of a Sociological Theory of Religion.* Garden City, NY: Anchor Books.

Berland, Gretchen K. 2001. "Health Information on the Internet: Accessibility, Quality, and Readability in English and Spanish." *Journal of the American Medical Association* 285 (March 23): 2612–2621.

Berlin, Brent, and Paul Kay. 1991. *Basic Color Terms: Their Universality and Evolution.* Berkeley: University of California Press.

Bernasek, Anna. 2006. "A Poverty Line That's Out of Date and Out of Favor." *New York Times,* August 14, p. 8.

Bernburg, Jón Gunnar, Marvin D. Krohn, and Craig Rivera. 2006. "Official Labeling, Criminal Embeddedness, and Subsequent Delinquency: A Longitudinal Test of Labeling Theory." *Journal of Research in Crime & Delinquency* 43 (1): 67–88.

Bernstein, Basil. 1962. "Social Class, Linguistic Codes and Grammatical Elements." *Language and Speech* 5: 221–240.

Bianchi, Suzanne M., and Daphne Spain. 1996. "Women, Work, and Family in America." *Population Bulletin* 51 (December).

Bianchi, Suzanne M., John P. Robinson, and Melissa A. Milkie. 2006. *Changing Rhythms of American Family Life.* New York: Russell Sage Foundation.

Bishaw, Alemayehu, and Jessica Semega. 2008. *Income, Earnings, and Poverty Data from the 2007 American Community Survey.* American Community Survey Reports, ACS-09. Washington, DC: U.S. Government Printing Office. Accessed June 20, 2009 (www.census.gov/prod/2008pubs/acs-09.pdf).

Bisi, Simonetta. 2002. "Female Criminality and Gender Difference." *International Review of Sociology* 12 (1): 23–43.

Black, Donald. 1995. "The Epistemology of Pure Sociology." *Law and Social Inquiry* 20 (Summer): 829–870.

Black, Thomas. 2009. "Mexican Factories May Cut Fewer Jobs Than in 2001." Bloomberg News June 1. Accessed June 15, 2009 (www.bloomberg.com/apps/news?pid=20601086&sid=aFT3Y.rFittM&refer=news).

Blaine, Tasha. 2009. *Just Like Family: Inside the Lives of Nannies, the Parents They Work for, and the Children They Love.* Boston: Houghton Mifflin Harcourt.

Blau, Peter M., and Marshall W. Meyer. 1987. *Bureaucracy in Modern Society,* 3d ed. New York: Random House.

Blau, Peter M., and Otis Dudley Duncan. 1967. *The American Occupational Structure.* New York: Wiley.

Blauner, Robert. 1972. *Racial Oppression in America.* New York: Harper and Row.

Bligh, Michelle C., and Jeffrey C. Kohles. 2009. "The Enduring Allure of Charisma: How Barack Obama Won the Historic 2008 Presidential Election." *Leadership Quarterly* 20 (3): 483–492.

Blinder, Alan S. 2006. "Offshoring: The Next Industrial Revolution." *Foreign Affairs* (March/April).

Blumer, Herbert. 1955. "Collective Behavior." Pp. 165–198 in *Principles of Sociology,* 2d ed., ed. Alfred McClung Lee. New York: Barnes and Noble.

———. 1969. *Symbolic Interactionism: Perspective and Method.* Englewood Cliffs, NJ: Prentice Hall.

Boaz, Rachel Floersheim. 1987. "Early Withdrawal from the Labor Force." *Research on Aging* 9 (December): 530–547.

Bogan, Jesse, Kerry A. Dolan, Christopher Helman, and Nathan Vardi. 2008. "Failing State." *Forbes* December 22. Accessed June 15, 2009 (www.forbes.com/global/2008/1222/058.html).

Bonilla-Silvia, Eduardo. 2004. "From Bi-Racial to Tri-Racial: Towards a New System of Racial Stratification in the USA." *Ethics and Racial Studies* 27 (November): 931–950.

Booth, William. 2009. "In Mexico, the U.S. Downturn Hits Home." *Washington Post,* June 14. Accessed June 15, 2009 (www.washingtonpost.com/wp-dyn/content/story/2009/06/14/ST2009061400169.html).

Bortolotti, Dan. 2006. *Hope in Hell: Inside the World of Doctors Without Borders.* Buffalo, NY: Firefly Books.

Bourdieu, Pierre. 1962. *The Algerians.* Preface by Raymond Aron. Boston: Beacon Press.

———. 1984. *Distinction: A Social Critique of the Judgment of Taste.* Cambridge, MA: Harvard University Press.

———. 1998a. *Acts of Resistance: Against the Tyranny of the Market.* New York: New Press.

———. 1998b. *On Television.* New York: New Press.

Boushey, Heather. 2009. "Gender and the Recession: Recession Hits Traditionally Male Jobs Hardest." Center for American Progress, Washington, DC. Accessed June 4, 2009 (www.americanprogress.org/issues/2009/05/gender_recession.html).

Bowles, Samuel, and Herbert Gintis. 1976. *Schooling in Capitalistic America: Educational Reforms and the Contradictions of Economic Life.* New York: Basic Books.

Brannigan, Augustine, and William Zwerman. 2001. "The Real 'Hawthorne Effect.'" *Society* 38 (Jan/Feb): 55–60.

Bray, Hiawatha. 2009. "Finding A Way Around Iranian Censorship." *Boston Globe,* June 19. Accessed July 1, 2009 (www.boston.com/business/technology/articles/2009/06/19/activists_utilizing_twitter_web_proxies_to_sidestep_iranian_censorship/).

Brenner, Elsa. 2008. "Everything You Need, in One Giant Package." *New York Times,* April 6. Accessed June 18, 2009 (www.nytimes.com/2008/04/06/realestate/06live.html).

Brewer, Cynthia A., and Trudy A. Suchan. 2001. *Mapping Census 2000: The Geography of U.S. Diversity.* Washington, DC: U.S. Government Printing Office.

Brewer, Rose M., and Nancy A. Heitzeg. 2008. "The Racialization of Criminal Punishment." *American Behavioral Scientist* 51 (January): 625–644.

Brown, David K. 2001. "The Social Sources of Educational Credentialism: Status Cultures, Labor Markets, and Organizations." *Sociology of Education* 74 (Extra Issue): 19–34.

Brown, George M. 2006. "Degrees of Doubt: Legitimate, Real and Fake Qualifications in a Global Market." *Journal of Higher Education Policy & Management* (1): 71–79.

Brown, Robert McAfee. 1980. *Gustavo Gutierrez.* Atlanta: John Knox.

Brown, Tyson H., and David F. Warner. 2008. "Divergent Pathways? Racial/Ethnic Differences in Older Womens Labor Force Withdrawal." *Journals of Gerontology Series B: Psychological Sciences & Social Sciences* 36B (3): S122–S134.

Bruce, Steve. 2000. *Choice and Religion: A Critique of Rational Choice Theory.* New York: Oxford University Press.

Buckle, Chris, Y. M. Lisa Chuah, Calvin S. Fones, and Albert H. C. Wong. 2007. "A Conceptual History of Koro." *Transcultural Psychiatry* 44 (1): 27–43.

Bucks, Brian K., Arthur B. Kennickell, Traci L. Mach, and Kevin B. Moore. 2009. "Changes in U.S. Family Finances from 2004 to 2007: Evidence from the Survey of Consumer Finances." *Federal Reserve Bulletin* 95 (February): A1–A55.

Budig, Michelle J. 2002. "Male Advantage and the Gender Composition of Jobs: Who Rides the Glass Escalator?" *Social Problems* 49 (2): 258–277.

Bullard, Robert D., ed. 2007. *Growing Smarter: Achieving Livable Communities, Environmental Justice, and Regional Equity.* Cambridge: MIT Press.

Bullard, Robert. 2000. *Dumping in Dixie: Race, Class, and Environmental Quality,* 3d ed. Boulder, CO: Westview Press.

Bulle, Wolfgang F. 1987. *Crossing Cultures? Southeast Asian Mainland.* Atlanta: Centers for Disease Control and Prevention.

Burawoy, Michael. 2004. "Public Sociologies: Contradictions, Dilemmas, and Possibilities." *Social Forces* 82: 1603–1618.

Bureau of Labor Statistics. 2007. "Labor Force (Demographic) Data." February 13. Accessed February 28 (www.bls.gov).

———. 2008. "Employment Characteristics of Families in 2007." Accessed May 26, 2009 (http://www.bls.gov/news.release/famee.toc.htm).

———. 2008. "Number of Jobs Held, Labor Market Activity, and Earnings Growth Among the Youngest Baby Boomers: Results From a Longitudinal Survey." *BLS News* June 27. Accessed May 6, 2009 (http://www.bls.gov/news.release/pdf/nlsoy.pdf).

———. 2008b. "Highlights of Women's Earnings in 2007." U.S. Department of Labor, October, Report 1008. Accessed June 17, 2009 (www.bls.gov/cps/cpswom2007.pdf).

———. 2009a. "Mexico: Hourly Compensation Costs for Workers in Maquiladora Manufacturing Export Industries, 1975–2006." Accessed June 14, 2009 (http://stats.bls.gov/fls/flshcindmaq.htm).

———. 2009b. "International Comparisons of Hourly Compensation Costs in Manufacturing, 2007." *Bureau of Labor Statistics News:* March 26. Accessed June 14, 2009 (www.bls.gov/news.release/pdf/ichcc.pdf).

Bureau of the Census. 1975. *Historical Statistics of the United States, Colonial Times to 1970.* Washington, DC: U.S. Government Printing Office.

———. 1994. *Statistical Abstract of the United States, 1994.* Washington, DC: U.S. Government Printing Office.

———. 1998. "Race of Wife by Race of Husband." Internet release of June 10.

———. 2004. *Statistical Abstract of the United States, 2004–2005.* Washington, DC: U.S. Government Printing Office.

————. 2005a. *Statistical Abstract of the United States, 2006.* Washington, DC: U.S. Government Printing Office.

————. 2005b. "Total Midyear Population for the World: 1950–2050." Updated April 26. Accessed June 1 (www.census.gov/ipc/www/worldpop.html).

————. 2005c. *Florida, California and Texas Future Population Growth.* Census Bureau Reports, CB05-52. Washington, DC: U.S. Government Printing Office.

————. 2005d. "International Data Base." Accessed April 26 (www.census.gov/ipc/www/idbnew.html).

————. 2007a. *Statistical Abstract of the United States, 2008.* Washington, DC: U.S. Government Printing Office.

————. 2007b. "American Community Survey 2006" (www.census.gov).

————. 2007c. "Current Population Survey, 2005 to 2007. Annual Social and Economic Supplements." Accessed December 29 (www.census.gov/hhes/www/income/income06/statemhi3.html).

————. 2008a. *Statistical Abstract of the United States.* Washington, DC: U.S. Government Printing Office.

————. 2008b. "Total Midyear Population for the World: 1900–2050." Data updated March 27, 2008. Accessed April 9 (www.census.gov).

Burkeman, Oliver. 2007. "Virtual World Wakes Up to Violent Protest." *Manchester Guardian,* February 16, p. 6.

Bush, Jason. 2006. "What's Behind Russia's Crime Wave?" *Business-Week,* October 19. Accessed Wednesday, May 20, 2009 (http://www.businessweek.com/globalbiz/content/oct2006/gb20061019_110749.htm).

Butler, Daniel Allen. 1998. *Unsinkable: The Full Story.* Mechanicsburg, PA: Stackpole Books.

Butler, Robert N. 1990. "A Disease Called Ageism." *Journal of American Geriatrics Society* 38 (February): 178–180.

C

Call, V. R., and Teachman, J. D. 1991. "Military Service and Stability in the Family Life Course." *Military Psychology* 3:233–250.

Callaway, Ewen. 2008. "Polygamy Is the Key to a Long Life." *New Scientist* August 19. Accessed May 26, 2009 (http://www.newscientist.com/article/dn14564-polygamy-is-the-key-to-a-long-life.html).

Cañas, Jesus, and Robert W. Gilmer. 2009. "The Maquiladora's Changing Geography." Federal Reserve Bank of Dallas, *Southwest Economy:* Second Quarter. Accessed June 14, 2009 (http://dallasfed.org/research/swe/2009/swe0902c.cfm).

Caplan, Ronald L. 1989. "The Commodification of American Health Care." *Social Science and Medicine* 28 (11): 1139–1148.

Caplow, Theodore, and Louis Hicks. 2002. *Systems of War and Peace,* 2d ed. Lanham, MD: University Press of America.

Carey, Anne R., and Elys A. McLean. 1997. "Heard It Through the Grapevine?" *USA Today,* September 15, p. B1.

Carmichael, Mary. 2007. "Troubled Waters." *Newsweek* 149 (June 4), pp. 52–56.

Carr, Deborah. 2007. "Baby Blues." *Contexts* (Spring): 62.

Carson, Rachel. 1962. *Silent Spring.* Boston: Houghton Mifflin.

Carty, Victoria, and Jake Onyett. 2006. "Protest, Cyberactivism and New Social Movements: The Reemergence of the Peace Movement Post 9/11." *Social Movement Studies* 5 (3): 229–249.

Casey, John. 2004. "Is Your Nest Too Full?" WebMD May 17. Accessed May 27, 2009 (http://www.medicinenet.com/script/main/art.asp?articlekey=52508).

Castañeda, Jorge G. 1995. "Ferocious Differences." *Atlantic Monthly* 276 (July): pp. 68–69, 71–76.

Castells, Manuel. 1997. *The Power of Identity.* Vol. 1 of *The Information Age: Economy, Society and Culture.* London: Blackwell.

————. 1998. *End of Millennium.* Vol. 3 of *The Information Age: Economy, Society and Culture.* London: Blackwell.

————. 2000. *The Information Age: Economy, Society and Culture* (3 vols.), 2d ed. Oxford and Malden, MA: Blackwell.

Catalyst. 2007. *2007 Catalyst Census of Women Board Directors, Corporate Officers, and Top Earners.* New York: Catalyst.

————. 2008. "Women and Minorities on Fortune 100 Boards." The Prout Group, the Executive Leadership Council, and the Hispanic Association on Corporate Responsibility. Accessed June 30 (http://www.catalyst.org/file/86/1-17-08%20abd%20study.pdf).

Cavalli-Sforza, L. Luca, Paolo Menozzi, and Alberto Piazza. 1994. *The History and Geography of Human Genes.* Princeton, NJ: Princeton University Press.

CBS News. 1979. Transcript of *Sixty Minutes* segment, "I Was Only Following Orders." March 31, pp. 2–8.

Center for American Women and Politics. 2009. "Facts on Women Officeholders, Candidates and Voters." Eagleton Institute of Politics, Rutgers University, New Brunswick, NJ. Accessed June 18, 2009 (www.cawp.rutgers.edu/fast_facts/index.php).

Centers for Disease Control and Prevention. 2007a. *HIV/AIDS Surveillance Report.* Revised June 2007. Atlanta, GA: CDC.

————. 2007b. "U.S. Public Health Service Syphilis Study at Tuskegee." Accessed April 25 (www.cdc.gov).

————. 2007c. "HIV/AIDS Among Women." Revised June 2007. Accessed March 21 (www.cdc.gov.hiv.topics/women/resources/factsheets/women.htm).

Centers for Medicare and Medicaid Services. 2009a. "National Health Expenditure Data: Historical—Table 1." Department of Health and Human Services. Accessed June 26, 2009 (www.cms.hhs.gov/NationalHealthExpendData/downloads/tables.pdf).

————. 2009b. "National Health Expenditure Data: Projected—Table 1." Department of Health and Human Services. Accessed June 26, 2009 (www.cms.hhs.gov/NationalHealthExpendData/downloads/proj2008.pdf).

Cevallos, Diego. 2009. "Indigenous Woman Fights for Rights." *Inter Press Service,* April 1. Accessed June 15, 2009 (www.ips.org/mdg3/mexico-indigenous-woman-on-the-offensive/#more-21).

Chambliss, William. 1973. "The Saints and the Roughnecks." *Society* 11 (November/December): 24–31.

Charter, David, and Jill Sherman. 1996. "Schools Must Teach New Code of Values." *London Times,* January 15, p. 1.

Chase-Dunn, Christopher, and Peter Grimes. 1995. "World-Systems Analysis." Pp. 387–417 in *Annual Review of Sociology,* 1995, ed. John Hagan. Palo Alto, CA: Annual Reviews.

Chen, Shaohua, and Martin Ravallion. 2008. "The Developing World Is Poorer Than We Thought, But No Less Successful in the Fight Against Poverty." Policy Research Working Paper 4703, The World Bank Development Research Group, August 2008. Accessed June 13, 2009 (www-wds.worldbank.org/external/default/WDSContentServer/IW3P/IB/2008/08/26/000158349_20080826113239/Rendered/PDF/WPS4703.pdf).

————. 2009. "The Impact of the Global Financial Crisis on the World's Poorest." April 30. Accessed June 13, 2009 (www.voxeu.org/index.php?q=node/3520).

Cheng, Shu-Ju Ada. 2003. "Rethinking the Globalization of Domestic Service." *Gender and Society* 17 (2): 166–186.

Cherkas, L. F., A. Aviv, A. M. Valdes, J. L. Hunkin, J. P. Gardner, G. L. Surdulescu, M. Kimura, and T. D. Spector. 2006. "The Effects of Social Status on Biological Aging as Measured by White-Blood-Cell Telomere Length." *Aging Cell* 5: 361–365.

Cherlin, Andrew J. 2009. *The Marriage-Go-Round: The State of Marriage and the Family in America Today.* New York: Knopf.

Cherlin, Andrew. 2004. "The Deinstitutionalization of American Marriage." *Journal of Marriage and the Family* 66: 848–861.

————. 2006. "On Single Mothers 'Doing' Family." *Journal of Marriage and Family* 68 (November): 800–803.

————. 2008a. "Can the Left Learn the Lessons of Welfare Reform?" *Contemporary Sociology* 37 (March): 101–104.

————. 2008b. *Public and Private Families: An Introduction,* 5th ed. New York: McGraw-Hill.

Chesney-Lind, Meda. 1989. "Girls' Crime and Women's Place: Toward a Feminist Model of Female Delinquency." *Crime and Delinquency* 35: 5–29.

Christensen, Kathleen. 1990. "Bridges over Troubled Water: How Older Workers View the Labor Market." Pp. 175–207 in *Bridges to Retirement,* ed. Peter B. Doeringer. Ithaca, NY: IRL Press.

Cigar, Norman. 1995. *Genocide in Bosnia: The Policy of "Ethnic Cleansing."* College Station: Texas A&M University Press.

Civic Ventures. 1999. *The New Face of Retirement: Older Americans, Civic Engagement, and the Longevity Revolution.* Washington, DC: Peter D. Hart Research Associates.

Clammer, John. 2009. "Sociology and Beyond: Towards a Deep Sociology." *Asian Journal of Social Science* 37 (3): 332–346.

Clark, Burton. 1960. "The 'Cooling-Out' Function in Higher Education." *American Journal of Sociology* 65: 569–576.

———. 1980. "The 'Cooling-Out' Function Revisited." *New Directions for Community Colleges* 32: 15–31.

Clark, Burton, and Martin Trow. 1966. "The Organizational Context." Pp. 17–70 in *The Study of College Peer Groups,* ed. Theodore M. Newcomb and Everett K.Wilson. Chicago: Aldine.

Clarke, Adele E., Janet K. Shim, Laura Maro, Jennifer Ruth Fusket, and Jennifer R. Fishman. 2003. "Bio Medicalization: Technoscientific Transformations of Health, Illness, and U.S. Biomedicine." *American Sociological Review* 68 (April): 161–194.

Clarke, Edward H. 1874. *Sex in Education; or, A Fair Chance for Girls.* Boston: James R. Osgood.

Clausen, Christopher. 2002. "To Have . . . or Not to Have." *Utne Reader* (July–August): 66–70.

Clinard, Marshall B., and Robert F. Miller. 1998. *Sociology of Deviant Behavior,* 10th ed. Fort Worth, TX: Harcourt Brace.

CNN. 2006. "Skinny Models Banned from Catwalk." September 13. Accessed June 7, 2008 (http://www.cnn.com/2006/WORLD/europe/09/13/spain.models/index.html).

———. 2008. "Exit Polls." CNN Election Center 2008. Accessed May 27, 2009 (http://www.cnn.com/ELECTION/2008/results/polls/#val=USP00p3).

Cognard-Black, Andrew J. 2004. "Will They Stay, or Will They Go? Sex-Atypical Work Among Token Men Who Teach?" *The Sociological Quarterly* 45:113–39.

Colby, David C. 1986. "The Voting Rights Act and Black Registration in Mississippi." *Publius* 16 (Fall): 123–137.

Cole, Elizabeth S. 1985. "Adoption, History, Policy, and Program." Pp. 638–666 in *A Handbook of Child Welfare,* ed. John Laird and Ann Hartman. New York: Free Press.

Coleman, James William. 2006. *The Criminal Elite: Understanding White-Collar Crime,* 6th ed. New York: Worth.

Collins, Gail. 2003. *America's Women.* New York: HarperCollins.

Collins, Randall. 1986. *Weberian Sociological Theory.* New York: Cambridge University Press.

———. 1995. "Prediction in Macrosociology: The Case of the Soviet Collapse." *American Journal of Sociology* 100 (May): 1552–1593.

Collura, Heather. 2007. "Roommate Concerns Fed by Facebook." *USA Today,* August 8, p. D6.

Commission for the Status of Women. 2009. "The Fifty-Third Session of the Commission on the Status of Women." Division for the Advancement of Women, Department of Economic and Social Affairs. March 2–13, Washington, DC. Accessed June 6, 2009 (http://www.un.org/womenwatch/daw/csw/53sess.htm).

Commission on Civil Rights. 1976. *A Guide to Federal Laws and Regulations Prohibiting Sex Discrimination.* Washington, DC: U.S. Government Printing Office.

Commoner, Barry. 1971. *The Closing Circle.* New York: Knopf.

———. 1990. *Making Peace with the Planet.* New York: Pantheon Books.

Congressional Budget Office. 2008. "Historical Effective Tax Rates, 1979 to 2005: Supplement with Additional Data on Sources of Income and High-Income Households." U.S. Congress, Washington, DC. Accessed June 6, 2009 (www.cbo.gov/ftpdocs/98xx/doc9884/12-23-EffectiveTaxRates_Letter.pdf).

Connell, R. W. 2002. *Gender.* Cambridge, UK: Polity Press.

———. 2005. *Masculinities,* 2d ed. Berkeley: University of California Press.

Conrad, Peter. 2007. *The Medicalization of Society: On the Transformation of Human Conditions into Treatable Disorders.* Baltimore, MD: Johns Hopkins University Press.

Cooley, Charles. H. 1902. *Human Nature and the Social Order.* New York: Scribner.

Coontz, Stephanie. 1992. *The Way We Never Were: American Families and the Nostalgia Trap.* New York: Basic Books.

———. 2005. *Marriage, a History: From Obedience to Intimacy or How Love Conquered Marriage.* New York: Viking.

———. 2006. "A Pop Quiz on Marriage." *New York Times,* February 19, p. 12.

———. 2008. "The Future of Marriage." *Cato Unbound,* January 14. Accessed June 9 (http://www.cato-unbound.org/2008/01/14/stephanie-coontz/the-future-of-marriage).

Cooper, Bruce S., and John Sureau. 2007. "The Politics of Homeschooling: New Developments, New Challenges." *Educational Policy* 21 (January and March): 110–131.

Cooper, K., S. Day, A. Green, and H. Ward. 2007. "Maids, Migrants and Occupational Health in the London Sex Industry. *Anthropology and Medicine* 14 (April) 41–53.

Corak, Miles. 2006. "Do Poor Children Become Poor Adults? Lessons from a Cross Country Comparison of Generational Earnings Mobility." Institute for the Study of Labor (IZA) Discussion Paper No. 1993, March. Accessed June 24, 2008 (http://papers.ssrn.com/sol3/papers.cfm?abstract_id=889034).

Corbett, Christianne, Catherine Hill, and Andresse St. Rose. 2008. *Where the Girls Are: The Facts About Gender Equity in Education.* Washington, DC: AAUW. Accessed May 29, 2009 (http://www.aauw.org/research/upload/whereGirlsAre.pdf).

Correll, Shelley J., Stephen Benard, and In Paik. 2007. "Getting a Job: Is There a Motherhood Penalty?" *AJS* 112 (5): 1297–1338.

Coser, Rose Laub. 1984. "American Medicine's Ambiguous Progress." *Contemporary Sociology* 13 (January): 9–13.

Côté, James E. 2000. *Arrested Adulthood: The Changing Nature of Identity and Maturity in the Late World.* New York: New York University.

Cox, Oliver C. 1948. *Caste, Class, and Race: A Study in Social Dynamics.* Detroit: Wayne State University Press.

Crosnoe, Robert, and Glen H. Elder, Jr. 2002. "Successful Adaptation in the Later Years: A Life Course Approach to Aging." *Social Psychology Quarterly* (4): 309–328.

Cross, Simon, and Barbara Bagilhole. 2002. "Girls' Jobs for the Boys? Men, Masculinity and Non-traditional Occupations." *Gender, Work, and Organization* 9 (April):204–226.

Croucher, Sheila L. 2004. *Globalization and Belonging: The Politics of Identity in a Changing World.* Lanham, MD: Rowman and Littlefield.

Crouse, Kelly. 1999. "Sociology of the Titanic." *Teaching Sociology Listserv,* May 24.

CTIA. 2009. "Background on CTIA's Semi-Annual Wireless Industry Survey." CTIA-The Wireless Association. Accessed May 2, 2009 (http://files.ctia.org/pdf/CTIA_Survey_Year-End_2008_Graphics.pdf).

Cullen, Lisa Takevchi. 2007. "Till Work Do Us Part." *Time,* October 8, pp. 63–64.

Cumming, Elaine, and William E. Henry. 1961. *Growing Old: The Process of Disengagement.* New York: Basic Books.

Currie, Elliot. 1985. *Confronting Crime: An American Challenge.* New York: Pantheon Books.

———. 1998. *Crime and Punishment in America.* New York: Metropolitan Books.

Curtiss, Susan. 1977. *Genie: A Psycholinguistic Study of a Modern Day "Wild Child."* New York: Academic Press.

D

Dahl, Robert A. 1961. *Who Governs?* New Haven, CT: Yale University Press.

Daisey, Mike. 2002. *21 Dog Years: Doing Time @ Amazon.com.* New York: Free Press.

Dalla, Rochelle L., and Wendy C. Gamble. 2001. "Teenage Mothering and the Navajo Reservation: An Examination of Intergovernmental Perceptions and Beliefs." *American Indian Culture and Research Journal* 25 (1): 1–19.

Dao, James. 1995. "New York's Highest Court Rules Unmarried Couples Can Adopt." *New York Times,* November 3, pp. A1, B2.

Darwin, Charles. 1859. *On the Origin of Species.* London: John Murray.

David, Gary. 2004. "Scholarship on Arab Americans Distorted Past 9/11." *Al Jadid* (Winter/Spring): 26–27.

———. 2008. "Arab Americans." Pp. 84–87 in *Encyclopedia of Race, Ethnicity, and Society,* vol. 1, ed. Richard T. Schaefer. Thousands Oaks, CA: Sage.

Davies, James B., Susanna Sandström, Anthony Shorrocks, and Edward N. Wolff. 2007. "Estimating the Level and Distribution of Global Household Wealth." Economic Policy Research Institute, Working Paper 2007–5, London, Ontario. Accessed June 12, 2009 (http://economics.uwo.ca/centres/epri/wp2007/Davies_05.pdf).

———. 2008. "The World Distribution of Household Wealth." United Nations University—World Institute for Development Economics Research, Discussion Paper No. 2008/03, Helsinki, Finland. Accessed June 12, 2009 (www.wider.unu.edu/publications/working-papers/discussion-papers/2008/en_GB/dp2008–03/).

Davis, Darren W., and Brian D. Silver. 2003. "Stereotype Threat and Race of Interviewer Effects in a Survey on Political Knowledge." *American Journal of Political Science* 47 (1): 33–45.

Davis, Gerald. 2003. *America's Corporate Banks Are Separated by Just Four Handshakes.* Accessed March 7 (www.bus.umich.edu/research/ davis.html).

———. 2004. "American Cronyism: How Executive Networks Inflated the Corporate Bubble." *Contexts* (Summer): 34–40.

Davis, James A., Tom W. Smith, and Peter V. Marsden. 2007. *General Social Surveys, 1972–2006: Cumulative Codebook.* Chicago: National Opinion Research Center.

Davis, James Allan, and Tom W. Smith. 2007. *General Social Surveys, 1972–2006.* Storrs, CT: Roper Center.

Davis, Joseph E. 2006. "How Medicalization Lost Its Way." *Society* 43 (6): 51–56.

Davis, Kingsley. 1940. "Extreme Social Isolation of a Child." *American Journal of Sociology* 45 (January): 554–565.

———. 1947. "A Final Note on a Case of Extreme Isolation." *American Journal of Sociology* 52 (March): 432–437.

———, and Wilbert E. Moore. 1945. "Some Principles of Stratification." *American Sociological Review* 10 (April): 242–249.

Dawson, Lorne. 2009. "Church-Sect-Cult: Constructing Typologies of Religious Groups." Pp. 525–544 in *The Oxford Handbook of the Sociology of Religion,* ed. Peter B. Clarke. New York: Oxford University Press.

Death Penalty Information Center. 2009. "Facts About the Death Penalty: May 1, 2009." Washington, DC. Accessed May 19, 2009 (http://www.deathpenaltyinfo.org/documents/FactSheet.pdf).

Deflem, Mathieu. 2005. "'Wild Beasts Without Nationality': The Uncertain Origins of Interpol, 1898–1910." Pp. 275–285 in *Handbook of Transnational Crime and Justice,* ed. Philip Rerchel. Thousand Oaks, CA: Sage.

DeMott, Benjamin. 1990. *The Imperial Middle: Why Americans Can't Think Straight About Class.* New York: William Morrow.

DeNavas-Walt, Carmen, Bernadette D. Proctor, and Jessica Smith. 2007. "Income, Poverty, and Health Insurance Coverage in the United States: 2006." *Current Population Reports,* Ser. P-60, No. 233. Washington, DC: U.S. Government Printing Office.

———. 2008. "Income, Poverty, and Health Insurance Coverage in the United States: 2007." *Current Population Reports,* P60–235. Washington, DC: U.S. Government Printing Office.

DeParle, Jason. 2007. "In a World on the Move, a Tiny Land Strains to Cope." *New York Times,* June, p. A1.

Department of Health and Human Services. 2007. "HIV/AIDS Surveillance Report." Cases of HIV infection and AIDS in the United States and Dependent Areas, Volume 19. Centers for Disease Control and Prevention, Atlanta, GA. June 25, 2009 (www.cdc.gov/hiv/topics/surveillance/resources/reports/2007report/pdf/2007SurveillanceReport.pdf).

Department of Homeland Security. 2006. *The Federal Response to Hurricane Katrina: Lessons Learned.* Washington, DC: U.S. Government Printing Office.

Department of Justice. 2000. *The Civil Liberties Act of 1988: Redress for Japanese Americans.* Accessed June 29 (http://www.usdoj.gov/crt/ora/main. html).

Devitt, James. 1999. *Framing Gender on the Campaign Trail: Women's Executive Leadership and the Press.* New York: Women's Leadership Conference.

Dickens, Charles. 1843. *A Christmas Carol.* London: Chapman and Hall. Accessed July 7, 2008 (www.gutenberg.org/dirs/4/46/46-h/46-h.htm).

Doeringer, Peter B., ed. 1990. *Bridges to Retirement: Older Workers in a Changing Labor Market.* Ithaca, NY: ILR Press.

Domhoff, G. William. 1978. *Who Really Rules? New Haven and Community Power Reexamined.* New Brunswick, NJ: Transaction.

———. 2006. *Who Rules America?* 5th ed. New York: McGraw-Hill.

———. 2009. "The Power Elite and Their Challengers: The Role of Nonprofits in American Social Conflict." *American Behavioral Scientist* 52 (7): 955–973.

Doress, Irwin, and Jack Nusan Porter. 1977. *Kids in Cults: Why They Join. Why They Join, Why They Stay, Why They Leave.* Brookline, MA: Reconciliation Associates.

Dorn, Stan. 2008. *Uninsured and Dying Because of It.* Washington, DC: Urban Institute.

Dressler, William W., Kathryn S. Oths, and Clarence C. Gravlee. 2005. "Racial and Ethnicity in Public Health Research: Models to Explain Health Disparities." Pp. 231–252 in *Annual Review of Anthropology 2005,* ed. William H. Durham. Palo Alto, CA: Annual Reviews.

Du Bois, W.E.B. [1903] 1994. *The Souls of Black Folk.* New York: Dover.

———. [1909] 1970. *The Negro American Family.* Cambridge, MA: M.I.T. Press.

———. [1940] 1968. *Dusk of Dawn.* New York: Schocken Books.

Dubner, Stephen J. 2007. "Everything You Always Wanted to Know About Street Gangs (But Didn't Know Whom to Ask)." Freakanomics blog, *New York Times,* August 6. Accessed June 10, 2008 (http://freakonomics.blogs.nytimes.com/2007/08/06/everything-you-always-wanted-to-know-about-street-gangs-but-didnt-know-whom-to-ask/).

Dugger, Celia. 2006. "Peace Prize to Pioneer of Loans for Those Too Poor to Borrow." *New York Times,* October 14, pp. A1, A6.

Dukes, Richard L., Tara M. Bisel, Karoline N. Burega, Eligio A. Lobato, and Matthew D. Owens. 2003. "Expression of Love, Sex, and Hurt in Popular Songs: A Content Analysis of All-Time Greatest Hits." *Social Science Journal:* 643–650.

Duneier, Mitchell. 1994a. "On the Job, but Behind the Scenes." *Chicago Tribune,* December 26, pp. 1, 24.

———. 1994b. "Battling for Control." *Chicago Tribune,* December 28, pp. 1, 8.

———. 1999. *Sidewalk.* New York: Farrar, Straus and Giroux.

Durden, T. Elizabeth, and Robert A. Hummer. 2006. "Access to Healthcare Among Working-Age Hispanic Adults in the United States." *Social Science Quarterly* 87 (December): 1319–1343.

Durkheim, Émile. [1887] 1972. "Religion and Ritual." Pp. 219–238 in *Émile Durkheim: Selected Writings,* ed. A. Giddens. Cambridge: Cambridge University Press.

———. [1893] 1933. *Division of Labor in Society,* trans. George Simpson. New York: Free Press.

———. [1897] 1951. *Suicide,* trans. John A. Spaulding and George Simpson. New York: Free Press.

———. [1925] 1961. Moral Education: A Study in the Theory and Application of the Sociology of Education. Glencoe, IL: Free Press.

———. [1895] 1964. *The Rules of Sociological Method,* trans. Sarah A. Solovay and John H. Mueller. New York: Free Press.

E

Ebaugh, Helen Rose Fuchs. 1988. *Becoming an Ex: The Process of Role Exit.* Chicago: University of Chicago Press.

Economic Mobility Project. 2007. *Economic Mobility of Immigrants in the United States.* Washington, DC: Pew Charitable Trust.

The Economist. 2008a. "Maharishi Mahesh Yogi." (February 16): 95.

———. 2008b. "A Ravenous Dragon: A Special Report on China's Quest for Resources." (March 15): 1–22.

EEOC. 2008. "Age Discrimination in Employment Act (ADEA) Charges FY 1997– FY 2007." Washington, DC: U.S Equal Employment Opportunity Commission. Accessed June 27 (http://www.eeoc.gov/stats/adea.html).

Ehrenreich, Barbara. 2001. *Nickel and Dimed: On (Not) Getting By in America.* New York: Metropolitan.

Ehrlich, Paul R. 1968. *The Population Bomb.* New York: Ballantine Books.

Ehrlich, Paul R., and Anne H. Ehrlich. 1990. *The Population Explosion.* New York: Simon and Schuster.

Ehrlich, Paul R., and Katherine Ellison. 2002. "A Looming Threat We Won't Face." *Los Angeles Times,* January 20, p. M6.

Elliott, Michael. 2005. "Hopelessly Divided: Being a Fan Is Like Having Your Own Personal Time Machine." *Time Magazine,* June 20, p. 76.

Ellison, Brandy. 2008. "Tracking." Pp. 301–304 in *Encyclopedia of Race, Ethnicity, and Society,* vol. 2, ed. Richard T. Schaefer. Thousand Oaks, CA: Sage.

Ellison, Ralph. 1952. *Invisible Man.* New York: Random House.

Ellul, Jacques. 1964. *The Technological Society.* New York: Knopf.

Eltman, Frank. 2007. "Wealthy Couple Charged with Slavery." Associated Press, May 24.

Ely, Robin J. 1995. "The Power of Demography: Women's Social Construction of Gender Identity at Work." *Academy of Management Journal* 38 (3): 589–634.

Emerson, Michael O., David Hartman, Karen Cook, and Douglas Massey. 2006. "The Rise of Religious Fundamentalism." *Annual Review of Sociology* 32: 127–144.

Energy Information Administration. 2008. "Emissions of Greenhouse Gases in the United States 2007." Office of Integrated Analysis and Forecasting, U.S. Department of Energy, Washington, DC. Accessed June 28, 2009 (www.eia.doe.gov/oiaf/1605/ggrpt/pdf/0573(2007).pdf).

Engels, Friedrich [1884] 1959. "The Origin of the Family, Private Property, and the State." Pp. 392–394 in *Marx and Engels: Basic Writings on Politics and Philosophy,* ed. Lewis Feuer. Garden City, NY: Anchor Books.

Escárcega, Sylvia. 2008. "Mexico." Pp. 898–902 in *Encyclopedia of Race, Ethnicity, and Society,* vol. 2, ed. Richard T. Schaefer. Thousand Oaks, CA: Sage.

Etaugh, Claire. 2003. "Witches, Mothers and Others: Females in Children's Books." *Hilltopics* (Winter): 10–13.

Etcoff, Nancy, Susie Orbach, Jennifer Scott, and Heidi D'Agostino. 2004. "The Real Truth About Beauty: A Global Repor—Findings of the Global Study on Women, Beauty and Well-Being." Commissioned by Dove, a Unilever Beauty Brand. Accessed June 28, 2008 (http://www.campaignforrealbeauty.com/uploadedfiles/DOVE_white_paper_final.pdf).

Etzioni, Amitai. 1965. *Political Unification.* New York: Holt, Rinehart and Winston.

———. 2007. "Are New Technologies the Enemy of Privacy?" *Knowledge, Technology & Policy* 20 (2): 115–119.

Eureka County. 2006. "EPA Hears Testimony on Proposed Radiation Rule." *Nuclear Waste Office Newsletter* (Eureka County Yucca Mountain Information Office) 11 (Winter).

ExecuNet. 2009. "2009 Executive Job Market Intelligence Report—Executive Summary." Accessed May 12, 2009 (http://www.execunet.com/promo/pdf/EUN2009Survey_summary.pdf).

F

Faith, Nazila. 2005. "Iranian Cleric Turns Blogger in Campaign for Reform." *New York Times,* January 16, p. 4.

Farley, Melissa, and Victor Malarek. 2008. "The Myth of the Victimless Crime." *New York Times,* March 12. Accessed May 20, 2009 (http://www.nytimes.com/2008/03/12/opinion/12farley.html).

Farr, Grant M. 1999. *Modern Iran.* New York: McGraw-Hill.

Fausto-Sterling, A. 2000. "The Five Sexes, Revisited." *The Sciences* (July/August): 18–23.

Fearon, James D., and David D. Laitin. 2003. "Ethnicity, Insurgency, and Civil War." *American Political Science Review* 97 (March): 75–90.

Featherman, David L., and Robert M. Hauser. 1978. *Opportunity and Change.* New York: Aeodus.

Federal Bureau of Investigation. 2009. "Organized Crime." Accessed May 20, 2009 (http://www.fbi.gov/hq/cid/orgcrime/ocshome.htm).

Felson, David, and Akis Kalaitzidis. 2005. "A Historical Overview of Transnational Crime." Pp. 3–19 in *Handbook of Transnational Crime and Justice,* ed. Philip Reichel. Thousand Oaks, CA: Sage.

Ferree, Myra Marx. 2005. "It's Time to Mainstream Research on Gender." *Chronicle of Higher Education* 51 (August 21): B10.

Ferree, Myra Marx, and David A. Merrill. 2000. "Hot Movements, Cold Cognition: Thinking about Social Movements in Gendered Frames." *Contemporary Society* 29 (May): 454–462.

Feuer, Alan. 2002. "Haven for Workers in Bronx Evolves for Their Retirement." *New York Times,* August 5. Accessed June 27, 2008 (http://query.nytimes.com/gst/fullpage.html?res=9D07E7D9133BF936A3575BC0A9649C8B63).

Fields, Jason. 2004. "America's Families and Living Arrangements: 2003." *Current Population Reports,* Ser. P-20, No. 553. Washington, DC: U.S. Government Printing Office.

Finder, Alan. 2006. "For Some, Online Persona Undermines a Résumé." *New York Times,* June 11. Accessed June 30, 2009 (www.nytimes.com/2006/06/11/us/11recruit.html).

Fine, Gary C. 2008. " Robbers Cave." Pp. 1163–1164 in *Encyclopedia of Race, Ethnicity, and Society,* vol. 3, ed. Richard T. Schaefer. Thousand Oaks, CA: Sage.

Finkel, Steven E., and James B. Rule. 1987. "Relative Deprivation and Related Psychological Theories of Civil Violence: A Critical Review." *Research in Social Movements* 9: 47–69.

Fiscella Kevin, and Kathleen Holt. 2008. "Racial Disparity in Hypertension Control: Tallying the Death Toll." *Annals of Family Medicine* 6: 497–502.

Fishman, Charles. 2006. *The Wal-Mart Effect: How the World's Most Powerful Company Really Works—and How It's Transforming the American Economy.* New York: Penguin Books.

Fitzgerald, Kathleen J., and Diane M. Rodgers. 2000. "Radical Social Movement Organization: A Theoretical Model." *The Sociological Quarterly* 41 (4): 573–592.

Flynn, Patrice. 2007. "Microfinance: The Newest Finance Technology of the Washington Consensus." *Challenge* 50 (March/April): 110–121.

Forsythe, David P. 1990. "Human Rights in U.S. Foreign Policy: Retrospect and Prospect." *Political Science Quarterly* 105 (3): 435–454.

Fortune. 2008. "Global 500: World's Largest Corporations." *Fortune* 158 (July 21): 165–174. Accessed June 12, 2009 (http://money.cnn.com/magazines/fortune/global500/2008/full_list).

Foy, Paul. 2006. "Interior Rejects Goshute Nuclear Waste Stockpile." *Indian Country Today* 20 (September 18): 1.

Franklin, John Hope, and Alfred A. Moss. 2000. *From Slavery to Freedom: A History of African Americans,* 8th ed. Upper Saddle River, NJ: Prentice Hall.

Freidson, Eliot. 1970. *Profession of Medicine.* New York: Dodd, Mead.

French, Howard W. 2000. "The Pretenders." *New York Times Magazine,* December 3, pp. 86–88.

———. 2004b. "China's Textbooks Twist and Omit History." *New York Times* (December 6), p. A10.

Freudenburg, William R. 2005. "Seeing Science, Courting Conclusions: Reexamining the Intersection of Science, Corporate Cash, and the Law." *Sociological Forum* 20 (March): 3–33.

Freudenheim, Milt. 2005. "Help Wanted: Oldest Workers Please Apply." *New York Times,* March 23, pp. A1, C3.

Frey, William H. 2007. "Mapping the Growth of Older America: Seniors and Boomers in the Early 21st Century." Living Cities Census Series, The Brookings Institution, May. Accessed June 18, 2009 (www.brookings.edu/~/media/Files/rc/papers/2007/0612demographics_frey/0612demographics_frey.pdf).

Fridlund, Alan. J., Paul Erkman, and Harriet Oster. 1987. "Facial Expressions of Emotion; Review of Literature 1970–1983." Pp. 143–224 in *Nonverbal Behavior and Communication,* 2d ed., ed. Aron W. Seigman and Stanley Feldstein. Hillsdale, NJ: Lawrence Erlbaum.

Friedan, Betty. 1963. *The Feminine Mystique.* New York: Dell.

———. 1993. *The Fountain of Age.* New York: Simon and Schuster.

Friedman, Thomas L. 2005. *The World Is Flat: A Brief History of the Twenty-first Century.* New York: Farrar, Straus and Giroux.

Friman, H. Richard. 2004. "The Great Escape? Globalization, Immigrant Entrepreneurship and the Criminal Economy." *Review of International Political Economy* 11 (1): 98–131.

Fulcher, James. 2004. *Capitalism: A Very Short Introduction.* New York: Oxford University Press.

Furedi, Frank. 2006. "The End of Professional Dominance." *Society* 43 (6): 14–18.

Furman, Nelly, David Goldberg, and Natalia Lusin. 2007. "Enrollments in Languages Other Than English in United States Institutions of Higher Education, Fall 2006." The Modern Language Association, November 13. Accessed May 3, 2009 (http://www.mla.org/pdf/06enrollmentsurvey_final.pdf).

Furstenberg, Frank F. 2007. "The Making of the Black Family: Race and Class in Qualitative Studies in the Twentieth Century." *Annual Review of Sociology* 33: 429–448.

Furstenberg, Sheela Kennedy, Jr., Vonnie C. McCloyd, Rubén G. Rumbaut, and Richard A. Setterstein Jr. 2004. "Growing Up Is Harder to Do." *Contexts* 3: 33–41.

Fuson, Ken. 2008. "Raid Mars Future for 3 Graduating Today from Postville." *Des Moines Register,* May 25. Accessed June 29, 2008 http://www.desmoinesregister.com/apps/pbcs.dll/article?AID=/20080525/NEWS/805250327/1001&theme=POSTVILLE_ICE_RAID).

Fussell, Elizabeth. 2006. "Leaving New Orleans: Social Stratification, Networks, and Hurricane Evacuation." Understanding Katrina: Perspectives from the Social Sciences, Social Science Research Council, Brooklyn, NY. Accessed June 10, 2009 (http://understandingkatrina.ssrc.org/Fussell/).

Fuwa, Makiko. 2004. "Macro-Level Gender Inequality and the Division of Household Labor in 22 Countries." *American Sociological Review* 69 (December): 751–767.

G

Gallup. 2008a. "Abortion." Accessed March 6 (www.gallup.com).
———. 2008b. "Homosexual Relations." Accessed March 6 (www.gallup.com).
———. 2008c. "Religion." Accessed March 14 (www.gallup.com).
———. 2008d. "Environment." Accessed March 18 (www.gallup.com).
———. 2009. "Military and National Defense." Washington, DC: Gallup, Inc. Accessed June 3, 2009 (www.gallup.com/poll/1666/military-national-defense.aspx).

Gallup Opinion Index. 1978. "Religion in America, 1977–1978." (January).

Gans, Herbert. 1971. "The Uses of Poverty: The Poor Pay All." *Social Policy* (July/August): 20–24.
———. 2009. "Reflections on Symbolic Ethnicity: A Response to Y. Anagnostou." *Ethnicities* 9(1): 123–130.

Garcia-Moreno, Claudia, Henrica A.F.M. Jansen, Mary Ellsberg, Lori Heise, and Charlotte Watts. 2005. *WHO Multi-Country Study on Women's Health and Domestic Violence Against Women.* Geneva, Switzerland: WHO.

Gardner, Gary. 2008. "Microfinance Surging." *World Watch* 21 (November/December): 30.

Gardner, Gary, Erik Assadourian, and Radhika Sarin. 2004. "The State of Consumption Today." Pp. 3–21 in *State of the World 2004,* ed. Brian Halweil and Lisa Mastny. New York: Norton.

Garfinkel, Harold. 1956. "Conditions of Successful Degradation Ceremonies." *American Journal of Sociology* 61 (March): 420–424.

Gaviria, Marcela, and Martin Smith. 2009. "The Madoff Affair." *PBS Frontline,* May 12. Accessed May 21, 2009 (http://www.pbs.org/wgbh/pages/frontline/madoff).

Geist, Claudia. 2005. "The Welfare State and the Home: Regime Differences in the Domestic Division of Labour." *European Sociological Review 2005* 21(1):23–4.

Gendell, Murray. 2008. "Older Workers: Increasing Their Labor Force Participation and Hours of Work." *Monthly Labor Review* (January): 41–54.

Gentleman, Amelia. 2007. "Police Ignore Serial Killings in Delhi Slum, Exposing Unequal Justice for India's Poor." *New York Times,* January 7, p. 8.

Gerhardt, Uta. 2002. Talcott Parsons: An Intellectual Biography. New York: Cambridge University Press.

Gerth, H. H., and C. Wright Mills. 1958. *From Max Weber: Essays in Sociology.* New York: Galaxy.

Gheytanchi, Elham. 2009. "Iranian Women Lead The Protests." *San Francisco Chronicle,* June 29. Accessed June 30, 2009 (www.sfgate.com/cgi-bin/article.cgi?f=/c/a/2009/06/29/ED8618EMUC.DTL).

Giandrea, Michael D., Kevin E. Cahill, and Joseph F. Quinn. 2007. "An Update on Bridge Jobs: The HRS War Babies." Bureau of Labor Statistics, Working Paper 407, May. Accessed June 18, 2009 (www.bls.gov/osmr/pdf/ec070060.pdf).

Giordano, Peggy C. 2003. "Relationships in Adolescence." Pp. 257–281 in *Annual Review of Sociology, 2003,* ed. Karen S. Cook and John Hagan. Palo Alto, CA: Annual Reviews.

Giroux, Henry A. 1988. *Schooling and the Struggle for Public Life: Critical Pedagogy in the Modern Age.* Minneapolis: University of Minnesota Press.

Gitlin, Todd. 1993. *The Sixties: Years of Hope, Days of Rage.* New York: Bantam Books.

Glaze, Lauren E., and Thomas P. Bonczar. 2008. "Probation and Parole in the United States, 2007 Statistical Tables." Bureau of Justice Statistics. Washington, DC: U.S. Department of Justice. Accessed May 19, 2009 (http://www.ojp.usdoj.gov/bjs/pub/pdf/ppus07st.pdf).

Glenn, David. 2007. "Anthropologists in a War Zone: Scholars Debate Their Role." *Chronicle of Higher Education* 54 (September 30): A1, A10–A12.

Global Alliance for Workers and Communities. 2003. *About Us.* Accessed April 28 (www.theglobalalliance.org).

Goering, Laurie. 2007. "The First Refugees of Global Warming." *Chicago Tribune,* May 2, pp. 1, 25.

Goffman, Erving. 1959. *The Presentation of Self in Everyday Life.* New York: Doubleday.
———. 1961. *Asylums: Essays on the Social Situation of Mental Patients and Other Inmates.* Garden City, NY: Doubleday.
———. 1963. *Stigma: Notes on Management of Spoiled Identity.* Englewood Cliffs, NJ: Prentice Hall.
———. 1979. *Gender Advertisements.* Cambridge, MA: Harvard University Press.

Golden, Frederic. 1999. "Who's Afraid of Frankenfood?" *Time,* November 29, pp. 49–50.

Goldstein, Melvyn C., and Cynthia M. Beall. 1981. "Modernization and Aging in the Third and Fourth World: Views from the Rural Hinterland in Nepal." *Human Organization* 40 (Spring): 48–55.

Gonzalez, David. 2003. "Latin Sweatshops Pressed by U.S. Campus Power." *New York Times,* April 4, p. A3.

Gottfredson, Michael, and Travis Hirschi. 1990. *A General Theory of Crime.* Palo Alto, CA: Stanford University Press.

Gottlieb, Lori. 2006. "How Do I Love Thee?" *Atlantic Monthly,* March, pp. 58, 60, 62–68, 70.

Gould, Elise. 2007. "The Health-Finance Debate Reaches a Fever Pitch." *Chronicle of Higher Education* (April 13): B14, B15.
———. 2008. "The Erosion of Employer-Sponsored Health Insurance: Declines Continue for the Seventh Year Running." EPI Briefing Paper No. 223, October 9. Washington, DC: Economic Policy Institute. Accessed June 26, 2009 (http://epi.3cdn.net/d1b4356d96c21c91d1_ilm6b5dua.pdf).

Gould, Larry A. 2002. "Indigenous People Policing Indigenous People: The Potential Psychological and Cultural Costs." *Social Science Journal* 39: 171–188.

Gouldner, Alvin. 1960. "The Norm of Reciprocity." *American Sociological Review* 25 (April): 161–177.
———. 1970. *The Coming Crisis of Western Sociology.* New York: Basic Books.

Government Accountability Office. 2003. *Women's Earnings: Work Patterns Partially Explain Difference Between Men's and Women's Earnings.* Washington, DC: U.S. Government Printing Office.

Gramsci, Antonio. 1929. *Selections from the Prison Notebooks,* ed. and trans. Quintin Hoare and Geoffrey Nowell Smith. London: Lawrence and Wishort.

Green, Alexander R., Dana R. Carney, Daniel J. Pallin, Long H. Ng´o, Kristal L. Raymond, Lisa I. Iezzoni, and Mahzarin R. Ban´aji. 2007. "Implicit Bias Among Physicians and Its Prediction of Thrombolysis Decisions for Black and White Patients." *Journal of General Internal Medicine* 9 (September): 1231–1238.

Greenblatt, Alan. 2005. "Upward Mobility." *CQ Researcher* 15 (April 29).

Greenhouse, Steven. 2007. "Low Pay and Broken Promises Greet Guest Workers in U.S." *New York Times,* February 28, pp. A, A14.
———. 2008. "Queens Factory Is Found to Owe Workers $5.3 Million." *New York Times,* July 23. Accessed June 20, 2009 (http://cityroom.blogs.nytimes.com/2008/07/23/a-queens-sweatshop-found-to-owe-workers-53-million/).

Greenspan, Alan. 2005. "Testimony." Hearing Before the Committee on Banking, Housing, and Urban Affairs, United States Senate One Hundred Ninth Congress, S. Hrg. 109–204. Accessed June 6, 2009 (http://frwebgate.access.gpo.gov/cgi-bin/getdoc.cgi?dbname=109_senate_hearings&docid=f:24852.pdf).

Grieco, Elizabeth M., and Rachel C. Cassidy. 2001. "Overview of Race and Hispanic Origin." *Current Population Reports,* Ser. CENBR/01–1. Washington, DC: U.S. Government Printing Office.

Gross, Jane. 2005. "Forget the Career. My Parents Need Me at Home." *New York Times,* November 24, pp. A1, A20.

———. 2007. "U.S. Joins Overseas Adoption Overhaul Plan." *New York Times,* December 11, p. A25.

Groza, Victor, Scott Ryan, and Sara Thomas. 2008. "Institutionalization, Romanian Adoptions and Executive Functioning." *Child & Adolescent Social Work Journal* 25 (3): 185–204.

Guerrera, Francesco, and Andrew Ward. 2007. "Women on March to Top of U.S. Companies." *Financial Times,* March 28, p.17.

Gutiérrez, Gustavo. 1990. "Theology and the Social Sciences," Pp. 214–225 in *Liberation Theology at the Crossroads: Democracy or Revolution?* ed. Paul E. Sigmund. New York: Oxford University Press.

H

Halle, David. 1993. *Inside Culture: Art and Class in the American Home.* Chicago: University of Chicago Press.

Hamilton, Anita. 2007. "Is Facebook Overrated?" *Time* 170 (December 3), pp. 46–48.

Hamilton, Mykol C., David Anderson, Michelle Broaddus, and Kate Young. 2006. "Gender Stereotyping and Under-representation of Female Characters in 200 Popular Children's Books: A Twenty-first Century Update." *Sex Roles* 55(11/12): 757–765.

Harding, Sandra, ed. 2003. *The Feminist Standpoint Theory Reader: Intellectual and Political Controversies.* New York: Routledge.

Harlow, Harry F. 1971. *Learning to Love.* New York: Ballantine Books.

Harrington, Michael. 1962. *The Other America: Poverty in the United States.* Baltimore: Penguin Books.

———. 1980. "The New Class and the Left." Pp. 123–138 in *The New Class,* ed. B. Bruce Briggs. Brunswick, NJ: Transaction.

Hart, Zachary P., Vernon D. Miller, and John R. Johnson. 2003. "Socialization, Resocialization and Communication Relationships in the Context of an Organizational Change." *Communication Studies* 54 (4): 483–495.

Haskins, Ron. 2008. "Wealth and Economic Mobility." Chap. 4 in *Getting Ahead or Losing Ground: Economic Mobility in America.* Washington, DC: Pew Charitable Trusts. Accessed June 20 (http://economicmobility.org/assets/pdfs/EMP _WealthandEconomicMobility_ChapterIV.pdf).

Hausmann, Ricardo, Laura D. Tyson, and Saadia Zahidi. 2008. *The Global Gender Gap Report 2008.* Geneva: World Economic Forum. Accessed June 18, 2009 (www.weforum.org/pdf/gendergap/ report2008.pdf).

Haviland, William A. 2002. *Cultural Anthropology,* 10th ed. Belmont, CA: Wadsworth.

Haviland, William A., Harald E. L. Prins, Dana Walrath, and Bunny McBride. 2005. *Cultural Anthropology: The Human Challenge,* 11th ed. Belmont, CA: Wadsworth.

Hayden, H. Thomas. 2004. "What Happened at Abu Ghraib." Accessed August 7 (www.military.com).

Hayden, H. Thomas. 2004. "What Happened at Abu Ghraib?" Accessed May 19, 2009 (http://www.military.com/NewContent/0,13190,Hayd en_090704,00.html).

He, Wan, Manisha Sengupta, Victoria A. Velkoff, and Kimberly A. DeBarros. 2005. "65+ in the United States: 2005." *Current Population Reports,* Ser. P-23, No. 209. Washington, DC: U.S. Government Printing Office.

Heilman, Madeline E. 2001. "Description and Prescription: How Gender Stereotypes Prevent Women's Ascent up the Organizational Ladder." *Journal of Social Issues* 57 (4): 657–674.

Henriques, Diana B., and Jack Healy. 2009. "Madoff Goes to Jail After Guilty Pleas." *New York Times,* March 12. Accessed May 21, 2009 (http://www.nytimes.com/2009/03/13/business/13madoff.html).

Herek, Gregory M. 2004. "Beyond 'Homophobia.' Thinking About Sexual Prejudice and Stigma in the Twenty-First Century." *Sexuality Research & Social Policy* 1(2): 6–24.

———. 2007. "Confronting Sexual Stigma and Prejudice: Theory and Practice." *Journal of Social Issues* 63(4): 905–925.

Heron, Melonie, Donna L. Hoyert, Sherry L. Murphy, Jiaquan Xu, Kenneth D. Kochanek, and Betzaida Tejada-Vera. 2009. "Deaths: Final Data for 2006." *National Vital Statistics Reports* 57 (14). Hyattsville, MD: National Center for Health Statistics.

Hertz, Rosanna. 2006. *Single by Chance. Mothers by Choice.* New York: Oxford University Press.

Higgins, George E., Richard Tewksbury, and Elizabeth Mustaine. 2007. "Sports Fan Binge Drinking: An Examination Using Low Self-Control and Peer Association." *Sociological Spectrum* 27 (4): 389–404.

Higgins, Michelle. 2008. "No Shoes, No Shirt, No Worries." *New York Times* April 27. Accessed August 5, 2009 (http://travel.nytimes. com/2008/04/27/travel/27nude.html).

Himes, Vristine L. 2001. "Elderly Americans." *Population Bulletin* 56 (December).

Hirschi, Travis. 1969. *Causes of Delinquency.* Berkeley: University of California Press.

Hirschman, Charles, and Irina Voloshin. 2007. "The Structure of Teenage Employment: Social Background and the Jobs Held by High School Seniors." *Research in Social Stratification and Mobility* 25: 189–203.

Hitlin, Steven, and Jane Allyn Piliavin. 2004. "Values: Reviving a Dormant Concept." Pp. 359–393 in *Annual Review of Sociology, 2004,* ed. Karen S. Cook and John Hagan. Palo Alto, CA: Annual Review of Sociology.

Hochschild, Arlie Russell. 1989. *The Second Shift: Working Parents and the Revolution at Home.* New York: Viking Press.

———. 1990. "The Second Shift: Employed Women Are Putting in Another Day of Work at Home." *Utne Reader* 38 (March/April): 66–73.

———. 2005. *The Commercialization of Intimate Life: Notes from Home and Work.* Berkeley: University of California Press.

Holden, Constance. 1980. "Identical Twins Reared Apart." *Science* 207 (March 21): 1323–1328.

———. 1987. "The Genetics of Personality." *Science* 257 (August 7): 598–601.

Holder, Kelly. 2006. "Voting and Registration in the Election of November 2004." *Current Population Reports,* Ser. P-20, No. 556. Washington, DC: U.S. Government Printing Office.

Hollingshead, August B. 1975. *Elmtown's Youth and Elmtown Revisited.* New York: Wiley.

Holmes, Mary. 2006. "Love Lives at a Distance: Distance Relationships over the Lifecourse." *Sociological Research Online* 11 (3).

Homans, George C. 1979. "Nature Versus Nurture: A False Dichotomy." *Contemporary Sociology* 8 (May): 345–348.

Home School Legal Defense Association. 2005. "State Laws" and "Academic Statistics on Homeschooling." Accessed May 12 (www .hslda.org).

Hondagneu-Sotelo, Pierrette, ed. 2003. *Gender and U.S. Immigration: Contemporary Trends.* Berkeley: University of California Press.

Horowitz, Helen Lefkowitz. 1987. *Campus Life.* Chicago: University of Chicago Press.

Horrigan, John B. 2007. *A Typology of Information and Communication Technology Users.* Washington, DC: Pew Internet and American Life Project.

———. 2008. "Home Broadband Adoption 2008." Pew Internet & American Life Project July. Accessed August 6, 2009 (www .pewinternet.org/~/media//Files/Reports/2008/PIP_Broadband_2008 .pdf).

Hout, Michael, and Claude S. Fischer. 2002. "Why More Americans Have No Religious Preference: Politics and Generations." *American Sociological Review* 67 (April): 165–190.

Howard, Russell D., and Reid L. Sawyer. 2003. *Terrorism and Counterterrorism: Understanding the New Security Environment.* Guilford, CT: McGraw-Hill/Dushkin.

Huang, Gary. 1988. "Daily Addressing Ritual: A Cross-Cultural Study." Paper presented at the annual meeting of the American Sociological Association, Atlanta.

Hughes, Everett. 1945. "Dilemmas and Contradictions of Status." *American Journal of Sociology* 50 (March): 353–359.

Hull, Victor. 2007. "100-and-Older Is Nation's Fastest Growing Age Group." Tampa Bay Online, September 2. Accessed June 19, 2009 (www.tbo.com/news/metro/MGBBR22Y26F.html).

Human Rights Campaign. 2009. "Maps of State Laws & Policies." Accessed May 27, 2009 (http://www.hrc.org/about_us/state_laws.asp).

Hunter, Herbert M., ed. 2000. *The Sociology of Oliver C. Cox: New Perspectives: Research in Race and Ethnic Relations,* vol. 2. Stamford, CT: JAI Press.

I

Ignatiev, Noel. 1995. *How the Irish Became White.* New York: Routledge.

Igo, Sarah E. 2007. *The Average American: Surveys, Citizens, and the Making of a Mass Public.* Cambridge, MA: Harvard University Press.

INEGI. 2009. "Mujeres y Hombres en México 2005. Anexo estadístico." Instituto Nacional de Estadística y Geografía. Accessed June 14, 2009 (www.inegi.org.mx/inegi/contenidos/espanol/bvinegi/productos/integracion/sociodemografico/mujeresyhombres/2005/anexo_2005.xls).

Innocence Project. 2009. "Innocence Project Case Profiles." Accessed May 20, 2009 (http://www.innocenceproject.org/know/).

Inter-Parliamentary Union. 2009. "Women in National Parliaments." Accessed June 3, 2009 (www.ipu.org/wmn-e/classif.htm).

Internal Revenue Service. 2008. "Fiscal Year 2008 Enforcement Results." Accessed June 6, 2009 (www.irs.gov/pub/irs-news/2008 _enforcement.pdf).

————. 2009. "The 400 Individual Income Tax Returns Reporting the Highest Adjusted Gross Incomes Each Year, 1992–2006." Accessed June 6, 2009 (www.irs.gov/pub/irs-soi/06intop400.pdf).

International Centre for Prison Studies. 2009. "Prison Brief—Highest to Lowest Rates: Entire World—Prison Population Rates per 100,000 of the National Population." School of Law, King's College, University of London, United Kingdom. Accessed May 19, 2009 (http://www.kcl.ac.uk/depsta/law/research/icps/worldbrief/wpb_stats .php?area=all&category=wb_poprate).

International Institute for Democracy and Electoral Assistance. 2009. "Voter Turnout Database." Accessed June 2, 2009 (www.idea.int/vt/view_data.cfm).

International Labour Organization. 2008. *World of Work Report 2008: Income Inequalities in the Age of Financial Globalization.* Geneva, Switzerland: International Institute for Labour Studies. Accessed June 12, 2009 (www.ilo.org/public/english/bureau/inst/download/world08.pdf).

International Monetary Fund. 2000. *World Economic Outlook: Asset Prices and the Business Cycle.* Washington, DC: IMF.

————. 2008. "IMF Helping Countries Respond to Food Price Crisis." *IMF Survey Magazine: In the News,* June 3. Washington, DC: IMF. Accessed August 12 (http://www.imf.org/external/pubs/ft/survey/so/2008/NEW060308A.htm).

International Telecommunications Union. 2009. "ICT Statistics Database." Accessed May 6, 2009 (http://www.itu.int/ITU-D/icteye/Indicators/Indicators.aspx).

Internet World Stats. 2009a. "Internet Usage Statistics: The Internet Big Picture." Accessed June 29, 2009 (www.internetworldstats.com/stats.htm).

————. 2009b. "Internet World Users by Language: Top 10 Languages." Accessed June 29, 2009 (www.internetworldstats.com/stats7.htm).

Ionescu, Carmiola. 2005. "Romania's Abandoned Children Are Still Suffering." *Lancet* 366 (9497): 1595–1596.

IRIN. 2008. "Burkina Faso: Food Riots Shut Down Main Towns." UN Office for the Coordination of Humanitarian Affairs. Accessed August 12 (http://www.irinnews.org/report.aspx?ReportID=76905).

Isaacs, Julia B. 2007a. *Economic Mobility of Families Across Generations.* Washington, DC: Economic Mobility Project, Pew Charitable Trusts.

————. Julia B. 2007b. *Economic Mobility of Men and Women.* Washington, DC: Economic Mobility Project.

————. 2007c. *Economic Mobility of Black and White Families.* Washington, DC: Economic Mobility Project.

————. 2008. "Economic Mobility of Black and White Families." *Economic Mobility Project,* Pew Charitable Trusts, November. Accessed June 21, 2009 (www.brookings.edu/reports/2008/~/media/Files/rc/reports/2008/02_economic_mobility_sawhill/02_economic _mobility_sawhill_ch6.pdf).

Isaacs, Julia B., Isabel V. Sawhill, and Ron Haskins. 2008. *Getting Ahead or Losing Ground: Economic Mobility in America.* Washington, DC: Pew Charitable Trust.

ITOPF. 2006. "Statistics: International Tanker Owners Pollution Federation Limited." Accessed May 2 (www.itopf.com/stats.html).

J

Jackson, Jerlando and Elizabeth O'Callaghan. 2009. "What Do We Know About Glass Ceiling Effects? A Taxonomy and Critical Review to Inform Higher Education Research." *Research in Higher Education* 50(5): 460–482.

Jacobe, Dennis. 2008. "Half of Public Favors the Environment over Growth." Accessed April 9 (www.gallup.com).

Jacobs, David, Zhenchao Qian, Jason T. Carmichael, and Stephanie L. Kent. 2007. "Who Survives on Death Row? An Individual and Contextual Analysis." *American Sociological Review* 72 (August): 610–632.

James, Susan Donaldson. 2008. "Students Use Civil Rights Tactics to Combat Global Warming." ABC News, January 19. Accessed August 12 (http://abcnews.go.com/Technology/GlobalWarming/story?id=2805553&page=1).

————. 2008. "Wild Child Speechless After Tortured Life: Abandoned by Doctors and Mother, Abused in Foster Care, 'Genie' Regressed." ABC News Online May 19. Accessed May 5, 2009 (http://abcnews.go.com/Health/Story?id=4873347&page=1).

Jamison, Andrew. 2006. "Social Movements and Science: Cultural Appropriations of Cognitive Praxis." *Science as Culture* 15 (1): 45–59.

Jargowsky, Paul A., and Rebecca Yang. 2006. "The 'Underclass' Revisited: A Social Problem in Decline." *Journal of Urban Affairs* 28 (1): 55–70.

Jenkins, J. Craig. 2004. "Social Movements: Resource Mobilization Theory." Pp. 14368–14371 in *International Encyclopedia of the Social and Behavioral Sciences,* ed. Neil J. Smelser and Paul B. Baltes. New York: Elsevier.

Jenkins, Matt. 2008. "A Really Inconvenient Truth." *Miller-McCure* 1 (March–April): 38–41.

Jenness, Valerie, David A. Smith, and Judith Stepan-Norris. 2006. "Pioneer Public Sociologist C. Wright Mills, 50 Years Later." *Contemporary Sociology* 35 (6): 7–8.

Jewison, Norman. 1971. *The Fiddler on the Roof.* Videorecording. Directed by Norman Jewison. 179 minutes. Santa Monica, CA: Metro-Goldwyn-Mayer.

Johnson, Allan G. 1997. *The Forest and the Trees: Sociology as Life, Practice, and Promise.* Philadelphia: Temple University Press.

Johnson, Tallese D. 2007. "Maternity Leave and Employment Patterns: 2001–2003." *Current Population Report,* P70–113. Washington, DC: U.S. Census Bureau.

Johnston, David Cay. 1994. "Ruling Backs Homosexuals on Asylum." *New York Times,* June 12, pp. D1, D6.

Jones, Nicholas A. 2005. *We the People of More Than One Race in the United States.* Census 2000 Special Reports, CENSR-22. Washington, DC: U.S. Government Printing Office.

Jones, Steven E. 2006. *Against Technology: From the Luddites to Neo-Luddism.* New York: Routledge.

Joseph, Jay. 2004. *The Gene Illusion: Genetic Research in Psychiatry and Psychology Under the Microscope.* New York: Algora Books.

Josephson Institute of Ethics. 2008. "The Ethics of American Youth—2008 Summary." Josephson Institute's 2008 Report Card on the Ethics of American Youth. Accessed May 2, 2009 (http://charactercounts.org/programs/reportcard/).

Jost, Kenneth. 2008. "Women in Politics." *CQ Researcher* 18 (March 21).

————. 2006b. "Where's Mao? Chinese Revise History Books." *New York Times,* September 1, pp. A1, A6.

Juergensmeyer, Mark. 2003. *Terror in the Mind of God: The Global Rise of Religious Violence,* 3d ed. Berkeley: University of California Press.

K

Kahn, Joseph. 2006. "Where's Mao? Chinese Revise History Books." *New York Times,* September 1, pp. A1, A6.

Kaiser Family Foundation. 2005. *Sex on TV: 2005.* Santa Barbara, CA: Kaiser Family Foundation.

————. 2009. "Trends in Health Care Costs and Spending." Kaiser Family Foundation Publication #7692–02, March, Menlo Park, CA. Accessed June 26, 2009 (www.kff.org/insurance/upload/7692_02 .pdf).

Kalev, Alexandria, Frank Dobbin, and Erin Kelly. 2006. "Best Practices or Best Guesses? Assessing the Efficacy of Corporate Affirmative Action and Diversity Policies." *American Sociological Review* 71: 589–617.

Kalish, Richard A. 1985. *Death, Grief, and Caring Relationships.* 2d ed. Monterey, CA: Brooks/Cole.

Kalita, S. Mitra. 2006. "On the Other End of the Line." *Washington Post National Week Edition,* January 9, pp. 20–21.

Kamp, Marianne. 2008. *The New Woman in Uzbekistan.* Seattle: University of Washington Press.

Kanter, Rosabeth Moss. 1993. *Men and Women of the Corporation.* New York: Basic Books.

Kapstein, Ethan B. 2006. "The New Global Slave Trade." *Foreign Affairs* 85 (November/December): 103–115.

Karney, Benjamin R., and John S. Crown. 2007. "Families Under Stress: An Assessment of Data, Theory, and Research on Marriage and Divorce in the Military." Santa Monica, CA: RAND Corporation.

Kasavin, Greg. 2003. "Real Life: The Full Review." GameSpot, July 11. Accessed June 3, 2008 (http://www.gamespot.com/gamespot/features/all/gamespotting/071103minusworld/1.html).

Katz, Jason. 1999. *Tough Guise: Violence, Media, and the Crisis in Masculinity.* Videorecording. Directed by Sut Jhally. Northampton, MA : Media Education Foundation.

Kavada, Anastasia 2005. "Exploring the Role of the Interest in the 'Movement for Alternative Globalization': The case of the Paris 2003 European Social Forum." *Westminster Papers in Communication and Culture* 2 (1): 72–95.

Kempadoo, Kamala, and Jo Doezema, eds. 1998. *Global Sex Workers: Rights, Resistance, and Redefinition.* New York: Routledge.

Kennickell, Arthur B. 2009. "Ponds and Streams: Wealth and Income in the U.S., 1989 to 2007." Finance and Economics Discussion Series, Divisions of Research & Statistics and Monetary Affairs, Federal Reserve Board, Washington, DC. Accessed June 7, 2009 (www.federalreserve.gov/pubs/feds/2009/200913/200913pap.pdf).

Kentor, Jeffrey, and Yong Suk Jang. 2004. "Yes, There Is a (Growing) Transnational Business Community." *International Sociology* 19 (September): 355–368.

Kerbo, Harold R. 2009. *Social Stratification and Inequality: Class Conflict in Historical, Comparative, and Global Perspective,* 7th ed. New York: McGraw-Hill.

Khorasani, Noushin Ahmadi. 2009. "How Social Movements Can Change Iran." *The Mark,* June 11. Accessed June 30, 2009 (www.themarknews.com/articles/290-how-social-movements-can-change-iran).

Kilbourne, Jean. 2000. *Killing Us Softly 3: Advertising's Image of Women.* Video. Produced and directed by Sut Jhally. Northampton, MA: Media Education Foundation.

Kim, Kwang Chung. 1999. *Koreans in the Hood: Conflict with African Americans.* Baltimore: Johns Hopkins University Press.

Kimmel, Michael. 2004. *The Gendered Society,* 2d ed. New York: Oxford University Press.

———. 2006. "A War Against Boys?" *Dissent* (Fall): 65–70.

———. 2008. *Guyland: The Perilous World Where Boys Become Men.* New York: HarperCollins.

Kinsella, Kevin, and David R. Phillips. 2005. "Global Aging: The Challenge of Success." *Population Bulletin* 60 (March).

Kirby, Emily Hoban, and Kei Kawashima-Ginsberg. 2009. "The Youth Vote in 2008." Fact Sheet, The Center for Information & Research on Civic Learning & Engagement, April. Accessed June 18, 2009 (www.civicyouth.org/PopUps/FactSheets/FS_youth_Voting_2008.pdf).

Kitchener, Richard F. 1991. "Jean Piaget: The Unknown Sociologist." *British Journal of Sociology* 42 (September): 421–442.

Klein, Stefan. 2006. *The Science of Happiness: How Our Brains Make Us Happy—And What We Can Do to Get Happier.* New York: Marlowe.

Kleinknecht, William. 1996. *The New Ethic Mobs: The Changing Face of Organized Crime in America.* New York: Free Press.

Kliewer, Wendy, and Terri N. Sullivan. 2009. "Community Violence Exposure, Threat Appraisal, and Adjustment in Adolescents." *Journal of Clinical Child & Adolescent Psychology* 37 (4): 860–873.

Klinenberg, Eric. 2002. *Heat Wave: A Social Autopsy of Disaster in Chicago.* Chicago: University of Chicago Press.

Knudson, Tom. 2006. "Promises and Poverty: Starbucks Calls Its Coffee Worker-Friendly—But In Ethiopia, a Day's Pay Is a Dollar." *Sacramento Bee,* September 23. Accessed June 12, 2009 (www.sacbee.com/502/story/393917.html).

———. 2007. "Investigative Report: Promises and Poverty." *Sacramento Bee* September 23. Accessed August 6, 2009 (www.sacbee.com/502/story/393917.html).

Kochhar, Rakesh. 2004. *The Wealth of Hispanic Households: 1996 to 2002.* Washington, DC: Pew Hispanic Center.

Kochhar, Rakesh, Ana Gonzalez-Barrera, and Daniel Dockterman. 2009. "Through Boom and Bust: Minorities, Immigrants and Homeownership." Pew Hispanic Center, May 12. Accessed June 22, 2009 (http://pewhispanic.org/files/reports/109.pdf).

Koerner, Brendan I. 2003. "What Does a 'Thumbs Up' Mean in Iraq?" *Slate* March 28. Accessed May 3, 2009 (http://www.slate.com/id/2080812).

Kohut, Andrew. 2007a. "How Young People View Their Lives, Futures, and Politics: A Portrait of 'Generation Next.'" Survey conducted in association with the Generation Next Initiative and documentary produced by MacNeil/Lehrer Productions. Washington, DC: Pew Research Center for the People & the Press. Acessed June 1, 2008 (http://people-press.org/reports/pdf/300.pdf).

———. 2007b. "Rising Environmental Concern in 47-Nation Survey: Global Unease with Major World Powers." The Pew Global Attitudes Project. Washington, DC: Pew Research Center. Accessed June 3, 2008 (http://pewglobal.org/reports/pdf/256.pdf).

Kokmen, Leyla. 2008. "Environmental Justice for All." *Utne Reader* (March–April): 42–46.

Korczyk, Sophie M. 2002. *Back to Which Future: The U.S. Aging Crisis Revisited.* Washington, DC: AARP.

Kosmin, Barry A., and Ariela Keysar. 2009. *American Religious Identification Survey: ARIS 2008 Summary Report.* Hartford, CT: Trinity College. Accessed June 1, 2009 (http://b27.cc.trincoll.edu/weblogs/AmericanReligionSurvey-ARIS/reports/ARIS_Report_2008.pdf).

Kottak, Conrad. 2004. *Anthropology: The Explanation of Human Diversity.* New York: McGraw-Hill.

Kozol, Jonathan. 2005. *The Shame of the Nation: The Restoration of Apartheid Schooling in America.* New York: Crown.

Kreider, Rose M. 2008. "Living Arrangements of Children: 2004." *Current Population Reports,* No. 114. Washington, DC: U.S. Government. Printing Office.

Kroll, Luisa, and Allison Fass. 2006. "The World's Billionaires." *Forbes* (March 9).

Kronstadt, Jessica, and Melissa Favreault. 2008. "Families and Economic Mobility." Washington, DC: Economic Mobility Project. Accessed August 13 (www.economicmobility.org/reports_and_research/literature_reviews?id=0004).

Kruttschnitt, Candace, and Kristin Carbone-Lopez. 2006. "Moving Beyond the Stereotypes: Women's Subjective Accounts of Their Violent Crime." *Criminology* 44 (2): 321–352.

Kübler-Ross, Elisabeth. 1969. *On Death and Dying.* New York: Macmillan.

Kuumba, M. Bahati. 2001. *Gender and Social Movements.* Lanham, MD: AltaMira Press.

Kwong, Jo. 2005. "Globalization's Effects on the Environment." *Society* 42 (January/February): 21–28.

L

Lacey, Marc. 2008. "Hunger in Haiti Increasing Rapidly." *International Herald Tribune,* April 17. Accessed August 12 (http://www.iht.com/articles/2008/04/17/news/Haiti.php).

Ladner, Joyce. 1973. *The Death of White Sociology.* New York: Random Books.

Lambert, Emily. 2009. "Nimby Wars." *Forbes* 183 (February 16): 98–101. Accessed June 29, 2009 (www.forbes.com/forbes/2009/0216/098.html).

Langhout, Regina D., and Cecily A. Mitchell. 2008. "Engaging Contexts: Drawing the Link Between Student and Teacher Experiences of the Hidden Curriculum." *Journal of Community & Applied Social Psychology* 18 (6): 593–614.

Lareau, Annette. 2003. *Unequal Childhoods: Class, Race, and Family Life.* Berkeley: University of California Press.

Larson, Edward J. 2006. *Summer for the Gods: The Scopes Trial and America's Continuing Debate Over Science and Religion.* New York: BasicBooks.

Lasker, John. 2008. "Inside Africa's PlayStation War." Toward Freedom, July 8. Accessed June 3, 2009 (http://towardfreedom.com/home/content/view/1352/1).

Lasswell, Harold D. 1936. *Politics: Who Gets What, When, How.* New York: McGraw-Hill.

Le Bon, Gustav. 1895. *The Crowd: A Study of the Popular Mind.* New York: Macmillan.

Leavell, Hugh R., and E. Gurney Clark. 1965. *Preventive Medicine for the Doctor in His Community: An Epidemiologic Approach,* 3d ed. New York: McGraw-Hill.

LeClaire, Jennifer. 2009. "Sixty Percent of the World Uses Cell Phones." *Mobile Tech Today.* Accessed May 6, 2009 (http://www.mobile-tech-today.com/story.xhtml?story_id=65006).

Leiserowitz, Anthony, Edward Maibach, and Connie Roser-Renouf. 2009. *Climate Change in the American Mind: Americans' Climate Change Beliefs, Attitudes, Policy Preferences, and Actions.* Yale Project on Climate Change and the George Mason University Center for Climate Change Communication. Accessed June 28, 2009 (http://envirocenter.research.yale.edu/uploads/climatechange-report2.pdf).

Lengermann, Patricia Madoo, and Jill Niebrugge-Brantley. 1998. *The Women Founders: Sociology and Social Theory, 1830–1930.* Boston: McGraw-Hill.

Leonhardt, David. 2007. "Middle-Class Squeeze Comes with Nuances." *New York Times,* April 25, pp. C1, C12.

Levine, Kenneth J., and Cynthia A. Hoffner. 2006. "Adolescents' Conceptions of Work: What Is Learned From Different Sources During Anticipatory Socialization?" *Journal of Adolescent Research* 21 (6) 647–669.

Levitt, Steven D., and Stephen J. Dubner. 2005. *Freakonomics: A Rogue Economist Explores the Hidden Side of Everything.* New York: William Morrow.

Lewis Mumford Center. 2001. *Ethnic Diversity Grows, Neighborhood Integration Is at a Standstill.* Albany, NY: Lewis Mumford Center.

Leys, Tony. 2008. "New Faces Endure Same Struggle." *Des Moines Register,* May 18, pp. 1, 11.

Ling, Peter. 2006. "Social Capital, Resource Mobilization and Origins of the Civil Rights Movement." *Journal of Historical Sociology* 19 (2): 202–214.

Lino, Mark. 2008. *Expenditures on Children by Families, 2007.* U.S. Department of Agriculture, Center for Nutrition Policy and Promotion, No. 1528–2007. Accessed May 27, 2009 (http://www.cnpp.usda.gov/Publications/CRC/crc2007.pdf).

Liptak, Adam. 2006. "The Ads Discriminate, but Does the Web?" *New York Times,* March 5, p. 16.

———. 2008a. "Damages Cut Against Exxon in Valdez Case." *New York Times,* June 26. Accessed April 27, 2009 (http://www.nytimes.com/2008/06/26/washington/26punitive.html).

Liptak, Adam. 2008b. "From One Footnote, a Debate Over the Tangles of Law, Science and Money." *New York Times,* June 26. Accessed April 27, 2009 (http://www.nytimes.com/2008/11/25/washington/25bar.html).

List, Justin M. 2009. "Justice and the Reversal of the Healthcare Worker 'Brain-Drain.'" *American Journal of Bioethics* 9(3): 10–12.

Logue, Susan. 2009. "Poll: More Newlyweds Met Online." *Voice of America News,* March 27. Accessed May 26, 2009 (http://www.voanews.com/english/archive/2009–03/2009–03–27-voa17.cfm).

Lopata, Helena Znaniecki. 1971. *Occupation: Housewife.* New York: Oxford University Press.

Lopez, Mark Hugo, and Paul Taylor. 2009. "Dissecting the 2008 Electorate: Most Diverse in U.S. History." Pew Research Center, Washington, DC, April 30. Accessed June 18, 2009 (http://pewresearch.org/assets/pdf/dissecting-2008-electorate.pdf).

Lorber, Judith. 1994. *Paradoxes of Gender.* New Haven, CT: Yale University Press.

Louie, Miriam Ching Yoon. 2001. *Sweatshop Warriors: Immigrant Women Workers Take on the Global Factory.* Cambridge, MA: South End Press.

Love, Orlan. 2009. "Postville Graduate, Once in Hiding, Gets into College." *Cedar Rapids Gazette,* May 9. Accessed June 19, 2009 (www.gazetteonline.com/apps/pbcs.dll/article?AID=/20090510/NEWS/705109992).

Lovgren, Stefan. 2006. "Can Cell-Phone Recycling Help African Gorillas?" *National Geographic News,* January 20. Accessed June 3, 2009 (http://news.nationalgeographic.com/news/2006/01/0120_060120_cellphones.html).

Lu Haoting. 2009. "Starbucks Pushes China Sales with Local Brew." *China Daily,* February 5. Accessed May 2, 2009 (http://www.chinadaily.com.cn/bizchina/2009–02/05/content_7447136.htm).

Lukacs, Georg. 1923. *History and Class Consciousness.* London: Merlin.

Lumpe, Lora. 2003. "Taking Aim at the Global Gun Trade." *Amnesty Now* (Winter): 10–13.

Lundquist, Jennifer Hickes. 2006. "Choosing Single Motherhood." *Contexts* 5 (Fall): 64–67.

Lyall, Sarah. 2002. "For Europeans, Love, Yes; Marriage, Maybe." *New York Times,* March 24, pp. 1–8.

Lymas, Mark. 2008. *Six Degrees: Our Future on a Hotter Planet.* Washington, DC: National Geographic.

Lynn, Barry C. 2003. "Trading with a Low-Wage Tiger." *The American Prospect* 14 (February): 10–12.

M

MacDorman, Marian, et al. 2005. "Explaining the 2001–2002 Infant Mortality Increase: Data from the Linked Death/Infant Death Data Set." *National Vital Statistic Reports* 53 (January 24).

MacEachern, Scott. 2003. "The Concept of Race in Anthropology." Pp. 10–35 in *Race and Ethnicity: An Anthropological Focus on the United States and the World,* ed. R. Scupin. Upper Saddle River, NJ: Prentice Hall.

MacFarquhar, Neil. 2008. "Resolute or Fearful, Many Muslims Turn to Home Schooling." *New York Times,* March 26, p. A1.

MacLean, Nancy. 2009. *The American Women's Movement: A Brief History with Documents.* New York: Bedford/St. Martin's.

Magnier, Mark. 2004. "China Clamps Down on Web News Discussion." *Los Angeles Times,* February 26, p. A4.

Maher, Timothy M. 2008. "Police Chiefs' Views on Police Sexual Misconduct." *Police Practice & Research* 9 (3): 239–250.

Malacrida, Claudia. 2005. "Discipline and Dehumanization in a Total Institution: Institutional Survivors' Descriptions of Time-Out Rooms." *Disability & Society* 20 (5): 523–537.

Malcolm X, with Alex Haley. 1964. *The Autobiography of Malcolm X.* New York: Grove.

Mangan, Katherine. 2006. "Survey Finds Widespread Cheating in M.B.A. Programs." *The Chronicle of Higher Education* (September 19). Accessed June 6 (http://chronicle.com/daily/2006/09/2006091902n.htm).

Mangum, Garth L., Stephen L. Magnum, and Andrew M. Sum. 2003. *The Persistence of Poverty in the United States.* Baltimore: Johns Hopkins University Press.

Mann, Horace. [1848] 1957. "Report No. 12 of the Massachusetts School Board." Pp. 79–97 in *The Republic and the School: Horace Mann on the Education of Free Men,* ed. L. A. Cremin. New York: Teachers College.

Mapel, Tim. 2007. "The Adjustment Process of Ex-Buddhist Monks to Life After the Monastery." *Journal of Religion & Health* 46 (1): 19–34.

Marijuana Policy Project. 2008. "State-by-State Medical Marijuana Laws: 2008." Washington, DC: Marijuana Policy Project. Accessed May 19, 2009 (http://www.mpp.org/assets/pdfs/download-materials/SBSR_NOV2008.pdf).

Marosi, Richard. 2007. "The Nation: A Once-Porous Border is a Turning-Back Point." *Los Angeles Times,* March 21, pp. A1, A20.

Marples, David R. 2004. *The Collapse of the Soviet Union, 1985–1991.* New York: Pearson Longman.

Martineau, Harriet. [1837] 1962. *Society in America.* Edited, abridged, with an introductory essay by Seymour Martin Lipset. Garden City, NY: Doubleday.

———. [1838] 1989. *How to Observe Morals and Manners.* Philadelphia: Leal and Blanchard. Sesquennial edition, ed. M. R. Hill. New York: Transaction.

Marx, Karl. [1845] 2000. "German Ideology." Pp. 175–208 in *Karl Marx: Selected Writings,* 2nd ed., ed. David McLellan. New York: Oxford University Press.

Marx, Karl, and Friedrich Engels. [1847] 1955. *Selected Work in Two Volumes.* Moscow: Foreign Languages Publishing House.

Massey, Douglas S. 1998. "March of Folly: U.S. Immigration Policy After NAFTA." *The American Prospect* (March/April): 22–23.

———. 2007. *Categorically Unequal: The American Stratification System.* New York: Russell Sage Foundation.

———. 2008. *New Faces in New Places: The Changing Geography of American Immigration.* New York: Russell Sage Foundation.

Massey, Douglas S., and Nancy A. Denton. 1993. *American Apartheid: Segregation and the Making of the Underclass.* Cambridge, MA: Harvard University Press.

Mayo, Elton. 1933. *The Human Problems of an Industrial Civilization.* London: Macmillan.

McAdam, Doug. 1988. *Freedom Summer.* New York: Oxford University Press.

McCabe, Janice. 2005. "What's in a Label? The Relationship between Feminist Self-Identification and 'Feminist' Attitudes among U.S. Women and Men." *Gender & Society* 19 (4): 480–505.

McCombs, Brady. 2009. "Death Count Rises with Border Restrictions." *Arizona Daily Star,* May 17. Accessed June 13, 2009 (www.azstarnet.com/sn/border/293256).

McDonald, Michael. 2009. "Election of a Century?" United States Elections Project. Accessed June 2, 2009 (http://elections.gmu.edu/Election_of_a_Century.html).

McDowell, David J., and Ross D. Parke. 2009. "Parental Correlates of Children's Peer Relations: An Empirical Test of a Tripartite Model." *Developmental Psychology* 45 (1): 224–235.

McGue, Matt, and Thomas J. Bouchard, Jr. 1998. "Genetic and Environmental Influence on Human Behavioral Differences." Pp. 1–24 in *Annual Review of Neurosciences.* Palo Alto, CA: Annual Reviews.

McGurty, Eileen. 2007. *Transforming Environmentalism: Warren County, PCBs, and the Origins of Environmental Justice.* Piscataway, NJ: Rutgers University Press.

McIntosh, Peggy. 1988. "White Privilege and Male Privilege: A Personal Account of Coming to See Correspondence Through Work and Women's Studies." Working Paper No. 189, Wellesley College Center for Research on Women, Wellesley, MA.

McKibben, Bill. 2003. *Enough: Staying Human in an Engineered Age.* New York: Henry Holt.

McLaughlin, Emma, and Nicola Kraus. 2002. *The Nanny Diaries: A Novel.* New York: St. Martin's Press.

McLellan, David, ed. 2000. *Karl Marx, Selected Writings,* rev. ed. New York: Oxford University Press.

Mead, George H. 1934. *Mind, Self and Society,* ed. Charles W. Morris. Chicago: University of Chicago Press.

———. 1964a. *On Social Psychology,* ed. Anselm Strauss. Chicago: University of Chicago Press.

———. 1964b. "The Genesis of the Self and Social Control." Pp. 267–293 in *Selected Writings: George Herbert Mead,* ed. Andrew J. Reck. Indianapolis, IN: Bobbs-Merrill.

Mead, Margaret. [1935] 2001. *Sex and Temperament in Three Primitive Societies.* New York: Perennial, Harper-Collins.

Meara Ellen R., Seth Richards, and David M. Cutler. 2008. "The Gap Gets Bigger: Changes in Mortality and Life Expectancy, by Education, 1981–2000." *Health Affairs* 27 (2): 350–360.

Mehl, Matthias R., Simine Vazire, Naírán Ramírez-Esparza, Richard B. Slatcher, and James W. Pennebacker. 2007. "Are Women Really More Talkative Than Men?" *Science* 317 (July 6):82.

Meier, Robert F., and Gilbert Geis. 1997. *Victimless Crime? Prostitution, Drugs, Homosexuality, Abortion.* Los Angeles: Roxbury Books.

Melby, Todd. 2007. "Exploring Why We Have Sex." *Contemporary Sexuality* 41 (October): 1, 4–6.

Mendez, Jennifer Bickman. 1998. "Of Mops and Maids: Contradictions and Continuities in Bureaucratized Domestic Work." *Social Problems* 45 (February): 114–135.

Merton, Robert. 1948. "The Bearing of Empirical Research upon the Development of Social Theory." *American Sociological Review* 13 (October): 505–515.

———. 1968. *Social Theory and Social Structure.* New York: Free Press.

———, and Alice S. Kitt. 1950. "Contributions to the Theory of Reference Group Behavior." Pp. 40–105 in *Continuities in Social Research: Studies in the Scope and Methods of the American Soldier,* ed. Robert K. Merton and Paul L. Lazarsfeld. New York: Free Press.

Meston, Cindy M., and David M. Buss. 2007. "Why Humans Have Sex." *Archives of Sexual Behavior* 36: 477–507.

Michels, Robert. [1915] 1949. *Political Parties.* Glencoe, IL: Free Press.

Milgram, Stanley. 1963. "Behavioral Study of Obedience." *Journal of Abnormal and Social Psychology* 67 (October): 371–378.

———. 1975. *Obedience to Authority: An Experimental View.* New York: Harper and Row.

Miller, David L., and JoAnne DeRoven Darlington. 2002. *Fearing for the Safety of Others: Disasters and the Small World Problem.* Paper presented at the annual meeting of the Midwest Sociological Society, Milwaukee, WI.

Millett, Kate. 1970. *Sexual Politics.* Garden City, NY: Doubleday.

Mills, C.Wright. [1959] 2009. *The Sociological Imagination.* New York: Oxford University Press.

———. [1956] 2000. *The Power Elite.* New edition with afterword by Alan Wolfe. New York: Oxford University Press.

Minnesota Center for Twin and Family Research. 2008. "Minnesota Center for Twins and Family Research." Accessed January 7 (http://mctfr.psych.umn.edu/research).

Minority Rights Group International. 2007. "World Directory of Minorities and Indigenous Peoples–Mexico: Overview." Geneva: United Nations High Commissioner for Refugees. Accessed June 14, 2009 (www.unhcr.org/refworld/docid/4954ce409a.html).

Mirapaul, Matthew. 2001. "How the Net Is Documenting a Watershed Moment." *New York Times,* October 15, p. E2.

Mishel, Lawrence, Jared Bernstein, and Heide Shierholz. 2009. *The State of Working America 2008/2009.* Ithaca, NY: ILR Press.

Mizruchi, Mark S. 1996. "What Do Interlocks Do? An Analysis, Critique, and Assessment of Research on Interlocking Directorates." Pp. 271–298 in *Annual Review of Sociology,* ed. John Hagan and Karen Cook. Palo Alto, CA: Annual Reviews.

Moen, Phyllis, and Patricia Roehling. 2005. *The Career Mystique: Cracks in the American Dream.* Lanham, MD: Rowman and Littlefield.

Mohai, Paul, and Robin Saha. 2007. "Racial Inequality in the Distribution of Hazardous Waste: A National-Level Reassessment." *Social Problems* 54 (3): 343–370.

Monaghan, Peter. 1993. "Sociologist Jailed Because He 'Wouldn't Snitch' Ponders the Way Research Ought to Be Done." *Chronicle of Higher Education* 40 (September 1): A8, A9.

Montagu, Ashley, 1997. *Man's Most Dangerous Myth: The Fallacy of Race,* 6th ed. abridged student ed. Walnut Creek, CA: AltaMira Press.

Moore, David W. 2002. "Americans' View of Influence of Religion Settling Back to Pre–September 11 Levels." *Gallup Poll Tuesday Briefing* (December 31).

Moore, Molly. 2006. "Romance, but not Marriage." *Washington Post National Weekly Edition,* November 27, p. 18.

Moore, Wilbert E. 1968. "Occupational Socialization." Pp. 861–883 in *Handbook of Socialization Theory and Research,* ed. David A. Goslin. Chicago: Rand McNally.

Morgan, Sue. 2009. "Theorising Feminist History: A Thirty-Year Retrospective." *Women's History Review* 18 (3): 381–407.

Morin, Rich, and Paul Taylor. 2009. Oldest are Most Sheltered: Different Age Groups, Different Recessions. Pew Research Center May 14. Accessed August 6, 2009 (http://pewsocialtrends.org/assets/pdf/recession-and-older-americans.pdf).

Morse, Arthur D. 1967. *While Six Million Died: A Chronicle of American Apathy.* New York: Ace.

Morselli, Carlo, Pierre Tremblay, and Bill McCarthy. 2006. "Mentors and Criminal Achievement." *Criminology* 44 (1): 17–43.

Mortimer, Jeylan T. ,and Michael J. Shanahan, eds. 2006. *Handbook of the Life Course.* New York: Springer Science and Business Media.

Moss, Michael, and Ford Fessenden. 2002. "New Tools for Domestic Spying, and Qualms." *New York Times,* December 10, pp. A1, A18.

Ms. 2006. "The Ms. Poll: Support High for Being a Feminist." *Ms.* 16(3): 44.

Murdock, George P. 1945. "The Common Denominator of Cultures." Pp. 123–142 in *The Science of Man in the World Crisis,* ed. Ralph Linton. New York: Columbia University Press.

———. 1949. *Social Structure.* New York: Macmillan.

———. 1957. "World Ethnographic Sample." *American Anthropologist* 59 (August): 664–687.

N

Nakao, Keiko, and Judith Treas. 1994. "Updating Occupational Prestige and Socioeconomic Scores: How the New Measures Measure Up." *Sociological Methodology* 24 (1994): 1–72.

Naples, Nancy. 2003. *Feminism and Method: Ethnography, Discourse Analysis, and Activist Research.* New York: Routledge.

National Center for Education Statistics. 2007. *Digest of Education Statistics: 2006.* Washington, DC: U.S. Government Printing Office.

National Center for Health Statistics. 2007. *Health, United States, 2007, with Chartbook on Trends in the Health of Americans.* Hyattsville, MD: National Center for Health Statistics. Accessed May 28, 2008 (http://www.cdc.gov/nchs/data/hus/hus07.pdf).

———. 2008. *Health, United States, 2008.* Hyattsville, MD: National Center for Health Statistics. Accessed August 6, 2009 (www.cdc.gov/nchs/data/hus/hus08.pdf).

National Geographic. 2005. *Atlas of the World,* 8th ed. Washington, DC: Author.

National Institute of Justice. 2007. "Transnational Organized Crime." U.S. Department of Justice. Accessed May 20, 2009 (http://www.ojp.usdoj.gov/nij/topics/crime/transnational-organized-crime/welcome.htm).

National Vital Statistics Reports. 2008. "Births, Marriages, Divorces, and Deaths: Provisional Data for June 2007." (January 28).

———. 2009. "Births, Marriages, Divorces, and Deaths: Provisional Data for July 2008." Accessed May 28, 2009 (http://www.cdc.gov/nchs/data/nvsr/nvsr57/nvsr57_13.htm).

Neiwert, David A. 2005. *Strawberry Days: How Internment Destroyed the Japanese Community.* New York: Palgrave Macmillan.

Netherlands Environmental Assessment Agency. 2007. "Industrialised Countries Will Collectively Meet 2010 Kyoto Target." UN Climate Conference, Bali, December 11. Accessed June 28, 2009 (www.pbl.nl/en/dossiers/COP13Bali/moreinfo/Industrialised-countries-will-collectively-meet-2010-Kyoto-target.html).

Neuman, W. Lawrence. 2006. *Social Research Methods: Qualitative and Quantitative Approaches,* 6th ed. Boston: Allyn and Bacon.

Neumark, David. 2008. "Reassessing the Age Discrimination in Employment Act." Washington DC: AARP Public Policy Institute. Accessed June 27 (http://www.aarp.org/research/work/agediscrim/2008_09_adea.html).

New York Times. 2006. "Questions Couples Should Ask (Or Wish They Had) Before Marrying." *New York Times* December 17. Accessed August 6, 2009 (www.nytimes.com/2006/12/17/fashion/weddings/17FIELDBOX.html).

Newman, William M. 1973. *American Pluralism: A Study of Minority Groups and Social Theory.* New York: Harper and Row.

Nicolas, Guerda, Angela M. DeSilva, Kathleen S. Grey, and Diana Gonzalez-Eastep. 2006. "Using a Multicultural Lens to Understand Illnesses Among Haitians Living in America." *Professional Psychology: Research & Practice* 37 (6): 702–707.

Nielsen, Joyce McCarl, Glenda Walden, and Charlotte A. Kunkel. 2000. "Gendered Heteronormativity: Empirical Illustrations in Everyday Life." *Sociological Quarterly* 41 (2): 283–296.

Nobles, Melissa. 2000. "History Counts: A Comparative Analysis of Racial/Color Categorization in U.S. and Brazilian Censuses." *American Journal of Public Health* 90: 1738–1745.

Nofziger, Stacey, and Hye-Ryeon Lee. 2006. "Differential Associations and Daily Smoking of Adolescents: The Importance of Same-Sex Models." *Youth & Society* 37 (4): 453–478.

Nolan, Patrick, and Gerhard Lenski. 2006. *Human Societies: An Introduction to Macrosociology,* 10th ed. Boulder, CO: Paradigm.

Norris, Poppa, and Ronald Inglehart. 2004. *Sacred and Secular: Religion and Politics Worldwide.* Cambridge: Cambridge University Press.

North Carolina Department of Environmental and Natural Resources. 2008. "Warren County PCB Landfill Fact Sheet." Accessed April 9 (www.wastenotnc.org/WarrenCo_Fact_Sheet.htm).

Norwegian Ministry of Children and Equality. 2009. "Women in Norwegian Politics." Norway, the Official Site in the United States. Accessed June 18, 2009 (www.norway.org/policy/gender/politics/politics.htm).

Novelli, William D. 2004. "2011 in America: A Blueprint for Change." *Harvard Generations Policy Journal* (Winter): 23–33.

O

Oakes, Jeannie. 2008. "Keeping Track: Structuring Equality and Inequality in an Era of Accountability." *Teachers College Record* 110 (3): 700–712.

Obach, Brian K. 2004. *Labor and the Environmental Movement: The Quest for Common Ground.* Cambridge, MA: MIT Press.

Obama, Barack. 2009. "Text of a Letter from the President to Senator Edward M. Kennedy and Senator Max Baucus." The White House, June 3, Washington, DC. Accessed June 26, 2009 (www.healthreform.gov/2009healthcareletterpres.pdf).

Oberschall, Anthony. 1973. *Social Conflict and Social Movements.* Englewood Cliffs, NJ: Prentice Hall.

O'Connell, Martin, and Daphne Lofquist. 2009. "Counting Same-Sex Couples: Official Estimates and Unofficial Guesses." Annual meeting of the Population Association of America, Detroit, Michigan, April 30–May 2, 2009. Accessed May 27, 2009 (http://www.census.gov/population/www/socdemo/files/counting-paper.pdf).

O'Connor, Anne-Marie. 2004. "Time of Blogs and Bombs." *Los Angeles Times,* December 27, pp. E1, E14–E15.

O'Harrow, Jr., Robert. 2005. "Mining Personal Data." *Washington Post National Weekly Edition* (February 6), pp. 8–10.

OECD. 2008. *Education at a Glance 2008.* Paris: Organisation for Economic Co-Operation and Development. Accessed June 13, 2009 (www.oecd.org/dataoecd/23/46/41284038.pdf).

———. 2009. "Society at a Glance 2009: OECD Social Indicators." Paris: Organisation for Economic Co-Operation and Development. Accessed June 7, 2009 (http://dx.doi.org/10.1787/550407525853).

———. 2009a. "Development Aid at Its Highest Level Ever in 2008." Organisation for Economic Co-Operation and Development March 30. Accessed June 13, 2009 (www.oecd.org/document/35/0,3343,en_2649_34487_42458595_1_1_1_1,00.html).

Office of Immigration Statistics. 2007. "2006 Yearbook of Immigration Statistics." Washington, DC: U.S. Department of Homeland Security.

Office of Justice Programs. 1999. "Transnational Organized Crime." *NCJRS Catalog* 49 (November/ December): 21.

Ogburn, William F. 1922. *Social Change with Respect to Culture and Original Nature.* New York: Huebsch (reprinted 1966, New York: Dell).

Ogburn, William F., and Clark Tibbits. 1934. "The Family and Its Functions." Pp. 661–708 in *Recent Social Trends in the United States,* ed. Research Committee on Social Trends. New York: McGraw-Hill.

Oliver, Melvin L., and Thomas M. Shapiro. 1995. *Black Wealth/ White Wealth: New Perspectives on Racial Inequality.* New York: Routledge.

Omi, Michael, and Howard Winant. 1994. *Racial Formation in the United States: From the 1960s to the 1990s,* 2d ed. New York: Routledge.

Onishi, Norimitso. 2003. "Divorce in South Korea: Striking a New Attitude." *New York Times,* September 21, p. 19.

Osberg, Lars, and Timothy Smeeding. 2006. "'Fair' Inequality? Attitudes Toward Pay Differentials: The United States in Comparative Perspective." *American Sociological Review* 71 (June): 450–473.

Ozawa, Martha N., and Young Choi. 2002. "The Relationship Between Pre-Retirement Earnings and Health Status in Old Age: Black-White Differences." *Journal of Gerontological Social Work* 38 (4): 19–37.

P

Padian, Kevin. 2007. "The Case of Creation." *Nature* 448 (July 19): 253–254.

Pager, Devah. 2003. "The Mark of a Criminal Record." *American Journal of Sociology* 108 (March): 937–975.

Pager, Devah, and Hana Shepherd. 2008. "The Sociology of Discrimination: Racial Discrimination in Employment, Housing, Credit, and Consumer Markets." *Annual Review of Sociology* 34: 181–209.

Pager, Devah, and Lincoln Quillian. 2005. "Walking the Talk? What Employers Say Versus What They Do." *American Sociological Review* 70 (June): 355–380.

Palm, Cheryl, Stephen A. Vosti, Pedro A. Sanchez, and Polly J. Ericksen, eds. 2005. *Slash-and-Burn Agriculture: The Search for Alternatives.* New York: Columbia University Press.

Park, Kristin. 2005. "Choosing Childlessness: Weher's Typology of Action and Motives of the Voluntarily Childless." *Sociological Inquiry* (August): 372–402.

Park, Robert E. 1922. *The Immigrant Press and Its Control.* New York: Harper.

Parker, Alison. 2004. "Inalienable Rights: Can Human-Rights Law Help to End U.S. Mistreatment of Noncitizens?" *American Prospect* (October): A11–A13.

Parsons, Talcott. 1951. *The Social System.* New York: Free Press.

———. 1966. *Societies: Evolutionary and Comparative Perspectives.* Englewood Cliffs, NJ: Prentice Hall.

———. 1975. "The Sick Role and the Role of the Physician Reconsidered." *Milbank Medical Fund Quarterly Health and Society* 53 (Summer): 257–278.

Parsons, Talcott, and Robert Bales. 1955. *Family: Socialization, and Interaction Process.* Glencoe, IL: Free Press.

Pascoe, C. J. 2007. *Dude, You're a Fag: Masculinity and Sexuality in High School.* Berkeley: University of California Press.

Passel, Jeffrey S., and D'Vera Cohn. 2009. "A Portrait of Unauthorized Immigrants in the United States." A Pew Hispanic Center Report, April 14. Pew Research Center, Washington, DC. Accessed June 21, 2009 (http://pewhispanic.org/files/reports/107.pdf).

Passel, Jeffrey S., and Paul Taylor. 2009. "Who's Hispanic?" Pew Hispanic Center, May 28. Accessed June 22, 2009 (http://pewhispanic.org/files/reports/111.pdf).

Passero, Kathy. 2002. "Global Travel Expert Roger Axtell Explains Why." *Biography,* July, pp. 70–73, 97–98.

Patterson, Thomas E. 2003. *We the People,* 5th ed. New York: McGraw-Hill.

Pattillo, Mary. 2005. "Black Middle-Class Neighborhoods." *Annual Review of Sociology* 31: 305–329.

Paxton, Pamela, Sheri Kunovich, and Melanie M. Hughes. 2007. "Gender in Politics." Pp. 263–285 in *Annual Review of Sociology* 2007. Palo Alto, CA: Annual Reviews.

Pear, Robert. 2008. "Gap in Life Expectancy Widens for the Nation." *New York Times,* March 23. Accessed June 26, 2009 (www.nytimes.com/2008/03/23/us/23health.html).

Peel, Lilly. 2008. "Matchmaker, Matchmaker Make Me a Match . . . If the Algorithms Agree." *Times Online,* October 6. Accessed May 26, 2009 (http://business.timesonline.co.uk/tol/business/industry_sectors/technology/article4887501.ece).

Perrow, Charles. 1986. *Complex Organizations,* 3d ed. New York: Random House.

Pershing, Jana L. 2003. "Why Women Don't Report Sexual Harassment: A Case Study of an Elite Military Institution." *Gender Issues* 21 (4): 3–30.

Peter, Laurence J., and Raymond Hull. 1969. *The Peter Principle.* New York: William Morrow.

Peterson, Karen. S. 2003. "Unmarried with Children: For Better or Worse." *USA Today,* August 18, pp. 1A, 8A.

Petrovic, Drazen. 1994. "Ethnic Cleansing—An Attempt at Methodology." *EJIL* 5: 1–19.

Pew Hispanic Center. 2009. "Mexican Immigrants in the United States, 2008." Pew Research Center Fact Sheet, April 15. Accessed June 21, 2009 (http://pewhispanic.org/files/factsheets/47.pdf).

Pew Research Center. 2006. "More Americans Discussing—and Planning—End-of-Life Treatment." The Pew Research Center for the People & the Press, Washington, DC, January 5. Accessed June 18, 2009 (http://people-press.org/reports/pdf/266.pdf).

———. 2007. "Optimism About Black Progress Declines: Blacks See Growing Values Gap Between Poor and Middle Class." Washington, DC: Pew Research Center. Accessed July 1, 2008 (http://pewsocialtrends.org/assets/pdf/Race.pdf).

———. 2007b. "Global Unease with Major World Powers: Rising Environmental Concern in 47-Nation Survey." Pew Global Attitudes Project. Washington, DC: Pew Research Center. Accessed July 4, 2008 (http://pewglobal.org/reports/display.php?ReportID=256).

———. 2008. "U.S. Religious Landscape Survey." Pew Forum on Religion in Public Life. Washington, DC: Pew Research Center. Accessed June 14, 2008 (http://religions.pewforum.org/pdf/report-religious-landscape-study-full.pdf).

———. 2008b. "Election-Year Economic Ratings Lowest Since '92: An Even More Partisan Agenda for 2008." Pew Research Center for People and the Press. Washington, DC: Pew Research Center. Accessed July 4 (http://people-press.org/reports/display.php3?ReportID=388).

———. 2009a. "Independents Take Center Stage in Obama Era." The Pew Research Center for the People and the Press, May 21. Accessed June 2, 2009 (http://people-press.org/report/?pageid=1516).

Pfeifer, Mark. 2008. "Vietnamese Americans" Pp. 1365–1368 in *Encyclopedia of Race, Ethnicity, and Society,* vol. 3, ed. Richard T. Schaefer. Thousand Oaks, CA: Sage.

Phillips, Katherine A., Katie A. Liljenquist, and Margaret A. Neale. 2009. "Is the Pain Worth the Gain? The Advantages and Liabilities of Agreeing with Socially Distinct Newcomers." *Personality and Social Psychology Bulletin* 35(3): 336–350.

Piaget, Jean. 1954. *The Construction of Reality in the Child,* trans. Margaret Cook. New York: Basic Books.

Pinderhughes, Dianne. 1987. *Race and Ethnicity in Chicago Politics: A Reexamination of Pluralist Theory.* Urbana: University of Illinois Press.

Pinkerton, James P. 2003. "Education: A Grand Compromise." *Atlantic Monthly* 291, January/ February, pp. 115–116.

Pinketty, Thomas, and Emmanuel Saez. 2008. "Tables and Figures Updated to 2006 for 'Income Inequality in the United States, 1913–1998,' *The Quarterly Journal of Economics,* February, 2003." Accessed June 6, 2009 (www.econ.berkeley.edu/~saez/TabFig2006.xls).

Pinnow, Ellen, Pellavi Sharma, Ameeta Parekh, Natalie Gevorkian, and Kathleen Uhl. 2009. "Increasing Participation of Women in Early Phase Clinical Trials Approved by the FDA." *Womens Health Issues* 19 (2): 89–92.

Planty, M., W. Hussar, T. Snyder, G. Kena, A. KewalRamani, J. Kemp, K, Bianco, and R. Dinkes. 2009. *The Condition of Education 2009* (NCES 2009–081). Washington, DC: National Center for Education Statistics, Institute of Education Sciences, U.S. Department of Education. Accessed May 29, 2009 (http://nces.ed.gov/pubs2009/2009081.pdf).

Planty, M., W. Hussar, T. Snyder, S. Provasnik, G. Kena, R. Dinkes, A. Kewal-Ramani, and J. Kemp. 2008. *The Condition of Education 2008.* NCES 2008-031. Washington, DC: National Center for Education Statistics, Institute of Education Sciences, U.S. Department of Education. Accessed June 14 (http://nces.ed.gov/pubs2008/2008031.pdf).

Popenoe, David, and Barbara Dafoe Whitehead. 1999. *Should We Live Together? What Young Adults Need to Know About Cohabitation Before Marriage.* Rutgers, NJ: National Marriage Project.

Population Reference Bureau. 1996. "Speaking Graphically." *Population Today* 24 (June/July): b.

———. 2004. "Transitions in World Population." *Population Bulletin* 59 (March).

———. 2008. *2008 World Population Data Sheet.* Washington, DC: Population Reference Bureau. Accessed June 13, 2009 (www.prb.org/pdf08/08WPDS_Eng.pdf).

Postman, Neil. 1988. "Questioning the Media." Videorecording. The January Series, January 12. Grand Rapids, MI: Calvin College.

———. 1999. *Building a Bridge to the 18th Century: How the Past Can Improve Our Future.* New York: Alfred A. Knopf.

Potts, John. 2009. *A History of Charisma.* New York: Palgrave MacMillan.

Pridemore, William Alex. 2003. "Measuring Homicide in Russia: A Comparison of Estimates from the Crime and Vital Statistics Reporting Systems." *Social Science & Medicine* 57 (8): 1343–1354.

ProCon.org. 2009. "Medical Marijuana: Votes and Polls, National." Accessed May 19, 2009 (http://medicalmarijuana.procon.org/viewadditionalresource.asp?resourceID=000151).

References

Progressive Student Labor Movement. 2008. "A Brief History of the Living Wage Debate at Harvard." Accessed July 7 (http://www.hcs .harvard.edu/~pslm/livingwage/timeline.html).

Provasnik, S., and Planty, M. 2008. *Community Colleges: Special Supplement to the Condition of Education 2008 (NCES 2008–033).* Washington, DC: National Center for Education Statistics, Institute of Education Sciences, U.S. Department of Education. Accessed May 31, 2009 (http://nces.ed.gov/pubs2008/2008033.pdf).

Prus, Steven G. 2007. "Age, SES, and Health: A Population Level Analysis of Health Irregularities over the Lifecourse." *Sociology of Health and Illness* 29 (March): 275–296.

Pryor, J. H., S. Hurtado, L. DeAngelo, J. Sharkness, L. C. Romero, W. S. Korn, & S. Tran. 2008. *The American Freshman: National Norms for Fall 2008.* Los Angeles: Higher Education Research Institute, UCLA.

Pryor, John H., Sylvia Hurtado, Jessica Sharkness, and William S. Korn. 2007b. *The American Freshman: National Norms for Fall 2007.* Los Angeles: Higher Education Research Institute, UCLA.

Pryor, John H., Sylvia Hurtado, Victor B. Saenz, Jessica S. Korn, José Luis Santos, and William Korn. 2006. *The American Freshman: National Norms for Fall 2006.* Los Angeles: Higher Education Research Institute, UCLA.

Pryor, John H., Sylvia Hurtado, Victor B. Saenz, José Luis Santos, and William S. Korn. 2007a. *The American Freshman: Forty Year Trends.* Los Angeles: Higher Education Research Institute, UCLA.

Q

Quadagno, Jill. 2005. *Aging and the Life Course: An Introduction to Social Gerontology,* 3d ed. New York: McGraw-Hill.

Quinney, Richard. 1970. *The Social Reality of Crime.* Boston: Little, Brown.

———. 1974. *Criminal Justice in America.* Boston: Little, Brown.

———. 1979. *Criminology,* 2d ed. Boston: Little, Brown.

———. 1980. *Class, State and Crime,* 2d ed. New York: Longman.

Quirk, Patrick W. 2009. "Iran's Twitter Revolution." *The Epoch Times,* June 24. Accessed July 1, 2009 (www.theepochtimes.com/n2/ content/view/18593).

Quisumbing, Agnes, Ruth Meinzen-Dick, and Lucy Bassett. 2008. "Helping Women Respond to the Global Food Price Crisis." IFPRI Policy Brief 7, October. Accessed June 18, 2009 (www.ifpri.org/ pubs/bp/bp007.pdf).

R

Rainie, Lee. 2001. *The Commons of the Tragedy.* Washington, DC: Pew Internet and American Life Project.

Rand, Michael R. 2008. "Criminal Victimization, 2007: National Crime Victimization Survey." *Bureau of Justice Statistics Bulletin,* December, NCJ 224390. Accessed May 20, 2009 (http://www.ojp.usdoj. gov/bjs/pub/pdf/cv07.pdf).

Rand, Robert. 2006. *Tamerlane's Children: Dispatches from Contemporary Uzbekistan.* Oxford: Oneworld Publications.

Ratner, Carl. 2004. "A Cultural Critique of Psychological Explanations of Terrorism." *Cross-Cultural Psychology Bulletin* 38 (1/2): 18–24.

Ravitz, Jessica. 2009. "Neda: Latest Iconic Image to Inspire." *CNN* June 24. Accessed June 30, 2009 (www.cnn.com/2009/WORLD/ meast/06/24/neda.iconic.images/).

Reddick, Randy, and Elliot King. 2000. *The Online Student: Making the Grade on the Internet.* Fort Worth: Harcourt Brace.

Reddy, Gayatri. 2005. *With Respect to Sex: Negotiating Hijra Identity in South India.* Chicago: University of Chicago Press.

Reid, Luc. 2006. *Talk the Talk: The Slang of 65 American Subcultures.* Cincinnati, OH: Writer's Digest Books.

Reinharz, Shulamit. 1992. *Feminist Methods in Social Research.* New York: Oxford University Press.

Reitzes, Donald C., and Elizabeth J. Mutran. 2004. "The Transition to Retirement: Stages and Factors That Influence Retirement Adjustment." *International Journal of Aging & Human Development* 59 (1): 63–84.

Relerford, Patrice, Chao Xiong, Michael Rand, and Curt Brown. 2008. "42 Students Questioned, 13 Disciplined." *Minneapolis Star-Tribune*

January 10. Accessed June 30, 2009 (www.startribune.com/local/ west/13663951.html).

Religious Tolerance. 2008. "Female Genital Mutilation (FGM): Informational Materials." Accessed March 1 (www.religioustolerance.org).

Ribando, Clare M. 2008. *CRS Report for Congress: Trafficking in Persons.* Washington, DC: Congressional Research Service.

Richtel, Matt. 2006. "The Long-Distance Journey of a Fast-Food Order." *New York Times,* April 11. Accessed May 13, 2009 (http://www .nytimes.com/2006/04/11/technology/11fast.html).

Rideout, Victoria, Donald F. Roberts, and Ulla G. Foehr. 2005. *Generation M: Media in the Lives of 8–18-Year-Olds.* Menlo Park, CA: Kaiser Family Foundation.

Ridgeway, Greg. 2007. "Analysis of Racial Disparities in the New York Police Department's Stop, Question, and Frisk Practices." Santa Monica, CA: RAND Corporation.

Rieker, Patricia R., and Chloe E. Bird. 2000. "Sociological Explanations of Gender Differences in Mental and Physical Health." Pp. 98–113 in *Handbook of Medical Sociology,* ed. Chloe Bird, Peter Conrad, and Allan Fremont. New York: Prentice Hall.

Rimer, Sara. 1998. "As Centenarians Thrive, 'Old' Is Redefined." *New York Times,* June 22, pp. A1, A14.

Ritzer, George. 2008. *The McDonaldization of Society 5.* Thousand Oaks, CA: Sage.

Roberson, Debi, Ian Davies, and Jules Davidoff. 2000. "Color Categories Are Not Universal: Replications and New Evidence from Stone Age Culture." *Journal of Experimental Psychology* 129 (3): 369–398.

Roberts, J. Timmons, Peter E. Grines, and Jodie L. Ma´nale. 2003. "Social Roots of Global Environmental Change: A World-Systems Analysis of Carbon Dioxide Emissions." *Journal of World-Systems Research* 9 (Summer): 277–315.

Robison, Jennifer. 2002. "Should Mothers Work?" Gallup, Inc., August 27. Accessed June 17, 2009 (www.gallup.com/poll/6676/Should-Mothers-Work.aspx).

Rodriguez, Richard. 2002. *Brown: The Last Discovery of America.* New York: Penguin Books.

Romano, Andrew, and Jessica Ramirez. 2007. "The Immigration Mess." *Newsweek,* June 18, p. 37.

Rootes, Christopher. 2007. "Acting Locally: The Character, Contexts and Significance of Local Environmental Mobilisations." *Environmental Politics* 16 (5): 722–741.

Rose, Arnold. 1951. *The Roots of Prejudice.* Paris: UNESCO.

Rosen, Ruth. 2007. *The World Split Open: How the Modern Women's Movement Changed America, Revised and Updated with a New Epilogue.* New York: Penguin.

Rosenthal, Robert, and Lenore Jacobson. 1968. *Pygmalion in the Classroom.* New York: Holt.

Rosin, Hanna. 2007. *God's Harvard: A Christian College on a Mission to Save America.* New York: Harcourt.

Rossi, Alice S. 1968. "Transition to Parenthood." *Journal of Marriage and the Family* 30 (February): 26–39.

———. 1984. "Gender and Parenthood." *American Sociological Review* 49 (February): 1–19.

Rossides, Daniel W. 1997. *Social Stratification: The Interplay of Class, Race, and Gender.* 2d ed. Upper Saddle River, NJ: Prentice Hall.

Rotolo, Thomas, and John Wilson. 2007. "Sex Segregation in Volunteer Work." *The Sociological Quarterly* 48: 559–585.

Rouvalis, Cristina. 2008. "Hey, Mom, Dad, May I Have My Room Back?" *Pittsburgh Post-Gazette,* August 31. Accessed May 27, 2009 (http://www.post-gazette.com/pg/08244/908416–51.stm).

Rowland, Christopher, ed. 2007. *The Cambridge Companion to Liberation Theology,* 2d ed. New York: Cambridge University Press.

Rubin, Alissa J. 2003. "Pat-Down on the Way to Prayer." *Los Angeles Times,* November 25, pp. A1, A5.

Ryan, William. 1976. *Blaming the Victim,* rev. ed. New York: Random House.

Rymer, Russ. 1993. *Genie: An Abused Child's Flight from Science.* New York: HarperCollins.

S

Saad, Lydia. 2004. "Divorce Doesn't Last." *Gallup Poll Tuesday Briefing,* March 30 (www.gallup.com).

Sachs, Jeffrey D. 2005a. *The End of Poverty: Economic Possibilities for Our Time.* New York: Penguin Books.

———. 2005b. "Can Extreme Poverty Be Eliminated?" *Scientific American* 293 (September): 56–65.

Sacks, Peter. 2007. *Tearing Down the Gates: Confronting the Class Divide in American Education.* Berkeley: University of California Press.

Sale, Kirkpatrick. 1996. *Rebels Against the Future: The Luddites and Their War on the Industrial Revolution* (with new preface by author). Reading, MA: Addison-Wesley.

Samuelson, Paul A., and William D. Nordhaus. 2005. *Economics,* 18th ed. New York: McGraw-Hill.

Sanday, Peggy Reeves. 2002. *Women at the Center: Life in a Modern Matriarchy.* Ithaca, NY: Cornell University Press.

———. 2008. Homepage. Accessed March 15 (www.sas.upenn .edu/~psanday).

Sandler, Ronald, and Phaedra C. Pezzullo, eds. 2007. *Environmental Justice and Environmentalism: The Social Justice Challenge to the Environmental Movement.* Cambridge: MIT Press.

Sarachild, Kathie. 1978. "Consciousness-Raising: A Radical Weapon." Pp.144–150 in *Feminist Revolution.* New York: Random House. Accessed June 30, 2009 (http://scriptorium.lib.duke.edu/wlm/fem/ sarachild.html).

Sargent, John and Linda Matthews. 2009. "China Versus Mexico in the Global EPZ Industry: Maquiladoras, FDI Quality, and Plant Mortality." *World Development* 37(6): 1069–1082.

Sassen, Saskia. 2005. "New Global Classes: Implications for Politics." Pp. 143–170 in *The New Egalitarianism,* ed. Anthony Giddens and Patrick Diamond. Cambridge: Policy.

Sawhill, Isabel V. 2006. "Teenage Sex, Pregnancy, and Nonmarital Births." *Gender Issues* 23 (4): 48–59.

Sayer, Liana C., Suzanne M. Bianchi, and John P. Robinson. 2004. "Are Parents Investing Less in Children? Trends in Mothers' and Fathers' Time with Children." *American Journal of Sociology* 110 (July): 1–43.

Scarce, Rik. 1994. "(No) Trial (But) Tribulations: When Courts and Ethnography Conflict." *Journal of Contemporary Ethnography* 23 (July): 123–149.

———. 1995. "Scholarly Ethics and Courtroom Antics: Where Researchers Stand in the Eyes of the Law." *American Sociologist* 26 (Spring): 87–112.

———. 2005. "A Law to Protect Scholars." *Chronicle of Higher Education* (August 12): 324.

Scelfo, Julie. 2008. "Baby You're Home." *New York Times,* November 12. Accessed June 29, 2009 (www.nytimes.com/2008/11/13/ garden/13birth.html).

Schachtman, Tom. 2006. *Rumspringa: To Be or Not to Be Amish.* New York: North Pointe Press.

Schaefer, Richard T. 1998a. "Differential Racial Mortality and the 1995 Chicago Heat Wave." Paper presented at the annual meeting of the American Sociological Association, August, San Francisco.

———. 1998b. *Alumni Survey.* Chicago, IL: Department of Sociology, DePaul University.

———. 2006. *Racial and Ethnic Relations,* 10th ed. Upper Saddle River, NJ: Prentice-Hall.

———. 2009. *Sociology: A Brief Introduction,* 8th ed. New York: McGraw-Hill.

Schaefer, Richard T., and William W. Zellner. 2007. *Extraordinary Groups,* 8th ed. New York: Worth.

Schaffer, Scott. 2004. *Resisting Ethics.* New York: Palgrave Macmillan.

Scharnberg, Kirsten. 2007. "Black Market for Midwives Defies Bans."*Chicago Tribune,* November 25, pp. 1,10.

Schelly, David, and Paul B. Stretesky. 2009. "An Analysis of the 'Path of Least Resistance' Argument in Three Environmental Justice Success Cases." *Society & Natural Resources* 22 (4): 369–380.

Schmeeckle, Maria. 2007. "Gender Dynamics in Stepfamilies: Adult Stepchildren's Views." *Journal of Marriage and Family* 69 (February): 174–189.

Schmeeckle, Maria, Roseann Giarrusso, Du Feng, and Vern L. Bengtson. 2006. "What Makes Someone Family? Adult Children's Perceptions of Current and Former Stepparents." *Journal of Marriage and Family* 68 (August): 595–610.

Schmidley, A. Dianne, and J. Gregory Robinson. 2003. *Measuring the Foreign-Born Population in the United States with the Current Population Survey: 1994–2002.* Washington, DC: Population Division, U. S. Bureau of the Census.

Schmidt, Peter. 2008. "A University Examines Underlying Problems After Racist Incidents." *Chronicle of Higher Education* 54 (March 14): A18–A21.

Schnaiberg, Allan. 1994. *Environment and Society: The Enduring Conflict.* New York: St. Martin's Press.

Schur, Edwin M. 1965. *Crimes Without Victims: Deviant Behavior and Public Policy.* Englewood Cliffs, NJ: Prentice Hall.

———. 1968. *Law and Society: A Sociological View.* New York: Random House.

———. 1985. "'Crimes Without Victims: A 20 Year Reassessment." Paper presented at the annual meeting of the Society for the Study of Social Problems.

Schurman, Rachel. 2004. "Fighting 'Frankenfoods': Industry Opportunity Structures and the Efficacy of the Anti-Biotech Movement in Western Europe." *Social Problems* 51 (2): 243–268.

Schwartz, Shalom H., and Anat Bardi. 2001. "Value Hierarchies Across Cultures: Taking a Similarities Perspective." *Journal of Cross-Cultural Perspective* 32 (May): 268–290.

Scott, Greg. 2005. "Public Symposium: HIV/AIDS, Injection Drug Use and Men Who Have Sex with Men." Pp. 38–39 in *Scholarship with a Mission,* ed. Susanna Pagliaro. Chicago: DePaul University.

Scott, Megan K. 2008. "Twentysomething, College-Educated and Moving Back In." *Washington Post,* May 17. Accessed May 27, 2009 (http://www.washingtonpost.com/wp-dyn/content/ article/2008/05/16/AR2008051601921.html).

Second Life. 2009. "Economic Statistics." Accessed May 13, 2009 (http://secondlife.com/statistics/economy-data.php).

Semuels, Alana. 2007. "Second Life Prove Hard Sell." *Chicago Tribune,* July 23, p.5.

Shah, Anup. 2009. "Poverty Facts and Stats." *Global Issues,* March 22. Accessed June 15, 2009 (www.globalissues.org/print/article/26).

Shaheen, Jack. 2006. *Reel Bad Arabs: How Hollywood Vilifies a People.* Videorecording. Directed by Sut Jhally. 50 minutes. Northampton, MA: Media Education Foundation.

———. 2009. *Reel Bad Arabs: How Hollywood Vilifies a People,* 2d ed. New York: Olive Branch Press.

Shaw, Clifford R., and Henry D. McKay. 1969. *Juvenile Delinquency and Urban Areas.* Chicago: University of Chicago Press.

Sheskin, Ira M., and Arnold Dashefsky. 2007. "Jewish Population of the United States, 2006." In *American Jewish Year Book 2006,* ed. David Singer and Lawrence Grossman. New York: American Jewish Committee.

———. 2007. "Jewish Population in the United States, 2007." Pp. 133–205 in *American Jewish Year Book 2007,* ed. David Singer and Lawrence Grossman. New York: American Jewish Committee.

Shipler, David K. 2004. *The Working Poor: Invisible in America.* New York: Alfred A. Knopf.

Shirky, Clay. 2008. *Here Comes Everybody: The Power of Organizing Without Organizations.* New York: Penguin Books.

Shostak, Arthur B. 2002. "Clinical Sociology and the Art of Peace Promotion: Earning a World Without War." Pp. 325–345 in *Using Sociology: An Introduction from the Applied and Clinical Perspectives,* ed. Roger A. Straus. Lanham, MD: Rowman and Littlefield.

Shupe, Anson D., and David G. Bromley. 1980. "Walking a Tightrope." *Qualitative Sociology* 2: 8–21.

Silicon Valley Cultures Project. 2004. The Silicon Valley Cultures Project website. Accessed February 3, 2005 (www2.sjsu.edu/depts/ anthropology/svcp).

Silver, Ira. 1996. "Role Transitions, Objects, and Identity." *Symbolic Interaction* 10 (1): 1–20.

Simmons, Robin. 2009. "Entry to Employment: Discourses of Inclusion and Employability in Work-Based Learning for Young People." *Journal of Education & Work* 22 (2): 137–151.

Simmons, Tavia, and Martin O'Connell. 2003. "Married-Couple and Unmarried-Partner Households: 2000." *Census 2000 Special Reports,* CENBR-5. Washington, DC: U.S. Government Printing Office.

Singel, Ryan. 2008. "FBI Tried to Cover Patriot Act Abuses with Flawed, Retroactive Subpoenas, Audit Finds." *Wired,* March 13.

Accessed June 30, 2009 (www.wired.com/threatlevel/2008/03/fbi-tried-to-co).

Sisson, Carmen K. 2007. "The Virtual War Family." *Christian Science Monitor,* May 29.

Smith, Adam. [1776] 2003. *The Wealth of Nations.* New York: Bantam Classics.

Smith, Craig. 2006. "Romania's Orphans Face Widespread Abuse, Group Says." *New York Times,* May 10, p. A3.

Smith, Denise. 2003. *The Older Population in the United States: March 2002.* U.S. Census Bureau Current Population Reports, P20–546. Washington, DC. Accessed June 18, 2009 (www.census.gov/prod/2003pubs/p20–546.pdf).

Smith, Tom W. 2003. *Coming of Age in 21st Century America: Public Attitudes Toward the Importance and Timing of Transition to Adulthood.* Chicago: National Opinion Research Center.

Snyder, T. D., S. A. Dillow, and C. M. Hoffman. 2009. *Digest of Education Statistics 2008* (NCES 2009–020). Washington, DC: National Center for Education Statistics, Institute of Education Sciences, U.S. Department of Education.

Social Security Administration. 2008. "Fast Facts & Figures About Social Security, 2008." SSA Publication No. 13–11785. Social Security Administration, Office of Research, Evaluation, and Statistics, Washington, DC. Accessed June 18, 2009 (www.ssa.gov/policy/docs/chartbooks/fast_facts/2008/fast_facts08.pdf).

Solove, Daniel J. 2008. "Do Social Networks Bring the End of Privacy?" *Scientific American* 299 (September): 100–106. Accessed June 30, 2009 (www.scientificamerican.com/article.cfm?id=do-social-networks-bring).

Sorokin, Pitirim A. [1927] 1959. *Social and Cultural Mobility.* New York: Free Press.

Sprague, Joey. 2005. *Feminist Methodologies for Critical Research: Bridging Differences.* Lanham, MD: AltaMira Press.

Stack, Carol. 1974. *All Our Kin: Strategies for Survival in a Black Community.* New York : Harper & Row.

Stalker, Peter. 2000. *Workers Without Frontiers.* Boulder, CO: Lynne Reinner.

Standish, Peter and Steven Bell. 2008. *Culture and Customs of Mexico.* Santa Barbara, CA: Greenwood Press.

Stark, Rodney, and William Sims Bainbridge. 1979. "Of Churches, Sects, and Cults: Preliminary Concepts for a Theory of Religious Movements." *Journal for the Scientific Study of Religion* 18 (June): 117–131.

———. 1985. *The Future of Religion.* Berkeley: University of California Press.

Starr, Paul. 1982. *The Social Transformation of American Medicine.* New York: Basic Books.

Stavenhagen, Rodolfo. 1994. "The Indian Resurgence in Mexico." *Cultural Survival Quarterly* (Summer/Fall): 77–80.

Steele, Jonathan. 2005. "Annan Attacks Britain and U.S. over Erosion of Human Rights." *Guardian Weekly,* March 16, p. 1.

Steidle, Brian. 2007. *The Devil Came on Horseback: Bearing Witness to the Genocide in Darfur.* New York: PublicAffairs.

Stein, Leonard I. 1967. "The Doctor-Nurse Game." *Archives of General Psychology* (Volume 16): 699–703.

Stelter, Brian, and Brad Stone. 2009. "Web Pries Lid of Iranian Censorship." *New York Times,* June 22. Accessed July 1, 2009 (www.nytimes.com/2009/06/23/world/middleeast/23censor.html).

Stenning, Derrick J. 1958. "Household Viability Among the Pastoral Fulani." Pp. 92–119 in *The Developmental Cycle in Domestic Groups,* ed. John R. Goody. Cambridge, UK: Cambridge University Press.

Steward, Samuel M. 1990. *Bad Boys and Tough Tattoos: A Social History of the Tattoo with Gangs, Sailors, and Street-Corner Punks.* Binghamton, NY: Harrington Park Press.

Stewart, Quincy Thomas. 2006. "Reinvigorating Relative Deprivation: A New Measure for a Classic Concept." *Social Science Research* 35 (3): 779–802.

Stratton, Terry D., and Jennifer L. McGivern-Snofsky. 2008. "Toward a Sociological Understanding of Complementary and Alternative Medicine Use." *The Journal of Alternative and Complementary Medicine* 14 (6): 777–783.

Strauss, Gary. 2002. "'Good Old Boys' Network Still Rules Corporate Boards." *USA Today,* November 1, pp. B1, B2.

Stretesky, Paul B. 2006. "Corporate Self-Policing and the Environment." *Criminology* 44 (3): 671.

Strudler, Michael, and Michael Parisi. 2009. "Individual Income Tax Returns, Preliminary Data, 2007." *Statistics of Income Bulletin* 28 (4): 110–120.

Sudan Tribune. 2008. "Darfur's Poorest Squeezed by Ration Cuts." (June 22). Accessed August 12 (http://www.sudantribune.com/spip.php?article27608).

Suitor, J. Jill, Staci A. Minyard, and Rebecca S. Carter. 2001. "'Did You See What I Saw?' Gender Differences in Perceptions of Avenues to Prestige Among Adolescents." *Sociological Inquiry* 71 (Fall): 437–454.

Sullivan, Harry Stack. [1953] 1968. *The Interpersonal Theory of Psychiatry.* ed. Helen Swick Perry and Mary Ladd Gawel. New York: Norton.

Sullivan, Kevin. 2006. "In War-Torn Congo, Going Wireless to Reach Home." *Washington Post,* July 9. Accessed May 6, 2009 (http://www.washingtonpost.com/wp-dyn/content/article/2006/07/08/AR2006070801063.html).

Sumner, William G. 1906. *Folkways.* New York: Ginn.

Sun, Yongmin, and Yuanzhang Li. 2008. "Stable Postdivorce Family Structures During Late Adolescence and Socioeconomic Consequences in Adulthood." *Journal of Marriage & Family* 70 (1): 129–143.

Sutcliffe, Bob. 2002. *100 Ways of Seeing an Unequal World.* London: Zed Books.

Sutherland, Edwin H. 1937. *The Professional Thief.* Chicago: University of Chicago Press.

———. 1940. "White-Collar Criminality." *American Sociological Review* 5 (February): 1–11.

———. 1949. *White Collar Crime.* New York: Dryden.

———. 1983. *White Collar Crime: The Uncut Version.* New Haven, CT: Yale University Press.

Sutherland, Edwin H., Donald R. Cressey, and David F. Luckenbill. 1992. *Principles of Criminology,* 11th ed. New York: Rowman and Littlefield.

Sutton, Philip W. 2007. *The Environment: A Sociological Introduction.* Malden, MA: Polity Press.

Swatos, William H., Jr., ed. 1998. *Encyclopedia of Religion and Society.* Lanham, MD: AltaMira.

Swidler, Ann. 1986. "Culture in Action: Symbols and Strategies." *American Sociological Review* 51 (April): 273–286.

Szasz, Thomas S. 1971. "The Same Slave: An Historical Note on the Use of Medical Diagnosis as Justificatory Rhetoric." *American Journal of Psychotherapy* 25 (April): 228–239.

Sze, Julie, and Jonathan K. London. 2008. "Environmental Justice at the Crossroads." *Sociology Compass* 2(4): 1331–1354.

T

Tafur, Maritza Montiel, Terry K. Crowe, and Eliseo Torres. 2009. "A Review of Curanderismo and Healing Practices Among Mexicans and Mexican Americans." *Occupational Therapy International* 16 (1): 82–88.

Taha, T. A. 2007. "Arabic as 'A Critical-Need' Foreign Language in Post-9/11 Era: A Study of Students' Attitudes and Motivation." *Journal of Instructional Psychology* 34 (3): 150–160.

Taylor, Dorceta E. 2000. "The Rise of the Environmental Justice Paradigm." *American Behavioral Scientist* 43 (January): 508–580.

Taylor, Jonathan B., and Joseph P. Kalt. 2005. *American Indians on Reservations: A Data Book of Socioeconomic Change Between the 1990 and 2000 Censuses.* Cambridge, MA: Harvard Project on American Indian Development.

Taylor, Verta. 1999. "Gender and Social Movements: Gender Processes in Women's Self-Help Movements." *Gender and Society* 13: 8–33.

———. 2004. "Social Movements and Gender." Pp. 14348–14352 in *International Encyclopedia of the Social and Behavioral Sciences,* ed. Neil J. Smelser and Paul B. Baltes. New York: Elsevier.

Telsch, Kathleen. 1991. "New Study of Older Workers Finds They Can Become Good Investments." *New York Times,* May 21, p. A16.

Tentler, Leslie Woodcock. 2004. *Catholics and Contraception: An American History.* Ithaca, NY: Cornell University.

Terkel, Studs. 2003. *Hope Dies Last: Keeping the Faith in Difficult Times.* New York: New Press.

Terry, Sara. 2000. "Whose Family? The Revolt of the Child-Free." *Christian Science Monitor,* August 29, pp. 1, 4.

Tertilt, Michèle. 2005. "Polygyny, Fertility, and Savings." *Journal of Political Economy* 113 (6): 1341–1370.

Thomas, Gordon, and Max Morgan Witts. 1974. *Voyage of the Damned.* Greenwich, CT: Fawcett Crest.

Thomas, William I. 1923. *The Unadjusted Girl.* Boston: Little, Brown.

Thomas, William I., and Dorothy Swain Thomas. 1928. *The Child in America: Behavior Problems and Programs.* New York: Knopf.

Thompson, Ginger. 2001a. "Chasing Mexico's Dream into Squalor." *New York Times,* February 11, pp. 1, 6.

Thornberg, Robert. 2008. "'It's Not Fair!'—Voicing Pupils' Criticisms of School Rules." *Children & Society* 22 (6): 418–428.

Tierney, John. 2003. "Iraqi Family Ties Complicate American Efforts for Change." *New York Times,* September 28, pp. A1, A22.

Tilly, Charles. 1993. *Popular Contention in Great Britain 1758–1834.* Cambridge, MA: Harvard University Press.

———. 2004. *Social Movements, 1768–2004.* Boulder, CO: Paradigm.

Tolbert, Kathryn. 2000. "In Japan, Traveling Alone Begins at Age 6." *Washington Post National Weekly Edition* 17, May 15, p. 17.

Tonkinson, Robert. 1978. *The Mardudjara Aborigines.* New York: Holt.

Tönnies, Ferdinand. [1887] 1988. *Community and Society.* Rutgers, NJ: Transaction.

Toosi, Mitra. 2007. "Labor Force Projections to 2016: More Workers in their Golden Years." *Monthly Labor Review* (November): 33–52.

Torres, Lourdes. 2008. "Puerto Rican Americans" and "Puerto Rico." Pp. 1082–1089, vol. 3, in *Encyclopedia of Race, Ethnicity, and Society,* ed. Richard T. Schaefer. Thousand Oaks, CA: Sage.

Traugott, Michael W. 2005. "The Accuracy of the National Preelection Polls in the 2004 Presidential Election." *Public Opinion Quarterly* 69 (5): 642–654.

Ture, Kwame, and Charles Hamilton. 1992. *Black Power: The Politics of Liberation,* rev. ed. New York: Vintage Books.

Twitchell, James B. 2000. "The Stone Age." Pp. 44–48 in *Do Americans Shop Too Much?* ed. Juliet Schor. Boston: Beacon Press.

U

Uchitelle, Louis. 2003. "Older Workers Are Thriving Despite Recent Hard Times." *New York Times* September 8. Accessed August 6, 2009 (www.nytimes.com/2003/09/08/us/older-workers-are-thriving-despite-recent-hard-times.html).

UNAIDS. 2007. *AIDS Epidemic Update December 2007.* Geneva: Author.

UNCTAD. 2009. "Mainstreaming Gender in Trade Policy." United Nations Conference on Trade and Development, March 10–11, Geneva. Accessed June 18, 2009 (www.unctad.org/Templates/WebFlyer.asp?intItemID=4760&lang=1)

UNICEF and World Health Organization. 2008. *Progress on Drinking Water and Sanitation: Special Focus on Sanitation.* UNICEF, New York and WHO, Geneva. Accessed June 28, 2009 (www.wssinfo.org/en/40_MDG2008.html).

United Nations. 2008. *The Millennium Development Goals Report 2008.* New York: United Nations. Accessed June 13, 2009 (www.un.org/millenniumgoals/2008highlevel/pdf/newsroom/mdg%20reports/MDG_Report_2008_ENGLISH.pdf).

———. 2009. *International Migration Report 2006: A Global Assessment.* Department of Economic and Social Affairs, Population Division. Accessed June 21, 2009 (www.un.org/esa/population/publications/2006_MigrationRep/report.htm).

United Nations Development Programme. 2000. *Poverty Report 2000: Overcoming Human Poverty.* Washington, DC: UNDP.

———. 2008. *Human Development Indices: A Statistical Update 2008.* New York: United Nations Development Programme. Accessed June 7, 2009 (http://hdr.undp.org/en/media/HDI_2008_EN_Complete.pdf).

United Nations Population Division. 2005. *World Fertility Report 2003.* New York: UNPD.

United States Department of Justice. 2008a. *Crime in the United States, 2007.* Washington, DC: United States Department of Justice, Federal Bureau of Investigation. Accessed May 20, 2009 (http://www.fbi.gov/ucr/cius2007/index.html).

———. 2008b. "Crime Clock: 2007." *Crime in the United States, 2007.* Washington, DC: United States Department of Justice, Federal Bureau of Investigation. Accessed May 20, 2009 (http://www.fbi.gov/ucr/cius2007/about/crime_clock.html).

U.S. Census Bureau. 1975. *Historical Statistics of the United States, Colonial Times to 1970.* Washington, DC: U.S. Government Printing Office.

———. 2004. *Current Population Survey (CPS)—Definitions and Explanations.* Washington, DC: U.S. Census Bureau. Accessed June 8, 2008 (http://www.census.gov/population/www/cps/cpsdef.html).

———. 2008. "Current Population Survey (CPS)—Definitions and Explanations." Washington, DC: U.S. Census Bureau. Accessed May 22, 2009 (http://www.census.gov/population/www/cps/cpsdef.html).

———. 2008a. "PPL Table 1B: Child Care Arrangements of Preschoolers Under 5 Years Old Living with Mother, by Employment Status of Mother and Selected Characteristics: Spring 2005 (Percentages)." Who's Minding the Kids? Child Care Arrangements: Spring 2005. Accessed May 6, 2009 (http://www.census.gov/population/www/socdemo/child/ppl-2005.html).

———. 2008b. *Statistical Abstract of the United States: 2009* (128th ed.). Washington, DC: Author.

———. 2008c. "Table PINC-03. Educational Attainment—People 25 Years Old and Over, by Total Money Earnings in 2007, Work Experience in 2007, Age, Race, Hispanic Origin, and Sex." Annual Social and Economic Supplement. Washington, DC: U.S. Census Bureau. Accessed May 29, 2009 (http://www.census.gov/hhes/www/macro/032008/perinc/new03_000.htm).

———. 2008d. "Historical Income Tables—Households." Accessed June 6, 2009 (www.census.gov/hhes/www/income/histinc/inchhtoc.html).

———. 2008e. "2007 Poverty Table of Contents." Current Population Survey 2008 Annual Social and Economic Supplement. Accessed June 8, 2009 (http://www.census.gov/hhes/www/macro/032008/pov/new46_100125_01.htm).

———. 2008f. "2008 National Population Projections: Tables and Charts." Accessed June 18, 2009 (www.census.gov/population/www/projections/tablesandcharts.html).

———. 2008g. "2007 American Community Survey 1-Year Estimates." American FactFinder. Accessed June 19, 2009 (http://factfinder.census.gov/home/saff/main.html).

———. 2009a. "Families and Living Arrangements." Washington, DC: U.S. Census Bureau. May 23, 2009 (http://www.census.gov/population/www/socdemo/hh-fam.html).

———. 2009b. "Educational Attainment." Washington, DC: U.S. Census Bureau. Accessed May 28, 2009 (http://www.census.gov/population/www/socdemo/educ-attn.html).

———. 2009c. "Tables of Alternative Poverty Estimates: 2007." Accessed June 8, 2009 (http://www.census.gov/hhes/www/povmeas/tables.html).

U.S. Department of Agriculture. 2007. "International Macroeconomic Data Set." Economic Research Service. Accessed August 6, 2009 (www.ers.usda.gov/data/macroeconomics).

U.S. Surgeon General. 1999. "Overview of Cultural Diversity and Mental Health Services." In Chap. 2, *Surgeon General's Report on Mental Health.* Washington, DC: U.S. Government Printing Office.

U.S. Trade Representative. 2003. *2002 Annual Report.* Washington, DC: U.S. Government Printing Office.

Urbina, Ian. 2004. "Disco Rice, and Other Trash Talk." *New York Times,* July 31, p. A11.

Utne, Leif. 2003. "We Are All Zapatistas." *Utne Reader* (November–December): 36–37.

V

Van Dijk, Jan., John van Kesteren, and Paul Smit. 2007. *Criminal Victimisation in International Perspective, Key Findings from the 2004–2005 ICVS and EU ICS.* The Hague, Boom Legal Publishers. Accessed May 20, 2009 (http://rechten.uvt.nl/icvs/pdffiles/ICVS2004_05.pdf).

Vanderstraeten, Raf. 2007. "Professions in Organizations, Professional Work in Education." *British Journal of Sociology of Education* 28 (5): 621–635.

Vasagar, Jeeran. 2005. "'At Last Rwanda Is Known for Something Positive.'" *Guardian Weekly,* July 22, p. 18.

Veblen, Thorstein. [1899] 1964. *Theory of the Leisure Class.* New York: Macmillan.

———. 1919. *The Vested Interests and the State of the Industrial Arts.* New York: Huebsch.

Venkatesh, Sudhir. 2006. *Off the Books: The Underground Economy of the Urban Poor.* Cambridge, MA: Harvard University Press.

———. 2008. *Gang Leader for a Day: A Rogue Sociologist Takes to the Street.* New York: Penguin Books.

Venter, Craig. 2000. "Remarks at the Human Genome Announcement, at the Whitehouse." Accessed June 30, 2008 (http://www.celera.com/celera/pr_1056647999).

Vidal, John. 2004. "One in Three People Will Be Elderly by 2050." *Guardian Weekly,* April 1, p. 5.

Villarreal, Andrés. 2004. "The Social Ecology of Rural Violence: Land Scarcity, the Organization of Agricultural Production, and the Presence of the State." *American Journal of Sociology* 110 (September): 313–348.

Vincent, John A. 2006. "Ageing Contested: Anti-Ageing Science and the Cultural Construction of Old Age." *Sociology* 40 (4): 681–698.

Virtcom. 2009. "Board Diversification Strategy: Realizing Competitive Advantage and Shareholder Value." A Whitepaper by Virtcom Consulting, prepared for CalPERS. Accessed June 22, 2009 (www.calpers-governance.org/docs-sof/marketinitiatives/initiatives/board-diversity-white-paper.pdf).

Vowell, Paul R., and Jieming Chen. 2004. "Predicting Academic Misconduct: A Comparative Test of Four Sociological Explanations." *Sociological Inquiry* 74 (2): 226–249.

W

Wais, Erin. 2005. "Trained Incapacity: Thorstein Veblen and Kenneth Burke." *KB Journal* 2 (1). Accessed May 13, 2009 (http://www.kbjournal.org/node/103).

Waitzkin, Howard. 1986. *The Second Sickness: Contradictions of Capitalist Health Care.* Chicago: University of Chicago Press.

Waldman, Amy. 2004a. "India Takes Economic Spotlight, and Critics Are Unkind." *New York Times,* March 7, p. 3.

———. 2004b. "Low-Tech or High, Jobs Are Scarce in India's Boon." *New York Times,* May 6, p. A3.

———. 2004c. "What India's Upset Vote Reveals: The High Tech Is Skin Deep." *New York Times,* May 15, p. A5.

Walker, Iain, and Heather J. Smith, eds. 2002. *Relative Deprivation: Specification, Development, and Integration.* New York: Cambridge University Press.

Wallerstein, Immanuel. 1974. *The Modern World System.* New York: Academic Press.

———. 1979a. *Capitalist World Economy.* Cambridge, UK: Cambridge University Press.

———. 1979b. *The End of the World as We Know It: Social Science for the Twenty-first Century.* Minneapolis: University of Minnesota Press.

———. 2000. *The Essential Wallerstein.* New York: New Press.

———. 2004. *World-Systems Analysis: An Introduction.* Durham, NC: Duke University Press.

Wallis, Claudia. 2008. "How to Make Great Teachers." *Time,* February 25, pp. 28–34.

Warner, R. Stephen. 2005. *A Church of Our Own: Disestablishment and Diversity in American Religion.* New Brunswick: Rutgers University Press.

———. 2007. "The Role of Religion in the Process of Segmented Assimilation." *The Annals of the American Academy of Political and Social Science* 612 (1): 100–115.

Warren, Patricia, Donald Tomaskovic-Devey, William Smith, Matthew Zingraff, and Marcinda Mason. 2006. "Driving While Black: Bias Processes and Racial Disparity in Police Stops." *Criminology* 44 (3): 709–738.

Wartella, Ellen, Aletha C. Huston, Victoria Rideout, and Michael Robb. 2009. "Studying Media Effects on Children: Improving Methods and Measures." *American Behavioral* Scientist 52 (8): 1111–1114.

Waters, Mary C. 2009. "Social Science and Ethnic Options." *Ethnicities* 9(1): 130–135.

Watts, Duncan J. 2004. "The 'New' Science of Networks." Pp. 243–270 in *Annual Review of Sociology 2004,* ed. Karen S. Cook and John Hagan. Palo Alto, CA: Annual Reviews.

Weber, Max. [1913–1922] 1947. *The Theory of Social and Economic Organization,* trans. A. Henderson and T. Parsons. New York: Free Press.

———. [1904] 1949. *Methodology of the Social Sciences,* trans. Edward A. Shils and Henry A. Finch. Glencoe, IL: Free Press.

———. [1904] 2009. *The Protestant Ethic and the Spirit of Capitalism,* trans. Talcott Parsons. New York: Scribner.

———. [1916] 1958a. "Class, Status, Party," Pp. 180–195 in *From Max Weber: Essays in Sociology,* ed. H. H. Gerth and C. Wright Mills. New York: Oxford University Press.

———. [1916] 1958b. *The Religion of India: The Sociology of Hinduism and Buddhism.* New York: Free Press.

Wechsler Henry, and Toben F. Nelson. 2008. "What We Have Learned from the Harvard School of Public Health College Alcohol Study: Focusing Attention on College Student Alcohol Consumption and the Environmental Conditions That Promote It." *Journal of Studies on Alcohol and Drugs* 69 (4): 481–490.

Wechsler, Henry, J. E. Lee, M. Kuo, M. Seibring, T. F. Nelson, and H. Lee. 2002. "Trends in College Binge Drinking During a Period of Increased Prevention Efforts: Findings from Four Harvard School of Public Health College Alcohol Surveys: 1993–2001." *Journal of American College Health* 50 (5): 203–217.

Weinberg, Daniel H. 2004. "Evidence from Census 2000 About Earnings by Detailed Occupation for Men and Women." Census 2000 Special Reports, CENSR-15. Washington, DC: U.S. Census Bureau. Accessed June 26, 2008 (http://www.census.gov/prod/2004pubs/censr-15.pdf).

———. 2007. "Earnings by Gender: Evidence from Census 2000." *Monthly Labor Review* (July/August): 26–34.

Weinstein, Henry. 2002. "Airport Screener Curb Is Regretful." *Los Angeles Times,* November 16, pp. B1, B14.

Weiss, Michael J. 2000. *The Clustered World: How We Live, What We Buy, and What It All Means About Who We Are.* Boston: Little, Brown, & Company.

Wells-Barnett, Ida B. [1928] 1970. *Crusade for Justice: The Autobiography of Ida B. Wells,* ed. Alfreda M. Duster. Chicago: University of Chicago Press.

West, Candace, and Don H. Zimmerman. 1983. "Small Insults: A Study of Interruptions in Cross Sex Conversations Between Unacquainted Persons." Pp. 86–111 in *Language, Gender, and Society,* ed. Barrie Thorne, Chris Kramarae, and Nancy Henley. Rowley, MA: Newbury House.

———. 1987. "Doing Gender." *Gender and Society* 1 (June): 125–151.

Western Interstate Commission for Higher Education. 2008. "Knocking at the College Door 2008." Accessed July 24 (http://wiche.edu/agendabook/May_08/presentations/MizePrescott.pdf).

Wethington, Elaine. 2000. "Expecting Stress: Americans and the 'Midlife Crisis.'" *Motivation & Emotion* 24 (2): 85–103.

Whyte, William Foote. [1943] 1981. *Street Corner Society: Social Structure of an Italian Slum,* 3d ed. Chicago: University of Chicago Press.

Wickman, Peter M. 1991. "Deviance." Pp. 85–87 in *Encyclopedic Dictionary of Sociology,* 4th ed., ed. Dushkin Publishing Group. Guilford, CT: Dushkin.

Wierzbicka, Anna. 2008. "Why There Are No 'Colour Universals' in Language and Thought." *Journal of the Royal Anthropological Institute* 14 (2): 407–425.

Wilford, John Noble. 1997. "New Clues Show Where People Made the Great Leap to Agriculture." *New York Times,* November 18, pp. B9, B12.

Wilkinson, Tracy. 2009. "Remittances to Mexico Down Sharply." *Los Angeles Times,* June 2. Accessed June 15, 2009 (www.latimes.com/news/nationworld/world/la-fg-mexico-remittance2–2009jun02,0,6255959.story).

Williams, David R., and Chiquita Collins. 2004. "Reparations." *American Behavioral Scientist* 47 (March): 977–1000.

Williams, Kristine N. and Carol A.B. Warren. 2009. "Communication in Assisted Living." *Journal of Aging Studies* 23 (1) 24–36.

Williams, Mike. 2008. "Rising Cost of Food Devastates Haiti." *Atlanta Journal Constitution,* June 17. Accessed August 12 (http://www.ajc.com/news/content/news/stories/2008/06/16/haiti_food_crisis.html).

Williams, Robin M., Jr. 1970. *American Society,* 3d ed. New York: Knopf.

Wills, Jeremiah B., and Barbara J. Risman. 2006. "The Visibility of Feminist Thought in Family Studies." *Journal of Marriage and Family* 68 (August): 690–700.

Wilson, Carl. 2007. *Let's Talk About Love: A Journey to the End of Taste.* New York: Continuum.

Wilson, Robin. 2007. "The New Gender Divide." *Chronicle of Higher Education* 53 (January 26): A36–A39.

Wilson, William Julius. 1980. *The Declining Significance of Race: Blacks and Changing American Institutions,* 2d ed. Chicago: University of Chicago Press.

———. 1987. *The Truly Disadvantaged: The Inner City, the Underclass and Public Policy.* Chicago: University of Chicago Press.

———, ed. 1989. *The Ghetto Underclass: Social Science Perspectives.* Newbury Park, CA: Sage.

———. 1996. *When Work Disappears: The World of the New Urban Poor.* New York: Knopf.

———. 1999. *The Bridge over the Racial Divide: Rising Inequality and Coalition Politics.* Berkeley: University of California Press.

Wilson, William Julius, J. M. Quane, and B. H. Rankin. 2004. "Underclass." *International Encyclopedia of Social and Behavioral Sciences.* New York: Elsevier.

Winseman, Albert L. 2005. "Religion in America: Who Has None?" (December 6). Accessed March 4, 2007 (www.gallup.com).

Wirth, Louis. 1931. "Clinical Sociology." *American Journal of Sociology* 37 (July): 49–60.

Withrow, Brian L. 2006. *Racial Profiling: From Rhetoric to Reason.* Upper Saddle River, NJ: Prentice Hall.

Witte, Griff. 2005. "The Vanishing Middle Class." *Washington Post National Weekly Edition,* September 27, pp. 6–9.

Wolf, Naomi. 1992. *The Beauty Myth: How Images of Beauty Are Used Against Women.* New York: Anchor.

Wolfe, Richard. 2008. "New Week, Bush's Agenda Is Africa." *USA Today.* February 15, p. 6A.

Women and Work Commission. 2006. "Shaping a Fairer Future." Presented to the Prime Minister by Baroness Prosser of Battersea, February 2006. Accessed June 18, 2009 (http://www.equalities.gov.uk/pdf/Shaping%20a%20Fairer%20Future%20report.pdf).

Word, David L., Charles D. Coleman, Robert Nunziator, and Robert Kominski. 2007. "Demographic Aspects of Surnames from Census 2000." Accessed January 2, 2008 (www.census.gov/genealogy/www/surnames.pdf).

World Bank. 2003a.*World Development Report 2003: Sustainable Development in a Dynamic World.* Washington, DC: World Bank.

———. 2006c. "India, Inclusive Growth and Service Delivery: Building on India's Success." Development Policy Review, Report No. 34580-IN. Accessed June 13, 2009 (http://siteresources.worldbank.org/SOUTHASIAEXT/Resources/DPR_FullReport.pdf).

———. 2007a. *World Development Indicators 2007.* New York: World Bank.

———. 2008. "Total GNI 2006 (Atlas Method)." Quick Reference Tables. Accessed June 16 (http://siteresources.worldbank.org/DATASTATISTICS/Resources/GNI.pdf).

———. 2008. *World Development Indicators 2008.* Washington, DC: World Bank.

———. 2009a. "Gross National Income per Capita 2007," Atlas Method and PPP." *World Development Indicators 2009.* Accessed June 11, 2009 (http://siteresources.worldbank.org/DATASTATISTICS/Resources/GNIPC.pdf).

———. 2009b. "Gross Domestic Product 2007." *World Development Indicators 2009.* Accessed June 12, 2009 (http://siteresources.worldbank.org/DATASTATISTICS/Resources/GDP.pdf).

World Development Forum. 1990. "The Danger of Television." (July 15): 4.

World Health Organization. 2002. The World Health Report 2002: Reducing Risks, Promoting Healthy Life. Geneva, Switzerland: WHO Press.

———. 2005. *WHO Global Atlas of Traditional, Complementary, and Alternative Medicine.* Geneva, Switzerland: WHO Press.

———. 2009. *World Health Statistics 2009.* Geneva, Switzerland: WHO Press.

Y

Yinger, J. Milton. 1970. *The Scientific Study of Religion.* New York: Macmillan.

Yoong, Nicholas, and Eric Young. 2007. "2007 Corporate Board Report Card: A Report on Directors of Asian Ethnicity on Fortune 500 Boards." A Project of the Corporate Board Initiative of the Committee of 100, Inc., New York. Accessed June 20, 2009 (www.committee100.org/initiatives/corporate_board/2007%20May%2C-100%20Report%20Card.PDF).

Z

Zarembo, Alan. 2004. "A Theater of Inquiry and Evil." *Los Angeles Times,* July 15, pp. A1, A24, A25.

Zellner, William M., and Richard T. Schaefer. 2006. *Extraordinary Groups,* 8th ed. New York: Worth.

Zetter, Kim. 2009. "FBI Use of Patriot Act Authority Increased Dramatically in 2008." *Wired,* May 19. Accessed June 30, 2009 (www.wired.com/threatlevel/2009/05/fbi-use-of-patriot-act-authority-increased-dramatically-in-2008).

Zimbardo, Philip G. 2007. *The Lucifer Effect: Understanding How Good People Turn Evil.* New York: Random House.

Zola, Irving K. 1972. "Medicine as an Institution of Social Control." *Sociological Review* 20 (November): 487–504.

———. 1983. *Socio-Medical Inquiries.* Philadelphia: Temple University Press.

Zweigenhaft, Richard L., and G. William Domhoff. 2006. *Diversity in the Power Elite: How It Happened, Why It Matters,* 2d ed. New York: Rowman and Littlefield.